Education of the Senses

Books by Peter Gay

Freud, Jews and Other Germans:
Masters and Victims in Modernist Culture (1978)

Art and Act: On Causes in History—Manet, Gropius, Mondrian (1976)

Style in History (1974)

Modern Europe (1973), with R. K. Webb

The Bridge of Criticism: Dialogues on the Enlightenment (1970)

The Enlightenment: An Interpretation, volume II,
The Science of Freedom (1969)

Weimar Culture: The Outsider as Insider (1968)

A Loss of Mastery: Puritan Historians in Colonial America (1966)

The Enlightenment: An Interpretation, volume I,
The Rise of Modern Paganism (1966)

The Party of Humanity: Essays in the French Enlightenment (1964)

Voltaire's Politics: The Poet as Realist (1959)

The Dilemma of Democratic Socialism:
Eduard Bernstein's Challenge to Marx (1952)

The Bourgeois Experience

VICTORIA TO FREUD

✍

VOLUME I

Education of the Senses

✍

PETER GAY

New York OXFORD UNIVERSITY PRESS Oxford

Oxford University Press

Oxford New York Toronto
Delhi Bombay Calcutta Madras Karachi
Kuala Lumpur Singapore Hong Kong Tokyo
Nairobi Dar es Salaam Cape Town
Melbourne Auckland

and associated companies in
Beirut Berlin Ibadan Mexico City Nicosia

Copyright © 1984 by Peter Gay

First published in 1984 by Oxford University Press, Inc.,
198 Madison Avenue, New York, New York 10016-4314
First issued as an Oxford University Press paperback, 1985

Oxford is the registered trademark of Oxford University Press.

Library of Congress Cataloging in Publication Data
Gay, Peter, 1923–
Education of the senses.
(The Bourgeois experience v. 1)
Bibliography: p. Includes index.
1. Sex (Psychology)—Social aspects—Europe, Western—
History—19th century. 2. Sex (Psychology)—Social aspects—
United States—History—19th century.
3. Middle classes—Europe, Western—History—19th century.
4. Middle classes—United States—History—19th century.
I. Title. II. Series.
BF692.G36 1983 306.7'094 83-8187
ISBN 0-19-503352-3
ISBN 0-19-503728-6 (pbk.)

Printing (last digit): 9 8 7 6 5
Printed in the United States of America

TO
VANN WOODWARD
WITH AFFECTION AND ADMIRATION

Contents

The illustrations will be found after pp. 182 and 342.

Les premières impressions ne s'effacent pas, tu le sais. Nous portons en nous notre passé; pendant toute notre vie nous nous sentons de la nourrice.

Gustave Flaubert to his mother,
November 24, 1850

An ample theme: the intense interests, passions, and strategy that throb through the commonest lives.

Thomas Hardy, note of May 1882

Abbreviations

BU-JHL   Brown University, John Hay Library.

DPT   David Peck Todd Papers

G.W.   Sigmund Freud, *Gesammelte Werke*, ed. Anna Freud, E. Bibring, W. Hoffer, E. Kris, O. Isakower, in collaboration with Marie Bonaparte, 18 vols. (1940–52).

LF   Lyman Family Papers

MLT   Mabel Loomis Todd Papers

MTB   Millicent Todd Bingham Papers

SC-WHA   Smith College, Women's History Archive

S.E.   Sigmund Freud, *The Standard Edition of the Complete Psychological Works*, translated under the General Editorship of James Strachey, in collaboration with Anna Freud, assisted by Alix Strachey and Alan Tyson, 24 vols. (1953–74).

SF   Silliman Family Papers

SS   Sophia Smith Collection

St.A.   Sigmund Freud, *Studienausgabe*, ed. Alexander Mitscherlich, Angela Richards, James Strachey, 11 vols. (1969–75).

Stabi   Staatsbibliothek

Y-MA   Yale University Library, Manuscripts and Archives

General Introduction

Orientations

1. A Sketch Map

Since this enterprise will extend over several substantial volumes, the reader has every right to know what to expect. As he moves along he will, I trust, come to agree with me that the bourgeois experience from Victoria to Freud deserves, in fact demands, symphonic treatment. My exploration will range from the early nineteenth century to the outbreak of the first World War. I have taken the 1820s and on occasion some years before as suitable points of departure, for the erotic reserve and moral earnestness of the middle classes which have seduced historians to wax sarcastic about "Victorians" were largely in place a decade or two before Victoria ascended the throne in 1837. And the year 1914, when Sigmund Freud was in mid-career as a psychoanalyst, imposed itself as my obvious terminal date: the first World War poisoned, with so much else, the kind of bourgeois culture that is my subject. Western culture experienced fundamental, irreversible, often traumatic changes in this span of time, far from synchronized, but leaving a pattern coherent enough to invite a few generalizations. I shall take account of them in succeeding chapters, but I want to say now, summarily, that I am dividing my nineteenth century between an early and a late phase, and will note a broad band of far-reaching cultural shifts between, for the most part, the 1850s and the 1890s. In those decades, patterns of courtship and ideals of education, fears about masturbation and notions about corporal punishment, portrayals of women and tastes in architecture, and many other cultural traits were transformed, sometimes imperceptibly and sometimes almost out of all recognition. I intend the names I have used for my subtitle to be nothing more than emblems of these changes.

3

Perceptive historians have noted more than once that Queen Victoria was not a Victorian; in the same sense, Freud was not a Freudian: they are not responsible for the myths that have been woven around their names. I want them to stand as reminders that bourgeois culture in the 1890s was quite different from bourgeois culture half a century before.

That word "culture," which I use in the comprehensive way of the anthropologist, requires some words of caution. Every human artifact that contributes to the making of experience belongs under this capacious rubric: social institutions, economic developments, family life, moral and religious doctrines, the anxieties of physicians, the tides of taste, the structure of emotions, even politics. But, while doubtless each culture displays striking dominant traits and a measure of coherence, its broad subdivisions develop with some degree of independence, sometimes in isolation, from one another. I have elsewhere suggested a little facetiously that "Vienna" was not a real city at all, but an invention of cultural historians in search of a basket large enough to comprehend the vigorous and varied literary, artistic, scientific, and philosophical life lived within a few square miles. This was more than a joke on my part: the culture of Sigmund Freud, shaped by the German classics, nineteenth-century positivist thought, and friendships with Jewish physicians, was not the culture of Hugo von Hofmannsthal or other civilized residents of that imaginary city. My point should be plain: culture is more complex, more discontinuous, and more astounding than students of modern Western civilization have recognized. The ebb and flow of cause and effect, especially when we include its unconscious dimensions, is refractory to the historian seeking to chart it.

What I mean by "bourgeois," no less elusive or elastic than "culture," will emerge from this introduction, from my cast of characters, and from the documents on which I shall principally draw. My leading men and women are physicians, merchants, teachers, housewives, novelists, painters, politicians, the occasional prosperous artisan who has secured a measure of economic independence and social respectability, and the rare aristocrat whose credentials are dubious and whose very posture is supremely bourgeois. My most rewarding documents are such confessions, often involuntary, as private diaries, family correspondence, medical texts, household manuals, religious tracts, and works of art. I will reproduce phrenological profiles, annotate intimate letters, interpret paintings, and analyze dreams. The nineteenth-century bourgeois experience was very rich, candid and secretive, patterned and chaotic, at the same time.

In exploring this broken and fascinating terrain, I have found my witnesses in America as well as Europe. In fact, Americans occupy something of a privileged though not a disproportionate place. Their prominence is a tribute to the accessibility of American archives, not solely in being convenient to me, but in other and more interesting ways. Their holdings in those posthumous revelations have proved abundant beyond my most buoyant expectations. And on the whole, some rare and striking European exceptions apart, the diaries, journals, and letters that Americans left behind—often earnestly begging that they be destroyed but, it would appear, half hoping that they would be preserved—have proved less circumspect and less defensive than their French or German or English counterparts. Moreover, my reading in these American materials has substantially confirmed the predictions of contemporary commentators that America, though indubitably European in its origins and most of its ideas, was also prophetic for European developments. From Alexis de Tocqueville in the 1830s to Sigmund Freud eighty years later, critics saw the United States as the quintessential bourgeois society, an incarnation, whether promise or threat, of the middle-class culture toward which European societies seemed to be irresistibly traveling. The United States was a country in which, as Stendhal and Dickens and countless other observers noted, the bourgeois appetite for material things, lack of higher ideals, and incompetence in love was most perfectly realized and most blatantly displayed. To be sure, as I have suggested and shall demonstrate in detail, nineteenth-century bourgeois culture was many as well as one: attitudes toward the show of affection, the discussion of ailments, the supervision of girls, the use of contraceptives, and other significant ingredients in middle-class life differed drastically from decade to decade, from country to country, from stratum to stratum. But for all these nuances and evolutions, for all these individual histories, the varieties of bourgeois ideals and conduct form a recognizable family of desires and anxieties. To take American testimony is to capture the nineteenth-century bourgeoisie at its purest or, perhaps better, at the edge of its destined future. Since the condition of women in nineteenth-century middle-class culture, whether political, educational, or sexual, is of supreme symptomatic interest, it is significant that the United States should have been the first country to admit women to colleges, the first to give women the vote, the first to license women as physicians, and the first (as impressionistic evidence strongly suggests) to encourage, or at least wink at, premarital erotic experimentation. Nineteenth-century America was what nineteenth-century Europe, more or less, must become.

The substantive argument of this work owes much to the thought of Freud. So does its overall outline. I have constructed my volumes on the fundamental building blocks of the human experience—love, aggression, and conflict. In this volume, I examine the bourgeoisie's sensual life, the shapes that its libidinal drives assumed under the pressures of its moral imperatives and physical possibilities; in the volume to follow, I will be examining middle-class ways of loving, bourgeois modes of erotic expression and concealment. I will, in that second volume, explore theories of love; the cultural fantasies that the fiction of the age enshrined; the disguises that erotic desire could assume in the so-called higher realms of culture; the forms of loving that divines called sinful and psychiatrists, perverse; and the price that bourgeois constraints on sexuality exacted, or were thought to exact, from the middle classes. In both volumes, love and sex are interwoven, just as they were interwoven as an ideal in bourgeois fantasies. My decision to separate these two volumes was purely tactical: the material is simply too rich to be contained in a single, manageable book.

I have chosen to begin this inquiry with bourgeois sexuality and with its mature form, love, to dramatize and, I trust, to complicate and correct, those tenacious misconceptions that have dogged our reading of Victorian culture as a devious and insincere world in which middle-class husbands slaked their lust by keeping mistresses, frequenting prostitutes, or molesting children, while their wives, timid, dutiful, obedient, were sexually anesthetic and poured all their capacity for love into their housekeeping and their child-rearing. This dominant, derisive, little-challenged perception is, to be sure, not wholly a fiction: I am, in fact, devoting sizable sections of this volume to ignorance about sexual matters and prejudices against women among educated professional men and less-privileged nineteenth-century bourgeois alike. There were, in the bourgeois century, impotent husbands, frigid wives, young men and women innocent of the most elementary facts of life; and scandalous reports of homosexual establishments or the illicit traffic in prepubertal girls sufficiently attest to the night side of middle-class sensual experience. Sailors, soldiers, rootless traveling salesmen, were not the only customers on which nineteenth-century prostitutes could count. Many of Sigmund Freud's patients seemed to him irrefutable proof that the bourgeois culture of his time had excessively constrained the sexual impulse. I am working to revise current views of the Victorian age, including some of Freud's, then, not for the sake of revision but in an attempt to recapture the conflicts, the ambivalence, the diversity of nineteenth-century bourgeois culture.

How conflict-ridden and diverse that culture was should emerge perhaps even more strikingly in the volumes I am devoting to aggression. Psychoanalytic definitions of aggression are anything but settled; however defined, it emphatically embraces more than the workings of hatred, more than the lust for destruction. Freud spoke more than once, in passing, of an instinct for mastery, and I am including under the rubric of aggression man's urge to control his environment by means of technological, political, aesthetic, and social inventions. I will be analyzing bourgeois styles as a way of adaptation, and will explore specialization, professionalization, social inquiry, the march of science, and the writing of history quite as intensely as such covertly hostile modes of behavior as humor or sanctioned severity with children, pupils, the poor, and foreigners.

In the concluding volumes, on the travail of liberal culture, I want to translate onto the social scene the theme of conflict, which psychoanalysts principally view as an experience of the individual with himself. Toward the end of the nineteenth century, the embattled bourgeoisie confronted three adversaries, none of them very much inclined toward compromise: surviving centers of aristocratic power and prestige; growing working-class parties spurred on by militant, often revolutionary, ideologies; and implacable avant-gardes in literature, the arts, the theatre, and philosophy, disdaining the bourgeoisie as bereft of taste, avid for money, and hostile to cultivation. Of these three adversaries the last, the avant-garde, remains the least understood. It was no more unified than the middle classes that its articulate, self-elected spokesmen were savaging; many good bourgeois actually welcomed the new art and patronized it without condescension while, on the other hand, many avant-garde artists and writers were solid bourgeois at heart. The historian's habit of taking Flaubert's or Marx's anti-bourgeois outbursts as though they were sober reports from the front has done little to clarify this complex and confused situation. I hope to revise, in these concluding volumes, our accepted perception of bourgeois life in a largely, noisily, adversary world, and to approximate more closely to its real, including its unconscious, experience.

To encompass historical experience in all its dimensions requires welding traditional historical attitudes and techniques to the psychoanalytic scheme of human nature and human development, each informing and criticizing its partner. The search for documentation, the construction of causal patterns, the vigilant, skeptical mistrust of speculation must go hand in hand with the analytical leap from the manifest contents of my evidence to its latent meanings. Certainly the historian can never duplicate, in his armchair or in the archives, the psychoanalytic situation, hermetic, regressive, designed to facilitate the communication of unconscious with unconscious. Yet the historian can at least in some measure approximate it. He can interpret dreams, especially if the dreamer has placed them within an associative texture; he can read the sequence of themes in a private journal as though it were a stream of free associations; he can understand public documents as condensations of wishes and as exercises in denial; he can tease out underlying unconscious fantasies from preoccupations pervading popular novels or admired works of art.

I am not issuing a call for historians to be psychoanalyzed, let alone to become psychoanalysts. The wisest in the historical craft have, without benefit of Freud, made allowance for the panoply of motives, the crosscurrents of influence, the subtleties of expression, the lessons that the slightest hints may impart. I have no wish to patronize the giants of the historical profession—Elie Halévy, Marc Bloch, or whoever our models may be—and to imply that they would have been better historians somehow if they had only been fortunate enough to undergo psychoanalytic training. Long exposure, trained intelligence, and highly developed empathy can uncover connections and justify conclusions that psychoanalysts might reach, with their professional techniques, far more laboriously if at all. Freud, we know, envied the poets because they grasped intuitively what it took him years to establish. The psychoanalyst may envy historians for the same reason.

He need not envy them excessively. The psychological theories that most historians casually adopt and apply capture only some of the rhythms and melodies of the past, while its overtones, its hidden resonances, its repetitions that are not merely repetitions, and its myriad surprises are not at their command. What psychoanalysis can contribute to the interpretation of experience is a set of methods and of propositions designed to wrest from the past its recondite meanings and to read its full orchestrated score. My aim is to integrate psychoanalysis with history. These volumes, then, are not psychohistory; they are history informed by psychoanalysis. There is a difference.

Perhaps the most distinctive quality of this kind of history lies in its receptivity to the conspicuous share of the social world in the making of minds, even in their unconscious workings. It will emerge soon enough that the cultural signals by which nineteenth-century bourgeois oriented themselves were often uncertain and anxiety-provoking. It was a time of progress and for confidence, but also one for doubt, for second thoughts, for bouts of pessimism, for questions about identity.

2. Dimensions of Experience

Nineteenth-century bourgeois culture, then, has not lost its capacity to astound. Much as we know, we know too little about it, and many wrong things: the middle classes from the days of Victoria to the days of Freud are underprivileged in this respect, if in few others. The general perception of those we have loosely, perhaps inescapably, called the Victorians certainly needs drastic revision, poised as it is, awkwardly, between amusement over their earnestness and disdain for their prudery, between indignation at their hypocrisy and a slightly patronizing nostalgia for their engaging quaintness. For all the dependable researches and discriminating analyses that serious students of the past have lavished on that culture, it continues to invite the historian to explore its familiar terrain and to wrest new interpretations from its inexhaustible materials.

This seems, in itself, an astonishing assertion. The massive bulk of surviving records should rather occasion fatigue and a certain helplessness.[1] No century surely, except our own, is more exhaustively documented than the nineteenth. It could hardly be otherwise; the century was, after all, the house of our fathers, and most of it, defying the ravages of war and heartless time, still stands, unrenovated, even untouched, open to inspection. The wallpaper has faded only a little, most family portraits are still in place. Yet that century is awash with questions unanswered and, for that matter, questions unasked. Its aristocrats, statesmen, artists, and poets have long been the property of entertaining gossips and exhaustive biographers, though even some of them continue to yield surprises; its working classes, especially when engaged in strikes or rebellions, and its rural populations have in recent years claimed the sympathetic attention of a small army of social historians.

Not so the middle classes: we have failed to take the measure of their experience, their reception of the economic, political, intellectual, and social changes that so radically transformed their lives. Did these changes make the century the bourgeois century? And how did they reverberate in the all-important but little-investigated realms of feeling, the domains of frustration and fulfillment, self-appraisal and social perception, confidence and anxiety? What explains the passion of the nineteenth-century middle classes for privacy, so pervasive and so irresistible as to enter the

1. Opening his *Eminent Victorians* (1918), Lytton Strachey, as always in search of paradox, treated the plethora of available information as an almost insuperable impediment: "The history of the Victorian Age will never be written: we know too much about it." This is witty, suggestive, and perverse.

very definition of the bourgeoisie? What did modern capitalism do for, and to, its most notorious beneficiaries? Was there a distinctive bourgeois style in sexuality, in aggression, in the solitude of prayer, the consumption of art, the management of social mobility? What, in short, was the bourgeois experience in the university, in the marketplace, in the polling booth, in the museum, in bed? It is Sigmund Freud who has impelled me to ask these questions, and left his mark on my answers.

On October 3, 1897, Freud wrote one of his uninhibited letters to Dr. Wilhelm Fliess in Berlin, then his closest friend and only confidant. It was to Fliess that Freud was transmitting all his startling discoveries without reserve. These were excited, not wholly pleasant days for him. His seduction theory of neuroses, which, Freud had hoped, would make his reputation as an innovative healer of nervous disorders, was on the verge of collapse from lack of credible evidence. The epoch-making victory he would snatch from this defeat—the recognition of the privileged part that fantasy plays in mental life—was still struggling for formulation. His self-analysis was at its most intense; Freud was dredging up deeply repressed memories and essaying the most far-reaching dream interpretations he had yet ventured to make. In this atmosphere of tense inquiry and unsparing self-confrontation, he recalled, as he told Fliess, that when he had been between two and two and a half, his "libido toward matrem had awakened" on the occasion of an overnight railway journey from Leipzig to Vienna, which had given him the opportunity to see her "nudam." And then, having unburdened himself of this long-repressed recall, Freud immediately added, in a telling association of which he seemed quite unaware, that he had welcomed the death of his infant brother, born a year after him, with "wicked wishes and genuine infantile jealousy."[2] Love and hate proved constant companions, intimate enemies.

With its very concealments and instructive mistakes, this is a resonant moment, for it condenses, with impressive economy, the overriding themes of my study: the propulsive power of erotic and aggressive urges, their continuous, abrasive entanglement, and a concealed conflict on an intimate stage. More than that, it exhibits the workings of civilization—the control of wishes and the delay of gratifications in the mind of man. And it

---

2. Freud to Fliess, October 8, 1897, Sigmund Freud, *Aus den Anfängen der Psychoanalyse: Briefe an Wilhelm Fliess, Abhandlungen und Notizen aus den Jahren 1887–1902*, ed. Ernst Kris et al. (1950), 233; *The Origins of Psycho-Analysis: Letters to Wilhelm Fliess, Drafts and Notes: 1887–1902*, tr. Eric Mosbacher and James Strachey (1954), 219.

demonstrates the persistence, the sheer vitality, of early encounters, the hold of psychological defenses over the shaping of memories. After the passing of half a lifetime, and in a letter to his best friend, like him a physician, Freud found it necessary to clothe his incestuous desires in the decent obscurity of a learned tongue; the Latin established a space of safety between himself and his forbidden arousal. And it is significant that Freud should have misplaced the date of his exciting, seductive glimpse: he had actually been four years old at the time. By making himself younger and smaller than he had really been, he denied the palpable eroticism of the oedipal stage he had reached, portrayed himself as less powerful, less dangerous, than he was, as scarcely able to conceive, let alone carry out, his aggressive and sexual intentions. When he told Fliess about them he was forty-one years old. The reverberations of his memory, its long, almost unimpaired reach from Freud's troubling current situation to his infantile passions, invite the historian to explore beyond the immediate occasion, to move outward to Freud's cultural environment and back to his early personal history. In a word, with its far-reaching implications for the study of man's most potent, yet markedly secretive, springs of action, this immensely suggestive vignette is the exemplar of an experience. In a very real sense, this book and its successors are an extended commentary on it.

An experience is an encounter of mind with world, neither of these ever simple or wholly perspicuous. Often commonplace on the surface, experience shows itself, especially when we trace its roots to the remote domains of the unconscious, uncooperative, evasive, taciturn; the creature of ambiguous impulses and unresolved conflicts, it often sows confusions and compels drastic misreadings. Far more than simply providing occasions for the stereotyped exercise of thought and action, experience participates in creating objects of interest and passion; it gives form to inchoate wishes and defends against besetting anxieties. Man's irrepressible appetite for experience reaches back to the child's earliest investigations in search of sexual knowledge and to the pleasure that mastery gives him, largely repressed and later sublimated into less primitive cultural activities. Both as unique event and as linked to others, an experience is thus more than a naked wish or a casual perception; it is an organization of passionate demands, persistent ways of seeing, and objective realities that will not be denied.

And it is also, in addition to being an encounter of mind with world, an encounter of past with present. Love and hate, those energetic makers of history, have extended and largely secret histories of their own: the pressure of the past is pervasive and insistent. To call man the cultural animal is to stress his nature as an animal that learns from experience, if often the wrong lessons. Experience, William James exclaimed in 1890, in his exuberant way, is "our educator, our sovereign helper and friend."[3] It emerges from the clash and collaboration of conscious reflection and unconscious need, blends memory and desire, none of them unalterable or ready-made. And while much of the potent instruction by which man lives takes place beyond the reach of his awareness, much of it is accessible to him: when Sigmund Freud cautioned his fellow psychoanalysts to attend, with even-handed impartiality, to the manifest presentations of dreams no less than to their latent contents, he might have been speaking to historians about the need to respect evidence both remote and accessible.

Experiences, then, testify to the uninterrupted traffic between what the world imposes and the mind demands, receives, and reshapes. This intercourse has long occupied, indeed troubled, professional historians. Precisely like the realities among which it is thrown, the mind, at once stable and changing, is almost never wholly passive. I am not arguing for incurable subjectivity. Minds are often strikingly efficient in their grasp on the contours and meanings of their perceptions. Most historians subscribe to the dubious critical proposition that every human being is the hapless victim of false consciousness, a mere partisan, an unwitting but incurable spokesman for his class, his faith, and his time. They like to say, with cultural anthropologists, that men construe their experience.[4] So they do. But that construction is an uneasy collaboration between misperceptions generated by anxiety and corrections provided by reasoning and experimentation. Most persons' view of reality is, for all its passionate and neurotic revisions, a recognizable representation of that reality, resembling the world quite as much as an eighteenth-century map approximated the actual configurations of the globe. Men, even madmen, do not simply invent their world. The materials they employ for its construction are, by and large, public property.

I shall have ample occasion in these pages to discover self-deceptions, correct misreadings, and analyze the unconscious meaning of conscious acts. But I want, at the same time, to make strong claims for the authority of external reality and for the competence of mind. The prevalence of

3. *The Principles of Psychology*, 2 vols. (1890), II, 620.
4. " 'All experience,' as Clifford Geertz puts it, 'is constructed experience.' " William H. Sewell, Jr., *Work and Revolution in France: The Language of Labor from the Old Regime to 1848* (1980), 10. He is quoting from Geertz, *The Interpretation of Cultures* (1973), 405.

partisan argumentation, irrational beliefs, and hostile projections through-out history offers disheartening evidence for the limits on human objectivity. The psychoanalytic persuasion notoriously holds that there is always more to men's ideas, speeches, and actions than meets the unschooled eye. But it does not commit the psychoanalyst—or the historian—to the view that things are always the opposite of what they appear to be. They are, paradoxically, at the same time not what they seem *and* what they seem. That is what makes them so interesting and so difficult. And Freud's thought, far from slighting these intricacies, recognizes, in fact celebrates them, and facilitates their study. This is one of its claims to the historian's attention and certainly one of the reasons why I find it so congenial.

Freud at forty-one, therefore, seeing his mother naked once again in his mind, would have been right to call this a second edition: it was a revised revival of commands and prohibitions, an unfolding of verifiable events around 1860 reshaped into the useful, indeed strategic, memory emerging in 1897. Freud's boyish desires recalled in adult anxiety were deeply personal, but they had general implications; they erupted as he was struggling to formulate a psychology in which all little boys' desire for their mothers would be a conspicuous element. That historians should generally have shunned the inaccessible dimensions of experience is perfectly comprehensible. The unconscious is intractable. At best, however tantalizing the traces it may leave behind, it is almost illegible to the un-trained observer. But, while the assignment of rendering it legible and accessible to historical inquiry is admittedly difficult, it remains a decisive truth of history—a truth the historian ignores at his peril and to his loss—that much of the past has taken place underground, silently, eloquently.

For all the intricate and energetic activity of the unconscious, the historical interpretation of experience must be sensitive to its conscious no less than to its unconscious dimensions, to the work of culture on mind—the world, in a word, in which the historian is most at home. It is only fitting that Sigmund Freud should have had his consequential erotic perception on a train, that supreme metaphor for a nineteenth century in motion. The intimacy of the compartment and the rhythmic pulsation of the journey helped to give rise, and particular form, to the four-year-old's imperious desires. The human mind hungers for reality; except for the largely encapsulated id, which is the depository of the raw drives and of deeply repressed material, the other institutions of the mind, the ego and the superego, draw continuously and liberally on the culture in which they subsist, develop, succeed, and fail. While the mind presents the world with its needs, the world gives the mind its grammar, wishes their vocabulary, anxieties their object. Man's superego is an accumulation of parental and other didactic injunctions; man's ego, endowed with capacities for thinking, calculating, and anticipating, encounters and tests realities. The mind levies on the world for its fantasies, its very dreams. And if these shadowy activities of the mind borrow so heavily from sights and sounds and smells, then the daytime experience of normal neurotics —the principal stuff of history—must cling still more tightly to the social, religious, economic, and technological imperatives which together define the possibilities and prescribe the limits of individuals and groups alike.

The reductionism that has bedeviled much psychohistory is therefore indefensible not merely because it slights the subtleties of the historical process, but, perhaps even more gravely, because it slights the subtleties of the psychoanalytic view of man in the world. Not all reduction, to be sure, is reductionist. In an essay of 1913, in which he speculated on the uses of psychoanalysis to historical studies, Freud adumbrated this distinction, and hinted at a way in which his individualistic psychology could make itself relevant to the study of collective experience, in which biography could become history. "Psychoanalysis," he wrote, "establishes an intimate connection" between the "psychical achievements of individuals and of societies by postulating the same dynamic source for both. It starts with the fundamental idea that it is the principal function of the mental mechanism to relieve the person from the tensions which his needs create in him. Part of this task can be fulfilled by extracting satisfaction from the external world; for this purpose it is essential to have mastery over the real world." But, he adds, "reality regularly frustrates the satisfaction of another part of these needs, among them, significantly, certain affective impulses. This produces the second task; that of finding some other way of disposing of the unsatisfied impulses." Persuaded that psychoanalysis had already thrown dazzling light on the origins of religion, morality, justice, and philosophy, Freud now concluded that "the whole history of culture only demonstrates which methods mankind has adopted to bind its unsatisfied wishes under changing conditions, further modified by technological progress, wishes sometimes granted and sometimes frustrated by reality."[5]

This little-known passage is nothing less than an ambitious agenda for historians, an invitation whose implications neither psychoanalysts nor historians have even begun to explore. Freud is clearly alert to the way in

5. "Das Interesse an der Psychoanalyse" (1913), [not in *St.A.*], *G.W.*, VIII, 415; "The Claims of Psycho-Analysis to Scientific Interest," *S.E.*, XIII, 185–86.

which mental operations, translated into inventions, institutions, and solutions to problems, emancipate themselves to lead an autonomous public existence. In that sense, even technology is, if traced back far enough, a rational method of gratifying unsatisfied wishes. But it is also an external, objective reality which, having freed itself from mind, now faces mind. It is a far from casual matter that men should use metaphors drawn from family life when they speak of religion, politics, or the factory. They invest their public environment with their intimate experience and that environment at once mirrors and acts upon that experience. Class consciousness, national loyalties, economic decisions, are all species of mental work making their mark on realities and being marked by them in turn. Cults of youth, or age, or nature, hopes for advancement or despair of mobility, commitments to parliamentary institutions or to charismatic leadership, the choice of business strategies, and a myriad of other sentiments and activities are partly rational, partly nonrational, the fruit of calculation and of ungratified wishes that the individual and his groups barely know and can hardly acknowledge. Psychoanalytic categories explaining these richly layered experiences are not prescriptive channels in which historical interpretations must run; they are descriptions of available and unavailable human options. They enormously enlarge the historian's opportunity to grasp all the dimensions of the past and their relative share in their precipitate, experience. That is why I closely analyze what I call the pressures of reality as varied as the introduction of the railway, the vulcanization of rubber, the conquest of childbed fever, the persistence of social hierarchies. They made the bourgeois experience what it came to be.

Strictly speaking, of course, there was no bourgeois experience in the nineteenth century or any other; there were only bourgeois experiences. The experience of any individual, as the psychoanalytically oriented historian has particular reason to know, differs, however slightly, from that of all others. To write the history of the bourgeois experience in the nineteenth century; to enter, as inquisitively as I can, into the mind of the middle class, is to hazard risky generalizations. Only the individual loves and hates, develops tastes in painting and furniture, feels content in moments of consummation, anxious in times of peril, and furious at agents of deprivation; only the individual glories in mastery or revenges himself upon the world. The rest is metaphor.

But it is a necessary metaphor. For all humans share at least their humanity—their passions, their paths to maturation, their irrepressible needs. And each develops social ties, belongs to part-cultures that expose him to predictable clusters of experiences, each bearing family resemblances close enough to seduce the historian into collective judgments. Religious denominations, urban neighborhoods, linguistic communities, and, in the nineteenth century, classes, mold the individual into a recognizable member of several societies. By the time a child is ready for school, he is a little living anthology of his particular culture—partial, indeed unique, a true individual, but still a highly instructive witness to his several worlds. That is why the ways of psychoanalysis, its theories and its techniques, can build the very bridge between individual and collective experience that most historians, deeply uneasy with the Freudian dispensation, have persisted in treating as problematic. For the psychoanalyst's individual is a social individual. Even that most private of internal, largely unconscious struggles, the repression of the Oedipus complex, Freud noted, operates under "the influence of authority, religious teaching, education, reading."[6] Other experiences, however personal and intimate, are no less cultural in their nature and their implications. This explains why Freud saw no essential difference between individual and social psychology.

Still, behind each of my psychological and historical generalizations there must stand the veritable and only center of experience: the person. It is to dramatize this conviction that I am prefacing each of these volumes with an analytical biography: I want to recall, with no pretense of imitating, Sigmund Freud's classic case histories which are, in the best sense of that word, histories. These psychological and social portraits are not perfect mirrors of, but eloquent clues to, culture. They lead to that vast, intricate mosaic, the bourgeois experience of the nineteenth century, that I propose to recover, reconstruct, and recount.

6. *Das Ich und das Es* (1923), *St.A.*, III, 302; *The Ego and the Id*, *S.E.*, XIX, 34.

✎ ONE ✎

The Strain of Definition

A WORRYING though often barely visible ingredient in the experience of the nineteenth-century bourgeoisie was anxiety over its very definition: its internal rank orders, its status in society, its relation to other classes, its political future, its moral character. "I appeal to the middle classes," Thackeray wrote in *Vanity Fair*.[1] But while both he and his readers thought the meaning of the appeal perfectly clear, neither could be quite sure. Much was in doubt: ideals, prospects, the meaning of terms not least of all. The shapes of the social pyramids which furnished grounds for aspirations and condescension were partially obscured by subtle social distinctions and conflicting claims, their upper and lower boundaries often lost behind the mists of desperate struggles to join, or leave, or rise within, the bourgeoisie. And the legends burdening the history of the middle classes, coupled with the long-standing debate over their reputation, helped to generate, in the midst of heady advances and sober optimism, an uncertain sense of identity, often verging on self-hatred. A capacious and persecuting bourgeois conscience bedeviled many in the nineteenth century, and would, in the twentieth, exacerbate historians' efforts at retrospective map-making.

But myths, contradictions, neurotic distortions often hold the key to historical realities. They will, in fact, prove essential elements in any meaningful definition of the nineteenth-century middle classes. I think of these classes as a family of desires and anxieties. Much else served to give them an appearance of coherence and unity that was only in part

1. End of ch. 9, in *The Works of William Makepeace Thackeray*, Centenary Biographical Edition, 26 vols. (1910–11), I, 104.

17

factitious: converging interests, political pressures, legal classifications, shared perceptions. But they were an extended family, ramified and quarrelsome. The bonds that held them together were often weaker than the strains that kept them apart. And the most telling symptoms of these strains are their names.

1. From Names to Things

The confusions infecting the vocabulary of nineteenth-century class did not escape its contemporaries. In 1893, the American scholar Charles K. Needham, translating a German physician's pamphlet against licensed prostitution, came upon the word *Bürger* and paused for some reflections. "The full meaning of this word," he said in a ruminative footnote, "can not be translated by the phrase *middle class*, altho' I have occasionally done so in previous pages. The conditions of life in England and America are different from those in Germany, so that there is nothing in English to convey the meaning in one word."[2] Needham was shrewd enough to see that these linguistic difficulties disclosed difficulties of substance. German terminology certainly recognized them: it differentiated, subtly but plainly, between *Bürgertum* and the fashionable import "bourgeoisie." When Thomas Mann, as late as 1918, praised the *Bürger* and denigrated the bourgeois, he was working in a rhetorical tradition at least a century old. Moreover, *Bürger* was at once a legal and a social label: it designated the citizen of a state or the member of a class, an ambiguity that German writers did not fail to exploit. Again, Germans used not only *Bürgertum* but *Mittelstand* as well, and the curious linguistic history of that name offers added evidence that instability of usage in the nineteenth century often bespoke instability in society and a measure of nervousness.

Early in the century, Goethe, Hegel, and their contemporaries saw the *Mittelstand* as respectable and prosperous, comprising in its upper reaches higher public servants and other educated men; by mid-century, the term designated small merchants and manufacturers. In the 1870s, with the founding of the new Reich and the turbulence of unbuttoned, often ruinous speculation, *Mittelstand* was demoted into a synonym for petty bourgeois, for shopkeepers trying to keep above the waters of bankruptcy and clerks crowding into the dismal jobs that new industrial and commercial empires were opening up to them. Most in both groups had every

2. Handwritten translation dating from 1893 of Dr. Theodor G. Kornig, *Die Hygiene der Keuschheit* (1890; 2nd ed., 1891), 166–67n. Zeta Collection, Yale Sterling Library.

cause to be gloomy about their social opportunities and their economic future. Economists began to distinguish between an old and a new *Mittelstand*, worrying about the decay of the first and the shabbiness of the second. And so, by the 1890s the name had come to stand for a social sector in persistent trouble, a problem in search of a policy.[3] The career of this name, with its irresistible downward propulsion, documents serious strains within the German bourgeoisie itself.

The English middling orders, for their part, were strikingly reluctant to separate themselves out by distinctive, aggressive class names. While the word "bourgeoisie" had been available to them since the late seventeenth century, they refused to naturalize it and preferred the native "middle class" or rather, with grave and sensible respect for pluralism, "middle classes." It was apparently quite acceptable for English writers to call the German middle classes "bourgeois"; George Eliot did so in 1856. But as late as 1873, J. A. Symonds noted that the adjective "bourgeois" was "a modern phrase." It was only cosmopolitan worldlings or those in search of a faintly denigrating label who would easily resort to this French loan word. "The great superiority of France over England," wrote Oscar Wilde in one of his scintillating, misleading epigrams, "is that in France every bourgeois wants to be an artist, whereas in England every artist wants to be a bourgeois."[4] And, recording in her diary in early 1890 that she had invited "Sidney Webb the socialist" to dine at her house, Beatrice Potter, soon to become Beatrice Webb, noted that he was "a remarkable little man," who was "somewhat unkempt, [with] spectacles and a bourgeois black coat shiny with wear."[5] Most of her compatriots had preferred the other names that had a more domestic ring: in 1834, John Stuart Mill could call the "three classes" dividing up English society "landlords, capitalists and labourers."[6]

This reluctance cannot be dismissed as linguistic chauvinism. It was the Marxists, after all, beginning in the mid-1840s with Engels's *Condition of the Working Class in England*, who made "bourgeois," if not their monopoly, certainly a distinctive habit of socialist discourse. It became, for the politically active, something of a polemical term: William Morris could recall the years of his youth as "a dull time oppressed with

3. Heinrich August Winkler, *Mittelstand, Demokratie, und Nationalsozialismus* (1972), 21–26.

4. Roger B. Henkle, *Comedy and Culture: England 1820–1900* (1980), 3.

5. Jeanne MacKenzie, *A Victorian Courtship: The Story of Beatrice Potter and Sidney Webb* (1979), 69.

6. Asa Briggs, "The Language of 'Class' in Early Nineteenth-Century England," in Briggs and John Saville, eds., *Essays in Labour History* (1967), 43.

bourgeoisdom and philistinism.''[7] Not even the presumably innocuous
choice of referring to the highly stratified middling regions of society
in the singular or the plural could escape political implications: assertive
Liberals like Richard Cobden emphatically employed "middle class" to
advertise their appeal for unity and their expectation of power.[8] The
language used to characterize that ill-defined, perhaps undefinable terri-
tory occupied by the middling orders was almost never wholly innocent,
almost never wholly unpolitical.

The Babel of definitions does not end here. The very profusion of
comprehensive descriptive labels like "bourgeois," *Bürger*, or "middle
class" exhibits the variety of social types gathered under these copious
umbrellas. Some historians, distinctly uncomfortable with such capaciousness, have separated out the great capitalists, whether patrician or
plutocrat, who hobnobbed with the nobility, and the poorest master
artisans, who lived no better than laborers, from the bourgeoisie, either
placing them into special categories of their own or assimilating them to
their neighbors. Others have taken the escape route of classifying as
middle class all those not laborers or peasants or aristocrats. They have
some legal warrant for their drastic simplifications: the Prussian *Landrecht*
gathered into the "bourgeois estate" (*Bürgerstand*) all those who "by
birth, can be counted neither among the nobility nor the peasant estate,
and were not later incorporated into either of these."[9] Yet the splendid
clarity of the Prussian code, summary and psychologically imprecise,
was not available in other countries, where historians felt compelled to
resort to economic or social criteria instead.

To compound these confusions further still: in the mid-nineteenth
century, Parisian proletarians used *bourgeoise* to designate respectable,
sober working-class housewives whose husbands were afraid of them.[10]
And landowners without noble titles proved no less difficult to place:
whether engaged in business, serving as magistrates in town, or living off
their rural investments, they had continuous, close dealings with urban
affairs and access to political power. These landlords—particularly
numerous and influential in France and Prussia, at least to the middle of
the century—fit the stereotype of the bourgeois least smoothly. "No one
wants to live in the countryside on his land," as the comte de Villèle,

7. Morris to Fred Henderson, alderman of Norwich, October 19, 1885, E. P.
Thompson, *William Morris: Romantic to Revolutionary* (1955), 878.

8. Briggs, "Language of 'Class,' " 59.

9. *Allgemeines Landrecht für die Preussischen Staaten von 1794*, ed. Hans Hatten-
hauer (1970), part II, title 8, page 452.

10. Denis Poulot, *Le Sublime, ou le travailleur comme il est en 1870, et ce qu'il
peut être* (1870; ed. 1980), 36.

brilliant financier and France's prime minister late in the Restoration, put it. "All our *gentilshommes* are turning themselves into bourgeois by spending six or nine months in town to enjoy social life, comforts, and the facilities to raise and place their children."[11] For most observers, a bourgeois was an urban animal. But non-noble landlords displayed enough of the characteristics normally associated with the bourgeoisie to be sometimes grouped with manufacturers and professional men.

Acknowledging such intricacies, contemporaries enlisted descriptive adjectives to mark subdivisions and trace movements: *haute, bonne, petite bourgeoisie*, upper and lower middle class. Yet even these, though helpful, proved too coarse a sieve to capture all the subtle distinctions and sweltering conflicts that pervaded middle classes everywhere, providing impulses for restlessness and change. In the mid-1830s, Michel Chevalier, traveler, observer, a lesser Tocqueville, later to become a distinguished French public official, published a book of reflections on the United States in which he compared American institutions with those of his own country. In America, he noted, the middle class was a coherent and comprehensive entity, consisting of "manufacturers, merchants, lawyers, physicians," as well as "a small number of cultivators and persons devoted to letters or the fine arts." In France, on the other hand, the "numerous middle class" was sharply divided between "the active class," engaged "in commerce, manufactures, agriculture and the liberal professions," and the "idle" bourgeoisie, "which consists of men without active employment, landholders who derive an income of $500 or $1,500 from their estates by rents or by sharing the produce with the cultivator without attempting to increase it." These two "divisions" of the middle class, Chevalier thought, "differ essentially from each other," even though, as he added on the next page, with scant regard for consistency, they "are not wholly and sharply separated from each other."[12] Plainly, defining and placing the middle classes was a task to daunt the most astute and confident of commentators.

Sometime near the end of the 1860s, Emile Zola, ever imaginative and often malicious, tried his hand at refining current vague and gross characterizations of the bourgeoisie by dividing French society into five worlds: *peuple*, among whom he included workers and soldiers; *commerçants*, described as "speculators on the demolitions" in Paris, industrialists and well-to-do tradesmen, "women of intrigue" and department

11. Robert Forster, "The Survival of the Nobility During the French Revolution," *Past and Present*, No. 37 (July 1967), 84.

12. Michael Chevalier, *Society, Manners, and Politics in the United States: Letters on North America* (3rd. enlarged ed., 1838), ed. John William Ward (1961), 380–83.

store owners; *bourgeoisie*, which he tersely defined as "sons of parvenus"; *grand monde*, which consisted of politicians and influential public officials; and *un monde à part*, consisting of whores, murderers, priests, and artists.[13] This is amusing and even penetrating, but it only reveals the general embarrassment with the definition of the middle orders. The upper middle class, for one, was never wholly coherent, rarely presented a united front; the personages Zola defined as *commerçants*, *bourgeoisie*, and *grand monde* often had conflicting if overlapping aims and values. Well-connected lawyers and higher civil servants, prominent clerics and distinguished physicians, often deserted one stratum of middle-class life for another. The Germans, in response to such facts of social life, enriched their sociological vocabulary by finding names for groups claiming consideration on grounds of property or educational attainments: they spoke of *Besitzbürgertum* and *Bildungsbürgertum*, both suggestive if still overly capacious categories. In particular *Bildung*, the secure possession of high culture, or, at times, its suave display, provided the educated middle classes with claims to status, even to authority. To know classical texts, to quote liberally from German literature, to show a cultivated interest in the arts and music allowed *Bürger* to temper their old servile adoration of the titled.[14] It was an impressive demonstration of the prestige *Bildung* could provide that many German aristocrats, in Prussia and in other states, should prudently equip their sons with a quantity, or at least the marks, of higher education—as if they were good bourgeois.

Government officials presented another acute problem, both for themselves and for social definition. The position of German civil servants, for one, the *Beamten*, especially in the higher reaches, was curiously ambiguous. And since in the German states, university professors or conductors of court orchestras were public officials as well, they, too, occupied a rather peculiar status. By the nineteenth century, their awkward posture had become something of a German tradition,[15] clearly perceived by Prussia's bureaucrats themselves: in his memoirs, Rudolf

13. Colette Becker, "Preface" to Zola, *Au bonheur des dames* (1883; ed. 1971), 14.
14. See John R. Gillis, *The Prussian Bureaucracy in Crisis, 1840–1860* (1971), 11. The same held true of France; see Theodore Zeldin, *France, 1848–1945*, 2 vols. (1973–1977), vol. I, *Ambition, Love and Politics*, part I, *passim*.
15. Speaking of the code that Frederick the Great had promulgated in the previous century, Alexis de Tocqueville noted that "between the noble and the burgher, an intermediate class, consisting of high functionaries who are not noble, ecclesiastics, and professors of learned schools, gymnasia, and universities, is placed." This was a true intermediate class, no longer quite bourgeois but not yet noble, and far from easy with its status. *The Old Regime and the Revolution* (1856; tr. Stuart Gilbert, 1955), 229.

von Delbrück, aristocrat and civil servant in Berlin, recalled that "bureaucratic circles, finding themselves between the tightly closed court society on one hand and the bourgeois community on the other, led a life of their own."[16] Elsewhere, in Belgium or in France, this kind of isolation seems to have been somewhat less sharp, the alienation of functionaries from middle-class life less complete, than in the German states. But it was there, and uncomfortable.

The same fluidity and, with that, controversy mark the conflict of claims to preeminence between competing bourgeois pyramids. Money gave power, and so did lineage, and the two did not necessarily coincide. They could be made to coincide, and often were: marriage negotiations between rich families and old families could take on the dimensions, and practically assume the importance, of diplomatic negotiations between states. There was some circulation within, as there was at the edges of, middle-class elites. Money could purify itself by marrying lineage, while lineage could replenish its coffers by marrying money. But such alliances were far from casual or easy: resistance to families in trade often frustrated matches that love, or sheer self-interest, would have dictated.

The few dependable studies of modern cities that have ventured to examine their social structure lend touches of specificity to these general observations. The struggles at the margins as well as within the middling orders were continuous, severe, and exhausting. In the German industrial town of Barmen, in 1861, the *Bürgertum*, ranging from men of economic power at one end to the embattled *Mittelstand* at the other, made up 9 percent of the population; forty-six years later, in 1907, that percentage had risen to over 23, though, not surprisingly, the most impressive gains had been scored near the bottom of the social scale. Even this fairly modest enlargement of middle-class cadres was far from universal: in the Ruhr town of Bochum, the numbers of middle-class *Bürger* increased, between 1858 and 1907, only slightly, from just over 13 to about 16.5 percent, with the real jump, as in Barmen, among the lowly ranks of civil servants and white-collar employees. Yet, even though they took their toll, such struggles could repay untold expenditures of energy and patience, despite galling and frequent setbacks. In Great Britain, the number of taxpayers assessed for £200 almost doubled in two decades, from slightly under 9,000 in 1851 to about 17,500 in 1871. This heady rate of growth held relatively steady until the assessment passed £800, when it markedly declined; the number of persons assessed for £2,000 and more rose, in the same span of time, from 235 to 356, or just over

16. Gillis, *Prussian Bureaucracy*, 33.

50 percent. While in mid-nineteenth-century Britain, the lower and, above all, the fairly affluent middle classes slightly closed the gap between themselves and their wealthier fellow bourgeois, the rich remained inaccessible, the source of envious fantasies.

Some segments of the middle classes enjoyed a prestige independent of their income. The liberal professions, notably the law, medicine, the church, and education, lifted their practitioners above the rank that mere money would have assigned to them. Their small numbers, and their self-perception as a corporate elite, protected their prestige from dilution: between 1851 and 1881, the proportion of lawyers in England and Wales slightly declined from four to three in a thousand, while physicians and clergymen retained their numbers, the former remaining at seven and the latter at four in a thousand; only educators, profiting from the recent diffusion of educational opportunities, rose from 1 to 1.6 percent. Money was far from irrelevant to these professional people: a struggling attorney, a penniless curate or teacher, was bound to have much trouble finding an eligible marriage partner. But their roads to advancement were at least not wholly blocked. In England, in Germany, and elsewhere, a diligent and alert young man could translate a university degree or a respectable diploma into a passport to preferment.

As the figures make painfully clear, bourgeois populations—high, middling, or low, active or idle, commercial or professional—swam in a sea of poverty. It is a crucial fact of nineteenth-century middle-class life, feeding their anxieties and shaping their consciences, that bourgeois were always, everywhere, even in commercial cities, in a minority. The middle classes made up in knowledge, power, and at times pretensions what they lacked in numbers. In nineteenth-century Bochum and Barmen, something like 10 or 12 percent could claim bourgeois status; in Paris, where at least two-thirds of the population were poor by any standard of measurement, perhaps 15 percent, if that many, could rightfully call themselves bourgeois. If, as some infatuated middle-class orators liked to say, the bourgeoisie was the nation, it was that only in a highly figurative sense.

But the most dramatic social aspect of the bourgeois experience in the nineteenth century was the economic, social, and political inequality that prevailed within the bourgeoisie itself; its hierarchical divisions were more telling than any class solidarity—except when outside pressures were brought to bear by a radicalized rural population or a militant labor movement. Whether *grand* or *petit*, old or new, bourgeois tried to live decently, educate their children, decorate their houses, and leave property. But the sources of their income, like its size, varied sharply. The distance between the top rung of the bourgeois ladder and its bottom rung was great, the ladder itself very steep and arduous to climb. If, in the Bochum of 1895, 93 percent of the population clustered at the lower end of the economic scale, earning 3,000 marks a year or less, often far less, they together accounted for only about two-thirds of the city's income. In pointed contrast, the elite of wealth in Bochum, about one in a hundred inhabitants, engrossed 15 percent of the whole. This meant that many bourgeois in that town crowded near the line that divides the merely impecunious from the downright poor, and that some of them crossed it. In Barmen, too, among those who were distinctly middle class, at least two-thirds were master artisans and salaried employees, struggling for the most part to make their way, while only a third were denominated "capitalists" and "merchants." And most merchants made modest incomes indeed.

Clerks, that rapidly swelling army of respectable and very badly paid bourgeois toiling for exporters, department stores, railway systems, and government offices were, by and large, even closer to the doom of sheer poverty than independent merchants. In England, after mid-century, a clerk in private industry might get his start at £70 a year and rise to perhaps £200 or, if he was capable or had social connections, to twice that amount. When, in September 1900, P. G. Wodehouse, the son of "reasonably solvent but certainly not wealthy parents," began to work in a London bank, his initial salary was £80 a year, a meager sum which his father supplemented with another £80 without thereby making young Wodehouse even mildly prosperous.[17] Government employees generally started at around £125 and might in the long run—the very long run—command over £1,000 a year, but those bureaucrats were rare, and their incomes distinguished. We know that the number of persons assessed at more than £2,000 amounted, in 1871, to a mere 356 in all of Great Britain, while the breathtaking stratosphere of taxpayers assessed at £5,000 and beyond was inhabited, in the same year, by a mere 80 individuals. This long stretch from £70 to £5,000 was a pressing, often oppressive reality in nineteenth-century middle-class culture, in Britain and elsewhere. In the Paris of 1817, more than half of all inhabitants paid rent at below 150 francs, and a quarter more paid between 150 and 400 francs. The large middling range (principally populated, near the bottom, by prosperous artisans) paying rent between 400 and 2,500 francs amounted to a fifth of the whole, while only 0.8 percent could afford more than 2,500 francs. Some among this handful

17. Benny Green, *P. G. Wodehouse: A Literary Biography* (1981), 11, 55.

of the rich, the narrow tip of the bourgeois pyramid, were very rich indeed. Like the Krupps, they could establish virtual dynasties and build castles; like the English merchant banker James Morrison, they could leave four million pounds to their heirs. These brewers, financiers, and munitions makers were the stuff of legend; to call these magnates "bourgeois" seems to make nonsense of the name.[18]

Nor is it easily rescued by a look at middle-class styles of conduct, most notably the pursuit of the finer things of life, which was marked by the most striking variations. Burghers living in court capitals depended on the taste and munificence of the ruling house. In contrast, burghers living in free cities or commercial capitals found themselves as active on the cultural as they were on the political front, achieving their aims almost exclusively through voluntary associations to which they devoted the same persistent energies they ordinarily devoted to making money. In nineteenth-century Munich, the theatre, the opera, the symphony orchestra, the museums, the university, were all the creations, and remained the creatures, of Wittelsbach largesse. Middle-class *Bürger* met in informal circles to read plays, exhibit paintings, and perform quartets. And they could, when they chose, exert pressure on the public servants who were in charge of high culture in Bavaria by lobbying for their tastes or displaying their preferences by crowding to some performances and staying away from others. But essentially, royal patrons set the tone and provided the means for all that was best in Munich's music, drama, art, and learning. Manchester provides a dramatic alternative. Its celebrated Hallé orchestra, its distinguished libraries, its university, conservatory, and art gallery were all private ventures drawing on private endowments. The blessings that royalty was asked to bestow would come later and were purely decorative. The conduct of middle-class citizens in search of high culture was not always wholly predictable: while Berlin was a royal and from 1871 an imperial capital, and while its magnificent museums were all built at the expense and on the orders of high Hohenzollern patrons, the splendid Berlin Philharmonic Orchestra, founded in 1882, was a private undertaking. There were Bavarians with initiative worthy of an Englishman, as there were Englishmen who would rather let the crown govern the arts, but on the whole the distinction

---

18. I have, in these paragraphs, principally drawn on Wolfgang Köllmann, *Sozialgeschichte der Stadt Barmen im 19. Jahrhundert* (1960), 94–131; David F. Crew, *Town in the Ruhr: A Social History of Bochum, 1860–1914* (1979), ch. 3, "Social Mobility"; W. D. Rubinstein, *Men of Property: The Very Wealthy in Britain since the Industrial Revolution* (1981), passim; Adeline Daumard, *Les Bourgeois de Paris au XIXe siècle* (1970), passim.

held: when the cornerstone was laid for the Alte Pinakothek in Munich, it was decorated with a copper plaque which listed the principal collections housed in the museum and gratefully concluded: "Bavaria owes the building and its art treasures to the noble disposition of its rulers, the House of Wittelsbach." A few years later, the founders of the Birmingham Art Gallery placed a memorial stone into the front hall of their museum which celebrated a very different bourgeois style, more laconically and more eloquently: "By the gains of Industry," read the inscription, "we promote Art."[19]

The middle classes, then, did not achieve unanimity even in their attitudes toward high culture. The bourgeois philistinism which furious commentators from Heinrich Heine to William Morris never tired of denouncing was certainly not so pervasive as they liked to think. But it was visible enough. Directors of opera houses complained that much of their public—including the educated public—obviously preferred the light diet of Johann Strauss to the heavier fare of Richard Wagner. This was true even in Munich, in the nineteenth century among the most dazzling capitals of music in Europe: prosperous *Bürger* were perfectly content with "musical-declamatory evening entertainments" consisting of frivolous popular duets, bravura pieces for solo instruments, and amusing recitations.[20] Henry James was not the only dedicated literary man to deplore the triviality of contemporary novels and the low level of reviewing which could hardly raise anyone above the popular taste for mere entertainment, with its melodramatic intrigues, psychological crudity, and predictable happy endings. And James was speaking not of the literate masses who had recently swelled the ranks of the reading public, but of middle-class readers, presumably educated consumers of the printed word.[21] He did not see, did not have the means to see, how much of this aggressive vulgarity was defensive, anxious self-protection against the stringent demands that serious high culture was prepared to make. While the coteries that sprang up late in the nineteenth century to cultivate avant-garde painting or esoteric poetry were exclusive by choice, they would have found it practically impossible to recruit new adherents to their circles, devoted as they were to the passionate pursuit of the difficult.

At the same time, apart from the favorite middle-class claim to

19. Peter Böttger, *Die Alte Pinakothek in München* (1972), 20; Asa Briggs, *The History of Birmingham*, vol. II, *Borough and City, 1865–1938* (1952), 100.

20. Heinrich Bihrle, *Die Musikalische Akademie München, 1811–1911* (1911), 28.

21. James, "Criticism" (1891), *Selected Literary Criticism*, ed. Morris Shapira (1963), 167–71.

respectability, the claim to cultivation is probably more characteristic of more bourgeois than any other of their cultural habits. Cultural critics, themselves as much a nineteenth-century phenomenon as the philistinism they were anatomizing, had an easy time scorning the pathetic mimicry of the lower middle classes, the anxious conformism of the better situated, the pretentious patronage of the rich. And, as I have already suggested, many bourgeois amassed attributes of cultivation not to flatter the eye, delight the ear, or move the soul, but to display, in the authentic manner of the parvenu, their recently acquired wealth and status. Charles Dickens's egregious Veneerings, in whose glittering, opulent house everything was "bran-new," everything was for show, were aptly caricatured types.

But while philistines and social climbers were, in the mobile and nervous nineteenth century, a palpable presence, there were many middle-class families that earnestly valued their cultivation. Few bourgeois households were complete without pictures on the wall, music in the parlor, classics in the glassed-in bookcase. Bourgeois, men and women, sang, sketched, faithfully attended concerts and literary readings, recited and even wrote poetry. Those splendid musical evenings in Vienna held at the hospitable house of the eminent German surgeon Theodor Billroth, who was himself an accomplished pianist and in whose drawing room much of Brahms's chamber music received its first performance, were exceptional only in their quality. And so the charge, however familiar, that these accomplishments were mere bait that young girls on the marriage market dangled before eligible bachelors was largely a canard. "To give an idea of the extent of dilettantism here," the Vienna correspondent of the *Leipziger Musikzeitung* wrote in 1808: "every cultivated girl, whether she is talented or not, must learn to play the piano, or to sing; first, it is the fashion, secondly it is the most convenient way of displaying oneself prettily in society and thus, if fortune smiles, to make a striking match."[22] Some decades later, this misogynistic joke had worn rather thin. Eligible middle-class girls were often talented and serious pianists. In 1884, the English periodical *Musical Opinion* reported that Germany could boast some 424 factories turning out about 73,000 pianos a year, and these pianos saw some serious action.[23] The middle classes' claim to cultivation, then, is a piquant and useful ingredient in a

22. Eduard Hanslick, *Geschichte des Konzertwesens in Wien*, 2 vols. (1869–70), I, 67.
23. E. D. Mackerness, *A Social History of English Music* (1964), 221.

possible definition of the bourgeoisie. However problematic, however mixed the motives of those making the claim, it was both widespread and largely authentic. And yet the ways of realizing it were distinctive and varied.

In this atmosphere of uncertainty and of a sprawling, uncontainable pluralism, hinting at clashes of political interests and irreconcilable social conflicts, it became, significantly enough, common practice to attach ingenious, picturesque, and, strictly speaking, illogical labels to important elements in the middle classes. Early in the July Monarchy, Stendhal set the pattern: "The banks," he wrote, "are masters of the state. The bourgeois has replaced the Faubourg Saint-Germain, and the bank is the aristocracy of the bourgeois class." Again, in 1843, Otto Camphausen, a Prussian bureaucrat, noted that his state was ruled by career civil servants, "a sort of aristocracy of experts."[24] The epithet "finance aristocracy," half envious and half derisive, spread across Europe; in Germany *Geldaristokratie* and in France *l'aristocratie financière* entered current usage. And Germans would refer to impecunious clerks who normally earned less than skilled factory workers as "proletarians in stand-up collars"—*Stehkragenproletarier*. Later, that ingenious Marxist invention "labor aristocracy," applied to artisans relatively well paid and usually moderate in their politics, underscored the tendentious possibilities inherent in such imaginative nomenclature and illustrates, quite by the way, the problem of defining the middle classes with any precision. It is symptomatic that this deliberate linguistic confusion should survive into the twentieth century, even in the speech of eminent historians. "Whether we fly high or low," Johan Huizinga wrote in 1935, "we Dutchmen are all bourgeois—lawyer and poet, baron and laborer alike. Our national culture is bourgeois in every sense that you can legitimately attach to the word."[25] Nor should it surprise anyone that an English journal should call King Louis Philippe in 1849, the year after his abdication, "the huge mercantile monarch, the great chapman and dealer."[26] In defiance of logic and orderliness, "bourgeois" seemed at once too narrow and too broad a name to characterize the middle classes.

All these mixed epithets capture clusters of ambiguous self-perceptions and fervent, normally frustrated fantasies. Independent artisans, though

---

24. Roger Price, *The Second French Republic: A Social History* (1972), 42; Gillis, *Prussian Bureaucracy*, 22.

25. Joel Mokyr, *Industrialization in the Low Countries, 1795–1850* (1976), 83.

26. *British Quarterly Review*, February 1849, Douglas Johnson, *Guizot: Aspects of French History*, 1787–1874 (1963), 223–24.

almost destitute, could be fierce in the defense of their status.[27] For their part, rich industrialists would encounter stiff, humiliating resistance from aristocrats, often far less wealthy than they, to their campaigns for membership in exclusive regiments or for coveted decorations and honorific titles. But many of them (though by no means all), no less desperate in their way than the lowly office clerk or half-starving craftsman, maneuvered to climb the pyramid of prestige.

These groups, to be sure, poised precariously at the edges of their class, were exceptionally susceptible to ambiguous destinies. But the very core of the bourgeoisie—the substantial burgher, whether factory owner, educated housewife, prosperous merchant, middling bureaucrat, distinguished physician or professor—was itself less than solid. General medical practitioners were at odds with surgeons and specialists. Academics wedded to the classical curriculum battled for scarce funds with innovating scientists. Merchants pushed for free trade while manufacturers lobbied for protection. Old money looked down on new money, genteel poverty on parvenu wealth. English merchants proclaimed their undying loyalty to their monarch no less fervently than did Russian merchants, but with the Russians this made part of their repertoire of servility, while among the English it was a cheerful tribute freely bestowed by self-respecting men. These conflicts, and others, often eclipsed bourgeois collaborations and alliances.

Nor can we count on even that old stand-by, the bourgeois character, to ease our way into a usable definition. For the implacable avant-garde, the matter was easy. Praising the deft and malicious caricatures with which Henry Monnier, the popular actor and cartoonist, satirized hapless French middle-class types, Théophile Gautier found them impressively lifelike: "His bourgeois characters—and no one has painted them more truly—bore you like actual bourgeois by endless floods of clichés and solemn asininities. This is no longer comedy; it is stenography."[28] Tenacious, orderly, prudent—later, cocktail party psychoanalysts would call him the anal character par excellence—the bourgeois was above all

27. The prominent German pedagogue and historian of Berlin Karl Friedrich von Klöden recalled many years later that when he came to work for his uncle, a goldsmith with a miserable workshop and no apprentices, he aroused the wrath of his aunt and her mother by referring to "the handicraft of the goldsmith." The women, he remembered, "bridled as though they had been stung by a wasp. It was no handicraft, they said, but an 'art' or a 'calling.'" Max Jähns, ed., *Jugenderinnerungen Karl Friedrich von Klödens* (1874), 174.

28. Donald Fanger, *Dostoevsky and Romantic Realism: A Study of Dostoevsky in Relation to Balzac, Dickens, and Gogol* (1965), 279.

boring. He was, or aspired to become, the rentier. But other critics of the middle classes gave them a very different character. In 1889, the influential Danish literary critic and biographer Georg Brandes denounced the bourgeoisie of his time as "the ruling Caliban," who had "inherited the characteristic defect of the old aristocracy, arrogance."[29] His bourgeois was the materialistic and hypocritical exploiter. And indeed, there was no single typical bourgeois: the unscrupulous entrepreneur or ingenious engineer stood model for him quite as much as the timid grocer or the pedantic bureaucrat. Daring was no less a bourgeois trait than caution. What nineteenth-century bourgeois had in common was the negative quality of being neither aristocrats nor laborers, and of being uneasy in their middle-class skins. But what divided them was almost as important, and a source of real strain. Those who, in the nineteenth century, undertook to characterize the bourgeois—and nearly everyone did—knew less than they thought they knew.

2. Tempting Simplicities

The need to live by secure, sharply etched classifications is buried deep in the human mind and one of its earliest demands; simplicity allays anxieties by defeating discriminations. Real situations are rarely clear-cut, real feelings often nests of ambivalence. This is something the adult learns to recognize and to tolerate, if he is fortunate; it is a strenuous insight from which he will regress at the first opportunity. That is why the liberal temper, which taught men to live with uncertainties and ambiguities, the most triumphant achievement of nineteenth-century culture, was so vulnerable to the assaults of cruder views of the world, to bigotry, chauvinism, and other coarse and simplistic classifications. "Every society," wrote Friedrich Nietzsche in one of his most brilliant aphorisms, "has the tendency to degrade and, as it were, to starve out, its adversaries—at least in its perception." The criminal, he thought, was one victim of such a regressive process; so was the Jew. And "among artists, the 'philistine and bourgeois' becomes a caricature."[30] And artists, the avant-gardes, Nietzsche might have added, only set the tone for the wider culture. Class consciousness, which emerged fitfully and then more

29. Henry J. Gibbons, "Georg Brandes: The Making of an Aristocratic Radical" (Yale Ph.D. diss., 1979), 203.

30. "Aus dem Nachlass der achtziger Jahre," *Werke*, ed. Karl Schlechta, 5 vols. (1972), IV, 188.

and more aggressively toward the end of the eighteenth and in the early nineteenth century, enshrined such a caricature: a mixture of social realities and unconscious needs.

Superbly disregarding all complicating evidence, dismissing all doubts, and employing what they thought objective indicators and subjective impressions, all equally problematic, nineteenth-century journalists, politicians, and novelists spoke and wrote as though the bourgeoisie were a solid, single, definable, and immensely important social entity. Their definitions defied such inconvenient facts as that the Nonconformist conscience in England tended to produce bourgeois of one sort and the Roman Catholic conscience in Tuscany bourgeois of another; or that upper-middle-class families in Lille arranged their daughters' marriages while equally respectable families in Washington, D.C., let their daughters marry for love; or that some bourgeois took the industrialist as the modern ideal while others derided him as a coarse upstart.

But everyone, or nearly everyone, used the language of class with abandon. In her authoritative study of the Parisian bourgeoisie in the first half of the nineteenth century, Adeline Daumard tells an amusing anecdote that demonstrates how such language imposed itself even on those who most fiercely denied its utility. Addressing the Chamber of Deputies in 1847, Garnier-Pagès argued that "there are no classes in our country any more" and denounced Guizot for his "detestable" theory that there are "different classes, the bourgeoisie and the poor." Then he continued, innocently, "I see many bourgeois here." There was laughter in the house.[31] The pressure of this vocabulary was apparently irresistible.

Poets and novelists were no less unequivocal in their choice of words. Heinrich Heine, in his late essay "Lutezia," derided the "new philistine world" he saw all about him as an "industrial, bourgeois age"; Henry James spoke freely of "large, fat bourgeois sofas"; Marcel Proust had his dandified Bloch renounce the watch and the umbrella as "insipid bourgeois implements."[32] It may be inconvenient that, taken together, all these applications of the charged adjective do not add up to a coherent portrait; they do not characterize, or lampoon, quite the same traits. Yet this seemed to disturb no one. Henry James, we know, chose his words with the utmost care; so did Heinrich Heine and Marcel Proust or, for that matter, Alexis de Tocqueville. Others, less fastidious, were more

31. Daumard, *Les Bourgeois de Paris*, 5.

32. Jeffrey L. Sammons, *Heinrich Heine: A Modern Biography* (1979), 324; Leon Edel, *Henry James: The Middle Years, 1882–1892* (1962), 160; Marcel Proust, *Du côté de chez Swann*, in *A la recherche du temps perdu*, ed. Pierre Clarac and André Ferré, 3 vols. (1954), I, 92.

oceanic in their epithets. Yet none had any trouble making himself understood. One could *see* the bourgeois deputies in the French Chamber, the
fat bourgeois sofas, the insipid bourgeois umbrellas, and attach clear
meanings to them, with sharp outlines.

And had the bourgeois not been highly visible for centuries? One way
that students of the bourgeois have taken toward defining him has been
to trace his history. It seems a most reasonable proceeding, particularly
since nineteenth-century evocations and characterizations of the bourgeois
seemed to have little in common beyond asserting that he had indeed
formed a class. But it has problems of its own. For what historians have
done with the bourgeois past, both recent and remote, has been to
elaborate the most persuasive and most durable of folk-tales, that of
the rising bourgeoisie. The spectacle of a class of assertive, low-minded,
shamelessly mercantile burghers elbowing others aside and pushing their
way up the ladder of wealth and power through the centuries must be
the most popular historical explanation ever invented. It has shortened
many inquiries and simplified many answers. What has made it particularly seductive is that it is not wholly false. But, adaptable, beautifully
vague, it has been pressed into service to account for the sweep of six
centuries of Western history and more: the emergence of the medieval
town, the birth of capitalism, the Protestant Reformation, the European
expansion overseas, the consolidation of absolute states, the English Civil
War, the breathtaking career of scientific thought, and, of course, the
eighteenth-century Enlightenment. As for the nineteenth century (to
pursue this acrobat among explanations to its most recent and most death-
defying feats), the bourgeoisie has been credited, or saddled, with the
Industrial Revolution, the political revolutions that inundated Europe
from 1789 onward, the rise of mediocre taste, and modern imperialism.
Those overpowering nineteenth-century realities: urbanization, industrialization, mechanization—all revolutions less dramatic but also less
ephemeral than the barricades built by workers and the constitutions
scribbled by politicians—were, we are told, the handiwork, and naturally
improved the position, of the middle class. It is no accident that Charles
Morazé's widely read survey of the nineteenth century should have been
titled *The Triumph of the Bourgeoisie*.[33] It could hardly have been
called anything else.

This triumph, the folk-tale suggests, was not confined to political or
economic spheres. The conquering bourgeois seemed as irresistible in
the realms of taste and ideas as in the legislature and on the stock ex-

33. *Les Bourgeois conquérants* (1957; English tr., 1966).

change. He impressed his way of thinking and feeling on the classes above and below him. In this account, that a reigning monarch, Queen Victoria, should have given the nineteenth century its name only proves how decisively the bourgeois had established his supremacy; she was, after all, as some of her contemporaries derisively or affectionately said, the greatest bourgeoise of them all. Until challenged by the radical movements of the late nineteenth century, the bourgeoisie had things its own way. The French Revolution and its offshoots elsewhere, we are told, provided immense, seemingly irreversible benefits to bourgeois forces in country after country; the Revolution of 1830 brought to the French throne that supreme bourgeois, Louis Philippe, complete with umbrella; the great Reform Act of 1832 secured political primacy for the English middle class. Later, we are told further, the bourgeoisie elsewhere completed its climb to positions of decisive influence, for all the temporary setbacks it experienced after the timid and mismanaged revolutions of 1848. Did not the very failures of 1848 provide evidence for the dizzying distance that the middle orders had come? Did their precipitous and anxious retreat in late 1848 and 1849 not provide a sardonic commentary on their stake in society? From having been, only half a century before, the party of movement, did the bourgeoisie not now turn into a party of order? And not long after, did not its interrupted ascent to the summit continue? In such appraisals, nineteenth-century observers anticipated and fed the verdict of later historians that the bourgeoisie had ever advanced and ultimately triumphed. "Today," Michel Chevalier summed it all up in the late 1830s, "it is universally recognized that the middle class rules in France."[34] In short, for a hundred and fifty years we have been told that the nineteenth century was the century of the bourgeoisie. No one could doubt it.

Or almost no one. Skeptical historians have been laboring, mainly in specialized monographs, to modify this sweeping verdict; a few have attempted to set it aside altogether. They have argued that it explains too much, and hence very little. They have questioned the description of the bourgeoisie as politically supreme in England after 1832, and argued that in Germany it was never dominant, whether in politics or in society, at all. They have even thrown doubts on the attractive and amusing description of Louis Philippe as a bourgeois king. Indeed, Friedrich Engels who, with his friend Karl Marx, was among the first to inflict the label of "bourgeois century" on his age, could near the end of his life take some distance from one of his own favorite formulations. In 1845,

34. Chevalier, *Society, Manners, and Politics in the United States*, 382.

he had asserted flatly that the "ruling class is, in England, as in all other civilized countries, the bourgeoisie." But in 1892, he wrote: "In England, the bourgeoisie never held undivided sway. Even the victory of 1832 left the landed aristocracy in almost exclusive possession of all the leading government offices. The meekness with which the wealthy middle class submitted to this" was, Engels confessed, "inconceivable to me."[35] His belated reversal has been consolidated in recent historical scholarship. But the notion that the nineteenth century was the century of the bourgeoisie, and much the worse for being so, continues to be a staple of accepted wisdom, indispensable to twentieth-century pieties about our recent past.

3. A Battle of Perceptions

All these efforts at definition amount to a battle of perceptions. But not all views have had equal representation. To judge by the current repute of the nineteenth-century middle classes, it seems that the most telling contemporary descriptions and later appraisals were written by its critics. Their often venomous though highly persuasive caricatures have become practically canonical—practically but not wholly so, for self-serving and self-confident bourgeois self-portraits were far from rare in their time and have not lacked some posthumous support.

Heinrich Heine, that fertile inventor of metaphors, demonstrates how imaginative, how funny, and how deadly the anti-bourgeois caricature could be. Walking through the Salon of 1843 in Paris, he noted with some disgust that whatever the ostensible subject of the pictures, each was dominated by the modern bourgeois spirit, the spirit of selfishness and greed. Most of the portraits, he wrote, "have such a pecuniary, egotistical, ill-tempered expression!" Even a painting of Christ being scourged awakened, in Heine, distasteful commercial associations; the Christ reminded him of the "director of a bankrupt corporation." And the historical paintings, grandiose though their announced theme might be, recalled "small retail stores, speculations on the stock exchange, mercantile values, bourgeois philistinism."[36]

Like other unfriendly commentators on what they thought the dismal bourgeois age, Heine considered those he derided as the masters of the

35. *The Condition of the Working Class in England in 1844* (1845; tr. Florence K. Wischnewetzky, 1885, ed. 1892), 95n; "On Historical Materialism," in Marx and Engels, *Basic Writings on Politics and Philosophy*, ed. Lewis S. Feuer (1959), 63.

36. *Henrich Heines Sämtliche Werke*, ed. Ernst Elster, 7 vols., (1887–90), VI, 392–93. Heine's word is *Spiessbürgerlichkeit*.

modern world the source of infinite boredom, a relatively innocuous-sounding term which, behind its overt meaning of tedium, concealed a good portion of sheer rage. Each critic had his favorite instance of the boring bourgeoisie: Stendhal despised all provincials; Flaubert, nearly all Frenchmen. Heine, for his part, detested the English middle classes who were, he thought, the very embodiment of vulgar materialism and egotistical piety. The disciple of Stendhal in this as in so much else, Heine mourned, with Napoleon's death, the age of true heroes; modern bourgeois, he wrote, admire "quite other heroes, like the virtuous Lafayette or James Watt, the cotton spinner."[37] Even more vehement than Heine, Gustave Flaubert had a consuming contempt for the bourgeoisie that amounted to a neurotic aversion: finding the bourgeois literally nauseating, he once signed a letter "bourgeoisophobus." It was a phobia he wanted taken seriously. Others happily joined Flaubert in the good fight, including that brash and gifted young Russian diarist, Marie Bashkirtseff who, irritated by Emile Zola's silent rejection of her overtures, told him, correctly anticipating that he would continue to ignore her: "I don't suppose you will answer this: I'm told that in actual life you are a complete bourgeois."[38] It was intended, and certainly taken, as an insult.

One powerful reason why Flaubert's phobia persisted through the nineteenth century and would resonate among later historians was the avant-garde's seemingly irrefutable demonstration that the middle classes were unable to feel, or to give, love sincerely. This indictment amounts to the charge that in their crassness, their mechanical rationality, bourgeois converted all of life into merchandise, all of experience into the cool operations of adding and subtracting. Certainly, being human, the bourgeois—at least the male of this unfortunate species—craved sexual satisfaction, but he could not merge his sensuality with affection. The lavish praise of love pervading the poetry the bourgeois liked to read and the letters he liked to write was denigrated as sheer sentimentality, as a cover for emotional incapacity and the grossest lechery. From this perspective, the very idea of romantic love and the much-advertised irregular private lives of many artists in the nineteenth century were so many reproaches to that monument to insincerity, that bland and deceptive facade, bourgeois marriage. What Sigmund Freud would later

37. Sammons, *Heine*, 324. That James Watt was, of course, not a cotton spinner but the famous modernizer of the steam engine may indict Heine's grasp on facts, but it would not mitigate his visceral detestation of the middling orders.

38. Dormer Creston [pseud.], *Fountains of Youth: The Life of Marie Bashkirtseff* (1937), 285.

discover to be a pathological symptom common among men fixated on their mothers came to be the bourgeoisophobes' diagnosis of prevalent bourgeois attitudes: "where they love they do not desire, and where they desire they cannot love."[39] As they liked to tell it, middle-class husbands saw their wives as competent housekeepers, doting mothers, and erotic disasters. Gavarni, the celebrated French caricaturist and social commentator, would entertain his friends, including the Goncourt brothers, novelists and indefatigable diarists, with horrifying tales of pedantic bourgeois women he had seduced: they were, to hear him tell it, obsessed with rules, martyrs to punctuality. They would chide him for being five minutes late, and one bourgeoise once made an assignation with him "five months and one week from now."[40] In one of his early notebooks, Leopold von Ranke, speaking of love, put the matter rather less frivolously: "Every relationship that does not emerge from insight or love is sinful: for apart from these ideas, it can be based only on a common worldly purpose, a low bourgeois advantage."[41] The classic denunciations by Marx and Engels therefore found cordial echoes among many who were not Marxists: "The bourgeois sees in his wife a mere instrument of production," they wrote in the *Communist Manifesto*; indeed, "our bourgeois, not content with having the wives and daughters of their proletarians at their disposal, not to speak of common prostitutes, take the greatest pleasure in seducing each other's wives."[42] The bourgeoisie, in sum, was as unlovable as it was unloving.

The historian must treat such verdicts with the utmost reserve. Some of them were the projection of the critics' neuroses onto an admittedly vulnerable public target; it was all too tempting to despise what one could not attain and to saddle the bourgeois with wishes and qualities that one feared to find in oneself. Some were the paradoxical tributes to a liberal culture, hospitable to its most impassioned slanderers as no culture had ever been. And some simply echoed ancient assaults that had acquired plausibility through sheer repetition. The cold intensity and inventive vocabulary that Heine, Marx, and their fellows placed at the service of their rage and contempt, their virtual nausea at the very

39. Freud, "Beiträge zur Psychologie des Liebeslebens, II, Über die allgemeinste Erniedrigung des Liebeslebens" (1912), *St.A.*, V, 202; "On the Universal Tendency to Debasement in the Sphere of Love (Contributions to the Psychology of Love)," *S.E.*, XI, 183.

40. July 22, 1856, Edmond and Jules de Goncourt, *Journal; mémoires de la vie littéraire 1851-1896*, ed. Robert Ricatte, 22 vols. (1956-58), II, 21.

41. Ranke, *Tagebücher* [1814], ed. Walther Peter Fuchs (1964), 138.

42. *Manifesto of the Communist Party* (1848; tr. Samuel Moore, 1888, intr. A. J. P. Taylor, 1967), 101.

thought of the bourgeois, have never been surpassed and rarely been equaled. Yet they were not new; they were the climax to a very long and, by mid-nineteenth century, very rich tradition of disparagement. It dates back at least as far as Jesus who, the Scriptures report, drove the money changers and the pigeon sellers from the temple, and pronounced himself pessimistic about the chances of a rich man entering heaven. That pessimism did not abate in pagan Rome or the Christian Middle Ages and was rescued for modern times by the ambivalence of the Protestant Reformers. The emergence of the modern state and modern society gave bourgeois splendid channels for advancement in wealth and power, but derisive satire and angry, often envious denunciations followed them, as before.

Late in the eighteenth century, indicters of the bourgeoisie added new counts and spoke with new urgency. The rebellious poets of the Sturm und Drang, with the young Goethe of *Werther* at their head, energetically urged the proposition that the bourgeoisie was ignoble not merely in status but also in style. And romantics of many persuasions, in many countries, carried this message into the nineteenth century. E. T. A. Hoffmann dramatized it with his famous ironic reversal: he gave his readers to understand that his favorite character, the mad musician Kreisler, was saner by far than his mundane and mediocre fellow-citizens whose cherished mental balance really amounted to lack of spiritual refinement, a mortal failure of aesthetic perception. Art—painting, poetry, music above all—was a kind of sacred sickness, often unto death; the rosy good health and good conscience of the respectable *Bürger* were the stigmata of an invincible obtuseness. The early-nineteenth-century German states, like early-nineteenth-century France and other civilized societies, came to be crowded with young, self-appointed Kreislers, pale with the boredom that is rage, and defying the philistine with their paintings, their compositions, their verses, and their manifestos.

Much of this was a rebellious pose, the revolt of the young against fathers who had engrossed power in politics and influence in the arts. But whatever its origins, its manifestations were electrifying. They put the bourgeoisie on the defensive in the very decades hailed, or deplored, as the time of its greatest triumphs. Heine and Flaubert were unrepresentative only in their addiction to excess, their sheer eloquence. Others, only less extravagant and less imaginative, took leaves from their book. By 1857, then, when Flaubert published *Madame Bovary*, such opinions were far from rare. When he died in 1880, his private vendetta against the reigning philistinism was practically a mass movement. The happy few, that cultural elite of which Stendhal had dreamed in the 1830s, had grown, half a century later, into many, though hardly happy. And while the most articulate crusaders were, by and large, French, Germans had been the pioneers, and Matthew Arnold's *Culture and Anarchy*, scarcely a neglected text, demonstrates that contempt for the middle-class philistine had, by the 1860s, reached England.

As the invective against the detestable philistine gained circulation, the epithet "bourgeois" lost most of its specificity. The enemies of light and beauty added up to all but a handful of select souls. "In speaking of the bourgeoisie," Friedrich Engels cautioned his readers in *The Condition of the Working Class in England in 1844*, "I include the so-called aristocracy."[43] Two decades later, in 1862, shortly after Flaubert had completed *Salammbô*, his strange, sanguinary novel about Carthage, he wrote to a friend expressing the hope that it would "annoy the bourgeois, that is to say, everybody."[44] But, polemical and partisan as the crusade was in its rhetoric, it was only too authentic in its sentiments. The crusaders saw themselves as forlorn champions of a vanishing culture which, they feared, was being swamped by a massive invasion of newly rich, politically powerful, aesthetically ignorant bankers and merchants and bureaucrats, with small traders and lowly clerks, if possible more vulgar than their betters, bringing up the bourgeois rear.

Yet with all their verve and their influence, the anti-bourgeois crusaders did not have a monopoly on public opinions about the middle classes. The age of Victoria did not want for genial observers, cheerfully celebrating what they perceived as impressive middle-class contributions to the progress of civilization. "The *Bürger* order," the influential conservative German cultural historian and sociologist Wilhelm Heinrich Riehl firmly said at mid-century, "has been, since the old days, the principal bearer of justified social movements, of social reform." And in Riehl's own time, he added confidently, the *Bürgertum* was "in possession of preponderant material and moral power. Our whole age bears a bourgeois character."[45] He spoke not without satisfaction, for he counted himself a *Bürger*.

This self-congratulatory perception was in a great tradition. For centuries, in proud city after proud city, middle-class magnates, presiding over trading enterprises, craft guilds, and family clans, had fostered the arts and supported the sciences. Merchant princes like the Medici, almost proverbial for their discriminating generosity to savants and poets, painters and sculptors, musicians and architects, had been merchants before

43. Engels, *Condition of the Working Class*, 276.
44. Philip Spencer, *Flaubert: A Biography* (1952), 160.
45. *Die bürgerliche Gesellschaft* (1851; 9th ed., 1897), 199.

they became princes. And what the high culture of Florence owed to its richest bourgeois, the high culture of other civilized centers—Bruges, Amsterdam, Nürnberg, Edinburgh—owed to their middle-class patriciate. The patricians who had dominated the great commercial cities of the early modern period, men who refused titles of nobility and found the vocation of trader not merely profitable but dignified, could not conceive of any reason why they should be embarrassed about their position in the world. We see them in the portraits, complete with the merchant's attributes—financial records, scales for weighing gold, money itself—in which painters like Hans Holbein the Younger excelled, and which lend immortality to an unapologetic, sturdy, wholly self-respecting social estate. And these middling orders found some persuasive and witty apologists: Addison in his *Spectator* and Voltaire in his famous letters on the English praised the peaceful, tolerant merchant precisely because he was untouched by the grandiloquent and destructive, essentially childish ideals of the aristocracy. Perhaps a little perversely, Addison and Voltaire even found something admirable in the stock market speculator.

More soberly, in societies where men of commerce gained great wealth and great reputations alike, middle-class ideologues took their order to be the very repository of civic virtue, destined to exercise power in the state and leadership in high culture. In the early years of the eighteenth century, Daniel Defoe proclaimed trade, in England, to be far from "inconsistent with a gentleman";[46] and this positive view found welcoming echoes in the nineteenth century. "The value of the middle classes of this country," wrote James Mill in 1826, "their growing number and importance, are acknowledged by all. These classes have long been spoken of, and not grudgingly, by their superiors themselves, as the glory of England." Four years later, in one of those inaccurate but impressive linguistic shifts I have noted before, the radical Lord Brougham confounded the English middling orders with the English nation itself. "By the people," he said, "I mean the middle classes, the wealth and intelligence of the country, the glory of the British name."[47] It is significant that Brougham, a peer of recent vintage, instead of seeking to conceal his middle-class origins, emphatically proclaimed their virtues. And bourgeois inclined to praise themselves less extravagantly than this still advanced the strongest possible claim to self-respect. Reflecting in 1885 on the character of "the lower strata of the German burgher estate,"

46. *The Complete English Tradesman* (1726), 376.
47. Both in Harold Perkin, *The Origins of Modern English Society, 1780–1880* (1969), 230.

the literary publicist Robert Prölss singled out their "honesty, perseverance, firmness, and strength of character."[48] Eight years later, Charles Needham defined the *Bürger* as a man with "some family pride in his ancestry without the feeling of exclusiveness belonging to the nobility." Whether his income be large or not, "he lives within his means" and is intent on maintaining, or if possible extending, "whatever marks of confidence and esteem are indirectly accorded to him" by his community. And this will hold true whether he is a "professional or mercantile" man, "an artist or an artificer, a banker or a manufacturer, an employee or an employer."[49]

It was perhaps inevitable that there were self-satisfied bourgeois in the decades after the French Revolution who would claim the century for their own. What many a disgruntled cultural critic detested as bourgeois vices, they hailed as bourgeois virtues: the drying up of the poetic vein as realism, the lack of exalted principle as practicality, the obsessive devotion to work as energy, the bovine conservatism of the prosperous as solidity. Even Marx and Engels, scarcely enamored of a class whose historic mission, they thought, was rapidly coming to an end, found expressive words of praise for it. "The bourgeoisie," they wrote in a famous paragraph in the *Communist Manifesto*, "has subjected the country to the rule of the towns. It has created enormous cities," it has "drawn all nations, even the most barbarian, into civilization," and thus "rescued a considerable part of the population from the idiocy of rural life."[50]

Their appreciation, stinted as it was, has not commanded general assent. One reason for this was the bourgeoisie's passion for self-criticism and for fostering a troop of unsparing social critics, nearly all drawn from its own ranks. "Balzac and his comrades," Henry James noted in a mordant diagnosis, hate the bourgeoisie "because they are almost always fugitives from the bourgeoisie. They have escaped with their lives, and once in the opposite camp they turn and shake their fists and hurl defiance."[51] Arthur Symons, Symbolist poet and critic, agreed. Considering the aesthetic rebels of the 1890s, he noted, with some disdain, "Nothing, not even conventional virtue, is so pro-

48. Prölss, "Zur 200-jährigen Geburtstagsfeier Georg Friedrich Händels," *Gartenlaube*, XXXIII, 7 (1885), 113.

49. Needham, handwritten translation of Kornig, *Hygiene der Keuschheit*, 167n.

50. *Manifesto*, 13.

51. "Honoré de Balzac," in James, *French Poets and Novelists* (1878; 2nd ed., 1884), 102–3.

vincial as conventional vice: and the desire to 'bewilder the middle
classes' is itself middle class."[52] Yet the historian in search of a definition
for nineteenth-century middle-class culture cannot overlook that this
furious hostility touched the realities of the time at many points. There
was, in important respects, something stifling about business civilization,
especially when heavily infused with evangelical fervor, something un-
congenial to elevated tastes, subtle discriminations, moral and artistic
freedom, let alone fine critical perceptions. The official art that continued
to garner prizes in the Salons across Europe, the pretentious interiors
of affluent German households in the early decades of the Empire, the
insensitive interference of censors with painting or poetry they judged
to be obscene or blasphemous—these and related cultural symptoms
strongly suggest that the travail of innovative spirits in literature, the
arts, and thought was by no means all self-imposed. The pain and rage
to which avant-garde writers and artists gave vent in their private letters,
their favorite cafes, and their ephemeral periodicals were something more
creditable than the posturing of aesthetes biting the hands that fed them,
infuriated only because they wanted to be fed still more. It was something
better, too, than the primitive need of the belligerent to divide the world
cleanly into friends and enemies. The range and rapidity of social change
threw up a very army of parvenus, most of them trembling with social
anxiety. In their bewilderment at finding themselves in the unfamiliar
country of high culture, they would with some notable exceptions cling
to the taste of generations just past and uphold traditional standards that
more secure consumers of culture had long since questioned and were
about to abandon. Art for the sake of self-display and of soothing reassurance dominated public exhibitions and private houses. What is more,
the mass production of cultural goods fostered by technical improvements in printing, photography, and, toward the end of the century, the
phonograph, raised alarming questions about the consequences of spreading culture across wider and wider populations. The acquisition by
bourgeois of new positions of power was rather less extensive and far
more nuanced than the legend has it, but it inevitably generated a certain
social and political defensiveness among the newcomers, which prominently included an obtuse, sometimes frantic, and normally self-serving
denial of social realities coupled with an equally obtuse, equally frantic
refusal to countenance aesthetic experimentation.

52. Holbrook Jackson, *The Eighteen Nineties: A Review of Art and Ideas at the
Close of the Nineteenth Century* (1913; ed. 1966), 134.

Nineteenth-century bourgeois, then, did much to deserve the criticisms lavished on them. And, as I have said, many bourgeois turned self-examination into self-laceration. They invited—virtually set the tone for—collective denunciations with an avidity that would have done honor to a tribe of masochists. No doubt, the nineteenth-century bourgeoisie produced some exquisite superegos. Though earnestly devoted to privacy, it would periodically indulge in well-publicized attacks of guilt feelings. "We— the middle classes I mean, not merely the rich—we have neglected you; instead of justice we have offered you charity, and instead of sympathy we have offered you hard and unreal advice." Thus Arnold Toynbee, addressing a working-class audience in 1883. "You have to forgive us," he continued, "for we have wronged you." He spoke at a time when "men of intellect and men of property," as Beatrice Webb was to recall later, acquired "a new consciousness of sin," a troubled awareness she described as "a collective or class consciousness."[53] George Bernard Shaw who, for his own reasons, did his best to fan such feelings, noted in 1912 that "the great conversions of the XIX century were not convictions of individual, but of social sin. The first half of the XIX century considered itself the greatest of all centuries. The second discovered that it was the wickedest of all the centuries."[54] Shaw, in his usual vein, overstated both halves of his proposition and deliberately slighted the coexistence of contradictory feelings in the early and the late years of the century alike. But his generalization, breezy and facile as it is, may serve as a reminder that the problems of defining the bourgeoisie was more than a question of accurate names, more than a task for sociological comparisons: it involved the problematic moral nature of bourgeois life itself. Perhaps the most severe hurdle impeding the enterprise of defining the nineteenth-century bourgeoisie is its troubled attempts at self-definition.

Despite all these obstructions to a definition at once comprehensive and differentiated enough, I am not suggesting that there is nothing to define. Coalescing under external pressure, the nineteenth-century bourgeoisie generated common styles of thinking about love and aggression. It was, without metaphysical implications, at once one and many. Shrewdly, Prince Metternich recognized this characteristic as early as 1820: "this intermediate class," the middle class, he wrote to Czar Alexander I, takes "all sorts of disguises, uniting and subdividing as occasion offers, helping

53. Peter d'Alroy Jones, *The Christian Socialist Revival, 1877–1914: Religion, Class, and Social Conscience in Late-Victorian England* (1968), 85–86n.
54. "Introduction" to Dickens, *Hard Times* (ed. 1912), in George H. Ford and Lauriat Lane, Jr., *The Dickens Critics* (1961), 126.

each other in the hour of danger, and the next day depriving each other of all their conquests."[55] Perhaps nineteenth-century English writers had the best of it: except in polemical or ironic moments, they clung, as I noted, to the term "middle classes," which deftly exhibits the invincible plurality within bourgeois culture coexisting with a measure of underlying unity.

55. "Confession of Faith: Metternich's Secret Memorandum to the Emperor Alexander" [December 15, 1820], *Memoirs of Prince Metternich, 1815–1829*, ed. Prince Richard Metternich, tr. Mrs. Alexander Napier, 5 vols. (1881), III, 468.

ꝥ TWO ꝥ

Architects and Martyrs of Change

1. The Sway of the New

The uncertainties besetting nineteenth-century bourgeois, which they bequeathed to their historians, were not confined to agonized questions about their duty to their inferiors or their reputation among poets and painters. More than any of its predecessors, their century was a time of unexampled hopes and unfamiliar anxieties. It was, as Gladstone said, "an agitated and expectant age."[1] For the poor, of course, it was more agitated than expectant; peasants and laborers, soldiers and sailors could testify that cruelty and callousness had not disappeared from the world. Extreme misery and noisome squalor continued to haunt untold thousands in the most advanced Western countries. Contemporaries saw this clearly; witness Goya's hair-raising *Disasters of War*, Florence Nightingale's appalling reports from the Crimean front, unvarnished official papers on the conditions of the laboring classes, or a walk through that oppressive, peculiarly modern horror, the industrial slum.

The bourgeois experience was, of course, by and large far more gratifying, at least on the surface. It is no accident that it was good bourgeois, conspicuous beneficiaries of early-nineteenth-century economic expansion and political upheavals, who pressed for further expansion, for more upheavals. The very language that Prince Metternich, troubled guardian of European traditions, chose in that famous secret appraisal of his time he submitted to Alexander I in December 1820, testifies to the dynamic energies at work in the bourgeoisie: he complained that "agitated classes" all across the Continent were subverting public order. The rapid "prog-

1. John Morley, *The Life of William Ewart Gladstone*, 3 vols. (1903), I, 4.

ress of the human mind" unaccompanied by equal progress in "wisdom" had led to the exercise of private judgment, and it was, he thought, "principally the middle class of society which this moral gangrene has affected." Those subversives, he noted, were led by such active bourgeois as "state officials, men of letters, lawyers, and the individuals charged with public education," all of them ridden, he feared, by "presumption."[2] In the course of the bourgeois century, this presumption was to be a prominent instrument for keeping the middle classes in motion. Only the shapers of change would have used a less invidious term: self-confidence. In ways unthinkable to most of their ancestors, those educated, or situated, to share in the enormous gains of capitalism found it possible to move from passivity to activity, to assert and, better, to exercise mastery over their world in exhilarating new ways. "Nobody who has paid any attention to the peculiar features of the present era," Prince Albert, addressing the Lord Mayor's banquet, said in 1850, "will doubt for a moment that we are living at a period of most wonderful transition, which tends rapidly to accomplish that great end, to which, indeed, all history points—the realization of the unity of mankind." Looking ahead to the forthcoming Great Exhibition, he told his listeners that "knowledge acquired becomes at once the property of the community at large," and so "man is approaching a more complete fulfillment of that great and sacred mission he has to perform in this world."[3] The Prince Consort's tone is a little self-satisfied, perhaps excessively hearty in its uncomplicated sunniness. But his message was not news to his listeners: it was a welcome commonplace, a representative view, sounding the dominant theme of the century. As E. B. Tylor, the pioneering cultural evolutionist, put it in 1867: "The history of man" is "the history of an upward development."[4] International fairs, like London's Great Exhibition of 1851, the mother of them all, were both documents and instruments of progress.[5]

2. "Confession of Faith: Metternich's Secret Memorandum to the Emperor Alexander" [December 15, 1820], *Memoirs of Prince Metternich, 1815–1829*, ed. Prince Richard Metternich, tr. Mrs. Alexander Napier, 5 vols. (1881), III, 458–67.

3. Nikolaus Pevsner, *High Victorian Design: A Study of the Exhibits of 1851* (1951), 16–17.

4. J. W. Burrow, *Evolution and Society: A Study in Victorian Social Theory* (1966), 248.

5. Not all of these, however, roused such optimism. Visiting Paris in the summer of 1889, the English jurist and positivist Frederick Harrison encountered a French friend who denounced the Exhibition celebrating the centennial of the French Revolution as a "wretched fair," as a "monster bazaar which the advertising shopmen have set up in the Champ de Mars as an imitation of the Empire in the race of vulgar display!" It struck him as no better than "a big tradesman's advertisement," which "all

Progress was not just a myth for the respectable. Political radicals, whether utopian or "scientific," clearly discerned the end of scarcity, which had been the source of the least appeasable social strife in the past. "We have measured the lands," as Heinrich Heine, animated by the persuasive verve of the Saint-Simonian dispensation, wrote in the mid-1830s, "weighed the forces of nature, reckoned the means of industry, and behold, we have found: that this earth can nourish us all decently if we all work and do not want to live at the cost of another."[6] If there was enough for everyone, the future could only be bright indeed, and its prospects were all implicit in the present. Change, for many, was not a threat but a promise.

I need hardly demonstrate that change is the law of life and that most ages are ages of transition. In the nineteenth century, though, the very nature of change underwent a change; it was more rapid and more irresistible than in the past. It was also strikingly uneven: advances in the natural sciences did not automatically generate improved medical treatment; the gathering of social information did not quickly eventuate in social reform. And time-honored social arrangements, like family life, were torn by the clash of new needs and old habits. Hence change in the nineteenth century was more often unsettling than exhilarating.

The age, I must say, was exceedingly sensitive and responsive to its supreme experiences; historians became the scientists of change from having been, by and large, its poets. And there was widespread agreement, even among those who deprecated his pessimism, with Carlyle's exclamation of 1829: "That great outward changes are in progress, can be doubtful to no one. The time is sick and out of joint."[7] Hence intelligent witnesses to their century would call it a time of transition without any sense of uttering a commonplace, convinced rather that they were stating a truth of some consequence, and distinguishing their age from its predecessors. John Stuart Mill spoke of his time, in 1831, as "an age of change," and, again, as "an age of transition." Three decades later, in 1860, Emile Zola informed a close friend that "our century is a century of transition."[8]

---

honest Republicans" see "with shame and indignation," while French workmen "regard it as the Golden Calf at whose shrine the *bourgeoisie* worship." "A Breakfast-Party in Paris," *The Nineteenth Century*, No. CL (August 1889), 173–74.

6. Jeffrey L. Sammons, *Heinrich Heine: A Modern Biography* (1980), 166.

7. "Signs of the Times," in *Latter-Day Pamphlets, Characteristics, etc.*, Library Edition (1885), 29.

8. Mill: *Essays on Politics and Culture*, ed. Gertrude Himmelfarb (1962), 3, 43; Zola: to his close friend Jean-Baptistin Baille, June 2, 1860. *Correspondance*, ed. B. H. Bakker, 3 vols. so far (1978–   ), I, 169.

And at the end of the nineteenth century, psychoanalysis, all its reputation to the contrary, though committed to the postulate of a fundamentally unchanging human nature, demonstrated that it, too, was hospitable to perceptions, and to the analysis, of change. The Oedipus complex, as Sigmund Freud recognized in the process of formulating it, had a history of its own, and it was a social history. Comparing Sophocles' *Oedipus Rex* and Shakespeare's *Hamlet*, Freud called attention to the "changed treatment of the same material" in the two tragedies; this underscored the "whole difference in the mental life of these two widely separated cultural epochs," a difference he interpreted as "the secular advance of repression in the emotional life of humanity."[9] In this recognition of change, psychoanalysis, subversive in so many other ways, was at one with its age.

Earlier, in the seventeenth and eighteenth centuries, traditional ways of thought had been stretched and bent, but innovative ideas in the social sciences had been fitted into inherited ways—with difficulty perhaps, but fitted none the less. One could, even in the eighteenth century, be a sound scientist and a good Christian at the same time, and while this dual allegiance remained a very lively possibility in the bourgeois century, it became harder and harder to sustain. Meanwhile the French and the industrial revolutions, accompanied and followed by no less consequential upheavals in the sciences of man, shook most structures of belief and authority and demolished some of them forever.

These great upheavals were looming presences in the minds of the nineteenth century, spawning hopeful dreams or nightmarish vistas, inviting optimists to predict the triumph of science, the liberation of women, or the renewal of culture and pessimists to foresee the ruin of religion, the subversion of family life, or the decay of order. For centuries, innovation had been feared in any form and had served as a term of vigorous disparagement; in the nineteenth century, it was elevated into an institution. In the time of the Reformation, Roman Catholics would taunt Protestant rebels with the rhetorical question, "Where was your church before Luther?" Later in the sixteenth century, English Puritans found themselves on the defensive for seeking "innovations in the state," while a century after that, Cotton Mather thundered against the founders of the new Brattle Street church in Boston as agents of "*Satan* beginning a terrible Shake" and as sinful "*Innovators*" making "a Day of *Temptation*" among the Massachusetts faithful. It was only after the men of the

9. *Die Traumdeutung* (1900), *St.A.*, II, 268; *The Interpretation of Dreams, S.E.*, IV, 264.

Enlightenment, with Locke in the vanguard, began to ask what rights the old had over the pressures of the new that innovation became, gradually, an acceptable idea.[10] The age of the fathers was yielding to the age of the sons. Movement became thinkable, commonplace.

Indeed movement in its most ordinary meaning was, in the nineteenth century, nothing less than spectacular. Migrants crossed frontiers, often oceans. During the decade of the 1820s, the United States received 150,000 immigrants; in the 1840s, the figure rose dramatically to 1.5 million. And during the 1880s, America absorbed the impressive—and to many, frightening—total of more than 5.2 million. Nor was the United States the only recipient of migrants: South America, eastern Russia, South Africa, Canada, Australasia were transformed by the swarms of newcomers. It has been estimated that between the early 1820s and the early 1920s, when restrictions choked off immigration into the United States and most other countries to a mere trickle, something like 62 million left Europe to settle abroad. While this vast *Völkerwanderung* was, of course, principally a migration of peasants, artisans, and laborers, many bourgeois too sought better lives elsewhere. Failed merchants, dissident political publicists, middle-class Jewish victims of bigotry, fled the Old World to try the New. And the economic and social life of bourgeois societies was affected by their immigrants, not always to the hosts' liking. Migration was an adventure, a way to freedom, to economic solvency or personal safety, but, principally for the migrants, it was also a pervasive, often crippling trauma.

The same holds true for the second, no less drastic kind of migration: from the farm to the factory, the workshop, the office. That movement, whether seasonal or, more often, permanent, aided natural increase to create the gigantic metropolitan centers of the nineteenth century. "The United States," as the late Richard Hofstadter put it in his *Age of Reform*, "was born in the country and has moved to the city."[11] All of Europe experienced the same massive translations. As Maxime du Camp, Flaubert's friend and historian of modern Paris, noted late in the nineteenth century: "England goes to India, Germany goes to America, France migrates to Paris."[12] He could have added that England also went to London, Germany to Berlin. While in 1800, just 21 percent of the population of England and Wales lived in towns of 10,000 or more, by 1850

10. Peter Gay, *A Loss of Mastery: Puritan Historians in Colonial America* (1966), II, 130–31.

11. Hofstadter, *The Age of Reform from Bryan to F. D. R.* (1955), 23.

12. Quoted by Paul Bourget, "Discours" to the Académie Française, *Oeuvres*, 9 vols. (1899–1911), I, 514.

that figure had reached nearly 40, and by 1890 more than 61 percent. Other countries, more tenaciously rural than England, nevertheless showed rises only slightly less dramatic: for Belgium, the figure rose, between 1800 and 1890, from 13 to 35 percent; for the United States, in the same time span, from less than 4 to more than 27 percent. The voracious metropolis was the most conspicuous target of this mobility. In 1800, Paris, already the undisputed center of French life, had fewer than 600,000 inhabitants; by 1850, it held more than a million and, by 1900, well over 2.5 million. Berlin leaped from 420,000 in 1850, when it was merely the capital of Prussia, to 2 million in 1900, when it was also the capital of imperial Germany. These cities changed out of recognition in one lifetime.

This flight from the land, the home of nearly all mankind since time out of mind, was not merely directed at a handful of capitals. Industrial and commercial centers like Birmingham and Manchester, small towns just a century before, exploded into sprawling, thriving, miserable, bustling urban agglomerations in a few decades. Some of these nineteenth-century towns were virtually stamped out of the ground: in 1801, Middlesbrough had 581 and Crewe 121 inhabitants; ninety years later, the first boasted a population of 76,135, the second one of 28,761.[13] It was more than the absolute growth of cities, it was the very pace of urbanization that most contemporaries found so astonishing and some worried observers so detestable. In Germany, the number of *Grosstädte*, defined as cities with more than 100,000 inhabitants, multiplied between 1871 and 1910 no less than six times, from 8 to 48. While the German cities gained, the country-side lost. In 1882, more than 42 percent of all Germans still lived on the land and about 35 percent worked in industry, building, and mining; only thirteen years later the urban working population was larger than the rural one, and by 1907 the agricultural sector had shrunk to 28 percent, while the industrial sector engrossed almost 43 percent. In France, too, towns were magnets. Every year, more than 100,000 Frenchmen left the farm to find work in town; between 1875 and 1881 alone, their numbers amounted to 840,000. By 1891, even France, that country of farms and hamlets, found itself with just 45 percent of the population working the land.

These are gross figures, in more ways than one. The experience of the nineteenth century requires distinctions more refined than these naked statistics. It was the age of the suburb, the *faubourg*, the *Vorort*, increasingly working class in composition as the century went on, but continuing

13. Guy Chapman, *Culture and Survival* (1940), 125.

to shelter the middle classes. Each suburb, whether outside Berlin, Rome, or New York, had its own history, and its beginnings often reached back into early modern times. But it was the nineteenth century, especially after the appearance of the railroad, that most assiduously fostered these refuges from the noise and crowds of the modern city, developed these little unpretentious, and sometimes pretentious, properties.

This startling phenomenon of burgeoning middle-class settlements invited some envy and a great deal of ridicule. No one was a readier target of satire than the suburbanite; the contemporary perception of his life, tastes, and aspirations was almost uniformly jaundiced, and produced a spate of lampoons. George and Weedon Grossmith's minor classic *The Diary of a Nobody*, first published in 1892 and steadily reprinted, is, with its benign, almost affectionate portrayal, only the least condescending exemplar of the literature. Yet, though an object of easy disdain, the suburb proved unconquerable everywhere; H. J. Dyos, the historian of the south London suburb of Camberwell, once shrewdly noted that observers would fall into military language when they talked about this awesome development: "Alexander's armies were great makers of conquests," Wilkie Collins wrote in 1861, when the pace of suburbanization was markedly quickening, "and Napoleon's armies were great makers of conquests, but the modern Guerrilla regiments of the hod, the trowel, and the brick-kiln, are the greatest conquerors of all; for they hold the longest the soil they have once possessed," complete "with the conqueror's device inscribed on it—'THIS GROUND TO BE LET ON BUILDING LEASES!'" Camberwell, a sparsely settled neighborhood in the early years of the nineteenth century, grew from 39,868 inhabitants in 1841 to 259,339 in 1901—a stunning sevenfold increase in sixty years.[14] While more and more of this quarter million were respectable working men commuting to London on rapid and cheap trains, and while Camberwell even developed its own slum, the middle-class element retained its foothold. The fantasies that middle-class Londoners enacted in Camberwell, middle-class Berliners enacted in Wilmersdorf. But as factories and working-class housing engrossed suburb after suburb—Argenteuil outside Paris, La Guillotière outside Lyon—some of these bourgeois dreams turned into nightmares. Here as elsewhere, the bourgeois experience was overtaken by ambivalence.

The suburbs, creatures and creators of change, loomed large in that experience as defenses from anxiety no less than as realizations of

14. H. J. Dyos, *Victorian Suburb: A Study of the Growth of Camberwell* (1961), 51, 54–55.

wishes. And the cities themselves provided ample material for gratification and uneasiness. The nineteenth century produced a lively pattern of shifting residence within towns, with the multiplication of factories, the invasion of railway tracks and terminals, the expansion of government offices, the rise and fall of fashionable neighborhoods. The figures reporting all these changes merely sum up, but fail to evoke, the experiences that every act of migration so intensely produced. The implications of these experiences, explored in fiction and in social criticism, were not fully understood, but they engaged the central concerns of human existence: sexual morality, work discipline, family cohesion, perceptions of time, space, and life chances.

The sway of change was aptly dramatized by the incantatory employment of the word "new." Jacob Burckhardt, great historian and principled conservative, detected this habit early. "Everybody wants to be *new*," he wrote in 1843, "but nothing else." Such a desire might be popular, but it required, Burckhardt thought, no mental effort: "To be liberal," he laid it down in 1841, "is the easiest thing of all."[15] More than half a century later, Holbrook Jackson characterized the 1890s as typified by books titled *The New Hedonism* and *The New Fiction* and by movements calling themselves the New Paganism, the New Voluptuousness, and, in obvious reaction, the New Remorse, but also the New Spirit, the New Humor, the New Realism, the New Drama, to say nothing of the New Unionism and the New Woman.[16] Shortly after 1890, indeed, the Austrian critic and essayist Hermann Bahr noted the repeated emergence of "young" schools of art and literature everywhere, even of "youngest" schools. "Every day," he wrote, "sees the appearance of a new aesthetic of the future. Everyone offers his particular formula for the novel." No question: "The old formulas have served their turn, there is an irresistible thirst after the new."[17] Samuel Johnson had already deplored, in 1783, the widespread "fury of innovation," but his was a tranquil, placid time compared to the vertiginous situation a century later. Certainly by the 1880s, a keen social observer like Emile Durkheim was confident that his was a new age, a new era.

Walter Bagehot earlier summed up this conviction authoritatively, in the opening paragraph to his *Physics and Politics*: "One peculiarity of this age is the sudden acquisition of much physical knowledge. There is scarcely a department of science which is the same, or at all the same, as

15. Burckhardt to Johanna Kinke, August 23, 1843; to Louise Burckhardt, April 5 [1841], *Briefe*, ed. Max Burckhardt, 9 vols. (1949–80), II, 42; I, 162.

16. *The Eighteen Nineties* (1913), 21–23.

17. *Studien zur Kritik der Moderne* (1894), 96.

it was fifty years ago. A new world of inventions—of railways and of telegraphs—has grown up around us which we cannot help seeing; a new world of ideas is in the air and affects us, though we do not see it."[18] And it was arguable that the new world of ideas, however invisible, was transforming nineteenth-century society at least as irreversibly as those most visible inventions, the railroad, the telegraph, or the international credit network. Certainly, when Bagehot published his appraisal of his age, the pace of change had been strenuous for some decades. Yet its tempo accelerated as the age of Victoria moved toward the age of Freud. The art historian Hermann Uhde-Bernays, looking back at the frantic pace animating the life of his city, Munich, in the early 1890s, remembered this speeding up by resorting, once more, to the familiar incantation: "The struggle was over a new art, a new drama, a new opera, new concerts in newly constructed halls, the rejuvenation of educational institutions, a new, fresh life in a dried-up, dusty atmosphere."[19] In 1912 Dr. Hermann Rohleder thought it right to introduce a book on sexual hygiene and pedagogy with yet another invocation to the overwhelming reality of his day: "Surely everyone knows that colossal upheavals in all domains are characteristic of our present-day culture, of today's generation, of the moderns. In the field of technology, we have lived through innovations that we could not have dreamt of fifteen, indeed ten years ago; the same holds true of commerce, industry and—last not least—the sciences." The ancient Greek saying that everything is subject to upheavals "has surely never been truer, or more justified, than in our time."[20] An age like this, dizzy with change, Rohleder implied, needs a new look at sexuality, which is of course changing in company with everything else.

Charles Péguy was doubtless exaggerating, but he beautifully captured this mood when he said, a year after Rohleder, "The world has changed less since Jesus Christ than in the last thirty years."[21] This pervasive passion for the new did not escape such specialized students of contemporary culture as Auguste Escoffier, possibly the most distinguished chef in the bourgeois century. In the preface to his classic cookbook he exclaimed: "But novelty is the universal cry—novelty by hook or by crook!" He was speaking of recipes and of dishes, but he might have been characterizing the world at large: "Novelty! It is the prevailing cry; it is

18. *Physics and Politics* (1872), 1.
19. *Im Lichte der Freiheit* (1947), 107.
20. Dr. Hermann Rohleder, *Grundzüge der Sexualpädagogik* (1912), xi.
21. Quoted as an epigraph to Roger Shattuck, *The Banquet Years: The Origins of the Avant Garde in France, 1885 to World War I* (1958; rev. ed., 1968), 1.

imperiously demanded by everyone."[22] But the time had its compensations. Emile Zola, who saw the terrors of his world passionately, often rather melodramatically, was still able to discover, with many others, "the pleasure of novelty, something," he went on, "that people are willing to pay for dearly in Paris."[23] They were willing to pay, it seems, in some of the provinces as well.

Probably the most pertinent contribution to the victory of the new came, as I have noted, from the middle class itself. The demands of industrial capitalism forged what came to be called a new middle class which altered the traditional contours of the bourgeoisie forever. Technological and administrative improvements in manufacture and banking, in transport, merchandising, and government called for, and got, troops of typists, secretaries, supervisors, bookkeepers, sales personnel—men and, increasingly, women, devoted not to growing or making things, but to rendering services. The railroad and the typewriter, the steamship and the telegraph, the easing of credit and of capital formation, made the savings of large-scale organization almost irresistible: the factory, the sizable law firm, the department store, were all hungry for help. In 1870–71, the average cotton mill in England employed 177 persons—workers, managers, and clerks. And in these very years the average counting house employed four clerks.[24] From the perspective of the twentieth century, this scale of enterprise seems modest enough, but for the mid-nineteenth century and later, such numbers were signs of a new age. The new middle class expanded unchecked, uncheckable. In 1851, the English census revealed 91,000 men in commercial occupations. A decade later the number was 130,000, and by 1911 it had risen to 739,000, an eightfold multiplication in only sixty years. And women participated in this explosion in ever-larger measure: if, in 1851, there had been almost no women clerks, by 1861 there were 2,000 of them, a scanty 1.5 percent of the whole. But in 1911, the share of women had risen to 157,000, making a rather more respectable 21 percent of all clerks in England.

These developments were by no means unique to England, the first industrial nation. In France, between 1856 and 1906, the administrative and commercial sectors of the economy grew from 21 to 28 percent, while industry grew, in that same time span, only 2 percent, less than one-third as rapidly. And in Germany, the most palpable shifts clustered at the end of the nineteenth century. Between 1882 and 1907, while the

22. Escoffier, A Guide to Modern Cookery (1903; 2nd ed., 1909), vii.
23. Zola, Salons, ed. F. W. J. Hemmings and Robert J. Niess (1959), 148.
24. B. G. Orchard, The Clerks of Liverpool (1871), 7.

number of employers and owners declined by 7 percent, that of workers rose by 110, and that of employees by 592 percent: in a quarter of a century, the industrial work force doubled, but that of secretaries, clerks, salesmen multiplied three times as fast.[25] The modern world was becoming a world of clerks; the base of the bourgeois pyramid was widening out of all recognition.

Among the most insatiable makers of the new middle class were governments. The amounts of money they found themselves obliged to spend, the numbers of employees they had to take on to fulfill their multifarious new functions of supervision and control, and the share of clerks among the burgeoning tribe of public servants, all grew at remarkable rates. In 1792, the English central government spent £7.7 million; in 1897, a little more than a century later, it spent ten times as much, £77.9 million. In 1797, it employed nearly 16,000 persons, of whom about 1,500, or less than 10 percent, were clerks; the figures for 1869 are 108,000 persons, with just under 17,000, or more than 15 percent, in clerical positions.[26] After mid-century, clerks were to become subjects of humorous comments in the periodicals, and even in novels. Sympathetic observers found them funny and poignant alike. Others, most mordant, were inclined to see them as petty tyrants or servile crawlers, or both—pathetic nobodies acting as if they were somebody.[27]

But the lives of the new middle class were lives not wholly without hope. The myth and, to a far lesser degree, the fact of social mobility animated many among them. Yet for most, their lot was inescapable: years of provisional employment followed by longer years of making ends meet with very little. It was notorious, in Germany and France especially, that such respectable personages as schoolteachers or postal clerks married late and had few children; they could rarely afford more than two, and often barely these. To make things more exasperating still, many civilian employments were infected by more than a touch of militarism. Public officials were enjoined to cultivate the virtues of discipline and submissiveness, of unslackening work and unquestioning loyalty.

---

25. Theodore Zeldin, *France 1848–1945*, 2 vols. (1973–77), vol. I, *Ambition, Love and Politics*, 105; Emil Lederer and Jakob Marschak, "Der neue Mittelstand," in *Grundriss der Sozialökonomik*, IX, 1 (1926), 127; figures rounded off.

26. Harold Perkin, *The Origins of Modern English Society, 1780–1880* (1969), 123.

27. "A body of men," wrote Benjamin Orchard, "with strong distinctive traits, yet uncounted, uncared-for, misunderstood, or not understood at all, even by those who mix most closely with them—indeed, not even by themselves." *Clerks of Liverpool*, quoted as an epigraph to David Lockwood, *The Black-Coated Worker: A Study in Class Consciousness* (1958), 12.

While, in many establishments, the relations of superior to inferior were patterned on those characteristic of family life, it was the authoritarian family that stood as model.

This authoritarianism and this crippled mobility, with its inflexible rank orders and resilient hierarchies, evoke memories of traditional society, of the old regime. Yet there was also much in it that was strictly modern: the sheer mass of the new *Mittelstand*, together with the misery of the old, demonstrate that the bourgeoisie in the age of Freud had changed significantly from what it had been in the age of Victoria.

2. An Age of Express Trains

All this motion took its toll. Architects of change also became, too often, its martyrs: the century's vertiginous mobility, headlong and not wholly predictable, exacted many of its sacrifices right at home. At times, this victimization was the consequence of mobility in the quite literal sense: in the early 1860s, the once prosperous merchants of Orléans impotently watched their former customers in the region passing them by, traveling to Paris by the railroad.[28] Physical events and mental states were, as always, inseparable. And the old commonplace that everything, even progress, must be paid for, held good for that progressive age, the nineteenth century, and that progressive class, the bourgeoisie—inexorably.

The late nineteenth century made the astonished discovery that even change for the better could, and often did, generate a deep-seated mental malaise. This recognition was first adumbrated by three of the most perceptive observers of their time—Nietzsche, Freud, and Durkheim— and then drifted down to the general reader. In his aphoristic reflections of the 1880s, Nietzsche laid it down that "in the inner mental economy of the *primitive* man, *fear* of *evil* predominates. *What* is *evil*? Three things: chance, the uncertain, the sudden."[29] Freud generalized this informal diagnosis of anxiety to all humans on the simple ground that all are, at bottom, primitive. Anxiety, as he put it in his later theory, is a warning signal released at the appearance of danger, real or imagined, and this permits man to deploy his defenses: fight, flight, denial, and the others. Durkheim's discovery of the phenomenon of anomie is wholly appropriate to its time, the mature bourgeois century. Anomie, Durkheim argued, arises in the absence of firm boundaries and recognizable rules of

28. Pierre Sorlin, *La Société française*, vol. I, *1840–1914* (1969), 79.

29. "Aus dem Nachlass der achtziger Jahre," *Werke*, ed. Karl Schlechta, 5 vols. (1972), IV, 217–18.

conduct, and this anguishing social disorientation can strike after sudden prosperity quite as fiercely as after sudden disaster.

These were important insights, shocking largely because they offended the canons of common sense: good news—a coup on the stock exchange, a promotion in the office, the completion of a difficult task, or the conquest of a skittish lover—should, one would suppose, produce nothing but euphoria. Actually, it often bred panic. Sigmund Freud analyzed this surprising phenomenon long after Durkheim had introduced anomie into the vocabulary of the social sciences: man's instinctual drives are conservative. Change, no matter how positive, requires expenditures of mental energy, acts of adaptation. Unless it is hedged about with precautions and accompanied by affectionate encouragement, unless it is assimilated step by step, it has all the risks of a venture into the unknown, where automatic responses and accustomed procedures lose their authority. Hence, Freud intimates, change, however desirable, however longed for, is both laborious and dangerous. What Proust, in *Du côté de chez Swann*, would later call, in a lovely phrase, "le bon ange de la certitude" lent its soothing presence to the bourgeois century only on rare occasions.

Bourgeois anxiety was, of course, not new when Nietzsche, Freud, and Durkheim diagnosed it. Earlier in the nineteenth century, during the decades of the bourgeoisie's most spectacular political and economic triumphs, it had left its telltale marks on the middle-class mind. By the 1880s, we know, it had been given shape by energetic adversaries: the demands of organized labor, the appearance of radical parties, the scorn of avant-garde intellectuals. There were others, notably feminist movements and literary or artistic dissenters, articulate, angry, not always just, and no longer satisfied with modest concessions. Implacably hostile to the bourgeoisie, all these critics exploited what George Bernard Shaw called, in 1891, "the guilty conscience of the middle class."[30]

Yet bourgeois anxiety, the sign and symptom of danger, was not simply a fear of specific enemies; it was diffuse and endemic. Visiting the imperial court at Compiègne in 1861, Théophile Gautier noted a general tenseness among the visitors there; only old aristocrats, he thought, seemed at all relaxed. "The *bourgeois* himself does not know too clearly just how he should behave. It is obvious that he is not sure of his role."[31] He might well have applied this sense of middle-class uneasiness to other, less trying situations. It was punctuated by sporadic efforts to

30. *The Quintessence of Ibsenism* (1891; ed. 1912), 3.

31. See November 28, 1861, Edmond and Jules de Goncourt, *Journal; mémoires de la vie littéraire 1851–1896*, ed. Robert Ricatte, 22 vols. (1956–58), V, 29.

master the environment or the self, by reiterated flights into wistful nostalgia and, increasingly as opportunities presented themselves and dangers seemed to escalate, by betrayals of liberalism. Change was the principal cause. Under its impulsions, the unconscious dimensions of experience assumed undeniable prominence, for while change resolves some conflicts, it generates and exacerbates others by removing the welcome signposts of social habits.

In earlier ages, anxiety had been endemic, recurrent, seasonal, and expected. Change had meant rare unanticipated good fortune or all-too-predictable disaster: cycles of good and poor harvests, the overthrow of ruling dynasties, the waning of old gods. Nineteenth-century change was, in contrast, harder to read, but its most elemental urge was toward the rationalization of life, away from the comforts of unquestioned belief and the sway of unresisted impulse. The rejection of the direct expression and public gratification of bodily needs, which had begun in the Renaissance with such cultural inventions as the fork and the pocket handkerchief, continued and intensified. The thresholds for feelings of shame and disgust were steadily lowered. Respectable nineteenth-century culture found the imagination a dangerous companion, and instead celebrated delay, modulation, control. Such restraint was, as a cultural posture, difficult to sustain, and often necessary to evade; as Freud said early and often, bourgeois morality, especially sexual morality, made harsh demands and placed unprecedented strains on middle-class minds. And the forms of delay and control were unstable, under steady attack from novelty and the passions on one side and the longing to repress inadmissible, illicit desires on the other. To make matters more unsettling still, change was often surprising, steadily accelerating, always far-reaching, and, as I have said, wholly irreversible. This is why there were such powerful reactionaries making such intense efforts to reverse it. The life of Metternich, a brilliant agent of regression, is a tribute to the changes he attempted to arrest, if not undo, until they undid him. And Metternich had many devoted followers.

One of the most conspicuous symptoms of the general uneasiness was a sense of drift and of confusion, a feeling of being overpowered by impulses too rich and varied to be easily absorbed. In 1897, Karl Storck, a German biographer, uttered a current cultural commonplace when he deplored "our noisy time, addicted to advertising, whose mercantile business manners have already invaded our artistic circles."[32] As early as 1848, Count Duchâtel, who had been King Louis Philippe's Minister

32. *Otto von Leixner. Eine Studie* (1897), 3.

of the Interior, had already characterized his age as one in which "things move more quickly than they did sixty years ago. Events, like travelers, move by steam."[33] He was speaking under the impress of an unforeseen political revolution. But all across the century, witnesses would record their sense of disarray in command, of philosophers at a loss and statesmen paralyzed. In 1844, thinking back on the years after the Napoleonic wars, Disraeli depicted them as a time of overriding helplessness: "The people found themselves without guides. They went to the ministry; they asked to be guided; they asked to be governed." But while the unenfranchised clamored for the vote and laboring men for their rights, "What did the ministry do? They fell into a panic." They had been content, in the old days, to administer; now they were being asked to govern. And this, Disraeli suggested, badly frightened them. "Like all weak men," he added perceptively, "they had recourse to what they called strong measures." It was not only the ruled, then, it was the rulers themselves who suffered anxiety attacks in the uncharted terrain of the nineteenth century. A few years after Disraeli drew this sketch, Alphonse de Lamartine, poet and politician, expressed his sense of France in very similar language: "These times are times of chaos; opinions are a scramble; parties are a jumble; the language of new ideas has not been created."[34] The intensifying passion for a science of society that would explain and solve everything, the humble return of venturesome rebels to the religion of their fathers, and the emergence of such modern cults as Christian Science and Theosophy all hint at the frantic need for guides through the jungle of modernity. The mixture of generosity and rationality that characterizes the liberal spirit was a hard-won acquisition for the few, and under persistent pressure.

In fact, the triumphs of the new, of the secular, of science, were far from complete or undisputed. The old ways, though under persistent assault, displayed an astonishing vitality. Religion regained much lost ground, especially among the respectable, especially in England. The age of Auguste Comte and Charles Darwin was also the age of Cardinal Newman and William James. Earlier, decades before Queen Victoria ascended the throne in 1837, it had become possible, indeed fashionable, for the literate and the affluent to reject the deism or atheism of the Enlightenment in favor of the faith of one's grandfathers. Marx's famous

33. Georges Duveau, *1848: The Making of a Revolution* (1965; tr. Anne Carter, 1967), 27.

34. Disraeli: *Coningsby* (1844; ed. 1948), 78 [Book II, ch. 1]; Lamartine: "Declaration of Principles," Clifford Geertz, "Ideology as a Cultural System," in Geertz, *The Interpretation of Cultures* (1973), 221.

observation that religion is the opium of the masses was a serious misjudg-
ment—certainly for the nineteenth century: religion remained, or rather
became once again, the opium of the middle classes, particularly in Great
Britain, the United States, and Germany. There were influential and outspoken clusters of unbelievers in these countries and elsewhere, modest
agnostics, philosophical theists, and dogmatic positivists; in France especially, the anti-clerical and anti-theological persuasions inherited from
Enlightenment and Revolution retained impressive strength and wide
appeal among the educated bourgeoisie. Yet in 1895, Emile Durkheim
could deplore "these times of renascent mysticism," and he included
France in his worried survey.[35]

But not even religion was an inviolable defense against despair. It was
rarely an untroubled faith. The dramatic, cumulative, and, to believers,
scandalous advances in the natural sciences, source of excited prognostica-
tions for many, were also the cause of fearful reaffirmations in others.
Science evoked the most ingenious sophistries, themselves symptoms of
anxiety, in defense of time-honored credos. Not surprisingly, it was
precisely the most unsettling developments characterizing the age,
notably industrialization and urbanization, that evoked gloomy appraisals
and portentous predictions from modern Jeremiahs. Blake was in good
company in denouncing the dark, Satanic mills, Metternich far from
eccentric in deploring the general loss of faith and stability.

In country after country, decade after decade, progressive and conservative voices alike lamented the unsettled, unsettling state of their age.
They detected an alarming lack of anchorage, a universal anarchy of
thought, an unhealthy speed of existence, a general uneasiness and vacilla-
tion in the very midst of irresistible scientific advance. Emile Zola, a
champion of progress and a partisan of modernity, spoke for them all
in an early letter. "Emerging from an abhorrent past," he wrote to a
close friend in 1860, "we are marching toward an unknown future. Since
we are French, that is to say, impatient *par excellence*, we are hurrying."
He thought that what characterized his time was "impetuosity, devouring
activity; activity in the sciences, activity in commerce, in the arts, everywhere: railroads, electricity applied to telegraphy, steam making vessels
move, balloons launching themselves in the air." Zola did not confine
his catalogue of "devouring activity"—an aptly brutal, oral metaphor—
to technical innovations. "In the domain of politics, it's far worse: nations
rise up, empires tend toward unity. In religion, all is unsettled; this new

35. "Author's Preface to the First Edition," *The Rules of Sociological Method*
(1895; tr. Sarah A. Solovay and John H. Mueller, ed. George E. G. Catlin, 1938), xl.

world about to emerge needs a young and vivacious religion. Thus the world is hurling itself into the path of the future, running and eager to see what awaits it at the end of its race."[36] The religion, young and vivacious, that Zola called for was the religion of progress, the energetic organization of natural and economic resources for the general welfare. Yet even in Zola's pulsating list, we hear the rhythms of anxiety, the barely perceptible fear that things are whirling out of control.

This strain of uneasiness surfaced in the most placid memoirs. In the early 1860s, when Lady Knightley was still the eligible Miss Louise Bowater, she sensitively captured this modern uncertainty in her rather genteel but highly intelligent journal. Contrasting with "the bustle and turmoil of town" a "glorious" morning drive in the English summer sun, glimpsing deer and woodpeckers and calm, lovely lakes, she observed how she felt "daily more and more the pace at which most people of the present age are living. Can we wonder at the increase of insanity? There is a wild look in the eyes of half the men I meet on the railroad," and that look, she added, "makes me shudder. There is no rest, no repose for anyone in the present day; you are always on the go, for pleasure or business. Is this preferable to the stagnation of former days? I do not know; it is difficult, almost impossible, to decide."[37]

Even John Stuart Mill found it difficult, almost impossible, to overcome his ambivalence about progress. It was Mill's lifelong, earnest effort to advocate improvement and to rescue what he found valuable in the new dispensations all around him. But, though receptive to change, he recognized that its very rapidity presented his time with massive problems. "The inferiority of the present age," Mill wrote in his diary early in 1854, in an apt paradox, "is perhaps the consequence of its superiority. Scarcely any one, in the more educated classes, seems to have any opinions, or to place any real faith in those which he professes to have." Sounding much like Disraeli a decade before, he added: "Those who should be the guides of the rest, see too many sides to every question." What the age needed was strength of character, but that was hard to find. The leaders "hear so much said, about everything, that they feel no assurance of the truth of anything."[38] This was not the prescription for confident mastery.

36. To Jean-Baptistin Baille, June 2, 1860, *Correspondance*, I, 169.
37. *The Journals of Lady Knightley of Fawsley*, ed. Julia Cartwright (Mrs. Ady) (1915), 39. This passage has also been noted by W. L. Burn, *The Age of Equipoise: A Study of the Mid-Victorian Generation* (1964), 101.
38. January 13, 1854, *The Letters of John Stuart Mill*, ed. Hugh S. R. Elliot, 2 vols. (1910), II, 359.

We hear, in Mill's pressing skepticism about both leaders and followers in his day, the accents of Alexis de Tocqueville's *Democracy in America*, a work that Mill had in fact studied with care and reviewed with admiration. Tocqueville was that rare phenomenon: a prophet honored in his own time. He had visited the United States in 1831 and recorded the results of his observations and reflections in four powerful volumes, published in 1835 and 1840. In America, Tocqueville had seen the future and had come away with mixed feelings. The United States, as I have noted before, made prophesying easy; it presented itself as the visible destination of a fateful voyage on which Europe had long been embarked. It demonstrated that the society of the future would be governed by bureaucracies under the sign of equality, with all the vulgarity, mediocrity, and contempt for intellect and excellence that this implied. But Tocqueville also saw much that was creditable in American society. If his last years were marked by increasing political disenchantment and private depression, that was the consequence as much of French politics, in which he took an active part, as of his musings on change. In any event, he disdained quarreling with the inevitable.

Tocqueville's admiring readers were often less discriminating and less resigned than their master. In 1851, after reading him, Henri-Frédéric Amiel, the Genevan professor, philosopher, and critic remembered more for his secret diary than for his published writings, noted that "Tocqueville's work provides the mind with a good deal of calm, but leaves a certain distaste. One recognizes the necessity of what is coming." Here was an Olympian posture that might not have displeased Tocqueville; Amiel, though, was too agitated to rest content with it: "One sees that the era of *mediocrity* in everything is at hand, and the mediocre freezes every desire. Equality engenders uniformity"; it sacrifices "the excellent, the remarkable, the extraordinary." Amiel feared that "melancholy—*spleen*—will become the malady of the *egalitarian* century," a fear that some egalitarians shared. Inevitably, "the useful will replace the beautiful; industry, art; political economy, religion; and arithmetic, poetry." In the coming age of individualism and increasing division of labor, "ideal individuals" will disappear; the "time of great men is passing, the epoch of crowds" is at hand. Society "will become everything and the individual man will be nothing. Statistics will register great progress, and the moralist a gradual decline." In a word, the "universal well-being" that the nineteenth century promised to achieve was being bought "at too high a price." Progress, however dramatic, was simply not worth the cost. Everything, the Goncourt brothers noted, was turned upside down. Pleasure was dead; business was king; a great purge was coming, for theirs, the Goncourts confided to their diary, were abnormal times.[39]

Pessimists found this congenial doctrine. Looking at his century with undisguised contempt, Jacob Burckhardt punctuated his correspondence with abusive exclamations at the dizzying, speeding, vulgar age into which an unkind fate had cast him. Old people, he wrote to a friend, are necessarily conservatives, and they "can hardly find much pleasure in the present-day world of rapid change." What makes this declaration notable is that it was made in 1873, when Burckhardt was only fifty-five. It was the rate of change, as much as its direction, that made him feel both old and conservative, wholly out of tune with his century. Modern man, he somberly wrote, had cheerfully and stupidly renounced the solid values of cultivation and diversity for the dubious blessings of the new: "People of today sacrifice, if they must, all their own particular literature and culture in favor of 'night through-trains.' "[40]

The railway, ever increasing in velocity as locomotives and railbeds and signals were constantly being improved, became a potent metaphor for the bewildering, anxiety-making speed of the nineteenth century. Hans von Bülow, brilliant conductor and piano virtuoso, expressed what was becoming a cliché among the cultured when, in 1874, he called his age "an age of express trains."[41] The erotic desires and fears stimulated by the rhythmic experience of the train ride were never far beneath the surface of such epithets. And the nervous feeling that speed was accelerating beyond reason was further exacerbated by the intimations that new sensations were crowding in. As another favorite, equally characteristic nineteenth-century metaphor had it, there was great danger of overloading mental circuits. "Life grows ever more complicated," Theodor Billroth wrote to his friend the Austrian music critic Eduard Hanslick, in 1876. Life, he added, "absorbs us more and more; the ever intensifying competition in economic, artistic, literary, social areas may be proof of intensified development of energy in our generation, but with all this work and unending haste after new tasks to do, there is also much that is lost. Art suffers most from this; the modern public has no time left for

39. September 6, 1851; January 18, 1857, *Journal intime*, ed. Bernard Gagnebin and Philippe M. Monnier, 4 vols. so far (1976–   ), I, 1063; II, 72–73.

40. Burckhardt to Bernhard Riggenbach, February 11, 1873; to Friedrich von Preen, July 20, 1870, *Briefe*, V, 190; 104–5.

41. Bülow to Luise von Weltz, 15/27 February, 1874, *Briefe*, ed. Marie von Bülow, 8 vols. (1895–96), V, 143. Bülow's term is *Courierzüge*.

looking and listening, for thought and feeling alike are forcibly pulled along in a predetermined path by the great wheel of time."[42]

The irresistible velocity of that wheel generated a poignant and pathetic nostalgia for the pre-railroad days. "We who have lived before railways were made," Thackeray wrote, "belong to another world." When men rode in coaches, "*then* was the old world." He allowed that "gunpowder and printing" had "tended to modernize" civilization. But, Thackeray insisted, it was the railroad that "starts the new era." And he pictured those who "lived before railways, and survive out of the ancient world" as being "like Father Noah and his family out of the Ark. The children will gather round and say to us patriarchs, 'Tell us, grandpapa, about the old world.' And we shall mumble our old stories, and we shall drop off one by one; and there will be fewer and fewer of us, and these very old and feeble." No question, "We who lived before railways are antediluvians—we must pass away."[43] Allowing for the hyperbole and archness of Thackeray's humor, the little scene he has conjured up embodies a very real sense of loss.

Thackeray was evoking a mood, not writing social history. The railway, with all its powerful capacity for revolutionizing the location of industry, the transport of goods, the configurations of cities, the pattern of holiday-making, was as much a product of the underlying economic and social revolution as its cause. It was a spectacular symbol, a welcome theme for nineteenth-century painting and poetry. Somewhat more resistant to dramatization, but even more influential, were the new forces in finance, factory building, the organization of labor that swept the century—in short, mature commercial and industrial capitalism. Bankers were as active in the making of nineteenth-century change as engineers and manufacturers. Together, they were constructing a world as precarious for its beneficiaries as it could be devastating for its victims.

For all its nervous reflections on status, power, and morality, the bourgeoisie was, by and large, the dynamic force in a dynamic age. It was a time, for many, of the kind of confidence for which Prince Albert spoke, a confidence as secure in their conscious as it was unproblematic in their unconscious minds. They could absorb many changes, though abrupt and unpredicted, and console themselves for their moments of uneasiness with occasional glances at their bank balances, their political ascendancy, or their social rewards. The bourgeois century was an age

---

42. Billroth to Hanslick, May 9, 1876, Hanslick, *Aus meinem Leben*, 2 vols. (1894), II, 314.

43. "De Juventute," *Roundabout Papers, The Works of William Makepeace Thackeray*, Centenary Biographical Edition, 26 vols. (1910–11), XX, 73.

of improvement, for bourgeois perhaps more than anyone else. Its dominant ideology of hope was less a cloak for despair than a sincere belief in progress. The myth that dominated the age, at least among its beneficiaries, almost had to be the myth of mobility. Heady pronouncements about careers open to talent and the marshal's staff carried in the common soldier's knapsack dramatized the general conviction that the social world of the educated and active bourgeois was a world with few barriers, in which hard work, shrewd intelligence, unwearied persistence, brought returns that an older status-ridden society had denied to all but the most fortunate handful. Steep social ascent was, to be sure, an old story; the biographies of statesmen, bishops, mercantile magnates, abounded in tales of humble origins overcome by courage, energy, and brains. And not all of these tales were imaginary: these were, after all, the men of whom one wrote biographies. But now, in the shifting sands of the nineteenth century, that "tempestuous and unstable epoch," as a French newspaper called it in 1878, this myth of mobility was democratized.[44] A highly popular success literature carried word of the myth to a wide and receptive reading public: Horatio Alger's stories and Samuel Smiles's biographies illustrated, for all who could read, the varied and brilliant possibilities of rising from rags to riches.

It is therefore anything but accidental that the traditional static names for social divisions—"estates" or, more graphic, "orders," or, more graphic still, *Stände*—gave way, in the nineteenth century, to names appropriate to a divided society open to the prospect of improvement: "classes," "parties," or, late in the century, "interest groups." In the same way, and with the same effect, the names once applied to groups sharing political, religious, or artistic convictions were, by and large, supplanted by dynamic language: "school," which suggests dependence on a master, and "sect," which suggests fierce lifelong loyalties, were set aside for "movement." In English, that term seems first to have been used in this modern sense in 1828, significantly in "labour movement." Soon after, it was generalized to other groups, all ready to produce, and to enjoy, change. The nineteenth century was an age of movement, and of movements.

This is not just a play on words. The covert point the new usage was making was that widening opportunities were impressive, that it was legitimate to accept their promise and, still more that the time was right to mobilize, organize, and steer the forces of change in a desirable direction. If change was a whirlwind, men could learn to master it. Modern disciplines like sociology perceived themselves as agents of

44. *Limoges*, May 23, 1878. I owe this reference to John Merriman.

social improvement, an improvement which prominently included upward mobility. "Active at once in aiding progress and in removing hindrance, the science of culture is essentially a reformer's science."[45] With these ringing words E. B. Tylor concluded his famous *Primitive Culture*. Karl Marx had some noted company in his time in arguing that the true task of philosophizing is to change the world rather than to contemplate it, to shift from passivity to activity.

For many centuries, of course, men had wrested a living from the soil, built bridges and roads and great cities, philosophized about their destiny, and applied scientific discoveries to technology. In the Renaissance, humanists highly praised and professed to see the quality of energy, pitted against wicked chance, embodied in exceptional individuals. The practical thought of Sir Francis Bacon, which looked to works rather than words, was less a description of accepted procedures than a prophecy, but the scientific revolution of the late seventeenth century and the intensification of technical imaginativeness beginning in the eighteenth turned some of Bacon's most excited prognoses into sober realities.

It was in particular the age of the Enlightenment that provided influential educated Europeans and Americans with a new perspective, an expansive sense of possibilities for mastery. To be sure, destitution continued its ravages, diseases continued to take their toll, bigotry and injustice flourished little less than before. With the gradual fading of protection and patronage, exploitation worsened as exploiters found new opportunities. But as the philosophes began to erode metaphysics and theology alike, they attempted to apply the critical methods of the sciences, so immensely fertile in their original sphere, to all reflection about the individual and society alike; this generated realistic expectations that the treadmill of human existence might yield to the application of intelligence, that age-old cycles of epidemics, famines, general poverty, and devastating war might cease at last. In the realm of human handiwork, the new atmosphere was symbolized by what Alfred North Whitehead has called the invention of invention.

The men of the Enlightenment underscored the shift from passivity to activity by reviving an ancient Roman saying, dormant through the Christian centuries, to the effect that man is master of his fate. Bacon had already said it, as had Descartes and Locke, before it became a favorite expression among the philosophes of the eighteenth century. By the nineteenth, it was widely accepted as truth. "Man," John Davies

45. E. B. Tylor, *Primitive Culture: Researches into the Development of Mythology, Philosophy, Religion, Art and Custom*, 2 vols. (1871), II, 410.

told the Manchester Mechanics Institution in 1827, "must be the architect of his own fame." This pleasing image did not quickly lose its popularity. In *David Copperfield*, Charles Dickens has Mrs. Micawber express the fervent hope that, as she and her family embark for Australia to make a new life there, Mr. Micawber may become "the Caesar of his own fortunes." And in 1878, in Newburyport, Massachusetts, the editor of the *Herald* praised two rich local worthies, both men of "humble origin" whom life had early thrown "on their own resources," and who were both "men of integrity, industry, and of indomitable perseverance," as successes—"of course." And both had been "architects of their own fortune."[46] For such men, in such an age, anomie was improbable and anxiety, if they experienced it at all, underground.

Collectively, then, the nineteenth-century bourgeois mood was a mixture of helplessness and confidence; endemic excitement was controlled by social devices and private defenses. Reflecting with an almost morbid longing on the heavenly peace granted the dead, William Gladstone mused that for the living, the "main element" of "earthly life" is "perpetual conflict."[47] He was speaking of the uncertainties attached to the human condition in any age, on all social levels. But he would have been justified in applying his observation, with special pertinence, to his own time and his own class. Everything was being called into question: religious teachings, political principles, social ideals and, very emphatically, sexual morality. And this often made even the profiteers of the age, a sizable and sturdy tribe, exceedingly nervous. When, toward the end of the nineteenth century, physicians, psychologists, and sociologists christened their time the Age of Nervousness, they were only codifying a pervasive and conspicuous complaint, extensively canvassed

46. Asa Briggs, *Victorian Cities* (1963; ed. 1968), 104; *David Copperfield* (1850; ed. 1966), 880 [ch. 57]; Stephan Thernstrom, *Poverty and Progress: Social Mobility in a Nineteenth-Century City* (1964; ed. 1969), 71. One did not need to be a philosopher to make such a claim; witness the comment of William Hutton, a printer at Birmingham, who said in 1780: "Every man has his fortune in his own hands." T. S. Ashton, *The Industrial Revolution, 1760–1830* (1948), 17.

47. May 9, 1840. *The Gladstone Diaries*, ed. M. R. D. Foot and H. C. G. Matthew, 8 vols. so far (1968–   ), III, 28.—In 1856, George Templeton Strong, distinguished New Yorker and witty diarist, hinted, quite artlessly, at the erotic foundations of the bourgeois experience. Walking in his city on a busy, snowy January day, observing the "city railroads" which he thought "insane vehicles," he saw the whole crowded and turbulent scene as a "wintry dionysiaca," nothing less than "an orgasm of locomotion." While it would be heavy-handed to take Strong's sprightly tropes at their face value, his metaphor condenses the conjunction of change and sensuality that is the theme of this and the following volume. January 8, 1856, *Diary*, ed. Allan Nevins and Milton Halsey Thomas, 4 vols. (1952), II, 251.

in the popular press and meticulously documented in the medical literature.

Yet, three or four brilliant diagnosticians apart, cultural critics concentrated on the impact of material realities on mental states: on speedy travel, crowded cities, accelerating inventions. Many of Gladstone's contemporaries had vague intimations that the perennial conflicts of which he spoke had remote, mysterious origins, but they were unwilling or unable to pursue these conflicts beyond their obvious manifestations—until Sigmund Freud postulated the overriding influence of elemental, largely unconscious forces in the shaping of human experience. It is into these inaccessible domains of sexuality and aggression that I propose to follow him.

Education of the Senses

BOURGEOIS EXPERIENCES, I

An Erotic Record

1. Mabel Loomis

For reasons that are only too obvious, sexual consummations, among the most intimate and the most important of all experiences, are also among the most scantily documented. This holds with particular force for a culture that takes exceptional pains to keep its private concerns private. Hence, when the historian finds someone like Mabel Loomis Todd, leisurely and uninhibited enough to keep an exhaustive record of her erotic life and leave it to posterity intact, he can only express his gratitude and quote at length. Her blessed precision, engaging garrulity, and never-flagging interest in herself are not Mabel Todd's only charms for the student of nineteenth-century middle-class culture. Cheerful, talented, sociable, popular enough to arouse jealous gossip, she was capable of sustaining affectionate and amorous ties; effective as a writer, lecturer, and editor, as wife, hostess, and lover, she constructed for herself, more than most, an enviably robust and resilient character. When she died in October 1932, at seventy-five, her daughter Millicent, her only child, mourned most of all Mabel Todd's indefatigable energy and her infectious gaiety.

Yet even she—and this makes Mabel Todd all the more interesting—had to wrestle in maturity with conflicts both concealed and open. A certain aroma of transference, of unfinished oedipal business, hangs over her adult loves: she found herself driven to act upon repressed emotions, inappropriate in their intensity and their targets—emotions that had survived from childhood and now intervened in her choice of attachments. But in success and in failure, Mabel Todd's encounters with her

unconscious wishes and her conscious ambitions link her to other—she
was inclined to think, lesser—mortals.

"On the morning of the fifteenth of May, 1879, my darling and I came
up from breakfast, at 1234, Fourteenth st., and had a very happy few
minutes of love in our room."[1] The diary may have become a commonplace in the bourgeois century, but this was not a commonplace entry.
It was an effort to recapture, in a retrospective journal, the moment
when a child had been conceived. The episode she was reconstructing
was certainly not esoteric; its vicissitudes are, of course, the subject of
this book. But the mind recording it was remarkable.

Admittedly, and instructively, Mabel Loomis was, in most respects,
wholly at home in the nineteenth-century middle class. Like other proper
young women, in the United States and across the Western world, she
played the piano and sang, wrote poetry and painted. Her accomplishments were, to be sure, more polished than those of the average amateur.
Drawing on a fund of seemingly inexhaustible yet patiently disciplined
animal vitality—she often practiced the piano two or three hours a day—
she played and sang well enough to perform in public, wrote well
enough to be published, and painted well enough to be paid for her
watercolors and screens. At times she felt flooded by words burning
"with the intenseness of their birth," by a "power," a "terrible sacred
flame" which "throbs so through my whole being,"[2] an erotic investment
in her gifts rare among girls of her time and station—or, at least, rarely
acknowledged. She was handsome without being beautiful; her eyes were
too prominent and her nose a little too heavy for that. But she radiated
vivacity and good health. When she lost weight, she worried; like most
of her contemporaries, she did not like to be too thin. Her waist, she
knew, would remain slim even when she was, as she put it with some
complacency, "fat." Her splendid figure, which she cultivated with care,
struck her and her many admirers as most satisfactory. But it was her
talents, her perseverance, her emotional energies, her artless sensuality
that made her exceptional.

Still, Mabel Loomis shared most of the aspirations, and many of
the prejudices, that characterized the nineteenth-century bourgeoisie. The
family in which she grew up in Washington, D.C., at the time of the
Civil War was, like thousands of other families, devoted, intrusive, proud
of its ancestry, ambitious far beyond its financial resources, socially

1. "Millicent's Life," I [p. 1], box 46, MLT, Y-MA.
2. Mabel Todd to David Todd, September 4, 1879, box 112, DPT, Y-MA.

anxious while professing freedom from anxiety—in short, average in its very claim to be above average. Mabel Loomis remains, for all her cherished individuality, with all her sacred flame, a recognizable specimen of the cultivated nineteenth-century middle class.

In the manner of other proper American girls, she indulged in fantasies of social success, voraciously devoured novels, idolized her father, and, unlike some of her Continental counterparts, married for love. She took romantic walks and moonlight rides, invited confidential conversations and exchanged noncommittal letters with eligible young men, staying by and large within the bounds of the permissible in her stumbling, awkward, touching rehearsals for life. Typically, she came through nearly all of these titillating trials unscathed. There was one brief, dangerous flurry with an "older man," one Ezra Abbot—he was thirty and she eighteen—from which she was rescued, much to her relief, by her parents' objections. But David Peck Todd, whom she married when she was twenty-two, was wholly eligible; like her father an astronomer, he was promising, busy, bursting with far-reaching schemes, and, she was delighted to discover, "thoroughly well bred." And precisely like thousands of nineteenth-century literates, both as a single girl and a married woman, she kept a diary for compressed, often highly charged accounts of her day's doings, and a journal for elaborated reflections and recollections, about flowers and forests, about her modest triumphs at the piano and in the drawing room, about her suitors and, principally, about her ever-fascinating self. In the manner of diarists everywhere, she addressed both her journals and her diaries as living beings, as trusted friends. Her very first effort, dating from 1871, a little stilted still in the early pages, experimental and tentative, is her "dear journal"; a year later, already freer, she can prepare her dear journal, jocularly, for a revelation: "I will tell *you* something, old journal." And she concluded her second journal in precisely the same manner: "Good bye little book—your loving and grateful friend, Mabel Loomis."[3] It was her wedding day.

While the stream of her autobiographical musings makes Mabel Loomis typical of her class and her age, their introspective candor and their fine lucidity set her apart, memorably. When, on the fifteenth of May, 1879, she came up from breakfast to have, with her "darling," those "very happy few minutes of love," minutes she recorded in precious detail, she had been married for three months. She was to have such happy episodes often, across the years, and not with her husband alone.

---

3. November 30, December 5, 1877, Journal II, box 46, MLT; July 16, 1871, November 7, 1872, Journal I, box 45, MLT; March 5, 1879, Journal II.

Mabel Loomis, I must repeat, was a most proper girl, of a most reputable family. The child of her parents in this as in so much else, she took marked pleasure in her family coat of arms, "which I have—a fine one on both sides, thank Heaven." She had a solid, slightly snobbish feeling for the fine distinctions that discriminated each level of the middle class from its neighbors. And, partly because money was not abundant in her parents' household, family and breeding were, for Mabel Loomis, the stigmata of authentic respectability. She worries, in 1873, still a teenage schoolgirl, over attending a sociable at the house of a family that "is not as high in the social scale as many in town, and we felt a natural repugnance to associating with them." At times, her verdicts reflect her own claims to cultivation: "I want to get out of this common-place Georgetown society as much as possible," she writes in early 1874; "I have grown far above any of them." As far as she could judge the matter, she belonged among the "best people."[4] Her efforts to distance herself from the ordinary American did not cease in her later years. In 1885, observing her countrymen on a trip to Europe, she makes her disdain emphatic: "I do not wish to be classed with the average American travelers, (who, I must say, are the vulgarest people we meet) and no amount of money, or even great kindness of heart, can cover up the vulgar & common tone of an American self-made business man." The show of money always irritated her: in 1890, when one of her oldest friends, Caro Andrews, presented some friends to her, she recorded, not without a touch of envy: "She introduced me to none of the women of my sort—but only to four large-breasted women who sparkled in diamonds." David Todd had, she quickly perceived, impressive assets to commend him, notably looks and brains, but it was his being "a perfect gentleman" which first raised him above the many men clamoring for her attention. "Aside from his mind," she wrote in her journal in the early spring of 1878, after she had come to admire him, "he is a direct descendant from Jonathan Edwards, so has good blood."[5] Such things counted.

Unlike her social certainties, her moral certainties yielded to the pressure of her experience—her erotic experience, to be precise. Indeed, as we shall see, it was the very firmness of her snobbery that permitted her to be flexible about her morality. But in her formative years, she was wholly conventional; as a girl, however sincere her pose of independence,

4. October 14, 1877, Journal II; May 2, 1873, January 21, 1874, Journal I; November 11, 1877, Journal II.

5. July 3, 1885, Journal IV, box 46, MLT; February 10, 1890, Journal V, box 46, MLT; April 14, 1878, Journal II.

she felt no impulse to defy, or even question, her family's view of things.[6] She recognized the boundaries fencing in bourgeois behavior, and respected them. After listening to a brotherly young man recount his "love affairs and flirtations," she reflected: "I suppose I do not know much about the world, but I have always supposed that any girl who considers herself a lady would resent any familiarities on a man's part until she was engaged to him. Promiscuous hugging and kissing is something I never could stand even to hear of, and I have always thought it an indication of a low tone in a girl to permit it, or a man to suggest it." She was sure that "it is only common girls, plebeian, truly, who indulge in such things." And she added, with one of those flashes of perception that make her introspection so rewarding: "I have always kept my circle of personal magnetism entire and to myself."[7] She was speaking of her vivid, expressive sensuality of which she became only too aware, and which gave her that striking ascendancy over social gatherings and, more dangerously, over men. To open the circle of her magnetism was to invite passionate declarations in response to her potent, if at least partly unconscious, invitations.

Her surviving narcissistic impulses, and her unalloyed enjoyment of men once she had discovered them, made it improbable that she would keep the magnetic circle of her sensuality permanently inviolate. It was in the summer of 1872, when she was nearing sixteen, that she first became fully conscious of her erotic needs and powers. "Every body stared at me," she noted in July 1872, after a picnic, "but I rather liked it." A month later, on vacation in Charlton, Massachusetts, she was bored until a "man" arrived: "Joy to the world, a boy has come." He was the brother of one of her friends, and a valuable acquisition. "Indeed scarcely in the whole village can there be found one of those wonderful creatures." By mid-November, after she had turned sixteen, she confessed the plain truth to her journal: "I begin to think that I am very fond of gentlemen." She was. In mid-winter, after rehearsing some musical pieces at church, she recorded ingenuously: "It was ever so much fun, for all the boys were there."[8] Her adolescence was, for her as for other normal human beings, a trying time, in more ways than one. These were years for

6. In November 1877, when she was just twenty-one, she was obliged to refuse an invitation to go to Europe with friends, even though she could have financed the cost—"only $400.00"—with money of her own, because "father would not consent to my going without either himself or mother being with me. . . . I had to give it up. But it was a trial. I wept quite profusely." She wept but she obeyed. November 30, 1877, Journal II.

7. September 22, 1877, Journal II.

8. July 5, August 9, November 21, 1872, February 8, 1873, Journal I.

experimentation, for playing with roles and identifications, and years of revived inner struggles with oedipal wishes, both amorous and aggressive. It was a time for repetitions and farewells.

For Mabel Loomis, adolescence proved an opportunity for discovering her talents as a gifted performer and her vocation as a passionate wife. During the three or four years that followed puberty, as she entered young womanhood, her diaries and journals increasingly center on men. She speculates whether she could be happy with any of her suitors, finds several of them attractive but all of them wanting—in refinement, taste, or intellectual freedom. Confident that she was special, she felt under obligation to choose with exceptional care. The man she sought must be "good, true, intellectual & tender,"[9] to say nothing of having a good family tree.

But Mabel Loomis's confidence was a little tremulous, for her impulsiveness spelled danger. Her appetite for love was insatiable; it seemed as though she was making up an old deficit, whose origins had long been forgotten. Like many other young women—and men—she was in the grip of unresolved conflicts, not acute enough to paralyze her, but endemic, vaguely troubling. "If people will only just *love* me," she had written a little pathetically when she was not yet sixteen, "I will do anything for them." She continued to insist that she wanted a career, and rejected the role of "clinging vine" to which some of her school friends were cheerfully submitting. "But," she mused, "I have such an immense capacity for loving that when I let ever so little a stream start out, & then check it, I am nearly suffocated with the overpowering rush of something indescribable which comes over me." These are florid if unintended metaphors. Love, Sigmund Freud once said, makes things wet. It also suffocates. On the day that Mabel Loomis confessed to her conflict over releasing and then checking the stream of her sensuality, she felt bound to note that while she had developed rather slowly, "I have come to a point now where the intensity of my feeling is simply immense." While she categorically denied that she could have married any of the men crowding about her, and complacently allowed that she was, at twenty-one, "all 'the fashion,' " she craved "affection so much, that I really believe a weak man would make me happier than no man at all." She recognized the risks to which her clamorous appetites exposed her: "I am not in a safe position, for the next man who comes to me lovingly would not find it hard to make me love him." As she frankly diagnosed her case, she was suffering from "a mental, or no an affectional

9. January 6, 1878, Journal II.

starvation."[10] She was waiting for the right man, but too impatient to wait long.

Mabel Loomis's neediness rose to the surface in her most innocuous encounters. Qualifying a Massachusetts fall day, with its glorious foliage, as "delicious," she falls afoul of a friend, John Garland, "uncultivated in the finer points of life & society," who argues for reserving this succulent adjective for "eatables or drinkables." She defends herself indignantly, with a rush of anger, citing "first class authors" in the *Atlantic* on her side, and the colorful facts, the red and yellow maples, themselves: "but they are *delicious*, & I will say so."[11] The squabble is pedantic, but her passion points less to her need to be right—though it points to that as well—than to her need to find expressive equivalents for her erotic emotions. It is no accident that other poetic nineteenth-century sensualists used her cherished adjective in precisely this metaphorical way. "What a delicious shiver," Charles Kingsley has his hero, Lancelot, say in his novel *Yeast*, "is creeping over those limes!"[12] That was the shiver Mabel Loomis had in mind, anticipating greater shivers to come.

Her keen-eyed search for a man and her pleasure in the pursuit itself were, if a little over-eager, appropriate and adaptive in her time, and not in themselves guarantees of bubbling, barely restrained sensuality. It was the assignment of respectable young women to settle down with an eligible young man. "I am becoming ardently matrimonial," Alice James, worthy sister to William and Henry James, sensitive, introspective, and intelligent to a degree, confessed to a friend in the mid-1870s, "and if I could get any sort of man to be impassioned about me I should not let him escape."[13] That sounds bold and is candid, but Alice James herself was rarely in a frame of mind, or shape of health, to be impassioned about any man. Mabel Loomis was quite different: her quest for a suitable partner was inextricably linked to her sensual awakening.

Her awareness of the erotic energy that inhabited her and the erotic ambiance that she generated made the inescapable conflicts between her impulses and her defenses acute. At times they rose to consciousness and gave her some uneasy moments about her conduct. "I wonder if I am a flirt?" she once asked herself in her journal—she was just under twenty —after a discarded admirer had accused her of being one, but comfortably decided, soon enough, that she was not; having seen a pretty

10. September 20, 1872, Journal I; January 6, 1878, Journal II.

11. October 14, 1877, Journal II.

12. *Yeast* (1851; ed. 1899), 25. For an anthology of that term, see below, xxx.

13. Alice James to Annie Ashburner, May 10 (1876?), Jean Strouse, *Alice James: A Biography* (1980), 164.

sixteen-year-old provoke the glances of men in the street, she concluded: "I myself am very fond of gentlemen, but not quite in the coarse way, she likes her 'beaux' I hope." It was not a self-satisfied posture she could always sustain. She was too excitable and too honest for that. Upon first meeting "Mr. Todd," whom she found "quite charming," she observed that he was "evidently thoroughly at home among *young* ladies, as indeed," she added, "is every man I know. They are all more or less flirts." Mr. Todd, she found, immediately fastening on his physical attractions, "is very good looking, a blonde, with magnificent teeth, pleasant manners, & immense, though innocent enough, powers of flirting. Well," she concluded, "so also have I."[14] Yet, with a certain youthful sagacity, she chose to observe the proprieties, often interpreting them in the most literal way possible. Once, after she had come to know David Peck Todd well, she took his arm on a walk and found her gesture unconventional enough to immortalize in her journal: to take a man's arm, she noted, was to acknowledge publicly that one considered oneself engaged, and she had little desire to be familiar out of season.[15]

Public circumspection did not inhibit private experimentation. Until she grew intimate with David Todd, Mabel Loomis seems to have confined much of her excitement to the enjoyment of the great outdoors; her journals swarm with entries recording her "intense happiness," her "great joy," not to speak of her regular "ecstasies," in the presence of wide meadows and dark woods, favorite flowers and dazzling moonlight, calm beaches and stormy seas. "Oh glorious! Oh delightful!" she exclaimed in the late summer of 1872, "to see the dear old ocean again." And, a little more than a year later: "The wind is blowing gloriously and the sky fills me with unspeakable longings and joy," she writes;

14. August 26, December 15, 1876, November 30, 1877, Journal II.—Flirting was a serious offense, and attractive young girls were often conscience-stricken when they discovered that they had led some infatuated male into making a futile declaration. Thus, Louisa Bowater, exceedingly popular with eligible men, resolved, thinking of a young Captain, "I must try and be a good child and not flirt," and again, "I cannot feel for him as he does for me, and he is worthy of something better than I can give him. But it has cost me very much, and at times I feel as if I had flung my happiness away. May God forgive me if I have flirted with him." June 6, July 14, 1864. *The Journals of Lady Knightley of Fawsley*, ed. Julia Cartwright (Mrs. Ady) (1915), 80, 86.

15. April 14, 1878, Journal II. She was obviously thinking of calling her new suitor by his first name: in her entry of March 21, 1878, she writes of him as "D Mr. Todd," a revealing struggle. Journal II.—In Europe, this gesture seems to have had far less significance: some time in 1878, a friendly young girl took Otto von Leixner's arm, as he duly noted in his journal, without drawing any consequences. *Tagebuch*, 1868, Leixner Nachlass, Stabi, Berlin. In England, it was a gesture of sheer politeness (see George Eliot, *Middlemarch*, ch. 29).

these entries are typical of her emotional style. Her ecstasies amount to more than the derivative, almost obligatory effusions of a gently raised girl with an ear for poetic prose; like other bourgeois, men and women alike, though more articulately than most, Mabel Loomis eroticized nature. It was only after she and David Todd were securely, as it were officially, in love that she could afford to discard these displacements and seek much of her gratification with a man. Even her journals, which she had "intensely enjoyed" and which had "often inexpressibly comforted" her became less necessary as she concentrated on a living erotic target.[16]

That target was anything but tame or tepid. "Drive in buggy with 'accommodating horse,' " David Todd wrote in his diary some four months before he was to marry Mabel Loomis. "Home about 9. Mabel will remember with pleasure the new sensation I caused her this evening. We may call this our engagement night." About a month later he noted tersely: "First long love—5–6." In her own diary, Mabel Loomis charted the progress of her love with mounting excitement. As early as April 1878, after taking the customary walk—"we walked, and walked & walked, & had a most congenial time"—David Todd came in to Mabel Loomis's house "for a few minutes"; the couple "walked up and down the room, and,—and he—well, I couldn't help it." But she insisted, some doubts lingering behind her defiant affirmation, "I woke up the next morning very happy though, & feeling not at all condemned." Almost two weeks earlier there had been what she called a "slight passage at arms in which I made a mistake—which worried me much, but the effect of that mistake has entirely disappeared, I'm happy to say."[17] Explicit as she normally was, there are times when Mabel Loomis compels her unauthorized reader to guess at her meaning.

Later, in August, when David Todd was away on one of his astronomical field trips, she confided to her "old friend, this faithful book," her pressing erotic needs: "His letters have truly a *physical* effect on me," and she confessed, with just a shred of genteel reticence, "I am going to tell something which I ought not to—I *know* David is necessary, not only to my happiness, but his presence is absolutely essential to my physical health." In early January 1879, after a long walk with her "David, blessed boy," she "sewed buttons on for him" and, after supper, had "another dear sweet few minutes with him & then he—blacked my shoes! At last."[18]

16. September 20, 1872, December 13, 1873, Journal I; November 9, 1878, Journal II.
17. October 27, December 5, Diary 1878, box 108, DPT; April 25, April 14, 1878, Journal II.
18. August 3, 1878, Journal II; January 5, Diary 1879, box 39, MLT.

This rather wry entry immortalizes what must have been something of an anticlimactic encounter. The pleasures that the engaged couple took with one another were, though intense, probably incomplete. For Mabel Loomis and David Todd, as for other betrothed couples across the Western world, the period of engagement gave opportunities for sexual experimentation. In 1843, when Julia Ward became engaged to her fellow abolitionist Samuel Gridley Howe, Longfellow wrote to him: "The great riddle of life is no longer a riddle to you; the great mystery is solved." A decade earlier, Elias Nason, a student at Brown, asked Mira Bigelow, whom he had been courting for two years, to visit him: "Can you come to me?" He could foresee much physical pleasure if she only would: "To see & hear & touch each other every day" and to talk intimately would "make things comfortable." But, evoking past meetings, Nason seemed more intent on recalling and generating excitement than comfort: "My heart loves to dwell on the scenes that we have passed together—all the walks and kisses and larks and sings and thoughts and meetings and partings and clingings." Whether many middle-class girls actually had intercourse before marriage or not—and it would seem not —the time of their betrothal was, for many, a time for exploring and being explored. The "promiscuous hugging and kissing" that Mabel Loomis firmly condemned was, as she cheerfully recognized, permitted to couples pledged to one another: "Of course you would expect it after you were engaged, but I think the line should be very distinct between the friendships which a girl may have with many men, and the one particular kind of affection which she gives the man she is to marry."[19]

This was the line of propriety. In his popular book The Physical Life of Woman, the American physician and reformer George H. Napheys laid it down as axiomatic that "the urgency of man and the timidity of woman are tempered by the period of courtship."[20] He was at least half right: while approved courtship often tempered the timidity of woman, it also, just as often, gave the man's urgency new opportunities. "Oh! that precious boy!" Mabel Loomis wrote in her diary a little more than a week after he had blacked her shoes. "If only he were here at this moment, how I would 'show' him!" What Mabel

19. Howe: Robert Latou Dickinson and Lura Beam, The Single Woman: A Medical Study in Sex Education (1934), 130; Nason: Ellen K. Rothman, "Sex and Self-Control: Middle-Class Courtship in America, 1770–1870," Journal of Social History, XV, 3 (Spring 1982), 409; Mabel Loomis: September 22, 1877, Journal II. Dickinson and Beam estimated that around the turn of the century, perhaps one-fourth of all respectable engaged young American women were no longer virgins (p. 135).

20. Physical Life of Woman (1869; ed. 1888), 65.

Loomis couldn't help doing, what happened during those dear sweet few minutes after supper, what she wanted to show her fiancé, must remain matters for conjecture. It is practically certain that, with all her excited premarital play, Mabel Loomis entered marriage at least technically a virgin: at the end of January 1879, when the Loomis family had decided that the wedding should take place early in the day, David Todd wrote his fiancée, with undisguised enthusiasm, that he liked the idea very much. "Then we could have our first night of love at once—*dearest one*! The day-time lighted gas and other things in accord therewith is quite to my notion, too." While this is hardly the letter of an established lover to his experienced mistress, it is also not the letter a man would send to an ignorant, blushing young thing. On March 10, 1879, five days after the wedding, Mary Loomis wrote to her just-married daughter in an excess of maternal ecstasy: "Never shall I forget the rapt expression of purity and peace which I caught in your face on the eventful evening, soon after the ceremony."[21] She sounds gushy, commonplace, and, in view of her daughter's erotic experimentations, a little obtuse, but Mabel Loomis's expression was doubtless perfectly sincere. She had got the man she wanted. As for her look of purity: innocence was for her—and, it will turn out, for other proper bourgeois—a relatively elastic thing.

2. Mabel Loomis Todd

Marriage, far from dimming the Todds' sexual ardor, or reducing it to pleasant, drowsy monotony, only enhanced it. The couple's appetite grew with its regular and lawful satisfaction; their early life together offers persuasive support for George Bernard Shaw's much-quoted observation that marriage is the most licentious of human institutions.[22] "David is more passionately my lover than he ever was before our marriage," Mabel Loomis Todd glowingly recorded in her journal after the first five months, "and I feel most deeply grateful to God for giving me in my husband a man whose fresh springs of deepest tenderness and love grow fuller & fuller every day, encompassing me with the sweetest life-fountains that a woman's life can ever know." As so often, so here, Mabel Todd's metaphors were more instructive than she could have guessed. It was not simple brutish sexuality, of course, that swept her away, but the happy combination of sensuality with affection: "His love

---

21. January 16, Diary 1879; David Todd to Mabel Loomis, January 30, 1879, box 3, MLT; Mary A. Loomis to Mabel Todd, box 31, MLT.

22. *Man and Superman*, Act III, *The Bodley Head Bernard Shaw: Collected Plays with Their Prefaces*, II (1971), 670.

for me is so passionate, & yet so pure."[23] Yet the sensuality was indispensable to her, as it was to her husband.

David Todd, adoring and avid at the same time, doubtless stimulated by his wife's delighted discoveries, generated a steamy domestic atmosphere that Mabel Todd enjoyed and fostered. From the outset of their married life, it seems, the Todds ended their evenings and began their mornings with a sensual routine, preface and postscript to a night spent with their arms around each other. "Every night," as Mabel Todd recalled it, "he undressed me on the bright Turkey rug before the fire, & then wrapped me up to keep warm while he put hot bricks in the bed. Then he took me in his arms & tucked me safely in bed, & kissed me over & over, while he went to his desk & studied an hour, or two longer. And after parties, when I came in cold, he did first the same for me—& loved me so!" Then, in the morning, "he would get up and brighten the fire, & spread all my clothes around it until they were warm, when he would come for me, & taking me in his arms, set me down on the rug close to the fire, where all my 'toasting hot' garments were awaiting me. Then would come the grapes or figs or apples on which he always regaled me before breakfast."[24] The Todds reveled in the whole menu of married pleasures: working, reading, making music, and taking walks; but their pleasure in marital sexuality transcended and infused all the others.

When they were together, they made love, it would seem, without troubling inhibitions and liked to link their intercourse to other gratifications. There were those figs and grapes in the morning, and, at times, even more suggestive foods. "Ice cream on the way home—," Mabel Todd noted in her diary after two months of marriage, "and the most rapturous & sacred night of all our love." When they were apart—she visiting her parents, he observing the stars—they could barely contain their hunger for one another's bodies: "David," Mabel Todd wrote to her husband, "it is just dreadful to sleep alone." And again, three years later, "I want you very much, dear, very much." She could almost taste his return: "The night of the fourth is our time, darling, and I am

23. August 24, 1879, Journal III, box 46, MLT.

24. December 11, 1881, Journal III. See Mabel Loomis Todd's letter to her mother, March 16, 1879, from her honeymoon: "As for David—well, he gets up and brings me apples or oranges to eat before breakfast every morning . . . ," a somewhat laundered but still highly suggestive account of her night life. Box 31. One may wonder if the Todds had learned some of these little practices from literature: Becky Sharp warms her husband's slippers (*Vanity Fair*, ch. 17), and so does Sophy Traddles for her husband (*David Copperfield*, ch. 61). But then, since the nights were very cold in their northern climate, life was probably the teacher here.

anticipating it with joy." For his part, David Todd would worry just how to contain his appetites alone: "Can I—Oh! can I, wait so long?" He would scheme to meet her so that they could make love without delay, and manfully tried to control his thoughts and his pen lest, by writing too ardently about love, he inflame himself and his wife too much: "I have tried to promise myself to write you a dispassionate letter this time, sweet love—," he wrote her after they had been married for almost three years, "but I've no idea of anything else that I may write, and I love you so that it is hard not to be writing to you all the time about it—but you know I oughtn't to be doing that. If I tell you how intolerably worthless and stupid life seems to me without you here to love me and to be loved, and that two days ago I had fully resolved to be this moment far on my way to Washington, to rest in your arms to-morrow night—notwithstanding that I should have to leave you before twentyfour hours had passed—I shall have said all that you need know, and all that it will be good for me to write."[25]

Then, when they met again, they made up for wasted time, night after night. "Tenderest thoughts of my lover-husband." This is Mabel Todd in her diary late in 1879. *"My own precious David* met me at the Grand Central, having come on by the limited express from Washington for that purpose. Oh joy! Oh! Bliss unutterable—my pure, own husband." For full measure, she noted the following day: "Last night was almost too happy for this world." The years after, her diary shows no slackening in her excitement: "This night, from 9 P.M. until about 12, was the happiest of my whole happy life, so far." And again, "The last was such a happy night! Oh! Oh!" Some of the entries are tantalizingly obscure: "Oh! my oriental morning," she writes in 1881, and, the next year, leaving rather less to the imagination, "We retired at seven & had a magnificent evening, David and I. I shall never forget it, so I'll not write about it." The entry is followed by two symbols signifying that the couple had intercourse twice that unforgettable night of February 28, 1882. These episodes of what Mabel Todd once called "a little Heaven just after dinner" are by no means tokens of sexual athleticism: they occur on the average somewhat less than once a week. And there were some disagreeable moments: "So, dearest," David Todd wrote to his wife from one of his astronomical expeditions late in 1882, "I can remain out here quietly away from you until the auspicious occasion arrives when I can come to you as we both desire after such a separation." He

25. May 12, Diary 1879; Mabel Todd to David Todd, August 1, 1879, December 18, 1882, box 12, DPT; David Todd to Mabel Todd, August 20, 1879, December 9, 1881, box 35, MLT.

was, he added, inclined to "save myself and mine own the experiences we have not infrequently had in past time and which are always disastrous & little short of torture"—presumably a reunion while Mabel Todd was menstruating.[26]

But the couple made up in orgasmic intensity what they missed in frequency or spoiled with bad timing. Sightseeing in Europe in the summer of 1885, with some friends but without her husband, Mabel Todd confided the pressures of her sensuality to her travel journal: "I am longing most uncomfortably for my husband," she wrote; "I am counting the days until I get to him for my own satisfaction. I was not made to live alone."[27] It is true, she was not made to live alone; if she wanted her own satisfaction, she had to get to a man.

She needed him—and he needed her—even after she had become pregnant. On September 10, 1879, after David Todd had returned from an expedition, she felt at first a certain shyness with her husband, which only disappeared with the evening: "The night brought us very near to each other. The physical effect of our close communion was unlike anything I ever experienced—it was enjoyment, and yet it was very hard for me to feel the same kind of intensity as before—it was a thrilling sort of breathlessness,—but at last it came—the same beautiful climax of feeling I knew so well, yet even in its intensity different from the spring's rapture." But as she went on with "my darling through all these happy weeks," she enjoyed "all the time our lovely intercourse—more, I think upon every occasion than the last, though we indulge but rarely & try to be particularly careful about the time in each month when I should have been ill, were it not for my little one."[28]

Mabel Todd recorded these intimate details in a journal she began shortly after her daughter was born. I have quoted the opening words of that journal before: "On the morning of the fifteenth of May, 1879, my darling and I came up from breakfast, at 1234 Fourteenth st., and had a very happy few minutes of love in our room." They had had them in fact very recently: "My darling had lost this wonderful part of himself three days before this Thursday morning, but not previously to that, for two weeks." But the encounter of May 15 held a special place in Mabel Todd's marital imagination: she had designed it explicitly to experiment with a favorite notion she had about fertility—or, rather,

---

26. September 10 and 11, Diary 1879; August 19 and December 12, Diary 1880, box 39, MLT; July 3, Diary 1881, box 39, MLT; February 28, March 21, Diary 1882, box 39, MLT; David Todd to Mabel Todd, December 8, 1882, box 35, DPT.

27. August 7, 1885, Journal IV.

28. "Millicent's Life," I [p. 20].

infertility. "I had been ill three times since my marriage, and by continuing to observe the same care which we had before exercised—viz: to restrain ourselves from the fulness of our intercourse at all times except from fourteen days after my sickness ceased, until three before the next time—we should undoubtedly have avoided the slightest danger of any result from that sweet communion." But on May 15, Mabel Todd had been "barely eight days over my illness," and, instead of practicing the coitus interruptus normal for the Todds at such times, she made herself into a guinea pig: "With me," she believed, "the *only* fruitful time could be at the climax moment of my sensation—*that* once passed, I believed the womb would close, & no fluid could reach the fruitful point." And so, "not at all from uncontrollable passion, but merely from the strongest conviction of the truth of my idea, I allowed myself to receive the precious fluid, at least six or eight moments after my highest point of enjoyment had passed, and when I was perfectly cool & satisfied, getting up immediately, thereafter, and having it all apparently escape."[29] This homemade biological theory was a special variant of the popular notion that conception can only take place if both partners experience orgasm, combined with the equally popular notion, endorsed by many fatally misguided medical specialists, that woman is least fertile at the mid-point of her menstrual cycle. The dramatic disconfirmation of this bit of imaginative science was complete nine months later, and was named Millicent.

For some months, the prospect of a baby in no way inhibited the Todds from continuing to enjoy what they enjoyed most; the last fairly explicit reference in Mabel Todd's diary to a "night of love" comes in December 1879, when she was in the seventh month of her pregnancy. At the beginning, before she acknowledged that pregnancy, though she was afflicted with occasional depression, loss of appetite, and some nausea, the couple's sexual pleasures became, if anything, more delicious than ever. In July, when they took a long vacation trip across upstate New York, she noted that "all this sweet month David's & my love for each other was most blessed & satisfactory." And she recalled "one of the happiest days of all," the day they "went in the steamer *Schuyler* from Geneva to Watkins, on the beautiful Seneca Lake—*oh*! how we loved each other! and what a glorious & beautiful evidence of it we had in our room, before dinner, at the Glen Mountain House!" She "enjoyed fully as much as ever, all this time, our happy love-embraces, seeing in myself not the slightest diminution of intensity of joy—and my nights

29. Ibid., [pp. 1–2].

were oft-times radiant, & my days glorified by this heavenly proof of our deep love for each other—never, however, often enough to weaken nor tire me—& sometimes carried to their fullest consummation—frequently not—only a moment of intense nearness—merely for the happiness of that, & wholly without the strongest passion."[30] To make love was, for the Todds, to play.

When, early in August, David Todd departed on one of his stargazing trips, he left behind a wife nervous, sleeping lightly at first, afraid of burglars, missing her husband's body beside her. Examining the state of her mind as she came into her fourth month, Mabel Todd discovered that her erotic appetite had in some measure—though only in some measure—abated. "I longed somewhat for David in a merely physical way, more or less during this whole month of August, but not as much as I feared I should—the passional part of my nature seemed to grow less strong, though still quite intense." What she mainly wanted now, she thought, was to be "merely loved and petted, than anything more passionate." As she advanced toward motherhood she regressed, not unnaturally, toward childhood. Then, to her delight, her mild depression lifted, and she was pervaded, as she had been at times before, by "a grand and free sense of power," which seemed to her "an all-embracing *genius* which took entire possession of me—not a genius for painting nor for music nor for writing alone—but as if I could do any of these things with perfect ease & glorious success if I but gave myself to any of them. A genius which overflooded me, & could be turned into one channel as easily as another."[31] After Millicent had been born, Mabel Todd liked to dwell on this revived sense of early omnipotence for, a firm believer in prenatal influences, she was certain that, much like her sexual happiness of July, her access of self-confidence must have done the burgeoning embryo a great deal of good.

Meanwhile, though, in the first months of her pregnancy, she was busy denying that she was pregnant at all. Even when a woman physician suggested that her failure to menstruate might be the result of her sweet communions with her husband, Mabel Todd persisted in ascribing it to emotional stress or an old tendency to indigestion. She duly reported her indisposition to her mother, only to be swamped with long, anxious epistles full of good counsel and marked by agitated underlinings. Mrs. Loomis told her daughter that taking good care of her body was a divine command, and that she must eat fruit, get lots of rest, and take

30. Ibid., [pp. 6–7].
31. Ibid., [pp. 13, 15–16].

healthful exercise. Her letter of August 3 is a minor hysterical tract; it appeared all the more annoying to its recipient by comparison with a letter that her "darling father" sent the next day, short, jovial, jocular Mabel Todd was already disconcerted by the prospect of motherhood, which must have seemed more and more inescapable to her as the month of August went by; this avalanche of home medicine, purveyed in repeated and repetitive doses, irritated her even more. "Now, my dear little Mother," she wrote on August 16, "you just stop scolding me!" She accused her mother of jumping to conclusions about her health: she was *not* abusing her body! "Another thing, please, when you have an important fact to tell me—*dont* say it over & over a dozen times."

The important fact that Mabel Todd came to acknowledge to herself was far more decisive than dyspepsia. Late in August, she noticed a "hard little protuberance" below her stomach and from that moment on, she could no longer sustain the theory of fertility on which she had acted on the morning of May 15. On September 3, she announced her pregnancy to her mother in a revealing letter. Its first two pages are filled with domestic minutiae, with purposeful and detailed information about clothes. Then comes the main event: "I am sorry, exceedingly, to be forced to tell you that the conviction is growing almost to a certainty upon me, that I am in what is sometimes known as an 'interesting situation.'" Her aversion to motherhood is palpable, not only in her candid regret, but also in her reluctance to burst out with the news, and her arch quoting of the prissy circumlocution for her pregnancy. "I know *just* the day the whole thing began," she confided, and then tried to exorcise whatever anxiety she might feel about her interesting situation by canvassing, at some length, her sturdy good health, which should make for an uneventful pregnancy and easy birth. But it was not yet definite, and she warned her mother, in tones rare in her voluminous correspondence: "But listen—if you so much as *intimate* this possibility to a *living soul*, I can *never* forgive you."[32]

But hints grew into certainty. Finally, in mid-September, Mabel Todd made it official, in one of her rare misspellings: "It is proven that I am *enciente*." The thought of having a child, having to care for it instead of devoting her time to herself, continued to depress her. She told her husband of feeling "almost trying grief" at the prospect of motherhood, and she examined what she called her "selfishness," with her usual lack of cant, in her journal. Having lived like a "butterfly," she would now

---

32. Mary A. Loomis to Mabel Todd, August 3 and 12, 1879; Mabel Todd to Mary A. Loomis, August 16, September 3, 1879. All box 31, MLT.

have to sacrifice time and attention to someone else, and this troubled her. "I have found my perfect & happy sphere in wifehood—I was *made* for a wife—for a mother, truly, *no*. My life is in my husband—a child or children will be merely incidental; yet," she immediately reassured herself, "I know I shall love this little one—yet not," she added, her honesty breaking through, "with the strength in that sort of love which I put in my wife love—the one is not necessary to me—the other is my air & food & water—without it I should perish."[33] As so often, Mabel Todd was writing, not as an exceptional woman, but as an unusually frank one: the fear of what children would do to their life haunted many women only less prepared to acknowledge the true state of affairs.

Yet once Mabel Todd was sure that she was pregnant, she adopted the new role of mother-to-be with her accustomed vigor and verbal facility. Interestingly enough, it was her husband who engineered this transformation by setting a tone of sheer ecstasy, coupled with the most unconditional worship, at receiving word that his wife was probably pregnant. He most fervently wished, he wrote her, that the news would prove true. "My beloved wife," he began his outpouring, "I must first tell you that my whole life for the past week has been one grand, unceasing tribute of glory in and worship of—*you*"; he assured her that he would spare her as much drudgery in the coming months as he could and that, in perhaps three years, they could leave their child with its grandparents and finally make a European tour—shrewd promises to soothe a woman afraid that a child would inhibit her clamorous talents. But above all, sustaining this rhapsodic strain for about twenty pages, David Todd told his wife that he adored "the perfect nobility" of her "womanly character," that her approaching motherhood was nothing less than "sacred," and that her letter had deepened, heightened, lengthened his "glorious love" for "thee —Mabel—wife—mother." He mildly reproached himself for not telling her earlier of his "deep longing for a fruitful embrace of my fascinating spouse—of you my own Mabel—of you my matchless, sacred, precious, true, loving, holy, darling, cheery, perfect, sweetest, lovely bride." He composed variations on the theme of her "exalted womanhood," called her, in one way or another, "sacred, holy mother," and acknowledged that he had long, though silently, regarded her as beautifully suited to the task that awaited her: "I've often thought how admirably your body is built for this sacred exercise—the hips so broad—to say nothing of the

33. September 12, Diary 1879; October 6, 1879, Journal III. We would do well to take the phrase about her life being in her husband with a good bit of reserve; it was a conventional expression, and she was too independent for so clinging a role, suitable to more ordinary mortals than she thought herself to be.

marvelous perfection of all those parts from never having been distorted by tight-lacing." Having enjoyed his moment of recalling the perfections of his wife's body, he returned to *his* responsibility for the happy forth-coming event: the day would come, he hoped, when she would "feel the power, in happy, blissful content and thankfulness, of that mysterious life-giving element—of which I have given to you abundantly, and which you have transplanted into the richness of your fertile, virgin soil." No wonder she found his letter to be "perfectly inspired & thrilling."[34] The high-pitched rhetoric that David Todd and his wife had used to praise the delights of sexual intercourse, he now used to praise its results. His "precious fluid," as his wife called it, had done its work, and that made him proud.

This letter is something of a historic document. David Todd, to be sure, was working in an ancient tradition when he endowed maternity with sanctity; it was certainly the common coin of respectable rhetoric throughout the nineteenth century. What is striking is that he joined piety about motherhood with enthusiasm for sexuality. The received wisdom has long been, we know, that the nineteenth-century middle-class male split his love life in two, that some of his women were angels, others were whores. But the conduct and the sentiments of the Todds contradict this prevalent perception. If David Todd took the lead in sexual intimacy, Mabel Todd followed rapturously and closely; in fact, their diaries and letters suggest that it was the wife who inspired the husband to his finer flights. At the same time, the couple's sensuality, though inventive and unapologetic, was thoroughly domesticated. David Todd was a tamed animal whose earthiness was welcome; Mabel Todd was neither angel nor whore. The salutation and signature they liked to employ—"husband-lover" or "lover-husband"—explicitly and emphatically join what critics of the bourgeoisie have insisted was normally separated. As late as June 1885, when they had been married for six years, David Todd concluded a letter to his wife: "Goodbye you sweet heartsweet. I love you. David Husband Lover." Mabel Todd used the same language in her diaries.[35] And this happy junction of eroticism and respectability included, and survived, the begetting of Millicent. There seemed to be no visible reason why it should not have endured. But then the Todds moved from Washington to Amherst.

34. David Todd to Mabel Todd [late August, 1879], box 3, MLT; "Millicent's Life," I [p. 18].

35. David Todd to Mabel Todd [June 1885?], box 36, MLT. See Mabel Todd, September 10, Diary 1879.

3. Mabel Loomis Dickinson

It was at Amherst that Mabel Loomis Todd translated her sense of power and genius into activities that give her a claim to a modest place in history; an intimate of the Dickinsons, Amherst's most prominent family, she was among the first to value, and the first to edit, Emily Dickinson's poems. But her intimacy, though the source of ecstatic happiness, also came to be profoundly problematic: for well over a decade, Mabel Loomis Todd, that reputable, socially ambitious wife and mother, and Austin Dickinson, Emily's brother, treasurer of Amherst College, local luminary, a married man with grown children, were lovers. They met in her house in the evening, upstairs, locking the door to husband and daughter alike; they went on unsupervised sentimental excursions into the countryside; they contrived to spend time together in Boston; they wrote one another lyrical love notes when they were both in Amherst, lyrical love letters when they were apart. Their affair was secret, involving melodramatic subterfuges and strenuous concealments, but it was a secret that everyone shared, a test case for the middle-class social style.

It is also an exhibition of Mabel Todd's needs; her affair with Austin Dickinson reads like the realization of insistent fantasies. David Todd took his young wife to Amherst in August 1881, where he became instructor in astronomy and director of the College Observatory. The couple were a catch for polite Amherst society, confined as it was to its quiet, unvarying menu of genteel entertainments and familiar faces. David Todd was a graduate of Amherst and considered handsome; Mabel Todd was accomplished and, as she well knew, "magnetic." Hence it was only natural for Susan Dickinson, the undisputed social arbiter of the town, and her husband Austin to appropriate the newcomers with hospitable imperiousness. For a time, all went well or, as Mabel Todd would have put it, "brilliantly." Some of the most sensual passages I have quoted from her journals and letters date from the Todds' first years at Amherst.

But then men other than her husband—I will not call them rivals—began to crowd Mabel Todd's erotic timetable. Late in 1881, while the Todds were still settling in, she undertook, or at least failed to discourage, a risky flirtation with Ned Dickinson, Austin and Susan Dickinson's son. He was twenty, an Amherst undergraduate, inexperienced, humorless, utterly oblivious of the proprieties once infatuation possessed him. As Mabel Todd confided to her journal and confessed to her husband, the whole wretched business was her fault; she had too much enjoyed her sleigh rides and waltz lessons with Ned, and even his amorous speeches, to check him when there was still time. She thought Ned good-looking, most enjoyable to be with; in February 1883, some months after she had tried to reason him into friendship, she admitted that she had for some time harbored an "especial feeling" for her suitor.[36] By then, in the normal way of disappointed men, Ned's frustrated love had turned to clear-sighted hate, and he denounced Mabel Todd to his mother as a flirt who had played with the son and, tiring of the game, was now aiming at the father. That old reproach of being a flirt, an epithet that carried a great deal of weight then, now came back to haunt her.

Mabel Todd's irresponsible, if (for her) inconsequential involvement with Ned Dickinson suggests that she was far more dependent on repeated doses of male devotion than her amply documented social successes and marital satisfactions would seem to indicate. Her narcissistic hunger would flare up whenever her supplies appeared to be threatened, even temporarily. In January 1882, visiting her parents in Washington, with her husband working at Amherst, she noted that she was having "a most brilliant time," with "magnetism enough to fascinate a room full of people—which I have done, actually." She added, guilelessly, that she had "flirted outrageously with every man I have seen—but in a way which David likes to have me, too." An old admirer, a Mr. Elliot, continued to call on her, and while she tormented him by telling him about her married happiness, she did not discountenance his visits. Frank with herself, she admitted that she more than welcomed, she needed all this attention.[37] Even when her husband was near, she kept her eyes open for new sources of admiration, for new men to succumb to her magnetism. In August 1882, just two weeks after her husband had returned from an expedition, with her diary recording repeated instances of a little Heaven after dinner, she could also tell that diary, "I became so interested in a new man, Mr. Robinson, a Cambridge man. . . ."[38] Again, poignantly enough, during her trip to Europe in the summer of 1885, though she accompanied a couple she knew well and was presumably secure in the adoration of her husband and that of her lover, she found traveling without a sympathetic male soul very trying; she was "strongly attracted" to a soulful Englishman, someone who valued the

36. February 3, 1883, Journal III.
37. January 20, 1882, ibid.
38. August 15, Diary 1882. The entry for July 28, just after her husband's return, records the ecstatic consequences—two orgasms for her: "## 28 and 29 f. m."

beauties of nature and the charms of cities as she did. "I wish," she wrote
naively, in London, "Austin were with me—or David."[39] Ned had been
virile on a sled, agile on the dance floor, and touching on his knees, but
he was only a boy. What Mabel Todd needed was a man, and Ned's
father was just such a man.

Mabel Todd's long love affair with Austin Dickinson was a source of
persistent strain and intermittent depression for them both; pointed death
wishes, not for themselves but for their partners, punctuate their letters.
A little slip of paper inserted into her diary for 1889 gives these wishes
definitive voice. It reads, in its entirety: "Mabel Loomis Dickinson/
Amherst, Massachusetts/August 14, 1889."[40] There are pathetic moments
of unappeased frustrations in her letters to her lover: "I love you," she
wrote to him in April 1890, "and I want you bitterly."[41] Yet the affair
continued from the early 1880s to Austin Dickinson's death in August
1895, at an unflagging fever pitch. The pair developed a code of private
abbreviations and enlisted dependable couriers, solemnly remembered
favorite poems and excursions, tenderly celebrated clandestine anniver-
saries. With their rage for converting memories into mementos, it is easy
to establish when they discovered that they loved one another. On
September 11, 1882, Austin Dickinson wrote into his diary, in his accustomed lapidary manner, "Not much going on," listed the names of a
card party concluding with "Mrs. Todd," and then added, gravely,
"Rubicon."[42] The Rubicon he crossed with Mrs. Todd, and fondly
recalled with her every year, was one of awareness; the Rubicon of
sexual consummation they crossed later at some undeterminable date.

They certainly crossed it: on the day of Austin Dickinson's funeral,
Mabel Todd saw his "dear, beloved body" for the last time, "kissed his
blessed cold cheek," and "held his tender hand. The dear body," she
added, "every inch of which I know and love so utterly, was there, and
I said good-bye to it." And Austin Dickinson seems to have known every
inch of her body, too: "I love you—and I love you," he wrote her in

39. June 17, July 3, 1885, Journal IV.

40. Diary 1889, slip inserted between August 14 and August 15, box 40, MLT. She
tried this imaginary married name twice, on one side with pencil, on the other with
ink.

41. Mabel Todd to Austin Dickinson, April 5, 1890, box 100c, MLT.

42. September 11, Diary 1882, box 101, MLT. The diary holds a slip of paper with
drafts for several entries later more or less approximately transcribed. Under the same
date, we read: ". . . and ev'g with M—— and the rubicon." Mabel Todd's diary for
that year has, on the same date, in pencil, in what looks like Austin Dickinson's
handwriting: "Rubicon."

the summer of 1885, "and I kiss you all over."[43] The near-hallucinations she experienced in those days also bear persuasive witness to complete physical intimacy. "Well, my beloved Austin," Mabel Todd wrote in her journal three months after his death, "there is no need to say good-night —you do not go away at all. I feel you here in me, enfolding me, this instant." She found the work of mourning formidable and almost unbearably slow; in March 1896, as she reached the end of another of her journals, with her lover's death more than seven months in the past, she still felt her unappeased despair and Austin's presence at all times. It was the greatest loss she ever suffered. What she told her husband in September 1895—"I never shall be the same again, of course"—may have been a little tactless but it proved a fairly accurate prediction.[44] And it is true: Mabel Todd outlived her elderly lover by thirty-seven years, but though she had one or two later passionate flings, she was no longer quite the same lively, erotically charged woman that she had been.

Mabel Todd's capacity for self-dramatization was highly developed, her taste for emotional effusions unabashed, but in this affair, the affair of her life, she drew on resources that owed little to conventional rhetoric. She was not posing, even to herself. On August 10, 1895, as her lover lay dying at home, inaccessible to her, she began a letter to which she added, day after day, pages of charged reminiscences and unreserved adulation—"Oh, my love, my darling, my own, own mate and owner, how I love you! And how I long for you and miss you, and feel in spirit your dear arms around me!"—concluding, four days later, with a little intimate apostrophe moving in its simplicity: "Good morning, my dearest love! My heart has been with you all night, and will be all day. I am going for a little excursion today. I cannot breathe or work here, so I am going away for the day. I love you."[45] One need only read this, and the heartbroken exclamation in her diary on the day after her Austin died, her facile, practiced eloquence all gone, to recognize the measure of her investment in her love: "My God, why has thou deserted me!" In paraphrasing, rather than quoting Christ, she kept her suffering individuality intact. Millicent Todd, then an observant and grave young adolescent, confirmed her mother's perilous state in her diary just after

43. August 19, 1895, Journal V; Austin Dickinson to Mabel Todd, [July 3, 1885], box 98, MLT.

44. November 15, 1895, March 31, 1896, Journal V; Mabel Todd to David Todd [September 2, 1895], box 12, DPT.

45. On the back of the last page she later wrote in pencil: "My last notes on earth to him, which he never had, in the body." Box 101, MLT.

the Todds learned of Austin Dickinson's demise. "Mamma is nearly dead."[46]

This was pardonable hyperbole. "The whole town weeps for him," Mabel Todd wrote on August 19. "Yet I am the only mourner." Her grief blinded her so much that she failed to see the company she had in misery—at home. Among the most sincere mourners for her lover was her husband. "My best friend died tonight," David Todd wrote in his diary on August 16, "& I seem stranded." Two days later he observed that he had "tried to work, but my heart is too heavy"; and the day after, with "the funeral of our best friend," was "The saddest day of my life." Millicent once again conveys the atmosphere in the Todd household, strikingly in her father's words. "This," she wrote the day before Austin Dickinson's funeral, "has been one of the very saddest days that I ever passed in my life. Mamma has been crying all day and Papa has cried some and has looked *so sad* that I have been perfectly bewildered."[47]

Millicent Todd, witness and sacrifice, had been bewildered for years, not wholly consciously. For, as she sensed to her embarrassment and shame, her father was not ignorant of his wife's affair, but had persistently and cheerfully connived in it. He had encouraged his wife to meet her lover and, if convenient, to prolong her assignations; he had carried messages between them; he had discreetly kept out of the way in the evenings, when the pair were together upstairs in his house, warning them that he was coming home by whistling a tune from *Martha*. More than sixty years later, so profound was her humiliation, Millicent could still hear that "little tune," and visualize her bedroom, "with bunches of violets on the wall paper." It would wake her up, "toward daybreak on a starry night." But, she added, her defensive stratagem of denial still firmly in place, she did not "remember wondering why he whistled before entering the house."[48] To wonder would have been to conjecture, and to conjecture would have been to know and thus be grievously injured in her self-respect.

Millicent Todd's father did more than facilitate the lovers' meetings. He would accompany them on trips and, when his wife was away, join her lover that both might praise the woman they adored. In early 1884, celebrating Austin Dickinson's "sacred" love for her, the heights and

46. August 17, Diary 1896, box 41, MLT; August 16, Diary 1895, box 132, MTB, Y-MA.

47. August 19, 1895, Journal V; August 16, 18, 19, Diary 1895, box 108, DPT; August 18, Diary 1895, MTB.

48. "Talk with Frances Hersey, 26 February 1957" [typescript], 2, box 132, MTB.

depths it had reached and the splendid resources it had liberated in her, Mabel Todd took the trouble to comment: "And all the time my dear David & I are very happy & tender & devoted companions. My married life is certainly exceptionally sweet & peaceful & satisfying, & his nature is just the one to soothe & rest me." When Austin Dickinson speculated, "I think we three would have no trouble in a house together in living as you and I should wish,"[49] he also voiced David Todd's readiness for such a cozy arrangement.

David Todd's complicity in his wife's infidelity covered infidelities of his own, but it had other rewards; he seems to have found vicarious participation in his wife's sexual adventures almost as satisfying as the real thing. And on the most obscure, most tenaciously defended levels of his unconscious, he must have taken considerable erotic pleasure in the emotional intimacy that Austin Dickinson's affair with his wife permitted him with her lover. Such matters are obscure; what is beyond doubt is that he had an undeniable "weakness" for women not his wife: in the midst of a prose poem about her spiritual union with Austin Dickinson, Mabel Todd recorded her disenchanted recognition that her husband was not "what might be called a monogamous animal."[50]

Sadly, her daughter Millicent was compelled to underscore her mother's verdict. Late in life her mother confided to her, she wrote, that "they had hardly been married three years when he began to make love to everybody that would accept his advances. He had most of the women guests who came to our house, even beginning on my friends when I grew up." David Todd was, as his wife put it in one of her pointed and perceptive aphorisms, "innocently unmoral." In his later years, in the 1920s, when he was confined to an insane asylum or a companion's care for his increasingly erratic behavior, he further justified his wife's appraisal in some lascivious reminiscences of women he could have had and of his suspect fondness for pubescent girls. Nor did he confine himself to expressive fantasies. Recalling a painful visit to her aged, unbalanced father, her memory jolted by her mother's recent death, Millicent dwelled with unconquerable disgust on the day: he had screamed at her, disowned her, maligned her mother, wept uncontrollably, and then, drastically reversing his field, switched from rage to sentiment. " 'Come, darling, come,' " he had sobbed, " 'I loved your mother so—and you, you, I love you because I loved her.' " Then, Millicent added, he "tried

49. March 30, 1884, Journal III; Austin Dickinson to Mabel Todd, July 12 [1885], box 98, MLT.
50. February 6, 1890, Journal V.

to kiss me on the mouth, and thrust his tongue into my mouth with all the accompaniments," filling her with "horror and loathing" until she turned away, "faint and nauseated."[51] In this repellent family scene, we recognize David and Mabel Todd's lovemaking, caricatured and debased, but a simulacrum of the ecstatic episodes that had filled the couple with such longing when they were apart and such contentment when they were together.

Feeling little if any conscious guilt for his susceptible and roving libido, David Todd had been innocently—and not so innocently—unmoral most of his life. The obscene talk and gestures of his last years only illustrate in retrospect how precarious his controls over his erotic passions— incestuous, polygamous, probably homosexual—had been earlier, in the very years that he and his wife had presented themselves to the world as a happily married couple, very much attached to one another, and brimming with erotic energies. All of this domestic theatre was far from being pure sham. David Todd, with all his vagaries, had been able to establish an enduring attachment to his wife, anchored in esteem and desire together. "Dear little precious heart," he wrote to her while she was on her European excursion, "how I love you! And how I want you, too!" And his wife reciprocated these sentiments, at once affectionate and passionate, beyond mere relief at having a husband who did not stand in her way. "I think of you, dream of you, long for you—*when* shall we see you?" she wrote to David Todd in the spring of 1883, seven months after she had crossed the Rubicon with Austin Dickinson. "Love me tremendously every minute, dear. Devotedly, worshipfully, grate- fully, lovingly & most tenderly your wife, Mabel."[52] This is not hypocrisy—there was, after all, little need for that in this marriage—but, rather, an emotional capaciousness for which the traditional treatment of nineteenth-century bourgeois domesticity has left us unprepared.

I am not suggesting that Mabel Loomis Todd's erotic experience was

51. Richard B. Sewall, *The Life of Emily Dickinson*, 2 vols. (1974), I, 301; No- vember 26, 1911, Journal XII, box 48, MLT; October 2, Diary, 1933, p. 13, box 131, MTB. On April 28, 1929, David Todd, writing from a mental hospital, recalled: "As a young father all little girls *except her* [Millicent] were very fond of me. *Why* has always been a mystery unsolved to me. Still is. What jealousy is I haven't the slightest conception, but I think I came near being jealous once of a friend whose own daughter—of 14 perhaps—he was fondling and necking and petting as she sat in his lap. Of course, quite as a matter of necessity, such a relationship is a mutual betterment for both, because a sexless love—purely platonic." David Todd to Emma Cecilia Thursby, typescript copy, box 112, DPT.

52. David Todd to Mabel Todd, July 14, 1885, box 36, MLT; Mabel Todd to David Todd, April 14, 1883, box 12, DPT.

in any way commonplace. She prided herself, after all, on her independence and her individuality, and she justified her extramarital excursion with a patrician contempt for the herd of middle-class pharisees.
She thought herself rare, and Austin Dickinson unique. In the summer
of 1884, looking through her old journals, she could "see through them
all touches of great thoughts, barely-indicated possibilities which are, I
hope, *blossoming* in me now. But the greatest proof I have *ever* had that
I am different from ninety-nine others, & that my girlish hope—that I
had something rare in me—was well-founded, lies in the great, the
tremendous fact that I own the entire love of the rarest man who ever
lived." It was not so much that her extraordinariness licensed her
adultery, but that her adultery confirmed her extraordinariness. That is
what I meant when I said that the firmness of her snobbery permitted her
to be flexible about her morality: cultural aristocrats like herself made,
and remade, the rules in obedience to some higher law.

To be sure, Austin Dickinson's intolerable domestic situation had given
him good grounds for seeking solace with one so vital, so cultivated, and
so understanding as she saw herself to be; he told her, and she duly wrote
it down, that his wife, vulgar, moody, and vindictive, had often refused
sexual intercourse with him for months and had, despite his earnest wish
for children, aborted four of them before she had allowed Ned to be
born, and she had tried to abort him, too. But even if this marriage had
been less of the hell he described it to be, Austin Dickinson's union with
Mabel Todd was, to their satisfaction, made in heaven. When, in the
winter of 1884, Mabel Todd's mother and grandmother objected to her
intimate friendship with a married man, she took the high line of disdain.
Her friendship with Mr. Dickinson, she insisted in a defiant journal entry,
had raised her to unimagined summits of spirituality. Instead of being
"perfectly satisfied with roast-beef & lager," she had been "supping upon
the nectar of the gods." The affair meant the realization of her finest
self, and she was glad to note that her husband understood this perfectly:
"David is large enough to see that if he does not answer to me at every
point & another does it's not his fault, nor mine, nor the other's."
Inescapably, this led her to a position of which a Nietzsche would not
have been ashamed: "It is dangerous doctrine for the masses, but one in
a thousand can understand it." She was neither wicked nor weak enough,
she wrote, even to "think of the conventional part of it." The one in a
thousand who could understand her was, of course, Austin Dickinson,
who shared this aristocratic vision and, in fact, had taught his young
mistress much of it. "The spirit," he wrote her early in 1883, "is greater

than the letter. Conventionalism is for those not strong enough to be laws for themselves, or to conform themselves to the great higher law where all the harmonies meet."[53] This was heady doctrine for two nineteenth-century bourgeois to adopt.

It was also most convenient: the sinners indicting, and thus rising above, those who castigate the sin. Certainly, the element of self-serving justification, of apologetics that do not apologize, occasionally surfaced in Mabel Todd's autobiographical musings. She indignantly defended George Eliot against what she thought small-minded reviewers who sermonized against her for living in unhallowed union with G. H. Lewes: "The law of God is to me far higher than calf skin & parchment." When "two noble creatures recognize each other through the confusion & mist which men throw over life, & know clearly that each is the fitting & perfect complement to the other, it behooves them to give as little pain to others as possible, but to follow the clear light from within & above which showed them to each other, and live out their highest together. This," she admitted, not without some complacency, "is undoubtedly revolutionary doctrine," here applied to George Eliot standing in for Mabel Todd.[54] But her antinomian defiance of the moral law that governs the multitude was not simply an attempt to lend intellectual respectability to her illicit adventure: it was the logical expression of her narcissistic investment in her own powers, her conviction that she was called to realize her potentialities including, and especially, her sexual passions.

The prominent share of sensuality in her self-image emerges in a striking rumination she put down after visiting Mrs. Laura Chant's Refuge for "Erring Women" in Chicago. This was in 1890. The sight of the "poor girls all about me" dissolved her in tears. It was "heartbreaking" to see these pregnant unmarried girls. "How *can* society combine to say that theirs is the one deadly sin?" she asked herself. "If it is something they have done for love of a man, then it is a sweet and pure thing, perhaps perverted, but not bad in any way." To see the perversion of the good as in no way bad was radical doctrine enough, but it was not merely heedless love that was justified in Mabel Todd's eyes. Lust, too, had its rights. "If it is out of mere passion, as I hear some girls go into that life merely to gratify lust, why I pity them, but it is an instinct given by nature and not to my mind half so bad as yielding to a craving for drink, because that is artificial & not born of nature."[55] She

53. August 3, 1884, January 6, 1885, Journal III; December 16, 1885, Journal V; Austin Dickinson to Mabel Todd [March?] 1883, box 98, MLT.

54. March 4, 1885, Journal III.

55. May 13, 1890, Journal V.

found the erotic passions common only in the sense that they were natural, which is to say universal.

Mabel Todd's love affair was, of course, anything but universal, though perfectly natural. She was right to suspect that most married women did not realize their potentialities in quite her dashing manner. Yet her affair was, for all its illicit nature and clandestine ways, a new edition of her life with her husband. There was something intensely respectable about Mabel Todd's defiance of respectability. Playfully, but with serious intent, she referred both to David Todd and to Austin Dickinson as her "owner," an epithet symbolizing humility and intimacy alike. Both men were, implicitly and explicitly, lover and husband at the same time, which is to say that both gratified far more than sheer sexual desire in her; they supplied her hunger for love and admiration and gave her a feeling of artistic and spiritual expansiveness, of a higher kind of purity. "Every charm—every fascination which I possess he notes & loves, & aids me in keeping. . . . he is so glad to have me constantly paint and practice—it would grieve him more deeply than even myself if I should give them up."[56] This was Mabel Todd's portrait of her husband five months after their marriage; with some slight shift of emphasis, notably an intensification of the religious undertone that is somewhat attenuated in her writing about David Todd, it could be a portrait of her lover. Both men gave her an almost undefinable sense of wholeness; neither permitted a split between passion and affection, between sexual and intellectual activity. And she did the same for them. That glowing name, "sweet communion," which Mabel Todd bestowed on intercourse with her husband applies to her experience as a whole, with David Todd and with Austin Dickinson alike. Beyond doubt, her absorption first in her husband, then in her lover, made her emotionally far less accessible to others than she needed to be, and it is painfully plain that her daughter was the principal victim of her own illicit happiness. But to herself, the benefits were enormous, a source of endlessly reiterated exclamatory surprise.

There was, to be sure, one marked difference between these two loves of her adult life: their age. Born in April 1829, Austin Dickinson was fifty-three when he crossed the Rubicon with Mabel Todd; he was, in short, old enough to be her father. He almost was, indeed, her father's age, for Eben Loomis had been born a year earlier, in 1828. And Mabel Loomis Todd idealized her father extravagantly, no less than when she had been just Mabel Loomis. "*Father* came!" she exclaimed joyfully in

56. August 24, 1879, Journal III.

her first journal, written when she was not quite fourteen. "He is splendid."[57] It was not an entry she would have written about her mother. In fact, her mother's serene readiness to do without her father during the long hot months when Washington was exposed to malaria and Mrs. Loomis fled north struck her as culpable indifference. In September 1879, when she was already irritated by her pregnancy and scarcely inclined to be charitable to her mother, she said so plainly: "I must say I would rather die outright, than come to such a practical feeling about this matter as you have with regard to your separation from father. You are perfectly contented to be away from him." As for herself, "six weeks" away from David was about as much as she could stand. Three decades later, in 1910, just two years before her father's death, she had his portrait painted because "he is too beautiful not to be perpetuated."[58] In thinking of him, she sounds the religious note throughout: her father leads a "holy life"; she berates herself when she keeps a youthful flirtation from him, her "blessed father"; when he turns fifty-six, just twice her age, she is moved to think of her "blessed saintly poetical father." And, just as this beloved father was, in her mind, assimilated to the divine Father in heaven, so her all-seeing, all-merciful God looked and acted suspiciously like Eben Loomis. Whatever the activities of the beneficent deity—and he rather faded as Mabel Loomis grew up—her earthly father was much available to his only child. She studied German with him; regularly, in Washington, she walked him part way to the office. In January 1878, when she was all of twenty-one, she recalled, with a nostalgia worthy of a mature woman, the "happy days" of her childhood, "when my handsome young father would come at one o'clock from the office" to work in the "blessed" garden all afternoon.[59] As enamored young men were to find out, it was ungrateful work competing with such a model of perfection. She drew comparisons and, until David Todd came along, they were invidious.

In many of her autobiographical jottings, she makes these comparisons explicit. Writing home from her honeymoon about the exquisite thoughtfulness of her new husband, she gives it the supreme accolade: "I have never seen any thing like it except in father's sweetness to mother." When "Mr. Dickinson" entered the scene, he, too, was held up to the

57. October 18, 1870, "Volume 1 of my youthful Journal," box 3, MLT. For other ardent entries, see October 19, 1871; September 26 and November 11, 1872; May 30, June 21, and July 18, 1873; June 30, August 14 and 30, 1874, Journal I.

58. Mabel Todd to Mary A. Loomis, September 3, 1879; April 11, 1910, Journal XII.

59. June 12, 1876, Journal II; November 9, 1876, the eve of her twentieth birthday; November 11, 1884, Journal III; January 12, 1877, January 18, 1878, Journal II.

same high standard. "He & I are the fastest friends. To think that out of all the splendid & noble women he has known, he should pick me out—only half his age—as the most truly congenial friend he ever had! There is no one in Amherst, or anywhere else, to compare with him, except my two dear men"—her husband and, of course, her father. This was at the very beginning of her discovery that she loved Austin Dickinson; two years later, thinking on her lover, she no longer subjected him to competition with her husband: "The thing which makes it certain that nobody ever approached him is, not only that he is noble & strong & true in character, nor that he is impressive in look & manner, (the finest looking man I ever saw) or that he comes from a staunch old New England family, nor that he is sensitive & tender & lonely, nor that he loves nature *exquisitely*—nor even all of these dear things together. But emphatically that his nature is lofty & spiritual beyond that of any one I ever met, unless it is my blessed father."[60] Indeed, Austin Dickinson was much like her father in salient traits: Eben Loomis, too, waxed lyrical over nature and over poetry.

Dazzled as she was by the radiance of her elderly lover, she found that her father's vivid presence never faded. In her infatuated submissiveness, in fact, she treated Austin Dickinson as though he were her father; she liked to call him, in her letters and to his face, "my King."[61] Nature and custom have decreed that, highly scandalous exceptions apart, girls must lose the initial oedipal combat and yield the father to the mother; for a young woman to carry off in triumph an older man, and a married man at that, was to win that combat doubly, if vicariously. In this way, too, Mabel Todd's affair with Austin Dickinson was a new edition of an earlier love, her love for Eben Loomis.

Mabel Loomis Todd's involvement with an older man was, of course, first and last her personal destiny. Its configurations were unique: grounded in her unflagging longing for her blessed father, foreshadowed in her single serious adolescent infatuation with a man twelve years her senior, and subtly implied in the profession of her husband who was, like her father, an astronomer. The sense of "affectional starvation" of which she had complained as a young girl, and which never wholly left her, was a markedly private symptom. But her transfigured incestuous invest-

60. Mabel Todd to Mary A. Loomis, March 16, 1879, box 31, MLT; September 15, 1882, August 3, 1884, Journal III.

61. For two of many instances, see November 10, 1886, her thirtieth birthday, and June 4, 1896, almost a year after her lover's death, Journal V. Her daughter later remembered that her mother called Austin Dickinson "My King" to his face, and in her house. Sewall, *Emily Dickinson*, I, 298.

ment had extensive cultural reverberations. The love for the father, unabated through the years, was a highly visible occupation of many women's lives in the nineteenth century, more visible probably in that autobiographical and contentious age than ever before. Some of Mabel Todd's most active contemporaries, like Louisa May Alcott or Catharine Beecher, never married, but carried their caring, maternal devotion through to the end. Others, like the embattled American birth-control advocate Margaret Sanger or the respected Swedish novelist Victoria Benedictsson, were saddled with their feelings for their father all their lives, drenched in arousing and frightening sexual fantasies never appeased and never forgotten.[62]

Such forbidden love, more or less sublimated, and often deftly concealed, became a prominent nineteenth-century reality. Even women who married and led strenuous lives long remembered their father's intervention in their young existence with a shudder of delight that has the erotic at its heart. For the prosperous especially, the father was the bringer of pleasure, the liberator from rules, and the maker of holidays. He brightened the children's hour. As the British suffragette Dora Montefiore recalled her early childhood in the 1850s, in a well-regulated and very sizable family: "Every evening we were dressed to go down to the drawing room for the children's hour, from six to seven, when my dear father had returned home, and we small people were made joyful by his sunny smile and the way in which he entered into our fun and games and devised glorious surprises for us." And on Sundays, anything but gloomy, there was "the pure pagan joy" of a walk with father.[63] Such men were unforgettable.

A girl's idealization of her father could have baneful consequences. It could stultify her erotic development, compel her into irrational, damaging comparisons between the perfect father and the imperfect suitor, and force her into service to an elderly tyrant, especially if the mother was an invalid or had died. Whatever a girl's triumph over the incompetent or absent mother, it was often paid for in lifelong slavery. But, suitably sublimated, it could also enrich a woman's experience of love as a satisfying compound of the physical and the spiritual, the erotic and the affectionate strands of passionate engagement. The oedipal period has finely been called a school for love, and it can be that, rather than a road to emotional shipwreck, for girls as much as for boys.

Critical psychologists have been inclined to denounce idealization as a

---

62. For Benedictsson, see below, pp. 112–17.
63. Dora B. Montefiore, *From a Victorian to a Modern* (1927), 12–14.

trap, as an obstruction to finding sexual satisfaction possible, or even conceivable, with worshiped beings. But it may also serve, for the fortunate, as a way of elevating the erotic experience by lending it the tinge of poetry. Mabel Todd, though not wholly unscathed, was among the lucky ones. Her erotic career, for all its poignancy, all its frustrated imaginative aspirations to becoming Mabel Loomis Dickinson, was precisely such an education in love. Her attachment to her father, imperfectly worked through and never abandoned, provided her with impulses for realizing her longings with an older man, on a high level of mental as much as physical gratification.

Like thousands of other respectable girls, then, Mabel Todd was something of a victim to her early erotic history; unlike thousands of others, she later acted where others only yearned. Her affair with Austin Dickinson is almost too good to be true, a compromise with her emotional needs as satisfactory as can be imagined. It was not typical of widespread bourgeois practices, but, rather, the realization of one bourgeois woman's fantasies. Marriage manuals of her time were uneasy with such fantasies, but their strictures against May-December marriages only underscore their frequency. An elderly man, these manuals insisted, should be as continent as he could manage to be, for, as one of them put it, "Each time that he delivers himself to this indulgence, he casts a shovelful of earth upon his coffin." Some apprehensive authors, in fact, could wax vehement on the subject: Dr. Augustus K. Gardner denounced marriages between "men bordering on decrepitude and poor young girls" as "repugnant to nature," as nothing less than "monstrous," dangerous to husband, wife, and if such a monstrous union ever bore fruit, to its children.[64] Some difference in age seemed appropriate: many manuals recommended, on economic as much as physical grounds, that the husband be several years older than his bride. And many widowers whose wives had died in childbirth promptly reentered the marriage market. Hence middle-class circles were thoroughly familiar with marriages made between mature men and barely nubile girls. And, worried preachments to the contrary, it seems that many young brides did not find such a fate very onerous. In a culture in which daughters' idealization of fathers was encouraged and the affection of fathers for daughters given fairly free rein, it could hardly be otherwise. Hysteria, that protean malady so widespread in the nineteenth century, presented as one of its prominent symptoms a retreat from adult sexuality to replicas of early objects. And

64. A Physician [N. F. Cooke], *Satan in Society* (1871), 169–70; Gardner, *Conjugal Sins Against the Laws of Life and Health and Their Effects upon the Father, Mother and Child* (1870), 171 and ch. II, "Marriage between Old Men and Young Girls."

Mabel Loomis Todd, with her ebullience and theatricality, with the air of animation that her visitors found so beguiling and her daughter so memorable, was a touch hysterical. Her choice of the most powerful older man in Amherst, Massachusetts, was thus at once a private and, as it were, a cultural act. Austin Dickinson's autumnal maturity goes far to explain his attractiveness to her, a woman who, though enormously energetic and filled to overflowing with the consciousness of her powers and her youthfulness, never denied that she was half his age.

In the severe, unforgiving memory of her daughter, Austin Dickinson appears as a snob who taught her mother to feel disdain for ordinary mortals, a humorless and remote figure who never smiled, never spoke to her, and who, worst of all, wore a red wig—this the finest-looking and most spiritual man her mother had ever known. Millicent Todd's retrospective assessment is bound to be, at least in part, a report from the interior; a girl, growing up as she did in a household with an unsavory secret, could hardly see the intruder in any other light. One of her earliest memories was "sitting between my young mother and stern, elderly Mr. Dickinson as he drove his high-stepping horse through the woods of Leverett in search of a small hemlock for a particular spot."[65] The sensation of being squeezed between this improbable pair, her vital youthful mother and that dour old gentleman, must have been intensely uncomfortable.

It was worse; it was destructive. Millicent Todd returned to her past obsessively, pursued by a riddle she had to solve and burdened by a duty she had to discharge. She volunteered that her particular preoccupations must have had their origins in her imposing lineage: "The weight of ancestry bowed me down—still does. I seem to feel a sense of obligation to them all." We know better and so, often, did she. It was her mother's infidelity and her father's disgrace that bowed her down in puzzlement and depression. At sixteen, she had written a long poem earnestly refuting Pope's dictum "Whatever is, is right." She had learned from her own experience that whatever was, was wrong. She felt "a deep-set drive toward an almost unattainable goal—inexorable today as it was then," a draining, compulsive weight of responsibility. "An integral part of it was a sensitiveness to injustice with a determination to do something to set things right."

We know from Freud that the guilt of the innocent is the hardest of all to bear. While Millicent Todd's mother went her way superbly dis-

---

65. Millicent Todd Bingham, *Emily Dickinson's Home. The Early Years, As Revealed in Family Correspondence and Reminiscences, with Documentation and Comment* (1955; corr. ed. 1967), 411.

dainful of the conventions and her father made himself into his wife's pander, she obscurely felt, in the way of the young, that the appalling and unvarying situation was her fault. She saw herself, Hamlet-like, doomed to repair the damage she had somehow done, and called to make the world see that there was nothing amiss. Her task seemed all the more urgent since she knew in her bones that everything was amiss, and that the world was a pitiless judge. She was afraid, she recalled, that "the sensibilities" of the "Amherst public" were offended, and she could never overcome her memory of having been snubbed by those who disapproved of her mother's conduct. That conduct, she was firmly convinced, had isolated Mabel Todd from her society: "When mamma chose her course of action, she chose along with it the ignominy which such a New England community heaps upon that sort of behavior."[66]

The discovery that these memories are tendentious, or at least overstated, is perhaps the most rewarding return that this introductory inquiry has yielded. Her experience could not help but color Millicent Todd's verdict on her mother's social situation. And her appraisal beautifully fits the picture normally painted of nineteenth-century middle-class society: secretly prurient and publicly prudish, hypocritical in condemning the missteps of others that one did not have the courage, or the opportunity, to commit oneself. Some scattered outbursts in Mabel Todd's journals against "narrow, uncharitable, self-righteous" members of the Amherst faculty, churchgoers all, suggest that she was made to suffer— or, perhaps, feeling some residual twinge of guilt, made herself suffer— at the hands of pious pharisees. And toward the end of his life, for once lucid and precise, David Todd remembered that when he and his wife returned from a long visit to Japan in 1896, Amherst was "buzzing with gossip," and "everybody" said that the Todds could not continue living in the town.[67]

This is probable enough: it was the year after Austin Dickinson had died, and those too timid to affront their local potentate could now loosen their tongues with impunity. But the evidence on the other side is more impressive by far. The Todds, after all, stayed on. There were some in Amherst who countenanced Mabel Todd's affair because Austin Dickinson, the local patrician, could do no wrong: power long held is not so quickly dissipated. Austin Dickinson, locally famous for his beautification of the Amherst College campus and intensely engaged in all the affairs of the town, was not universally beloved certainly, but

66. "Talk with Frances Hersey," 1–2, *MTB*; Sewall, *Emily Dickinson*, I, 298–99, 295.
67. November 12, 1890, Journal V, MLT; October 2, 1933, Diary, MTB.

generally respected. He was, in the memory of one who knew him well, a "tower of strength," a "tall, slender, commanding figure" with "somewhat martial bearing" and "a voice like thunder."[68] This was the man who, in one of his early love letters, could unselfconsciously call himself "Narcissus."[69] Some of his ostentatious strength was a cover for deeper weaknesses. It was in obedience to his family that he had married Susan, gone to law school, and remained in Amherst; such pliancy suggests that Austin Dickinson was more complex, less in calm control, than he appeared to others. But with his figure, his voice, his bearing, not to forget his local prominence, he could, within limits, do more or less what he wanted. And there seem to have been some citizens of Amherst, including his sister Emily, who took an indulgent view of his affair with a married woman because they thought that after all his marital misery, Austin Dickinson deserved a little pleasure.

But far more important than the town's complaisance about the man was its toleration of the woman in the affair. Though only half-heartedly preserving the appearances, Mabel Todd found herself lionized while Austin Dickinson lived, and little less after he died. Her diaries are filled, tantalizingly, with laconic, heartfelt entries like "Austin in the evening," and at the same time with invitations to the most select social occasions that the town and college had to offer. She was invited to exclusive teas, to commencements, to professors' and deans' houses; she was a favorite chaperone at fraternity dances. At one point in May 1889, the DKE fraternity, compelled to choose between her and her arch-enemy Susan Dickinson, chose the adulteress rather than the wronged wife: after Mrs. Dickinson and her daughter had publicly snubbed Mabel Todd, a representative of the DKEs apologized to her and told her, "they will no more be invited."[70] It was Mabel Todd, the unrepentant sinner, who entertained dozens of visiting dignitaries across the years; who sang at funerals, for charity, and in the First Congregational Church on Sundays; who presided over teas for Smith girls; who was chairman, first of the committee that established a Faculty Club for Amherst, then, a little later, of the committee that established an Amherst Woman's Club; who founded the Amherst Historical Society; who gave years of highly publicized efforts to keep Amherst and its surroundings beautiful—as late as 1913, she was made chairman of the local Forestry Association. Even more impressively, beginning in 1894, she undertook to bring to

68. MacGregor Jenkins, *Emily Dickinson, Friend and Neighbor* (1930), 70–72.

69. Sewall, *Emily Dickinson*, I, 108.

70. For this incident, see Mabel Todd's Diary 1889, May 15 and 18. Sharon White drew my attention to this revealing story.

Amherst a chapter of the Daughters of the American Revolution—an organization as relentlessly respectable as any that bourgeois society has spawned—became its first Regent, and remained in that commanding post until 1903, eight years after Austin Dickinson's death. These are not the activities of an outcast frantic to rehabilitate a ruined reputation; they depended for their success on the willingness of Amherst society, notably its ladies, to work with and to be presided over by Mabel Loomis Todd. And they were all at least moderately successful. It was one thing to invite respectable women to tea; it was another for them to come. And most of them came.

From this perspective, Mabel Todd's erotic experience throws unexpected light on nineteenth-century bourgeois culture. Amherst society may not have been the most censorious in the Western world; one visiting journalist, writing during Mabel Todd's residence there, found that its citizens had "a fine independence about them," and praised "its whimsicality and culture and its freedom."[71] At the same time, Amherst was scarcely a sink of licentiousness; its definition of proper behavior was more or less typical of its age and its society.

All cultures, we know, place boundaries around the passions; they construct powerful defenses against murder and incest, to say nothing of derivative transgressions. In complex cultures like nineteenth-century Europe and America, these boundaries are sure to be complex as well, broken through by facilitating openings and strengthened by special obstructions. Segments of culture, like religious denominations or classes, add prohibitions of their own. These boundaries and these obstructions are far harder to map than self-appointed spokesmen for morality and restraint, the border guards of civilization, would make it appear; their regulations and their pronouncements tend to depict wishes rather than realities. They are wide, often ambiguous bands of prohibitions, accommodating an impressive variety of conduct.

The nineteenth-century bourgeoisie appears to have set its ideal boundaries rather narrowly. But not even the wider boundaries that historical research reveals were easily legible or in any way definitive. They permitted escapes to pleasure that many respectable people in search of sensual gratification could take in safety. One such route was secrecy; another, observance of the conventions. What contemporary moralists were all too quick to call "hypocrisy" was actually a way of carving out space for the passions—within reason. Doubtless, Mabel Loomis Todd paid a price for her illicit sweet communions; she forfeited

71. Jenkins, *Emily Dickinson*, 12–13.

her wholehearted ease of mind and the unstinted approval of her peers. She damaged, with the best will in the world, her husband and her daughter. But routes of evasion were available to her, and she traveled them. It is significant for an appraisal of the nineteenth-century bourgeois experience that the price was one she could afford to pay.

❧ ONE ❦

Sweet Bourgeois Communions

THE RETICENCE of the bourgeois century raises intractable questions about its erotic life. In 1898, surveying the sexual morality dominant in his time, Sigmund Freud found it at once appalling and puzzling. "In matters of sexuality," he wrote, "we are, all of us, the healthy as much as the sick, hypocrites nowadays."[1] Freud was, of course, striking at what he thought the irredeemable dishonesty of the bourgeoisie, but at the same time acknowledging defeat in the face of impenetrable obscurities. It is certain that Mabel Loomis Todd's sexual self-portrait is exceptional in copiousness and candor; not even George Sand descended, or rose, to such instructive detail. It is far less certain that it was exceptional in nature as well; the historical, as distinct from the anecdotal, value of the record that Mabel Todd so diligently compiled requires further investigation. She could recall, over and over, that "same beautiful feeling of climax I knew so well." She could reexperience, with an intensity that repetition could not dim, her "sweet communions."[2] It remains to ask how many other middle-class wives, or for that matter husbands, even those on the most intimate terms with their passions, could have filled their diaries with remembrances of communions quite so sweet, quite so often.

The answer can never be conclusive. Nineteenth-century bourgeois culture, as we know, varied markedly across time, place, rank, and hence, in attitudes. Moreover, each sexual experience is necessarily so closely linked

1. "Die Sexualität in der Ätiologie der Neurosen" (1898), *St.A.*, V, 18; "Sexuality in the Aetiology of the Neuroses," *S.E.*, III, 266.
2. See "Millicent's Life," I [p. 21], box 46, MLT, Y-MA.

to physical endowment, early gratifications, and later opportunities, it is so dependent on the chances of birth order, first seduction, traumatic encounters, that no individual erotic history can fully represent any other. The very survival of sexual testimony is a mixture of accidents, almost bound to distort the collective past. For what happens to have been preserved and what the historian has managed to study may invite conclusions quite different from those implicit in the far larger body of past sexual experiences forever lost or inadvertently ignored. The documents I have used are soundings in a vast intimate literature buried in attics or in archives unvisited, to say nothing of those destroyed by indifferent or shocked heirs. The very act of confiding one's sexual history to paper, as Mabel Todd did with such admirable abandon, makes the writer somewhat suspect as a witness: the vast majority of bourgeois, certainly in the nineteenth century, even those most assiduous in keeping their diaries, remained stonily silent about the delicate matter of sexual love.

The historian of their erotic life need not follow them into silence. Nor is he condemned to biography. But the peculiar and fragmentary nature of his materials compels him to interrogate as diverse a set of witnesses as he can find and induce to testify. Indirect, unintentional disclosures may prove as valuable as obviously pertinent testimony. I have explored three kinds of evidence in asking how much and what sort of company Mabel Loomis Todd had in her time: the journals, diaries, letters of others which, together, have partially corroborated and amply complemented, but sometimes openly contradicted her recorded experiences; the extremely rare, not very reliable, but still informative investigations into collective sexual behavior; and the pervasive nineteenth-century attitude toward female sexuality, which turns out to be the public precipitate of shared private fantasies. All of these materials are illustrations, none are proofs: they are points on a sketch map of culture. There can be no proof in this kind of history; the map must remain a sketch. Its test must be whether other illustrations would have suggested a different map.

By definition, the historian can only use the records he has been able to mobilize for his work, and can only use them as he uses all of his materials: skeptically. If anything, his suspiciousness needs to be most pronounced in that tender region of experience, sexuality, in which pride, shame, or embarrassment guide the pen, inventing conquests and denying defeats, distorting feelings and, only too often, copying formulas. Few diarists or autobiographers, no matter how sensitive or intelligent, really understand all of their impulses or are conscious of all of their ambivalence. They often do not remotely know how much they are really saying. That is why suspicion, though indispensable as a professional posture, is not enough. The methods and theories of Sigmund Freud, which, as I have already noted, have been indispensable to me, provide ways of digging beneath the surface of the written word to underlying sexual needs and conflicts. To read unconscious fantasies in their expressive manifestations is one way, and an important one, of enlarging the scope of an individual's report on himself, at once linking him with his fellows in his time and in his past. Such reading is not easy, but I have been buoyed throughout by Freud's observation that try as one may to conceal one's innermost desires and aversions, confession oozes from every pore. The point is to recognize the confession for what it is and understand what it means.

1. A Paradise for Two

Explicit erotic notations like Mabel Todd's journals are rare, but not unique. Similar entries, whether shamefaced confessions or glowing memories, punctuate the diaries and correspondence of others, now and then, here and there. True, not all of the experiences they record were gratifying. Communions could be solitary, and at times the very thought of them appeared as a threat to moral integrity or bodily health rather than a promise of pleasure. "Now," the German journalist and editor Otto von Leixner wrote in his journal in 1867, when he was a student at Graz, "sensuality is beginning to stir within me, more powerfully than before, although I struggle against it. Up to now, I have not embraced any female being,—but I do not know whether I will have strength enough to offer resistance much longer. May this fruit remain untasted by me as long as possible!" Plainly he was afraid, and fed his fear by observing the baneful symptoms of sexual indulgence all about him. "I see what sensuality has worked with many of my acquaintances; they are not just physically, but emotionally enfeebled." For Leixner, the road to erotic satisfaction presented itself as devious, rough, and possibly not worth taking. Yet in the end it was: after some unhappy affairs, he found the "proper balance between spirit and sensuality" he had long sought, and married his "beloved Tilda," to whom he would write yearning letters from his trips, and compose an affectionate "Little Travel Diary."[3]

Others, men and women alike, never took that road all the way. Henri-Frédéric Amiel, that superbly introspective Genevan diarist, espe-

3. *Tagebuch* begun June 10, 1867, p. 3; *Tagebuch II*, September 16, 1869; *Kleines Reisetagebuch*, June and July 1887. All box 2, Leixner Nachlass, Stabi, Berlin.

cially in his young years often confessed, both to his physician and to his journal, "a dangerous habit," involuntary nocturnal emissions fueled by rich food or lascivious fantasies. "Monday, in the morning," he wrote in May 1841, "a seminal emission, through a dream, abundant and exhausting." He reveled in erotic daydreams; innocent games of forfeit at parties, discussions on marriage, or talk of Victor Hugo's marital infidelities could arouse him, as could the perusal of relevant chapters on marriage in the canon law, including such heady items as "*fornicatio, concubinatus, raptus, adulterium, incestus, virginitas*," to say nothing of "*debitum conjugale*" or "*usus naturalis et contra naturam.*"[4] For his part, Hans Christian Andersen satisfied some of his sexual longings by evoking in fantasy the women he professed to love, all of them happily unavailable, and by masturbating. "My blood," he noted in early 1834, during a visit to Italy, "in strong motion. Enormous sensuality and struggle against myself. If it is really a sin to satisfy this mighty lust, then I will fight against it. I am still innocent, but my blood burns. In dreams all my innards boil. The South certainly claims its rights. I am half ill.—Happy the one who is married, is engaged!"[5] It was not a happiness that Andersen, or Amiel, would ever know.

Yet marriage in itself—need I say it?—did not guarantee sexual felicity. One nineteenth-century document to this melancholy fact, far more poignant than the revelations of the suffering and frustrated bachelors I have cited, is the candid, enormously detailed autobiographical record of the Swedish novelist Victoria Benedictsson, better remembered by posterity, much like Amiel, for her diaries and her journals than for her published work. Her cherished Big Book—her *Stora Boken*—became her confidante, her "dear old book," the trusted repository of her most intimate feelings and her most intense encounters. She found both agonizing, for all her life she oscillated between the extremes of ambivalence: from her youth on, she had had a recurrent dream in which the same man appeared at once as her friend and her enemy. Born in 1850, she had, at twenty-one, married a widower more than twice her age. Far from a happy union, her marriage was partly a fulfillment of a rash promise, partly an act of liberating herself from her parents, partly a desperate repetition of her campaign for love from her father. "I have affection for you, Christian," she warned the man she was to marry, "but

4. August 20, 1839, May 31, 1841, November 21, 1848, *Journal intime*, ed. Bernard Gagnebin and Phillipe M. Monnier, 4 vols. so far (1976–   ), I, 133, 189, 375. And see March 5, October 16, November 1, 1840, I, 146, 164, 178.

5. February 23, 1834, *Aus Andersens Tagebüchern*, ed. and tr. Heinz Barüske, 2 vols. (1980), I, 189. Andersen's true sexual tastes remain somewhat obscure.

I have never experienced what one calls love, and will perhaps never experience it"—hardly an auspicious beginning.[6]

Once married, Victoria Benedictsson felt trapped in her dull environment, restless in the expected role of submissive housewife, parched for intellectual company. She did not quarrel with her husband, but enclosed herself more and more in her troubled and ambitious fantasies. She read voraciously, and she began to write—reviews, sketches, stories. In 1884, she published a highly regarded collection of short stories, *Från Skåne*, which launched her career, in the appreciative words of Edmund Gosse, as "perhaps the most original of the many women writers of modern Sweden."[7] She was launched but miserable: she virtually separated from her patient and indulgent husband, traveled extensively, and ventured into a more ambitious genre, the novel, not without applause—all under her male pseudonym, Ernst Ahlgren.

The adoption of a transparent masculine disguise was a conventional gesture for women writers in the bourgeois century, but for Victoria Benedictsson it had a particular and pathetic relevance: it underscored her self-contempt, her "shame at being a woman." That shame seized her, almost daily, throughout her life: "Damnation! That I should be a woman with the brain of a man!" she exclaimed in her diary in 1887, the year before her death. "A woman is nothing for herself or by herself, and I am only a woman."[8] The memory of early traumatic moments never faded: she could not forget her father letting her know how much he despised the cowardly female sex. Her ailments and her intermittent suicidal depressions were overdetermined; they had physical and more important social as well as psychological origins. In 1876, after she had given birth to a daughter who died in infancy, she was very ill. And she had much to be dispirited about: a loveless marriage; disappointment in her older daughter who, she said derisively, was growing up to be like her husband; and, above all, the fate of an intelligent, sensitive, and enterprising woman trying to find her way in a restrictive, male-dominated culture. She did not reject all her middle-class values: throughout her life, she professed belief in marriage and rejected the free-love doctrine of the Scandinavian avant-garde. But nothing was enough, nothing satisfied

6. March 31, 1871, Lucien Maury, *L'Amour et la mort d'Ernst Ahlgren (Victoria Benedictsson). Le roman vécu d'une romancière suédoise* (1945), 72, 24.

7. E[dmund] G[osse], "Swedish Literature," *Encyclopaedia Britannica* (11th ed., 1911), XXVI, 220.

8. "Shame": Maury, *L'Amour*, 18–19. On male pseudonyms, see below, p. 179. "Damnation" (March 2, 1887): Fredrik Böök, *Victoria Benedictsson och Georg Brandes* (1949), 147.

her. And this dissatisfaction invites a search beyond physiology or sociology.

Victoria Benedictsson was, after all, to the extent that she chose to rebel, impressively successful. Her husband let her live her life as she pleased; she enjoyed considerable literary éclat. Hence her intermittent depressions, her delicate health, her toying with thoughts of suicide, must have sprung from her unconscious, from obscure wishes and obscure sources of guilt. Benedictsson could never extricate herself from her first love for her remote, difficult, adored father; her choice as a husband of a forty-eight-year-old widower with five children—and he was emphatically her choice—attests to that. Once established as a writer, she began to make friends with literary men whom she treated, significantly, as brothers, at times as sons. She thought herself ugly, bony, of account, if at all, only as a failed man with a good mind. There is no hint that she ever experienced anything resembling sexual pleasure with her husband.

Then, on October 1, 1886, she met Georg Brandes: her Big Book is movingly precise on this fateful encounter. A brilliant outsider, the self-appointed gadfly of conventional literature and philosophy, a vehement (if bourgeois) enemy of the bourgeoisie, Brandes had by that time a European reputation. He knew every writer worth knowing; he wrote incessantly and was read widely. A celebrated literary critic, discoverer and shaper of talent, champion of the new realism, about to launch his biographies of great men—Disraeli, Lassalle, Caesar—he gave public lectures that were exhilarating and exasperating events. His radical pronouncements, grating on the conservative literary and academic establishment of his Denmark, only made him all the more irresistible. Women threw themselves at him, and Brandes, philandering husband, doting father, and experienced man of the world, as often felt inclined to accept their advances as he thought it prudent to reject them. Victoria Benedictsson, pathetically in search of emotional stability and intellectual approval, was no match for his confident judgments and his suave ironies. Brandes made Benedictsson's fraternal stance, her favorite escape from erotic involvement, untenable and, indeed, largely undesirable. As early as December 16, 1886, after knowing Brandes less than three months, she could note in her journal: "I am head over heels in love." Often she wrote in code, as if to conceal the inconvenient but irresistible sensual truth even from herself. And on the same day she recorded "the long-awaited moment: Georg Brandes kissed Ernst Ahlgren." But she confessed, always in code and normally in the third person, that she liked Brandes to touch her and to kiss her hand, and she deliciously tortured herself with fantasies of having him really kiss her: "He would bend over her as she lay on the divan and his face would be close to hers." Nor could she wholly deny the oral erotic pleasure that his visits gave her: "I hope to eat myself to satiety with the presence of Brandes."[9] It was a great awakening for her, at thirty-six.

All was not kisses, real or imagined. The two had much to talk about: the avant-garde movement in Scandinavian fiction, the politics of literature, the ethics of libertine love, and their pasts, not excluding their erotic entanglements. On this last point, Brandes had much more to tell than she did and, not surprisingly, he hoped to add Victoria Benedictsson to his long list of conquests. He had never cajoled any woman into bed, he told her proudly, and had never been refused. But she proved elusive and difficult. When he had first kissed her, she had not felt responsive at all; she was inundated by her craving for spiritual intimacy, for tranquil affection. She "thirsted" for the familiar address, *du*, which Brandes perversely denied her for months. When the two were apart, they wrote quick informal notes or sent cryptic telegrams; when they met, they experimented with intimacy: "He kissed me on the mouth," she noted late in January 1887, "lightly and dispassionately as if we were two women."[10]

These games proved too tame for Brandes, who soon grew more passionate and more exigent. On March 15, 1887, Victoria Benedictsson noted in her diary, once more in code, "The first time he asked me." He asked her repeatedly, "Do you want to?" or, argumentatively, a little defensively, "Why don't you want to?" He embraced her vehemently, fumbled with the buttons on her underwear, and offered to strike her—a threat that she, in her guilt-ridden, masochistic way, welcomed and playfully encouraged. From then on, the two engaged in a painful and protracted *pas de deux*, interrupted by frequent absences and markedly inconclusive quarrels. They kissed warmly, sparred verbally, debated whether she wanted to or not. Often Brandes grew angry at her prevarications; he could, it seems, cool down as rapidly as he could be aroused. Throughout their intimate colloquies, more a form of combat than real conversations—all meticulously recorded in the *Stora Boken* and Benedictsson's other diaries—one senses how she was steeling herself for that ultimate ordeal, sexual intercourse. Finally, on November 13, 1887, as Brandes once again asked her to sleep with him, she replied in the affirmative for the first time, but demurred, "Not this evening." She

9. Ibid., 42, 46, 44, 99.
10. Ibid., 171, 163, 83.

was menstruating. His self-possession and composure immediately in place, Brandes told her, " 'Well, whenever you wish, then!' And he left." But six days later, her excuse evaporated, the pair consummated their affair. Somewhat to her surprise, she felt clean, happy, peaceful, innocent, and unashamed.[11] But the good feeling was evanescent. Almost two months later, she tried to commit suicide by taking morphine, and early on July 22, 1888, she was found dead, her throat slashed, the victim not of her single late love affair but of her lifelong self-hatred.

This self-hatred was largely shaped by, and in turn gave shape to, her sexual conflicts. Unlike Mabel Loomis Todd, Victoria Benedictsson had never enjoyed sweet communions; she had no doubt, and often confessed, that intercourse repelled her. "In sleepless nights," she noted late in 1886, during her early acquaintance with Brandes, "she had imagined for herself a certain kind of physical contact"; but her imagination made that contact light and delicate, wholly free of crudity. She recognized that "she would be disappointed" by sexual consummation. Reflecting on her principled reserve with Brandes, she found holding back "refreshing" and added, "that other thing I don't really much care for at all." After she had rejected his early advances, she explained to him in March 1887 what he must have known all along: "To be loved in that way is disgusting; at least it is for me."[12] Perhaps he did not believe her; certainly he did not like to admit defeat. It is precisely because she loved him, she told Brandes, that she did not want to surrender to him. It was a logic that the impatient Brandes found a little bizarre, but which makes perfect psychological sense for someone like Victoria Benedictsson, who sharply separated sex from love, and who did not much care "for that other thing."

Her frigidity was entangled in fundamental sexual confusions and in her ultimate grievance: she felt herself to be a castrated man, furious and, even more, depressed at being enslaved in a woman's body. She once noted in a puzzled and contradictory entry that she dreaded only one thing: "to be deprived of!" We are entitled, I think, to complete that sentence: it was dreadful to be deprived of a penis, source and symbol of power. For instantly she denied what she must have thought: "be deprived of?" she went on and, moving to safer ground, associated her malaise to fears of darkness and death. It is revealing that she should have linked thoughts of self-destruction to thoughts of irreparable mutilation: "I begin to think about suicide," she wrote in April 1887, and,

11. Ibid., 162–63, 243, 248–49.
12. Ibid., 68, 105, 162.

directly after, "I am not unhappy but inadequate, a woman without a woman's calling." And she asked despairingly, "I am also a writer; am I not also then in some sense partly a man?" Sigmund Freud, we know, postulated an essential penis envy among girls: when a girl "utters the wish, 'I would rather be a boy,' we know what deficiency her wish is supposed to set right."[13] Most girls learn to reconcile themselves to their biological destiny, resigning themselves to or even reveling in their femininity. But Benedictsson was not among them; often her envy of the male, and the irretrievable injustice of her fate, overwhelmed her.

She found her lot particularly galling because the world, especially the world that most mattered to her, did not want to accept her wishful self-definition as being part man. That is why she could not recover from Brandes's unconcealed disdain for her novel *Fru Marianne*, her "hymn to marriage." Shortly after it was published, a scathing anonymous review by Edvard Brandes, Georg's brother and, she feared, his spokesman, moved Benedictsson to write, laconically: "Despair." And she added, without any sense of hyperbole, that she had "received the death sentence of my work, perhaps of me." Georg Brandes himself proved even more devastating. When, in June 1887, she sent him a copy of *Fru Marianne*, he told her cruelly, choosing the very vocabulary that was sure to wound her most deeply: "It is too much of a ladies' novel. This between us."[14]

We know that her suicidal impulses were endemic and had risen to the surface repeatedly over the years. And, as Byron told Shelley after Keats's death, one does not die of a review.[15] But this contemptuous rejection from the one man she had ever loved, and in words that banished her irrevocably to the women's quarters, left her defenseless. Her guilt and rage at what she was and at what she wanted to be rose up in her. Her long farewell letter to Brandes, written just before her last and successful attempt to put an end to her life, concludes with words that, once again, insist on separating love from sensuality: "How dear you were to me!"[16]

Fortunately, few nineteenth-century loves ended as tragically as this. Published autobiographies, like confidential journals, offer rich and

13. Ibid., 240, 192, 262. Freud: "Über infantile Sexualtheorien" (1908), *St.A.*, V, 178; "The Sexual Theories of Children," *S.E.*, IX, 218.

14. Maury, *L'Amour*, 145–46; Böök, *Victoria Benedictsson*, 136, 201.

15. On April 16, 1821, Shelley had written Byron that "Young Keats" had died "from the consequences of breaking a blood-vessel, in paroxysms of despair at the contemptuous attack on his book in the *Quarterly Review*." Byron, who had himself criticized Keats, reasonably replied, "I did not think criticism had been so killing." Leslie A. Marchand, *Byron: A Biography*, 3 vols. (1957), II, 905.

16. Böök, *Victoria Benedictsson*, 201, 281, 287.

persuasive evidence that there were, in the bourgeois century, successful middle-class marriages which elevated shared sensuality into an indispensable element. The charming autobiographical volumes by Molly Hughes, for one, disclose a young London girl and wife of the late century, affectionately passionate, a little reticent, but sensible and warm, calm and happy with her husband Arthur.[17] Again, the life of the Kingsleys, Charles and Fanny, was at least for some years an uninterrupted celebration of sexual gratification within the sacred confines of marriage. Nathaniel and Sophia Hawthorne found the married estate a license for freely felt, though not freely expressed, erotic pleasure.[18] And, to judge from occasional entries in her diary and passages in her letters, Elizabeth Cady Stanton, nineteenth-century America's most influential feminist, enjoyed, at least at first, a most gratifying married life with Henry B. Stanton, the celebrated abolitionist orator.

The Stantons would intermittently navigate through serious conflicts later, and the two, both busy, went their own way much of the time. Her statements about marital felicity, then, were as much the expression of wishes as they were recollections of realities. But the realities had left their deposits. In 1853, a phrenological analysis declared her "able to enjoy the connubial relationship in a high degree"—able and willing.[19] The couple had seven children in fairly rapid succession, and Elizabeth Cady Stanton, engaged from her youth in feminist organization and propaganda, led a life of cheerful domesticity and intense commitment, combining housework, child care, and political action without slighting any of it. Votes for women were her mission, but marriage was important to her in her very role of feminist reformer. "I hold that it is a sin," she wrote to her close friend Susan B. Anthony in 1853, when she had been married for a dozen years, "an outrage on our holiest feelings, to pretend that anything but deep, fervent love and sympathy constitute marriage. The right idea of marriage is at the foundation of all reforms." She looked for legal, political, economic, and sexual equality, and quoted, with high

17. Recalling his tragic death after two decades of marriage, she wrote: "In fact, we never did attempt to put our love for one another into words—until the end." He "was run over at the foot of Chancery Lane and taken into Barts to die. I reached him in time for half an hour of life, which he spent entirely in pouring out all the pent up expressions of love that he had strength to utter, in which the word 'glorious' was incessantly repeated. In my own anguish I hadn't the sense to reply in the same language, but could only keep on imploring him to fight for life. 'No, Molly, I'm done for,' he said, and began again on his chant of triumph." M. Vivian Hughes, *A London Girl of the Eighties* (1936), 202–3, 261.

18. For the Kingsleys, see my next volume, *The Tender Passion*, ch. 4; for the Hawthornes, below, pp. 456–58.

19. Lois W. Banner, *Elizabeth Cady Stanton: A Radical for Woman's Rights* (1980), 35.

approval, one of the last pronouncements of Lucretia Mott, friend and fellow feminist: " 'In the true marriage relation, the independence of the husband and wife is equal, their dependence mutual and their obligations reciprocal.' " Surely, she commented, "this is a good definition of marriage." In the following year she noted, "I have come to the conclusion that the first great work to be accomplished for women is to revolutionize the dogma that sex is a crime, marriage a defilement and maternity a bane." She obviously did not live as though sex were a crime: "I have never been a man-hater," she confessed. In late 1883, she recorded that she had been reading *Leaves of Grass*. She admired Whitman for his frankness, but deprecated his perception of the female of the species: "Walt Whitman seems to understand everything in nature but woman. In 'There is a Woman Waiting for Me,' he speaks as if the female must be forced to the creative act, apparently ignorant of the great natural fact that a healthy woman has as much passion as a man, that she needs nothing stronger than the law of attraction to draw her to the male."[20] She was, at sixty-eight, speaking out of her own early satisfactory passionate experience.

Sexuality could be problematic for men as for women, a contest with private devils often lost. The memoirs of James Hopkinson, English cabinet maker, ingenuous, earnest, but unsentimental, a little uncertain in their spelling and touching in their didacticism, condense such characteristic conflicts in the recital of a striking dream. "I have had some remarkable dreams in my time," Hopkinson begins, and in many of them he seems "to have the power of flight." Sigmund Freud notes in his *Interpretation of Dreams* that such dreams are often, though not always, a symbolic wish for sexual prowess. So they probably were for Hopkinson who, in his young years, lonely and frustrated, had sexual longings much on his mind. And indeed the dream he was moved to recount in his autobiography in exhaustive detail, which had Satan for its protagonist, was precisely about these longings. Dreamt when he was about twenty, it reaches into the depths of Hopkinson's troubled and unfulfilled sexuality. He dreamt that he was walking in a park in Nottingham, "with a little dog. I had just reached the lowest part of the valley, when who should make his appearance but his *Satanic* Majesty, clothed in all his terrors." Hopkinson, in his dream, did not want to appear frightened by running away, but instead "kept my eyes steadfastly upon him. He said

20. March 1, 1853; November 13, 1880; February 22, 1881; August 28, 1884; September 6, 1883, *Elizabeth Cady Stanton, As Revealed in Her Letters, Diary and Reminiscences*, ed. Theodore Stanton and Harriot Stanton Blatch, 2 vols. (1922), II, 48, 178, 183, 220, 210.

I have come to stop your goings on. I thought he meant because I went
to chappel. He said I intend to fight you. I replied very well with the
greatest of pleasure." Satan made an appointment to meet Hopkinson the
next day at 12, and then "slowly disappeared, drawing his enormous tail
after him which looked like an immense serpent, covered with scales."
This left Hopkinson pondering, still in his dream, how to face this
adversary and he "decided to go to the work shop and make a heavy
club and drive a lot of long nails into it so as to project out and form
a formidable weapon wherewith to meet him. I also decided to take the
terrier dog with me that he might bite his tail behind while I met him in
the front." At last, the time for the duel came, and Hopkinson was at the
meeting place at twelve sharp. "In another minute he arrived looking
more terrible than ever, and his eyes looked as red as if they had been
stitched in with red worsted. Not a word was spoken, but just as I was
going to tell the dog to begin with his tail, all at once he changed into
a most beautiful woman with jet black eyes."

Unsophisticated as Hopkinson may have been, he is most perceptive
in recalling the day's residues that provided fuel for his dream. "Upon
this I awoke, and," lapsing into the rhetoric of the Puritan literature he
had been reading, "behold it was a dream." And he confidently adds:
"I can account for that dream. I have been reading about Christain in the
Pilgrims progres going through the valley of humiliation," appropriate
reading for a good Baptist and assiduous chapel goer. And in fact, in the
course of Christian's "Dangerous Journey and Safe Arrival at the Desired
Country," he meets, in the Valley of Humiliation, the hideous monster
Apollyon, flatterer, tempter, and mortal enemy to the Christian faith,
"clothed with scales like a fish (and they are his pride)," much like
Satan's "enormous tail" in Hopkinson's dream. Christian and Apollyon
engage, first in furious palaver and then in deadly combat, just as Satan
proposed to duel with the dreaming Hopkinson; the sword flies out of
Christian's hand but as Apollyon is about to finish him off, the Pilgrim
deftly recovers his sword, wounds Apollyon, and drives him away. For
Hopkinson, this dramatic encounter, this decisive struggle between good
and evil, purity and sin, was overdetermined. He had long been fond of
Bunyan, he noted, as of "Miltons paradise lost," in which he particularly
enjoyed "Miltons description of Adams first meeting with Eve," as well
as "the fight between the good and bad angels, and how the bad angels
were ultimately driven out of heaven by the triumphant Son of God."
This great battle, which occupies much of Book I in *Paradise Lost*, is on
a gigantic canvas what Christian's duel with Apollyon, and Hopkinson's
struggle with Satan, are in miniature: the acting out of man's unending

inner conflict over good and evil, restraint and impulse. As for "Adams first meeting with Eve," Hopkinson must have been thinking of Satan's first glimpse of mankind's progenitors, happy and innocent still,

> Godlike erect, with native honour clad
> In naked majesty.

Milton's Eve especially must have supplied a memorable picture for the young man's erotic fantasies:

> She, as a veil down to the slender waist,
> Her unadorned golden tresses wore
> Dishevelled, but in wanton ringlets waved
> As the vine curls her tendrils, which implied
> Subjection, but required with gentle sway,
> And by her yielded, by him best received,
> Yielded with coy submission, modest pride,
> And sweet, reluctant, amorous delay.
> Nor those mysterious parts were then concealed;
> Then was not guilty shame,

intoxicating stuff for an apprentice avid for worldly experience.

If there is any doubt that Hopkinson's dream canvassed his sexuality, his needs, anxieties, and confusions, it is settled by the very next entry in his episodic memoirs, following hard upon the melodramatic encounter in the dream like an association on the psychoanalyst's couch: "A few months before I was out of my time I really began to think it was time I had a *sweetheart*. I had a feeling of loneliness and I had a vacancy in my heart which required filling." He was not to fill it permanently until a dozen years later, after some episodes with one "nice looking young woman" and another, and was to be, apparently, a happy and contented husband.

But in his youth, at least, Hopkinson found sexuality as dangerous as it was enticing. The dream vividly dramatizes his mixed feelings, his inconclusive struggles with Eros. At one level, the dream presents an oedipal scene, David bravely confronting Goliath: "I always am brave when I am dreaming," Hopkinson sardonically comments, barely veiling his wish for admirable potency. The lone apprentice, accompanied only by his terrier and armed with his heavy club alone, stands ready to challenge the towering devil who sports his enormous phallic tail. This adversary seems formidable enough, but Satan shows himself more formidable yet: he turns into a beautiful black-eyed woman. Unconsciously, Hopkinson was echoing a long tradition, which was to experience a remarkable revival in the nineteenth century: the devil as a woman, which is only another way of seeing woman as devil. And this miraculous transformation of the terrible Satanic majesty into a lovely female suggests a complicating though not contradictory interpretation: a measure of uncertainty about sexual identity or, at least, masculine strength; Hopkinson had, as we know, some self-deprecating comments to make about his bravery. And behind all of this there may lurk the memory of a primal scene, recovered and distorted in the manner of a dream: the combat, as Hopkinson imagines it, is a confused melee, Hopkinson striking at the devil with his nail-studded club from the front while his terrier bites Satan's tail. It is reminiscent of the rape, ugly and violent, that the threshing about of sexual intercourse often appears to be in the eyes of the small child witnessing it, in helpless excitement and fear. No wonder that the dream "made a deep impression" on Hopkinson when he first dreamt it, and that it stayed with him until he recaptured it for his autobiography half a century later.[21]

There were times, indeed, when conjugal provocations reached for a perverse luxuriance more commonly encountered in pornographic novels. In May 1904, Godfrey Lowell Cabot, Boston patrician and prominent industrialist, sent a sensual confession—and invitation—to his wife, Minnie. He was in West Virginia on a business trip and had evidently just awakened, aroused beyond bearing. It was 4:12 in the morning. "I have had a dream, I can't sleep for longing." Then, lapsing into German, he reported it: "I dreamt that you urinated into my mouth, much, very much, and that I had swallowed down your urine greedily." He added, in German, that he loved her "so much," and then, immediately, returning to English, that the weather was very warm and that he was working on his mail.[22]

This was evidently a repetitive fantasy for Godfrey Cabot. A year later, again away on business in West Virginia, he rehearsed it once more: "You do not know," he wrote to Minnie, "how I long for you. I was almost wild with desire as I came along hither in the train today." Then, he told her his wild desire, again in German: "I wished that your bladder were filled with urine to bursting, and you could, to save your life, relieve yourself only by urinating into my mouth until you had

---

21. *Victorian Cabinet Maker: The Memoirs of James Hopkinson, 1819–1894*, ed. Jocelyne Baty Goodman (1968), 55–56. In view of Hopkinson's limited education, it is worth recording that he thought himself thoroughly middle-class, indeed called himself, in his will, a "Gentleman" (p. 110).

22. Leon Harris, *Only to God: The Extraordinary Life of Godfrey Lowell Cabot* (1967), 228. Harris provides both the originals and a translation, but I have made my own.

entirely emptied yourself and I was totally filled with your urine to bursting." Continuing in German, he moved to another fantasy, more extravagant still: "Or, if you were a large giantess, who was utterly starved, with a great yearning to devour a human being, how gladly I would be the victim, if only you would swallow me alive, if you would pull through your beloved lips over your slimy tongue first my feet then my legs my hips my whole body my head, one after the other, through your beautiful throat into your dear belly where I could sense your heartbeat and your breathing so sweetly and quietly as I fell asleep in bliss and little by little disappeared in you through digestion." It would appear that his imaginative yearnings troubled Cabot a little, but not enough to stay his pen: "You would best destroy this silly letter," he told his wife, back in English, "or if you cannot understand it, with the help of a German dictionary, I will translate it to you when I return." And he signed himself, a man who had been married for almost fifteen years, "Your lover."[23]

In the absence of Cabot's associations to these opulent fancies, it is risky to venture interpretations. Cabot had been deeply attached to his mother, who had kept his youthful environment as "wholesome" as she could manage; for all his collegiate amorous adventures, he claimed to have entered marriage, at twenty-nine, a virgin. Earlier, beset by self-doubt, and in rapid succession, he had proposed to three young women, almost as though to reassure himself that he was manly enough for the rough world of business and industry in which he was beginning to maneuver with a good eye for profitable opportunities. And later, he presented himself to those who knew him well as a prude and a prig; he would thunder against couples seeing one another in the nude. "What he practiced," his son-in-law remarked, "was legalized rape."[24] What he practiced in his mind was more scandalous still, if far less palpable.

Cabot's two successive fantasies are pendants to one another. In the first, he is filled with his wife's substance; in the second, she is filled with his whole being. Both seem to represent regressive wishes, the

23. Ibid., 229–30. One of the Goncourt brothers had a strikingly similar dream half a century before. He finds himself in an immense, beautifully decorated salon, style Louis XV, and meets a woman there: "I put my mouth on the mouth of the woman and married my tongue to her tongue. I experienced an infinite pleasure, as if all my soul rose to my lips and was inhaled and drunk by that woman. Special pleasure during the dream, beyond real pleasure. Ideal coitus." November 1854, Edmond and Jules de Goncourt, *Journal; mémoires de la vie littéraire 1851–1896*, ed. Robert Ricatte, 22 vols. (1956–58), I, 157.

24. Apparently, as Minnie Cabot told her daughter, the couple's honeymoon had been a horrifying disaster. Harris, *Only to God*, 33, 137. For his son-in-law's comment, p. 323.

second far more drastic than the first. Cabot seeks nourishment, fanta-sizing like a small child about the character, the very source, of his supplies. He yearns to return to his mother's womb, reversing the natural progression of things, even entering her head last, as though a film of his birth were being played backwards on the screen of his mind, and then imaginatively enjoying the quiet subsistence of the foetus in its mother, only to dissolve into her as he had been before conception. Both fantasies are linked in still other ways. Cabot's urinary and urethral images are both frequently symbols of sexual desire, and his vision of his body being swallowed up is akin to those dreams of intercourse in which the body as a whole takes the place of the penis, and the woman's mouth that of the vagina.

These psychoanalytic speculations may be plausible, though they throw more light on Godfrey Cabot's peculiar needs than on the contours of bourgeois sexuality. But his willingness to fix his fantasies on paper and forward them to his wife invite larger inferences. Minnie Cabot was an utterly proper New England matron, an incurable snob and an in-veterate complainer, anxious about money, reputation, social position. The prospect is improbable, but, as Godfrey Cabot's letter reveals, far from unthinkable: Minnie Cabot, the very model of middle-class recti-tude, laboriously deciphering her husband's sexual fantasies, or, even better, her husband, this impeccable Boston Brahmin, translating them for his wife's benefit. That Godfrey Cabot should have been an alert and active member of Boston's censorious Watch and Ward Society only makes the idea of such reading all the more appalling. His work for the Watch and Ward gave Cabot some enviable opportunities to read obscene books and study obscene photographs.

In general, it is safe to say, bourgeois married bliss was at once less infantile and less inconsistent than it was with Godfrey and Minnie Cabot. At times, as the letters and occasional writings of Joseph and Laura Lyman testify, it could achieve an allusive, playful freedom proving that habituation need not produce tedium, that repetition could enhance pleasure, even among bourgeois. Joseph Lyman was a graduate of Yale, class of 1850, a lawyer, journalist, and in the late 1860s, after eking out a scanty and precarious living for some years, a respected editor and writer on agronomy. As a young man he had been a friend to Emily Dickinson and a suitor of her sister, Lavinia. In 1858 he married Laura Baker, a young woman who had literary pretensions that almost matched his own, and trusted phrenologists as enthusiastically as he did. While the husband had a phrenologist draw up a profile of his character, in-cluding his sexuality, the wife wrote for the phrenological press: in

October 1865, Joseph addressed Laura Lyman from New York, with the jocularity that the two enjoyed, as "MY BELOVED CONTRIBUTOR To the American Phrenological Journal Known by the immortal Signature 'L.E.L.' "[25] Evidently, the couple perceived themselves as partners, of the pen quite as much as in bed: "I wish I could get some writing that would let us work together a week," he wrote to her two weeks later. "The intellectual partnership between us is as delightful & perhaps as fructiferous as the physical."[26]

From early 1864 on, their partnership, both intellectual and physical, was temporarily disrupted as Joseph Lyman went to New York in search of stable employment, while his wife and their children remained behind in Easthampton, Massachusetts. He was doing hack writing and publishing occasional editorials in the *New York Times*, and would visit his family on as many weekends as he could afford. He missed his wife sorely, and not only her mind: "I wish you *could* be taken up bodily (I insist upon the fleshly transition)," he wrote to her on February 14, 1865, "and set down here with me a day and a night. . . ." His plans were grandiose and, in the unbuttoned intimacy of his correspondence with his wife, sound rather purposefully mad, like the boasting of the boy who wants to win his adored mother with unexampled feats: "Haven't you slept 7 years with a Lawyer & if you *are* a woman you are such a woman as Lord Brutus took to wife—so *mothered* & so husbanded what cant you do. Hear me Portia. I am hatching a tremendous plot to murder Ben Butler & Abe Lincoln & take both their heads in a bag to Richmond & get appointed Confed.Ag't by Davis to go to Europe & negotiate a universal & perpetual Peace! & become myself Prime Minister to the Kingdom of Mexico. You shall have a silver bedstead!"[27] When he was apart from his wife, Joseph Lyman gave his luxuriant and florid imagination its head.

The frustrating arrangement that kept the couple separated made them both intensely uncomfortable. "I anticipate unspeakable delight in your embrace," Joseph Lyman wrote to his Laura on March 11, 1865. But for the time being anticipation was all he had. Two days later, he had whipped himself up still further, wishing he could "feel close around

25. October 17, 1865, box 4, LF, Y-MA.

26. November 1, 1865, box 4, LF. In 1867, the couple published a popular and substantial treatise, *The Philosophy of Housekeeping: A Scientific and Practical Manual for the Preparation of All Kinds of Food, the Making Up of All Articles of Dress, the Preservation of Health, and the Intelligent and Skilful Performance of Every Household Office*—the subtitle deftly summarizing its contents and suggesting its tone.

27. February 14, 1865, box 3, LF; [March 11, 1865], box 4, LF.

me the caressing hands & be soothed by the voluptuous touch! But soon we will have it—all—full measure." Not soon enough, it would seem. "I love you ver——y much indeed my dear wife," he told her ten days later. "How kindly you would put your white arms all around me and make me sink to sleep sweet as asphodel with the exquisite contact of your smooth body. How the dreams would be of summer winds." Laura Lyman, for her part, did not hang back. "Oh how I love you," she wrote him during the same month, happily joining sexuality to religion. "How I long to see you—how I long to 'be all night in the hollow of my husband's shoulder' as Dr. Breen used so felicitously to express it in his sermons. How I long to feel the contact of my mind against yours"— and not, if I may repeat my formulation, only of his mind. A little later she grew more explicit still, downright earthy. "I'll drain your coffers dry next Saturday I assure you."[28] The Lymans had been married for seven years when they exchanged such sentiments; they had undergone distressing financial hardship, mourned the loss of a daughter, solemnly canvassed the correct pedagogy for their two little sons. In the midst of recitals of daily woes and little triumphs, social snubs and ambitious programs for the future, sexual delights engrossed their thoughts, and found unabashed expression in their letters.

Their tantalizing, enforced separation in fact generated a teasing seductiveness that might seem more appropriate in young romantic lovers than in a safely married bourgeois couple. Nor is it always easy to establish the Lymans' real feelings. Joseph Lyman wrote indefatigably: a philosophical treatise on beauty (which turned out to be an excuse for a close study of woman's body), essays on health and happiness, on agriculture, politics, and history, most remaining in manuscript, some published; Laura Lyman tried her hand at highflown evocations of her bucolic honeymoon and papers on housekeeping.[29] The couple's prose abounds in shared mannerisms—the elongation of "ver——y" and other emphatic vocables is only one of them—in poetic flights, classical allusions, grand thoughts, and elevated, sometimes elephantine diction. But their partnership in sensuality, their joint pleasure in the physical

28. Joseph to Laura Lyman, [March 11], 13, 23, 1865; Laura to Joseph Lyman, March 11, 23, 1865. Both in box 4, LF.

29. Laura Lyman, "Locust Hill and our Life There." It begins: "Never to a more delightful retreat went lovers to sip the golden goblet of newly consummated Love than Locust Hill. Hidden far away among lonely hills in the very heart of a mountainous country, no rude or careless eye of a rude and careless world could mark the natural transport and overflowing delight of a newly married pair in the Eden of their united lives. . . ." The reader who wishes to read further can find the manuscript in box 11, LF.

aspects of eroticism, remains unmistakable; it survived their style. They liked to go bathing nude in the ocean, and there is no evidence that she was more timid about her nakedness than he was about his. And when in 1863 Joseph Lyman compiled what he called a "Historia Erotica," a loose, informal gathering of miscellaneous observations on sex in Greek and Latin, he particularly noted that he had undertaken this experiment in explicitness for the eye of his wife Laura alone: "Oculis Laurae Solae Scripta." And the initiative in seduction was by no means reserved to Joseph Lyman. On March 11, 1865, "Saturday Night 10½," Laura Lyman offered herself, as it were, as food for her husband's fantasies: "I have just bathed in warm water here before the fire and am just as sweet as a rosebud." And she added, in blatant invitation: "Don't you wish you were here? or by some mysterious Arabian hocus pocus, I could put my ring on the table & wake up *there* in your arms, your two room-mates being supposed to be absent or buried in a profound & magical sleep? How much would you give? Nay, such delights are not bought with silver or gold." It must have occurred to her poor husband that such delights could indeed be bought with silver or gold, for it was after all their deplorable lack that kept the couple apart. He replied ten days later, in a forlorn little apostrophe: "You *will* talk about those baths of yours and how ravishingly sweet you make yourself on Saturday nights and the heaven which is not mine *now*." Not a bit repentant, only varying her seductive image slightly from enticing cleanliness to enticing dirtiness, Laura Lyman took up her husband smartly: "I am *not* bathed," she wrote on March 24, "the sheets are not clean—my under garments are not fresh—you shall not be tantalized any longer—but this isn't Saturday night—and tomorrow night I won't write a word to you—nor Sunday until the freshness of the bath is all gone & all the attractiveness with it." Not a little proud of her innocent and intimate provocativeness, she concluded affectionately: "*Now* how do you like it my cat? Good bye—I love you better & better & better."[30] They continued to love one another, better and better and better, it appears, making more money and more children, until his sudden early death in 1872, of smallpox. He was only forty-two.

Another, very different happy couple, in marriage and even before, were Lester Ward and Lizzie Vought. Ward charted the progress of their intimacy in a journal he kept from 1860 to 1870, in French—to practice the language, he said, but also, it would seem, to give elbow room

30. Historia Erotica, box 8, LF; Laura to Joseph Lyman, March 11, 1865, Joseph to Laura Lyman, March 21, 1865, Laura to Joseph Lyman, March 24, 1865, all in box 4, LF.

to his daydreams and his experience of wooing the young woman to whom he referred, invariably, as "the girl." It is an instructive journal, for Ward, then a poor young man tenaciously educating himself to become one of America's most distinguished sociologists, wrote with enviable inner freedom, moving from theme to theme, quite unself-conscious about revealing associations.

In the summer of 1860, Ward came to know and to love *la fille*, but at first confined himself to holding hands and covering her face with kisses.[31] By early October, his "soul" was "full of dreams" about the future and love and marriage. "I cannot believe," he wrote, "that I shall ever really be happy without marrying the girl, my first choice and the sole object of my affections." He would "envisage the happiness of a union with her and the sweet sensations of my spirit are not to be described." He was sure that she loved him and that they had much in common. "With her tender and affectionate disposition I can be the happiest of mortal beings. O yes! to be embraced in her arms of love is like entering the gate of heaven." He reproached himself with yielding to such imaginings, but continued to cultivate them and to describe the indescribable: late in October, he noted that she had admitted that she loved him, kissed him on the mouth, and called him affectionate names. One evening, as they settled down together, reclining on a bench, he unfastened his shirt and put her hands on his bare chest; she was willing but a little shy, wondering if she was doing wrong. "O I am mad with love," he commented, his desire outrunning opportunity: "O if your sister were not here!"[32]

Fortunately, Lizzie Vought's sister would not always be in the way, but consummation was still some time off. In late November, Ward gave pathetic, if unconscious, utterance to his longing and his frustration. He had, he noted, just "finished a letter, or rather a page, to the girl," and added, "I had a horrible dream last night concerning her. I dreamt that she married a man named McCarty and she wrote me a letter and what sensations of horror and despair it produced in me!" He was ready to interpret this response as a favorable signal: "This assures me that I truly

31. August 5 and 19, 1860. The original French diary, called "Journal des affaires particulières et générales," from which I quote here, is unpaginated. In 1935, Bernhard J. Stern brought out a translation entitled *Young Ward's Diary*. It is serviceable and generally accurate, so I have appended references to that volume in parentheses (here, 6–7). But Stern's text frequently omits sentences and makes some distracting slips. Hence I have uniformly resorted to the French original, in the Lester Frank Ward Papers, BU-JHL.

32. October 11, 1860 (13); October 21, 1860 (14–15). In his excitement, Ward wrote *"insensensé."*

love her. O if she died I would want to die too! Her sweet little figure is at present very dear to me." Then he jumped, as he often did, in the manner of nineteenth-century diarists, to mundane details about the weather: "It snowed last night and it is very cold this morning. The barometer is holding steady at around 29." But his love for the girl, and her sweet little figure, hovered in his mind, and he returned to them, though in symbolic form: "I strained to push my steel pen into my pencil case a moment ago, and it became stuck so that I broke my pencil case to get it loose."[33] The steel pen was obviously not the only pointed object that Ward wanted to activate, the pencil case not the only thing he wanted to break.

But he had to wait. Ward saw much of the "girl" during the winter, and in early 1861 the couple groped for new levels of physical intimacy with one another: "The girl and I have had a very sweet time. I kissed her on her sweet breasts and took too many liberties with her sweet person and we are going to stop. It is," he added, "a very fascinating practice and instills very sweet, tender and familial feelings in us, and consequently makes us happy." But, happy as they were, he was afraid that they might go too far and offend against "the laws of virtue." Their resolutions held firm for a while, and it was not until October 25, 1861, more than a year after Ward had discovered that he loved the girl, that he could report to his diary: "Being obliged to discontinue writing rather brusquely last Tuesday, I must take up the story where I left off. When I arrived at the house of the sweetness, she received me in her arms of tenderness and pressed me to her form of honey, and our lips touched and our souls entered Paradise together." It was the moment they had been inching toward for more than half a year. "Her mother was ill, but her sister had gone away and all was well. That evening and that night we experienced the joys of love and tasted the felicity which belongs to married life alone. On Sunday I stayed all day in the soothing regions of felicity. In the interval I wrote a letter to my mother which I have not yet mailed. At about eight o'clock I forced myself from her breast of honey and lips of sweetness."[34] At the moment of reaching his erotic goal—*their* erotic goal, I should say—Ward, to judge by the intrusive appearance of that letter, found boyish wishes, once repressed,

33. November 23, 1860 (22).

34. February 9, 1861 (35); October 25, 1861 (80–81). It is of some interest that the sixteen-year-old James Boswell used very similar language for sexual consummation, as he conducted a heady love affair with a woman of good family, eleven years his senior: "Tea," he wrote in his journal on December 16, 1761, "paradise. Think on this evening." Frederick A. Pottle, *James Boswell: The Earlier Years, 1740–1769* (1966), 79.

rising up to haunt him. To think of his mother at this supreme moment of sexual consummation, so ardently desired and so patiently planned, to remember a filial duty not yet completed, was to exhibit the subterranean persistence of tenacious oedipal longings in Lester Ward. This was the masculine pendant to Mabel Todd, presumably absorbed in her sensual marriage, struggling with her feelings for her father and for Austin Dickinson, her father's surrogate, all her life. We are never wholly done with old childish loves.

But absolute concentration on the sensual was not given to Lester Ward, as it is given to few. In August 1862, he enlisted to fight in the Civil War, and fixed this, and another important event, in his diary: "All men who can are going to war, and all is excitement. But one more event is needed to crown the catalogue, and yesterday was the day. Wednesday August 13, 1862. I had to register my marriage! What? I, married? True enough. The cherished of my heart, whom I have loved for so long, so constantly, and so frantically, is mine. We are keeping it a secret, but people have guessed it without discovering it. O how sweet it is to sleep with her! I paid $3.00 fee."[35] Life, embracing love and war, was at this moment very exciting, and Ward recognized that. But he also recognized, in the midst of his felicity, that everything, including excitement, exacted its tribute.

The fee proved far from excessive. Married life wholly matched the Wards' high expectations; his diary swarms with breathless exclamations about his "darling Lizzie" or his "sweet wife" who, he puts it summarily, is "perfect." They studied and played together, as a compatible pair. He found, with his angel of a wife, the bonds of marriage sweet, and they were physical bonds, experienced in her arms and on her breast. On March 4, 1866, he noted happily that it was his wife's birthday—and his mother's. But he did not dwell on the coincidence, preferring, rather, to recall the blessings of his marriage. To be away from his wife was torture: "How I love her!" he wrote in the summer of 1867, while his Lizzie was off on a visit. They had then been married for five years. "How can I wait another week?" It was the kind of question that David Todd and Joseph Lyman and thousands of other bourgeois husbands across the Western world would ask in similar circumstances.[36] When Lizzie Ward died in 1872, Lester Ward was desolate—not desolate enough to remain single but, despite all the frantic efforts of his second wife to erase the blissful memories of his first marriage, his thoughts of Lizzie, and their

35. August 13, 1862 (114).
36. See August 19, September 6, November 3, 1863 (118, 121, 124); March 12, 1865 (64); March 4, 1866 (193); August 4, 1867 (236).

dozen years together, never left him. The two had, after all, been the first to enter, and explore, their sexual paradise—together.

Ward's memories are deeply implicated in his sociological writings. Desire was central to his view of man's place in society. It is desire that pushes man to action, and every desire is, in and of itself, good. "All desires are alike before nature—," he wrote in his discussion of modesty, "equally pure, equally respectable. All are performed with the same freedom, the same publicity, the same disregard for appearances. Nature knows no shame. She affects no modesty." And he explicitly included sexual desire in his sweeping thesis: "The acts which are necessary to the perpetuation of a species possess no special quality which distinguishes them from those necessary for its preservation." As long as the gratification of one's desires does not compromise that of others it is permissible. The less modesty, the less false shame, the more pleasing such natural activities as sexual intercourse will become. Like so much else that deluded men think natural and unchangeable, modesty is a purely social, a conventional acquirement; it is a "remarkable sentiment," a "mass of absurdities and irrationalities."

This was philosophical utilitarianism informed and colored by personal experience, equating pleasure with happiness and, at the same time, exculpating pleasure from the charge of immorality. Hence, both implicitly and explicitly, Ward was a sexual egalitarian, mirroring once more the bliss he had enjoyed, jointly, with his Lizzie. In a strikingly original explanation of female sexuality, he argued that it is an "anomaly"; in other animal species, the female is passive, her passion periodic. But species man possesses both imagination and reason, and thus the anomaly of female sexual desire becomes normal in humans. True, women affect to flee the man; they are shy and timid where the man is aggressive. But this is a purely social, long-inherited convention. It is mere modesty. "Unless the functions of the body are in harmonious operation nothing worthy of the name happiness can exist," Ward wrote in 1893, in his *The Psychic Factors of Civilization.* It is true, on evolutionary grounds, that woman is the repository of intuition. But it does not follow, certainly not for Ward, that her reason is weaker than man's, or that the two sexes should be unequal in any respect, least of all in their need for, and right to, sensual gratification.[37] Ward's "philosophy of desire" was a sophisticated argument about pleasures and pains, the search for satisfaction and the restoration of equilibrium after gratification. But at its

37. *Dynamic Sociology, or Applied Social Science as Based Upon Statical Sociology and the Less Complex Sciences,* 2 vols. (1883), I, 632–33, 639; *Psychic Factors,* 72 and chs. 9 and 26. See also *Dynamic Sociology,* 602–9.

heart his sociology was a celebration, a poignant, glowing portrait of the
paradise Lester Ward had shared with his wife.

Other correspondence of married couples survives haphazardly, tantalizing but in its incomplete way eloquent testimony to a good portion
of erotic satisfaction, in the most proper surroundings, for both partners.
The well-known American economist and prolific writer on railroad
affairs Henry Varnum Poor told his wife in June 1842, after they had
been married for nine months, upon their "first separation of any considerable length of time since our marriage," that he could not go to
sleep at night, and could hardly tolerate "going *to bed all alone*." His
wife reciprocated the feeling, and continued to deplore any occasion
that tore them apart; almost twenty years later, she wrote her husband
an impassioned plea, displaying concern, loneliness, and the most unmistakable desire for physical closeness: "Henry my darling, Why *did* you
not come home yesterday? I try not to be anxious. If you are sick, I
can come to you in a moment. The children are all well," she reassured
him, and added: "I can leave them *just as well as not*."[38] Tersely but
passionately Mrs. Poor, faced with a choice between husband and children, chose her husband, without hesitation.

Students of nineteenth-century bourgeois culture have often discounted
the effusive vocabulary of intimate correspondence as empty formulas,
specimens of unvarnished and unmeaning sentimentality. Actually, the
flowery words often expressed not more but less than they meant. They
were tokens of powerful emotions, hints at uninhibited fantasies. The
eminent German botanist Karl Heinrich Emil Koch, whose expeditions
took him to the Caucasus and southern Russia, lived out his sensual
fantasies in long letters to his fiancée. "Dearest Beloved," he wrote from
St. Petersburg in the spring of 1838, on his way back home, "when these
lines reach you, give your yearning free play and yield wholly to the
sweet hope that you will soon clasp me in your loving arms." He
reminded her that their "time of heavy trials" was nearing its end, and
that the "morning sun of our friendly life together glows in the fiery
East of our reunion." His longing for her, he told her, was "gnawing" at
him, "sighs all go to you," as he anticipated pressing his girl "to my
heavily beating heart"—all well-worn but precise poetic evocations of his
unsatisfied emotional and erotic appetites. Seven years later, now married
to his Therese, as he went off on another botanical expedition he reminded his "Dearest," his "All," that their earlier farewell had been quite

38. June 5, 1842, box 8, Poor Family Papers, Radcliffe College, Schlesinger Library;
August 11, 1861, box 9, ibid.

different; then they had already loved one another "ardently," but the feeling they now had for one another was really "inexpressible and boundless"; it has seized the "most serious, the deepest life of the soul."[39] Gratified desire did not diminish love but often intensified it.

The bourgeois record is rich in such passions, and they traverse lovers' lives, from adolescence to elderly maturity. When business or family affairs forced them apart, wives rushed to join husbands and husbands, wives; children are, in much of this middle-class correspondence, as in middle-class diaries, interesting, amusing, often cherished footnotes, the source of lighthearted anecdotes and the targets of earnest advice. The bond that mattered, surpassing all others, was that between spouses. The nineteenth-century middle-class wife who pours all her affection into her children and denies her husband all sexual warmth is largely a myth —a pathological though certainly not uncommon exception. It could have arisen only because the gap between public conduct and private feelings was very large; fastidiousness and decorum denied the erotic most avenues of expression. But there were many bourgeois communions in that age which produced, for wife and husband alike, that beautiful feeling of climax which Mabel Todd knew so well.

2. The Dubious Certainty of Numbers

Elusive and baffling as the quality of sexual experience must be to its historian, its quantity, the distribution and intensity of erotic pleasure and pain across culture, is more elusive, more baffling still. Yet the question whether the marital felicity of the Todds, the Lymans, the Wards was in any way representative of their class and time is worth asking. The nineteenth century, addicted to surveys and comparisons, did not fail to include sexuality in these inquiries, and to draw conclusions about its incidence by subjecting it to the dubious certainty of numbers. These studies, fragmentary, partial, sorely in need of skeptical interpretation as they are, permit at least some informed guesses about bourgeois sexual life in the years that Lester Ward and Mabel Todd recorded their repeated visits to Paradise, enjoyed a little heaven after dinner. In 1907, the German sexologist Dr. Iwan Bloch, more celebrated as a publicist perhaps than a medical specialist in sex, brought out a comprehensive survey on modern erotic life in which he did not slight the vexed question of female sexuality. After rehearsing the conflicting views of prominent sexologists,

39. April 22, 1838, box 1, Karl Koch (1809–79) Nachlass, Stabi, Berlin; May 17, 1843, box 2, Koch Nachlass.

he reported the results of a highly informal, regrettably imprecise survey that he had undertaken on his own: "I have myself questioned a considerable number of educated women on this point." And "*without exception*," these middle-class women—evidently not a servant girl or dairy maid among them—had "declared the theory of the inferior sexual sensitivity of woman to be incorrect; many even thought that it is greater and more persistent than in the man."[40] Impressionistic as Dr. Bloch's investigative methods were, he was confident that women are probably quite as sensual as men.

Some two decades before, an eminent Scottish gynecologist, J. Matthews Duncan, far more taken than Iwan Bloch with the value of statistics, had reached almost identical conclusions. Lecturing on sterility to the Royal College of Physicians in 1883, he acknowledged that female sexuality was a "delicate" matter, and that usable definitions of terms, which would ease inquiry, were hard to establish. He found it helpful to differentiate sexual desire from sexual pleasure—excitement from orgasm —but even this distinction did not permit that conscientious investigator to proffer really conclusive generalizations. Indeed, among 504 sterile women whom he questioned about their erotic experience, only 196 would, or could, report on their sexual pleasure, and 191 on their sexual desire: Dr. Duncan's tight-lipped majority added up to more than 60 percent of his sample. But an impressive number among those of his patients uninhibited, or boastful, enough to answer his indiscreet questions asserted, or admitted, that they were sensual beings: 152 said that they felt sexual desire, while only 39 recorded its absence; 134 reported orgasms, while 62 did not.[41] It was not much, but it was enough to permit Duncan to think of sensual women as normal.

Dr. Duncan's lectures are in fact a tribute to the varieties of sexual experience. "Desire and pleasure," he wrote, "may be excessive, furious, overpowering, without bringing the female into the class of maniacs; they may be temporary, healthy, and moderate; that may be absent or null"; some, even married women who regard their husbands with affection, may feel aversion or pain. Artificial stimulants or inhibiting forces can fundamentally transform the very nature of desire and pleasure alike; the passage of time, too, brings its alterations. The "influence of society and its amusements, of diet, of special kinds of reading, of association with males, is well known and recognized in the increase

40. *Das Sexualleben unserer Zeit in seinen Beziehungen zur modernen Kultur* (1907; 5th enlarged ed., 1908), 90.

41. *On Sterility in Women* (1884), 90; see table, p. 99.

of sexual desire." Perhaps even more far-reaching was Duncan's conviction that sexually anesthetic virgins can, and after a time often do, learn
to enjoy the erotic embraces of their husbands: "Pleasure is frequently
absent at marriage, and gradually developed during the continuance of
that state."[42] The capacity for sexual arousal and for sexual satisfaction
is inherent in women as it is, only more obviously, in men.

As a specialist in women's disorders, Duncan was professionally surrounded by sexual malfunctioning, and he took the ailments he treated
very seriously; they were both "numerous and important." But they
were *ailments*; Duncan was prepared to lend his authority to what he
called the "almost universal opinion" that "in women desire and pleasure
are in every case present, or are in every case called forth by the proper
stimulants. The opinion is founded on experience, and it is, no doubt,
nearly true." Duncan epitomized these complicated realities in one
vignette: "A robust healthy woman is married at eighteen; she bears
three children and has four miscarriages before she has passed twenty-
three years of age. Up to the birth of her last child, and for five years
subsequently, she experiences no sexual desire, and has no pleasure. Five
years after her last pregnancy she almost comes to have intense desire
and pleasure, but remains sterile for four additional years before she
seeks a cure of her sterility. Fertility present, while desire and pleasure
are absent: sterility present, while desire and pleasure are present."[43] The
passionate female in tune with her husband was, for Dr. Duncan, no rarity.

The Mosher Survey, probably the most thoroughgoing inquiry into
middle-class sexual behavior in the bourgeois century, forcefully invites
the same conclusions. Beginning in 1892, Clelia Duel Mosher investigated
the erotic feelings and habits of about four dozen American women.
Her first venture was suggested by a Mother's Club at the University
of Wisconsin, some of whose members she used as guinea pigs; but later
she cast her net more widely. A zoologist who took a medical degree,
practiced as a physician, and ended up as Professor of Personal Hygiene
at Stanford University, Clelia Mosher straddled the boundary of two
ages. Reserved by upbringing but inquisitive by profession, she was
prudish about the display of sensuality and hesitant about its meaning
for her. In Europe just after World War I, she deplored the way
Americans had adopted "Latin standards." For herself, she noted, the
constant dwelling on sex "disgusts and revolts me—I like to keep away—

42. Ibid., 90–91, 92, 94.
43. Ibid., 96, 100.

Sex has its place but not for constant contemplation—There are so much more interesting things—."[44] She never married. A self-described and self-controlled Victorian, her "sense of decent reticence" served her well as she asked her respondents the most uninhibited questions to get some memorable, if generally laconic, answers.[45]

Dr. Mosher was both fortunate and unfortunate in her respondents. The very character of her sample, making it unrepresentative of the general, even of the middle-class, population of the United States, also provided her with respondents willing to discuss their most private lives. Most of the forty-five women who returned usable answers had gone to normal school or attended college, in decades when it still took exceptional energy and enterprise for a girl to seek higher education. And most of these respondents had, naturally enough, married educated men. Dr. Mosher's population, then, serves to map the upper limits of Victorian sensual flexibility and liberalism. Victorian: for, while Clelia Mosher took her questionnaires into the twentieth century, the overwhelming majority of her respondents were at home in the nineteenth. Seventeen of them had been born before the Civil War, sixteen more before 1870; a clear majority, in short, were very much members of Mabel Todd's generation, and had absorbed their erotic ideals and inhibitions before the notorious "new woman" came onto the scene. And they were like Mabel Todd also in that, as I have indicated, all were middle class, all were educated, and most had had some experience earning their own money. While Mabel Loomis Todd had given piano lessons, sold her paintings, and later made presentable sums giving slide lectures and writing for the periodical press, these women had worked mainly as teachers. Had any of them met Mabel Todd, they would have had much to talk about and agree on.

Possibly the weightiest matter they would have agreed on, though they might not have talked about it, was the pleasure of married sex. More than a third of these forty-five women claimed that they reached orgasm "always" or "usually"—nine, or one in five, said "always." Another forty percent replied, sounding only marginally less satisfied, that they experienced it "sometimes" or "not always." Although some

44. Kathryn Allamong Jacob, "Clelia Duel Mosher," *Johns Hopkins Magazine*, XXX, 3 (June 1979), 16.

45. "These lectures in personal hygiene," she wrote in 1926, two years before her retirement from Stanford at sixty-five, "are exhausting me more than they should. Where should I draw the line? My Victorian sense of decent reticence is constantly shocked although my secretary says I have given no sign." Carl N. Degler, "Introduction," *The Mosher Survey: Sexual Attitudes of Forty-Five Victorian Women*, ed. James MaHood and Kristine Wenburg (1980), xviii.

among Dr. Mosher's questions were ambiguous, these numbers invite the reasonable inference that only one woman in four among her sample was more or less sexually anesthetic—I say more or less because even in this last group several occasionally felt the stirrings of sensual arousal. In at least one instructive instance, the confession of sexual pleasure subverts a most emphatic denial. No. 23, asked, in Mosher's somewhat stilted formulation, "Do you always have a venereal orgasm?" firmly answered, "Never." Logically, she should have skipped the next question, which inquiries, "When you do" have an orgasm, what is the "effect immediately afterwards?" But No. 23 calmly chose to respond to it as well: "Keyed up after and more stimulated."[46] Plainly, some women who enjoyed orgasms would rather not admit that they had any, ever. The sensuality of these educated married women was shot through with hesitations and conflicts, but it was fairly active and alert and, with rare exceptions, unapologetic. There is nothing extravagant about imagining matrons like these, before 1900, taking the initiative in bed.

The capacity to reach orgasm implied, for many of Dr. Mosher's respondents, the right to expect it. Some took failure to experience it as a regrettable episode to be overlooked in the glow of the next, more satisfying, erotic embrace; a few treated it as something of an intimate catastrophe. One, who happily had an orgasm nearly every time, found its absence "depressing and revolting." A second said about her failures, if "I remain unsatisfied the result is bad, even disastrous, nerve racking, unbalancing, if such condition continues for any length of time." She even attributed a fibroid tumor she developed during the menopause to her repeated inability to reach a satisfying sexual climax. Yet a third, who found intercourse agreeable without achieving an orgasm every time, suggested that when she did not, she was philosophical about it: "Every wife submits sometimes when perhaps she is not in the mood, but I can see no bad effect. It is as if it had not been. But my husband was absolutely considerate. I do not think I could endure a man who forced it." And this, her husband's gentle regard for the tides of her sexual appetite, was necessary to her pleasure. Many respondents, indeed, recognized that male and female sexual rhythms could vary greatly, and their husbands' patience and forbearance were therefore necessary to their erotic economy. Most in Dr. Mosher's sample seem to have been married to considerate husbands; some say so emphatically, and many others imply it. The average frequency of intercourse was around once a week, often declining over time, with a few couples indulging much more often,

46. *Mosher Survey*, 263.

or much more rarely, than this—a rate that seems to have satisfied the husbands practically as much as the wives. There were differences in desire: while at least thirteen of these women continued sexual intercourse during pregnancy at the same intervals as before, and about twenty more had intercourse at a somewhat reduced rate, their eagerness for sex decreased, whether in obedience to physiological signals or to cultural proscriptions. Intercourse during these months was largely in obedience to the husband's wishes; though, while not desired by most wives, it also seems not to have been painful or revolting to them. Few respondents found themselves yoked to insatiable sexual athletes: one, No. 27, felt victimized; she reported intercourse three times a week, or "oftener if she would submit," even though she found sexual relations only intermittently agreeable and her sexual desire arising about once in two weeks. She submitted, when she did submit, because it was "necessary to keep home together and keep man satisfied."[47] A few others also noted that their desire for intercourse arose rather more rarely than their husband's. But most respondents were blessed with husbands who waited for them—had, in fact, waited for them at the very outset of their married life: one had not consummated the marriage for ten days, another for two weeks, still another for a whole year.[48] Only two respondents explicitly, bitterly characterized sexual pleasure as reserved to the male. The gratification from intercourse, as one of these women graphically put it, is the preserve of "man—occasionally. Like animal once or twice a year."[49] It was perhaps characteristic of this respondent to acknowledge little desire on her part and only occasional orgasms. But she was in a vanishing minority, at least in this sample.

True to their upbringing, their whole culture, Dr. Mosher's respondents found their sexual feelings running well ahead of their conventional vocabulary. They had been raised, nearly all of them, as good Christian girls, and the pious conviction that God had intended intercourse for procreation alone retained its hold on their moral imagination. Thirty, or two-thirds of them, called "reproduction" the principal goal of sexual relations, but their glosses, terse and often touchingly inconsistent, disclose that many among them also saw pleasure as justifying the sexual act, even if conception was not intended or not possible. No. 24, the most

47. No. 12, 138; No. 47, 453; No. 41, 415; No. 27, 302–4. No figures in this survey are harder to extract than the ones relating to intercourse during pregnancy. Nine did not answer that question at all; only five said more or less categorically that it did not occur. The responses of many others are inconclusive.

48. See, in order, No. 22, 251; No. 43, 426; and No. 15, 174.

49. No. 32, 351. No. 9 (102) is not wholly clear on this point.

dogmatic of the purists, had second thoughts. "I cannot recognize as true marriage," she wrote bluntly, "that relation unaccompanied by a strong desire for children. Platonic love from this point of view is almost as far removed from my standard as marriage, that is, a form of so called legalized prostitution." This phrase was a weary cliché by the 1890s, and had been one long before; No. 24 could have read it in any number of tracts on marriage, or, for that matter, in such anti-sexual fictions as Tolstoy's *Kreutzer Sonata*.[50] Yet she was open to doubts and discriminations and had done her bit toward strengthening her own happy marital bond. Being "very much in love with husband," she ingenuously confessed, she had "rather cultivated the passion." Even now, after years of marriage, she was experiencing orgasm less than half the time. When she did she found it exhausting, admittedly, but it also made "intercourse in a sense more agreeable."[51] Upon examination, "legalized prostitution" turned out to be a highly tendentious description of her experience.

Most of Dr. Mosher's other respondents did not need to go through such tortuous reasoning to discover the sexual relation to be agreeable indeed. One, who had orgasms "generally," noted that she "would have hated to have omitted the experience." Another, who thought intercourse "usually very delightful," found it "a sedative," for it made her "very sleepy and comfortable. No disgust, as I have often heard it described." The ideal, she proposed, would be "once a month, when both are well, and during the menstrual period, and," she added, "in the daylight."[52] Her erotic imagination was alive and unembarrassed.

Sexual intercourse was, for many of these women, healthy and health-giving. They wanted it, but wanted it, as some of them firmly stressed, in moderation: "I consider this appetite as ranking with other natural appetites," as No. 14 put it, "and like them to be indulged legitimately and temperately."[53] But within these limits of legitimacy and temperance,

---

50. No. 24, 277. The Goncourts, ever cynical, called married households a "proclaimed concubinage." May 24, 1858, *Journal*, II, 237. More poignantly, and more indirectly, Mary Chesnut, that observant Confederate diarist, saw slavery as prostitution, and then commented: "There is no slavery after all like a wife," and, later, "All married women, all children and girls who live in their father's houses are slaves." The inference to be drawn is obvious. May 9, 1861, and February 25, 1865 (1880s version), *Mary Chesnut's Civil War*, ed. C. Vann Woodward (1981), 59, 729; see also Woodward's Introduction, li.

51. No. 24, 276–77.

52. No. 5, 66; No. 11, 126–27.

53. No. 14, 162. She added, significantly: "I consider it illegitimate to risk bringing children into the world under any but most favorable circumstances." She had three children of her own.

intercourse seemed natural, necessary, salutary. One respondent, No. 2, divorced and remarried, who thought intercourse "necessary to complete harmony between two people," attributed a significant improvement in her mental and physical health to her happy second marriage: "My husband," she wrote, "is an unusually considerate man; during the earlier months of marriage," when she was fifty, "intercourse was frequent—two or three times a week and as much desired by me as by him." The day after an orgasm, one woman, No. 41, born six years after Mabel Loomis Todd, would experience "a general sense of well being, contentment and regard for husband. This," she underscored her point, as though Clelia Mosher might not believe her, "is true Doctor." Her little exclamatory appeal suggests, once again, the divorce of private experience and public discussion in the bourgeois century. It seems as though large numbers of middle-class couples enjoyed sexuality; but, taught that this was wicked, and ignorant about the pleasures of the others, they were timid about their own. Though she did not always reach orgasm, this respondent was lucid, almost urgent, in her appreciation of sensuality in a good marriage. "I think women as well as men need this relation during middle life. It makes more normal people." While she had four boys of her own, the procreation of offspring did not, as far as she could see, need to enter into sexual congress at all: "Even if there are no children, men love their wives more if they continue this relation, and the highest devotion is based upon it, a very beautiful thing, and I am glad nature gave it to us."[54] Her quiet gratitude to nature was a tribute to bourgeois sexuality.

For all its unforced enthusiasm, there is in this response just a hint of manipulativeness or, perhaps, of resignation. If they consent to sex, "men love their wives more." The readiness of many among Dr. Mosher's respondents to have intercourse during pregnancy when their own level of erotic desire had significantly abated suggests nothing less. And several other women in Dr. Mosher's sample acknowledge as much. "Bond between the sexes," commented one, "a man more fond of his wife than other women, makes people fond and tender." This same respondent defined love as the quality "which binds the sexes together." The notion of sexual intercourse as the solder of marriage is a fairly common motif in these replies. "A close bond," No. 5 wrote, "making marriage more stable"; and again, "binds people together and holds family together—is a bond." Another was no more verbose: "Relation brings man and woman closer." Sometimes, the orgastic enjoyment of the husband radiated out to gratify the wife and to confirm a sense of closeness: "Pleasure man

54. No. 2, 24–25; No. 41, 415–16.

gets—and the pleasure of the intimacy with the one you love." The very monotony of this rhetoric, and its occasional illogic, testify to the eagerness of the respondents. Intercourse for purposes other than reproduction had its own justification. "A sense of intimacy not to be had in any other way; especially when people cannot be affectionate without going full course. Serves as a bond above even physical pleasure."[55] This anxiety to please, to fit smoothly into the role that biology had assigned to her, propelled at least one woman into a revealing slip. Asked to specify her ideal sexual situation, No. 19 said: "In prime of life: for a man well developed & vigorous about twice a week. For a woman, half as often—twice a month"—which, of course, amounted only to a quarter, not half, as often. "I was always well," she hastened to add, "and it did not hurt me and I always meant to be obliging."[56] Yet many of Dr. Mosher's respondents did not find it too onerous to be obliging; it brought rewards, not all of them purely spiritual. I am reminded of the charming French *mot* that Dostoevsky gives to a buxom young beauty, an inveterate sinner, at confession: "Ça lui fait tant de plaisir et à moi si peu de peine!" Had not many husbands, and even more of the wives, been so innocent in the ways of sexuality, Dr. Mosher's statistics on orgasm would have been even more favorable than they already were. Ignorance was not bliss.

But there was much bliss, even so. The Mosher Survey persuasively suggests that many educated bourgeois women in the nineteenth century valued—some even craved—a sexual commerce that brought an equal measure of gratification to both partners, and did not hesitate to include it in the list of qualities essential to a good marriage. Few of them could manage the rhetoric of eroticism very deftly; they plainly found it easier to perform the act of sex than to talk about it, even to an inquirer as judicious and unthreatening as Clelia Mosher. Their responses are often single words or broken phrases; lyricism is rare and more often intimated than exhibited. All the better: it means that these respondents formulated their answers not by borrowing from poetry but by listening to experience. What emerges from these comments is the felicitous conjunction, in the marital experience of these women, of affection and passion, the joining of what Sigmund Freud called the two strands of eroticism. What they all prized, and for the most part got, was temperance in practice, mutuality in demands, and spirituality in love-making.

It is this last theme, spirituality, that punctuates the Mosher survey like an insistent leitmotiv. Asked, as all were, what warranted sexual intercourse beyond the generation of offspring, one, No. 45, replied, "Affection much. One man & one woman spiritual significance most vital." And another, less breathless and more articulate: "It seems to me to be a natural and physical sign of a spiritual union, a renewal of the marriage vows." This elevating of sexual intercourse into the thin air of purity was a commonplace in bourgeois culture. Pleasure in sexuality serves "a higher purpose," as No. 29 put it, "than physical enjoyment." Sexual intercourse produces "oneness," No. 44 said; it is "uplifting like music."[57] And No. 17 found that love-making gives a "sense of complete-ness, a spiritual completeness, which is not gained in [any] other way." Then she moved, without hesitation, from mind to matter: "Physically necessary to the woman as well as the man for a complete life." Testify-ing to the delights of her sexual rapport with her husband, practicing intercourse temperately but reaching orgasm "almost invariably," No. 12 called it "not sensual pleasure, but the pleasure of love," an appealing confusion which meant, of course, that she enjoyed sensual pleasure accompanied and facilitated by warm, exclusive, and shared affection. Sexual intercourse, she added "is only warranted as an expression of true and passionate love." One respondent, No. 10, rare in this company, brought in the deity to justify sexual intercourse: "I think the man and woman married from love, it may be used *temperately* as one of the highest manifestations of love, granted us by our Creator." But her ideal was firmly planted in human equality: "Occasional intercourse," con-trolling conception, and "everything to be absolutely mutual."[58]

Love was central, indispensable, to these women, the ground, the crown, the rationale of sexuality. Intercourse, one told Clelia Mosher in 1897, is the "expression of love between man and woman," an act that is "frequently simply the extreme caress of love's passion." Eleven years younger than Mabel Todd, she confessed, after she had been married for a year, that once she had thought children to be the sole legitimate object of intercourse. But she had come to see, through "experience," that "the habitual bodily expression of love has a deep psychological effect in making possible complete mental sympathy, and perfecting the

57. No. 45, 442; No. 3, 44; No. 29, 328; No. 44, 435. No. 15 is no less eloquent: "In general terms the ideal habit would be that which should most perfectly and com-pletely serve as the physical expression of the spiritual union of husband and wife." She noted that she and her husband had not yet found the "ideal habit" for them, after four years. But she went on: "We believe in intercourse for its own sake—we wish it for ourselves and spiritually miss it, rather than physically, when it does not occur, because it is the highest, most sacred expression of our oneness" (p. 176).

58. No. 17, 197; No. 12, 138–39; No. 10, 113–14.

spiritual union that must be the lasting 'marriage' after the passion of love has passed away with years."[59] This woman expected the pleasures of sexual intercourse to outlast her immature infatuation and to cement the "spiritual union" that was her ideal of marriage.

There is more than one way of reading these fervent declarations of faith in love, of the wish to believe in the higher meaning of married sexuality. The Mosher Survey, after all, opens the door to such dramatic revisions of traditional theories about nineteenth-century sexuality that the historian might be tempted to over-interpret its fragmentary and sometimes contradictory evidence. Considering how many respondents wished to be obliging, before and during pregnancy, to their husband's importunities, perhaps even the optimistic figures on orgasms deserve to be read with some circumspection. Yet even if they were overstated, even if the respondent was as eager to please Dr. Mosher as she was her husband, this implies a certain bias in favor of sexual gratification, even for the woman, in the bourgeois century. At least some of these respondents resorted to the rhetoric of spirituality as a denial of the body, a way of coming to terms with masculine erotic demands that would leave them neither exhausted nor disgusted, and give them a gratifying sense of a marital duty well performed, worthy of a husband's gratitude. But many among Dr. Mosher's respondents were like No. 41, who was glad that nature had given human beings this beautiful sexual impulse. For them, sexuality offered itself, not simply as an instrument of married love, as an adjunct to peaceful domesticity, but as an autonomous pleasure. Their sheer worship of the spiritual licensed the gratifications of the physical. Often, intercourse was a moment of paradise, and paradise for two. What I have called the dubious certainty of numbers is not quite so dubious on this crucial point.

Dr. Mosher's investigation is at once flawed and fascinating. The women she selected and the questions she posed make it vulnerable to the charge of involuntary distortion; her small number of respondents, their very willingness to talk, and their educational level invite the objection that her results were far from representative. Certainly the answers of those who refused to participate in Clelia Mosher's bold experiment in social inquiry, or a cluster of Victoria Benedictssons, would have yielded a radically different profile of bourgeois sexuality in the nineteenth century. At the same time, the answers Dr. Mosher elicited carry conviction and have meaning beyond her group of forty-five. Hesitant, unrehearsed, inconsistent, they have the authenticity of awkwardness. Their

59. No. 22, 254.

artless and earnest candor is a clue to desires and fulfillments of which they were only partially aware; it points to erotic felicities they felt it necessary to clothe in the current vocabulary of pious respectability—this emerges most strikingly with intercourse for its own sake and their moral posture that it ought to have procreation for its purpose. Moreover, there were enough failures in the sexual lives of Mosher's respondents to make her pioneering survey a tribute to the varieties of sexual experience. The Mosher Survey is the best, indeed the only, effort at the scientific charting of bourgeois sexuality in the nineteenth century. It is all we have. But it is congruent with other, more informal testimony, and beautifully complements the letters of the Lymans and the jottings of Lester Ward. Mabel Todd, in short, spoke for a substantial population of married middle-class women. What was rare about her meticulous documentation was not her experience but her eloquence.

3. The Problematic Sex

This inquiry into the bourgeois erotic experience is, as these pages demonstrate, inseparable from the nineteenth-century debate over female sexuality. As Dr. Iwan Bloch, the noted if notoriously slipshod sexologist, summed up the wisdom of a century in 1907, the "expressions of male sexual desire and sexual lust" appeared to be "fairly unequivocal." Hence they were generating little debate—considering men's dread of impotence and anxiety about their wedding night, rather less than they merited. But for Bloch, as for many students of erotic life in his time, it was the "old controversy" over the nature and strength of woman's sexual appetites that had "not been resolved even today."[60]

The controversy had indeed, as Bloch said, a long history, but not a very lively one. Ancient Romans, medieval Christians, men of the Renaissance and the Enlightenment, would have agreed that the matter had been largely settled in the often-retold vignette about Zeus and Hera squabbling over the relative share of sexual pleasures granted males and females. Zeus, to excuse his inveterate philandering, had pleaded that woman was the lustier sex and his infidelity only a substitute for her gratifications; Hera, the angry, wronged wife, had pointedly countered that his conduct only proved the opposite. They had consulted the seer Tiresias, who had experienced sexual intercourse in both male and female incarnations, and he had unhesitatingly awarded the palm of pleasure to woman, nine to one. There might be some, in antiquity or later, to

60. *Das Sexualleben unserer Zeit*, 89.

question Tiresias's improbable specificity, but few would have denied that his verdict contained an essential truth. When, around the time of Christ, the influential Jewish philosopher Philo Judaeus interpreted the Fall of Man as an allegory, he read Adam as the embodiment of reason led astray by Eve, the incarnation of sensuality. The great moralists from Montaigne onward never doubted that woman is, indeed, an eternal Eve. One did not have to be a misogynist fulminating against Woman as the source of all moral corruption to see her as the vessel of lust. And this is how she appeared through the centuries—until the nineteenth.

Bloch, then, was being imprecise as usual when he suggested that the question of female sexuality was still unresolved in his day; more accurately, it had been reopened a hundred years or so earlier. Much like the intensive, panic-stricken crusade against masturbation, the doubts that physicians and preachers threw on woman's native sensuality were highly characteristic phenomena of the time.[61] The bourgeois century made Woman problematic.

This rather curious debate made a decisive difference to nineteenth-century women in all their roles—and to men as well. After all, whether female sexual responsiveness was an inborn drive or an acquired task, a natural right or a legal duty, mattered: the answer one gave helped to shape the extent, the very character, of woman's marital obligations and, more obliquely her aptitude, if any, for higher education and the liberal professions. To define the nature of female sexuality was to do nothing less than to define the nature of marriage itself and to supply instructive clues to the quality of bourgeois communions.

In the light of the certainty that had governed medical and theological discourse on this important matter through the centuries, nineteenth-century hesitations and contradictions are arresting. Some physicians, awed by what they perceived to be the intricacy of sexual impulses, called for more research. "The question whether the man or the woman covets the joys of sexual commerce more," Dr. Friedrich Siebert, a skin specialist and sexologist in Munich, wrote in 1901, "has been much canvassed and answered in various ways. We lack a really dependable standard of judgment." Similarly the French physician Paul Moreau, in his treatise on aberrations of the "sense of generation," noted—justly enough for the decade in which he was writing, the 1880s—that "there is a genital sense generally acknowledged but not scientifically explored." In the same vein of restraint, the Swedish specialist Dr. Seved Ribbing maintained in the early 1890s that the "strength of the human sexual drive,

61. See below, pp. 295-318.

its demand for an object of satisfaction, shows great differences under exceptional circumstances," and he listed celebrated individuals, including women, "equipped with a truly enormous sexual drive." He detected subtle differences between men and women, but thought both beyond doubt erotic in their very nature. Dr. Siebert thus spoke for a respectable body of opinion when he expressed skepticism about the popular belief that "the *naturae frigidae* is far more widespread among women," and instead ventured the suggestion that while many women display a certain aversion to intercourse, they probably do so because a clumsy husband "has used up his forces before his wife has reached the moment of highest voluptuous pleasure." But, he added, this delicate question needed to be investigated further.[62]

Other nineteenth-century commentators on sexuality saw no such need. Cynic, idealist, and scientist could meet on the proposition that woman craves intercourse as much as man. French students of love like Stendhal or Balzac certainly took this for granted. Candid prosecuting attorneys or lawyers of women in the dock for crimes of passion—for murdering an inconvenient husband or a cooling lover—publicly noted what many privately believed: that woman often takes the initiative in starting an affair, and that she needs regular doses of sexual pleasure to keep her sanity. "Deprived of certain pleasures," one such lawyer wrote about his client in 1882, woman will suffer, "and the mind becomes troubled when the senses have not been satisfied."[63] Numerous physicians unhesitatingly endorsed this point of view, and not just for murderesses. In 1855, Dr. Félix Roubaux, a specialist in French mineral waters and something of a medical historian, argued in his bulky treatise on impotence and frigidity that "in normal coitus, the role of the woman is not wholly passive." And he energetically defended the woman's right to sexual desires and "venereal pleasures."

Often enough, this defense was swathed in elevated rhetoric. In his treatise on the sexual instinct, the noted obstetrician Dr. James Foster Scott acknowledged that woman is endowed with erotic desire, but he hailed it as a servant to higher duties: "A clean, pure, undefiled sexual feeling" is a "fundamental law in woman's nature, for love is her element; and her sexual feeling is by no means a light thing, but an inflexible yearning, normally, toward an honorable maternity, which impulse is

62. Siebert: *Sexuelle Moral und Sexuelle Hygiene* (1901), 47; Moreau: *Des aberrations du sens génésique* (1880; 3rd ed., 1883), 317; Ribbing: *Sexuelle Hygiene und ihre ethischen Konsequenzen* (1892), 43.

63. Mary S. Hartman, *Victorian Murderesses* (1977), 192.

infinitely higher in rank than the sensual passion of the libertine and seducer." In an ingenuous—and, for the nineteenth century, far from uncommon—reversal, Dr. Scott argued that the sexual appetites of the woman actually raise her above the man; finer than the male, she is "the Mother—the Generatrix—of all animate beings."[64] For many in the bourgeois century (though by not means all) it was one thing to see a truth, quite another to publish it without moralizing embellishments.

Men of the world had arrived at the same conclusions, by experiment, though they were inclined to state them without genteel frills. "I would say to a bachelor, his face young and his heart old, stripped of foolish illusions," the sophisticated and heartless Goncourts confided to their journal, "eager to use women, seeking not to secure his pleasure but to make his way: always, and fearlessly, set upon the woman of thirty-eight, plethoric and tormented in her blood. With her, he can do everything, and dare everything very quickly; and once the woman is his, he possesses her entirely: he can make her the instrument of his ambition or the tool of his passions." The scene that the Goncourts here conjure up is ugly in the extreme. It anticipates a number of Maupassant's iciest tales: the panting, sexually unsatisfied female, no longer young—in the mid-nineteenth century, thirty-eight was distinctly middle-aged—debasing herself before the stud who gives her regular orgasms. But whatever its amorality, this bit of paternal counsel from two experienced roués to apprentice roués leaves no doubt that in the Goncourt circle at least, woman was known to be a fully sexual animal—if little better than an animal.

The brothers, of course, knew what they were talking about. With surgical precision and detachment, they recorded the orgasmic outbursts of their mistresses: "Today, here is the murmuring, the breathing, and the *grunting* of love. It's the woman who speaks and who moans: 'This is hitting my nerves ... Oh! Bibi, I'm coming ... Hum ... hum ... hum ... Do it! ... Hum ... hum ... hum ...' Here the woman is done enjoying; the man continues. The woman: 'Oh! One of my legs is hurting ... Do it, say, pig! ... Oh! everything's wet ...'" Again: "Study of love from nature. Noise of the sheets.—'Hi! hi! hi!'—Snuffly breathing. In low tones: 'That's tickling me nicely ... Push hard ... Ah! oh! ...' The bed squeaks; breathing is speeding up: 'I want to go on top of you

64. Roubaux: *Traité de l'impuissance et de stérilité chez l'homme et chez la femme, comprenant l'exposition des moyens recommandés pour y remédier*, 2 vols. (1855), II, 449–50; Scott: *The Sexual Instinct: Its Use and Dangers as Affecting Heredity and Morals* (1899), 126–27, 119.

. . . Oh! my Bibi . . . Hum! hum! hum! . . . Oh! you're going too far,
my God! . . . Your heart was beating under my buttocks . . .' "[65] The
Goncourts needed no surveys to tell them that woman was as capable of
sexual excitement as any man.

Amiel agreed with the Goncourts though, of course, in far more decent
tones: "Fundamentally it is the same thing for each sex," he wrote. "In
their reciprocal attraction, *each searches for his complement*. One may
say that Don Juan himself seeks only one woman; and that the whole
life of each woman is spent in seeking *one* man, *her* man."[66] At times this
affirmation had a rather raffish, if professional, provenance. Some time in
1865, John Bartlett, phrenologist in New York, drew a character profile
for Joseph B. Lyman. Doubtless aware of Lyman's pride in his physical
prowess and his ambition as a writer, Bartlett took care to note Lyman's
"sustained power for a long chase," and described Lyman's "animality"
as "partly that of the eagle & partly that of the horse." Lyman, he asserted, was certainly "a natural writer—the pen is as natural as a talon on
an eagle's claw." It was a most encouraging appraisal. Bartlett's comments
on Lyman's erotic situation, enclosed with his report, were even more
encouraging: "Your prick is either down or up—mostly down but when
it is up you do vigorous work—so thorough that no sane woman would
hanker for a change." Bartlett added: "If your wife is in fine health &
your equal physically, you can let things have their way; but a full
cavalry charge draws on you as much as two or three leaders in your
columns." And he suggested, "You ought not to fire a broadside oftener
than once a week. That will content her & not hurt you. If your life were
either more muscular or more epicurean you could indulge more copiously. You want things right, just right about your bed and it pays to
have them right." Bartlett took particular care to reassure Lyman about
his wife's stake in his sexual performance. "Your wife," he concluded,
"has no occasion to feel jealous of you. You are a gentleman and you
don't want food unless it is flavored right & served in a proper dish. If
you do it once to a woman you will do it a great many times, for two
reasons, first because you dont want variety and second because she
could not possibly gain anything by a change."[67]

There is much to be said about this little diagnosis, evidently drafted in

---

65. June 13, 1858; November 1 and 16, 1859, *Journal*, II, 246–47, III, 161, 168.
(Suspension dots in the original.) The very next entry on November 16 echoes the
sexual rhythms just recorded: "Civilization goes from the Orient, from South to
North: it is like the pulse of the globe rising again."

66. August 22, 1849, *Journal intime*, I, 514.

67. Titled "Sexually," this is Bartlett's appraisal in its entirety. Box 10, LF.

careless haste and labeled "obscene." The pungency of Bartlett's language, his military metaphors and broad advice on how to satisfy a woman suggest a certain camaraderie between expert and client, or the kind of coarseness often characteristic of man talking to man about woman. It is impossible to know what Laura Lyman would have thought about being likened to a proper dish even if, as we know, she enormously enjoyed her sexual life with her husband. But what matters here is Bartlett's calm confidence in woman's sensuality. It evidently required no discussion, let alone proof. In describing Joseph Lyman's sexual capabilities as so vigorous and thorough that "no sane woman would hanker for a change," he meant to say that sane women enjoy intercourse as much as do men. In postulating that if Lyman's wife is "in fine health & your equal physically," Bartlett reasonably implied that women's sexual appetites often differ for physical as much as for psychological reasons; in arguing that if Lyman's own life were "more muscular or more epicurean," he could indulge in sex more than once a week, he suggested, just as reasonably, that men's appetites, too, vary with their circumstances.

The materials that reached the general public, whether facile popularizations or carefully researched treatises, often took this line, at once expected and liberal. Gustave Droz, a prolific Parisian journalist, stated the argument for the passionate woman in his *Monsieur, madame et bébé*, which was first published in 1866 and ran through 121 printings in eighteen years. The book is a set of linked, strenuously informal essays leading from courtship to marriage to parenthood, complete with lubricous bachelor, intrusive mother, and blushing bride. Droz's tone seems intolerably arch today, but it was calculated: it was his way of disarming what he thought to be prudish social ideals that made women dread marriage in his day. The wedding over, the bride's mother "says a few words into her daughter's ear, speaks to her of sacrifice, of the future, of necessity, of obedience . . ."; no wonder the first night is a succession of timid approaches on the husband's part and equally timid encouragements on the wife's, until at last she lets him, poor shivering fellow, join her in bed and kiss her. Finally she confesses that she loves him, "but so softly and so slowly that she seems to be dreaming." Yet all goes well: that erotic happiness is natural in marriage was, after all, Droz's message. "How many times, my God, have we laughed in recalling these memories now so far away!"[68] Madame's sexuality needed only to be awakened to meet monsieur's halfway.

There were authoritative, or at least plausible, voices in the French

68. *Monsieur, madame et bébé* (1866), 137, 154.

medical profession who shared Droz's conviction that a happy marriage must not neglect sensual felicity for both partners. The most notable among these was Dr. Auguste Debay, a retired army surgeon who became a popular author on all sorts of subjects, including the hygiene of bathers and the mysteries of magnetism. But what he called his "studies on love, happiness, fidelity," on "jealousy, adultery, divorce, and celibacy," always remained his favorite terrain. His *Hygiène et physiologie du mariage*, first published in 1848, rivaled Droz's popular journalism in sales and, doubtless, in influence; it reached its 125th printing in 1881 and continued to find new readers after that. Debay volubly inveighed against sexual abstinence, and deplored its consequences, especially for women, as nothing short of disastrous: "Celibacy," he writes, "exercises so baneful an influence on the intellectual faculties of the woman that, in all lunatic asylums, the number of girls and unmarried women is entirely out of all proportion" to the general population; he noted that "hideous neuroses attack the majority of girls who consecrate themselves to chastity despite the ardor of their temperament." Such a girl turns pale and languishes; give her a man and her cheeks will bloom again.[69] For all his vaunted professionalism, Dr. Debay did not disdain folksy remedies.

Marriage is, therefore, in Debay's book, a blessing, physical and mental, for both sexes. The "sharing of pains and pleasures," the affectionate mutual aid, tender caresses, and sweet consolations, make marriage a rare resource in an egotistical world. And, for Debay, these shared activities emphatically included sexual intercourse: marriage is "that happy commerce of body and soul which aids the couple to bear the burdens of life." The much-agitated question of whether man or women experiences the livelier pleasure in bed is an idle one, for it has been resolved "by the physiological experiments" of modern researchers. The truth is that such pleasures vary, and for many reasons. "The imagination and genital sensitivity influence one another reciprocally. Subjects endowed with erotic imagination, just like those endowed with genital superactivity, experience very frequent desires which they constantly seek to satisfy. It is in town and among the idle"—among the bourgeois, one might say, especially prosperous ones—"that one encounters this category of individuals."[70] Debay echoed a dominant view of his age in perceiving rural sexuality as brutality in the male and more or less marked indifference in the female. The middle classes, he intimated, literate, sensitive, schooled

69. Debay, *Hygiène et physiologie du mariage* (1848), 14–15. See also Debay, *Philosophie du mariage. Etudes sur l'amour, le bonheur, la fidélité, les sympathies et les antipathies conjugales. Jalousie—adultère—divorce—célibat* (1849).

70. *Hygiène et physiologie du mariage*, 101–2.

to patience, enjoy a more gratifying, literally more human, sexual life than that.

In pursuing his exposition of refined sexuality, Debay rehearses the varieties of genital sensations with almost voluptuous precision. When intercourse is short, he notes, woman "shows herself passive in the act." But when, on the other hand, intercourse is prolonged, then "the friction of the labia minora, the titillation of the clitoris, the soft rubbing experienced by the vagina, raise the excitation of her whole genital apparatus to the highest degree." Voluptuous pleasure is sure to follow swiftly. The woman's "sexual system" is more "extensive" than the man's; her imagination is livelier, her sensitivity greater. Hence she "trembles, shudders under the amorous embrace and savors pleasure during the whole time that sexual excitement lasts." Man's arousal may rise higher but is shorter. And man, after intercourse, is more exhausted than woman, susceptible to a kind of "momentary impotence"; at best he can perform no more than five or six times in seven to eight hours—an athletic rate that Debay evidently found neither excessive nor extraordinary. Woman, in contrast, is ready for intercourse at all times, on a moment's notice. Much, Debay implies, depends on the technique and the sensitivity of her lover: "Woman resists amorous combats longer than man, and it is always foolish or imprudent for him to try to prove the contrary by physical means." In fact, Debay balks at some sexual practices as unkind to the female, and unnatural into the bargain: to "approach a menstruating woman" is revolting; men who do so display "disgusting lubricity and depraved tastes."[71] There were some styles of sexual gratification that Debay, liberal and debonair as he was, found unacceptable.

Debay was scarcely a revolutionary. He counseled women to sham a sexual arousal they did not feel, especially simultaneous orgasm: "Man likes to have his happiness shared." True, a man can be a beast in bed, but if he is, Debay told his women readers, "you can extinguish in your caresses the ardors of his sexual fever." It was only fitting that Debay should single out the missionary position as the "normal" one for intercourse; woman astride the man might produce a voluptuous experience, but it constitutes a reversal of the natural order. For all his suggestive tone and confident posture, Debay was a counselor in conflict; the familial hierarchy he honored was at war with his advocacy of erotic enjoyment for both sexes. When all was said, man, for him, belonged on top. Yet the twenty-odd pages Debay devotes to aphrodisiacs only underscore his commitment to sensuality and his conviction that woman is an erotic

71. Ibid., 103–4, 221–25, 80.

creature in her own right, rather than the passive victim of the lustful male, or a mere biological instrument for the perpetuation of the race.[72] It says much about Debay's culture—educated, largely liberated from the moral authority of religion, and French—that his book should have enjoyed such immense and lasting popularity.

While others, Germans or Englishmen, liked to ascribe such relaxed views on sexual conduct to proverbial French immorality, one could find sexologists across the Western world who took the same position, implying that a married man need not seek his sexual gratifications outside the marriage bed. Dr. Anton Nyström, for one, a distinguished Swedish physician who also dabbled in cultural history and philosophy, and whose writings were widely translated, insisted that "in woman, as well as in man, it is undoubtedly the sexual instinct, and not the problematical desire of propagation, which attracts the one to the opposite sex. The sexual instinct belongs to the female organization just as much as to that of the male, even if ascetic principles and social conditions to a great extent suppress them." Nyström was one of the few medical experts of his day to distinguish between woman's original nature and her social situation. Because both her asceticism and her submissiveness in society have been taken as fundamental to her being, he wrote, "many have proclaimed that the sexual instinct plays no important role whatever in woman, and if it is strong in some individuals it is a sign of moral degeneration or improper voluptuousness." Like other critics of prevailing notions about female sexuality, Nyström was inclined to hold religion responsible for such blatant misconceptions: "The dominant sexual ethics of Christian countries has forced woman to suppress her sexual instinct." And, unlike most other writers on the subject, Nyström actually consulted women, "many educated and refined," including the German pacifist and sex reformer Helene Stöcker, on their views of female sexuality. Not surprisingly, he found their "candid and well prepared articles" most useful documents, in which "the sexual instinct and the desire of love are declared to be just as decisive for woman as man, and motherhood is given a secondary importance." Mabel Loomis Todd could have enthusiastically subscribed to both of these propositions. The brief case histories, nothing more than vignettes, that he offered from his own medical experience amply confirmed what these educated and refined women had already said in print: sexual abstinence, in which Dr. Nyström included masturbation, induces insomnia, headaches, hallucinations; moreover, the sexual impulse

72. Ibid., 106, 108–9, 354–78.

had a way of breaking through the most formidable inner obstructions.[73] Droz and Debay had some impressive allies.

But their camp, though far from timid, isolated, or eccentric, was for some decades increasingly outnumbered, and its opinions partially drowned out, by far more somber voices denying the healthy and respectable woman any natural erotic inclinations whatever. The opposing parties lined up against one another across time and place; Bloch himself quotes half a dozen or more experts, most of them recent and most of them German, fundamentally at odds. There was no national consensus: Italians and Frenchmen, Germans, Englishmen, and Americans found themselves on both sides of the question. Nor did a consensus ever emerge; advocates of sexual purity, who invariably portrayed the natural woman as shrinking and passive in the sexual relation, seem to have become more diligent as the century progressed. But they never monopolized the field. Nor did eminent specialists agree with one another; early in the century and late, and into the twentieth century, some diagnosed woman to be as passionate as man, others insisted on her natural frigidity.

Probably the best-known—and certainly the most literary—critic of the long-dominant perception of woman as a passionate being was Dr. William Acton, whose gospel of female sexual anesthesia was approvingly quoted in his time and achieved international circulation. Acton was nothing if not blunt: "The majority of women (happily for them) are not very much troubled with sexual feelings of any kind. What men are habitually, women are only exceptionally." And he added that such exceptional women were essentially aberrant creatures, nymphomaniacs and other potential, or actual, inmates of insane asylums. Interestingly enough, Dr. Acton intended this cardinal fact of life to be reassuring, rather than depressing, to men: "No nervous or feeble young man need, therefore, be deterred from marriage by an exaggerated notion of the duties required from him. The married woman has no wish to be treated on the footing of a mistress." Her natural coldness should permit him to shed his apprehensions. "In the majority of cases," Dr. Acton reinforced his point, "the modest English female, who has just gone through all the anxieties and fatigues of the marriage ceremony and its attendant leave-takings, and finds herself in a position so new, so anxious, and so apparently isolated, as that of a newly married woman, would be generally only too happy for the first few days to dispense with what in most

73. *The Natural Laws of Sexual Life: Medical-Sociological Researches* (1904; tr. Carl Sandzen, 1906), 150–51, 157–61.

instances is to her, at least, a most painful and distressing climax to her other agitations." She was, to Dr. Acton's mind, too much of an angel to be treated like a "courtezan."[74]

Those engaged in the business of religious exhortation found Acton's pronouncements most welcome. But many medical specialists, often with decades of practice behind them, also rushed to endorse his terse and dogmatic conclusions. In the mid-1880s, Dr. Richard Freiherr von Krafft-Ebing lent them his imposing authority in his widely read and repeatedly revised *Psychopathia Sexualis*. He acknowledged the erotic foundations of high culture: "What would the plastic arts and literature be without their sexual base!" But he did not grant that much to women. As late as 1894, in the ninth edition of his classic, he insisted that "without doubt," the man has "a livelier sexual need than the woman. Heeding a powerful natural drive, he desires a woman from a certain age onward. He lives sensually." The woman is different: "If she is normally developed mentally and well brought up, her sensual desire is small. Were it not so, the whole world would be a bordello, and marriage and the family unthinkable. At all events, the man who flees woman, and the woman who pursues sexual gratification, are abnormal phenomena." Women crave love more than men do, but theirs is a spiritual rather than an erotic need. In a "medical-psychological study" of sexual perversion first published in 1890, Krafft-Ebing reiterated what he had already said in his masterpiece: woman is naturally passive. "With woman, docile subordination to the other sex is a physiological phenomenon." Her lot is at once biological and social: the female is passive in the process of generation and "in the social conditions that have always existed."[75] On this showing, the most revolutionary upheaval in the social order could never strike off the shackles that nature had fastened on woman's erotic desires.

This became the prevalent though, as I have noted, by no means universal view of the matter. In his authoritative textbook *The Human Body*, first published in 1881, H. Newell Martin, biologist and physiologist, cites a knowledgeable physician to the effect that not merely is the act of sexual intercourse at best a "nuisance to the majority of women belonging to the most luxurious classes of society," but very many of them suffer acute pains from this presumed pleasure, and often break down in their general

---

74. *The Functions and Disorders of the Reproductive Organs, in Childhood, Youth, Adult Age, and Advanced Life, Considered in their Physiological, Social, and Moral Relations* (1857). Revised several times with trifling changes in the subtitles and substantially enlarged. I am quoting from the 3rd ed. (1865), 133–35, 103.

75. *Psychopathia Sexualis, mit besonderer Berücksichtigung der conträren Sexualempfindung* (1886; 9th ed., 1894), 11, 14; *Neue Forschungen auf dem Gebiete der Psychopathia Sexualis. Eine medicinisch-psychologische Studie* (1890; 2nd ed., 1891), 38.

health. Martin evidently shared Dr. Acton's conviction, expressed some decades earlier, that women consent to intercourse only to please their men. "A loving woman, finding her highest happiness in suffering for those dear to her, is very unlikely to let her husband know this, so long as she can bear it."[76]

Others, though less doctrinaire, were little less sure. In the mid-1850s William A. Alcott, the American educational reformer and a licensed physician, condemned lewd publications for spreading the "very erroneous impression" that the woman is "naturally sensual, like the other sex." And he asked, rhetorically, whether any "slander can be greater than the affirmation that she is constitutionally, or by natural inclination, impure?" Alcott conceded that there are some "shameless women," but most occupy "a sphere but little lower than that of angelic excellences." Some years before, in his famous article on prostitution in the *Westminster Review*, the English publicist W. R. Greg lifted women into the same exalted sphere: "Women's *desires* scarcely ever lead to their fall." With the exception of the lower orders which are continuously exposed to stimulation and lasciviousness, "the desire scarcely exists in a definite and conscious form" in women "till they *have* fallen." While in men, "in general, the sexual desire is inherent and spontaneous, and belongs to the condition of puberty," in women "the desire is dormant, is non-existent, till excited." And so, "women whose position and education have protected them from exciting causes, constantly pass through life without ever being cognizant of the promptings of the senses. Happy for them that it is so!"[77]

Greg was inching his way toward a striking compromise: women have, like men, sexual impulses implanted in them, but while the male feels them powerfully and displays them hungrily, the female senses them obscurely and may never act on them at all, until she is seduced into lubricity. Many writers on sex and marriage, in fact, maneuvered themselves into some intermediate position on woman's erotic constitution: man must be the active initiator of sexual commerce, while woman

76. *The Human Body: An Account of Its Structure and the Conditions of Its Healthy Working* (8th ed., 1904). Martin was professor of biology at The Johns Hopkins University and of physiology in its medical faculty. Dr. Alexandre Mayer, a leading French authority, expressed himself in very much the same way, in a long chapter on "Woman," in his *Des rapports conjugaux considérés sous le triple point de vue de la population, de la santé et de la morale publique* (1848; 4th ed., 1860), esp. 210, 215.

77. Alcott: *The Physiology of Marriage* (1855), 45–46; [W. R. Greg]: "Art. VII— I. De la prostitution dans la ville de Paris, par Parent-Duchâtelet . . . ," *Westminster Review*, LIII (June 1850), 456–57. Greg does acknowledge that women obscurely feel at least something resembling sexual arousal.

remains a mysterious being; but woman has her sexual feelings, too. Thus, in his tract *Queenly Womanhood*, drenched in citations from Scriptures, Smith H. Platt argued that while the "most obvious" purpose of the sexual instinct is the perpetuation of the human species, "there are strong reasons for believing that it ministers to another purpose," namely "the growth or fervor of the natural affections." And these are shared by both sexes. "This conclusion," he thought, "is greatly strengthened by the otherwise unaccountable frequence and persistence of the desire," though he quickly added, rushing back to the safety of conventional wisdom, "particularly among males of the human species." Platt enjoined wives to sacrifice their health to their husbands' sexual needs, "even though the sacrifices may *seem* to be a species of immolation, abhorrent to the sensibilities of her nature." But he added, for balance, that "no true husband will behold such sacrifice for *him* without feeling the noblest instincts of his manhood stirred to their profoundest depths," and he will restrain himself. Thus he will "nullify to the last possible degree the necessary infliction, and in that which seems inevitable to deepen his love and tenderness for the noble woman who not only has given herself to him, but *given herself for him*."[78] It may not have seemed much of a concession to feminist sensibilities, but it was the most a solid phalanx of male writers on sex could bring themselves to offer late in the nineteenth century.

Pious female publicists, for their part, though no less critical of the woman's movement than the most patriarchal of men, sometimes lapsed into a kind of defensive feminism: they would argue that in this highly developed, and sadly decadent, civilization it was woman's supreme task to rescue man from the sensual morass to which his worldly activities steadily exposed him, and which imperiled his soul. Mrs. Sarah Stickney Ellis, whose influential books reiterated over and over that women must sacrifice themselves and live for others, argued in *The Women of England* that women want education for a number of reasons: to "invest material things with the attributes of mind," to "give interest to our familiar and necessary occupations," but "especially, that we may assist in redeeming the character of English *men* from the mere animal, or rather, the mere

78. *Queenly Womanhood. A private treatise; for females only, on the sexual instinct, as related to moral and Christian life* (1875; 2nd ed., 1877), 13–14; 132–33. For a very similar view, see Dr. William A. Hammond: "Women as a sex exhibit far less intensity of sexual desire than do men. As an English writer [doubtless Dr. Acton] has remarked, it is well for the sanctity of the family that it is so." *Sexual Impotence in the Male and Female* (1887), 278. At the same time, Dr. Hammond felt constrained to treat frigidity as a disorder.

mechanical state, into which, from the nature and urgency of their occupations, they are in danger of falling."[79] This was modest and straightforward enough; Mrs. Ellis had no intention of urging the educated woman to redeem her man's character from its animal condition by becoming an adept in the animal passions. A quota of robust good sense is mixed in with exhortation in tracts like hers; the purity literature is not so prudish or constrictive as it has been painted to be. But the ideal of domesticity is never far from the surface, and such literature belongs, more or less manifestly, under the rubric of wishes.

Indeed, the improving literature of the day, a vast and interminable outpouring of clerical and pedagogic polemics, would not let the women be. Apart from the exceptions I have noted, it denigrated or minimized woman's sensuality, or denied it outright. The fear of facts distorted, and dictated, conclusions as blatantly as did the vocation of uplift or the lust for notoriety. In many authors, it is impossible to distinguish among these motives, largely because avowed principles screened unconscious conflicts. The insistence that man remain on top which, as we have seen, haunted even books written to praise sexuality obliquely discloses widespread anxieties about the danger of man being relegated to the bottom. The moralizing about sex positions symbolized other, more primitive concerns.

By and large, the intentions of marriage manuals were naively on the surface; they copied convenient and unproved bits of folk wisdom about the relations between the sexes as they unashamedly copied one another, the better to denounce female immodesty, male brutality, and general decadence. It is tempting to suggest that these moralists needed a corrupt society, since one less wicked, less given over to erotic debauch, would have rendered them unemployed. But in fact, most improving manuals were candidly religious in inspiration and tone, and it was by no means only the evangelicals who liked to quote, and quote again, those pious pronouncements calling women vessels of wrath and bidding them to fulfill their destiny, obediently, at home, surrounded by children and oblivious to sexuality. August Bebel's famous polemic *Woman under Socialism* pays wry tribute to such tenaciously held Christian views; he quotes some of St. Paul's most notorious sayings about woman's necessary subjection to man as well as some about the incurable sinfulness of the female sex from the most rabid misogynists among the Church Fathers.

79. *The Women of England, Their Social Duties, and Domestic Habits*, 2 vols. in 1 (1839), II, 197.

In the 1880s, when Bebel wrote his effective piece of socialist propaganda, calling for woman's equality with man in all respects including the sexual one, the nineteenth-century notion of female erotic anesthesia was still very much alive.

The medical literature, as we have seen, is no less problematical than the manuals compiled by pastors or educators. It is less predictable and certainly seemed, at the time, more authoritative than its clerical or didactic competitors. Dr. Eugène Becklard, to take an early example, held, in a tract on sexual physiology first published in 1838, that women may be "amorous" or not, precisely like men. When he notes that "the laws of Hymen" do not "restrict but actually promote sexual pleasures," he is referring to man's and woman's pleasures alike. But this evenhandedness does not prevent Dr. Becklard from regarding "the female sex," whom he considers to be "naturally adepts in love-making," as being at the same time "the passive principle, which has little to do in the affairs of courtship, but to respond to the action of another."[80] His little book, an early but characteristic representative of the modern genre, portrays natural inclination and social constraint as interacting, a view that suggests once again, like W. R. Greg's, a possible compromise on the vexing question of female sexuality: one might think of it as inborn, as strong as any man's, yet restrained for good reasons by society, which imposes on women the roles of diffidence and receptiveness in the interest of familial harmony.

It was not a compromise that a Krafft-Ebing would have accepted, but it evidently seemed a satisfactory strategy to both moralists and medical specialists who deplored the selfishness and animality of husbands without at the same time having a taste for equality between the sexes. One physician who found this intermediate position agreeable was Dr. Elizabeth Blackwell. A well-known pioneer in medical education, she was the first woman to receive a medical degree in the United States. Though a rebel, her rebelliousness was severely circumscribed by her religious convictions; she described herself as a "Christian physiologist," and her writings on marriage reflect her dual overriding preoccupations—woman and God. In her *Counsel to Parents*, she sternly argued that a highly developed Christian civilization justly insists on "*some* limit to the indulgence of natural instinct" as "necessary in both sexes." But this was a restraint on excess, rather than a check on inherent viciousness. "Physical passion is not in itself evil, on the contrary it is an essential part of our

80. *The Physiologist: Or Sexual Physiology Revealed* (4th ed., tr. 1846), 68, 82.

nature. It is an endowment which like every other *human* faculty, has the power of high growth."[81] Again, in *The Human Element in Sex*, Dr. Blackwell warned against the manifold degradations to which modern society tempts the sexual impulse, and reiterated that "The physical pleasure which attends the caresses of love is a rich endowment of humanity, granted by a beneficent Creative power." Beyond question, "The sexual act itself, rightly understood in its compound character, so far from being a necessarily evil thing, is really a divinely created and altogether righteous fulfillment of the conditions of present life." By demoting it below mental pleasures, and surrounding it with cautions against abuses, Dr. Blackwell did not precisely wax lyrical about sexual intercourse, but her very reserve must have made her case all the more impressive to its respectable readers, readers much like the respondents to Dr. Mosher's survey. By stressing the "mental element," she, like so many others, saw marital love as an amalgam of tenderness and desire. "The severe and compound suffering experienced by many widows who were strongly attached to their lost partners," she wrote sympathetically, is "well known to the physician; and this is not simply a mental loss that they feel, but an immense physical deprivation."[82] The measure of that physical deprivation was, in the mind of this Christian physiologist, proof of the innate sexual sensibility of woman.

A few writers had the wit to glimpse, at or least some obscure inclination to exhibit, the extraordinary paradoxes that female sexuality posed to nineteenth-century middle-class society, self-conscious as it was, committed to decorum, anxious for and even more anxious about change. The short-lived, widely respected American physician George H. Napheys, who died in 1876 in his early thirties, is a case in point. His sexual politics were distinctly progressive; he could argue (as Defoe and Diderot had before him) that woman's manifest "inferiority" to man was caused by her role in reproduction, and that woman's "faculties in which she is superior to man have been obscured and oppressed by the animal vigor and selfishness of the male." Once she has time and opportunities to unfold her powers, this inferiority will disappear. Nor was frigidity a virtue for him. "It is a false notion, and contrary to nature," he wrote, "that this passion in a woman is a derogation to her sex. The science of physiology indicates most clearly its propriety and dignity." Those wives

81. *Counsel to Parents on the Moral Education of Their Children, in Relation to Sex* (1879; 4th rev. ed., 1881), 62, 76.

82. *The Human Element in Sex: Being a Medical Inquiry into the Relation of Sexual Physiology to Sexual Morality* (1884; ed. 1894), 14, 49–51.

who boast of "their repugnance or their distaste for their conjugal obligations," of "their coldness" and the "calmness of their senses," fail to
see these manifestations for the very "defects" they are. Women who can
"withdraw themselves from the operations of this mysterious law without
suffering and with satisfaction, show themselves by that fact to be incomplete in their organization."[83]

But while Napheys, this alert and generous woman's specialist, knew
what he wanted for women, he did not know very clearly what women
actually experienced. "The vast majority of women," he wrote, endorsing
some unnamed medical authority, enjoy a "moderate" sexual appetite.
At the same time he also said, in print, that "only in very rare instances
do women experience one tithe of the sexual feeling which is familiar
to most men. Many of them are entirely frigid, and not even in
marriage do they ever perceive any real desire." The opposite view, that
women are "creatures of like passions with ourselves," is decidedly "a
vulgar opinion."[84] It would take a gifted casuist to reconcile these
conjectures with each other.

It would, on the other hand, surpass all that casuist's talents and training
to make sense of Dr. Otto Adler's grave and circumstantial treatise on
woman's defective sexual susceptibilities, published in 1904. This extraordinary work provides access more to the mentality of nineteenth-century
physicians than to the sexuality of nineteenth-century women. One of
Dr. Adler's authorities was Dr. J. Matthews Duncan who, we will recall,
had plainly stated that women's sensuality is perfectly normal and that
there was a medical consensus to that effect. Now, summing up his
conclusions on female lustfulness, Dr. Adler called on his professional
experience as well as on other gynecologists. "Practically all authors agree
in this," he wrote, apparently forgetting that Dr. Duncan had thought
practically all authors agreed on the opposite, "that *the sexual drive
(desire, urge, libido) of the woman is markedly smaller, in its first
spontaneous origins as in its later manifestations, than that of the man*";
often, indeed, the woman's "libido must be awakened in suitable fashion
and often it does not arise at all." He appealed to men of experience:
how often do husbands complain of their frigid wives! Men's irregular,
if commonplace, adventures among passionate prostitutes did not shake
Dr. Adler's confidence in his conclusions. Nor did the absence of
dependable statistics. Recalcitrant as he knew the witnesses to be, he

83. *The Physical Life of Woman: Advice to the Maiden, Wife and Mother* (1869;
3rd ed., 1888), 21–22, 96–97.
84. *The Transmission of Life. Counsel on the Nature and Hygiene of the Masculine
Function* (1871), 173.

boldly estimated that sexual anesthesia afflicts "certainly not less than ten percent" of all women, and he thought it probable that the figures were far more portentous: "twenty, thirty, indeed perhaps as many as forty percent!" It is this last figure that appealed to Dr. Adler most, and which he proffered as probably accurate.[85]

But if at least three out of five women have been "awakened" to sexual enjoyment, and if a goodly portion of these, in turn, have experienced orgasm, biology cannot be the principal cause of frigidity, and the female sexual drive, however else it might be described, cannot be "defective." On Dr. Adler's own showing, even if one grants him estimates so ill grounded and so grossly inflated to suit his case, passionate middle-class marriage is anything but an aberration from some depressing norm. The very cases which Dr. Adler adduces to buttress his argument demolish it conclusively; most of his patients were potentially Mabel Loomis Todd's sisters. Among fifteen relevant vignettes, at least ten record intense sexual interest: either orgasms reached through masturbation, or unconsummated but none the less voracious appetites. Two of Dr. Adler's patients, in fact, dramatized their excitability in his office, one of them to orgasm, in response to his examining their sexual organs and his touching their clitoris. These presumably anesthetic women resemble the patients reported by other nineteenth-century physicians, women who sought out examination of their genitalia by means of the speculum, because it aroused them sexually. Most of Dr. Adler's other patients visibly suppressed, or unconsciously repressed, their erotic susceptibilities from prudence or anxiety: one feared that sexual arousal might harm her husband who was suffering from heart disease; another, a widow with eight children, sought refuge in masturbation after her happy marriage had ended, and found to her surprise that her programmatic, self-conscious seduction of an eighteen-year-old had brought her no sexual pleasure. These case histories abound with hysterical conversion symptoms which indicate, not some fundamental deficiency in sexual endowment, but a neurotic incapacity to tap the sources of erotic pleasure, or—and this often—a libido insulted by thoughtless, egotistical, or impotent lovers. In a book devoted to demonstrating the defective sexual capabilities of the female, Dr. Adler instead provides impressive evidence for the prevalence of marital maladjustments and of infantile neuroses revived: childhood sexual conflicts driven underground with the passage of years, left unresolved, and returning to awareness in early

85. *Die mangelhafte Geschlechtsempfindung des Weibes: Anaesthesia sexualis feminarum. Dyspareunia. Anaphrodisia* (1904), 124 (Adler quotes Duncan on 67–69), 13–15.

adult life. Whatever the precise diagnosis for each of Dr. Adler's cases, they all testify to a brimming reservoir of unsatisfied female desire.

One of Dr. Adler's patients, "Case XIV," is exceptionally instructive, for she illustrates, once again, the disjunction between experience and expression that also afflicted most respectable society, a disjunction that reveals sexual passions which middle-class culture screened from awareness or articulation. Hers is a particularly vivid case, for the inability to draw inescapable inferences from unambiguous materials is shared here by patient and physician. Case XIV was a woman of thirty-one who had learned to masturbate before puberty, achieving "full satisfaction" which was "always combined with wetness." As an adult, she continued to secure sexual gratification by masturbating or being masturbated. She had had her first true love affair at twenty-two, with "an educated man, a higher officer, whom she sincerely loved"; but intercourse with him, she told Dr. Adler, took place *"without any feeling."* And to her *"greatest astonishment it did not arise in all later attempts, although the patient was sexually excited to a high degree and passionately desired the embraces and caresses of the man."* Since that time, this lack of feeling continued to shadow her love affairs, though she had been intimate with about ten men. "She is regularly excited, strongly, by the caresses of the man, especially when he kisses her and strokes her breasts. She then immediately feels a wetness in her genitals; however, she reaches satisfaction only when a certain place of the vulva is manually stimulated by herself or by her lover. In coitu normali she had not the slightest voluptuous feeling, not even with protracted attempts." At first deeply distressed, she had come to accept her frigidity, especially after meeting a number of other women resigned to the same erotic fate.[86]

But precisely what was that fate? Case XIV is not a woman "without any feeling," but one whose powerful sexuality required special conditions for its full gratification. Whatever this patient's psychological history—and Dr. Adler was not the physician to elicit it from her—there is nothing in her case, or in any of the others he cites, to substantiate his conclusion that female sexuality is, by its nature, "inferior" to that of the man. In his disregard of the evidence, Dr. Otto Adler is a worthy heir to Dr. William Acton, who had argued several decades before that "the best mothers, wives, and managers of households know little or nothing of sexual indulgences. Love of home, children, and domestic duties, are the only passions they feel." There were, in truth, many middle-class women in the nineteenth century who felt none but the homely passions that Dr. Acton lists, but who took this to mean that there was something seriously wrong with them. Otherwise, they would hardly have sought out Dr. Acton, Dr. Adler, and others of their clan, except, perhaps, for infections. It is questionable if such physicians, with such preconceptions, relieved their patients' sufferings. As far as Dr. Acton could see, a married woman tolerated sexual intercourse only because it was her husband's legal right, and because she could not help seeing how much pleasure she gave him. "As a general rule, a modest woman seldom desires any sexual gratification for herself," Dr. Acton wrote, and "but for the desire of maternity, would far rather be relieved from his attentions."[87] Actually, it is far more probable that if a nineteenth-century bourgeois couple was not sexually compatible, the wife wanted more, or different, attentions from her husband rather than fewer, especially once the period of child-bearing was past or precautions against conception had become part of the domestic routine. There were many reasons why married women in the nineteenth century failed to seek out a gynecologist for sexual problems. But it is not necessary to ascribe their professions of well-being to timidity or ignorance, to a low level of expectation or sheer resignation to their sexual slavery. They were less timid than they had long been and expected more than they had long done. Fewer and fewer of them were slaves. Their professions of erotic contentment were realistic, partly accurate reports.

Medical publications increased in volume, bulk, and the trappings of objectivity as the century progressed, graduating from tract to treatise. In the 1820s and after, physicians from Scandinavia to Great Britain, the Germanies to the United States, produced a very avalanche of books of advice for the young, for those about to be married, and for those keeping house. They were usually short, quickly written, quickly translated, and just as quickly revised, so that the credulous reader was confronted with an instant success: a second, or an eighth edition. In these productions, physicians (and often their imitators, men of the cloth) exploited their titles and academic degrees to retail popular superstitions—redheads are more amorous than brunettes, and the like—or to recall words of wisdom from such time-honored authorities as Montaigne. After mid-century, while books of this sort continued to flourish, the books on sexuality written by physicians were more often addressed to other physicians than to the general public; these volumes were heavy with charts, explicit drawings, and clinical vignettes about suffering patients; when they came to detailing the varieties of sexual

87. *Functions of Reproductive Organs*, 134.

intercourse, especially its "perverse" modes, they would lapse decorously into the thinly veiled and easily penetrable obscurity of Latin. Usually they brought to their formidable task a great deal of learning and, less often, a portion of common sense. Dr. George M. Beard, the famous American physician who coined the term "neurasthenia," could, in the midst of a diatribe against coitus interruptus, condoms, and other "unnatural methods of intercourse," relax his guard enough to describe "normal sexual intercourse, when not carried to excess," as "a sedative and tonic. It promotes sleep," he thought, "calms and strengthens the nervous system, and assists the digestion and all the other functions." Beard was ready to be flexible about his definitions. While he believed that most couples indulged their sexual appetites too freely, he acknowledged that "excess in intercourse is a relative term."[88] Rigidity and censoriousness were not Beard's specialty.

Yet when all is said, few of the physicians pronouncing in this delicate area of human experience were wholly disinterested, or even very perceptive. Their books were dictated more by unexamined preconceptions and unconscious fears than by medical observations. The medical literature of the bourgeois century, right down to 1914 and even beyond, runs counter to the revelations of the sexual pleasure that diaries, journals, fictions, and surveys disclose and that psychoanalytic investigations can substantiate. Certainly the palpable contradictions in which a specialist like Dr. Otto Adler entangled himself for all his clinical experience, all his parade of case histories, or the irresolute guesses of Dr. George Napheys, do not awaken confidence in their ability to draw rational inferences from the confessions they were uniquely privileged to hear.

By the end of the nineteenth century, the controversy over female sexuality, which obscured rather than illuminated the larger puzzle of bourgeois marital relations, had become wholly unproductive. Claim met counterclaim; all sides refurbished trite arguments and served them up as original. Only someone predisposed to be convinced could be persuaded by such stale material. And, beyond becoming intellectually bankrupt, the debate also came to seem remote and abstract, as the real world left the debaters behind. The modern woman was posing concrete and pressing questions to statesmen, educators, and physicians, with her push for liberal and professional education, for equal treatment in property rights and divorce, and for the vote. While the woman's

88. *Sexual Neurasthenia*, ed. A. D. Rockwell (1884; 5th ed., 1900), 126–27. For Beard, see my next volume, *The Tender Passion*, ch. 5.

movement left the great issue of sexuality largely implicit and decently covered, it could hardly ignore the erotic sphere; the battles over contraception and abortion were too obviously linked to woman's sexuality on one side and to woman's legal and economic emancipation on the other. It was the endless succession of babies that so many husbands seemed eager to father on their wives or the persistence of old patterns of domestic authority that kept so many middle-class women exhausted with housework and child care, prevented them from improving their minds or realizing their talents, and doomed them to a premature old age. In this atmosphere, heavy with issues of incalculable consequences, the repetitious arguments over woman's natural erotic inclinations came to seem both offensive and unnecessary.

What was urgently wanted was a fresh start, and Sigmund Freud would provide that around the turn of the century, both by developing radically new methods of inquiry and by returning to ancient wisdom. From his first psychoanalytic papers on, he had postulated woman's inborn capacity for sexual arousal and full gratification; as early as 1895, he published a paper on anxiety neurosis in which he spoke flatly of the *"artificial* retardation and atrophy of the female sexual drive."[89] In his first masterpiece, *The Interpretation of Dreams*, completed before 1900, he adumbrated his revolutionary ideas of human sexuality; five years later, in the first edition of *Three Essays on the Theory of Sexuality*, he elaborated that theory and proposed ways of integrating it into a general account of mental development. Before the outbreak of World War I, Freud's psychoanalytic ideas had reduced the nineteenth-century controversies on sexuality to irrelevance.

The age was at once ready for Freud and not ready. It was ready in that much of the ammunition that would serve him in making his revolution lay scattered—inchoate, often half-understood—in medical monographs and among philosophical speculations unencumbered by facts. Some intrepid sexologists, including that incurable romantic Havelock Ellis, were finding ways of propagating daringly positive notions about sexuality, including female sexuality. The inaccessible unconscious, the power of erotic impulses, even the infantile origins of the sexual drives, all have their prehistory before psychoanalysis. But in most respects, the age was not ready for Freud: it is symptomatic that Dr. Iwan Bloch could call the controversy over woman's erotic endowment

---

89. "Über die Berechtigung, von der Neurasthenie einen bestimmten Symptomenkomplex als 'Angstneurose' abzutrennen" (1895), *St.A.*, VI, 43; "On the Grounds for Detaching a Particular Syndrome from Neurasthenia under the Description 'Anxiety Neurosis,'" *S.E.*, III, 109. Italics mine.

"unresolved" as late as 1906. And physicians and educators continued to wrangle over the possible damage that higher education might do to the vulnerable bodies of adolescent girls, and to rehearse, evidently without fear of getting bored, that perennial question of woman's amorousness.[90] To read these controversies is to take the measure of Freud's originality.

Almost without exception, Freud's precursors had failed to pursue the implications of the sexual information they had such ample opportunities to gather; they had taken for genetic and universal what was really acquired and local. Not even that sizable minority of specialists who had detected a potent erotic drive in woman ever ventured far beyond anecdotes; if they were right, when they were, they were right largely by accident. Gentle, intelligent, and observant as physicians often were, many of them learned from their patients what they already believed on other grounds. "The error of judgment commonly made," one intrepid woman wrote to a London newspaper in 1889, "is to assume that women are less susceptible than men to the great passion."[91] Too many men, including those in positions of authority, simply did not know how to listen. Freud, in contrast, was one of the great listeners in history. Dreams, slips, gestures, symptoms, silences, served him as unwitting but, once recognized, informative guides to the retreats of inner life where sexual desires had taken refuge. He came to see what previous students of sexuality had failed to see: the feelings and experiences his patients could not remember constituted not the most trivial but the most important incidents in their erotic history. Emphatic conduct or noisily trumpeted convictions were, for Freud, distorted expressions of wishes that could be, and often were, the precise reverse of their overt manifestations. Thus it became possible for Freud to diagnose frigidity in a female patient not as the confirmation of an innate defect, but as the condensation of a conflict that had sexual passion at its core. The freedom for interpretation that his decoding of mental messages granted—in fact imposed—on healers and researchers provided a historic opportunity to read erotic experience, in all its complexity, more completely than it had ever been read before.

One momentous consequence of Freud's work, then, was the discovery —or better, the rediscovery—of sensuality in women behind its contemporary cultural disguises of shame, reticence, and crippling frigidity.

90. There was, in those years, an international debate over young men's ability to withstand the rigors of education, and a widespread fear of overburdening young minds. But women were always regarded as the truly vulnerable sex.

91. *New York Herald* (London ed.), August 14, 1889, in Hartman, *Victorian Murderesses*, 252.

Still, Sigmund Freud was far from resolving the controversy over Woman. The question was to occupy him all his life; as early as 1905 he noted, with evident regret, that the love life of woman "is still veiled in impenetrable obscurity," in part because of her insincerity; and as late as 1932 he felt obliged to concede that psychology will "not solve the riddle of femininity."[92] By then he had complicated his categorical view of the prewar years that the sexual development of boys and girls runs in parallel ways. But early and late Freud had some sense of the confusion, and the implicit value judgments, concealed in such terms as "masculine" and "feminine," and in the common identification of the first with activity and the second with passivity.

Inconsistent and surprisingly conventional as Freud's ideas on female sexuality sometimes were, he never wavered in his conviction that, whatever differences between the sexes further biological and psychoanalytic research might ultimately disclose, the potent fact of female sexuality was beyond rational challenge. And, whatever contemporary psychologists or later social historians would make of them, Freud's theories of infantile sexuality and developmental stages permitted him to integrate the study of respectable sexuality, its modest successes and pathetic failures, with the study of its neighbors, the neuroses and perversions. It permitted him, further, to speculate fruitfully on the unconscious sexual foundations of the arts, literature, politics, and religion. Freud supplied the erotic experience of the adult with its history. And his ideas on the sexual drive suggested explanations for a host of phenomena that, while in no way peculiar to the nineteenth-century bourgeoisie, came to characterize it, at least in the minds of its critics: the angel in the house, the worship of the mother, the idealization of the father, the middle-class craving for privacy, the attempt to purify Shakespeare and the Bible. Freud even provided materials that might explain the myths manufactured to stigmatize the nineteenth-century bourgeoisie.

Beyond all this, Freud's discovery of the unconscious and its workings provided a solid basis for analyzing men's emotional investment in woman's problematic sexuality. For psychoanalytic explorations of men's —and women's—defensive stratagems reached to the dynamic sources of that investment, all the more risky and elaborately disguised amid the dramatic upheavals of the age. The most sarcastic or most technical arguments asserting the feebleness or nonexistence of female sexuality

92. *Drei Abhandlungen zur Sexualtheorie*, St.A., V, 61; *Three Essays on Sexuality*, S.E., VII, 134; "Die Weiblichkeit," *Vorlesungen zur Einführung in die Psychoanalyse, Neue Folge*, St.A., I, 547; "Femininity," *New Introductory Lectures on Psycho-Analysis*, S.E., XXII, 116.

were rooted in widespread wishes and anxieties rather than in biological or physiological facts. Behind men's blustering claims to a monopoly of sensuality or, at least, to their undisputed superiority in that department, there lurked a lifelong, ineradicable anxiety, man's fear of woman.

That fear deserves, and will get, a chapter to itself. Here I only want to note that whatever Sigmund Freud did to make it comprehensible, his intervention in the debate over woman's sexuality proved something of a paradox. He offered most of the solution but, at the same time, perpetuated some of the problem. Freud was, after all, not simply the subverter of his culture; he was also its child. Discovering year after year unsuspected sources for sexual misery, it seemed plausible to him that man's archaic and endemic fear of woman, coupled with other, no less devastating fears, would necessarily contaminate married erotic pleasures. And, seeing only the victims of sexual maladjustments in his consulting room, Freud was inclined to underestimate the opportunities for erotic happiness available in the bourgeois world, for women and men alike. Some of the responses to Clelia Mosher's questionnaire, and many of the entries in Mabel Todd's journal, would have come as a surprise to him. But that makes them no less real, no less powerful a presence in bourgeois culture.

TWO

Offensive Women and Defensive Men

MAN'S FEAR of woman is as old as time, but it was only in the bourgeois century that it became a prominent theme in popular novels and medical treatises. It engaged the attention of journalists, preachers, and politicians; it invaded men's dreams and gave them subjects for their poems and paintings. Woman's increasingly open display of her power seemed the public counterpart of that private power that men evoked, more and more anxiously, in the second half of the nineteenth century: both furnished them with formidable arguments against woman's emancipation. For most males luxuriating in dominance, a woman deserting her assigned sphere not only became something of a freak, a man-woman; she also raised uncomfortable questions about man's own role, a role defined not in isolation, but in an uneasy contest with the other sex.

Men's defensiveness in the bourgeois century was so acute because the advance of women all around them was an attempt to recover ground they had lost. In earlier centuries, women had participated in running small family shops, helped to direct craftsmen's enterprises, and played highly visible roles as midwives. Then came, gradually but irresistibly, the modern professions and large-scale manufacturing and merchandising, in which women were denied any posts of command; and the diffusion of prosperity allowed many respectable couples to exempt women from the workplace. Reminiscing at mid-century about the Boston of around 1800, Harriot Hunt, America's first successful woman physician, recalled that "those were the days when women were not stigmatized for having an interest in the National housekeeping, as well as the domestic."[1] Patronizing, often slandering women, men tried to keep not only what they had long possessed but also what they had recently acquired.

One favorite instrument of men's self-defense was the tired yet indefatigable cliché about woman being the mysterious sex. Like other modern commonplaces, this had its roots in antiquity; it had been reinforced through the centuries by the very traits that men had first fostered in woman and then declared to be beyond comprehension. Her blushes and her coquetry, her bashful ways and her proverbial inconstancy in love, were adduced as proof of her essential mysteriousness. In the eighteenth-century Enlightenment, devoted to the unmasking of secrets, mysterious woman became a matter of humane, almost scientific speculation. But even then, even David Hume, the most open-minded skeptic of the age, found it necessary to declare woman a subject "little to be understood." The theme was too rewarding to be quickly discarded in the rubbish bin of baseless superstitions and survived into the nineteenth century intact. Attributing to woman confusing and contradictory traits, men found to their astonishment that she was at once timid and threatening, desirable and frightening. With time-honored roles of woman under severe pressure, nineteenth-century men indulged in this projective activity more freely and more desperately than ever. In 1905, Franz Lehar regaled enthusiastic audiences with a rousing new number, "Yes, the Study of Women Is Hard," in *The Merry Widow*. Most men at the première, like most men of two or three generations earlier, could readily assent.

Amiel's ruminations in his journal are thus characteristic of his time and class. "Since the apple of Eden," he wrote in 1849, after reading in Casanova's *Mémoires*, "woman has always remained man's enigma, his temptation, his hell and his paradise, his dream and his nightmare, his honey and his gall, his rage and his felicity." Early in the following year, he had a long, interesting conversation with a young lady of his acquaintance in which he canvassed, among other topics, "feminine nature, the impotence of objective analysis before women," and insisted that there is some mystery in every woman's fate. Alexandre Dumas fils, playwright and moralist, said the same thing rather more ominously in print: in a polemical pamphlet on female infidelity, he refers to "that charming and terrible X, *Woman*." Collectively and individually, it seemed to him, mankind continues to be agitated about her. "We are always born of her, we often die of her, for if, under present circumstances, she gives

1. *Glances and Glimpses, or Fifty Years Social, Including Twenty Years Professional Life* (1856), 4.

life to the infant, she takes it back from man as much as she can." In his anonymous *Satan in Society*, an exhaustive treatise on masturbation, marriage, and religion first published in 1870, the American physician Nicholas Francis Cooke put the matter summarily: "The temperament of woman exposes her to the most singular inconveniences and inconsistencies. Extreme in good, she is also extreme in evil. She is inconstant and changeable; she 'will' and she 'won't'." What is more, she "is easily disgusted with that which she has pursued with the greatest ardor. She passes from love to hate with prodigious facility. She is full of contradictions and mysteries." Not even Sigmund Freud was wholly immune to the charm of this pervasive old theme. As late as 1926, after three decades of psychoanalytic practice and innumerable observations on women both in and out of his consulting room, he could speak of the sexual life of adult women as a "dark continent."[2] No wonder others found woman hard to understand.

Men's highly charged construction of the mysterious sex in art, in literature, in society, in bed, supports my definition of experience as an encounter of mind with world, as a struggle between conscious perceptions and unconscious dilemmas. For the shifting realities of women's situation confronted most middle-class men, and for that matter most middle-class women, with a need to clarify attitudes, test prejudices, and make decisions. Men's very self-perception was at stake. The exasperated feelings all this aroused and the venomous controversies it generated should astonish only those who fail to recognize the commanding share of subterranean feelings in the making of social postures and political ideologies.

1. Women on the March

The laws and social habits regulating the traffic between the sexes in the nineteenth century exemplified and exacerbated the uncertainty and uneasiness reigning in bourgeois culture. Increasingly urgent calls for reform were matched by intensifying resistance. Partisan, downright punitive as biology seemed to be, bearing down as it did on women's health, needs, and desires, its consequences were showing themselves far from inexorable; the pressures of pregnancy, childbirth, constricted careers, and the rest could be partially alleviated by ingenious technology, gentle sabotage,

2. Hume: to William Mure of Caldwell, November 14 (1742), *The Letters of David Hume*, ed. G. Y. T. Greig [pseud.], 2 vols. (1932), I, 45; Amiel: December 3, 1849, February 4, 1850, *Journal intime*, ed. Bernard Gagnebin and Phillippe M. Monnier, 4 vols. so far (1976–   ), I, 584–85, 648; Dumas: *L'Homme-Femme* (1872), 3–4; Cooke: *Satan in Society*, 280–81; Freud: *Die Frage der Laienanalyse*, St.A., XI, 303; *The Question of Lay Analysis*, S.E., XX, 212.

and thoughtful husbands. In his melodramatic, somewhat hysterical manner, Jules Michelet continued to portray the female of the human species as the walking wounded of life; "*woman*," he wrote emphatically in his popular book on love, "*bears the weight of a great fatality*." She displays her injury during menstruation, confirms it during childbirth. "Nature favors the male." Woman's periodic bloodletting gave him sufficient reason to exclaim: "How severe nature is on woman!"[3] But it was becoming somewhat less severe as the century went on; the burden woman had to bear came to appear less a destiny than a long-standing bias, proclaimed by men and exploited in their favor. Indeed, the accepted customs of bourgeois culture, though displaying a crusty vitality, proved less than immortal. Ideas, ideals, relationships unchanged since time out of mind were vulnerable to attack and open to amendment.

Yet every advance, in the household, in law, at school, at work, had to be dearly bought, and the more remediable the plight of woman appeared to the judgment of strenuous reformers, the more impatient many women became with their lot. The struggle for women's rights came to be seen as the campaign to recognize, and repair, women's wrongs.[4] There were many of them, and acute. Indeed, the catalogue of women's grievances in the nineteenth century is by now amply and forcefully documented. Setting out both women's highly visible disabilities and their subtler complaints, it points to dissatisfactions that caused tensions, at times open warfare, between men and women. This war between the sexes was much debated in the popular press, in the fiction, the theatre, the painting of the day. Yet its full significance for the bourgeois experience retains much of its mystery, buried as feelings often were in intimate correspondence and private jottings.

In 1880, a housewife of Hallam, Connecticut, kept a terse but revealing diary. We know that she was thirty-three at the time, but no other records of her life have reached posterity, no earlier or later diaries, no letters, not even her name. But her laconic laments about her situation, mixed in with the customary notations about the weather, expenditures, and health, achieve a kind of mordant poetry. Bored, frustrated, and very angry, she condenses the exasperation of her sex in a few happy—or, rather, unhappy—turns of phrase. On March 28, she "did not attend church." An "unpleasant Easter day," she noted. She stayed at home on

3. *L'Amour* (1858; 4th ed., 1859), 16, 351.
4. See *Women's Rights* (1867) by John Todd, a Congregational minister much in demand on the lecture circuit, and Mary A. Dodge, writing under the pseudonym Gail Hamilton, *Women's Wrongs: A Counter-Irritant* (1868).

many Sundays; when she did attend services, she could be energetically repelled: "Went to Baptist church in the evening," she wrote on June 20. "Mr. Knapp ranted." She was fearfully busy cleaning the house, over and over. "One by one," she wrote on April 27, "the mountains diminish into molehills," and, on the following day, about her kitchen: "'The worst is over' now." Her quotation marks testify to a certain self-awareness; the commonplace phrase of relief she was adopting for the occasion seemed like a sarcastic comment on the Sisyphean nature of her task. No wonder she would curtly note at times, as she did on September 12: "Monotonous day," and, again, on September 19, another Sunday on which she did not go to church: "Monotonous day."

Hers was the monotony of unending domestic slavery, rather than of time begging to be wasted. "A day of hard work," she wrote on November 13, "but I am accustomed to that." Even sickness was a luxury she could not really afford: "An invalid today," she noted on October 8. "But if I am sick I only have to work the harder so it does not pay." When illness compelled her to be idle, she was half apologetic, half defiant: "Unable to work," she wrote on June 15. "An iron horse *can* wear out." These pithy entries, often resigned, sometimes sardonic, sound the note of gentle rebelliousness. But now and then her dissatisfaction mustered the resonance of outright protest. "A home day," she noted on June 18. "The figure-head looked on while the slaves labored." Help from supportive relatives was welcome but did not reduce her rage: "Pleasant" —this on September 6. But the weather was all that was pleasant. "Aunt Sophia came up and assisted me at the wash-tub. Very romantic life." What fantasies—of freedom, of leisure, of travel—this woman had to set aside for the unvaried routine of her life, as exhausting as it was uninteresting! "A day of days," she noted on May 5. "I believe I shall be insane if there is not a change some day." June 12 was another "day of days," and one, she added, giving voice to her depression, "that makes one long for eternal rest." She felt her intelligence rotting away: "Pleasant. Chained in my cell," she wrote on August 10. "Mrs. Snuff, alias Parmelee came to see her fellow-idiot." Her life seemed to her an interminable gray corridor of chores and more chores. "Shall I ever forget these dreary days?" she asked, rhetorically, on September 10, and again, on the next day: "Clear and cool. Perfect weather. But oh! What wretched, wearisome days are appointed unto me."[5] Such days were appointed unto untold thousands of middle-class women in her time. That kind of life was, as the combative English journalist Mrs. E. Lynn Linton recalled to her

5. Vol. 12, box 1, Diaries, Miscellaneous, Y-MA.

sister, at once "frightfully full to us, and wholly without colour or interest."[6] Many women, doubtless, knowing no better, welcomed this routine.
But many other women drew very different conclusions from the tedious
drudgery of their lives. They did not like it and said so, more and more
loudly as the decades went by. They had to say it often, and emphatically,
before anything changed.

Throughout much of the bourgeois century, all across the Western
world, women remained virtual chattels in the hands of their fathers and,
later, of their husbands. The double standard, defined and defended by
men, reigned almost unchallenged. In 1869, when John Stuart Mill published that cardinal document in the history of feminism, *The Subjection
of Women*, a modern law of divorce had been on the English statute books
for only a dozen years, and its provisions treated men and women with
characteristic inequity. The Matrimonial Causes Act of 1857, even after
earnest tinkering and frequent amendments, gave the disaffected husband
the right to sue for divorce on grounds of his wife's adultery; a wife, on
the other hand, had to adduce, in addition to adultery, some other heinous
offense like cruelty, rape, or sodomy. Like England's prostitutes, who
had to submit to the indignity of medical inspection while their customers
went unmolested by the police, England's married women were made to
feel their inferiority to the male, in divorce proceedings as elsewhere.

There were countries, including Scotland and Sweden, where the laws
of marriage treated the partners more or less as equals; yet for all their
conservatism, English statutes were, by the 1860s, relatively liberal for
their time. In France, the right to divorce had briefly and timidly flowered
during the heady years of the Revolution; Napoleon's regime, though
markedly regressive in family law, had not repealed this legislation. Then,
promptly in 1816, soon after the restored Bourbons had returned to
France, divorce was abrogated, not to be reinstituted until 1884. But even
after, in France as in England and in other countries, the doctrine of male
supremacy continued to govern legislation and practice, inviting imperiousness toward women on the part of government officials or bank clerks,
and generating delicate efforts on the part of sympathetic men to evade
the rules and social habits designed to infantilize women. Almost without
exception, woman stood under the sign of Jesus's dictum, as recorded in
the Gospel of Mark, that in marriage the couple become "one flesh," and
under its corollary, by which the husband speaks for that legal entity:
"My wife and I are one," they would say in the nineteenth century, "and

6. Duncan Crow, *The Victorian Woman* (1972), 21.

I am he." In England, this complacent attitude was firmly embedded in the common law, and everywhere it provided potent arguments against women managing their own inheritances, appearing in court as their own agents, opening their own bank accounts, and incurring debts on their own responsibility. The most scandalous, neglectful, and brutal of husbands could obtain custody of his children, affronting the facts of the case and the promptings of common sense. "Criminals, idiots, women, minors, is the classification sound?" the influential English feminist Frances Power Cobbe asked rhetorically in 1868, and her grouping graphically condensed English law and English practice as then in force.[7]

This was the state of things when, in the following year, Mill published his *Subjection of Women.* "The wife," he wrote, "is the actual bond-servant of her husband: no less so, as far as legal obligation goes, than slaves commonly so called." And he catalogued each link in the English-woman's chain: "She vows a lifelong obedience to him at the altar, and is held to it all through her life by law." She can perform "no act whatever but by his permission, at least tacit. She can acquire no property but for him; the instant it becomes hers, even if by inheritance, it becomes *ipso facto* his." Even the legal device of marriage settlements, open to the prosperous alone, proved only a limited impediment to the husband's squandering his wife's money; and in any event, "in the immense majority of cases there is no settlement: and the absorption of all rights, all property, as well as all freedom of action, is complete." Mill reminded his readers that the designation of the married couple as "one person in law" only meant one thing: "whatever is hers is his." The "parallel inference is never drawn that whatever is his is hers." And while the "degradation" of woman as wife was appalling, the degradation of woman as mother was worse: "They are by law *his* children. He alone has any legal rights over them." In short, the Englishwoman is no better than "the personal body-servant of a despot," a voluntary drudge, a pathetic victim.[8]

Mill's indictment was responsibly drawn and, considering his passionate engagement, soberly presented. But dramatically enough, in 1870, the very year after its publication, some of it was invalidated by the passage of the Married Women's Property Act. And in succeeding years a series of enactments, including supplementary Married Women's Property Acts of 1882 and 1893, the Guardianship of Infants Act of 1886, and others like them, began to dismantle England's time-honored patriarchal system. Influential men, lawyers, judges, and statesmen, many of them far from

7. "Criminals, Idiots, Women, and Minors," *Fraser's Magazine for Town and Country*, LXXVIII (1868), 777–94.

8. *The Subjection of Women* (1869), 55, 57–59.

being feminists, found the laws regulating marriage, inheritance, and financial dealings inequitable in the extreme and moved to repair the injustices these laws produced. And the woman's movement, truly international from the 1850s on, with feminists in one country taking courage from feminists in others, scored impressive successes here and there, as in Sweden, where a string of laws, beginning in 1845, granted women the right to hold and keep their property, and came to acknowledge them as fully responsible legal beings.[9] On the other hand, as I have noted, in France the *Code civil* treated women as minors, preventing them from disposing of their property or exercising authority over their children, during marriage or (once it was revived in 1884) after divorce. The angry description, by reformers, of Frenchwomen as entities without legal existence was and remained, strictly speaking, accurate.

The new German Empire was no different. As late as 1907, Marianne Weber, surveying woman's position in law, could say that "in the family law of our German civil code, the patriarchal and the individualistic ideal of marriage are wrestling for supremacy."[10] Helene Lange, the energetic lifelong advocate of women's rights, especially in the teaching profession, recalled that when Mill's *Subjection of Women* appeared in German in 1880 (translated by Sigmund Freud) its reviewers tried to dismiss it with cheap and inferior arguments.[11] Even its translator, far from demonstrating the intellectual independence with which he would later complicate men's perception of women, told his fiancée that Mill lacked the "sense of the absurd"; he had, in his argument that women can earn as much as men, overlooked that women are fully occupied with managing their household, with caring for husband and children. "He has simply forgotten all that, like everything else concerning the relationship between the sexes." Mill might find women as oppressed as black slaves, but "any girl, even without a suffrage or legal competence, whose hand a man kisses and for whose love he is prepared to dare all, could have set him right." The notion of throwing women into the struggle for life struck Freud as "stillborn." He conceded that "law and custom" owed women much they had withheld from them, but it remained true, for him, that "nature had determined woman's destiny through beauty, charm, and sweetness."[12] Martha Bernays's reply to this conven-

9. Rosalie Ulrica Olivecrona. "Sweden," in *The Woman Question in Europe. A Series of Original Essays,* ed. Theodore Stanton (1884), 211, 211n.

10. *Ehefrau und Mutter in der Rechtsentwicklung. Eine Einführung* (1907), 413.

11. *Lebenserinnerungen* (1921), 112.

12. Freud to Martha Bernays, November 5, 1883, Ernest Jones, *The Life and Work of Sigmund Freud,* vol. I, *1856–1900, The Formative Years and the Great Discoveries* (1953), 176.

tional appraisal of woman's nature and mission is not extant, but there is no reason to suppose that she resented it: nineteenth-century women were as hard to move into the feminist camp as men, sometimes harder.

That the prospects of German feminists were indeed unpromising emerges vividly from the angry glosses that Marie Calm, poet, pedagogue, and activist, supplied to a few salient provisions in the Prussian and Bavarian codes. "Here is the law of Prussia," she wrote in 1884: "Children may not marry without the consent of the father.—¶45. (So the mother is of no account when it comes to giving up her daughter!) By marriage the husband obtains control of the wife's fortune.—¶205. Whatever the wife earns during her marriage belongs to the husband.—¶221. The wife may not contract any debts on the fortune she has brought to the husband.—¶318 and 319. (He has the right to squander the whole of it, but she may not spend a farthing of what was once her own!) In regard to divorce: Bodily ill treatment may be a cause of divorce, if it endangers the health or life of the wife(!).—¶685." Calm then offered some specimens from the Bavarian statute book: "By marriage the wife comes under the authority of the husband and the law allows him to chastise her moderately(!)—¶2. Women, with the exception of the mother and grandmother, are unfit to be guardians.—¶90. (So are minors, lunatics, and spendthrifts!)"[13] As Frances Power Cobbe had already shown, such humiliating classifications rankled, but they injured more than feelings. And they were painfully slow to disappear. By 1911, the *Encyclopaedia Britannica* allowed that "Chastisement of a wife by a husband, possibly at one time lawful to a certain extent, would now certainly constitute an assault."[14] It had taken generations of feminists, women and men together, outpourings of articles and petitions, lobbying, and testifying, to enforce such revisions in the statute books and in human consciousness.

To the energetic, tenacious, often frustrated partisans of reform, the pace of improvement seemed glacial. The call of organized women for change in laws and habits grew more active, their voices more strident, toward the end of the nineteenth century. But increased publicity and occasional victories only whetted appetites, fed impatience, and made the forces of resistance appear more irritating than ever. In 1890, Havelock Ellis insisted in his first book, *The New Spirit*, that the march of science, of democracy, and of women was irresistible. "The rise of women," he noted confidently, to "their fair share of power, is certain."[15] But more

13. Marie Calm, "II, The National Association of German Women," in Stanton, *Woman Question*, 159n.

14. "Women," vol. XXVIII, 785.

15. Ellis, *The New Spirit* (4th unchanged edition with new prefaces, 1926), 10.

seasoned feminists, tested in the field, were not quite so sanguine. Certainly the causes of votes for women, which many feminists took to be the critical issue, their supreme test, had made little headway in almost half a century of agitation. In 1890, the year of Ellis's *New Spirit*, the newly minted American state of Wyoming was the first to grant women the vote. But after that, the march of women into politics slowed to a shuffle. Women had voted in school elections in a few American states for some decades, while in England they had been entitled to vote for, and permitted to sit on, school boards since 1870. Certain local franchises followed. But parliamentary or Congressional suffrage was quite another matter: at this vital point, male resistance hardened. In 1893, Colorado gave women the vote, followed in 1896 by Idaho and Utah, and then (but not until 1910) by the state of Washington. Meanwhile, woman suffrage had come to a handful of outlying lands—to New Zealand in 1893 and South Australia in 1894—far from European culture. The principal countries of the Western world were obviously indifferent to these examples; they had to undergo devastating wars and revolutions, disagreeable, even sanguinary suffragist campaigns, interminable debates and delays, before they, too, limped into the camp of universal suffrage, mainly in the 1920s. France held out until 1944. Interestingly enough, that generous nineteenth-century battle cry "universal suffrage" was restricted to manhood suffrage. Even the radical Dutch polemicists who, in the 1880s, called for the "Algemeen Stemrecht" or "Algemeen Kiesrecht," did not include women in their program. Even Mary A. Dodge, teacher, poet, publicist, an energetic exposer of women's wrongs, indignant as she was about the patronizing tone of males, did not believe in woman suffrage.[16] For most men, and many women, the thought of extending the vote in national elections to females was almost literally unthinkable.

The economic prospects of women were somewhat more cheering than this, but not much. The ideal that equal work should be rewarded by equal pay was still a remote fantasy; women's struggle to enter respectable and remunerative occupations was, though still very exhausting, a slightly less hopeless cause. The autobiographies of woman physicians and lawyers are laden with bravery and discouragement. The triumph of a single individual had to go a long way, but it did generate public atten-

16. E. H. Kossmann, *The Low Countries, 1780–1940* (1978), 327; Aristide Astruc, "Le Suffrage universel en Belgique," *La Nouvelle Revue*, XXI (1883), 39–63. For Dodge, see also note 4 above.—Not all the opposition to woman's suffrage was conservative: radicals in Roman Catholic countries like France or Italy feared that women, notoriously under the influence of their priests, might swell the ranks of reactionary parties in national elections.

tion out of all proportion to its immediate significance: a woman doctor or woman lawyer had reached an eminence easy to ridicule but impossible to overlook.

In striking though perfectly understandable contrast, women prized invisibility in writing for money, the one activity in which they had achieved a good deal of prominence. More often than not, women novelists or journalists came before the public under male pseudonyms: Ernst Ahlgren in Sweden, George Sand and Daniel Stern in France, George Eliot and Currer Bell in England, to say nothing of the ambiguous A. M. Barnard in the United States and E. Marlitt in Germany. In France, as the student of woman's situation, Theodore Stanton, observed in 1884, "several of the most popular contributors of the *Revue des Deux Mondes, Temps, Figaro*, and other leading Parisian periodicals, are women who sign their stories and articles with a masculine or fanciful name."[17] It was as though the adoption of such names could somehow appease the rage of male writers at the invasion of unwelcome, downright unnatural strangers. The device did not appease anyone; as disguises they were flimsy and rarely protected the identity of woman authors for more than a year or so. Nor did they spare the woman's contingent irritable protests, tinged with envy, from their male competitors.

Meanwhile, as I have noted, the industrializing nineteenth century, with its burgeoning office forces and international commercial networks, found women more and more useful. It was not feminism that brought girls flocking to the lower echelons of sales forces or bureau employees, to posts where both pay and prestige were low; it was the rational, complex, modern capitalist economy. The daughters of artisans and petty shopkeepers went out to become clerks, typists, secretaries. Young genteel women, impoverished and unmarriageable, often took engagements as governesses, an occupation so poignant, so redolent with prospects of gross exploitation, subtle cruelty, and (very remotely) romance, that by mid-century novelists had taken up the governess's lot as a promising theme. And women, whether of working-class or bourgeois origins, almost came to engross the teaching profession, at least in the primary schools.

Teaching, of course, was an almost preordained choice. With the dizzying expansion of primary and secondary schools everywhere, especially after the 1860s, the appetite for teachers became insatiable, and women were, of course, available. What was more, women were all too prepared to accept far lower pay than men—an irresistible temptation

17. Theodore Stanton, editorial note to Kristine Frederiksen, "Denmark," in *Woman Question*, 230n.

for employers, in teaching as in other occupations, to overcome their prejudices in the service of their profits. The female teacher did not affront accepted stereotypes about woman's true character and true office: was she not a natural teacher at home, only extending to the schoolroom the part she had always played in the nursery? Yet her lot as teacher was more dismal than her vocation as mother. Reflecting on her own pioneering medical career and on the strains that professional life imposed on other women, Dr. Harriot Hunt commented in 1856: "The miserable remuneration commonly given to female teachers sadly cripples their usefulness. It weakens their own estimation of the worth of their services" and, beyond that, it "saps their self-respect." No wonder they would flee into loveless marriages: "her services underrated, and underpaid,—her importance, a cipher,—her self-respect gone—her toil thankless—her life disgusting—herself an underling—pinched, degraded, contemned, accused, weary, and miserable"—she is bound to escape from "her daily heartbreak into private civility and public respect, by marrying an imbecile! Who blames her?"—certainly not Harriot Hunt.[18]

This was a little flamboyant, but the outburst hints at some dismal facts of middle-class women's lives in the nineteenth century. Still, their outlook was not wholly depressing; if women generally clustered on the lowest rungs of the ladder of rewards and authority, some made their way closer to the top. Zola's adroit and ruthless Madame Aurélie, the feared and powerful *chef du rayon* efficiently superintending her domain in his fictional department store "Au Bonheur des Dames," was not an implausible character. If Havelock Ellis's sturdy prediction that women would soon rise to their "fair share of power" struck many of his readers, as late as 1890, as rather naive, it was not wholly groundless.

Yet, as the medical profession demonstrates, business and professional women like Madame Aurélie remained the exception. When, in 1856, Harriot Hunt predicted that "in a few years the medical profession will be equally shared between men and women" the paternity of that thought was a wish. "Public opinion," she insisted, "is fast tending to bring this about."[19] In fact, though it regularly outran the modest and reluctant reformers in the medical establishment, public opinion would do nothing of the kind. Yet it was open to discuss the matter. In 1890, the *Gartenlaube*, Germany's most popular family magazine, an occasional, innocuous, strenuously cheerful advocate of progressive causes, printed an article by a Swiss physician, Professor Dr. Hermann von Meyer, who patiently

18. Hunt, *Glances and Glimpses*, 102–4.
19. Ibid., 153.

and judiciously refuted the three standard charges against women as physicians—their presumed physical weakness, intellectual incompetence, and emotional susceptibility—and advocated their unrestricted admission to medical schools and medical practice.[20] Most of Dr. von Meyer's professional colleagues thought otherwise.

Indeed, medicine, a coveted prize in the long campaign for women's access to prestigious professions, offers some eloquent evidence for female determination and male defensiveness. The physician's calling seemed a natural one for women, as natural as teaching, for wives and mothers were in the nineteenth century, as they had always been, superintendents of health and nurses of the sick at home. There was nothing incongruous, unfeminine, about the amiable picture of a soothing hand administering medicine, wiping the fevered brow, and comforting the dying. Moreover, the notion that women could best care for women pleased many of the prudish and the squeamish, worried lest a male doctor violate his female patients' modesty. But, although women began to elbow their way into medical schools by mid-century, displaying tenacity and, if possible, wielding influence, the number of woman physicians remained small and their impact in the profession severely circumscribed. In 1883, Holland could boast Dr. Aletta Jacobs, who specialized in women and children; she claimed to feel fully accepted by her professional colleagues and came to see herself as an inspiration to future women doctors. But for some years she was, literally, unique in her country.[21] There were, during the early 1880s, no female physicians in Norway or the Austro-Hungarian Empire, a handful in Italy and perhaps a dozen, no more, in France. By 1900, the number of woman doctors in France had grown to 95, still a vanishingly small percentage of its medical population. It was reserved to England and the United States to take the lead, such as it was, in admitting women not merely to medical school but to medical practice. The English and American medical establishments were timid enough; they compromised their occasional gestures of good will by quibbling about women's qualifications and by excluding them from professional societies, hospital posts, and international congresses; by 1882, only 26 women had been entered on England's medical register. Eighteen years later, the number had multiplied tenfold, amounting to a pathetic 258. In the United States, to which feminists looked admiringly for cues, the situation was only marginally more favorable. By 1880, there were 2,432 woman physicians in the country, or 2.8 percent of the total; twenty years

20. "Die Frauen und der ärztliche Beruf," *Gartenlaube*, XXXVIII (1890), 654–56.
21. Elise van Calcar, "Holland," in Stanton, *Woman Question*, 165, 165n.

later, the number had grown to 7,387, or 5.6 percent.[22] Though its curve was upward, the woman's share remained unimpressive.

As so often, the figures barely hint at the aspiring woman physician's heartbreak, her persistence in the face of humiliating rejection and organized chicanery. The heroines of the campaign to enter medical school and medical practice—Harriot Hunt, Marie Zakrzewska, Elizabeth Blackwell—had to muster an endurance, a self-confidence, a wily patience that their adversaries were quick to label unfeminine and would offer as yet another reason for denying women an opportunity for higher education, let alone professional schools.

It was, in general, access to the universities in the late nineteenth century that proved the key to the woman's cause, more than access to the vote. And it was around this issue that the most emphatic, often ill-tempered disputes would swirl. The facts are quickly rehearsed: American educators pioneered in conceding that women possessed the kind of intelligence and physical stamina that could profit from advanced education. Oberlin College admitted women from the day of its founding in 1833, and its first woman students to have undergone the regular course of study graduated in 1841. This seemed a substantial step in providing the mysterious sex with the education hitherto strictly reserved for males. But Oberlin, at least in its first years, did not aim at full equality, or identity, of opportunity: its founders, though obviously sympathetic to what they called the "misjudged and neglected" sex, continued to believe, with the rest of society, that a respectable woman's principal task remained what it had always been—that of homemaker. But it did not follow, for them, that a wife and mother must be frivolous, ignorant, empty-headed.

These relatively modest aspirations for young females evolved with the times. Just as educational institutions left their mark on their society, so society transformed these institutions. Mount Holyoke opened in 1837 as a seminary after extraordinary efforts at persuasion and fund-raising by a pioneer in American woman's education, Mary Lyon, and grew into a self-respecting, full-fledged college after some decades. Meanwhile, Iowa State College opened its doors to women in 1858; other state universities followed Iowa's lead. Cornell established, six years after its founding, a small, special woman's division, Sage College, in 1874. For some years, Cornell was a trying college for young women to attend, requiring much

22. Mary Roth Walsh, *"Doctors Wanted: No Women Need Apply": Sexual Barriers in the Medical Profession, 1835–1975* (1977), 181, 187; Millicent Garrett Fawcett, "Women in Medicine," in Stanton, *Woman Question,* 63–89.

Antoine Wiertz, *La Belle Rosina*, also called *Two Young Girls*, 1847. This canvas was left by the painter (notorious for his gigantic machines and his macabre allegories) to the state upon his death in 1865. It is uniquely suggestive for this study. In posing a strapping young nude contemplating a skeleton her size, Wiertz vividly confronts the two fundamental forces, love and aggression, Eros and death, which, according to Sigmund Freud, unceasingly battle for supremacy over the human mind. In giving a peculiarly nineteenth-century form to a favorite medieval and early modern theme, Wiertz underscores the persistence of significant symbolic expressions. And in using a very naked model to dramatize his *memento mori*, he illustrates what I am calling the doctrine of distance, which gave artists in Victoria's time an opportunity to display attractive nudes without offending the discreet and the respectable.

Mabel Loomis Todd, February 1882. She is twenty-five, at Amherst, Massachusetts, her slender figure and magnetic eyes much in evidence.

The men Mabel Loomis Todd loved.

(1) Eben J. Loomis, her father, to whom she remained ever faithful, in 1895.
(2) David Peck Todd, her husband, who did not remain faithful to her, any
more than she did to him, ca. 1890. (3) William Austin Dickinson, her lover,
the most handsome man she ever met, ca. 1890.

I

2

3

I

2

3

Die Frau Professorin.

4

(1) Sir John Tenniel, *Women's Emancipation, Punch*, 1851. A crude but characteristic satire on "Bloomerism." (2) Edward L. Sambourne, *The Angel in "The House"; Or, The Result of Female Suffrage, Punch*, 1884. The punning title is, of course, an allusion to Coventry Patmore's immensely popular poem extolling married love. Note the blue stocking she is knitting. (3) *Modern Hothouse Plants, Fliegende Blätter*, 1845. One in a series depicting fantastic versions of emancipated women, she is an obvious allusion, with her attire and her cigar, to George Sand. (4) *Mrs. Professor, Fliegende Blätter*, 1846. From a series entitled *Emancipated Women*, placing a female into as unlikely a profession as men could imagine women occupying at mid-century.

1   2

(1) *The Poetess, Fliegende Blätter,* 1846. (2) Honoré Daumier, *"Pardon me, Sir, If I disturb you a little,"* 1844. In his series *Les Bas-bleus,* Daumier lampooned a familiar type, the disheveled female intellectual; the German version adds, for good measure, a modestly shrinking, housewifely husband in the background. (3) Heinrich Hoffmann, *History of a Thumb-Sucker, Struwwelpeter,* 1844–45. Three illustrations from one of Hoffmann's celebrated cautionary tales which, translated (a little crudely) into psychoanalytic language, warns that masturbation leads to castration.

3

1

2

3

(1) *Phyllis Riding Aristotle*, bronze Mosan aquamanile, before 1300. An artistic representation of man's slavery to woman popular in medieval and early modern art. There is a mid-fifteenth-century Florentine panel, now in the National Gallery in London, underscoring this theme by showing Phyllis astride Aristotle on one side and Delilah shearing Samson on the other. It is ironically called *The Triumph of Love*. (2) Dante Gabriel Rossetti, *Venus Verticordia*, 1864. A portrait of Woman unusually sensual even for Rossetti's sensual work, with her seductive apple and luscious naked breast, and her suggestive gesture grasping Eros's arrow. (3) Dante Gabriel Rossetti, *Pandora*, 1879.

I

(1) Max Liebermann, *Samson and Delilah*, 1902. A brilliant modern, highly explicit rehdering of this Biblical theme, extremely rare in Liebermann's large impressionist *oeuvre*. (2) Franz von Stuck, *Sin*, 1893. One of several versions that Stuck did of this rather blatant symbol of woman's sinful authority; the phallic snake coiled around Eve's lascivious body and staring at the viewer in company with its victim only underscores the erotic message. (3) Edvard Munch, *Harpy*, 1894. Munch's powerful, neurotic depictions of destructive Woman were an obsessive *leitmotiv* in his work.

DIE SUENDE

2

3

I

2

3   4

(1) Edvard Munch, *Vampire*, 1895. (2) Edvard Munch, *The Death of Marat*, ca. 1905–7. One needs to see the original to get a sense of the violent scene, blood spattered all over the canvas. (3) Edvard Munch, *Salome II*, 1905. (4) Aubrey Beardsley, *The Climax*, 1894. Illustration for Oscar Wilde, *Salome*. Beardsley's title, tying erotic consummation to extinction, seems deliberately teasing; the whole is a debased heritage of the romantic love affair with death.

I

(1) Aubrey Beardsley, *The Battle of the Beaux and Belles,* 1895–96. Designed
for Alexander Pope's *Rape of the Lock.* (2) Gustave Moreau, *Oedipus and the
Sphinx,* 1864. An impressive success at the Salon of 1864, most probably based
on the Heine poem I examine in the text, as translated into French by Gérard
de Nerval. (3) Franz von Stuck, *The Kiss of the Sphinx,* 1895. Another of
Stuck's murky contributions to the theme of devouring woman. (4) Edvard
Munch, *Sphinx,* ca. 1927. Possibly the most troubled of Munch's many self-
portraits, hinting at terrifying sexual ambiguities.

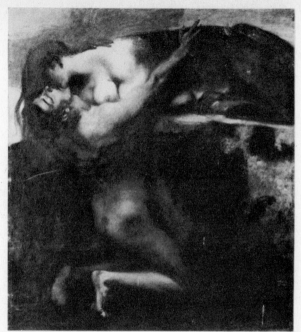

3

4

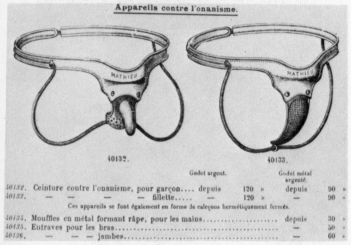

(1) Four-Pointed Urethral Ring, from J. L. Milton, *Pathology and Treatment of Spermatorrhoea* (London, 1887). No comment. (2) Apparatuses against onanism, from Maison Mathieu catalogue, 1904.

self-confidence and more self-control; they were only too conspicuously an "annex" to the men—and the woman's division at Harvard bore that slighting name for years. Yet the overall gains for women were far from shabby. The estimates for the 1890s vary drastically, from 20,000 to 50,000; in 1893, with a brave effort at specificity, Lida Rose McCabe counted 36,329 women as students in "all institutions in the United States affording a higher education to women," an impressive total that doubtless included teachers' seminaries.[23] Discrimination against women continued, but the first door, that to advanced education itself, had been forced.

It had been forced in Europe as well. In England, from the 1850s on, a handful of respectable girls' day schools, like Cheltenham Ladies' College, founded by Dorothea Beale in 1858, and the institution of extramural lectures in several cities had done indispensable spade work for the cause of woman's higher education. In the 1870s, England's two ancient foundations gingerly and tentatively made room for women students in Girton and Newnham colleges at Cambridge and at Lady Margaret Hall and Somerville College at Oxford, but would not grant them degrees. The University of London had opened its doors to women in 1878, and three years later Cambridge admitted women to examinations. France was not far behind. In 1879, in a stroke typical of French centralization, all *départements* opened teachers' training colleges. These new institutions essentially codified, and improved upon, an old ideal—woman as teacher. But in the following year, the august Sorbonne admitted women to lectures. Another fortress had fallen. Elsewhere, male bastions surrendered more slowly: German universities did not admit women to full-time study until well after 1900.

It is instructive but not surprising that most women students in Europe, especially in the German universities, were foreigners: Americans in search of what their own country was reluctant to provide; Russians wanting scope for their political even more than for their intellectual activities. Female outsiders sitting in the same lecture hall with men seemed more tolerable to the all-male university establishment than having one's sister, or one's friend's sister, sitting there. As in art, so in higher educa-

23. McCabe, *The American Girl at College* (1893), 108. She also notes that 11,718 women students were attending coeducational colleges, most of them state universities (pp. 108–9). Perhaps most to the point are the percentages of woman graduates: in 1870, about 15 percent of all to obtain the B.A. degree in American colleges and universities were women; by 1890, they made up 17 percent; and by 1910, almost a quarter: 23 percent.

tion: the exotic licensed what would have been unacceptable in the
familiar.

Exceptions do not prove the rule. But, having reached and perhaps
redefined the limits of the possible, the extraordinary individual illuminates the travail and the hesitations of ordinary mortals and the terrain
of progress which they can traverse only in fantasy. It is in this way that
the spectacular career of M. Carey Thomas dramatizes the struggle of
late-nineteenth-century women for self-respect, independence, a life of
their own.

Being an American, Carey Thomas also dramatizes that remarkable
timetable governing the evolution of bourgeois culture in the nineteenth
century: the lead that the middle classes of the United States were taking
in moving toward a future that Europeans, too, were bound to experience.
"Europe is Americanizing itself"—with this ringing statement C. de
Varigny in 1889 opened a comprehensive pair of articles on "Woman
in the United States" in the *Revue des Deux Mondes*. "Each race," he
wrote, "has developed a particular conception of woman." For the
Frenchman, "woman personifies the ideal"; for the Spaniard, "she is still
a madonna in a Church"; for the Italian, "a flower in a garden"; for the
Turk, "a utensil of happiness"; for the Englishman, "the mother of his
children and the manager of his household."[24] But now the American,
educating his girl and showing her the way to equality, has made her
flirtatious and powerful. The likes of M. Carey Thomas, then, less flirtatious certainly than powerful, were for Europeans fascinating portents.

And M. Carey Thomas beautifully demonstrates yet something else,
the psychological benefits of activity as against passivity. More intelligent,
more determined, and more fortunate than most—her father, and still
more strongly her mother, favored higher education for women—she
made herself into a success beyond the most extravagant predictions of
anyone but herself. Looking back at her career on her forty-first birthday
in 1898, after she had been president of Bryn Mawr college for four years,
she told a close friend, not without poignancy, that she wanted "to amount
to something more."[25] In the end she did not, but she transformed the
college over which she was to preside for twenty-eight years into the
most difficult school in the United States to enter and the most difficult
to graduate from; in a superb gesture of disdain for commonplace honors,

24. "La Femme aux Etats-Unis," *Revue des Deux Mondes*, XCIII (1889), 349-74,
432-64; quotations at 353-54.
25. To Mary Garrett, January 2, 1898, *The Making of a Feminist: Early Journals
and Letters of M. Carey Thomas*, ed. Marjorie Housepian Dobkin (1979), 16.

she rejected a chapter of Phi Beta Kappa for her campus, on the ground that *any* graduate of Bryn Mawr must be good enough to earn that coveted mark of scholarly distinction.[26] Males were invited to draw the inference that Carey Thomas thought women, far from being inferior to men, superior to them. Barely suppressed rage at slights that women had long experienced at the hands of men could not have been sublimated more splendidly than this. Excellence was the best revenge.

Born in 1857 in Baltimore into an educated Quaker family, Carey Thomas was an eldest child compelled to endure the clamorous rivalry of nine brothers and sisters; later she translated her sibling jealousy into a Malthusian principle: "If people realized," she wrote into her journal late in 1877, when she was almost twenty-one, "that to have more children than they can afford to train and support properly was a greater crime than anything else I am sure it would be better." Freud has taught us that the thirst for knowledge is, in part, a derivative of the child's urgent and anxious need to discover where babies come from—a need urgent and anxious because more than scientific interest is in play; it mirrors the nagging concern whether the parents' love will now be withdrawn and bestowed on the newborn rival. Certainly Carey's fertile mother gave her eldest daughter's appetite never-waning incentives. From infancy, that daughter showed herself clever, spirited, and imperious. She insisted on her rights because they were often threatened. Her conscious plan for her life was never to be obliged to yield. A "girl certainly [should] do what she chooses as well as a boy," she noted in her journal in early 1871, when she was barely fourteen. "When I grow up—we'll see what will happen." She wanted, above all, to be active: "My, I intend to study my Classics and Mathematics next year," she wrote later that year, "because I do so want to finish at Vassar and then come to Philadelphia and study for a doctor. I can't stand being dependent on anybody, even mother and father, and I want to do something besides eating, reading and dressing."[27] For her, passivity was the supreme crime.

This meant, as she early recognized, schooling and more schooling. "I ain't a tomboy but I ain't *ladylike* and I'm everything that's disagreeable and I do want a little excitement and I do want to go to Vassar," rather than to some gentle ladies' seminary. She was still fourteen, still at home. "I *do so want* to, and I am *perfectly determined* to get a good education."[28] At boarding school, a teacher who shared Thomas's energetic

26. Dobkin, "Introduction," ibid., 17.

27. December 17, 1877; First month, 1860; January 6, June 20, 1871, ibid., 123, 32, 48–49, 55.

28. October 1, 1871, ibid., 58.

desire to demonstrate woman's capacities talked her out of Vassar—a mere girls' college after all—and suggested she attend Cornell instead. And so she went to Sage College, and graduated after two years. Her determination to demonstrate at least one woman's gifts propelled her forward.

Then came graduate school, and her first serious setback. Even as a fourteen-year-old schoolgirl, she had earnestly attended feminist lectures and impatiently endured complacent male sermons about the "sacred shrine of womanhood." One evening, she had listened to such a lecture by Anna Dickinson, an eloquent advocate of woman's rights, and applauded Dickinson's fable about a brother and sister, both equally endowed with "genious and tallent"; the brother, intent on going out into the world to "do his part elevating the human race," would get his parents' tearful blessing, but his sister, quite as gifted, could never realize the same ambition: "They would put her in her chamber lock the door and put the key in their pocket and think they had done their duty." The tale incensed Carey Thomas, the youthful feminist: "Oh my how terrible how *fearfully* unjust." To make matters worse, a friend of her father's, a Dr. Morris, walked her back to her house and expatiated on woman's true place—at home, of course: "No matter what splendid talents a woman might have she couldn't use them better than being a wife and mother." Then, she indignantly recorded, Dr. Morris "went off in some high faluting stuff about the strength of women's devotion completely forgetting that all women ain't wives and mothers and they I suppose are to fold their hands and be idle waiting for an *ellgable* offer." That was too much: "Bah! Stuff and nonsenses!"[29]

Carey Thomas was exposed to stuff and nonsenses of this sort over and over again. It was in the air. Not long after the Dickinson lecture, she had to sit still for "an English man Joseph Beck," at dinner in their house. "He don't believe in the Education of Women. Neither does Cousin Frank King and my such a disgusson as they had"—*they*, suggesting that she sat by, listened, and kept her comments to herself. "They said that they didn't see any good of a womans learning Latin or Greek it didn't make them any more entertaining to their *husbands*. A woman had plenty of other things to do sewing cooking taking care of children dressing and flirting." Marriage, it seemed to the party—her mother a noble and notable exception—was "that *greatest state of earthly bliss*" in which woman could fulfill her "duty to amuse her husband and to learn nothing; never to exercise her powers of her mind so that he might have the

29. January 6, 1871, ibid., 48–49.

exquisite pleasure of knowing more than his wife." Her sardonic under-linings testify to the diarist's intense irritation. And her glosses, reserved for her journal, also testify to her perceptiveness, only sharpened by suppressed fury. She refused to be impressed, or appeased, by what she called "the usual cant," that woman "is too *high* too *exalted* to do any-thing but sit up in perfect ignorance with folded hands and let men worship at her shrine." Such cant must be read to mean only that women "ought to be *mere dolls* for men to be amused with, to fondle, pet and love maybe, but as for associating with them on terms of equality they wouldn't think of such a thing." It was maddening: "I got perfectly en-raged."[30] The only appropriate response, as Thomas believed even then, was to make her life a refutation of current prejudice.

But as Carey Thomas enrolled at Johns Hopkins University late in 1877 to do graduate work in classics, she discovered that she could study there only under special and inconvenient circumstances: she was sup-plied with reading lists and admitted to some lectures, but had to depend, for her real work, on personal tuition by individual professors. Classes were closed to her. After a year, in a dignified letter to the Board of Trustees, she withdrew, and went to study at Leipzig. German universities were still only inching toward coeducation: as Andrew Dickson White, president of Cornell and American minister to Berlin, told Carey Thomas's father, while a few women in Germany attended lectures in a few classes, "it would make a great uproar if a lady were to go into the lecture rooms of any great University." Berlin seemed almost impenetrable.[31] Leipzig, on the other hand, already had one American woman student, and some professors there appeared sympathetic. Accordingly to Leipzig she went, accompanied by her friend Mamie Gwinn, and studied there for more than two years.

Her experience was pleasant, her position precarious. Some professors and their wives were hospitable, and the students, if often embarrassed, rarely rude.[32] One danger came from Russian women students, looked upon, she reported home, "as a scourge." Clear-eyed as usual, she saw this political fear as a mere anxiety attack, "the panic felt by an absolute gov-ernment." German universities, she told her mother, "live in fear—the great opposition to women consists in the terror inspired by the Russian women and their anarchy inaugurated at Zürich until they were banished.

30. February 26, 1871, ibid., 50–51.
31. See M. Carey Thomas to Mary Garrett, July 1879, quoting or paraphrasing A. D. White; Andrew Dixon White to Dr. James Carey Thomas, July 4, 1879, ibid., 163, 164.
32. To her mother, February 7, 1880, ibid., 208.

I really think the application of one Russian woman would be sufficient to close Leipzig's doors to women." A rumor had circulated that there were now six Russian women studying in Leipzig and making propaganda for socialism. This was palpable nonsense: "Of course it was a libel as there is not one Russian in the University."[33] Carey Thomas found all this very instructive.

While she was not forced to leave Leipzig, she took her degree in Zürich; such academic peregrinations were far more usual for the Continent than the United States. Coming to Zürich principally to write her thesis and take her final examinations in philology, compelled to work up new subjects and make new acquaintances, she felt overwhelmed though moderately confident. She was near her goal; she almost held the key to what she wanted most: influence. "I would not give up my Ph.D. for anything," she wrote to her mother, who had encouraged her through it all, in 1882. Her final examinations, written and oral, were an arduous and prolonged affair, but she felt sure of a cum laude and could even imagine a magna cum laude. But, her exacting orals over, as she reported to her mother in a detailed and dramatic letter, she was congratulated by the dean on achieving the highest honor in the university's gift, "SUMMA cum laude."[34] No woman, and very few men, had ever taken such a degree. Not long after, on holiday at Spezia, the glow of her coronation as vivid as ever, she confessed her true ambition: "I should love to have the presidentship of Byrn Mawr."[35] She was to have it, within twelve years. Her career was a triumph of will and intelligence over unpromising realities. But how many women had Carey Thomas's energy, brains, purposefulness—and support?

2. Manhood in Danger

The first organized effort to free women from the cage of dependence and to rewrite dominant ideals of domesticity was, significantly enough, a delayed response to a wounding, gratuitous insult. While unsympathetic contemporaries would denounce the woman's movement as one act of aggression after another, it was in reality an offensive born of reiterated slights and intolerable frustrations. In 1840, Elizabeth Cady Stanton, Lucretia Mott, and other women delegates to the World Anti-Slavery Convention in London had been refused seats and compelled to follow

33. To her father, February 29; to her mother, February 1, 1880, ibid., 211–12, 207.
34. To her mother, no date, ibid., 257, 260–64.
35. To her mother, November 30, 1882, ibid., 265.

the proceedings as spectators. Even then, it is worth noting, some men recognized the incongruity of reformers presumably dedicated to righting the wrong of inequality treating women as inferiors: William Lloyd Garrison, for one, joined the ladies in the gallery. It was a historic but by no means isolated gesture; the woman's movement was propelled forward by loyal and assertive male supporters, by some consistent liberals, by a number of Freemasons who took their teachings seriously, and by impassioned devotees of the eccentric and percipient social theorist Saint-Simon. Dr. George R. Drysdale, that doughty English propagandist for birth control, demanded "justice for women" in his journal at mid-century;[36] a quarter of a century later, Josef Breuer, one of the two dis-coverers of psychoanalysis, thought his epoch-making patient "Anna O." as intelligent and as quick as any man, who needed, could readily digest, but had never got, solid mental food.[37] No general rule about man's fear of woman can stand without careful qualifications. Not all men inter-preted feminism as being directed against them.

Like Garrison, though obviously with a more personal interest, Stanton and Mott resented the Anti-Slavers' controversial decision to exclude them; they found it alike illogical and infuriating. But it was not until eight years later that they acted. In July 1848, Elizabeth Cady Stanton called a convention at Seneca Falls, New York, to take counsel and per-haps action on women's wrongs and women's rights. There had been polemics in behalf of woman's claims, and some recognition of their merits, before this. The classics of modern feminism, Mary Wollstone-craft's *Vindication of the Rights of Women* and Olympe de Gouges's *Les Droits de la femme*, date back to the revolutionary years at the end of the eighteenth century. Several cultivated salons in Berlin, presided over by such intelligent, emancipated Jewish women as Dorothea Veit, Henriette Herz, and Rahel von Varnhagen, flourished around 1810. Those fearless American propagandists, the Grimké sisters, gave their feminist lectures and published their feminist pamphlets in the late 1830s, bringing down upon their heads, in 1837, a Pastoral Letter from the Council of Congregationalist Ministers of Massachusetts chiding them for entering the sphere of public disputation. A handful of women's periodicals, like *La Femme Nouvelle* and *La Gazette des Femmes*, enjoyed short, if inter-esting, lives in the France of the mid-1830s. And the flamboyant, con-

36. See *The Political Economist; and Journal of Social Science*, No. 11 (January 1857), 85.

37. See Breuer, "Case Histories . . . Case 1, Fräulein Anna O." (1895), in Freud, *S.E.*, II, 21.

spicuous George Sand—a most unsettling model for other women, however unconventional—flaunted her love affairs, her male attire, her cigars, and her liberated convictions long before 1848. It was in the year of Seneca Falls, finally, that F. D. Maurice founded Queens College in London designed to provide some professional training for aspiring governesses, to give them, as Maurice put it in his inaugural lecture, not merely information to impart to their charges, but a "correct apprehension of principles."[38] When Elizabeth Cady Stanton and Lucretia Mott convened their little band of feminists, they could count on small communities of protest and swollen, if largely untapped, pools of talent for the cause.

The meeting at Seneca Falls adopted a stirring "Declaration of Sentiments and Resolutions," explicitly patterned on the Declaration of Independence. It was orderly, logical, modest, much like the conclave that produced it: the resolution calling for woman suffrage appeared so daring that it was almost not offered and, once offered, was almost not passed. Typically, men took a prominent part in the proceedings: James Mott, Lucretia's husband, presided, and the black abolitionist Frederick Douglass persuaded the assembly to demand votes for women. With all its circumspection, then, this convention saw the birth of the organized woman's movement, the first stirring of feminism to be taken seriously. Feminists in other countries borrowed courage from this American beginning to write manifestos, formulate demands, and organize associations.

While moderation was in quiet control at Seneca Falls, the response of the opposition was instantaneous and furiously irrational. Eloquent orators and editorial writers made broad fun of the feminists, male and female, and questioned their sexual credentials. Haranguing a feminist convention at Rochester in 1852, one Mr. Mandeville, a Protestant pastor at Albany, characterized woman activists as a "hybrid species, half man and half woman, belonging to neither sex." In the following year, again at Rochester, a Professor Davis took the floor right after Susan B. Anthony had addressed a teachers' convention to protest that "woman belongs on a pedestal." And, also in 1853, the *New York Herald* spat a venomous editorial at "unsexed women," insinuating that they had become activists because they were too repulsive to find a husband: some, for visible reasons, could never get a man; others, for equally visible reasons, had lost theirs. "These women are entirely devoid of personal attractions. They are generally thin maiden ladies, or women who perhaps have been

38. Rosalie G. Grylls, *Queens College, 1848–1948* (1949), 2–3.

disappointed in their endeavors to appropriate the breeches and the rights of their unlucky lords."[39] The male supporters of the movement fared no better; in 1854, the *Albany Register*, after describing "feminine propagandists" as "unsexed women" who "make a scoff of religion," turned on the men. They were "weak-minded," deluded whether "honest or dishonest," but in any case "tied to the apron-strings of some 'strong-minded woman'"; they were "restless men" who "comb their hair smoothly back, and with fingers locked across their stomachs, speak in a soft voice, and with upturned eyes." Insinuations, certainly in a respectable nineteenth-century newspaper, could hardly go further, though at times they did. In 1852, the *New York Herald* had already denounced "mannish women, like hens that crow," and "the majority of the male sex" who attended feminist conventions as "hen-pecked husbands" fit "to wear petticoats."[40] Perhaps the first success of the young feminist movement was to bring talk of sexual aberrations almost into the open—almost and, of course, with malicious, slanderous intent.

Such polemicists doubtless took pleasure in their wit, but anxiety lurks behind their aggressive jokes. In 1866, the *Albany Evening Journal* reported that Senator Lane of Kansas had presented a petition of "one hundred and twenty-four beautiful, intelligent and accomplished ladies from Lawrence" asking for a constitutional amendment prohibiting disfranchising citizens on grounds of sex. "That trick," the *Journal* commented, with ponderous sarcasm, "will not do. We wager a big apple that the ladies referred to are not 'beautiful' or accomplished. Nine out of every ten of them are undoubtedly *passé*. They have hook-billed noses, crow's feet under their sunken eyes, and a mellow tinting of the hair. They are connoisseurs in the matter of snuff." Should such a female happen to be married, the editorialist proposed to breathe "a fervent aspiration of pity for the weaker vessel who officiates as her spouse." In the same year, the *New York Tribune* ridiculed a petition for the vote by women from New England in the same language: "The sure panacea

---

39. Mandeville: *History of Woman Suffrage*, ed. Elizabeth Cady Stanton, Susan B. Anthony, and Matilda Joslin Gage, vol. I (2nd ed., 1889), 486; Davis: ibid., 515; *New York Herald*, September 7, 1853, ibid., 556–57.

40. *Albany Register*, March 7, 1854, ibid., 608–9; *New York Herald*, September 12, 1852, ibid., 852, 854. In its own special way, the *Herald*, in the same editorial, tied the abolitionist and feminist movements together: "How did woman first become subject to man as she now is all over the world? By her nature, her sex, just as the negro is and always will be, to the end of time, inferior to the white race, and, therefore, doomed to subjection" (p. 854). I shall explore the sexual innuendo against feminists in the next volume.

for such ills as the Massachusetts petitioners complain of, is a wicker-work cradle and a dimple-cheeked baby."[41]

On occasion, anti-feminists dropped all pretense at humor, or good humor, to disclose man's fear of woman in all it primitive force. Addressing the House of Representatives on May 30, 1872, Stevenson Archer of Maryland warned that "Woman Suffrage" was "not to be tolerated although Advocated by the Republican Candidate for the Vice Presidency." The movement had become a menace, Archer warned; "these innovators" were no longer "mere petticoated harlequins." In fact, "a monstrous army is now coming down upon us—a hundred thousand 'whirlwinds in petticoats'—which we must meet firmly, or be overwhelmed by the storm. The little wife has attained to such size and strength that her blows now make the big man wince; the wee finger-nails have grown to talons, and tear now where they only tickled before; and if the big, good-natured fellow does not look well to his guard, he will be throttled, stretched on his back, and brought to such terms as he dreamed not of a short while ago."[42] Woman, created by God to be gentle, has grown enormous, hard-hitting, with tearing talons, and capable of throwing man on his back. The little boy concealed in the nineteenth-century man looked up at his powerful unpredictable mother and was afraid.

Such hysteria, as notable for the quickness as for the vehemence of its response, was by no means confined to the United States. In France, men deplored the intellectual and political woman as an unsexed, unnatural female from mid-century on; while Saint-Simonian publicists dreamed of the day when women would achieve equality with men, panic-stricken sociologists and historians, cartoonists and novelists, paid wry tribute to the bloodthirsty nature of women, showing them stirring up excited crowds to acts of cruelty. These did not exclude castration: the notorious scene in Zola's *Germinal*, in which a troop of enraged miners' wives cut the penis off a usurious and lecherous grocer, only dramatized a common perception. So did the procession of seductive and fatal females with whom Zola populated his novels from the late 1860s on. He depicted them as responsible for fleeting erotic happiness and permanent destruction. Still, not even Zola in his most misogynous mood could quite rival the

41. *History of Woman Suffrage*, vol. II (1881), 101n.—The same line was taken by the author of *Satan in Society*, Dr. Nicholas F. Cooke: the strong-minded woman is a "sort of mistake of Nature. Such women are generally wanting in the qualities which inspire the love of man, and so, as in the harmony of things force must be united to weakness, these masculine women nearly always ally themselves with blanched males, weak physically and mentally, capable of receiving the authority which their wives needs must exercise" (p. 280).

42. Copy in box 2, Anti-Suffrage, SS, SC-WHA.

condescension, or fear, of his friends, the Goncourt brothers, who were convinced that "women have never done anything remarkable except by sleeping with many men and sucking their intellectual marrow: Mme Sand, Mme de Staël." As they saw it, there was "not a single virtuous woman whose intelligence is worth two sous. A virgin has never produced anything."[43] Woman as vampire, man as victim: that was, if not the general consensus, a strong current of male feeling in nineteenth-century France.

Only less blunt than the Goncourts, Daumier made straggle-haired, pretentious lady novelists and menacing-looking female socialists easy targets of his scorn. And as late as 1896, when feminist claims had been widely disseminated among the educated in France, Dr. Edouard Toulouse could, in a book on the causes of insanity, claim to recognize "degenerate women" by "their low voices, hirsute bodies, and small breasts."[44] During that half century, la femme-homme became a specter for terrified men to conjure with: she was the supreme enemy of the family, ruinous to man's self-confidence, and destructive of woman's real vocation. "It is not necessary for the political emancipation of women to be applied in its full extent," Count Agénor de Gasparin argued in a chapter on "La Femme-homme" in his L'Ennemi de la famille, "to produce a great deal of harm. The very idea is enough to unsettle the family; this false ideal falsifies positions, falsifies relationships, falsifies affections."[45] It did violence to experience, nature, and Christian teachings, and it foolishly slighted woman's invisible domestic influence.

English observers agreed. The slogan of the masculine woman scarcely needed to be imported from the United States or France; it had a rich domestic provenance. "The one thing men do not like is the man-woman," Montagu Burrows, Chichele Professor of Modern History at Oxford, warned in the Quarterly Review in 1869, and offered "the University-woman" as an exemplar of the hybrid. "Keep the male and female types essentially distinct. For those young ladies who cannot obtain 'a higher education' through their parents, brothers, friends, and books at home, or by means of Lectures in cities, let a refuge be provided with the training governesses; but for heaven's sake, do not let us establish the 'University-woman' as the modern type." The rhetoric—"for heaven's

43. February 19, 1862, Edmond and Jules de Goncourt, Journal; mémoires de la vie littéraire 1851–1896, ed. Robert Ricatte, 22 vols. (1956–58), V, 57.

44. Les Causes de la folie (1896), 53, in Susanna Barrows, Distorting Mirrors: Visions of the Crowd in Late Nineteenth-Century France (1981), 49n.

45. (1874; 4th ed., 1875), 313. And see Dumas fils, L'Homme-Femme, and Jules Bois, L'Eve nouvelle (1896), 8.

sake"—discloses the fear behind the manly pose. Women ought, rather, to "entice our 'golden youth' into matrimony, not by wiles and plots and match-making warfare, but by the exhibition of a true, modest, retiring, useful, womanly character."[46] Burrows did not need to add that these were qualities in which the man-woman was notoriously deficient.

Not to be outdone in the face of so vulnerable and so accessible a sexual target, *Punch* for years conducted a tireless, tiresome campaign against "Bloomerism" and "strong-minded women"; it did not lag behind its models, such as the *New York Tribune*, in its snide innuendos. Parodying a political female's address to the "electresses" in her district, *Punch* had the improbable candidate advocate a variety of trivial "womanish" causes, and describe herself as regular in features, with fine teeth: "My hair is dark chestnut; my moustachios are rather lighter."[47] The most obtuse of its readers could hardly miss the sly imputation of this gross caricature. But in its very reach for the nadir of bad taste, this campaign was a measure of nineteenth-century man's anxiety in the face of "strong-minded" women.

While *Punch* could bring itself to support the rights of girls to a higher education, it drew, in righteous outrage, the line at women voting, let alone sitting in Parliament; its cartoonists would entertain, and frighten, its readers with depictions of appalling masculine harridans lecturing the House of Commons.[48] The male citadel was under siege, and there was no point pretending that the besiegers were either gentle or pretty.

The sense that manhood was in danger deepened as the campaign for women's rights picked up momentum. In 1882, Sir Walter Besant, essayist, social commentator, and prolific novelist, published a transparent fable, *The Revolt of Man*, which took woman's emancipation to its logical (or, rather, illogical) limit: in that England of Besant's imagining, placed in the near future, traditional roles are completely reversed—women alone are enjoying the privileges of higher education, the suffrage, and public office, while men are reduced to abject dependence and humiliating domesticity. But love conquers this anti-Utopia at the end of Besant's thinly disguised tract for the times: a beautiful young cabinet member marries her rebellious, assertive lover; the unnatural reversal is repaired and the old order restored. There were a few exceptional social prophets, notably George Bernard Shaw, who could depict woman as Nature's

---

46. "Female Education," *Quarterly Review*, CXXVI (1869), in Patricia Hollis, *Women in Public, 1850–1900: Documents of the Victorian Women's Movement* (1979), 144–46.

47. *Punch*, XXI (1851), 20, 22, 35, 141, 155, 157.

48. Sambourne, "The Angel in 'the House,'" ibid., LXXXVI (1884), 279.

masterpiece, requiring man only to help her fulfill her biological destiny, and at the same time welcome their discovery of how much power she concealed behind her demure presence and hobbling skirts.[49] And there were, of course, English lawyers and educators who found female subjection in any sphere distasteful and unjust. But most publicists were rather like Sir Walter Besant: troubled at woman's advance, and not a little afraid.

The response of German anti-feminism strongly confirms the experience of other countries: the woman's movement touched a raw nerve, and slight actions in its behalf could produce fierce reactions. In Germany, feminism rose later and was far less outrageous, rather more conventional, than its American and English counterparts. And yet, the German male sprang to his own defense with nervous speed, almost before he was challenged. As in other countries, sermons, editorials, often mindless caricatures, were favorite weapons. In the very first year of its appearance, 1844, *Fliegende Blätter* produced four sketches ridiculing the active modern woman. A satirical magazine published in Munich that rapidly spread across the German states—which were parched for at least a modicum of disrespectful humor—it most pleased its readers with its "Modern Hothouse Plants." Both wicked and innocuous, they depicted emancipated women emerging from flower pots, flourishing a pen or other "mannish" implement, which, one must assume, they had taken from men. The most hostile of these skillful drawings is of a frowning and disheveled female holding a swagger stick in one hand and a cigar in the other. Not long after, *Fliegende Blätter* returned to the attack, less charmingly this time, with a series tersely called "Emancipated Women." It caricatured, among other recent anomalies, a dowdy woman at the lectern addressing male students—the "Woman Professor"—and, perhaps most pointedly, a woman writer, an unprepossessing, unkempt female, complete with spectacles and with pen intently clamped between her teeth; her husband, back from market with his basket and greeted by two ragged children, hovers modestly in the background.[50]

No comment was offered, and none was necessary. German public opinion was, after all, generally behind these anti-feminist illustrators. When Otto von Leixner, still a young student, found that women liked his poems, he noted in his journal, ungratefully and derisively: "But my God, praise from woman's mouth has rarely been of special value for

49. The most notable instance of Shaw's feminist reading of Darwinism is, of course, *Man and Superman* (1903); the "Epistle Dedicatory" to Arthur Bingham Walkley, though partly tongue-in-cheek and partly perverse, remains worth reading.

50. I, 6 (1844), 46; IV, 85, 89 (1846), 102, 135.

me." And when he met a lively seventeen-year-old girl, Toni, who impressed him with her deep thoughts, her original mind, and her atheistic convictions, he found no higher words of praise than to call her character "almost masculine." But he, like other Germans, was far from denying the female's superior powers: "Woman's tears," he noted in his diary in 1877, "are for the most part stronger than man's words."[51] Wilhelm Heinrich Riehl devoted a whole chapter of his widely read *Die Familie* to what he called, with pointed offensiveness, "Emancipation from Women." It is in times of cultural decay, excessive refinement, political stalemate, and enervating nervousness, he argued, that women leave the sacred precincts of the family to push forward into the public realm, meddling, as adored dilettantes, with matters that belong to the male of the species. The Germans, Riehl proudly boasted, had been the first to recognize the profound differences between man and woman, not to enslave her but to recognize her true value, her gift to rule at home. Riehl wrote to restore this happy domestic condition in a time out of joint, sicklied o'er with feeble men and feminist women.

In this atmosphere, any attempt to promote the professional advancement of women met with gentle or, more often, with fierce derision. In 1878, Wilhelm Raabe, master of the German novella, ridiculed the idea of an association of literati planned to include women writers: he found it, he wrote to his friend Ernst Eckstein, "really a little comical. It sounds a little like a certain fear of the good little women."[52] Dr. Max Runge, professor of obstetrics and gynecology at Göttingen, spoke for a solid majority of German opinion when, in a published lecture analyzing woman's nature, he said once again what others had said so often before: "Let us take it, then, as settled that the vocation of woman is to be wife and mother, and that all the rest lies more or less beyond her reach."[53] If German feminists—and there were German feminists—did not take this as settled, they must be, obviously, eccentrics or radicals. As late as 1912, anti-feminists thought it worth their while to found a German Society for the Prevention of Woman's Emancipation.[54]

51. Diary 1867–1868, pp. 7, 14; *Tagebuch* III, December 16 [1877], box 2, Leixner Nachlass, Stabi, Berlin. He does concede, in all fairness, that women seem to possess unusual sensitivity: "I must acknowledge that girls often found beauties in my verses that men did not notice at all, or barely noticed." But this does not reverse the contemptuous cliché—it only confirms it.

52. Raabe to Ernst Eckstein, August 10, 1878, *Briefe Wilhelm Raabes (1848–1910)*, ed. Wilhelm Fehse (1940), 162–63.

53. *Das Weib in seiner Geschlechtsindividualität* (1896; 2nd rev. ed., 1897), 18.

54. Richard J. Evans, *The Feminists: Women's Emancipation Movements in Europe, America and Australasia, 1840–1920* (1977), 112.

The nineteenth-century fear of woman, then, was an international and highly emotional issue. Even a female murderer aroused fearful self-questioning: when, in 1865, young Constance Kent was tried for cutting her little half-brother's throat, one newspaper was moved to comment that hers "was a wanton murder, not done by the hand of a man, for there is a *finesse* of cruelty about it that no man, we believe, however depraved, could have been guilty of," for a woman in whom the worst passions have overpowered the best is "morbid, cruel, cunning."[55] Many would agree with Rudyard Kipling that "the female of the species is more deadly than the male."

This pervasive sense of manhood in danger is, of course, the counterpart to that notorious nineteenth-century fiction, woman lacking all sexual appetites: this now appears as a reaction formation, as powerful as it was unconscious. Reaction formations are part of the arsenal of psychological defenses that Sigmund Freud was the first to discover and describe; they are maneuvers that convert impermissible or horrifying thoughts into their opposite: sadism into pacifism, fear of effeminacy into ostentatious toughness. The denial of female sexuality emerges as a tremulous self-fulfilling prophecy. To deny woman native erotic desires was to safeguard man's sexual adequacy. However he performed, it would be good enough. She would not—would she?—ask for more. Dr. Acton's reassurances to timid men about to face their young and, they feared, possibly demanding brides are thus an invaluable clue to distressing preoccupations in his culture. And if woman's erotic urges should prove merely dormant, it seemed all the better to leave them undisturbed. For what might woman not do to man once she was aroused? Many men, unwilling to face this fantasy, and shifting their surviving childish fears of maternal retaliation to all women in general, experienced feminism in all its forms as nothing less than a threat of castration.

3. The Castrating Sisterhood

Castration was in the nineteenth-century air, early and late, often as a telling metaphor. Amiel once defined the depressive mood of *spleen* as *"the equivalent of a castration."* And in 1887, the Swedish critic Oscar Levertin told the Danish playwright and politician Edvard Brandes that in Sweden, prudish censorship and boycotts were imperiling imaginative

---

55. *Bath Express*, April 29, 1865, in Mary S. Hartman, *Victorian Murderesses* (1977), 126.

literature: "A black death of castrating morality is sweeping over this country."[56] This morality was by no means kept out of children's reach. In 1845, the German physician Dr. Heinrich Hoffmann wrote and illustrated a little picture book for his children, *Der Struwwelpeter*, which immediately secured, and long continued to enjoy, an immense popularity. Adorning them with crude and highly explicit illustrations, Hoffmann offered his laconic cautionary tales as both cheerful and funny. His vast German public shared Hoffmann's benign appraisal of his work. But his warnings to children not to play with matches, refuse to eat their soup, or venture out into bad weather when good little boys and girls stay indoors are unrelieved in their savagery. The famous title figure of Struwwelpeter, with his disordered uncut hair and improbably long fingernails, is exposed only to obloquy. But the boy who will not eat his soup starves to death, the girl who obsessively plays with fire is burned to a crisp, and Konrad, the thumb-sucker, suffers irreparable damage. When Konrad proves incapable of obeying his mother's earnest monition to stop sucking his thumbs, the tailor cuts them off at the root with his enormous scissors —a young child's perception of an adult tool. Mutilation seemed a perfectly appropriate lesson in a didactic story for small boys. But just because Hoffmann seemed lighthearted about it, and his readers did not shrink from it in horror, does not mean that the thought was not frightening—even, at some deep level, terrifying. Neither masturbation nor castration, however disguised, is really amusing.

While in *Struwwelpeter* the principal agents of castration are men, other literature demonstrates that women were often prominent in the sport. On July 14, 1883, Bastille Day, Edmond de Goncourt recorded this dream in his journal: "I dreamt last night that I was at a party, in white tie. At that party, I saw a woman come in, and recognized her as an actress in a boulevard theatre, but without being able to put a name to her face. She was draped in a scarf, and I noticed only that she was completely naked when she hopped onto the table, where two or three girls were having tea. Then she started to dance, and while she was dancing took steps that showed her private parts armed with the most terrible jaws one could imagine, opening and closing, exposing a set of teeth. The spectacle had no erotic effect on me, except to fill me with an atrocious jealousy, and to give me a ferocious desire to possess myself of her teeth—just as I am beginning to lose all my good ones. Where the devil could such an outlandish dream come from? It's got nothing to do with the taking of the Bastille."[57]

This dream, like all dreams, is a privileged personal document. Edmond de Goncourt was a connoisseur of art, society, and politics; a lifelong bachelor, in his early days he frequented prostitutes and kept mistresses, but his real love was his brother Jules, with whom he virtually merged. The two brothers wrote books together on eighteenth-century French society, self-conscious and shocking realistic novels, and a much-cited journal, an indiscreet record of the social, political, artistic, and sexual life of their day. The two, it seems, also shared a mistress for some years, thus in a way restoring, and markedly improving upon, their first shared childhood love. When Jules died in 1870, a shattering event that his surviving half fixed forever in his journal, at engrossing length and in clinical detail, Edmond carried on alone, wounded, melancholy, more waspish than ever. Sensitive and observant, neurotic and in some ways proud of his neuroticism, Edmond de Goncourt was out of tune with his time, the chronicler of a world invaded by vulgarity, threatened by democracy, and blighted by Jews. The manifest dream displays him as the desolate bon vivant, at a party, in white tie, alone.

The latent dream thoughts capture even more of him. Goncourt's associations and implicit interpretations are all denials, somewhat forced efforts at devising innocuous explanations for threatening materials: the naked dancer writhing on the table does *not* excite him sexually, he had dreamt of teeth *only* because they reminded him of his own dental decay. These denials cannot conceal the castration fears lurking behind Goncourt's panicked vision of the *vagina dentata*, quite apart from his rueful hint—"just as I am losing all my good ones"—at the loss of his potency. But his fear was the child of a wish: the dream, we may conclude from his disclaimer, had everything to do with Bastille Day. His denial was doubtless overdetermined, but his wording suggests that "July 14" was the day's residue from which he constructed his dream. The holiday celebrating the storming of the Bastille, that looming emblem of paternal power, is the most meaningful day in the French calendar, no matter what the Frenchman's politics; it condenses, more than any other, the decisive rebellion against authority, the son symbolically slaying the father: a concrete piece of historical material that illustrates a permanent ingredient in human experience. But this daring oedipal wish apparently awakened in Goncourt a mortal fear of retaliation, castration being threat-

57. July 14, 1883, *Journal*, XIII, 45–46.

ened here not by the father but by the mother, so that his very wish was compromised in the wishing: even if the fantasy had been imagined to completion, the triumphant boy would have encountered the biting mother.

This was not the first time, I should add, that the Goncourt journal records dreams of castration. In November 1855, it notes, one of the brothers, almost certainly Jules, had dreamt of seeing a woman in a stone cage, a kind of bear cage. "I entered," and, "hardly inside, a chambermaid took hold of me and squeezed my nose between two fingers, like a barber, and with her other hand, thrust something into my mouth which was something on paper. The idea came to me that this was to prevent me from sensing the stench emanating from the place, and from the lady." Still, however radical his hostility to stinking woman, the dreaming Jules remembered his manners, telling the caged lady that he had come to present his respects, and then took a walk with her in the garden. The woman's aggression on his body is unmistakable; so is his hatred for the gentler sex. A year later, the journal records a mere fragment, less revealing but very much in character: "In a dream, a man whose nose drops to the ground and serves as a wick for lighting cigars."[58] No wonder that the Goncourt brothers could invent the all-devouring female protagonist of their novel *Manette Salomon*—and a handsome, rapacious Jewess at that. No wonder that the two never married.

The fear of woman has taken many forms in history. It has been repressed, disguised, sublimated, or advertised, but in one way or another it seems to be as old as civilization itself. Historical and anthropological research has turned up evidence of it in ancient myths and primitive folktales. Edmond de Goncourt's dream of the vagina armed with teeth sums up a picturesque if hardly reassuring tradition of lethal genitals reported across centuries and cultures. Murderous females appear in Greek mythology, medieval German poems, and Trobriand Island lore. The fear of woman thus seems endemic and permanent. It is born of man's early total dependence on his mother, and his longing, frustrated love for her, his defenseless lassitude after intercourse, and the frightening aspect and portentous implications of the female genitals: for the boy who is likely

58. November 5, 1855, November 22, 1856, ibid., I, 231; II, 56.—Anthropologists have discovered that the primitive fear of the *vagina dentata* is enshrined in the myths of many nations. And the vague and terrifying notion of the vagina armed with teeth ready to castrate any man rash enough to penetrate the woman also appears, usually covertly, in the dreams and fantasies of adults in Western civilization.

to see woman as a castrated male, the absence of her penis reads like a threat to his own. The Medusa and all the dangers to man's virility she stands for are a very old story.

There were centuries when this touchy theme did not enlist the interest of painters or poets, but when it did, it could find lurid expression. The temptress Eve had long been a staple in homiletic and pastoral literature; Phyllis who imperiously rode Aristotle and Delilah who pitilessly cut Samson's hair occasionally appeared in late medieval and early modern art; in the eighteenth century, Giovanni Battista Tiepolo painted the seductive and murderous Cleopatra gaily presiding over dinner with Antony, her breasts bare. Before 1800, in his brilliant and devastating *Liaisons dangereuses*, Choderlos de Laclos had imagined the magnificent, devouring Madame de Merteuil, who uses her intelligence, her charms, and her sexual seductiveness to revenge herself on a cruel world dominated by men, by ruining everyone within her reach. The nineteenth century reduced this female to a type, embodying her in recognizable, diverse, yet almost interchangeable figures. Painters and poets and novelists revived and elaborated fatal females from the distant past, from religious myth and historical legend, or invented *femmes fatales* of their own: Keats, *la belle dame sans merci*; Swinburne, his Lady of Pain, Dolores. The dangerous woman came to constitute one of the leading themes in the literary and artistic imagination of the century.

It succeeded another manifestation of the romantic malaise, the fatal man. While, until mid-century, demonic and destructive men like Byron held the center of the stage, they were succeeded by demonic and destructive women.[59] The division is far from absolute: Keats's dreamlike, enthralling vision of the merciless beauty captivating the isolated, pale, passive male; Heinrich Heine's seductive siren, the Lorelei; and Prosper Mérimée's diabolical gipsy, Carmen, each of them a killer of men, all antedate 1850. But what had been a trickle in the first half of the nineteenth century rose to a flood in the second half, though the cast of characters did not materially change: the vengeful female, the murderous courtesan, the immortal vampire all retained their grip on the nineteenth-century imagination. So did the castrating sisterhood: Salome beheading John the Baptist, Judith punishing Holofernes in the same irrevocable fashion, Delilah, more circumspect though no less effective, cutting Samson's hair.

59. I am, in this and the preceding paragraph, much indebted to Mario Praz's justly esteemed *The Romantic Agony* (1930; tr. Angus Davidson, 2nd ed., 1951), esp. chs. 2 and 4.

There was room, in these tributes to potent woman, for evasion and circumlocution. Not all the voluptuous women painted and sculpted in these decades had knife in hand. But they are innocent less often than men found agreeable, or safe. Dante Gabriel Rossetti's women, for one, are almost all the same, no matter how many models he employed. Ostensibly derived from diverse literary sources, sacred and secular, they tell one story, that of overwhelming, disarming, embracing female power. They are big, a little heavy, with long columnar necks, rounded lips swelling as if they had been stung by bees, and with immense entangling quantities of hair. Other artists, like Edward Burne-Jones, immortalize the same trauma, only with blander models. Galatea, in Burne-Jones's narrative quartet, is brought to life by a musing Pygmalion, androgynous rather than virile, and, in the end, worshipped by her kneeling maker, the creature having won, effortlessly, complete ascendancy over her creator.[60] In Walter Pater, the menace of woman is more direct, though still swathed in perfumed rhetoric. Analyzing—if that is the word—"Leonardo's masterpiece," the Mona Lisa, Pater rhapsodizes over her archetypal meaning; she "is expressive of what in the ways of a thousand years men had come to desire." Her beauty is "wrought out from within upon the flesh, the deposit, little cell by cell, of strange thoughts and fantastic reveries and exquisite passions." She had lived forever, but her immortality hints at suspect mysteries; "older than the rocks among which she sits; like the vampire, she has been dead many times, and learned the secrets of the grave."[61] Such women lure men to passionate suffering and perhaps an early death. In *La Colère de Samson*, a moody personal poem—most of these inventions allude to deep private losses—Alfred de Vigny generalizes this fatal type by depicting the war between the sexes as unending, with man ever the victim of woman: "More or less," he concludes, not without some pleasure, it seems, "woman is always DELILAH." Amiel had come to the same nervous conclusion: "Like Delilah," he told his journal, women "only enmesh the man of tender heart to ravish his powers," and he cautioned man to close his ears to seductive chants, to guard his heart: "Watch out!"[62]

Max Liebermann's modern *Simson und Delila*, which he painted, after

60. The art critic and historian Quentin Bell has a characteristic modern response to this quartet, finding it repulsive and unconsciously obscene. The *Pygmalion* paintings are, he writes, "a kind of hymn to sexuality in art. The sculptor creates an image of marble, he adores it and the goddess turns into a real live woman—made of soap. Pygmalion is also made of soap and one recoils at the idea of their sad, cold, slimy, saponaceous embraces." *Victorian Artists* (1967), 68.

61. Pater, *The Renaissance: Studies in Art and Poetry* (1873; Modern Library ed., n.d.), 103.

62. Vigny: "La Colère de Samson," written April 7, 1839, *Poèmes*, ed. Robert Abichard (1966), 251; Amiel: November 1851, *Journal intime*, I, 1110-11.

making preliminary sketches for two decades, in 1902, could serve as an illustration of Amiel's warning. Liebermann, then the best-known German painter by far, was something of a rebel in the Imperial artistic establishment with his love for Manet and his luminous impressionist canvases. He was not a painter of nudes, let alone of suggestive scenes. But his slender, magnificent Delilah, holding up her shorn victim's hair in a strained, declamatory gesture of victory, is as naked as Samson, his defenseless body slack, his head in her lap. Liebermann, a Jew, chose the moment of the Philistines' triumph and the Israelites' defeat, and he may have been thinking of his adversaries among official German artists, some of whom did not shrink from anti-Semitic innuendos. But whatever his polemical or symbolic intentions, the risky conjunction of sexual consummation and male vulnerability has never been pictured more expressively than in this stunning composition, all the more telling for being so rare in Liebermann's work.

These writers and painters discovered Delilahs in many women. In Dostoevsky's stories, the fatal female is a manipulative virgin tormented by contradictory needs and intolerable passions who drags men into the abyss; in stories by Pushkin and Gautier, Cleopatra, that irresistible and cruel queen, appears as a royal nymphomaniac who prostitutes herself to men only to order them killed the morning after they have enjoyed her. "You great voluptuary!" so Gautier apostrophizes her after describing her death-dealing habits, "how well you know human nature, and how profound is your barbarity!"[63] In such company, Eve, who seduced man into sin, and Helen, whose beauty caused the deaths of untold virile heroes, almost pale by comparison. Yet they too are vessels of wickedness: Franz von Stuck, a celebrated German painter around the turn of the century, painted Eve a number of times, complete with her emblem, the snake, and, lest anyone miss the message, inscribed the painting in large letters, "Sin."

Stuck did not confine his repertory of potent and injurious women to the figure of Eve. He painted Judith and Salome; he painted men fighting one another to the death over a gloating female; he painted Orpheus, headless, the blood gushing from his neck, after his fatal encounter with the Bacchae. Many of Stuck's women, whether they are Eve, the first tempter, or Vice, the universal temptation, triumphantly wear the phallic snake as a token of conquest. When he wishes to render bad conscience pictorially, Stuck has a strong but frightened man fleeing all-too-female furies in a panic.

Edvard Munch, a far more considerable artist, displays in his art a

63. Praz, *Romantic Agony*, 204.

very similar anxiety over biting, tearing, murderous women. In addition to Salomes and Sphinxes, he shows vampires at work, madonnas with death in their eyes, harpies rising from their meals. When Munch delineates jealousy, he has the woman drive the man to blank despair and depression; when he depicts mutual sexual attraction, it is the woman who entangles the man in the fatal web of her hair. In his brilliant oil, *Death of Marat*, he has Charlotte Corday standing naked by the bed of the dead Marat who bears Munch's features, as naked as she, his sheets spattered with blood; the terrifying sexual implications are as palpable as if Munch had painted the woman killing the man after their embrace. In the war between the sexes, at least for Munch, as it had also been for Vigny, the victor is invariably woman.

Aubrey Beardsley's females—his Messalina, his Helen, and his Venus— are bound to intimidate and quite ready to destroy the men who fall into their hands. With almost coarse directness he titled his illustration of Oscar Wilde's Salome floating, voluptuously holding the head of John the Baptist, "The Climax." It was, we understand, her climax, hardly his. And Beardsley's Belinda, from Pope's *Rape of the Lock*, may be charming in her anger, but she towers over the man as she launches her assault:

> To arms, to arms! the fierce virago cries,
> And swift as lightning to the combat flies.
> All side in parties, and begin th' attack
> Fans clap, silks rustle, and tough whalebones crack.

With Beardsley, woman, deadlier than she ever was in Pope, has the whip hand.

There was one fatal woman of ancient fable, the Sphinx, whose tale modern men could contemplate with some satisfaction. For years she had wantonly killed her hapless interrogators, and then Oedipus had vanquished her with his superior intelligence or, in another version, his unmatched masculine prowess. It is true that the end of Oedipus's career was rather less dazzling than its beginning; as the archetypal boy wishing to possess his mother, Oedipus had—untypically—realized his wish and was made to pay for his unconscious audacity. But his remorseful symbolic self-castration in no way diminished his stature; he remained the legendary hero who had subdued the female monster, half woman and half beast, the very incarnation of lustful, lethal woman.

That is how Ingres painted the *Oedipus* he exhibited in the Salon of 1827—strong, handsome, intelligent, a splendid body to add to the

roster of nudes available to respectable nineteenth-century eyes.[64] But
then another, more pathetic version of the fateful encounter between
Oedipus and the Sphinx invaded the scene, first employed in a strange
and beautiful poem by Heinrich Heine. The poet describes himself
wandering through a fairy-tale forest, enchanted by the aroma of the
lime blossoms and the wondrous glow of the moonlight. A nightingale
sings of love and tears, of the conflicted love that was the signature of
romantic poetry and of Heine's, filled with an ineffable mixture of
libido and aggression, joy and misery. Deliberately jumbling his adverbs,
Heine has the nightingale rejoicing sadly and sobbing happily—so sadly
and so happily that she prods him into recalling forgotten dreams. He
walks on to a large castle, shuttered, silent, as though death dwelt within
its desolate walls. And there sits a marble Sphinx, that monstrous hybrid,
compounded of horror and lust; she is beautiful, her very gaze eloquent
with wild desire, her silent smile promising sensual surrender. Once again
it is the nightingale that goads the poet into action—without her impulsion, it would seem, he would only wander and muse; her sweet song
overcomes his resistance and he leans forward to kiss the Sphinx's lovely
face. This awakens the statue, and she thirstily drinks the poet's kisses,
almost unto his last breath. Then, lusting for erotic pleasure, the Sphinx
embraces him and tears his poor body with her lion's paws, leaving the
poet to marvel at this coupling of rapturous torment and delicious woe.
His pain, like his pleasure, is beyond calculating; while her kisses make
him happy, her paws wound him grievously:

> Entzückende Marter und wonniges Weh!
> Der Schmerz wie die Lust unermesslich!
> Derweilen des Mundes Kuss mich beglückt,
> Verwunden die Tatzen mich grässlich.

And the nightingale sings a question to the Sphinx, seeking to solve, not
the riddle that Sigmund Freud thought was at issue between her and
Oedipus—where do babies come from?—but the romantic puzzle over
the fatal ambiguities of love. What does it mean, it sings, that love should
mix its bliss with mortal torment:

> O Liebe! was soll es bedeuten,
> Dass du vermischest mit Todesqual
> All deine Seligkeiten?

64. Robert Rosenblum, *Ingres* (1967), 80–81.

Heine's poet resolves the conflict between desire and defense not through virile action but in passive endurance, by surrendering to the clawing, man-eating woman.[65]

Heine imagined this modern Sphinx in 1839. A quarter of a century later, first in 1861 in a sketch and then, three years after, in a painting, Gustave Moreau identified the Sphinx's victim as Oedipus. Fascinated by castrating females, obsessed with Delilah, Salome, and beheaded Orpheus—and the Sphinx, Moreau painted Oedipus as no weakling; but, apart from staring at the horrid statue come to life to claw him, Oedipus does nothing. "We are rather pleased," wrote Théophile Gautier, "to find a little Hamlet in Oedipus." It is a shrewd appraisal of the dynamics underlying this scene. Oedipus had punished himself for acting, Hamlet for merely wishing; the literature and art of the nineteenth century depicting man's fear of woman had more of Hamlet in it than of Oedipus.

The Sphinxes that Franz von Stuck painted are far closer to the vision of Moreau than to that of Ingres; they do not look as though they are about to be vanquished by any man. And in a poignant self-portrait, Edvard Munch played with the theme once again, more ambiguously than any of his predecessors: the Sphinx, the man-killer, equipped with powerful arms and large heavy breasts, is Munch himself, advertising confusions over identity and his self-destructive urges: as the Sphinx, Munch is at once killer and victim.

It is tempting to reduce such poignant self-exposure to purely private testimony. We know that Munch, much like Moreau and Beardsley, suffered from severe personality disorders and that he endured largely unsatisfactory, often pathological relations with women. The charges that "Antis" liked to level against male feminists like John Stuart Mill—that they were unduly attached to their mothers and mortally afraid of women—seem far more appropriate diagnoses for these artistic innovators. The creative anxieties they poured into their troubling portrayals of fatal females appear less as the precipitate of ominous political news, or the oppressive presence of bluestockings, than of their inner states. Seeing them defy rather than represent the bourgeois, seeing their disturbing themes and unconventional techniques, one might plausibly argue that they speak only for themselves.

Such a posture is doubtless attractive to most historians of our day, who have reversed traditional hierarchies of historical significance in the conviction that the major artist or the first-class novelist is a less de-

---

65. "Vorrede zur dritten Auflage," *Buch der Lieder*, in *Sämtliche Werke*, ed. Oskar Walzel et al., 11 vols. (1911–20), I, 3–4.

pendable witness to culture than his mediocre fellows. It is certainly true enough that insignificant painters or popular novelists disclose common perceptions with relatively little distortion, and remain fairly close to the raw wishes and anxieties of their culture. They mouth the common-places and enact the feelings of their time. But the great painter or poet, however isolated he may be from the vulgar herd he professes to despise, often sees more sharply, feels more precisely, and reveals more accurately contemporary currents, including their unconscious dimensions, than his less-gifted contemporaries.

Still, it is one thing to assert that Heine, Moreau, and Munch speak, in their portrayal of woman, for others; quite another to recover what they are saying. One thing is certain: no century depicted woman as vampire, as castrator, as killer so consistently, so programmatically, and so nakedly as the nineteenth. And the familiar dialectic of action and reaction unquestionably marked the age: the rapid and intemperate response of male publicists to women's conclaves and women's demands strongly suggests that feminist activity gave shape to men's anxieties just as men's anxieties fostered, and shaped, feminist activity.

But this explanation, though defensible, is both incomplete and reductionist. The nineteenth-century attitude toward the self-assertive woman was heavily overdetermined; besides, it was varied in expression and allied to other feelings. By no means all male anti-feminists resorted to manifestly anxious slanders; many of them might be critical of the new woman but did not seem particularly afraid of her. Again, as we know, far from all men were anti-feminists: some were not critical of aggressive women, nor did their support of the cause appear to be motivated by timidity before the ferocious female. Finally, not all anti-feminists were men, and female opposition to the woman's movement once again confirms the inference that such opposition cannot have arisen from fear of the castrating woman alone. In all these three camps, anxiety might be latent, but its manifestations were far subtler than those cruel jokes about hens that crow and roosters that lay eggs. In his authoritative summary of the case against votes for women in England, Brian Harrison has shown that the most persistent and vociferous "Antis" were often not misogynists. Few of them echoed Thomas Carlyle's churlish dictum that *"no woman has any right to complain of any treatment whatsoever,"* but should, rather, "patiently undergo all misery."[66] On the contrary, they did much to foster the rights and opportunities of women in the realms of education, marriage, and even the professions.

66. Carlyle is reported as having said this by John Everett Millais, writing to Mrs. George Gray (May 10, 1854), Mary Lutyens, *Millais and the Ruskins* (1967), 210.

What is more, many "Antis" rejected woman suffrage by resorting to the fairly sober-sounding religious or scientific argument that the creator, whether divine or natural, had set up a division of labor that would be violated if women were granted access to politics. This case, simple and superficially attractive, was as international as the more openly anxious contention that woman's rights equaled man's mutilation. Suavely, these Antis held that while man is preeminent in some domains of life, woman is preeminent in others: the sexes occupy, in a word, separate spheres. Women already held the scepter of domestic sovereignty in one hand; need they hold the ballot in the other? This line of argumentation, which I have canvassed before, was less blatantly self-serving than would appear to the twentieth-century reader; it was something a little better than an unconscious defense mechanism or a conscious ideological distortion. After all, religious doctrine and scientific knowledge, as generally understood during this debate, were more or less in harmony on this point, at least as far as the Antis read them. "Progress," so the *Anti-Suffrage Review* succinctly summarized the case as late as 1913, "involves specialization rather than duplication."[67]

It is indeed reasonable to suspect hidden anxieties behind such reasoned statements; the moderate opponents of women's rights may have been simply more adept at concealing, or denying, their fear of castration by woman than their more candid, or more hysterical, brethren. Some fear was certainly in play here: leading anti-feminists lived in what Harrison has called "clubland," in the privileged enclaves of men's colleges, men's holidays, men's professional brotherhoods, all symbolized and perpetuated in men's clubs, and they found it painful to contemplate their boyish world being invaded by the females whom their favorite institutions had deliberately, and so far successfully, excluded. Sports, the army, government, the higher reaches of trade and industry, and the rest of the all-male preserves like the universities and the professions, only perpetuated this boyish segregation. But the fears of clubland were in important respects the reverse of fears unwittingly disclosed in the editorials I have quoted and the paintings I have discussed. They were fears not of being castrated but of being compelled to grow up, of having to abandon persistent adolescent ties, with their distinctly, though largely unconscious, homoerotic pleasures. A man did not need to suffer mortal fear of woman to see her, conveniently, as an inherently domestic animal; insistence on the male monopoly in the professional or political

67. Brian H. Harrison, *Separate Spheres: The Opposition to Women's Suffrage in Britain* (1978), 59, and passim.

world was not always a symptom of men's feelings of inferiority. At least one reason why the case against emancipated women was respectable was that it was complicated. It could draw on a varied repertoire of habits, fears, and expectations.

The educated and outspoken women who shared the views of the Antis and supported woman's continued dependent legal and low professional status as natural, even desirable, complicated the case further. Some of these women signed petitions against woman suffrage, others denounced their "mannish" sisters for wanting to crash the universities or the medical and legal professions, or wrote plays to lampoon the bluestockings of their time. Thus in 1889, Anna P. See, a desperately obscure playwright, published a crude little two-act farce, *When Women Vote*, in which the anti-heroine, a militant suffragette, forgets all her duties, including those to "her poor invalid husband," in the intoxication of her Cause. Her child comes to think that her mother, unnatural creature that she is, does not love her. But Anna See wanted to combine didacticism with cheer, and in a quickly manufactured happy ending she intimates that this wayward suffragette is about to learn her lesson, recognize her duty, and return, chastened, to her proper domestic sphere.[68] A weightier document dating from the same year makes the same point with more becoming gravity. In June of 1889 the influential English journal *The Nineteenth Century* published an "Appeal Against Female Suffrage," supported by the editors and signed by 104 women, some well known for their own exertions like the novelist Mrs. Humphry Ward, and others bearing the names of famous husbands, like Mrs. Matthew Arnold and Mrs. H. H. Asquith. This triumph of untroubled traditionalism stressed woman's "true dignity" and her "special mission," which, it argued, both flourished best outside the sordid struggles of public life; once in politics, woman's particular virtues of "sympathy and disinterestedness" would be fatally impaired.[69] Adhering to the document aroused some inner conflicts: one of the signers who repented of her "false step" was the brilliant young social investigator Beatrice Potter, later famous as Beatrice Webb. Conservative in upbringing, as she later put it, anti-democratic in sentiment, spoiled by her father's "overevaluation" of women, troubled by the "narrow outlook and exasperated tone of some of the pioneers of woman's suffrage," she had found it easy to

68. Copy in box 2, Anti-Suffrage, SS.

69. *Nineteenth Century*, No. CXLVIII (June 1889), 781–88. Separate reprint in box 2, Anti-Suffrage, SS. In the July number, *The Nineteenth Century* published "The Appeal Against Female Suffrage: A Reply," by the feminists Millicent Garrett Fawcett and M. M. Dilke (No. CXLIX, pp. 86–103).

join Mrs. Ward. Moreover, "at the root of my anti-feminism lay the fact
that I had never myself suffered the disabilities assumed to arise from my
sex."[70] This is an important confession: if so ambitious and self-possessed
a young woman as Beatrice Potter could declare herself content with
the scope that the world allowed her, other women, far more conventional, were likely to discover even fewer reasons for needing to protest
their subjection and improve their position.

Told over and over again that woman's weakness was her strength,
they professed to be satisfied with concentrating on enhancing their
sexual attractiveness and improving their domestic skills. If they protested at all, they would do so in the despairing and protected privacy
of their diaries, like that anonymous housewife in Hallam, Connecticut,
who hated her "romantic life" at the washtub. Much of this female
resignation or outright anti-feminism was, of course, a defensive maneuver, the stratagem that Anna Freud has christened "identification with the
aggressor."[71] Uneasy in their situation, and even more anxious at the
rage that it often aroused in them, women could master their anxiety by
adopting the opinions, imitating the very formulations, of men. Such
identifications could greatly reduce, and even eliminate, the strain a
woman would experience at finding herself in a minority and at
repudiating time-honored values that she had been taught to accept in
her childhood, at home. Women's ignorance of larger possibilities joined
women's identification with the aggressor in strengthening barriers to
their legal emancipation and their economic independence. What feminists
discovered they must do was not just soothe the fears of men, but arouse
the discontent of women, persuade them that true femininity was
compatible with participation in politics or the professions, before they
could discredit the preachments of pastors and politicians, anthropologists
and editorial writers.[72]

But in any event not all female critics of the "modern woman" simply,
or wholly, joined the forces of the enemy; a number of them were capable
of holding discriminating positions. Witness Eliza Lynn Linton, possibly

70. *My Apprenticeship* (1926; ed. 1971), 354. The enormous complexities of anti-
feminism emerge strikingly in August Strindberg's early work. Often cited for his
venomous (and anxious) portrayal of fatal woman in his plays and stories, often
quoted as a scornful adversary of Ibsen the feminist (as Strindberg made him out to
be), he could, at the same time, develop a kind of bill of rights for women, vigorously
advocating a series of measures that would have assured women many of the rights
that the most energetic feminists were asking for. See *Getting Married*, esp. his
Preface, 19–50.

71. *The Ego and the Mechanisms of Defense* (1936; tr. Cecil Baines, 1937), ch. 9.

72. For the "family ideology," see below, pp. 429–36.

the most quoted adversary of emancipated women in the late nineteenth century. Linton's career would have made her a natural recruit for the most aggressive feminism. Daughter of an impecunious and inaccessible country vicar, she fled to London as a young woman to make her own way with her pen: a diligent producer of fiction and a facile journalist, she wrote both for daily newspapers and for such prestigious weeklies as the *Saturday Review*. Anti-clerical and anti-Christian in her opinions, a declared agnostic, an active philo-Semite, widely traveled, she was the independent woman incarnate. An interesting companion, she enjoyed the acquaintance of distinguished writers and public figures. Her marriage to the widowed W. J. Linton, a prominent engraver, collapsed, and after he left her, she indulged herself discreetly in tender, highly emotional friendships with women. And her sympathy with the oppressed female informs her writings: "The most desolate creature in the world," she noted in one of her novels, "is a married woman whose husband has ceased to be her support." And in some early essays for Dickens's *Household Words*, as in the characteristically entitled "Rights and Wrongs of Women," she acknowledged that "women have grave legal and social wrongs," among which she classed "the laws which deny the individuality of a wife, under the shallow pretense of a legal lie; which award different punishments for the same vice; the laws which class women with infants and idiots, and other legal lies"—these are "the real and substantial Wrongs of Women." She had no use for brainless dolls, inveighed against the cult of female incompetence, and demanded that women "hold their own property free from their husband's control," enjoy a good education, and obtain the custody of children in divorce suits.[73]

Significantly, though, Linton owed her celebrity not to her rather predictable laments over the wrongs done to women and her equally predictable demands for reform, but to her highly colored, invective-splattered attacks on the wrongs committed *by* women. The essay that made her famous—though, for a time, that fame was anonymous—was "The Girl of the Period," published in the *Saturday Review* in March 1868. It was applauded, parodied, caricatured, reprinted, endlessly discussed, and followed up by Linton, an opportunist who recognized a profitable issue when she saw it, with a rash of later essays, all slight variations on her original onslaught. The astonishing vogue of "The Girl of the Period" is another window into the troubled mind of the nineteenth-century bourgeoisie. After all, the article is little more than

73. Herbert Van Thal, *Eliza Lynn Linton: The Girl of the Period* (1979), 47, 74.

a vituperative, unoriginal attack on the advanced girl who has given up those lovely, old-fashioned ideals of womanly womanhood that had placed the English girl above her less fortunate rivals: "something franker than a Frenchwoman, more to be trusted than an Italian; as brave as an American, but more refined; as domestic as a German, and more graceful." Cherished ideals of woman's trustworthiness and domesticity were now, to Linton's mind, in serious danger, for "the girl of the period is a creature who dyes her hair and paints her face, as the first articles of her personal religion; whose sole idea of life is plenty of fun and luxury; and whose dress is the object of such thought and intellect as she possesses." The girl of the period is vain, frivolous, a slave to fashion, neither very decent nor very clean, addicted to "slang, bold talk, and fastness," disdainful of respect for parents or traditional morality, and downright envious of gorgeously attired "queens of the *demi-monde.*" Such a creature, so young and already so decadent, has no use for the love of husband or children. She marries for money, for glitter, for shallow sociability. Her husband is the unfortunate victim of this modern monstrosity: "She has married his house, his carriage, his balance at the banker's, his title." In short, she justifies man's fear of woman: "Men are afraid of her; and with reason."[74] Linton's middle-class readers must have been very unsure of themselves to take "The Girl of the Period" as seriously as they did, exceedingly vulnerable to her energetic rant spraying random shots at a largly imaginary target. But then, they lived in an age so unstable that it was easy to believe almost anything. Very different pictures of modern woman seemed equally plausible and proved equally popular.

Yet the evidence is overwhelming. E. Lynn Linton's flirtatious and outrageous modern English female has much in common with Munch's murderous Charlotte Corday or Beardsley's voluptuous Salome: "Men are afraid of her; and with reason." What gives the painters' and poets' intimate confessions cultural resonance is that their self-revelations were congruent with the vituperation of editorial writers, the innuendos of newspaper cartoonists, the sentimental displacements of painters and sculptors. Anti-feminism, I repeat, was not solely a symptom of castration fears. It was a display of ignorance, of misplaced chivalry, or of a timid clinging to tradition—other kinds of fear. It was, in short, a set of adaptations to changing demands. The Sphinxes of Stuck and the viragos of *Punch*, the Delilahs of Gautier and the harridans of the

74. "The Girl of the Period," in E. Lynn Linton, *Modern Women* (1888), 25–30.

Fliegende Blätter, occupied very different aesthetic universes, but they inhabited one psychological world.

4. Sex in Mind and Body

To nervous men incapable of formulating their fear of woman in verse or translating it onto canvas, the more prosaic, if disputed, domain of higher education for females offered almost unlimited opportunities for self-expression. Carey Thomas was only one among many forced to swallow arguments against university training for women ranging from the subtle to the gross, from patronizing tactlessness to rude dismissals. Women did not need it; they could not use it; they might not survive it. There were, to be sure, some dissenting voices. In 1865, Joseph Payne, an eminent English pedagogue and active proponent of woman's education, told the annual meeting of the National Association for the Promotion of Social Science: "The mind has properly no sex."[75] Payne was a persuasive and respected publicist, soon to become England's first professor of education. But his views represented a distinct minority. Many men, and indeed many women, vociferously objected to what they thought the unsexing of the human female by advanced education, her departure from her true calling. In his notorious, controversial tract *Sex in Mind and in Education*, published in 1874, the eminent English specialist in mental disorders Dr. Henry Maudsley explicitly attempted to refute the proposition that the mind is sexless: "There is sex in mind as distinctly as there is sex in body." Hence, Maudsley reasoned, "if the mind is to receive the best culture of which its nature is capable, regard must be had to the mental qualities which correlate differences in sex."[76] All that remained to be established was what these differences were and what they entailed.

Maudsley was a sniffer of trends, a commentator on fashionable concerns; the intemperate debate he helped to heat up exhibits in miniature the intensity with which educated nineteenth-century men felt it necessary to defend themselves against clamorous females. The acrimony had been initiated by Dr. Edward H. Clarke, on whom Dr. Maudsley drew heavily and for whom he professed considerable respect. In 1873 Clarke, who had thought out loud about women's capacity for medical education for some time, gathered his thoughts into a little book, *Sex in Education*, subtitled, with no attempt at sarcasm, *A Fair Chance for the*

---

75. "The Education of Girls," *Transactions of the National Association for the Promotion of Social Science*, 1865, in Hollis, *Women in Public*, 143.

76. *Sex in Mind and in Education* (1874), 7–8.

Girls. While Clarke had earlier ventured to predict that women might in time become respectable physicians, he now offered what must have been the bleakest assessment of the effects of advanced schooling on young women to appear in the nineteenth century. The pioneering Boston doctor Marie Zakrzewska was one of Clarke's friends; the rowdy anti-feminism of medical students in Philadelphia some years earlier had aroused his irritation. But now, having had time to reflect, he allowed his fears as a male to conquer his observations as a physician. To expose woman to higher education, he argued, was to ruin her health, most fatally her capacity to reproduce her kind. "If these causes should continue for the next half-century," he concluded, darkly invoking the cautionary tale of "unwived Rome and the Sabines," it "requires no prophet to foretell that the wives who are to be the mothers in our republic must be drawn from transatlantic homes."[77] Anticipating the panic-stricken opponents of small families who wrote a decade or so later, Dr. Clarke foresaw race suicide, caused not by birth control but by woman's education.

The dread physiological upheaval that set woman apart, stigmatized her definitively, and exemplified her weakness was, in Clarke's view, the advent of menstruation. Unfortunately, the years of puberty were the very years during which educators subjected young women to the ravages of intensive schooling, and many girls never recovered from the irrational overwork that ill-advised pedagogues had imposed on them. To manage that "process of elimination" called "the catamenial function" irresponsibly, "during the epoch of development, that is from the age of fourteen to eighteen or twenty," not merely "produces great evil at the time of the neglect" but leaves "a large legacy of evil to the future." In a long, ostentatiously documented chapter, "chiefly clinical," Clarke buttressed his forebodings with half a dozen appalling case histories of young women, all perfectly healthy until they took the punishment of excessive educational labor, and ended up in his consulting room with "prolonged dyspepsia, neuralgia, and dysmenorrhea," to say nothing of more far-reaching ailments including—of course—severe nervousness and hysteria.[78]

The case in Clarke's repertory that attracted the widest attention was that of Miss D——, who had entered Vassar at fourteen, perfectly well and cheerful, the roses in her cheeks. She began menstruating when she was a sophomore, at fifteen, showing at first no sign of abnormality. But

77. Clarke, *Sex in Education* (1873), 63. See Walsh, *"Doctors Wanted,"* 117–28.
78. *Sex in Education*, 47, 69, 84.

then, misled by appearances, she continued her exacting schedule as though nothing drastic had happened to her body. "She studied, recited, stood at the blackboard, walked, and went through her gymnastic exercises, from the beginning to the end of the term, just as boys do." Then she began to have fainting fits during her exercises and developed painful, skimpy, and irregular menstrual periods. While she graduated with acceptable grades, her physique was imperiled. Indeed, the damage that Vassar had done to her lasted and intensified; Miss D—— lapsed more and more into invalidism. For two or three days each month, her period was nothing less than a torment to her; she became, in general, "pale, hysterical, nervous in the ordinary sense, and almost constantly complained of headaches." When, after consulting several physicians in vain, she finally came to Dr. Clarke, he diagnosed the roots of her troubles with ease. "The evidence was altogether in favor of an arrest of the development of the reproductive apparatus," evidence supported by his examination of her breasts, "where the milliner had supplied the organs Nature should have grown." Dr. Clarke was evidently no Podsnap; he took pride in his bluntness, his freedom of expression. As his critics did not fail to point out sardonically, he seemed not to know that milliners attend to women's heads rather than their breasts.

In any event Clarke found the lessons to be drawn from Miss D——'s case to be only too obvious. Vassar was certainly culpable. "Subjected to the college regimen, she worked four years in getting a liberal education," wholly "out of harmony with the rhythmical periodicity of the female organization." Applying the economic, quantitative analysis that the nineteenth century found so irresistible, Clarke argued that the "vital and constructive force" at work in Miss D—— had gone to her brain instead of to "the ovaries and their accessories." The baleful consequences were foreordained: "Her parents marvelled at her ill-health; and she furnished another text for the often-repeated sermon on the delicacy of American girls."[79] The conclusion imposed itself: the modern ideal of what Clarke called "identical co-education" was supremely misguided, an obtuse violation of the laws governing human physical development.

Dr. Clarke's little treatise caused a sensation. As late as 1908, thirty-five years after its publication, after the controversies it had spawned had come to seem almost quaint, Carey Thomas could still recall "the clanking chains of that gloomy little specter," Clarke's injection of sexual prejudices into education. His suavely written polemic, with its array of

79. Ibid., 79–84.

case histories and appeal to physiology, had come at the worst possible time. Higher education for women was in an experimental phase; no one, as Carey Thomas remembered only too clearly, really knew whether women's health could stand up under its stresses. The uncertain health of American girls and women had, after all, prompted worried comment by physicians and laymen alike for some years. *Sex in Education* was, therefore, calculated to weaken the feminists' resolve. "With trepidation of spirit," Carey Thomas recalled, "I made my mother read it, and was much cheered by her remark that, as neither she, nor any of the women she knew, had ever seen girls or women of the kind described in Dr. Clarke's book, we might as well act as if they did not exist."[80] Still, it was impossible to dismiss Clarke. His pessimism might have been as uninformed as it was unrelieved, but it generated many supportive echoes in his day. He was a prominent Boston physician, a familiar figure on the lecture circuit; he had been a Harvard Overseer. No wonder that his critics, however much he outraged them, treated Clarke with a kind of uneasy deference, acknowledging his "flowing, graceful," his "pungent and popular style," and taking note of his "residence, rank, and former official position."[81] He was, after all, neither a quack nor a crank, and his Harvard connections were impeccable.

Yet Clarke's critics were outraged, and the evident success of his book made them angrier still. By 1874, the year after its publication, *Sex in Education* had gathered a sheaf of favorable reviews and was in its eleventh printing; unfavorable notices, it seemed, only increased its sales. And, worse, Clarke's polemic appeared to have secured the endorsement of Dr. Marie Zakrzewska: "I hold substantially the same views," she was helpfully quoted as saying, "and have, during my practice of more than twenty years, taught to my patients identical principles of health."[82] Delighted, Dr. Clarke returned, in 1874, to do battle once again in behalf of the sickly, over-educated American girl in a new book, *The Building of a Brain*, in which he substantially reiterated the claims he had made a year before, and once again called for special—which is to say: inferior —education for girls, lest they end up as barren invalids. Quoting Dr. Maudsley's statement on sex in mind, Clarke amended it slightly: "Because there is sex in body, there must be sex in mind, and sex in

80. "Present Tendencies in Women's College and University Education," *Publications of the Association of Collegiate Alumnae*, III (February 1908), in William L. O'Neill, *The Woman Movement: Feminism in the United States and England* (1969), 170.

81. George F. Comfort, A.M., and Anna Manning Comfort, M.D., *Woman's Education, and Woman's Health: Chiefly in Reply to "Sex in Education"* (1874), vii.

82. Facing title page of Edward H. Clarke, *The Building of a Brain* (1874).

education."[83] He had no difficulty enlisting reputable support for his views: his first book, which had started the debate, had after all originated in a talk he had been asked to give to the New-England Women's Club in Boston; the second, in an address he had been invited to deliver before the National Educational Association on the "Education of Girls." He had, in short, much of the educated public with him. Let the radicals rave; the establishment was willing to listen.

But Clarke's adversaries were not at all the utopian, sexless, old-maidish feminists of savage contemporary caricature. They had notable intellects, respected orators, and, perhaps best of all, distinguished educators in their camp. They included George F. Comfort, Dean of the College of Fine Arts of Syracuse University and his wife, Dr. Anna Manning Comfort. In their *Woman's Education and Woman's Health*, they disputed Dr. Clarke's facts, assailed Dr. Clarke's logic, and condemned Dr. Clarke's taste. They noted, rather ruefully, that his book "has received marked attention at the hands of the periodical press, from the fugitive daily newspapers, up to the more elaborate and critical quarterly reviews," that the notices had often been uncritical, and that a number of parents had already "withdrawn their daughters from school through fear of the direful consequences which Dr. C. predicts."[84] In one short year, then— the Comforts were writing in 1874—*Sex in Education* had had a marked effect.

This was most unfortunate, for if Clarke's argument were followed through to the end, "the average American woman could not rise above the educational status of the peasant women of Germany." But, the Comforts hoped to show, Clarke's examples were far-fetched and should carry no one with them: thousands of young women had undergone the most strenuous educational experiences without suffering any of the symptoms Dr. Clarke had so lovingly detailed. Even his physiology, especially his analysis of the menstrual cycle, was slipshod and often markedly inaccurate. Far from prudish about physiological processes, the Comforts devoted some twenty pages to menstruation, and concluded that girls needed to be instructed in its significance, its discomforts, and the best way of managing it during its most intense days. All that was needed was good sense and more exercise. Beyond this, the Comforts found Dr. Clarke's prognostication that college-educated women would turn into Amazons, bellicose, unfeminine, domineering, to be as offensive as it was absurd: "Those women of New England and of America,

83. *Building of a Brain*, 64.
84. Comfort and Comfort, *Woman's Education*, vii–viii.

who have enjoyed the blessings of a liberal education, are as chaste, gentle, and feminine as any women in the world." Clarke, then, was alarmist, uninterested in the truth, and often coarse. "As far as the general subject of the higher education of- woman is concerned," the Comforts confidently concluded, "there can be no question but that its tendency is to promote the physical health of her sex, and consequently of the human race in its entirety."[85] The Comforts were an impressive team, and they were right against Clarke. But the Clarkes of their time went their way undismayed.

Another response to *Sex in Education*, edited, also in 1874, by Julia Ward Howe, was perhaps more telling. Howe was the ideal editor for such a counteroffensive: abolitionist, philanthropist, feminist, pacifist, and, best of all, author of "The Battle Hymn of the Republic," she was a national celebrity, a voice hard to dismiss. The authorities she gathered into her little battery of indignation differed in style and opinion. But, as Howe noted, most were "experienced in the office of tuition, and in the observation of its effects"; they were professionals in the field in which Dr. Clarke was, after all, an amateur. And they all agreed that "the facts and experience of their lives" invited conclusions far from his. They agreed, too, that Clarke was neither an objective nor a sensitive judge. He had written *Sex in Education*, as its subtitle proclaimed, to secure "a fair chance for the girls." But to "most" of Howe's authors, "his book seems to have found a chance *at* the girls, rather than a chance *for* them. All could wish that he had not played his sex-symphony so harshly, so loudly, or in so public a manner."[86]

In her own essay, Howe waxed sarcastic at Dr. Clarke's expense: what he attributed to the effects of exhausting education had other causes, what he thought he saw in girls was also true of men, what he found unfortunate in American women was highly visible in European women as well. Other writers in her anthology attacked Clarke's indelicacy and, drawing on their experience as educators, denied his assertions. More than one fastened on Miss D——, his hapless hysterical patient from Vassar. "Why, if he had an hysterical patient who happened to have been a pupil at Vassar," Caroline H. Dall, an outspoken Boston feminist, asked rhetorically, "did he trust, without examination, to her statements?"

85. Ibid., 17, 91, 155.
86. Julia Ward Howe, "Introduction," in *Sex and Education. A Reply to Dr. E. H. Clarke's "Sex in Education*," ed. Julia Ward Howe (1874), 6. Three decades later, the eminent American psychologist G. Stanley Hall could still approve of that symphony: even though "he may have 'played his sex symphony' too harshly," he wrote, "E. H. Clarke was right." Walsh, *"Doctors Wanted,"* 124n.

It was a good question. Vassar girls, Dall noted, after consulting the college physician, were well known for their excellent health. Moreover, it was simply untrue that—as Clarke had asserted—any girl was ever admitted at fourteen, not even for the preparatory courses. It was equally untrue that—as Clarke had also asserted—Vassar girls paid no attention to their menstrual periods: they were carefully instructed in "periodic precautions" and "positively forbidden to take gymnastics," to go on horseback rides, or strain their bodies in any other untoward way. And Howe published an open letter to Dr. Clarke from Alida C. Avery, Resident Physician at Vassar, earnestly protesting against the case history of Miss D—— and supporting Caroline Dall on every point.[87]

Clarke's critics never accused him of inventing Miss D——; they generously professed to believe that he had allowed a real patient to mislead him. They were probably right: Dr. Clarke would not be the last physician to credit a hysteric's fantasies. But it seemed beyond question to them that he had been so credulous because Miss D——'s story conveniently supported a conviction he had already reached. *Sex in Education*, weak in its reasoning, unreliable in its facts, and mistaken in its conclusions, was—on this all of Howe's authors were at one—nothing better than the all-too-felicitous expression of a popular superstition. Writing in 1874 and then again three years later, Dr. Mary Putnam Jacobi exhaustively demonstrated that the very basis of Dr. Clarke's case rested on an error: menstruation did not significantly affect and should therefore not significantly inhibit woman's serious reading or solid study.[88] There was, in these feminist polemics, a measure of denial: the most active days of the period could be disagreeable, debilitating, and painful; reticent about a subject that men themselves were, by and large, unwilling to discuss, and intent on making the strongest possible case for woman's competence, the feminist literature touching on menstruation sometimes took a rather cavalier tone. Yet in drawing its broad conclusions, that literature had the facts on its side: to argue that woman's periodic flow made her into a physical and intellectual cripple was a superstition enshrining a male anxiety.

Yet the superstition survived and the anxiety deepened. Women's high schools improved, women's colleges came to rival men's colleges in excellence, more and more universities admitted women on terms less and less humiliating. In 1894, just two decades after Howe had launched her counterattack on Dr. Clarke, Charles F. Thwing, President of the College

87. Howe, *Sex and Education*, 99, 102–4, 191–95.
88. Mary Putnam Jacobi, *The Question of Rest for Women During Menstruation* (1877).

for Women at Western Reserve University, said flatly: "The old and
tiresome question . . . whether women have intellectual abilities sufficient
to receive and profit by a college education, is closed."[89] He was unduly
optimistic. The question, however tiresome, was not wholly closed in
the United States; it continued to bedevil English higher education; and
it was very much alive on the Continent. National styles and the spectrum
of opinion differed on this matter as on so many others, but the very
proclamation of its death paradoxically underscored its continuing vitality.
In 1890, a brilliant Newnham girl, Philippa Garrett Fawcett, daughter
of a leading English feminist, placed first on the Mathematics examinations but, strictly speaking not being a student at Cambridge, she could
not get the coveted title of Senior Wrangler; instead she was, with a
characteristic mixture of fairness and illogic, placed above him. Hearing of this ambiguous triumph, Frances Mary Buss, the celebrated
headmistress and educational reformer, joyfully announced the event to
her students, and commented: "Thank God, we have abolished sex in
education!"[90] Not quite, not yet, not until the Philippa Garrett Fawcetts
of the Western world could be Senior Wranglers—not until French
opinion rejected the complacent dictum of Jules Rochard, a pundit who
was pleased to say, peremptorily, in 1888, "Women today have, in society,
all the share of influence that belongs to them."[91]

Certainly sex had not been abolished in German education, and
Germany in the late nineteenth century was of particular interest: no
other country drew so many eager foreign students, no other country
took such inordinate pride in its universities, as the Wilhelmine Empire.
In Germany, women were, according to a handbook compiled under
the auspices of Bryn Mawr in 1896, "as a rule admitted only as hearers
in the Philosophical Faculty," though, in addition, "they have also attended lectures in the Faculties of Law and Medicine." Isabel Maddison,
compiler of the handbook, drew some pitiless conclusions: the moral
strain on women applying for an opportunity to study at a German
university was formidable. "The seriousness of purpose and the ability
of individual women who have studied in Germany has, it is believed,
done much towards destroying the prejudice against women students in
the minds of the professors under whom they have worked." It followed,
the editor soberly noted, that "each woman who applies for permission to

89. Charles F. Thwing, *The College Woman* (1894), 10.

90. Josephine Kamm, *How Different from Us: A Biography of Miss Buss and Miss
Beale* (1958), 97.

91. Rochard, "L'Education des filles," *Revue des Deux Mondes*, LXXXV (1888),
645.

attend lectures should bear in mind the great responsibility she incurs in thus becoming, as it were, a test case, by which other similar cases in the future will be judged." The anxious desire of studious women to do better than men was yet another pressure that nineteenth-century reality made them bear.

German opinion, though, was in flux. "The whole question of the admission of women in the universities," Maddison commented, "has given rise to much discussion in Germany and is still far from settled."[92] That was an accurate appraisal. In 1897, Arthur Kirchhoff, a Berlin journalist, gathered a sheaf of authoritative opinions on the question of higher education for women into a fascinating compendium. Kirchhoff's inquiry had been spurred on by newspaper reports, dating from November 1896, that two professors at the University of Berlin had expelled women auditors from their lecture halls. The two, Heinrich von Treitschke and Erich Schmidt, the one a famous German historian and the other an only less famous German literary historian, later denied it, but the incident gave Kirchhoff the impetus to ask some scores of prominent professors and directors of museums and scientific institutes, and a handful of litterateurs, whether they thought women able, and entitled, to be admitted to universities.

The answers that Kirchhoff got and printed—120 of them usable—are hard to interpret. Kirchhoff himself thought the results "surprising," in that the number of professors arguing for the admission of women "had increased in the last few years in striking ways." One conclusion that Kirchhoff felt entitled to offer was that opponents were now "in a significant minority." In the absence of comparable inquiries from earlier decades, such an inference must remain speculative, though it seems reasonable. But the answers he elicited are far more puzzling than their editor suggests; many of the little essays he reprints are rambling and vague, clouded in qualifications, evasive with their allusions to special circumstances and future contingencies. Thirteen of the answers came from literary men and these, not surprisingly, identified themselves overwhelmingly with the future: ten of them flatly advocated the unrestricted admission of women to higher education. One or two echoed the optimists of England and the United States in wondering out loud why anyone thought the question still unsettled. The attempt to demonstrate woman's intellectual capacities or moral rights in this day and age, the conservative religious novelist Dagobert von Gerhardt-Amyntor wrote,

92. Isabel Maddison, *Handbook of British, Continental and Canadian Universities with Special Mention of the Courses open to Women, for the Graduate Club of Bryn Mawr* (1896; 2nd ed., 1899), 62–64.

was to carry coals to Newcastle. And Ludwig Fulda, realistic playwright and translator of Molière, was almost offended by the inquiry: "How a human being who deserves the name of modern," he wondered, "can dispute woman's right to, and ability for, academic study is totally incomprehensible to me."[93] Other novelists and poets were just as astonished.

Yet the 107 academics who made up the bulk of Kirchhoff's sample found his questions perfectly comprehensible. Thirty-five had no doubt that women should join men in all universities, as equals; thirty-six were quite as sure that they should not; thirty-six ranged from advocating admission with reservations to rejection with exceptions. It is this middle group that is most resistant to quantification: some argued that a few brilliant women should have access to the universities, but not set the pace for the rest; some, that selected specialties were proper for them but not others—not medicine but dentistry; not surgery but internal medicine; not theology but literature; not art history but curatorial work in museums. Still others suggested that women could grow ripe for university studies once they had adequate preparation in secondary schools. And a few offered self-fulfilling prophecies, suggesting that while women were certainly entitled to higher education physically and intellectually, it was only cruel to offer it to them since they would never get appropriate employment after graduation. Condescension is rife in these answers: in many of them women appear as strenuously studious, their fair heads bent over books long after the men have left for their fraternities and their beer; they appear as intense, forever asking earnest questions but lacking the gift, or the drive, for that unusual achievement that makes for future greatness.

These replies range across a wide spectrum of argumentation; many of them old, sometimes very old. One of them came from a veritable antique: Professor Dr. Ferdinand Wüstenfeld, a philologist at Göttingen, wanted it reported that, at eighty-eight, he needed the assistance of others to write down his views, but he did wish to be put on record as being decidedly in the negative. The famous and the relatively obscure appeared on all sides of the question. Otto von Gierke, the celebrated legal historian and theorist of political community, conceded in his lengthy answer that he might well admit a few women to his lectures; indeed he would gladly assist them in "decking themselves out in the degree of doctor of laws"— scarcely a reassuring tone of voice. And indeed, Gierke thought that what

93. *Die Akademische Frau. Gutachten hervorragender Universitätsprofessoren, Frauenlehrer und Schriftsteller über die Befähigung der Frau zum wissenschaftlichen Studium und Berufe*, ed. Arthur Kirchhoff (1897), x, 322, 320.

mattered far more than whether women sat in his classes or not was whether they would retain their foreordained place as wives and mothers. There was little point—in fact it would have "pernicious social consequences"—to having "female physicians indiscriminately loosed on suffering humanity just for the sake of competition." The same, he believed, held true for teachers. As for his own field, he saw no possible career for women in the law at all. "Our times are serious," he concluded. "The German people has something better to do than to engage in risky experiments with women students. Let us take good care above all"—and here Gierke's principal anxiety finally breaks through—"that our men remain men! It has always been a sign of decadence when masculinity was lost to men and took refuge among women!"[94]

That was plain enough. Other eminent professors were rather less dogmatic. Ulrich von Wilamowitz-Moellendorf, the great Greek philologist at Göttingen, begins his statement (from the feminist perspective) unpromisingly enough: "The difference between the sexes has often become inconvenient to tyrannical world improvers"; but nature will not be denied. "Most university teachers," Wilamowitz thought, "applaud the exclusion of women from universities," and it would be unfortunate if institutions of higher learning were to become the plaything of radical women lusting after "emancipation." At the same time, he conceded, a few women have already demonstrated that they can profitably participate in advanced education. And modern society has an obligation to further the secondary education of such women, to teach them to the limits of their capacities.[95] Like many others in Kirchhoff's survey, Wilamowitz feared the massive invasion of German universities by women, denounced the political machinations of outside agitators, advocated better education for girls, and acknowledged the claims of the exceptions.

A few of these professors were forthright in their support of equality. "Is that which we all consider the principal task of woman," Hermann Freiherr von Soden, a Berlin theologian, asked, "anchored so shallowly in her nature that she could lose her taste for it through scientific study and public activity?" And a surgeon, Professor Czerny of Heidelberg, thought that "women have already proved through numerous examples that they are capable of academic study and have therefore, in my view, proved their right to such study." But the tone that dominated this survey was one of doubt, of skepticism, if not of such outright, terse

94 Ibid., 225, 23, 27.
95. Ibid., 222–23.

rejection as that expressed by Professor Dr. med. Ernst von Bergmann, director of a Clinical Institute for Surgery in Berlin, who told Kirchhoff, "I consider women wholly unsuitable for academic studies and for activity in the professions to which these studies lead—unsuitable both physically and mentally." Many respondents liked to think, with Professor Dr. med. Franz Riegel, at Giessen, that, able as some women might be, "the public practice of the medical profession is never compatible with the role of woman, that of wife and mother." Another professor, Dr. med. Georg Lewin, director of a clinic for syphilis in Berlin, archly paraphrased the conclusion of Goethe's *Faust*, to the effect that "true femininity, which not merely draws us upward, but above all moves us to love—which is to say, marriage—is, if not wholly ruined, at least damaged by strenuous, concrete studies."[96] Domesticity was, in a word, paramount.

The very repetitiveness of this formulation only underscores its importance to these men, these highly successful and often talkative guardians of their profession. Home was, after all, woman's natural castle. If a girl left it, for a time and perhaps forever, she offended against the social and divine order—and these two orders were, for most of these respondents, the same. University study for women was, as one museum director argued, in fact a double violation of the rules by which the game of human life must be played: advanced education removed woman from her designated sphere and, by depriving a man of employment, kept him from founding a home of his own. It is significant, I think, that very few of Kirchhoff's respondents touched on what must have been in their minds: the impact of menstruation on woman as student and professional. The few who ventured to advert to those "certain days" noted explicitly that the menstrual period did not interfere with physical or mental labor. The others, who seemed to take the taboo against discussing menstruation seriously, apparently subscribed to the ancient apprehensive superstition about women's periods as a kind of special stigma, making women unfit for a man's world. In consequence, the genial and consoling notion that a highly educated woman would make for a more interesting wife and more effective mother enjoyed little popularity.[97]

This, then, was the rough consensus around which a solid majority

96. Ibid., 13, 95, 77, 73. Germans loved to cite, or quote, that last line of Goethe's *Faust*, Part II, about the elevating eternal feminine.

97. Prof. Dr. phil. Julius Lessing, director at the royal Kunstgewerbemuseum in Berlin, ibid , 231; Prof. Dr. med. Ottomar Rosenbach, an internist at the University of Breslau, ibid., 82–83; Prof. W. Panzerbeiter, who taught at a woman's Realgymnasium in Berlin, ibid., 297; and Prof. Dr. Julius v. Sachs, Director of the Botanical Gardens at the University of Würzburg, ibid., 280–81.

could form: the segregation of the sexes as enacted in the differential education and separate spheres assigned to men and women mirrored the needs of society and the prescriptions of nature. Max Planck, soon to become one of the world's leading physicists and already Director of the Institute for Theoretical Physics at the University of Berlin, spoke for that consensus, sounding much like any average academic of his time and country: it is only fair to make room in advanced educational institutions for the rare, remarkable female who has demonstrated her scientific gifts. But "one cannot emphasize enough that nature itself has prescribed to woman her vocation as mother and housewife," and that the laws of nature are ignored, or contravened, only at exorbitant cost.[98] Planck's rhetoric and Kirchhoff's survey as a whole demonstrate once again how elaborately men at ease with words could disguise their most primitive anxieties. In the anguished and inconclusive debate over woman's true place, the fear of woman and the fear of change met and merged.

98. Ibid., 256–57.

⋟ THREE ⋞

Pressures of Reality

WHILE characteristic nineteenth-century attitudes developed under the impulsion of unconscious urges and anxieties, pressures from the worlds of economics and medicine, among others, claimed their share in the making of the bourgeois experience. And that experience proved a crowded and intrusive setting for sensuality. It structured the openings for sexual feelings and actions, and imposed constraints on both. Women's struggles were among these public and powerful realities; less public certainly but perhaps even more powerful were realities directly tied to erotic processes: the strains of pregnancy, the risks of childbirth, the availability of modern methods of birth control. In short, the ego, that part of the mind turned toward external reality, was flooded with far more material than it could safely handle.

The ego is continuously, zealously, in search of the world. Compelled to navigate among beacons emitting conflicting and fragmentary signals and exposed to internal pressures of its own, it seeks to extract as much information from its sensations and perceptions as it can. It works to ward off dangers and to repeat pleasures. It organizes, with impressive efficiency, the individual's capacities for response and his encounters with men and things. It reasons, calculates, remembers, compares, thus equipping men to grope their way toward the future. Its appraisals are never beyond suspicion; they are bound to be distorted by conflicts and compromised by traumas. Thus, the outside world never really enters the mind unscathed; the impressions with which the individual must work are so many mental representations of the real thing. But the ego, obeying its appetite for experience, bravely continues to determine what is and, more difficult, what can be.

Psychoanalysts have been extremely cool to interpretations of experience that grant external influences any prominence. One can see why. It seems like an irreversible first step toward the social psychiatries of Harry Stack Sullivan and of Erich Fromm, systems which put the burden of responsibility for human character on society and largely discount those instinctual drives, sexuality and aggression, on which Sigmund Freud built his psychology. But the historian is forced into no such choice. Freud never questioned the powerful participation of objective realities in the very constitution of human experience. Love, as he put it late in life, seeks for objects. So does hatred. And those objects are external, not internal, agents of experience. Psychoanalysts like to say that the ego is the enemy of the drives. It must appear so from the vantage point of the compelling instincts which press only for gratification and treat each invitation to postpone or modify their demands as a hostile act. But from the larger perspective of the human being, the ego is the true friend of the drives, the great negotiator and compromiser, which induces the individual to give up lesser and riskier pleasures now for greater and safer pleasures later. The ego's ultimate task is to reach accommodation with the world and, at best, to manipulate and to master it.

The one apparent exception to the mind's continuous engagement with the world—the blissful oblivion of lovers to the scene around them—is no exception at all. Living in their cunningly constructed cocoons, lovers seem to need nothing and no one, inhabiting an autonomous realm of their own. But theirs is a privileged moment in human existence, fragile and transient, far from impervious to the pressures of reality. Lovers' rituals of celebration and delight, the very conditions of their splendid isolation, are indebted to the larger world for their form, their vocabulary, their meaning. All versions of the erotic life, passionate or affectionate or both, vibrate to surrounding facts of life—and death.

1. Facts of Life and Death

Writing from Cincinnati on April 27, 1885, "from my bed," earnestly enjoining the strictest secrecy, Eleanor Rogers informed her sister Susan Wright, in New Haven, that she had just suffered a most painful miscarriage. "PRIVATE," she put at the head of her letter, underscoring the forbidding word twice for emphasis. "*To be burned when read,*" she added and again, at the end, scribbled across her first page, to reinforce her plea: "Remember you are not to tell and you are to destroy this letter AT ONCE." The passion for privacy has rarely been expressed more poignantly than this.

Eleanor Rogers in fact seemed more than a little reluctant to confide this news even to her trusted sister; she was only fulfilling a "promise" to let her know "how matters ended with me." They had ended "with a vengance in pain and anguish." The memory of it, and her continuing discomfort, made her rebellious: "If a body has to suffer in having a child more than I suffered in having a miscarriage then Heaven prevent me from having children!" She confided that she was "still weak and full of pain." The day was Tuesday, four days after the catastrophe, but her physician had ordered her not to get up for another day or so. Her ordeal had begun the previous Friday noon, when she went to bed, "and from then on ever increasing pain and distress culminating at from eight to nine in everything coming away. Nobody was with me and so I could howl to my hearts content." Her mother-in-law was fortunately away, her "girl" occupied with a caller, and her husband Will in the city. He returned at ten-thirty that night, "when I was still in such pain that he sped for the Doctor who was busy with a labor case and did not get here until one o'clock. He had to remove the after birth a not altogether painless operation." Then she struck the note of rebelliousness again, more resoundingly than before, with an energetic oath: "By Jove would any woman marry if she knew what awaited her! I feel as if I must go off on a crusade to warn girls to remain unmarried." She added judiciously, "My husband has been everything and more than everything as a tender and most efficient nurse and has in every way behaved in a most exemplary manner. I am quite conscious that I am not being at all the submissive angel that I ought to be. I groaned all Saturday and cried all Sunday and last night and today I have some little outward controll of myself but of the tempest within we wont speak. But enough!" And she turned briefly to other family news, only to resume her impassioned ruminations. Evidently, it was not enough. "Yes I am glad Alice has a boy if she is," she wrote about Alice Belknap, another sister, "but I am glad after the manner of a cold shudder and an inward prayer that Heaven spare me such a joy if I have got to take the pain along with it. You will think I am gone stark mad perhaps I have." She had persuaded her domestic to give her pencil and paper, even though she was not supposed to be exerting herself; she expected that when her husband got home, "I shall get a scolding but you will get your letter and I will have fulfilled my promise."[1]

It was a promise that Eleanor Rogers would probably not have made to anyone but her "dear Sue," the oldest of the Silliman sisters and the family confidante. Writing to her again a month later, Eleanor Rogers made her reticence even more explicit. She was still far from well: "I do not like my internal economy at all. I have not been free of a discharge more than two days at any time and for the last week I have been unable to keep tidy do what I would so Will became alarmed and sought Dr. M. who gave me orders for injections twice a day, so far I see no effect." In her predicament she missed, and needed, her sister more than ever: "I have more faith in you than fifty Doctors so tell me what to do and I'll try and do it." But all of this was completely confidential: "Burn this up please, you are my safty valve but I dont want such communications as this left on record."[2]

Fortunately for the historian, these communications *were* left on record. Their very sequence of themes, their web of associations, their breathless pace rarely checked by punctuation, pulsate with Eleanor Rogers's animation over her unwonted expressiveness and over her tremulous courage. She wants to go on a crusade against marriage, but she quickly adds that her husband's tender attentiveness is beyond praise. She is inclined to be severe on what she reads as an unseemly parading of her travail—"But enough!"—yet cannot so easily set it aside: her happiness in her sister's new son is overshadowed by a cold shudder and a prayer for immunity from pain. And her boldness frightens her: "You will think I am gone stark mad," for she finds her little manifesto most inappropriate for a submissive angel: "perhaps I have." She bravely voices her distrust of that sacred household totem, the doctor, only to plead, once again, for privacy: "Burn this up please." But these hesitations and self-criticisms cannot disguise her message, the prodding of her ambivalence. Eleanor Rogers's manifest affection for her husband—who was, after all, the author of her ordeal—is beyond doubt. But so is her rising up against the consequences of acting on sexual urges. She loves Will, but she hates what he has done to her. It is nothing less than intercourse that her crusade

1. Box 53, SF, Y-MA. Alice Belknap herself, as one of her letters to Susan Wright of the previous year shows, had had more than one miscarriage of her own. "I am on my back but hope to be up tomorrow. I have had another miscarriage at two months, rather more serious this time than before as the membranes did not come away & had to be taken with forceps. Fortunately I escaped both blood poisoning & flooding & hope I am on the road to better condition than before." July 1884, ibid.

2. May 28, 1885, ibid.

against marriage is intended to check. The risks of pregnancy put the pleasures of sex into question.

In one decisive respect, of course, Eleanor Rogers was lucky. She lived to tell the tale. Thousands of other women in her day died in performing their marital duty. Its ravages are spread across letters and biographies and family Bibles. Karl von Holtei, German actor, playwright, novelist, curtly notes at the beginning of his garrulous autobiography: "My mother died after she bore me; my father, officer in the Hussars, did not know what to do with a screaming infant."[3] Often, these victims of sex lingered. Gustave Flaubert's adored sister Caroline died in March 1846, two months after she had given birth to a daughter, her first child, following prolonged and atrocious suffering. More often, though, they went quickly. The family register in the Chauncey family Bible, a sumptuously bound and elegantly printed folio, records one family's history tersely. "Nathaniel Chauncey of Philadelphia and Elizabeth Sewall Salisbury of Boston" were married on June 8, 1836, and the event was duly noted in their Bible. In the following year, as the family register discloses with the distancing restraint of Latin, the Chaunceys had a stillborn son: "Filius *mortuus* Nathanaelis et Elizabethae Sewall Chauncey natus est June 17, 1837." Two sons came after, in rapid succession, one in August 1838, another in August 1840: speedy impregnation was a way of cheating death.

But death would not be cheated. On May 19, 1850, ten years after her second living son had been born, Elizabeth Chauncey, then going on forty-three, gave birth to yet another son. The family register notes on the following day: "Francis Gardner Chauncey, son of Nathaniel and Elizabeth Sewall Chauncey, died May 20th 1850, about ten minutes before 7 o'clock P.M." The next entry completes the tragic story: "Elizabeth Sewall Chauncey, died on Wednesday, the 22nd day of May 1850, about five minutes before 5 o'clock P.M. Her remains and those of her infant son were removed to Newton Corner on Friday the 24th & Saturday the 25th and committed to the earth, at Mount Auburn, on Sunday the 26th of May 1850." The stately cadences and disciplined language of these entries and their air of devout acceptance of divine decrees cannot conceal the devastation that the lethal work of sensuality had left in its wake among the Chauncey family.[4]

3. *Vierzig Jahre*, 8 vols. (1843–50), I, 1.
4. For the Bible, printed in 1836, evidently a wedding present, see box 21, Chauncey Family Papers, Y-MA. The widower's distraction is no speculation. On the day of Mrs. Chauncey's death, W. H. Dillingham wrote to his friend Theodore Dwight Woolsey: "Our mutual excellent friend N. Chauncey Esquire, has met with the

There were thousands of Elizabeth Chaunceys in her time; the waste of human vitality, of flourishing and energetic young women's lives, was enormous. Early death hung like a capricious plague over the proper and the prosperous. Isabella Beeton, author of England's favorite book of household advice, an active and appealing journalist, lost her first child at three months and her second at three years; she herself died in 1865 of puerperal fever after the birth of her fourth child, at the age of twenty-eight.[5] Through the nineteenth century, then, the processes of pregnancy and giving birth were attended by severe pain and often by excruciating sufferings, and the ever-present threat of death to child and mother alike. It is true that from 1847 on, chloroform became available to ease the pangs of labor and parturition, and as early as 1853 so distinguished a personage as Queen Victoria availed herself of this blessed new conqueror of pain. The queen's authority as a setter of trends was unquestioned, though opposition to chloroform, as to other beneficent procedures, did not wilt without resistance. A disorderly array of medical, theological, and ethical arguments continued for some time to agitate physicians and intimidate laymen. Chloroform could kill, and, in clumsy hands, it sometimes did; moreover, its detractors never grew tired of intoning God's warning to disobedient Eve that henceforth she would bring forth in sorrow.[6] "It is an outrage upon the fundamental laws of adaptation," Robert Barnes, a lecturer in midwifery, wrote in *Lancet* in 1850, "to assume that a beneficent Creator has associated pain with the parturient process for other than a wise and necessary purpose." The middle classes especially, in general more susceptible to such religious argumentation than their richer or poorer counterparts, gave it a sympathetic hearing. But before long the wish for relief won out. When, in March 1855, Mrs. Sophia Gray, John Ruskin's mother-in-law, had a boy —she was then going on forty-seven—"that wonderful agent Chloroform," her daughter reported, spared her "all sense of suffering for two

---

greatest of earthly afflictions, in the loss of his dear wife. . . . Our friend, of course, is overwhelmed with the shock; he requests me to communicate this melancholy intelligence, at the earliest moment, to the family of the cousin of his departed wife." Box 12, Woolsey Family Papers, Y-MA.

5. Sarah Freeman, *Isabella and Sam: The Story of Mrs. Beeton* (1978), 137, 140, 222–23, 233–34. Such stories can, of course, be multiplied ad infinitum, among aristocrats and royalty as among the bourgeoisie: Princess Charlotte, the only child of the future George IV of England, died in November 1817, after giving birth to a stillborn son, at the age of twenty-one. See Cecil Woodham-Smith, *Queen Victoria: From Her Birth to the Death of the Prince Consort* (1972; ed. 1974), 16.

6. *Genesis* 3:16. The German version is blunter still; it speaks of pain: "Du sollst mit Schmerzen Kinder gebähren."

hours."[7] While the sufferings of many women continued unabated, it came to seem no longer impious, let alone unfashionable, to bear children in consciously limited discomfort.

The case against the use of chloroform to ease childbirth, made by those who believed a mother's pain to be natural, beneficial, and theologically correct, opens access to the deeper recesses of erotic life. Men rationalized their subterranean pleasure in the pain of women by arguing that it speeded the process of labor; besides, had it not always accompanied childbirth? Such defenses point to what the late nineteenth century was learning to recognize as a certain underlying sadism. And they betrayed also a certain fear of sensuality. Some obstetricians who reported that women under anesthesia broke into lewd and lascivious language were borne out by other healers: Tyler Smith observed that chloroform "metamorphosed" pain "into its antitheses" and aroused the "excitement of sexual passion." The tale gained a certain popularity and even credibility from repetition, but its bearers found themselves vulnerable to counterattack. James Simpson, the great Scottish surgeon who was one of the discoverers and most ardent advocates of chloroform, acidly commented in 1848 that those who "repeated and gloated over" this prurient report only disclosed, "apparently unconsciously on their part, the severest self-inflicted censure upon the sensuality of their own thoughts." Simpson's fellow Scot, James Syme, another celebrated surgeon, echoed this indictment a year later: these stories, he wrote, were "the results of impressions harboured in the minds of the practitioners, not in the minds of the chloroformed."[8] These are passionate and far from disinterested responses, but they shrewdly link perceptions of pregnancy with the realm of sexuality from which it had, of course, taken its origin. They detect projection at work half a century before Sigmund Freud inserted this psychological mechanism into the ranks of defenses and offered an explanation for its genesis and its manifestations.

Simpson's and Syme's blunt talk, combined with the undeniable effectiveness of chloroform, carried the day. But while women's terror or

7. Barnes: *Lancet*, II (1850), 39: A. J. Youngson, *The Scientific Revolution in Victorian Medicine* (1979), 111; Euphemia ("Effie") Ruskin: to Rawdon Brown, March 21, 1855, Mary Lutyens, *Millais and the Ruskins* (1967), 254. As late as 1882, the German philosopher Eduard Haeckel found it necessary to sing the praises of anesthesia in France, as though acceptance were still not complete. See Dr. Edouard Heckel, "Les Anesthésiques et la douleur," *La Nouvelle Revue*, XIV (January–February 1882), 80–90.

8. Dr. Tyler Smith, quoted in F. B. Smith, *The People's Health 1830–1910* (1979), 21; Simpson, *Anaesthetic Midwifery: Report on its Early History and Progress* (1848), 19, in Youngson, *Scientific Revolution in Victorian Medicine*, 125, 114.

pain, anticipated and actual, diminished in the second half of the nine-teenth century, the far more ominous specter of death continued to haunt them. Giving news of their friend Elizabeth Cady Stanton, Martha C. Wright told Susan B. Anthony in March 1859: "Mrs. Stanton has another son. I am glad that ordeal is safely past."[9] An ordeal it remained, and a danger: the vital statistics for the Western world are, from our late-twentieth-century perspective, appalling, though in the early days of Victoria their true import was only vaguely surmised. In 1841, when Dr. Christoph Bernoulli, professor of industrial sciences at Basel, pub-lished one of the first demographic studies conducted on modern statis-tical principles, he lamented the general ignorance: "Numerical estimates are not wanting, but the results gleaned from most investigations have been quite uncertain and are scarcely comparable." He cited a number of authorities on infant mortality, whose estimates differed widely though they were, at best, grim. The new science of population supported the guesses of common sense: "a large part" among the young, Bernoulli concluded, "die very early, for the most part in the very first years of life." He could also assert with some confidence that class and income were directly, though not invariably, related to the incidence of infant mortality; in the Paris of his time, he concluded, the children of the poor died at about twice the rate of the children of the comfortably off. And among the offspring of the poor, foundlings were most at risk.[10] The wise infant chose parents who were married and well-to-do, though even then his chances for reaching adulthood were precarious.

In the years that Bernoulli was compiling his treatise, the feverish ap-petite for precise social information was spreading from country to country, rapidly mounting to a beneficent epidemic. Adolphe Quetelet in Belgium, William Farr in England, laid the groundwork for medical and sanitary reform by initiating the quantitative study of social phe-nomena and by interpreting their numbers in seeking for significant comparisons. That is why Farr, for one, separated England into healthy and insalubrious districts, to discover the scourges devastating the latter and, if possible, reduce their death rates to the less heart-rending inci-dence in the former. Speaking of infant mortality in the decade of the 1860s, Farr wrote with a mixture of indignant sympathy and utilitarian calculation: "It is found that of 10,000 children born alive in Liverpool 5,396 live five years; a number that in the healthy districts could be pro-vided by 6,544 annual births. This procreation of children to perish so

9. March 29, 1859, Folder 1028.1, Garrison Family Papers, SS.
10. *Handbuch der Populationistik oder der Völker- und Menschenkunde nach statistischen Erhebnissen* (1841), 233–34, 244–48, 301.

soon—the sufferings of the little victims—the sorrows and expenses of their parents—are as deplorable as they are wasteful." But expense and waste, dismaying as they were, paled, in the mind of this humane demographer, before the grief of a mother: "The mother when she looks at her baby is asked to think of its death." Something must be done.

Something was done, but, for decades, with no visible results. "The high rate of infant mortality," Farr commented in the mid-1870s, "continues to occupy the earnest attention of medical statists." It continued to do so because the facts gave little ground for optimism. On the contrary: in the England of 1875, Farr wrote, the death rate of infants under one year was "158 per 1,000 or 4 per 1,000 above the average rate in the 10 years 1861–70. This implies that the mortality among infants is increasing." Mortality rates varied markedly and remained rather puzzling. If, in Liverpool between 1873 and 1875, infant mortality stood at the terrifying rate of 218.9 per thousand, in Portsmouth, which boasted England's most favorable statistics, it was 145.9, while all of Scotland, long famous for its medicine, could proudly point to a rate of 125.7 per thousand. This was the reality that every pregnant woman had to confront in the nineteenth century: to live in a country where "only" one baby in eight died within the year was cause for reassurance. Among the variables that Farr and his colleagues noted, and that offered hope of explaining high rates of infant mortality, were "the use of opiates, early marriages, and debility of mothers," to say nothing of "bad sanitary arrangements."[11] But abstention from drugs, delay of marriage, healthy mothers, and sanitary improvements, all solemnly recommended in those decades, did little to reduce infant mortality. And women everywhere, of course, knew—or felt—this in their bones.

International comparisons were just as suggestive but no less inconclusive. In the Sweden of the 1860s where infant mortality was enviably low, lower even than in Scotland, eleven out of every hundred babies died; in Prussia, France, and Spain, in the same years, it was about double that figure. And these dismal reports did not fully disclose all the realities. England, as we know, recorded the average incidence of infant deaths as hovering around sixteen out of a hundred, but, with thousands of deaths going unreported, the true figures were a good deal higher. And even a country like England, which took pride in its scientific accomplishments, did not significantly reduce this mortality until the end of Queen Victoria's reign: it was only after 1900 that it began to drop, and

11. *Vital Statistics: A Memorial Volume of Selections from the Reports and Writings of William Farr,* ed. Noel A. Humphreys (1885), 186, 190, 191–93.

only after 1910 that it finally reached the level of which Sweden had boasted half a century before.

To survive the perils of infancy was no small triumph, but did not guarantee long life: quite as many nineteenth-century children died between the ages of one and five as died in their first year. And even five was no threshold of safety. Physicians stood largely helpless before childhood diseases and had to trust luck—they liked to call it Nature—to pull their little charges through. In 1847, in the space of a few weeks, three younger sisters of Effie Gray, Ruskin's wife, died of scarlet fever; in 1852, several of her younger siblings were stricken and survived. It was a much-needed respite for the Grays who, of their fifteen children, saw only eight live beyond the age of seven. Such grim figures were by no means exceptional. The parents of Michael Zeno Diemer, a minor German painter and composer, did no better than the Grays: married in 1861, they had seven children, of whom the first two, both girls, died at a few months while two of their boys died of diphtheria, one at three and the other at nine. The death of children was an expected, but remained for most a dreaded, event. At times, some indifference—or, better, numbness —insinuated itself to permit parents to tolerate their bereavement: in an early, heavily autobiographical story, "My Boys and Girls," Walt Whitman mentions a child dead in infancy and comments: "It was not a sad thing—we wept not, nor were our hearts heavy."[12]

This bland tone bespeaks not callousness, but the self-control that habituation often brings; it helps to conceal the suppressed suffering. When, in 1890, Georg Brandes, that worldly philanderer, lost his cherished ten-year-old daughter, he was prostrated with his sense of irreparable loss for many months.[13] Whitman to the contrary, bourgeois, pious or irreligious, allowed themselves to find a child's death sad; most of them wept, with heavy hearts—wept, and worried about the others. In the spring of 1854, John Leech, the well-known English illustrator and cartoonist, and his family were visiting John Everett Millais. "Leech is here with his wife, sister, and baby, nurse, and maid," Millais reported. "The child takes up the attention of the 5 nearly all day. They lost their first and are dreadfully anxious about this second and only one, a pretty

12. Grays: Lutyens, *Millais and the Ruskins*, 7n; Diemer (1867–1939): Michael Zeno Diemer Papers, Aba 433, folder I, 1, Handschriften Abteilung, Stabi, Munich; Whitman: Justin Kaplan, *Walt Whitman: A Life* (1980), 85–86.

13. Brandes to Alexander L. Kielland, December 19, 1890, and to Jonas Lie, January 8 [1891], *Georg og Edvard Brandes, Brevveksling med nordiske Forfattere og Videnskabsmœnd*, ed. Norten Borup, 8 vols. (1939–1942), IV, part 2, 364–65, 451–52. I owe this reference to Henry Gibbons.

little girl with blue eyes, 5 months old."[14] The Leeches' luck held: their girl lived, and in the following year, in the customary nineteenth-century manner of "repairing" a child's death with a quick pregnancy, they added yet another hostage to fortune, this time a boy.

Class, as usual, told in the distribution of death, but not enough to spare the bourgeoisie. Nineteenth-century statisticians investigating the incidence of infant mortality amply confirmed the obvious: the poor, unable to nourish and shelter themselves adequately, unable to command trained attention, and treated with the utmost callousness in public institutions, saw about twice as many of their infants die as the prosperous, often more. This, we saw, Bernoulli noted in 1841, held true for Paris. And in the Lancashire town of Preston, around 1860, the "upper classes" lost around eighteen out of every hundred children under five; the "middle classes," twice as many—thirty-six—and the poor almost twice as many again, well over sixty.[15] Even the rich and the sheltered, then, must expect to bury some of their offspring. In the nineteenth century, middle-class families thought themselves most fortunate if they lost no more than one child out of five.

Unless a woman had been permanently disabled by medical intervention—far from rare—the loss of an infant was, speaking coolly, a reparable loss. And a wife, too, was a renewable resource. Many nineteenth-century widowers, sincerely mourning a wife dead in childbirth, did not hesitate to marry again, often a younger woman, thus exposing yet another female to the risks of sanguinary miscarriages, puerperal fever, or those lingering illnesses that often beset mothers of large families, eventually to defeat their vital energies. Franz Josef Lenbach, architect for a small Bavarian town and father of Franz von Lenbach, who became the most sought-after, most highly paid portrait painter of the German Empire, had eight children by his first wife in nine years, and the last, which soon died, took his mother with him: an invalid from late 1830 on, Frau Lenbach died in November 1832. Six weeks later, Lenbach found himself another wife with whom he had, in the space of ten years, eight more children, and who died, much like the first, a year after her last-born.[16] The dangers were great, and many husbands thoughtless,

14. Millais to Effie Ruskin, July 26, 1854, in Lutyens, *Millais and the Ruskins*, 238.
15. Bernoulli, *Handbuch der Populationistik*, 301; Smith, *People's Health*, 65–69.
16. Siegfried Wichmann, *Franz von Lenbach und seine Zeit* (1973), 8–10. William Millais, the painter's brother, married in 1860 and was widowed two years later when his wife, Judith, died in childbirth with her second child. Lutyens, *Millais and the Ruskins*, 259n. The long-term effect of pregnancy, even when the mother survived, was often severe and prolonged pain. Cecilia Bishop, a friend of Effie Ruskin's, was still suffering severely a year after giving birth. Ibid., 116.

especially those in search of second wives to superintend the brood they had made with the first. But even tender-hearted men, especially in the first half of the nineteenth century, had no dependable way of sparing their wives this mortal peril at regular intervals.

The figures are hard to read, for nearly everywhere they were imprecise or unreliable. Greedy physicians unwilling to attend those too poor to pay, or incompetent physicians losing their heads when faced with a difficult birth, were shielded by coroners and defensive fellow-professionals. Lying-in hospitals protected their reputations by shifting the cause of patients' deaths from ignorance, dirt, or negligence to some unspecified malady unrelated to the pregnancy. Midwives were often experienced and able, but many of them were ill-trained, even drunken, and plied their risky trade with inadequate supervision. And medical diagnoses remained vague, generally ill-informed, down to the end of the nineteenth century. All this combined to make inquiries into the incidence of childbed mortality something of a disheartening guessing game. But some figures were available, and, undependable, essentially evasive though they proved to be, they disclosed some worrisome facts. In Prussia between 1820 and 1834, as Bernoulli reported in his treatise, there was one mother's death to every 108 births. In the Swiss canton of St. Gallen, childbed fever and related "accidents" were more devastating still: between 1830 and 1837, the ratio between infants' births and mothers' deaths was only 88 to one. Württemberg offered a cheerful contrast: there, the ratio was 175 to one. These statistics puzzled Bernoulli, and others. He recognized that "a number of women died only a long time after giving birth, and yet in consequence of it," and he conjectured that around one hundred births entailed one mother's death. In 1870, in England, the figure was one in 204; it was scarcely improved in the 1880s, when it was one in 211 births.[17]

As with infant mortality, so with the mortality of mothers, comparative studies proved intriguing. The most celebrated of these comparisons was made in the early 1840s in Vienna's busy Lying-In Hospital; it was here that Dr. Ignaz Semmelweis gathered his facts and developed his hypotheses that would lead to his controversial discovery of antisepsis. Between 1841 and 1846, there were 2,680 deaths among the 37,833 treated in the Vienna Lying-In Hospital, a toll of 7 percent. In the notorious First Division of the hospital, where patients were dying at inexplicable rates that contrasted sharply with the deaths recorded in the Second Division, the average was around 10 percent and in some disastrous months would

17. Bernoulli, *Handbuch der Populationistik*, 283; Farr, *Vital Statistics*, 269–81.

rise to 14 and even 18 percent,[18] a toll hard to tolerate even for a century always nervously prepared to expect the death of a mother.

The death toll in lying-in hospitals, even that recorded in their least lethal wards, hints at the ravages of class among pregnant women. In decisive respects, middle-class women were naturally far better off than their working-class or peasant counterparts. They escaped the ordeal of going to a hospital to have a baby, their food was nourishing, their rooms relatively clean and their medical care reasonably attentive—at least much of the time. Yet, paradoxically enough, sophisticated modern techniques favored by fashionable physicians, or recently invented and still little-understood instruments, exposed bourgeois women to infections and other "accidents" which working-class women were too impecunious to en-counter.[19] Every pregnancy, even among the prosperous middle classes, even a birth eagerly, prayerfully awaited, brought its quota of anxiety.

That anxiety is difficult to document and impossible to measure, but it makes fleeting, if impressive, appearances in the confessions that women kept to themselves. On December 20, 1852, Hannah Smith, M. Carey Thomas's aunt, noted her second pregnancy with dismay and the merest hint of rebelliousness: "I am very unhappy now. That trial of my womanhood which to me is so very bitter has come upon me again. When my little Ellie is 2 years old she will have a little sister or brother." An abortion was clearly unthinkable. "It is all the more heavy a trial," she added, "because my husband agreed with me in thinking that I am too young for such cares and such suffering and he promised me I should not again be so tried at least until I was 25." Evidently, the Smiths had discussed birth control and Mr. Smith had undertaken to protect his wife from impregnation—in vain. "And this is the end of all my hopes, my pleasing anticipations, my returning youthful joyousness. Well, it is a woman's lot and I must try to become resigned and bear it in patience and silence and not make my home unhappy because I am so. But oh, how hard it is." Her niece, who read this passage with riveted attention and transcribed it into her own diary late in 1878, obviously thought it very hard, too: laments such as this, brave and helpless, only strengthened Carey Thomas's resolution to devote herself to her career and never to

18. Sir William J. Sinclair, *Semmelweis: His Life and His Doctrine; A Chapter in the History of Medicine* (1909), 29–33, 45, 51.

19. Analyzing mothers' death rates in England and Wales in the 1880s, F. B. Smith notes that in London, "wealthy parishes such as Hampstead and St. George's, Hanover Square, had higher puerperal fever and general maternity mortality rates than wretched St. Giles and St. George in the East." He concludes that "the servant-employing classes who retained expensive *accoucheurs* bought greater peace of mind, but no real lessening of their vulnerability." *People's Health*, 14, 56.

be married—never, in short, to go through the ordeal of bearing children.[20]

Hannah Smith spoke for more respectable women than she could have imagined. There was Eleanor Rogers after her miscarriage, with her gallant one-woman crusade against the married state. There was Mabel Loomis Todd, denying for months that she was pregnant: she adopted the stance of impatient, eager mother-to-be only after her husband provided her with an acceptable sexual identity complete with script for a mother's role. Then there was Elizabeth Dwight Cabot of Massachusetts. She had been married in 1857 and, after a wedding trip to Europe, settled down to family life. Late in 1858, when she was pregnant for the first time, she contemplated her condition in a confidential letter to her sister. She acknowledged that her morale was excellent, but quickly berated herself for being so "frivolous." Her situation, after all, called for seriousness; it might even become perilous. And so, she decided to adjust her behavior, if not her feelings, to the demands of the rather solemn society in which she lived. "I have made my will and divided off all my little things and don't mean to leave undone what I ought to do, if I can help it."[21] Her anxiety, real enough, translated itself into moral earnestness, no less real; her guilt feelings for her frivolousness activated her sense of responsibility to a world she just might have to leave prematurely.

But then, doing what ought to be done, writing her testament and the rest, Elizabeth Cabot felt compelled to confess that her pregnancy had put her in good spirits. And there were good reasons, biological and cultural, why pregnancy was, for her and thousands of other young women, ground for solid satisfaction. Once the local disruptions of the first months had passed, increases in hormonal and metabolic levels normally generated feelings of energetic well-being, a sense of competence and accomplishment. In 1823, in a letter to Emilie de Wismes, a good friend from convent days, George Sand analyzed her state of expansive happiness, modulated by an honest confession of discomfort, that matched the experience of thousands of other, only less articulate, pregnant women. She had suffered a minor accident and was keeping to her bed, but she reassured her friend that her pains were entirely bearable. "On the contrary, there is no sweeter suffering than that which announces that you are with child." She added frankly that "the uneasiness, the vexations which this causes you are quite real." But while doctors, nurses, and

20. Diary, September 1, 1878, *The Making of a Feminist: Early Journals and Letters of M. Carey Thomas*, ed. Marjorie Housepian Dobkin (1979), 149.

21. Carl N. Degler, *At Odds: Women and the Family in America from the Revolution to the Present* (1980), 60.

pharmacists frightened her, she was confident that all this was transient, and the happiness lasting. "I think that the little caresses of the new-born will make one forget all this. While waiting, you can't imagine what a pleasure it is to feel one's child stirring in your womb." There is a hint in this letter, no more, of ambivalence: George Sand had prefaced this cheerful report on her pregnancy with some rather tepid praise of marriage: "I won't preach to you to give you a taste for marriage, for that will come to you as to others, and besides, your situation is so agreeable and so prosperous that I don't see why you should hurry to change it. I only want to reassure you about *the pains attached to my condition*."[22] She was too perceptive to overlook the cause of those pains, her married state, and too honest to suppress it. But she could luxuriate in her biological blessing, the sweetest of sufferings. Certainly, for many other women like her, even those more anxious and more afraid than George Sand, the joy was worth the travail; late in the nineteenth century, as the pain was reduced, the balance shifted even more toward pleasure.

Pregnancy, of course, had never been, and in the nineteenth century did not become, a matter of pure endocrinology. Social needs, economic imperatives, family pride—pressures of reality all—invited, and often imposed, a limited range of permissible feelings; they would screen out all but the most determined and independent-minded women's protests and stifle their expression in all but the most guarded forums. Husbands wanted both to father an heir and to exhibit their potency; offspring could be used as counters in family alliances. It was an unquestioned truth that to be fertile was to be blessed; to be barren, cursed. The potent emotions implicit in these very adjectives betray the heavy cultural bias in favor of the woman who could become a mother, the stigma attaching to the one who could not.

Moreover, prescribed feelings about pregnancy were colored, sometimes blighted, by insistent sentimental, quasi-theological refrains reiterated in religious homilies, family gatherings, and popular novels. There was much cant about the sacredness of creating new life, about the "miracle" of birth, most of it retailed by men. In his little book *The Marriage Gift*, James Petrie, pastor of the Presbyterian Church at Phillipsburg, New Jersey, sounded the characteristic refrain: "I will not speak of the joy excited by the birth of the first-born, or of the peculiar emotions connected with the name father, mother: these are mysteries known only to those who have experienced them. Even the mother soon forgets her

22. January 30 (1823), *Correspondance*, vol. I, *1812–1831*, ed. Georges Lubin (1964), 103.

anguish for joy, that a man is born into the world."[23] The Lord had given;
that should erase all pain.

Even Havelock Ellis, by his own estimation a serious and unblinking
student of the ruder facts of sexual life, could not escape this dominant
style. Concluding his essay "The Psychic State in Pregnancy," he pointed
to questions surrounding the condition that medical science had still left
unsolved, and celebrated what he insisted on calling "the mystery of
pregnancy," with which, he portentously and rather obviously suggested,
"the future of the race is bound up." Contemplating that mystery he
lapsed, in his peroration, into the religious rhythms much favored in his
time: "We are here lifted into a region where our highest intelligence
can only lead us to adoration, for we are gazing at a process in which
the operations of Nature become one with the divine task of Creation."[24]
If even Havelock Ellis, presumably speaking for advanced opinion around
the turn of this century, could let himself go, one could hardly fault conventional publicists or preachers for adopting such hysterical hyperbole.

But the inauthenticity of this deification does not mean that the active
and happy feelings buoying up pregnant women were spurious, sheer
obedient repetitions of prevailing social myths. And the desire for a child
could strike the most surprising women, at the most surprising moments.
In March 1899, thanking her lover Leo Jogiches for an adroitly chosen
birthday present, Rosa Luxemburg gave way to fantasies of domesticity.
Jogiches had sent her the works of the German economist Karl Johann
Rodbertus, which made her, intelligent political theorist and activist that
she was, very happy: "You simply cannot imagine how pleased I am
with your choice. Why, Rodbertus is simply my favorite economist and
I can read him a hundred times for sheer intellectual pleasure." But Rosa
Luxemburg had another, maternal—I am tempted to say bourgeois—side
to her. Expressing her delight with her dear Leo's long letter, she began
to ruminate about their possible domestic arrangements, longing for "our
own little room, our own furniture, a library of our own, quiet and
regular work, walks together, an opera from time to time," and similar
joys. "And perhaps even a little, a very little, baby? Will this never be
permitted? Never? Darling, do you know what accosted me yesterday
during a walk in the park?" she asked, and answered her own question:
"A little child, three or four years old, in a beautiful dress with blond
hair; it stared at me and suddenly I felt an overpowering urge to kidnap
the child and dash off home with him. Oh darling, will I never have my

23. *Marriage Gift* (1864), 76.
24. "The Psychic State in Pregnancy" (1906), *Studies in the Psychology of Sex*,
2 vol. ed. (1936), II, 229.

own baby?"[25] If even an uncompromising intellectual and committed revolutionary could long for a baby, the cant about the irresistible maternal instinct that swirled about her had at least some evidence on its side.

To be with child, especially for the first time, is to take a step in emotional evolution; it works a complex reordering of woman's attachment to her mother and to her husband, a revival, in a new setting and with new consequences, of earlier, long-repressed feelings. Pregnancy is what psychoanalysts have called a normal crisis that leads, in the right circumstances, to increased mastery of the world and oneself and, through the byway of increased temporary dependency, toward a sense of adult autonomy.[26] The meaning of pregnancy distinctly includes the fulfillment of the promise of woman's biological endowment and psychological possibilities.

This promise might ring hollow for the nineteenth-century woman too poor to feed and clothe yet another child, or too worn with child-bearing to welcome new claims on her. It was no more pleasing for the wife— and, it is fair to add, the husband—too childish or too intent on other pleasures gladly to give up the social circuit or foreign trips. But particularly for women who could afford the enforced leisure, expected to be spoiled by attentive husbands and hovering mothers, and knew that they would be allowed to rest for some time after giving birth, the promise of pregnancy was glowing. It was compromised for the expectant mother mainly by her well-grounded fear of losing her child, or possibly her own life. This was an anxiety-making reservation, to be contemplated soberly, but in the clash of conflicting emotions, hope normally won out over fear. Besides, sexual desire—the woman's as well as the man's—was not so lightly ignored.

There was one famous occasion, as historians of psychoanalysis have particular cause to remember, when pregnancy became the signature of love: Josef Breuer's case of Anna O., the severely stricken hysteric whom he treated from 1880 to 1882 and who is the ancestor of all other psychoanalytic cases. With Anna O., this erotic engagement was one-sided, a sheer fantasy; the signature was, as it were, forged. When her father,

---

25. J. P. Nettl, *Rosa Luxemburg*, 2 vols. (1966), I, 143–44.

26. I borrow this felicitous phrase, "normal crisis," from Grete Bibring et al., "A Study of the Psychological Processes in Pregnancy and of the Earliest Mother-Child Relationship," *Psychoanalytic Study of the Child*, XVI (1961), 9–72. It is instructive to scan the footnotes to Havelock Ellis's essay "The Psychic State in Pregnancy": while some authors—Ellis included—wasted a good deal of space on the vexed question of "maternal impressions," serious and responsible studies of the psychological aspects of pregnancy were clearly entering the medical literature of Europe and the United States from the late 1880s onward.

whom she had devotedly nursed, died after a long illness, Anna O., then twenty-one, developed hysterical paralyses, found herself unable to speak in her own language, lost sensation in parts of her body, and often appeared delirious, even deranged. In months of close listening and intense hypnotic sessions, Breuer persuaded his patient to talk out her symptoms, recall their origins, and trace their symbolic language; slowly he recaptured her for normal life. But in the course of his long treatment, Breuer unwittingly made Anna O. fall in love with him. And for his own part, if only through being fascinated by this most unusual patient, Breuer became attached to Anna O., a fascination that Breuer's wife could not fail to notice and began to resent. Suddenly aware of this domestic complication, Breuer abruptly broke off the treatment and told Anna O. farewell. That night, he was called back to her bedside: her improvement had vanished and she was in the midst of hysterical childbirth. For months she had been nourishing an imaginary pregnancy which, when her "lover" deserted her, issued in parturition, just as imaginary. Pregnancy was, for Anna O., both a secret victory and a desperate invitation.[27] That it was a pure fantasy only enhances its symbolic significance; it hints at the larger meaning of all pregnancy for the economy of love.

2. From Conscience to Control

The prospect of motherhood, then, was much like an English sky: sometimes glorious, sometimes threatening, usually both at once, and in any event steadily changing. Pregnant women who wanted nothing more than to carry their child were not free from apprehension; pregnant women who wanted nothing less still experienced intervals of energy and euphoria. Society, as we know, was of course eloquently and insistently on the side of motherhood, and compliance with the imperatives of fertility, whether desired or feared, was general. Well into the time of Victoria, most middle-class couples faced frequent pregnancies with marked passivity, accepting all their perils, even though these perils predictably increased as some mothers kept bearing children into their late thirties and early forties. It was only gradually that this submissiveness came to be subverted. Women developed fantasies of flight from home and of forcing their husbands into a regimen of sexual continence or, at the least, into exploring the possibilities of birth control.

The evidence is notoriously fragmentary, but there were scattered in-

27. For Anna O., see Breuer, *Studies on Hysteria* (1895), *S.E.*, II, 21–47; Freud's comments in "On the History of the Psychoanalytic Movement" (1914), *S.E.*, XIV, 11–12.

cidents—little more—of bourgeois wives locking the bedroom door on their husbands, of bourgeois husbands thoughtfully protecting their wives from unwanted pregnancies, and of shamefaced discussions about limiting the number of offspring. These discussions became more frequent and less shamefaced as the century went on. But rigorists continued to declare motherhood to be woman's principal reason for existence. At least until mid-century, the bourgeois conscience, whether religious or secular in temper, found it hard to grasp that continuous child-bearing might not be a woman's highest duty. Before such passivity was challenged—and this challenge constitutes one of the authentic dramas of the nineteenth century —the cultural superego of the bourgeoisie emphatically included reverence for the decrees of Providence. And yet, for all this devout passivity, and for all the looming omnipresence of fatal diseases, bourgeois continued to perceive the death of a child or of a wife as a tragedy. Their capacity for mourning was scarcely dampened by its frequency. The bourgeoisie did not dip into some fixed reservoir of misery that could be diluted or divided up among a numerous family. But while many humbly blessed the name of the Lord, who, after He had given, had taken away, some at least came to wonder at the ironic results of sexual desire—the instrument of life turning into an instrument of death.

Still, Christian stoicism helped thousands of families to tolerate their bereavement. The thought of heaven gave relief, however temporary— however helpless it proved in the long run against the sense of loss. The soothing fantasies that belief in immortality and trust in a beneficent God could generate pervade letter after letter in the bourgeois century. In July 1849, Mary Anna Gibbs, member of a prosperous and cultivated Connecticut family, sent her brother Horatio Van Cleve some characteristic reflections on the death of their sister, their "dear Maggie." She recalled her as a delightful little child "with her guileless and winning ways," and as a grown woman, "amiable, intelligent and pious," yet "improving until the close of life." She had died a month after bearing a child and losing it after two hours; "a pretty little baby," prematurely born, "extremely small but perfectly well formed" and "sweet and harmless." It was "the loss of a sweet infant" that had "sent her to her saviour," for since that loss, Mary Anna Gibbs wrote, Margaret had "felt a new and strong attraction to heaven." She had come to stay with her sister, hoping to have the pure country air strengthen her and "to have with the divine permission some pleasant intercourse with a few friends here." But she had been "extremely feeble," though apparently happy, and almost wholly silent all the while. Her reticence was not a matter of genteel choice but of physical condition: "It was very trying to both herself and to us that she could so very seldom express her own feelings, or allow us to express ours." Yet her satisfaction in God was complete and visible: "Occasionally she expressed her enjoyment of that peace of mind and satisfaction in divine dispensations towards her which have comforted and supported us through this affliction. She felt the presence of her saviour and that God did all things well." But then she died, leaving her bereft family to express its satisfaction in turn: "And now she is gone from us to dwell forever with the beloved ones who preceded her, in the presence of her God."[28]

It is a poignant document which only a positivist could have thought groveling and just a touch masochistic. There were many others like it. Early in February 1865, Hattie, third child of Joseph and Laura Lyman, fell ill. On the twelfth, Joseph Lyman, writing from New York, could still paint an idyllic picture for his wife: "You have dressed & washed the baby," and in the early afternoon "Hattie is solacing her baby sorrows with 'rag titty' or asleep." But her baby sorrows were soon desperately grave. Two days later, having advised her husband of Hattie's illness, Laura Lyman exclaimed: "She lives still & is now likely to recover. Again & again I thought the soul had parted from the body," and, she added, "I was resigned and submissive to the will of God—hard as it was to give up my darling—It might be best for her to go now & I would not keep her contrary to the will of God." The next day, February 15, Joseph Lyman, addressing his "Dear Worn Wife," kept up the religious strain: "Your letter has made me sad & anxious"; he contemplated joining her, but "by this time she is better or—*better!*" Even for this exuberant, sensual couple, literary to a fault and addicted to the optimistic philosophizing of phrenology, the life of the blessed in heaven seemed a far better state than anxious existence on this earth. Indeed, only a few hours after Lyman wrote these lines, after a day and night of almost continuous spasms, the child died. Joseph Lyman later noted in his sparsely kept diary under that date, with a certain sense of irony: "8 o'cl. My little girl died. I was at the moment writing for the Times."[29]

On the next day, Laura Lyman wrote in some detail. "We thought she was better and I watched beside her feeding the flame of her little life— but the disease had reduced her too low." While Hattie had had a good day earlier, at night she took a turn for the worse and "at half-past eight

28. Mary Anna Gibbs to Horatio P. Van Cleve, July 5, 1849, box 13, Ebenezer Alfred Johnson Family Papers, Y-MA.

29. Joseph to Laura Lyman, February 12, 1865; Laura to Joseph Lyman, February 14, 1865; Joseph to Laura Lyman, February 15, 1865, all box 3, LF; February 15, Diary 1865, box 6, LF, Y-MA.

last evening she breathed her last." Then, almost as if to justify her care and stress her unremitting vigilance: "everything that medical attention, everything that nursing could do to prolong her little life was done—but 'God's finger touched her & she slept.' "[30] This gentle euphemism did not heal Laura's pain.

In fact, the correspondence between the Lymans, as the month proceeded, was a wrestling with the event, an attempt to find some meaning in it and some solace. On February 17, when the final news reached Joseph Lyman at his boarding house, he abruptly left the lunch table to be alone with himself. "Philosophy is all very well," he wrote to his wife that day, "it is the course of human events. I could go over to Astor Library & find the gloomy statistics that would prove how many millions of parents are peirced by similar greifs. Homer may say 'I shall bear this as I have borne everything else since it pleased the Gods to curse me with life.' Religion brings higher & deeper consolations. She has gone before; she is translated." Still, though he did not quite say it, religion, like philosophy, was all very well; it too did not reach the heart of loss: "And yet the gloomy fact remains that our little tender babe our flesh and blood lies dead & cold under the frozen earth and the thought cuts like the peircing of steel, & the spirit sings in pain and grief."[31]

The Lymans' two little boys were immediately included in this community of mourning. Thus, to "Allie," Joseph Lyman wrote: "I am ver——y sorry Hattie died. But she will be a fair angel up in Heaven. God has given her an angel mother." And, on the same day, in the same vein, to "Cha'," Lyman wrote: "Hattie has gone up to Heaven. An angel took her & she will be an angel too." Not neglecting the opportunity to make a didactic point at a moment of intense emotion, Lyman added: "Cha, be good and love your bro. Allie and don't be selfish. If you are selfish you will not be an angel. Angels are not selfish."[32] It took some time, and a sheaf of letters back and forth, before daily life claimed the Lymans, adults and children, once again.

Children in general were taught this sort of resignation early. They had to learn in good time that, as Alice Belknap told her sister Susan Wright in June 1884, "the Lords ways are not our ways." Thus, when M. Carey Thomas was eight, still too young to write in her diary, she dictated some of her feelings about early death—patently the echo of familial teachings —to her mother for transcription. On March 5, 1865, she had noted that "this morning I saw my sweet little baby brother for the first time." But

30. Laura to Joseph Lyman, February 16, 1865, LF.
31. Joseph to Laura Lyman, February 17, LF.
32. Joseph to Laura Lyman and their two sons, February 22 [1865], LF.

on September 6, she had a sadder message to transmit: "Dear little Jamie died at the Grove cottage—the sweetest and dearest little baby that ever could be." And on the following day, her proper sentiments were in place, though not wholly free from conflict. "I could not bear to see my darling, beautiful little brother shut up in that dark coffin and put in the ground. I should have screamed out loud when they did it if it had not been for the thought that he was so happy, and that I should see him in Heaven."[33]

The diary of young Edward Tallmadge Root who was born in Ohio the son of a Protestant minister and would become an eminent preacher himself, suggests that such lessons were absorbed thoroughly and well. In March 1881, shortly before he turned sixteen, his younger brother Willie died. "Tomorrow morning at seven," he noted on March 18, "(if I live) I shall be 16 years old. How fast I am becoming a man! But it will be sad, sad birthday to us all for the light and joy of our household, dear brother Willie is in Heaven; and we are so lonely." He missed Willie terribly. "No soft little arms will enfold me to night no dear voice will whisper 'Tell story.' No brother will give me birthday greetings in the morning; or entertain us with his merry sayings. O Willie, Willie, how can I live without you." For all the elegiac tone of this outpouring, Edward Root was too much the unblinking observer to spare himself the most clinical description of his younger brother's last illness. Edward himself had had an attack of scarlet fever and of "dropsy" earlier, and six weeks after being exposed, "Willie came down. This was Friday. On Tuesday it went to his brain and for three days he was out of his head. This was finally relieved and he seemed improving, but the disease then went to his right leg and then to the lungs. Then he was blistered" and his pain "kept him continually moaning. He became so deaf as not to understand a word and his throat was so bad he could not speak." At the end he was "unconscious and his breath was become shorter as I kissed him for the last time. He did not know me. his eyes were staring wildly his hand clinched my cheek—At a quarter past 10 he closed his eyes turned his head one side and fell asleep."

This momentous event called for all the resources of his piety. "Asleep in Jesus blessed sleep," he wrote, "From which none ever wake to weep." The "shattered bark," he concluded, "had reached port." The wording was borrowed; the feeling, his own. As the weeks went by, Edward Root confided to his diary how intensely he was mourning: "O precious brother Willie how can I live without you!" he wrote on March 25, and for

33. June 14, 1884, box 53, SF; *Making of a Feminist*, 38.

April 8, which would have been Willie's fourteenth birthday, he composed a touching reminiscence, a paean of praise to his departed brother, "studious and talented," who "gained honors at home and abroad." But, he added, "The Master needed him and has taken him to himself. O Lord help us to say 'Thy will be done.'" It was, then, not easy to say, even for a minister's son. "Dear Willie, your journey was short and happy; how much of sorrow and pain you have escaped!"[34] The young were sometimes, in the bourgeois century, old beyond their years, bearing a heavy load of conscience.

Possibly the most exacting conscience of the age, certainly the one that has left the most usable traces, inhabited William Ewart Gladstone. He came by his punitive evangelical superego naturally, through identification with his intensely religious, obsessively observant mother, who set the tone of the Gladstone household while her husband was busy with his mercantile and political affairs. An incurable hypochondriac, a chronic worrier, Mrs. Gladstone wielded more power than the most active of mothers; she imprinted on all her children, and on William most of all, the need for frequent prayer and continual self-abasement before the deity, a lively sense of sin, and a commitment to spiritual discomfort as a spur to useful and charitable Christian activity. Gladstone's diaries bulge with rich and fascinating material showing the bourgeois conscience at work on matters of domestic life and death. God, we know, was a vital presence both for William Gladstone and for his wife Catherine, and His mercies, like His wrath, were particularly obtrusive during Catherine Gladstone's frequent occasions of child-bearing. The Gladstones were guided—or, rather, terrorized—by two stringent demands: for submission to Providential decrees, and for unremitting dutiful labor. The Gladstones' God was like a strict, capricious, often cruel, yet adored father who could do no wrong: He dealt out pain and pleasure, death and life, unbearable suspense and surprising deliverance, yet had to be praised, unstintingly, for all He decided in His wisdom. He was, with all His exalted distance, a pressure of reality on domesticity, a true household God.

The Gladstones' first child, Willy, was born on June 3, 1840, and his father witnessed it all. Early in the morning, "C. awakened me & sent for Dr. Locock," who came promptly. "The whole day was consumed in a slow but favourable labour. Till 11 the pains were slight—till 3 quite ineffectual. about 7½ they began to assume the expulsory character." This invited Gladstone to prayer: "Praise & thanks be to God for his

34. Root Family Papers, Y-MA.

mercies to her & for the fortitude he gives her." The sight astonished him: "This is to me a new scene & lesson in human life. I have seen her endure today—less than the average for first children, says Dr L, yet, six times as much bodily pain as I have undergone in my whole life." Not surprisingly, the inevitable verse from Genesis sprang to his mind, with a commentary of his own, equally spiritual: " 'In sorrow shalt thou bring forth children' is the woman's peculiar curse, & the note of Divine Judgment upon her in Adam: so 'she shall be saved in childbearing' is her peculiar promise in Christ." Gladstone found that the elemental spectacle he was witnessing gave him nourishing food for rumination on causes and effects. "How many thoughts does this agony excite: the comparison of the termination with the commencement: the undergoings of another for our sakes: the humbling & sobering view of human relations here presented: the mixed & intricate considerations of religion which may be brought to bear upon the question of the continuation of our wayward race." As Gladstone reasoned it out, woman is peculiarly privileged; she has "the blessing that she may as a member of Christ behold in these pains certain especially appointed means of her purification with a willing mind."

Finally, "at 11¼ all was happily ended by the birth of a vigorous little boy. Catherine's relief & delight were beyond anything." He noted, with visible pride, that "she has been most firm & gallant," even though the two women friends who had attended her, and Dr. Locock, had encouraged her to scream. And he added, quite as proudly, that after the boy's birth his wife's "first wish" had been that "I should offer a prayer." On the following day, his diary reflects an immense relief and records a revealing confession. "Today all is smooth & happy. The child vigorous, quiet & (says nurse) very sweet tempered: Catherine in the best possible state of body, & absolutely melted in the penetrating sense of maternal love & delight, passing all expression.—But she allows the pain was awful."[35] It had been awful, but, for the sake of that penetrating sense of maternal love, it was bearable, almost welcome.

Gladstone's conviction that woman, willing her pain, was a chosen creature in the eyes of God sounds like special pleading, but his wife accepted it as an irrefutable truth. Her sense of maternal duty emerges even more emphatically with her second child, Agnes, born a little more than two years later. Serious labor pains began at three in the afternoon, and then "increased gradually till 6½: then quicker & quicker, 1½ hour

35. *The Gladstone Diaries*, ed. M. R. D. Foot and H. C. G. Matthew, 8 vols. so far (1968–   ), III, 33–34.

very sharp & a girl was born at 8. She was even bigger than Willy had been," and Catherine bore the last pains with perfect fortitude. "I could not but observe how exceedingly beautiful she looked while this suffering so severe but without bitterness was upon her"—without bitterness, that is, against her husband, or against sexuality itself. "She desired that we should offer together our prayers and thanksgivings just after the birth: and not only are all the outward circumstances as favorable as possible, but surely she has the higher gift of elevating this anguish, the burden of her womanhood, into a discipline of assimilation to her Lord. So likewise was her sense of the reward keen & strong: for she said within an hour she was ready to go through the same again for such another daughter."[36] She did go through the same again, both for sons and daughters, six more times. Catherine Gladstone bore the burden of her womanhood in happy resignation.

If birth was, for William Gladstone, mantled in awesome mystery, death called out all his talent for filial submissiveness, not untouched by Biblical erudition. When his sister-in-law, Lavinia Glynne, had a boy only to lose him on his first day, Gladstone drew upon his Christian convictions to assimilate the tragedy: "At 10 A.M. Lavinia had a boy: & all Hawarden was alive with joy on the birth of the heir. Between five & six it died: in the mother's bed—the death was not discovered till past seven." He added, in mixed dismay and trust, "It had not been baptized: but He who spared Nineveh for the sake of four score thousand who knew not their right hand from their left, has, as I trust & pray, mercies for this poor infant in that mighty Name, not a sound, but a power, which saves even of them who know it not." A little more than two years later, when Lavinia Glynne herself died in childbirth, he conscientiously noted down "the sad account" that her brothers had given him, and commented, with the purest admiration at his command: "Lavinia was a soul singularly pure and sweet though quite mature: she was infancy and womanhood together. It is well with her: Earth has lost, and Paradise has gained."[37] The consolation soothed him because Gladstone took it literally.

When the time came to witness the agony of one of his own children, Gladstone could continue to draw on his religious rhetoric, but his heart-rending diary entries reveal that he found his habitual meek compliance harder to mobilize than ever before. They are a poignant reminder that piety could insulate sufferings only so far. It channeled the work of mourning, but did not reduce, let alone eliminate the need for it. Jessy

36. Ibid., 231–32.
37. Ibid., IV, 2, 242.

Gladstone, less than five years of age, died of meningitis in April 1850. The girl's torments, cruelly deceptive periods of improvement interspersed with stretches of moaning and screaming in her parents' arms, lasted nearly two weeks. On March 31, Easter Day, Gladstone found "Jessy thank God better in the night under C's affectionate & unwearied care." Again on the next day he could report: "In the morning thank God she was better." But by April 2, her death had become thinkable: "And now O Father can we readily yield her up to Thee? O how much better will she be cared for than in this sad & evil world. His will be done. My Catherine bears up wonderfully." Her sublime fortitude kept Gladstone afloat. Then, on April 3, there was what Dr. Locock interpreted as a substantial improvement. "Let us with God's grace in our patience," Gladstone noted, "possess our souls until He declare His will." For the next four days there were gains, feverishly welcomed, and losses, soberly acknowledged. But by April 8, all hope was gone: "As the evening drew on all the signs grew worse, and our hearts again very sick yet I trust neither of us are so blindly selfish as to murmur at the Lord's being about to raise one of our children to Himself." Along with Dr. Locock, the Gladstones watched the "death battle," and early on April 9 it was lost: "It is all over, and all well. The blessed child was released at two o'clock in the morning compassionately taken by her Saviour into the fold of His peace."

Gladstone resolved to write about Jessy no more in his diary, but to compile "a few recollections of her little life." So he did, but his diary, though showing the strain of a heroic effort at self-command, continues to record the history of Jessy's parents' bereavement: Catherine Gladstone waking her husband with her weeping and later kissing the "cold features of our Jessy" for the last time; William Gladstone, three days after her death, thinking, in self-imposed solitude, "of her who seems incessantly to beckon me & say 'Come Pappy Come': & of the land whither she is gone." He could and would not forget her. "Aftn got flowers for Jessy's coffin, which I visit daily," we read on September 17, more than five months after the little girl's death.[38] With such tragic temptations, it was hard, even for a well-schooled Christian like Gladstone, to practice the obedience that his faith enjoined. He could pronounce the proper words, but the proper feelings almost eluded him.

There had been a moment, in fact, three years before, when Gladstone had reached the frontiers of his faith and looked beyond. In September 1847, his second child, Agnes, came down with erysipelas. Heartfelt

38. Ibid., 196–201, 239.

prayers filled the pages of Gladstone's diary, and he sought to arm himself with his accustomed submissiveness, his accustomed philosophy: "The struggle of death & childhood is fearful." The disease, Gladstone recalled, had killed his mother, and now threatened his daughter's life. But, he noted, "We have not a fear for her. She is full of the glory of Christian childhood," by which he meant that Agnes was an obedient little girl; she had not been "in any way naughty for one half minute at a time." But then Gladstone's inner struggle erupted: "Her dear and pure and gentle soul wants nothing as it were but to be in the presence of its Lord: yet we would keep the Lamb from the Shepherd's arms that she may grow into a greater fulness of his image." And this earnest desire made him reproach himself. "My heart is hard & unquiet & not willing to give back my child, and it rebels even when I say with what strength it is given me Thy will be done in earth as it is in heaven. It is easy to say may she never live but for the glory of God—it is not so easy to make Him only the judge of what is for His glory." The family offered prayers and hymns; little Willy Gladstone, then seven, added prayers of his own devising. Catherine Gladstone was more "courageous," her husband thought, than he: "Everyone," wrote Gladstone severely, "behaves well but me. I have talked & thought of union of the will with God: but have not attained to it." Yet Scriptures were there to heal, soothe, and strengthen: "The treasures of His holy Word come however to my aid."

When little Agnes gradually recovered, sleeping sweetly under her parents' watchful eyes, Gladstone could only interpret her improvement as a sign of providential grace. Yet his pious gratitude could not conceal the conflict at work; Gladstone was scourging himself for his irrepressible wish to have his daughter live, thus taking the ultimate disposition of her future out of God's hands. "He doth not afflict willingly nor grieve the children of men," Gladstone wrote, characteristically shouldering the burden of human misery. "And his way is in the sea, & his paths in the great waters, & his footsteps are not known. And He will comfort us again for the days wherein he hath plagued us & for the years wherein we have suffered adversity. And his supper is ready: but some of the dishes are bitter."[39] Gladstone could scarcely forgive himself for trying to sweeten some of life's dishes without divine authorization.

One recipe for such sweetening was, of course, contraception, which would have saved Gladstone, and his wife, much anguish. But it was one to which he remained obdurately opposed. He did not even want to talk about it; in 1873, when his wife was long past child-bearing, there was

39. Ibid., 648–57.

some public interest in a memorial to John Stuart Mill, who had just died—interest and resistance, for as a young man, Mill had strongly advocated birth control. Gladstone, though sympathetic to Mill's liberalism, found the whole matter a "painful controversy," his way of saying that it was an embarrassment, best left undiscussed.[40] It was too late; everyone was discussing the matter by then. But many among the bourgeois who did discuss the provocative issue of contraception, which obviously impinged on sexuality in the most pervasive and fundamental way, found their obligations—to themselves, their families, their country, and their God—by no means clear. Late in the century, the call to duty had become practically unintelligible. For families who took the Bible as their final arbiter, for families who listened to their priest or pastor, the issue raised no difficulties—except physical and psychological ones: God's command to employ the voluptuous passion for procreative purposes alone was unmistakable. But that passion had ways of pressing for gratification wholly unrelated to populating the world; it sought to justify itself by hunting for respectworthy apologies and medical sophistries but, failing them, it worked in secrecy and in silence. By mid-century, alarm at impious conduct on the part of the pious reached Rome: in 1849, Jean-Baptiste Bouvier, bishop of Le Mans, reported to Pope Pius IX that "practically all young couples do not want a numerous progeny and yet cannot morally abstain from the conjugal act." When their confessors interrogate them "on the way they employ the rights of marriage," the couples are visibly shocked, but even after receiving warnings, they "do not abstain from the conjugal act, nor can they be brought to the indefinite multiplication of the species." The consequences are appalling. "Grumbling against their confessors, they abandon the sacrament of penitence and the eucharist, offering a bad example to their children, their servants, and other Christian faithful."[41] In short, faced with the alternative of devout compliance and birth control, French Catholics, including sober bourgeois couples, often chose birth control.

So, it would seem, did American Protestants. Abortion, that drastic and often dangerous second defensive maneuver called in when contraception had failed, became almost modish in the United States around mid-century, the very time that the bishop of Le Mans was lamenting the spread of birth control in France. Its high incidence points to an

40. See John Morley, *The Life of William Ewart Gladstone*, 3 vols. (1903), II, 543–44.

41. Hélène Bergues, "L'Attitude de l'église: Respect de la vie et de la nature," in Bergues et al., *La Prévention des naissances dans la famille, ses origines dans les temps modernes* (1960), 229–30.

even higher incidence of efforts at contraception, for many who were willing to employ a condom or a sponge were unwilling to seek an abortion. A series of inquiries across the United States, conducted in the main by local medical associations, agreed that American women were resorting to abortion not only to destroy the consequences of an illicit misstep, but also to control the size of their legitimate families. "Now we have ladies," the Medical Society of Buffalo exclaimed in 1859, "yes, *educated and refined ladies*," undergoing abortions. In 1872, a special committee of the New York Medico-Legal Society confirmed this appraisal: abortion, it noted, was most prevalent "in our own day and city among the well-to-do—the socalled respectable classes." Physicians reporting unusual cases of abortion to their colleagues in the professional journals would identify the patient involved, more often than not, as the "wife of a wealthy banker," or as "belonging to a respectable family," or even as a "physician's wife." Most of these case histories were the work of doctors and publicists viewing with alarm rather than pointing with pride. But in 1889 an advocate of legalized abortion (a bold spirit in those censorious days of Anthony Comstock) praised, in the *Medico-Legal Journal*, "the educated, refined, cultured women of this country" for driving up the abortion rate in the United States to unprecedented heights.[42] As H. S. Pomeroy, a doctor in Boston, a sensible and not unkindly man, put the matter in 1888, "It must not be supposed that the physician has the most trouble with those who belong to the lower classes. These give comparatively little trouble in this way. They seldom apply to the reputable physician, and when they do they are easily refused"—a rather bland, offhand way of summing up the sexual realities of class society in Pomeroy's day. "The real difficulty comes from socalled highly respectable people, even from leaders in social and religious movements. We never know when some one of these may not implore one of us, as a family physician, to do that which is a sin before the law of God and man; and when to the entreaty there are added the tears and pleading of a charming woman, the situation becomes embarrassing and unpleasant in the extreme."[43]

While abortion, in America as elsewhere, was by no means a middle-class prerogative, the spread of anti-abortion legislation from the 1860s on drove up the price of abortions, and thus increasingly reserved them for the prosperous and the enterprising. More and more bourgeois women were taking their fate into their own hands. Yet many families, all across

42. I have borrowed the telling quotations from James C. Mohr, *Abortion in America: The Origins and Evolution of National Policy* (1978), 93–99, 101.
43. *The Ethics of Marriage* (1888), 57.

the Western world, continued to do their duty, and not only unquestioning Christians: if, around mid-century, the Gladstones produced eight children in fourteen years, four decades later the Freuds had six children in eight years. But by then, so large a brood was no longer characteristic for the educated middle classes. Speaking, in 1898, of "Malthusian tendencies to limit the number of conceptions within marriage," Freud himself acknowledged, "it seems to me beyond doubt that these designs are gaining increasing ground in our middle class."[44] In the great nineteenth-century struggle between conscience and control, it was control that was winning out, preparing the way for a triumph of secular will over religious compliance. The nineteenth-century sense of mastery, far from absolute and always precarious, was to register some among its greatest conquests with contraception, especially after the 1860s and 1870s, as devices and techniques became more dependable and less expensive, and appeared less wicked, than ever before.

3. The Struggle over Malthus

The shift in the emotions attaching to the potent name of Malthus is an instructive episode in the history of hope in the bourgeois century. It was Malthus's brilliant, persuasively written essay on population, with its dire prophecies of people inevitably outrunning their food supply at a fixed rate, that gave the first impetus, in the beginning still rather circumspect, to the modern debate on population and, with that, on birth control. First published in 1798 and then revised, reinforced, and expanded, Malthus's *Essay on the Principle of Population* somberly allowed only two kinds of restraints on the ever-increasing inundations of hungry humans pressing up against the limits of subsistence: positive checks like famine and war, and preventive checks, little more ingratiating, like abortion and infanticide. Beginning with the second edition of his controversial assault on what he had perceived to be shallow Enlightened optimism, Malthus added to his roster of preventive checks a new, slightly less devastating technique for regulating population: moral restraint. It amounted to continence during the bachelor years yoked to the patient postponement of marriage. Malthus objected to other forms of birth control as immoral, but "moral restraint," though unpalatable and largely unworkable, introduced at least a modicum of human participation in natural processes. The birth controllers who braved public opinion in the 1870s and after, as they founded their Malthusian leagues across

44. "Die Sexualität in der Ätiologie der Neurosen" (1898), *St.A.*, V, 27; "Sexuality in the Aetiology of the Neuroses," *S.E.*, III, 276.

Europe, modified the teachings of their patron to present a coherent, very simple policy for family planning. And their amendments to Malthus's portentous scenario were all in the direction of hope and activity. They recommended early marriage and methods of birth control less frustrating than continence. One of the little tracts that the Malthusian League of London issued two years after its founding in 1877 put the matter plainly. The League exhorted its readers to see that "To you it is given to fix the limits to the number of children you can wisely and honestly undertake to rear."[45] And the slogans that crusaders from Annie Besant to Margaret Sanger coined for the cause are all redolent with the exhilarating prospect of curbing the arbitrary and often cruel exactions of biology through rational, willed planning on the part of husband and wife. They spoke of "*volitional* limitation" and "*voluntary* motherhood," of "birth *control*" and "family *planning*," or "*willkürliche Geburtenbeschränkung*" and, picturesquely, of "*grève des ventres*."[46] These were calls to, and celebrations of, action.

In 1892, in Paris, when the French neo-Malthusian propagandist Marie Huot called for that "strike of the bellies," modern techniques of birth control had been in place for nearly half a century. They had emerged amidst delicate probing of the taboos encircling respectable sexuality, in an atmosphere compounded of erotic desire, mortal fear, social reticence, and religious resignation. In 1839, Charles Goodyear had vulcanized rubber, and in 1844 he obtained his first patent on an invention that had eluded earlier, less fortunate tinkerers. These are cardinal dates in the calendar of modern sexuality. By 1850, Goodyear and rival inventors had improved on the original procedures, and fairly reliable condoms and diaphragms were for sale across the Western world. This was the time that the age of conscience began to confront the age of control.

Considering the opposition, control conquered with impressive rapidity. Resistance, drawing indiscriminately on religious, sociological, political, biological, and strategic reasoning, remained tenacious and became, by the end of the century, more strident than before: the dialectic of controversy, which dictates that the greater the advances of one party, the stronger the counterattacks of the other, was visibly at work in the sensitive area of contraception. But resistance could not withstand the plausible, even obtrusive perception that to limit the size of one's family had immense advantages, to parents and to their wanted children alike.

45. C. R. Drysdale, ed., *Malthusian Tracts*, No. 2 (1879).
46. In 1891, George Noyes Miller published a little feminist fantasy, a modern *Lysistrata*, in which the whole female sex has denied access to its bodies: *The Strike of a Sex*.

The ancient and deeply felt desire for this kind of rational domesticity, which had produced an arsenal of often ineffectual and sometimes destructive folk remedies, was now on the verge of realization.

Not without hesitations, uncertainties, and circumlocutions. In 1837, Catharine Beecher wrote about her younger sister Harriet Beecher Stowe, mother of two and pregnant with her third, that the "poor thing" was bearing up "wonderfully well." But she wondered at her sister's calm prediction that "she shall not have any more children, *she knows for certain* for one while. Though how she found this out," Catharine Beecher added, "I cannot say, but she seems quite confident about it."[47] Such confidence, as many couples discovered, was often misplaced. Dickens, whose allusions to these touchy matters are sparse and prudent, and therefore all the more valuable, records one such instance in the brief family history that Eugene Wrayburn in *Our Mutual Friend* reels off for his friend Mortimer Lightwood: he had had two elder brothers, expected and welcomed, more or less. But then "my third brother appeared, considerably in advance of his engagement to my mother."[48] And some of the modern devices, which promised to be more dependable, seemed to many unpalatable. Writing to her friend Helena Gilder from San Francisco, Mary Hallock Foote told her of a "sure way of limiting one's family" that she had learned from a local beauty. It struck her as "a delicate thing to speak of in a letter," and the device as "dreadful," but, she commented philosophically: "Every way is dreadful except the one which it seems cannot be relied on." It was a dilemma that many fastidious middle-class couples faced. Mary Foote was speaking of "shields of some kind," to be "had at some druggists." It sounded "perfectly revolting" to her, but, she added, "one must face anything rather than the inevitable results of Nature's methods." These things will injure neither husband nor wife, and are "called 'cundums' and are made of either rubber or skin."[49]

This abashed confidentiality was better, much better, than nothing. But it grew from, and perpetuated, a certain half-knowledge about sexuality, an atmosphere of mystery which the most candid reformers could not dissipate. Indeed, pockets of ignorance remained sizeable and troublesome: in July 1884, Alice Belknap reported to her eldest sister, Susan Wright, that she had just had a miscarriage, more serious than

47. Catharine Beecher to Mary Perkins, Fall 1837, Kathryn Kish Sklar, *Catharine Beecher: A Study in American Domesticity* (1973), 320.

48. Book I, ch. 12 (1865; ed. 1908), p. 138.

49. December 7, 12 [1876], Mary Hallock Foote Papers, Stanford University Library (Carl Degler has already used the same passages in *At Odds*, 224).

the previous one. Her physician had therefore insisted that she must not permit herself "to get in this condition again for a year & then he thinks I will be all right. I am to go to him for hints when I get well. Would you like to know them?" Then, her confidential bulletin and sisterly inquiry out of the way, Mrs. Belknap turned to the weather. Her need for "hints" to prevent pregnancy without stopping intercourse discloses her own state of innocence—in 1884. And her thoughtful question implies that she had some reason to think her sister, wife of a Yale professor of chemistry, to be as innocent about contraception as she was.[50] But Alice Belknap was scarcely the incarnation of the genteel Victorian woman in the legend; her physician, after all, volunteered to instruct her in birth-control technology, and she was not merely interested in it, but willing to share it with her sister.

There is, though, much persuasive evidence, deposited in a handful of tantalizing diaries and spread across the population statistics, that certainly by the mid-1880s and probably for some decades before, most bourgeois couples knew about some form of contraception and quite a few employed it. Adults in the Western world who could read, frankly canvass marital strategies, pay for techniques that required some expenditures, and bring themselves to apply them could get what they needed when they needed it. Lester Ward and his wife Lizzie discussed and experimented with a variety of birth-control techniques; among Clelia Duel Mosher's forty-five women interviewed in the 1890s, no fewer than thirty-seven confessed to practicing at least one form of birth control, including withdrawal, the sponge, and the "cundum." And David Todd schemed and calculated with his wife how to keep her from becoming pregnant. On November 11, 1881, the day after her twenty-fifth birthday, Mabel Todd firmly declared in her journal, thinking of her little daughter Millicent: "I will *never* have another unless David has a salary of at least three or four thousand." Economics and sexuality were now firmly linked in many minds. Exactly two years later she noted in some dismay that she might be pregnant. "David & I are waiting & waiting. I am afraid it was not intentional."[51] She promised herself that she would not complain if

50. Box 53, SF.
51. Journal III, box 46, MLT, Y-MA.—In view of her earlier failure in birth control —Millicent Todd, we must remember, was at least in part the result of a misapplied rhythm method—it is important to stress that Mabel Todd had company in ignorance: most nineteenth-century physicians were hopelessly confused about women's menstrual cycle. Assuming that women are like animals in heat, they counseled against intercourse immediately after the period and pronounced it safe at mid-way. "A time about midway between the monthly recurring periods is best fitted for the

she were to have another child, but her resolve was not put to the test: her failure to menstruate eventually turned out to have some other, less consequential cause.

France was universally acknowledged to have been the first country in which birth control was accepted in respectable circles, though practically all its notorious advocates published their pamphlets in England and in the United States: to judge by the contemporary literature, the French practiced birth control without writing about it; the English and the Americans wrote about it without practicing it. That anomaly was to adjust itself in the closing decades of the nineteenth century, as Britain and the United States almost caught up with France in reducing their birth rates, at least among the middle classes. The propagandists, with their handbills, pamphlets, marriage manuals, reprinted, revised, excerpted, translated, pirated, did their work among those hungry for birth-control information. And the authorities, the defenders of order, reticence, and large families, unconsciously colluded with the enemy by bringing birth-control advocates to trial and thus to the attention of a public still largely innocent of their subversive teachings.

By far the most notorious of these miscalculations was the Bradlaugh-Besant trial. In 1877, Charles Bradlaugh and Annie Besant were prosecuted for publishing and distributing Charles Knowlton's *Fruits of Philosophy*, a tract then forty-five years old. The press, whether sympathetic or hostile to the cause of contraception, seized on the trial and helped to convert a trickle of sales into an avalanche: "A few hundred purchasers in the course of many years," the London *Daily News* wryly commented in June 1877, "have been converted into more than a hundred thousand purchasers in a few weeks."[52] This was no exaggeration; within three years of the trial, Bradlaugh and Besant had sold nearly 200,000 copies of their new edition of Knowlton, and each copy could count, of course, on several readers. To provide such free, unexpected, and unsurpassed publicity for a birth-control manual was a bit of stupidity so gross as to invite speculation that it was intentional, if unconscious, an unwitting yet somehow desired piece of self-sabotage.

---

consummation of marriage." Dr. George H. Napheys wrote in the 1860s. "This is the season of sterility." *The Physical Life of Woman* (1869; ed. 1888), 91. One wonders how many children were born in the nineteenth century on the basis of such advice.

52. J. A. Banks, *Prosperity and Parenthood: A Study of Family Planning Among the Victorian Middle Classes* (1954), 153.

The principal and most forceful argument running through Knowlton, and indeed the entire literature, was that large families provoked the doom of miserable, unredeemed poverty. Jeremy Bentham had, as early as 1797, vaguely hinted at the use of the vaginal sponge on Utilitarian grounds, to reduce the charges on England's poor rate. And the pioneering handbills preaching contraception that Francis Place, master tailor, self-educated intellectual, political reformer, scattered through London in 1823 spoke of a "great number of children" as "a never failing source of discomfort and apprehension," generating "a state of bodily, mental, and pecuniary vexation and suffering, from which there is no escape." Addressing the lower orders quite directly, Place reminded them that an excessive number of working people only served to depress wages and that, once income has been reduced, "working people can no longer maintain their children as all good and repectable people wish to maintain their children." Interestingly, another leaflet, which Place aimed at *The Married of Both Sexes in Genteel Life*, had the same message to convey: "In the middle ranks, the most virtuous and praiseworthy efforts are perpetually made to keep up the respectability of the family; but a continual increase of children gradually yet certainly renders every effort to prevent degradation unavailing, it paralizes by rendering hopeless all exertion, and the family sinks into poverty and despair."[53] Place's radical follower, the editor Richard Carlile, was to adopt the same line of reasoning in his journal, *The Republican*. It was an ingenious reversal of traditional doctrine: true respectability lay not in the patient acceptance of pregnancy but, on the contrary, in its active prevention.

Writing a few years later, Robert Dale Owen dramatized this argument in his famous tract *Moral Physiology*, at once fervent and reasoned. Its frontispiece was a pathetic engraving showing a young mother covering her face with her hands, as she turns away from her illegitimate baby which she has just abandoned under the statue of the merciful Virgin; it bears the legend, "Alas! that it should ever have been born!" Owen was a Malthusian revisionist: he shared Malthus's pessimism about threatened overpopulation but rejected his remedies as impractical: "Population, unrestrained, *must* increase beyond the possibility of the earth and its produce to support. At present it is restrained by vice and misery. The only remedy which the orthodoxy of the English Clergyman permits him to propose, is, late marriages." But, Owen objected, "the most enlightened observers of mankind are agreed, that nothing con-

53. *To the Married of Both Sexes of the Working People* and *To the Married of Both Sexes in Genteel Life*, reproduced in facsimile in Norman E. Himes, *Medical History of Contraception* (1936; ed. 1970), 214–16.

tributes so positively and immediately to demoralize a nation, as when its youth refrain, until a late period, from forming disinterested connexions with those of the other sex. The frightful increase of prostitutes, the destruction of health, the rapid spread of intemperance, the ruin of moral feelings, are, to the mass, the *certain* consequences." The final issue was, to Owen, plain: "*unless some less ascetic and more practicable species of 'moral restraint' be introduced*, vice and misery will *ultimately* become the inevitable lot of man upon earth." This prospect, gloomy but not inescapable, would remain the leading theme of the birth controllers throughout the bourgeois century and beyond. By the time the Malthusian League published the *Malthusian Handbook*, it could bluntly describe its purpose on the title page, "to induce Married People to Limit their Families within their Means,"[54] without any sense of novelty.

The reasons why contraception swept the middle classes in the last quarter of the nineteenth century are not far to seek and were earnestly explored at the time. The diffusion of prosperity among the middling orders made a small family seem supremely attractive; it promised better education, better clothing and housing, better opportunities for social and economic advancement. For the lower middle classes—married clerks, lesser government officials, and their like—family limitation came to appear as almost a necessity; each additional child meant a calculable cut in their standard of living. The waning influence of religious sanctions, even among the religious, partially relieved feelings of guilt over preventing conceptions or, in an emergency, birth. The spread of information about birth control and its improving technology made it first a thinkable, then a seductive, and finally an irresistible proceeding for many. And the widening repertoire of birth-control methods allowed the most fastidious couples to select the technique they found most agreeable on aesthetic, medical, and even athletic grounds. The vigorous, generally polite debates among the birth controllers as to the least distracting and most effective technique proved a splendid education for their readers. Whether the husband proffered economic advantage and the wife her health as reasons for family limitation, they could always agree on the *need* for contraception.

Rubber products like the condom and the diaphragm, fervently advertised and just as fervently denounced, were only the most spectacular modern aids in the anti-fertility pharmacopeia, and they made their way slowly against time-honored competitors. Francis Place had

54. *Moral Physiology; Or, A Brief and Plain Treatise on the Population Question* (1831; 8th ed., 1835), 27, 28; *Malthusian Handbook* (1893; 5th ed., 1911), 1.

recommended a vaginal sponge and, next, coitus interruptus, giving the sponge strong preference "as it depends upon the female."[55] In contrast, Robert Dale Owen, in his *Moral Physiology*, advocated coitus interruptus alone. He was in a long tradition. This technique required no devices, no medicine, no outside interference, and very little training, and it was therefore, throughout the nineteenth century as it had been for ages, the most popular method for preventing conception. The Todds, as we know, used it, and so did millions of other couples, educated or uneducated. "Among the modes of preventing conception which may have prevailed in various countries," as Owen put it, "that which has been adopted, and is now universally practised, by the cultivated classes on the continent of Europe, by the French, the Italians, and I believe, by the Germans and Spaniards, consists of complete withdrawal, on the part of the man, immediately previous to emission." Owen was satisfied that this method was flawless; it "is, in all cases, effectual."[56]

Owen was wrong. Medical inquiries, occasional private references, and the intense Roman Catholic campaign against what its moral theologians chose to call "conjugal onanism" testify to the continuing popularity of coitus interruptus. But its lasting vogue owed more to long-standing habits and cherished preferences than to its proven dependability; its effectiveness was severely limited, more unimpressive even than that of the rhythm method. It required a certain knowledge of physiology, a measure of cooperation, and above all a self-possession and self-control, at the very moments when rationality was at a discount, that few men could muster. All that could be said for it realistically was that it was somewhat less ineffective than post-coital douching. Those willing and able to employ modern condoms or diaphragms, nineteenth-century inventions both, were safer from unwanted pregnancies than those practicing withdrawal—safer by far. But they did not know that.

Owen was, however, right to say that coitus interruptus was easy to attempt. "It may be objected, that the practice requires a mental effort and a partial sacrifice. I reply, that, in France, where men consider this (as it ought ever to be considered, when the interests of the other sex require it), a *point of honour*—all young men learn to make the necessary effort; and custom renders it easy and a matter of course." The "sacrifice" of pleasure it entailed was, Owen thought, "trifling," in fact "very trifling," especially when compared with the "permanent welfare of those who are the nearest and dearest to us." The slight gain in

55. *To the Married of Both Sexes of the Working People*, in Himes, 214.
56. *Moral Physiology*, 61–62.

"physical enjoyment" available to those who refused to practice coitus interruptus should not outweigh "the comfort, the well-being—in some cases the *life*, of those whom we profess to love." Owen's cosmopolitanism is engaging. An Englishman living in the United States, he appealed to the "cultivated young Frenchman," who would be appalled to learn that some men might be less honorable and more selfish than he. "A Frenchman belonging to the cultivated classes, would as soon bear to be called a coward, as to be accused of causing the pregnancy of a woman, who did not desire it," even when "the matrimonial law had given him legal rights over her person."[57] And this, for Owen, was conclusive; he had no doubt that the French were authorities in such matters.

Owen's *Moral Physiology* went through more than a dozen editions, authorized or unauthorized, in the United States and at least as many in Great Britain; it was surpassed only by Dr. Charles Knowlton's *Fruits of Philosophy; or, The Private Companion of Young Married People*, first published in 1832. Knowlton was Owen's rival in ideas as in sales; he was uncomfortable with the method Owen had recommended, and advocated douching after intercourse instead. This was, he argued, safe, accessible, and (though he only hinted at this) sexually most satisfying. The "*female syringe*," he noted, at once "simple and cheap," could be bought in any "apothecary's shop," and its employment put the act of controlling conception into the hands of the woman, "where for good reasons it ought to be."[58] Owen and Knowlton agreed that the sexually active woman should be cherished; it was on the best way of cherishing her that they parted company.

The disagreement between Owen and Knowlton set the terms on which birth controllers would discuss contraception down to Sigmund Freud and beyond. The emergence of the cheap condom and, later, the diaphragm did not essentially change the issue. Effectiveness was, of course, the supreme consideration, and here the public was confronted, and confused, by the birth controllers' honest doubts and their perhaps no less honest but self-deluded claims. Their fervor of advocacy and their impatience with competing techniques raised questions to which no definitive answers could then be obtained. Confusions over the safety of rival techniques was compounded by the subsidiary but far from insignificant question of pleasure. Advocates of douching suggested that their method was superior to coitus interruptus not merely in the protection it provided after, but also in the enjoyment it permitted during

57. Ibid., 61n.
58. Charles Knowlton, M.D., *Fruits of Philosophy; or, The Private Companion of Young Married People* (2nd ed., ca. 1833), 34.

intercourse. Preachers and physicians who condemned every form of birth control argued, with barely concealed and indiscriminate glee, that all were ultimately noxious. The French physician L. F. E. Bergeret found that the various methods of "conjugal onanism" produced, in women, metritis (both acute and chronic), leucorrhoea, menorrhagia, haematocele, fibrous tumors, polyps; hyperaesthesia, colics, neuroses, and cancer in the uterus; hysteralgia, neuralgias, mammary congestion, diseases of the ovaries, and sterility, to say nothing of accidental pregnancy. Men could count on urethritis, diseases of the prostate, and of course impotence; while both sexes using birth control were susceptible to ailments of the nervous system, the circulation, the organs of respiration, and the digestive tract. Contraception ruined family life and corrupted society.[59] And Bergeret had followers, like the English obstetrician C. H. F. Routh, who uncritically adopted Bergeret's list and added suicidal mania and nymphomania for good measure.[60]

Advocates of birth control were naturally rather less sensational and a good deal more discriminating. In his early psychoanalytic speculations of the mid-1890s Sigmund Freud thought well of "free sexual congress between male youths and girls of respectable status" if only there were "innocuous methods to prevent conception." Unfortunately, the methods then available struck Freud as compromised by unpalatable side effects. Significantly, he derived these "noxae"—hysteria and anxiety neurosis— from a failure of sexual gratification, whether on the part of the man or the woman. This, I must repeat, was a radical departure, not from private nineteenth-century bourgeois practice as from governing medical and theological ideology. Freud treated man and woman in intercourse as equal partners: women, he wrote, "whose husbands suffer from *ejaculatio praecox* or from markedly diminished potency" will fall ill with anxiety attacks, and so will women "whose husbands practice *coitus interruptus* or *reservatus*." There are escapes. "She is spared a neurosis if the man afflicted with *ejaculatio praecox* can immediately repeat sexual congress with better success." Again, "*congressus reservatus* with a condom brings no injury to the woman if she is very quickly aroused and the man very potent; otherwise, this kind of preventive intercourse is no less pernicious than the others." As for coitus interruptus, that, Freud notes, "is nearly

59. *Des fraudes dans l'accomplissement des fonctions génératrices* (1868). The English translation, by Dr. P. de Marmon, from the third edition, bears the alarming and exhaustive title *The Preventive Obstacle, Or Conjugal Onanism. The Dangers and Inconveniences to the Individual, To the Family, and to Society, of Frauds in the Accomplishment of The Generative Function* (1870).

60. Banks, *Prosperity and Parenthood*, 155, 155n.

always pernicious." But it proves so for the woman only "if the man practices it inconsiderately; that is, if he breaks off coitus as soon as *he* is close to ejaculation, without troubling his head about the course of excitement" characteristic for her. There was, though, still another side to it: "If, in contrast, the man waits for the satisfaction of the *woman*, such coitus has the significance of a normal one for her; but then the man will fall ill with an anxiety neurosis."[61] As Freud clearly perceived, people who practiced birth control were taking new psychological risks. But when birth control worked satisfactorily, it improved life and even, whatever the priest might say, saved lives.

Population figures, gathered with increasing accuracy across the Western world in the course of the nineteenth century, confirm that birth control in fact worked very well.[62] And the nagging anxieties that the adversaries of contraception displayed offer added, if ironic, evidence for its efficacy. The French, who as I have said took the lead in using contraception, were also the first to analyze and deplore its consequences. The campaign against "depopulation," which grew ever more anguished in the 1870s, was, on the part of alarmists, an exercise in imaginative nostalgia. C. M. Raudot's *De la décadence de la France* of 1849 set the tone of regret for a golden past, a vanished time when families had been religious, harmonious, uncomplaining—and large. Frédéric Le Play, the versatile engineer, social scientist, and politician, lent his enormous authority and his vast empirical researches to the same cause: the restoration of sound—that is to say, pious and sizable—families. And it was true that many more Frenchmen seemed to be controlling the size of their families than anyone else. Beginning in the 1830s, at an accelerating pace with rare intervals of letup, the French birth rate dropped faster than the

61. "Manuskript B: Die Ätiologie der Neurosen" (February 8, 1893), *Aus den Anfängen der Psychoanalyse: Briefe an Wilhelm Fliess, Abhandlungen und Notizen aus den Jahren 1887–1902*, ed. Ernst Kris et al. (1950), 81; "Draft B: The Aetiology of the Neuroses," *The Origins of Psycho-Analysis: Letters to Wilhelm Fliess, Drafts and Notes: 1887–1902*, tr. Eric Mosbacher and James Strachey (1954), 72. "Über die Berechtigung, von der Neurasthenie einen bestimmten Symptomenkomplex als 'Angstneurose' abzutrennen" (1895), *St.A.*, VI, 36; "On the Grounds for Detaching a Particular Syndrome from Neurasthenia under the Description 'Anxiety Neurosis,'" *S.E.*, III, 100. Writing to Fliess later in 1893, Freud offered this terse diagnosis of a woman patient, aged twenty-four, with two young children: "Husband traveling salesman; was at home in the Spring, as well as recently, for some time. In the summer, during travels of husband, perfect well-being. Coitus interruptus and great fear of having children, hence hysteria." "Manuskript B," 88; "Draft B," 78.

62. Demographers explored, and continue to explore, other possible causes for the decline of the birth rate—decreasing natural fertility, the damaging effect on fertility rates of living in industrial cities, and so forth. But all substantially agree that contraception was the most significant factor in the drop of the rate, by far.

death rate; by mid-century, natality exceeded mortality just enough to provide for a natural increase of less than 5 percent. Many French *départements*, in fact, actually showed, and would continue to show, a deficit. Between 1800 and 1805, as the distinguished French economic historian Emile Lavasseur later noted, French couples had produced 4.3 legitimate children; between 1851 and 1855, that number dropped to 3.1, while, in the late 1880s, it passed a depressing milestone by declining to a mere 2.9—a fraction below the magic figure of three legitimate children per family.[63]

The backdrop to the anguished discussion was, of course, the war that France had lost in 1870, a wound that Frenchmen obsessively probed in the decades that followed. Quite naturally, the military argument against contraception stood at the center of many jeremiads. The marquis de Nadaillac's *Affaiblissement de la natalité en France, ses causes et ses conséquences*, published in 1885, is a characteristic specimen. Its epigraph is a laconic plea for energetic acts as against rhetoric: *Facta non verba*. And its preface places Nadaillac's case bluntly in the service of national defense, or, rather, national revenge. He proposes to offer comparisons of French natality with that of other nations, "our rivals today, perhaps our enemies tomorrow"; and he calls giving the facts general circulation "a patriotic duty." Like many critics of what they severely christened "conjugal frauds," Nadaillac was worried about a shortage of future soldiers for future wars: "The fate of a nation depends on its military preponderance, and that preponderance, all too often, on the number of men it can muster for the field of battle." This field was larger than the arena of military combat: "In the battles of industry, no less ardent, no less implacable, one must produce rapidly, one must produce a great deal, and the number of young and vigorous arms will assure the economic victory."[64]

The prospect of such a victory seemed, to the marquis de Nadaillac, a utopian fantasy in view of the unwillingness of French couples to produce children. He returned to the familiar figures once again; a total of 380 births per 10,000 in 1770 had ominously dropped a century later to 245. And he found comparisons with other countries extremely disturbing: the Russian figure was 507 births to 10,000 inhabitants; the Hungarian, 416; the Prussian, 384; the English, 337, and so down to France, which stood last, even behind Belgium, whose decline had been

63. Levasseur, *La Population française*, 2 vols. (1889–92), I, 215, 222.
64. *Affaiblissement* (1885; 2nd ed., 1886), v–vi, 2.

halted in recent years. This panoply of statistics served as a useful comment on the single comparison that interested and troubled Nadaillac most: the German birth rate. "Despite the gaps caused by emigration," he wrote, "German population is growing rapidly. Every German household is a *famille nombreuse*; every French household is a small family: there is the fact in all its brutal realism." It assured German hegemony over Europe, a grave danger which it would be imprudent to minimize.

Agreeing with the birth controllers in their causal analysis though not in their cheerful verdict, Nadaillac thought the grounds for the French population crisis all too palpable: an excess of willfulness, an "egotistic desire" for material goods amounting, at its worst, to decadence: "Of all the causes acting on the will of man, which stop natality from soaring and which threaten nations and races with destruction, doubtless the most powerful is the growing demoralization we witness every day. The immoderate development of luxury, the frenzied taste for enjoyment, the thirst for pleasure and the desire to subordinate all else to them, the contempt for duty all proceed from this single cause." This lust for pleasure—and *jouissance* encompassed sexual pleasure—was generated, and viciously fanned, by the sensual excitement to which modern Frenchmen were constantly subjected. Nadaillac listed "the most audacious nudes" in exhibitions, "scandalous titles" in bookstalls, "even more scandalous engravings" in shop windows, plays advertising "guilty passions," and "the most depraved" novels, replete with "the most daring descriptions" selling by the thousands; together they subverted authority in family and state alike and were scarcely designed to foster an atmosphere in which married couples had sexual intercourse for the sake of making more Frenchmen.[65] Clearly, the attack on contraception was, quite directly, an attack on pleasure, with sexual pleasure the central target.

Early in the 1890s, Arsène Dumont, an ambitious and eloquent demographer, developed the theory of "social capillarity" to account for the perceptible drop in the size of French families. Couples, he held, were regulating the number of their children in obedience to their aspirations, imitating the social stratum into which they hoped to rise. Far more than fear of poverty, expectations of social and economic advancement had proved an irresistible incentive to birth control. Other demographers, even those who did not find Dumont's theory wholly persuasive, joined the anti-Malthusian cause; the distinguished statistician Jacques Bertillon

65. Ibid., 6, 8–9, 17–19, 20, 70–71, 110–12.

presided over the Alliance nationale pour l'accroissement de la population française, while others founded the Ligue contre le crime de l'avortement. The campaign against birth control was well financed and well organized.

Indeed, the alliance of those who would purify what they thought the dangerous French commitment to selfish pleasure was influential and diverse. Theologians both Catholic and Protestant were naturally in the vanguard, tirelessly inveighing against the inroads that Neo-Malthusianism had made among the French bourgeoisie. Moralists condemned the neglect of duty consequent upon the search for enjoyment, and patriots its insidious dangers to French military strength. Physicians offered specialized diagnoses of their own: Dr. H. M. Gourrier, of the Faculty of Medicine at the University of Paris, argued in 1871, in his *L'Avenir du mariage*, that abstention from sexual intercourse, coitus interruptus, and mechanical devices were all unhealthy for both husband and wife. What he calls "truncated practice" or "discarding the seminal matter outside," or, for that matter, "stocking it in the condom," is excusable only if the wife is in very frail health or if other really weighty circumstances make pregnancy inadvisable. Otherwise unrestricted sexual intercourse is supremely desirable, not only for the sake of future generations but also for the participants; the "local bath by the semen" lubricates the wife's internal organs, much to her advantage. Besides, "motherly love" is the most vital of loves, the "desire for maternity" the most natural of feelings. And, during pregnancy, the wife's desires "calm down, since the aim of nature has been satisfied, has been attained."[66]

When it came to population, everyone was an expert. Emile Zola, who had treated sexuality as a dark and brooding passion in most of his novels, persuaded himself in his later years into an extravagant secular celebration of motherhood. It became, for him, the gateway to salvation in this world. Literary critics have noted the religious adjectives that Zola came to apply to love-making in his last novels—love-making, be it understood, sanctified by the making of a child. On May 23, 1896, he joined the debate with an article in *Figaro*, significantly entitled "Depopulation," in which he laid it down, bluntly, that "Every love which does not have a child for its aim is fundamentally only a debauch." *Fécondité*, one of his last, most tendentious, and least impressive novels, translates this maxim into fiction. The families in the novel all experience the predictable fate

---

66. Gourrier, *L'Avenir du mariage ou l'Usage et l'Abus dans l'union des sexes. Propositions et développements rédigés aux points de vue médical, philosophique, et théologique* (1871), 30, 38, 77, 89. Gourrier, far more credulous than most physicians of his time, seems to have believed that "the population is growing noticeably"; but, he warned, "the species is degenerating" (p. 97).

that their inventor's thesis imposes upon them: those who deliberately limit the size of their brood, whether through voluntary sterilization, abortion, or other means, come to a bad end: they go mad, commit murder, die in poverty. In contrast, the principal couple populate the world with twelve children, nearly all of whom grow to healthy and happy maturity.

Facing such a show of hostile opinion, and a vigilant French state eager to prosecute Neo-Malthusian publicists, advocates of birth control moved warily. And indeed, while the French birth rate did not recover, the activities of the *procréatomanes* definitely slowed down the dissemination of contraceptive propaganda and devices. The voices of religion, morality, social science, and patriotism were loud and seemed authoritative; but the principle of the two-child family, working quietly, continued to win its recruits.

In view of the shame of 1870, the agitation of the French "procreation maniacs" is easy to understand. But the Germans, who had, after all, won their war against France and built a formidable empire around their victory, sounded only marginally less worried. They acknowledged that the French were not reproducing, but they feared French schemes for revenge, schemes for encircling Germany by allying themselves with such nations as the Russians among whom the *famille nombreuse* remained the standard. German laments on threatened depopulation, beginning around 1870 with scattered essays in learned journals, swelled to a minor flood after 1900, the years of an aggressive German foreign policy and equally aggressive naval armaments; they are a graphic index of German anxieties, fantasies of flabbiness in the midst of muscle-flexing, for they were imprecise, confused, and largely unjustified. Thus in 1913, when the theologian and church historian Reinhold Seeberg published his "social-ethical" study of the declining birth rate in Germany, he could draw not only on official statistics—and he did, lavishly—but on a score of German pamphlets and treatises, all on the same theme and in the same tenor, all prophesying a "national calamity" and registering "that uncanny phenomenon that one must call 'the beginning of the end.'" Seeberg cited, with approval, Elias Schrenk's "signal of distress to the German people," also of 1913, a signal that prominently included a call for the founding of a German League for the Preservation of the People. He also cited, borrowing some dismaying figures, J. Wolf's study entitled, interestingly enough, *The Decline in Births: The Rationalization of the Sexual Life in Our Time*, published just the year before. And he referred, as well, to Felix Theilhaber's painstaking investigation into the population of Berlin published, like Seeberg's brochure, in 1913, and entitled, with the kind of ominous hyperbole that populationists liked to employ, *Sterile Berlin*.[67] Reinhold Seeberg was a voice in an insistent chorus.

Seeberg's alarmist refrain was that the decline in the German birth rate was marked and seemed to be continuing; the figures which he followed back to the 1860s established a downward drift that all Germans had to view with dismay, just as the "sad conditions" in France tore at the heart of all French patriots. While Germans were still far ahead of Frenchmen—in 1911, there were under twenty live births per thousand in France, and Germany showed more than thirty-one—the tendency toward German depopulation was a slide toward disaster. "We are threatened by a situation in which we, as a people, no longer progress but are retreating. But every people visited by such a fate is, as far as its political position in the world goes, condemned to decay, or compelled to receive foreign blood in larger and larger numbers." He cited the "great French political economist Leroy-Beaulieu" as predicting "that within six to eight generations a purely French population will have ceased to exist, and that there will be in its place a mixture of Flemish Belgians, Germans, Spaniards, Italians and Poles. We too, in Germany, will gradually have to resign ourselves to a similar conglomerate of alien peoples, above all Slavs and probably East European Jews as well." And that would spell the end of Germany as world power. All this because "increasing prosperity" had generated the wish to share in the wealth; the "two-child system" had become overwhelmingly popular, even shouldered aside, here and there, by the "one-child" and worse, the "no-child system." The radical teachings of Social Democracy only abetted the cause of depopulation, and the lure of luxurious, intoxicating big cities did its part. Most devastating of all, though, for Seeberg, was the new spirit that had gripped the "broad middle strata of the population," a fatal infatuation with individualism and materialism. Doom was at hand, if not immediately then soon, and it was the middle classes who were leading the way to disaster.[68]

This, then, was the temper of the anti-Malthusian literature across countries and decades: indignant, tense, approaching panic around the turn of the century. There were special, local variants, but adversaries

67. Seeberg, *Der Geburtenrückgang in Deutschland. Eine sozialethische Studie* (1913), 75–76, 1. The title of Schrenk's book was *Notsignal für das deutsche Volk* (1913); the name of his proposed organization, "Deutscher Bund für Volkserhaltung." And see Felix A. Theilhaber, *Das Sterile Berlin. Eine volkswirtschaftliche Studie* (1913).
68. Seeberg, *Geburtenrückgang in Deutschland*, 12, 20, 33–38.

of contraception formed an international family. Crusades against the dissemination of birth control information perhaps reached their climax in the United States, but they were conspicuous features in the cultural landscape of Europe as well. While eugenic speculations were particularly rife in Great Britain and Germany, proposals for population control and "race improvement" were also adumbrated in other countries. The most extreme of the eugenicists are hard to place: they were rarely quite certain whether it was more urgent to encourage the intelligent and the prosperous to reproduce their number or to prevent the idiotic and the indigent, who were breeding like rabbits, from swamping, and conquering, the world with their inferior brood. Compared with their inflammatory proposals, the publications of the Neo-Malthusians, though often naive and inevitably repetitive, were sobriety itself. The statistics that the anti-Malthusians spread so lavishly over their pages were an armor for anxiety. They were admittedly hard to interpret confidently, but they gave little cause for rational concern. Yet they did not relieve the helpless sense that the world was spinning out of control. The fall in the birth rate must have struck many anti-Malthusians as a reflection on their own potency.

Publications on birth control are windows on nineteenth-century bourgeois sexuality, and on the culture of privacy in which it was compelled to maneuver. This was true whether they were tendentious or scientific —and it was, as must have emerged, often impossible to distinguish the one from the other. Dogmatists of all persuasions displayed no conscious hesitations in their pronouncements, but their writings, taken together, read like commentaries on pervasive perplexities within the nineteenth-century bourgeoisie. They disclose the intractable conflict between self-interest and duty, desire and defense. The official prescriptive position, articulated by theologians, demographers, and politicians, amounted to a strident reminder that traditional values were in danger, a reminder that many bourgeois found persuasive. Hence their conflict. It was not just political and religious pressure, not just the terrors of hell or of legal retribution threatened by priests or censors, that gave good bourgeois reasons for bouts of guilt feelings as they contemplated condoms or reflected on coitus interruptus. The frantic calls to patriotism and the sentimental depictions of large happy families touched cherished chords in the middle-class mind. They had the magical appeal that reawakened childhood memories usually have. The bourgeois families that continued to populate the Western world with their sizable broods were so many tributes to ideals that the respectable had always professed and continued to teach their offspring. From their perspective, birth controllers appeared as tempters to unregulated hedonism, as irresponsible propagandists for the pleasure principle.

The perspective of the tempters was naturally very different. They found themselves compelled to work more quietly than they would have liked, and indeed contraception was scarcely the staple diet of casual conversation between average married couples, even when they were alone. It is no wonder that bourgeois diaries and letters are normally so unrevealing on this vital matter. But birth controllers acted, as it were, as psychoanalysts to the bourgeoisie by exposing unrelieved and uncontrolled child-bearing as an irrational reenactment of old superstitions, and arguments in its behalf as neurotic obstructions to reasonable conduct. To them, the official position appeared as a defensive maneuver. It grew increasingly futile as the nineteenth century went on, as it advertised and urged respectable attitudes that most bourgeois mouthed but fewer and fewer found credible.

While contraception opens windows on nineteenth-century bourgeois sexuality, it was, of course, not the private preserve of the middling orders; prostitutes, aristocrats, many peasants had been practicing it since time out of mind. The prevalence of abortion and epidemics of infanticide —incalculable since so much child-murder was disguised as the handing over of infants to professional care—strongly suggests that the contraceptive techniques these groups normally employed were often ineffective. But whether they were superstitious gestures or highly touted herbs, prolonged lactation or coitus interruptus, birth control methods were of course known to centuries other than the nineteenth, and to classes other than the bourgeoisie. What makes nineteenth-century bourgeois birth control unique is that broad segments of an influential class enlisted it in a systematic policy of rational family planning. And it was this concerted response to what I am calling the pressures of reality that makes middle-class birth control an indispensable ingredient in the bourgeois sensual style in the age of Victoria, years before anyone had heard of Freud.

The class character of birth control, and the trickling down of contraceptive technology from the upper to the lower reaches of society, seemed incontrovertible facts to nineteenth-century publicists. In 1886, the marquis de Nadaillac had already insisted that the "desire not to have children," an "evil that is growing year by year," was "descending from the rich to the middle classes," and from them to small proprietors in the countryside and to working people in the towns. Seven years later, Sigmund Freud wrote to Wilhelm Fliess: "The lower strata of the population, which do not know Malthusianism are pushing after," along the same path; they would in due time, Freud thought, fall victim to the neuroses at the moment principally plaguing the middle classes.[69] From the earliest days of birth-control propaganda, in the broadsides of Francis Place and others, it seemed evident, at least to the propagandists, that while the bourgeoisie needed contraception, the lower orders needed it more, but would come to it later than the middle class, and through its example. Contraception required both knowledge and willingness, and the bourgeoisie showed itself increasingly ready to deploy the one and preach the other.[70] The negative attitude of socialists toward birth control underscores the common perception that it was heavily a middle-class affair. Marxists, even the women among them, viewed the campaign for contraception with immense suspicion; it struck them as just another bourgeois device to evade the need for drastic social reform, an essentially reactionary legacy of individualism. To limit the number of proletarians was to deny not cannon fodder to the capitalists, but soldiers to the revolution. "The social question," Rosa Luxemburg said in 1913, "can never be solved by self-help, but only by mass help. As a weapon for the proletariat, child limitations must be rejected categorically."[71]

Contraception in all its forms, then, was irrevocably intertwined with bourgeois culture at decisive points. But its impact on nineteenth-century bourgeois sexuality is hard to assess. The material is scanty and the links are largely inferential. Common sense strongly suggests that these links were close. Once women had significantly reduced their very realistic fear of exposing themselves to lethal puerperal fever every time they were impregnated, once men and women together could largely forget the scarcely less traumatic fear of being condemned to deprivations as a result of unwanted but unstoppable pregnancies, sexual activity could be enjoyed with greater abandon than ever before. The very fact that

69. *Affaiblissement*, 111–12; "Manuskript B," 81; "Draft B," 72.

70. Writing in 1895, in the *Journal de la Société de Statistique*, Jacques Bertillon noted that in contemporary France, the very poor had 108 children per thousand, the poor, 95. Those in the prosperous ranks ranged from 72 to 75; the rich had 53, and the very rich, 43 per thousand. These figures were subjected to skeptical scrutiny by K. A. Wieth-Knudsen a little more than a decade later in *Natalité et Progrès: Synthèse économique, démographique et biologique* (1908; French tr., 1938), 152–53, and it is true that Bertillon had ignored important variables—married versus unmarried women, religious allegiances, and so forth. There were then, as there have continued to be, pockets of large rich families with strong ties to the Church, whether Protestant or Catholic.

71. R. P. Neuman, "Working Class Birth Control in Wilhelmine Germany," *Comparative Studies in Society and History*, XX, 3 (July 1978), 414.

couples were converting their sexual life from acquiescence to planning must have lent their intercourse a gratifying access of energy and freedom.

But on the deepest level of inner experience, the matter was not quite so simple. Certainly birth control brought, and was felt to bring, inestimable benefits. But the lifting of enormous anxieties over sexual activity was achieved at the cost of arousing other, though certainly less crippling, anxieties. To limit the number of one's offspring was to raise insistent, though largely unconscious, questions about cherished capacities to make, or bear, children. Birth-control techniques and devices, whether withdrawal, condoms, or any other, were rehearsals of impotence and sterility; that this impotence and this sterility were deliberate and reversible must have reduced their ability to arouse anxiety, but in the most intimate inward experience, their threat retained some of its force. Moreover, there was the sacrifice of pleasure that protective activities before, during, or after intercourse entailed, a sacrifice which, as Sigmund Freud sensibly warned, could provoke neurotic suffering. Hence, while such intercourse enhanced feelings of freedom in some respects, it inhibited them in others. It compromised the spontaneous gratification of desire by bringing calculation to bear on the passions; it imported the ego into the domain where the id had once reigned more or less supreme, and invited the reality principle to intervene in the working of the pleasure principle.

But these reservations aside, the available nineteenth-century evidence speaks convincingly of contraception as an aid to sexual gratification, for both partners. Tellingly, its contemporary opponents denounced birth control as a means to unchecked, wicked self-indulgence, while its advocates rejected Malthus's call for voluntary celibacy as an unrealistic appraisal of, indeed an insult to, the sexual passion. Moreover, the enterprise of planning the size of one's family acted to reduce, if perhaps not to eliminate, inequalities between husband and wife. For it was hospitable to discussion. Inequities remained; they were implied by biological imperatives and reinforced by social conventions. It was not men, after all, but women who found themselves propelled into a campaign for the control of their own bodies; it was not women, but men who would imperiously remind their partners of their marital duties. But the practice of contraception in any form required a modicum of cooperation between lovers.

Birth controllers in the nineteenth century liked to say that some devices, like the condom, gave power of decision to the husband, while others, like the douche, put the matter into the hands of the wife. But this is a little mechanical. Even when it was the husband who put on the device, or withdrew before ejaculation, he was likely to do so not merely out of deference to his wife but after agreeing with her about this delicate matter. Late in the eighteenth century, French confessors had already criticized "the excessive obligingness of husbands towards their wives," dealing as they did "too gently with their excessive delicacy" by sparing them the trouble of bearing children without renouncing the pleasure of intercourse itself.[72] And in the nineteenth century it was sometimes men who spoke for the ideal of total sexual equality in marriage, clearly envisioning frank discussions between the partners. In his paeans to "marriage-love," a series of fictive letters, the American reformer Henry C. Wright laid it down emphatically, at mid-century, that *The wife must decide how often, and under what circumstances*" her husband may enjoy "*the passional expression of his love.*" It is, Wright argues, only on the basis of genuine mutual respect that a marriage should be concluded and consummated. "Passional indulgence, *demanded as a right*, is a rape upon the person whom the husband has promised, before God and man, to cherish, honor and protect." Wright hints, gently, that such voluntary renunciation of "enforced maternity" will produce intensified and prolonged sexual pleasure for both partners. "You have truly said," he has the wife tell her husband, "that woman must regulate those relations in which her whole nature is put under such severe requisition. The pleasure of a moment may take a year out of her life; and shall she have no voice, and never be consulted, as to the functions of her body, the emotions of her soul, and the changes which may, by the birth of her children, be made in her eternal destiny?" Let the lover turn away "when his too ardent gaze is met by a look of pain or embarrassment," and let "the husband, under all circumstances, be thus observant and thus tenderly considerate." Then, "old age will find a love still young. Love will then be the memory of the present life, as it will be the joyful anticipation of the future."[73] It would not do, even for Wright, radical publicist that he was, to be too explicit about the erotic dividends of birth control.

Henry C. Wright was a propagandist, not a reporter, and his *Marriage and Parentage* went far beyond practice common at mid-century. But the population figures suggest that his views became commonplace, or at least

72. Jean-Louis Flandrin, *Families in Former Times: Kinship, Household and Sexuality* (1976; tr. Richard Southern, 1979), 225.

73. Wright, *Marriage and Parentage: or, The Reproductive Element in Man, as a Means to His Elevation and Happiness* (1854; 2nd ed., 1855), 243, 246, 248, 255.

widely available emotionally, three or four decades later. One anonymous birth controller had said precisely this as early as 1855: if women knew that they could dictate the number of their offspring, "with what pleasure they could yield themselves to the sexual embrace." Dr. Elizabeth Blackwell, Christian and scientist in equal measure, largely concurred: "in healthy loving women, uninjured by the too frequent lesions which result from child-birth, increasing physical satisfaction attaches to the ultimate physical expression of love."[74] Certainly the rewards of sex without procreation are written across the responses to Clelia Mosher's questionnaire. And the prospect of such gratifications, perhaps not central but far from insignificant, haunts those tremulous expressions of some nineteenth-century women's desire, rarely voiced but deeply felt, not to have children. There was pleasure in safety.

We cannot read Mabel Todd's erotic autobiography in any other way. Her memories of the day she was impregnated against her intentions are unequivocal on that score. We know how unjustified her theory of contraception proved to be. But what matters here is the attitude it implies. Biology might be destiny, but the Todds, and a great many other couples, sought ways of avoiding its most stringent decrees and enjoying its most delicious gifts. And if it was not to be evaded, one could at least dream. While Freud was writing his *Interpretation of Dreams*, one of his friends reported to him: " 'My wife has asked me to tell you that she dreamt yesterday that she was having her period. You will know what that means.' Of course I know it," Freud admitted. "If this young woman dreamt that she was having her period, she had missed her period. I can imagine that she would gladly have enjoyed her freedom for some time more before the hardship of maternity began. It was a clever way of announcing her first pregnancy."[75] It was also, I am persuaded, a clever way of announcing her desire to remain sexually available and sexually active.

This woman was only one bourgeoise of many for whom the moral conflicts of the nineteenth century could not be resolved with ease, not even by the churches, which had no persuasive answers. Higher standards of living, spreading patterns of leisure, improved expectations of longevity, intensifying and purposeful concern with the future of one's children, all, especially among the middling orders, made Neo-Malthusianism more attractive than ever. And technology, coupled with information, made it accessible. More and more bourgeois as the century went on therefore

74. Both in Degler, *At Odds*, 195–96, 268.
75. *Traumdeutung*, St.A., II, 144; *Interpretation of Dreams*, S.E., IV, 126.

found ways of minimizing, and even of changing, the pressures upon their sensuality. At the same time, intractable realities, physical, economic, and cultural, remained as forceful reminders of curbs upon their choices. As their ways with contraception show, they lived in a remarkable halfway house, poised between a kind of innocent wisdom and cultivated naiveté, between knowledge and ignorance. They knew much, but there was much that they did not want to know.

⋊ FOUR ⋉

Learned Ignorance

1. An Age of Factitious Innocence

Human beings are ignorant more than once. While they make their debut
in life with an impressive array of mental and physical endowments, all
these are wholly unrealized, possibilities waiting for experience. Then,
immediately, the world undertakes to inscribe on their minds knowledge
of sorts. The infant's initial encounters are so many lessons in its extended,
often trying, sexual education; its mother's breast, the warmth of her embrace, her soothing voice, her inexplicable and frightening absences, are
all authoritative, sometimes very harsh preparations for the career of the
adult lover.

They are authoritative but largely unconscious. As the child begins to
sort out inner urges from outward impressions, establishes boundaries
between self and world, and engages in his intensely solitary, not always
happy affair with his parents, he amasses the raw material from which he
will construct his erotic agenda. Then comes the oedipal phase, that
poignant domestic triangle, the first far-reaching crisis in the child's
history of loving, as decisive for the girl as it is for the boy. But these
instructive early phases of development are, though forever retained,
almost wholly forgotten; having traversed the Oedipus complex, the
child comes to repress much of what he has learned. There are good
reasons for these intense acts of forgetting: the little boy would just as
soon not be reminded of open or fancied threats to his cherished penis;
the little girl as soon deny her dismay at discovering that she has no
penis to lose.

But out of sight is not out of mind. While the child's sexual investigations and his often outlandish sexual theories, to say nothing of his sexual

experiences, are overtaken by an irresistible amnesia, they are not lost, only unavailable. They will reemerge in later years, disguised and elaborated, in the form of a loving disposition, a special taste, a distorted memory, and, often, a neurotic symptom. There is, after the long sexual moratorium of the latency years between five and six and the onset of puberty, a privileged second phase in man's erotic education, adolescence, the time when sexuality, pressing for recognition with a peculiar physical urgency, will not be denied. The adolescent's sexual experiments and troubles are something of a repetition of his infantile ventures. But amnesia intervenes yet again, less thoroughgoing this time, but no less intrusive, to deplete the young man's or woman's store of accessible carnal knowledge. One might wonder if the loss is really substantial; most of the explanations of sexual processes that the young work out for themselves or appropriate from their friends are, after all, inaccurate, and, in their earliest versions, downright fantastic.[1] But the repressions, first in the years of latency and then after puberty, are quite unselective in this regard; the inexperienced groom and bride on their wedding night have probably forgotten both what they had correctly observed and what they had anxiously invented. Innocence once forfeited can never be reclaimed, but in the nineteenth century respectable young men and women often entered the married estate with what I would call a factitious innocence.

This simulacrum of innocence necessarily followed, in part, from man's unique psychosexual development, a history that nineteenth-century bourgeois shared with all mankind. Man's budget of rousing yet frightening incestuous wishes and his disrupted growth into maturity make massive repressions inevitable and, often, beneficial. They protect his capacity for maneuvering in intimate human engagements, help to safeguard his very sanity. And some of these repressions could be lifted, most gratifyingly in the marriage bed. "Pleasure," the distinguished Scottish

---

1. While documentation of real castration threats is fairly hard to come by, the psychoanalytic literature provides some usable instances. "Little Hans," the five-year-old boy whom Freud treated in 1908, almost wholly in absentia, had been warned quite directly by his mother: "At the age of three and a half, his mother encounters him, his hand on his penis. She threatens him 'If you do that, I'll send for Dr. A.; he'll cut off your pee-pee maker'"—Little Hans's word for his penis. " 'What will you make pee-pee with then?'" Little Hans, obviously far from devastated: " 'With my bottom.'" "Analyse der Phobie eines fünfjährigen Knaben [Der kleine Hans]" (1909), St.A., VIII, 15; "A Phobia in a Five-Year-Old Boy [Little Hans]," S.E., X, 7–8.— Other patients of Freud's, notably the "Rat Man," reported similar threats, but what makes the incident involving Little Hans so significant is that his parents were declared, enlightened followers of psychoanalysis, and yet could not forego the traditional menaces.

obstetrician J. Matthews Duncan noted in 1884, "is frequently absent at marriage, and gradually developed during the continuance of that state."[2] A decade and a half later, the German specialist Dr. Friedrich Siebert noted the same happy phenomenon: "It must be declared as completely unjustified to let a girl marry, as happens not rarely, without preparing her for what is to come. Yet," he added, reasonably enough, "women for the most part do not run away from their husbands on that account"; nor do they scream for help. "They know how to adjust themselves without that and discover the cheerful side. But a few elderly ladies have told me that they look back at the first night of their marriage with horror and with regret."[3] But the horror was curable—sometimes.

The emergence of an exhilarating ability to enjoy sexual satisfaction was not simply an efflorescence of new insights; it was also a liberating of repudiated knowledge, a kind of memory. And this helps to explain what I have insisted on: happy sensual marriages among the middle class in the nineteenth century. They acquired their savor after childish passions found adult targets worthy of whole-hearted investment, and with the support of sensitive spouses—always supposing the absence of crippling sexual traumas.

Yet this advanced education or, rather, reeducation of the senses was often sabotaged, and sometimes doomed, by the obstructions that respectable nineteenth-century society deliberately placed in its way. Influential spokesmen for that society were intent on imposing postures of ignorance on its young. Many physicians, clergymen, and teachers, with the physicians setting the style, closed their eyes to the sexual facts about them and invented, or exaggerated, threats to physical and mental health attendant on sexual indulgence, threats that confused and frightened the public they had been trained to serve. When it came to providing information and shaping attitudes about sexuality, the learned professions often limped behind the sensible and educated middle-class public of their day, spreading obscurity rather than light. But these professions, as we shall see, were wholly implicated in, and representative of, their culture.

Its innocence was not a deliberate policy; it was an unplanned, if highly adaptive defense. The cultural style of the age fostered what A. J. Munby, barrister, poet, and compulsive lover of working-class women, called "that *ignorance* of vice which one desires in a lady."[4] Its cult of privacy and its timidity in naming physical acts, let alone sexual relations,

2. *On Sterility in Women* (1884), 94. See above, pp. 134–35.
3. Siebert, *Sexuelle Moral und Sexuelle Hygiene* (1901), iii.
4. Diary, February 1, 1859, Derek Hudson, *Munby: Man of Two Worlds* (1972), 19.

in public were only the most conspicuous, and remain the best remembered, manifestations of what I am calling learned ignorance. It was an ignorance unconsciously desired, informally imparted, and assiduously fostered. The bourgeois century repressed better than it knew.

The appalling tales conjuring up tight-lipped, one-sided, miserable domestic sexuality or properly raised young men and women pathetically uninformed about sex in all its ramifications remain ever-popular ingredients in the received wisdom about the middle classes in the age of Victoria. Many have been discredited as myths or unwarranted generalizations. Queen Victoria, her reputation to the contrary, was often amused; she even drew, and bought, male nudes and gave her adored husband Albert just such a drawing as a present.[5] But some of these tales are true; they are enshrined in psychiatrists' case reports, public scandals over suppressed books, and poignant confessions in autobiographies. "I was an inquisitive child, especially about the facts of sex," Lady Lutyens wrote, recalling the days in the early 1880s when she was still Emily Lytton, "but it never occurred to me to ask my mother any questions on the subject. I pestered the servants with questions, however, and pretended to know more than I did in order to draw them out. A cousin and I made a bargain to find out all we could and report our discoveries to each other." Neither the servants nor the cousin apparently provided her with the physical or psychological information she sought; it did not protect her, she later discovered, when she wanted protection most. In 1893, when she was eighteen, she fell in love with Wilfrid Scawen Blunt, celebrated explorer and unprincipled womanizer, whom she thought "the handsomest man I have ever met, and I think the most physically attractive," even though (or precisely because) he was more than three times her age: Blunt was fifty-three when he tried, manfully but in vain, to coax her into bed with him.

Emily Lytton was clear-sighted enough to recognize the source, and the risks, of her infatuation, and she blamed the polite evasions, along with those helpless silences, for failing to arm her against sexual temptation: "Our late experience has brought prominently before me," she wrote to a confidant, "the folly of the conventional protection which is relied on for shielding women from corruption. A particular passion is the cause, directly or indirectly, of perhaps half the vice and misery of the world. This passion is implanted for beneficent purposes in the

5. It was by Mulready. See Kathryn Moore Heleniak, *William Mulready* (1980), 158; the nude is on 154.

constitution of man, and with this indwelling informer, besides the thousand hints, or more than hints, that are continually cropping up, it is assumed that innocence will be preserved by an impossible ignorance." She asked, in some indignation: "What sort of safety can there be in a fictitious barrier that has rarely any existence? And it is a little short of madness when people keep up the hollow pretence, and trust to it."[6] I know few passages evoking as precisely and as delicately as this the importunate demands that sexual passion, the "indwelling informer," makes on the adolescent. It so happened that Emily Lytton escaped Blunt's enticements with her self-respect and her virginity intact, and in 1897, after she had freed herself from her fatal entanglement at last, she married the rising architect Edwin Lutyens. She got over Blunt, but she always remained convinced that had she known more, she would have suffered less.

As it was, she suffered a great deal. Her marriage was close and, with all its vicissitudes, successful. As she exclaimed to her husband in 1929: "32 years!! Isn't it wonderful. How happy we have been in spite of ups and downs." These ups and downs had included her refusing herself to her husband for years, and Edwin Lutyens engaging in a long-drawn-out affair. Her honeymoon, as Emily Lutyens wrote to her husband years after, was, even in memory, "a nightmare of physical pain and mental disappointment." The larger nightmare—a long fling with Theosophy and that firm, complete severance of any physical relationship after seventeen years of marriage and three children—was inevitable not because Emily Lutyens was frigid but precisely because she was passionate. "Remember that I married you," she told her husband, "loving you and wanting you physically as much as you wanted me. I don't reproach you one instant for what happened after because you were just selfish and did not think and I was silly too." Edwin Lutyens had come into marriage as inexperienced as his wife; exigent and highly sexed, he would evidently ejaculate quickly without satisfying her and leaving her, as she frankly told her daughter Mary later, "night after night unappeased and resentful." She wanted a share in his thoughts, his reading, his work. But even as she expressed her pathetic yearning for intellectual intimacy, she did so in vivid physical metaphors that called attention to her frustrated sexual appetites: "It is not that I don't love you—I love you so much I want more of you—not your body but your soul, your intellect, something big to take hold of and share." That something big to take hold of

6. *A Blessed Girl: Memories of a Victorian Girlhood, 1887–1896* (1953), 10; Emily Lytton to the Rev. Whitwell Elwin, September 2, 3, 1893, ibid., 228–29.

looked remarkably like his penis: "Do try and bring me near while there is still time—" she wrote in the same letter, "be patient and gentle—and give me a little bit of your life. I am not exacting—if only you would but make me equal to your pipe!"[7] He begged her to forgive him, to be patient with him, but his pipe was his pipe, and he never quite discovered how he might share it with her, how to satisfy her. The two were deeply invested in one another; they loved each other more, for all their ups and downs, as their years together passed. But ignorance about sex was an invitation to trouble, if not tragedy, and their shared ignorance made that invitation all the more pressing.

To judge from the travail of others, as uninformed as Emily Lutyens and her husband, her appraisal of the middle-class girl's situation in her century is neither eccentric nor subjective. In the autobiography she published in 1893, Annie Besant, Christian ritualist, skeptic, atheist, sexual radical, legal reformer, socialist and Theosophist in turn, put the matter with the lucidity of the experienced publicist. Her book itself partly draws the sting of her indictment, for in it she censured, candidly, the lack of candor all around her. During the summer of 1866, she became engaged to a clergyman whom she knew little and idealized beyond merit. The pair had taken walks and drives together but done little else, and on this fragile basis she accepted him; while she repented soon enough, her mother would not let her break the solemn engagement, and in the winter of 1867 Annie Besant was married, "with no more idea of the marriage relation than if I had been four years old instead of twenty. My dreamy life," she added, "into which no knowledge of evil had been allowed to penetrate, in which I had been guarded from all pain, shielded from all anxiety, kept innocent on all questions of sex, was no preparation for married existence, and left me defenceless to face a rude awakening."[8]

Thinking back on her predicament a quarter of a century later, she soberly concluded that "no more fatal blunder can be made than to train a girl to womanhood in ignorance of all life's duties and burdens and then to let her face them for the first time away from all the associations, the old helps, the old refuge on the mother's breast." If " 'perfect innocence' " was a "very beautiful" possession, it was also, she knew, a "perilous" one. And she urged that "Eve should have the knowledge of good and evil ere she wanders forth from the paradise of a mother's love."

---

7. Mary Lutyens, *Edwin Lutyens* (1980), 242–96, 97, 77–78. "They were both physically passionate, but Ned had had no experience and Emily had received no guidance from her mother beyond instructions not to refuse her husband anything and always to keep a pot of cold cream by the bed" (p. 56).

8. *An Autobiography* (1893), 70.

She was quick to generalize from her own experience: "Many an unhappy marriage dates from its very beginning, from the terrible shock to a young girl's sensitive modesty and pride, her helpless bewilderment and fear." With a superior erotic education acquired in school or in life, men might find it hard to imagine the "possibility of such infantile ignorance in many girls," but she assured her readers that it existed, even if its precise incidence must remain uncertain: "Such ignorance is a fact in the case of some girls at least, and no mother should let her daughter, blindfold, slip her neck under the marriage yoke." Annie Besant escaped that yoke within six years; with characteristic enterprise and bravely facing distasteful consequences, she obtained a separation in 1873. But she warned that other women, less spirited and less rebellious, would bear the yoke all their lives, victims of false delicacy and misplaced shame, their sensuality ruined beyond all hope of recovery.[9]

Actually Effie Ruskin's—or, better, Effie Gray's—story, often recited in the annals of nineteenth-century sexuality, suggests that a healthy libido could overcome the most genteel innocence and survive the most arrant neglect. On March 6, 1854, Effie Ruskin revealed to her parents, in a circumstantial and straightforward letter, that for six long years, her marriage had never been consummated: "I do not think I am John Ruskin's Wife at all—and I entreat you to assist me to get released from the unnatural position in which I stand to Him." She recalled the circumstances of her life with her brilliant but eccentric husband, including his readiness to talk intercourse for days on end without any intention of engaging in it. "He alleged various reasons, Hatred of children, religious motives, a desire to preserve my beauty, and finally this last year told me the true reason (and this to me is as villainous as all the rest), that he had imagined women were quite different to what he saw I was, and that the reason he did not make me his Wife was because he was disgusted with my person the first evening 10th April," of 1848, their wedding night.[10] She was much affected by her final breach with her husband, "ruined and nervous in both mind and body," but in the course of her plausible and sober recital, she never blamed her parents for failing

9. Ibid., 71.

10. Effie Gray (as she deliberately signs herself here, though, of course, still officially married to John Ruskin) to her father, Mary Lutyens, *Millais and the Ruskins* (1967), 155–56. Originally Mary Lutyens, and the many others who have dwelt on this almost irresistible affair, thought that Ruskin was disgusted by his wife's pubic hair, for which, Lutyens writes, "nothing had prepared him" (p. 156n). But she tentatively corrects this in her later *The Ruskins and the Grays* (1972), 108n, where she notes that at Oxford, Ruskin had "the opportunity" of "seeing erotic pictures," which would have revealed the whole truth about an adult woman's body.

to prepare her for sexual life and thus leaving her vulnerable to John Ruskin's sophistries. All she said, almost in passing, was: "I had never been told the duties of married persons to each other and knew little or nothing about their relations in the closest union on earth."[11] She was fond of her parents, and, though intelligent and self-assured, not inclined to be rebellious or to carry grudges. It says much about the prosperous middle-class culture from which she came that she did not resent, at least not openly, the ignorance in which her father and mother had left her. And it says something about her latent sexual passion, aching to be awakened, that she had at last come to recognize her situation as "unnatural"; upon gaining an annulment, a laborious and humiliating procedure, she married the painter John Millais to enjoy a long, sometimes stormy but largely satisfactory marriage, and to bear eight children.

Ignorance might be poor preparation for a happy marriage, as Emily Lytton and Annie Besant discovered to their sorrow. But it was not fatal. When Mollie Hughes, as she recalled in her autobiography, her sole claim to fame, became engaged in the 1880's, her mother said to her "casually one day, appropos of nothing, while she was writing a letter and I was busy over some Latin, 'I suppose you realize that you will have to sleep with Arthur?' 'Oh yes,' I replied, with the same appreciative smile that I had given to all her other remarks on a happy married life. I think now that she must have been puzzled as to how much or how little I knew." Nor will we ever know what she knew, for her mother "probed no further," and Molly Hughes does not tell us.[12] But whatever she knew she had not learned at home.

There is scattered evidence that the French were little better off. Recall Gustave Droz's imaginative reconstruction of French bourgeois marriage around mid-century. The few words that he has the bride's mother whisper into her daughter's ear after the wedding are manifestly words to a blushing ignoramus, and the maternal instructions about "sacrifice" and "necessity" were both very late in coming and wholly unhelpful in import. Some years before, in 1843, George Sand sent a "sermon," full of feeling, to her half-brother, Hippolyte Chatiron, in order to be helpful and on time. She had just learned that a friend had died in childbirth, and the news led her to reflect about men's marital conduct. Chatiron's daughter was about to be married, and she thought

---

11. Lutyens, *Millais and the Ruskins*, 155.—Something very similar happened to the famous American sex reformer and birth controller Marie Stopes, who discovered some months after she was married that her husband had failed to consummate their marriage. Keith Briant, *Marie Stopes: A Biography* (1962), 66–77.

12. M. Vivian Hughes, *A London Girl of the Eighties* (1936), 303.

that this was the proper moment for him to say a few words to his child's future husband: "Prevent your son-in-law from brutalizing your daughter on their wedding night, for among delicate women many organic weaknesses and painful childbirth have no other cause. Men are not sufficiently aware that this amusement is a martyrdom for us." She advised him to tell the young man he would do well to "temper his pleasure a little and to wait until he has brought his wife little by little to understand it and respond to it. Nothing is so horrifying as the terror, the suffering, and the disgust of a poor child who knows nothing and who finds herself raped by a brute. We bring them up," she added tartly, "as much as we can, as saints, and then we hand them over like fillies. If your son-in-law is a man of intelligence, and if he really loves your daughter, he will understand his proper role and will not object if you talk to him about it the night before."[13] There, she said, was the end of the sermon. She was obviously a little self-conscious about lecturing her half-brother, but she also felt compelled to let the voice of experience speak. George Sand, the notorious liberated female who, the genteel thought, changed lovers as other women changed their wardrobe, seems to have come to marriage little better prepared than Effie Ruskin, and discovered the pleasures of sensuality through experience, through sometimes painful experiments. As with other women, so with George Sand: innocence proved a curable condition.

It was not simply that road maps to orgasm were hard to come by in the bourgeois century; the whole country of the senses was befogged by delicacy. Proper married women waited for older sisters to instruct them in the mysteries of birth control; proper mothers "enlightened" their daughters about menstruation with so many euphemisms that the information thus imparted was more traumatic than sheer ignorance would have been. This, for one, is how Natalie Barney, celebrated international beauty and flamboyant lesbian, learned about her forthcoming menses around 1886: her mother pointed to fish in an aquarium who were "giving off red fibers: 'You will have them too when you are older. You must not be too surprised.'" At twelve, when Natalie Barney began to menstruate, she was not surprised so much as appalled: she fainted.[14] A few years later, Dr. Helen P. Kennedy questioned 125 American high school girls who had begun to menstruate as to whether they had "received instruction from your mother or talked freely with her on this matter." Thirty-six of her respondents had not talked with their mothers at all; 39 *had* discussed the matter, but in a constrained way; and 50 had canvassed menstruation in all frankness. Dr. Kennedy found these results sorely disappointing: "Less than half of the girls felt free to talk with their mothers of this most important matter! This is almost criminal ignorance," a "dangerous ignorance," she thought, "in which daughters are left by scarcely less ignorant mothers."[15] This was the anguished and demanding voice of the reformer. We shall encounter it again soon.

There are other fragments, to the same effect, with the woman invariably cast as the victim. Indeed, the brute in the bedroom, the sensual husband raping his shrinking, wholly uninformed bride, became a staple in the literature of bourgeois self-criticism, notably toward the end of the century, as the age of Victoria merged into the age of Freud. It makes for a plausible—and, I must add, titillating—scene in a melodrama for two: the timid, frightened girl torn from the arms of her mother and thrown on the mercy of this stranger who is her husband. And now that exigent male, unshackled at last, overcome with lust and impatient to taste the carnal delights that the conventions have compelled him to postpone, is bound to cast tenderness aside and to assert his "marital rights" with callous disregard of the physical pain and the mental anguish racking the fragile prize he has won. It seemed only too obvious why so many women should be afflicted with distasteful and terrifying maladies. "In one patient of mine," Dr. Mary Wood-Allen wrote ominously in her compendious *Ideal Married Life*, "I found a vaginismus that had existed since the wedding night, when the bride shrank with great dread from an experience for which she was wholly unprepared. Whenever her husband approached her the vagina closed with a spasm." Dr. Sicard de Plauzoles, a French feminist who eloquently advocated woman's right to dispose over her own body—emphatically including her right to "accept or refuse the sexual act, and maternity"—also evoked the image of rape: "The brutal exercise of the husband's power over the body of his wife revolts the conscience of every man of free thought and delicate feelings."[16]

This rhetoric, at once gloomy and bellicose, strongly implying marital initiation to be a hostile and pitiless act, was congenial to sex reformers. But the vocabulary of unimpeachably conservative texts was, though more temperate, no less suggestive; licensed rape on the wedding night

---

15. Dr. Helen P. Kennedy, "Effect of High School Work upon Girls During Adolescence," *Pedagogical Seminary*, III (June 1896), 469–82.

16. *Ideal Married Life* (1901), 155; de Plauzoles, *La Fonction sexuelle. Au point de vue de l'éthique et de l'hygiène sociales* (1908), 344, 347.

seemed to be something of an epidemic. These tracts speak of the "sacrifice" that the bride undergoes on her supreme occasion, of her "necessary ordeal," and often of her "surrender." In his much-discussed article on prostitution, published in 1850, the English publicist W. R. Greg bluntly asserted that married or unmarried, the "decorously educated" young woman finds that "the first sacrifice is made and exacted, *in both cases*, in a delirium of mingled love and shame."[17]

I have no doubt that such traumatic domestic dramas occurred, and that they took their toll. But there is as much wishful fantasy in these vignettes as gross reality, perhaps more: however widely credited they were, and are, they read like the anxious desire of men to assert confident mastery, supported by some women's desire to submit to the lash of a dominant male. We know, after all, that nineteenth-century bridegrooms were often patient and tactful: I have already cited the husbands of the women whom Dr. Mosher interviewed, some of whom postponed all attempts at consummating their marriage anywhere from three days to a year. Moreover, young men were often no more knowledgeable than the virgins they married. True enough, as Annie Besant was quite right to point out, adolescent boys had far better opportunities to gather sexual experiences than adolescent girls; the double standard, which encouraged the young man to collect such experiences while his future wife passively waited to benefit from his researches, reflected and encouraged at least some manifest sexual behavior.[18] At the same time, young men were often burdened with misinformation, or restrained from serious experiments by a view of woman that made her almost as untouchable as their own mothers—at least in their conscious minds.

As usual, sexual education seemed better on the other side of the Channel. "With us," so Sir Lawrence Jones recalled his prewar days at Oxford, "curiosity lingered to an age when the youth of the Continent were connoisseurs of women to a man." The lives of these Oxford undergraduates around 1905 were largely "woman-free." Sir Lawrence concedes that he and his fellows had "day dreams; I had my own aching fantasies," but "pretty girls were idealised beyond their deserts, plain ones were pitied beyond their needs, and the notional gap between man and girl made it difficult for either to regard the other as a simple fellow-creature." Inevitably, relations with girls "were formal and mannered, a prescribed distance was kept, and topics for talks limited." When Sir Lawrence and his friends took courage to inquire about sex, they were

17. [W. R. Greg], "Prostitution," *The Westminster Review*, LIII (July 1850), 473.
18. On the other hand, the "purity literature" often insisted that men be as virginal upon entering marriage as women.

handed the prevailing cultural pieties, even by experts. He recalled one
dinner party of undergraduates with a physician they all knew well;
when one of his friends asked "whether women enjoyed sexual intercourse," the doctor, "speaking as a doctor," told the youthful gathering:
" 'I can tell you that nine out of ten women are indifferent to or actively
dislike it; the tenth, who enjoys it, will always be a harlot.' " In long
retrospect, Sir Lawrence recognized this dictum, so dogmatically asserted,
as unsettling, even pernicious: "We accepted this, from such an authority,
as gospel. It is hard to imagine a more mischievous message to young
men," for it both "reproached all ardent bridegrooms and slandered all
willing brides." That doctor, he adds, "was the kindest of men, and the
most honest, and it is a measure of the false shame demanded of his woman
patients by the conventions . . . that a doctor could be so ignorant."[19]
This is apologetics rather than diagnosis; most doctors felt perfectly comfortable with the false shame their woman patients brought to the consulting room, and most of them, had their patients been less reticent,
would not have heard their message.

On the Continent, whatever repressed English undergraduates like Sir
Lawrence might think, the situation was only superficially different. It
was a cardinal point in the schoolboy code and of French fiction that at
the age of sixteen or so, the adolescent would have visited a house of
prostitution. But not all such ventures lived up to expectations; Flaubert's
Frédéric Moreau who, overcome by embarrassment in the bordello,
turned and ran, is more than a fiction: he is a collective portrait. The
daughters of pious and prosperous French middle-class families who attended convent schools were systematically kept in the dark about physiology, let alone sexuality. And Frank Wedekind's pioneering expressionist
play Frühlings Erwachen, completed in 1891, suggests that German youth
was no better off: some adolescent girls were still being told that the stork
brought babies, and schoolboys suffered the "spring's awakening" of
puberty as a flood of unmanageable feelings and a torment of insoluble
conflicts. Wedekind's avant-garde animus against the Enemy, bourgeois
hypocrisy, is so potent and so single-minded that his hysterical satire is
far from being a measured appraisal of available sexual knowledge. But
he is not wholly unjust to the atmosphere pervading the German Empire,
in which a serious novelist like Theodor Fontane was criticized for introducing adultery into his fictions.

The éducation sentimentale of the young certainly included frustrating
fantasies, furtive and embarrassing masturbation, and some lasting humili-

19. L. E. Jones, An Edwardian Youth (1956), 162, 37, 163.

ations. In the United States, as one wide-ranging survey of college boys disclosed around 1914, most young men learned about sex from servants or from their friends, which was often no improvement: of 677 who answered the question from whom they had acquired sexual information, no fewer than 544 listed "boy associates," 33 "girl associates," and 40 such varied sources as hired men, maids, talk, and observation of animals. As M. J. Exner, author of the survey, concluded, a little severely, "91.5 per cent received their first permanent impressions about sex from unwholesome sources." And, appropriately enough, nearly four out of five respondents thought that this way of learning about the mysteries of sexuality had had "a definitely bad effect" on them. A few years earlier, around 1910, German physicians estimated that about a fifth, or perhaps as many as a third, of *Gymnasium* pupils in the upper classes had had some sexual experience.[20] These are informed guesses, no more, and in any event they are silent about the quality of that experience, or the failed experiments recollected with shame. Neither carnal knowledge nor carnal activity was a guarantee of adequate, let alone triumphant sexuality.

How little Continental men knew, or how incompetent they could prove at the decisive moment, emerges from what one of Sigmund Freud's patients, an obsessional neurotic, told him about her initiation. "Her husband," as Freud sums up her account, "had during the wedding night suffered a not unusual mishap. He found himself impotent, and in the course of the night he came rushing from his room into hers many times, to repeat the attempt and see whether it would not work after all. In the morning he said he should feel ashamed before the hotel maid who made the beds, grabbed a little bottle of red ink, and poured its contents over the sheet."[21] This ludicrous incident, which would be funny if it were not so sad, suggests once again that the virginity of the bride was highly prized, indeed assumed, among the middle classes in Freud's time, and that a husband could be, if anything, more clumsy, more anxious, more uninformed, than his wife. The victim of the wedding-night trauma, though often the wife deflowered in pain and terror, was perhaps just as often the husband condemned to a show of potency.

Contemporaries, indeed, were more alert to the humiliations threatening the new bridegroom than later historians have been. Describing the appearance of a relative just before his wedding, Alice Belknap reported

20. M. J. Exner, *Problems and Principles of Sex Education: A Study of 948 College Men*, Y.M.C.A. pamphlet (1915), 6, 7; and see Dr. Hermann Rohleder, *Grundzüge der Sexualpädagogik für Ärzte, Pädagogen und Eltern* (1912), 15, 85.

21. "Zwangshandlungen und Religionsübungen" (1907), *St.A.*, VII, 16; "Obsessive Actions and Religious Practices," *S.E.*, IX, 121.

to her sister Susan Wright in 1883 that he "really shows his approaching marriage as most girls do, thin and pale." The men themselves sometimes frankly acknowledged the apprehensions that such pallor betrayed. Having decided not to consummate their marriage for a month, the Kingsleys anticipated their wedding night easy in mind: "I have been thinking over your terror at seeing me undressed," Charles Kingsley wrote to Fanny Grenfell several months before the great day, "and I feel that I should have the same feeling in a minor degree to you, till I had learnt to bear the blaze of your naked beauty. You do not know how often a man is struck powerless in body and mind on his wedding night." The risk of what, early in the century, Stendhal had called a "fiasco" was so great that some men found it most prudent to deny their anxiety altogether. "Here is *the* day at last," John Millais wrote to his close friend Charles Collins on his wedding day. "I find myself positively *not* in the least nervous, and very happy." His very negation was an affirmation. He was open enough to confess that much was at stake: "I feel feverish, and slightly out of sorts"; and he added, "How strange it is. I am hopeful it may be the right course I have taken which can only be known from experience." He well understood, he told Collins, that this was "a trial," and concluded, choosing his metaphors not without unconscious aptitude: "There are some startling accomplishments, my boy, like the glimpse of the dentists instruments—My poor brain and soul is fatigued with dwelling on unpleasant probabilities so I am aroused for the fight." His evocation of the dentist's instruments, those castrating tongs, set out his fear in its most radical form; his dwelling on "unpleasant probabilities" put it more realistically. Effie Gray had been legally certified *virgo intacta* by the country's most distinguished physicians; it was now up to him, not merely to be aroused for the fight, but to perform.[22] But he was *not* nervous.

His wife's diary tells a different story. She describes herself as confident and happy as she signed the marriage contract, but her husband as "more agitated. He said afterwards," she wrote, "he felt very much inclined to throw down the pen and ask what play he was performing in and refuse to sign." Once they were safely off on the train for their honeymoon, he

22. Belknap: May 27, 1883, July 1979 addition, box 53, SF, Y-MA; Kingsley: Susan Chitty, *The Beast and the Monk: A Life of Charles Kingsley* (1975), 86; Millais: July 2, 1855, Lutyens, *Millais and the Ruskins*, 260, 261. Mary Lutyens believes that Millais was, like his bride, a virgin. Effie Gray Ruskin's annulment required her to be examined by two physicians, who then certified that "the usual signs of virginity are perfect and that she is naturally and properly formed. . . ." Describing the procedure to her mother (May 20, 1854), she said, sensibly enough: "I will reserve further particulars" (pp. 263, 218).

broke down altogether. "He got very agitated and when the Railway had started the excitement had been so much for him that instead of the usual comfort I suppose that the Brides require on those occasions of leaving, I had to give him all my sympathy. He cried dreadfully, said he did not know how he had got through it, felt wretched; it had added ten years to his Life, and instead of being happy and cheerful, he seemed in despair." In a reversal of accepted roles, almost motherly in her tender concern, Effie "bathed his face with Eau de Cologne, held his head and opened one of the windows and he soon began to get better."[23]

This was more than the extreme response of a sensitive artist about to consummate a love he had so patiently and so discreetly pursued. It was perhaps not a typical experience, but it was far from rare. On October 20, 1869, when Louisa Bowater was married to Sir Rainald Knightley, she noted in her journal that she "did not feel in the least nervous—at least I felt there was too much to be done and thought of, to allow myself to give way." Her husband, on the other hand, "dear Rainald," was "very nervous." By the time the couple arrived at his estates, with the tenants drawn up, the church bells ringing, and a "very pretty and touching address" read out, "my darling husband spoke well and clearly in reply, and did not break down as I feared he would."[24] In the conflict between anxiety and obligation, obligation had gained the upper hand. Yet when all is said, it was probably more likely that a woman would yield to panic than a man. "I'm afraid, I'm afraid," a young girl told the Goncourt brothers in 1856, speaking of her future wedding night. "I'd like to have myself chloroformed!"[25]

Doubtless men, as ill-prepared for marriage as the most sheltered girl, wished not for the drugged haven of insensibility so much as for positive relief that would secure, or restore, their potency. The medical literature on male impotence published before psychoanalysts began to study the syndrome is unimpressive but revealing enough. Its most spectacular case histories involve men with physical impediments, or fiascos sustained by sexual inverts programmatically attempting heterosexual relations they really did not want. But, scanty as they are, the relevant medical papers lay bare beyond cavil the psychological component in some nineteenth-century men's futile efforts to satisfy a mistress or consummate a marriage. Jean-Martin Charcot and Valentin Magnan collected a number of such

23. Ibid., 262–63.

24. *The Journals of Lady Knightley of Fawsley, 1856–1884*, ed. Julia Cartwright (Mrs. Ady) (1915), 171–73.

25. September 22, 1856, Edmond and Jules de Goncourt, *Journal; mémoires de la vie littéraire 1851–1896*, ed. Robert Ricatte, 22 vols. (1956–58), II, 32.

cases of which one, a nightcap fetishist, would have interested Freud. It certainly interested William A. Hammond, a distinguished neurologist who had been Surgeon General of the United States Army. His *Sexual Impotence in the Male* is a veritable anthology of the current literature.[26] Hammond added related cases from his own practice and from other authorities. But, being perversions, they are, of course, by definition special and uncharacteristic of the age.

Far more prevalent and more representative were cases of temporary impotence, of which Hammond selected two specimens. The first was that of "a married man," the "picture of robust health," recently married and "much attached to his wife." Yet "for a year past whenever he had attempted sexual intercourse some thought often of a ludicrous character would take possession of his mind, and extinguish all desire at the very moment that the orgasm was beginning." The second case was not dissimilar: a young man, a professional gambler, whose "mind was severely taxed" by his occupation, discovered when he sought to gratify his "strong sexual desires" after work that he could not do so: "Some technical matter connected with the business was sure to come up in his mind with the effect of extinguishing all desire and with it all power." The diagnostic category of obsessional neurosis being unavailable to him, Hammond instead diagnosed both of these patients to be exceedingly impressionable: the repetition of strong perceptions generated a loss of confidence which, in turn, induced impotence. Hammond accordingly advised the first to move to a separate bedroom and refrain from intercourse for three months, and the second to take a long sea voyage and not contemplate sexual relations until his return. "The treatment," Hammond was pleased to report, "was so perfectly successful with both subjects that there was not the least difficulty when the periods of probation had expired."[27] There were times when this kind of primitive psychotherapy worked very well. But whether it worked or not, the point is that the need for it was recognized.

These cases, and the humiliating spectacle of the impotent bridegroom which Freud declared to be fairly common, have implications beyond the psychic disasters they delineate. That theatrical and menacing figure, the male beast in the marital bed, was real enough; Mrs. Eliza Duffey, in her widely read and, to many innocent girls, frightening book of advice, *What Women Should Know*, said as much in the 1870s: "One is often led to wonder if a large class of men are not simply brutes, in all that con-

26. William A. Hammond, *Sexual Impotence in the Male* (1883), 40–42.
27. Ibid., 16–19.

cerns the physical relations of marriage. Women do not readily make confidential complaints to other women against their husbands. So that when a word—an incompleted sentence smothered before it is fully uttered—is spoken, it must be wrung from the lips by extreme marital brutality. That women, many women, so suffer at the hands of husbands, brutal in this respect, though kind in all others, does not admit of doubt."[28] Yet this lusty animal is not a composite portrait drawn solely from women's experience; he is also a projection, mainly by men, denying male fiascos. Marriage was a trial for men as it was for women, in more senses than one. And, ironically but significantly, it was not made less of a trial, for either, by the doctors of the day.

2. A Profession of Anxiety

The spectacle of professional purveyors of knowledge functioning as accomplices of ignorance was by no means new. Charges against the learned professions for selfishness, exclusiveness, and licensed quackery go back to classical times; more recently, toward the end of the Enlightenment, Condorcet had centered his sociological interpretation of history on his perception that professional establishments, clerical and lay, had always been far more intent on securing their privileges and maintaining their monopolies than on diffusing their wisdom to the general benefit. In the nineteenth century, this spectacle only became more obtrusive, and in a way more pathetic, than before. The natural sciences were making spectacular strides; and medicine, increasingly if hesitantly borrowing from chemistry and related disciplines, was hard pressed to follow. If the railroad was the most dramatic exemplification of science in the service of technology, medicine registered innovations almost as visible and possibly more far-reaching. The names of Joseph Lister and Louis Pasteur, Ignaz Semmelweis and Sir James Simpson, are enduring reminders of how close nineteenth-century medicine came to the conquest of infection and pain.

For all these triumphs, massive numbers of respected physicians, many among them ornaments to their profession, credited and spread superstitions about the body that stamp them as Quixotic knights of learned ignorance. They tilted at their windmills in good company. The alliance that doctors, pastors, and educators would forge late in the nineteenth century to press for sex education had its forerunner in a common front

28. Eliza Duffey, *What Women Should Know* (1873), 116–17.

informally established decades earlier to combat masturbation, a sexual practice they found to be as troubling as they feared it to be epidemic. It is a revealing campaign, admirably condensing nineteenth-century middle-class anxieties, especially about sexuality, in a world in which less and less seemed settled, more and more was strange.

Throughout the nineteenth century, the vice of "self-abuse" or "self-pollution" propelled learned men, and some learned women, into postures of perspiring alarm; they flooded the literatures of medical advice and moral uplift with macabre case histories and desperate, repetitive pleas for action before it was too late. The credulity of well-educated divines in medical matters even exceeded their theological will to believe; and nervous fears paralyzed the mental powers of physicians who, in other areas of their expertise, knew better. "The subject of onanism," as Sigmund Freud put it in 1912, "is practically inexhaustible."[29] It had been inexhaustible for a century or more.

Appropriately enough, the father of the modern fear of masturbation embodied the learned alliance in one person: he seems to have been a clergyman dabbling in quackery. Whoever he was, before 1710 he published a book that set the stage for, and invented the vocabulary of, the craze to come: *Onania, or the Heinous Sin of Self-Pollution, And all its frightful Consequences, in both Sexes, Considered.* It was often reprinted and soon translated.[30] In coining his euphonious name for an established practice, the anonymous author cleverly claimed dubious Biblical authority for his diagnosis; in designating masturbation as a sin, and a heinous one, he skillfully mixed religious gravity with his pseudo-medical argumentation; in describing "onanism" as "self-pollution," he made it appear not merely dangerous to health and to the prospects of salvation, but filthy into the bargain. That the author of *Onania* also touted a secret remedy which, he promised, would provide relief from masturbation as well as such other sexual woes as sterility and impotence rather compromised his work but did not hurt its sales.

Onania must have responded to a measure of latent anxiety, for it enjoyed a certain vogue in the first half of the eighteenth century. The distinguished Swiss physician Samuel-Auguste-André-David Tissot found

---

29. *Die Onanie, Diskussionen der Wiener Psychoanalytischen Vereinigung* (1912), [not in *St.A.*], *G.W.*, VIII, 345; "Concluding Remarks, to a Discussion on Masturbation", *S.E.*, XII, 254.

30. By 1736, there was a German version retaining, in its title, all the lurid innuendos of the English original: *Onania oder die schröckliche Sünde der Selbstbefleckung mit allen ihren entsetzlichen Folgen.*

"The English *Onania* a true chaos," and only its "observations" worth anything; "all the author's reflections are nothing but theological and moral trivialities." But for a physician it was, after all, the observations that counted; and Tissot's own book, *De l'onanisme*, first published in 1758, would give the name, and the punishments annexed to the practice, a credibility that its anonymous predecessor could never have secured. Quite uncritically, Tissot copied down the ills to which, according to *Onania*, English masturbators fell victim: a general deterioration of mental faculties and physical strength, an accumulation of pains across the body, the spreading of pus-filled boils, a variety of ailments besetting the sexual organs including impotence, premature ejaculation, and gonorrhea, and a total disorder of the bowels.[31] Nor did Tissot, faithfully echoing *Onania*, omit insanity, though he noted that it was likely to be relatively mild and far from general. This dread effect of masturbation was to make medical history, with the cautious qualifications listed in *Onania* dropping away. In light of the fears that learned men would spread in the nineteenth century, the quack who wrote that text of texts appears moderate and humane.

While the author of *Onania* was obscure and anything but disinterested, Tissot was a physician with a European reputation. A leading figure in the Swiss Enlightenment, he corresponded with celebrated healers like Théodore Tronchin and Albrecht von Haller and celebrated authors like Voltaire and Rousseau; he was an early advocate of inoculation against smallpox, and a prolific, respected writer on a wide variety of medical subjects. In the manner of eighteenth-century physicians, Tissot was inclined to be subjective and anecdotal in his case histories. At the same time he was endowed with exemplary common sense; his book on the health of literary men recommends that they take exercise and cultivate cheerfulness as antidotes to the sedentary and often gluttonous life they normally lead.[32] It was only with masturbation that his good sense deserted him. Yet his little treatise on onanism enjoyed all the success of his more rational writings, perhaps more; a translation of the original Latin into French by his own hand in 1759 was so rapidly snapped up that seven more printings appeared in the space of a few months, while translations into several languages, including English, Italian and German, followed within the next decade. Indeed, Tissot's enormous prestige outlived him for a century. As late as 1834, thirty-seven years after his death, there was call for a new, "considerably augmented" edition. In

31. Tissot, *De l'onanisme* (1758; ed. 1834), 17–20.
32. Tissot, *De la santé des gens de lettres* (1768).

the next decade, Amiel could still cite Tissot as an unquestioned authority, and he was not the last to yield to the persuasive powers of *De l'onanisme*.[33]

While for Tissot the torments following masturbation were by and large those he had copied from *Onania*, later, more troubled physicians grew more expansive still. In 1812, Benjamin Rush included among the "morbid effects" of onanism, in addition to insanity, "seminal weakness, impotence, dysury, tabes dorsalis, pulmonary consumption, dyspepsia, dimness of sight, vertigo, epilepsy, hypochondriasis, loss of memory, manalgia, fatuity, and death."[34] In the course of the nineteenth century, as this learned mania spread across the civilized landscape, the list of symptoms shifted, burgeoned, and contracted with no discernible logic.

Weighty specialists lent their prestige to keep the issue alive and nervousness acute. In 1855, Dr. George R. Calhoun, surgeon of the Howard Association in Philadelphia, a philanthropic group devoted to the dissemination of medical information to sufferers from sexual ills, wrote a report on "Spermatorrhoea, Sexual Weakness, and Impotence" that confirmed its instigators' most extravagant fears and their most tremulous hopes. The first consequence of "Self-Abuse," he wrote, with a careless printer unwittingly underscoring the gravity of the matter, is "a total extinction of the emotions natural to the sexual extinct"; masturbation "demoralizes the whole character, and utterly destroys the sexual faculty." The child grows pale, his cheek sunken, his mind indolent, his movement slow, his temper obstinate, his mood irritable, his conduct sluggish, his comprehension dull, and his resistance weak. Life becomes a torment to the masturbator; "Self-Abuse," in short, "is the most certain road to the grave."[35] And, of course, Dr. Calhoun did not omit insanity from his catalogue.

Yet Dr. Calhoun held out hope that all but the most inveterate addicts could be cured with medicines and psychological treatments like "cold baths, douches, cold hip baths several times a day, moderate and cooling diet and drinks," to be supplemented by "hard mattresses with little

33. June 13, 1841, Henri Frédéric Amiel, *Journal intime*, ed. Bernard Gagnebin and Philippe M. Monnier, 4 vols. so far (1976–   ), I, 193. As late as 1870, Dr. N. F. Cooke invited those of his readers who thought his picture of "male and female self-abuse overdrawn" to procure Tissot's book. "A Physician," *Satan in Society* (1870), 17.

34. *Medical Inquiries upon Diseases of the Mind* (1812), in E. H. Hare, "Masturbatory Insanity: The History of an Idea," *Journal of Mental Science*, CVIII (January 1962), 4.

35. Calhoun, *Report of the Consulting Surgeon on Spermatorrhoea, or Seminal Weakness, Impotence, the Vice of Onanism, Masturbation, or Self-Abuse, and Other Diseases of the Sexual Organs* (ca. 1858), 4–6.

clothing" and by milk rather than coffee or tea or other stimulants. Dr. Calhoun's threats and promises alike were in line with the wisdom current at mid-century, and the grateful Directors of the Howard Association ordered 5,000 copies of his report to be "printed for gratuitous distribution." Three years later they voted for a new edition, again to be disseminated free of charge.[36] The anti-masturbation campaign was not just an exhausting, it was an expensive affair.

While insanity was long a favorite entry in the medical literature on masturbation, followed closely by lassitude and epilepsy, it was also controversial; in his conscientious survey of the medical literature on the subject, Havelock Ellis in 1900 noted a bewildering diversity of opinions.[37] And some doctors, like Henry Maudsley, exacerbated the general indecisiveness about the etiology, the symptomatology, the very significance of masturbation. In 1867, in his textbook on the physiology and pathology of the mind, Maudsley refers only in passing to "continued self-abuse," saying it "gives rise to a particular and disagreeable form of insanity."[38] In the following year, in an important article published in his *Journal of Mental Science*, Maudsley took a closer look at onanism and did not like what he found. It is in puberty, he argued, a time of psychological and physiological upheavals, that young men and women fall victim to the "vicious habit" of "self-abuse," and lay the groundwork for mental breakdowns then or later. Like other students of this scourge, Maudsley confounded prescription with analysis; he plainly detested what he professed to be describing. The masturbator is a moral pervert whose insanity is disagreeable in the extreme; it makes him morbid, egotistical, self-centered, downright amoral. Should he marry, he will be impotent or cruel and inevitably become insane, haunted by delusions and megalomania. "The sooner he sinks to his degraded rest the better for himself, and the better for the world which is well rid of him."[39]

36. Ibid., 6–7, 16, 23.

37. Ellis, *Studies in the Psychology of Sex*, vol. II, *The Evolution of Modesty, the Phenomena of Sexual Periodicity, Auto-Eroticism* (1900), 199–231.

38. *The Physiology and Pathology of the Mind* (1867), 248. Maudsley defined madness as a kind of regression, as the uncontrollable return of fundamental "instincts, appetites, or passions" (pp. 281–83).

39. "Illustrations of a Variety of Insanity," *Journal of Mental Science*, XIV (July 1868), 155, 152, 155, 153, 161. Maudsley was a Victorian but certainly no prude. One of his case histories concerns a "gentleman" who would energetically denounce the "wicked thing which it was that so many of the most beautiful women should be degraded to gratify the worst lusts of men." His prescription for curing "so much vice and misery" was to eliminate semen, the agent of corruption, from the world, and his way of doing it—one he followed himself and recommended to all others—was to "masturbate every morning into a tumbler of water and then to drink it."

With the passing of time, Maudsley's crusading fervor abated. He continued to argue that masturbation causes insanity, but he now removed the stigma of individual responsibility for this "moral perversion" by noting the possible influence of heredity. Perhaps such a sufferer from a "tainted neurosis" could be cured once "suitable persons" removed the patient from his family.[40] Whatever the prospects, his vice was no longer the masturbator's sole fault.

Maudsley was reluctant to doff the prophet's mantle but his views, once under revision, continued to evolve. In the 1890s, he conceded that the insanity characteristic of adolescents might accompany masturbation without being caused by it. In the sensible if bullying manner that characterized the later Maudsley, he now recommended "the inculcation of a more manly tone of thought and feeling."[41] But his old habits of mind died hard; as late as 1895, Maudsley could reiterate that if masturbatory mania has gone far, there is little the physician can do to save the patient's life. His education had not led to conversion. It proves, if proof be needed, that the craze for eradicating this vice was deep-seated.

Maudsley's last word on masturbation came after skeptics had made themselves heard, and when the passion for ascribing the most degrading sufferings to autoeroticism had passed its peak. As early as 1881, in a strategically placed article on "Onanisme" in the *Dictionnaire encyclopédique des sciences médicales*, Dr. Jules Christian had firmly denied observing any ill effects following upon masturbation; and in 1899, even a zealous worrier like Dr. Hermann Rohleder, who was haunted by the specter of German youth swamped by epidemics of onanism, did not include insanity among its baneful consequences.[42]

Still, the macabre imagination of physicians had shown an impressive staying power. For many of them, after all, beginning with Tissot in mid-eighteenth century, insanity was not the worst that the masturbator could expect: the ultimate penalty was premature death. Benjamin Rush had strategically placed death at the end of his catalogue, and by the 1830s and 1840s, there were others to carry the frightening message. Dr. Léopold Deslandes, whose book on onanism and related sexual abuses

---

That patient was, of course, an inveterate masturbator who, Maudsley proposed, was obsessed with "sexual subjects" and had concocted, "not designedly, but with unconscious hypocrisy an excuse for the vice which wrecked his life" (p. 160). This diagnosis is a splendid mixture of shrewd, empathetic understanding and residual dogmatism.

40. *The Pathology of the Mind* (the first edition of 1879 is the third edition of part II of *The Physiology and Pathology of the Mind*, 1867), 276, 453, 462.

41. *The Pathology of the Mind* (ed. 1895), 399, 407.

42. See Rohleder, *Die Masturbation. Monographie für Ärzte und Erzieher* (1899).

was, like most Continental literature on this theme, soon translated into English, coolly advised the physician to frighten masturbators under his care out of their habit. To tell the onanist, "in three months you will be a dead man," is often very effective: he "trembles and becomes pale: his heart beats quickly, his strength fails. Do not regret it, it is not by encouragement that you will save him from himself." But the stick should be followed by the carrot: "Add however that in a few months he will be a well man, provided he will renounce his bad habits." This procedure, Dr. Deslandes believed, must be followed invariably; in the most intractable cases, in fact, it should be graphically illustrated: when neither frightening books nor the physician's advice proves efficacious, "there is still one resource, which is the sight of an onanist dying."[43] Poisonous vices called for radical antidotes.

For these retailers of anxiety, the masturbator's demise, though often early, was never merciful. At mid-century, in his *Higiene del matrimonio*, the Spanish physician Pedro Felipe Monlau y Roca noted, characteristically, that frequent and inveterate "self-abuse" will produce "phthisis or consumption, aneurysm, palpitations, trembling, convulsions, eclampsia, epilepsy, paralysis, gibbosity or deviations of the spinal column, disturbance of the senses like loss of memory, diminution and even loss of intellectual faculties, idiocy and brutalization." Should the onanist happen to survive, he will face "precarious health, a short life," and "the most shameful impotence."[44] Fleeting, convulsive pleasure—thus went this literature of terror—was followed by irrevocable disgrace, excruciating pain, and untimely death.

In full accord with the bulk of the medical fraternity, indeed reaching back to *Onania*, Dr. Monlau y Roca asserted that the masturbatory scourge was as prevalent among the female as among the male sex, and no less disastrous. Some physicians in fact specialized in the female masturbator or wrote treatises explicitly addressed to that particular audience. One of these, Dr. Samuel Gregory, opened his primer on "self-pollution" for young women like other nineteenth-century writers on touchy subjects: he denounced the "prudish delicacy" that had "covered up the subject" and "seemed shocked at the bare mention of it." Gregory noted that "silence and ignorance have been tried," but had only been "found

43. Deslandes, *Manhood: The Causes of Its Premature Decline* (1835; tr. 1843), 231–32.

44. Monlau y Roca, in a free translation and revision by Dr. Paul Emile Garnier, *Hygiène de la génération. Le Mariage dans ses devoirs, ses rapports et ses effets conjugaux au point de vue légal, hygiénique, physiologique et moral* (1853; 4th ed., 1885), 614.

to favor the evil." The one reasonable course left, he believed, was "to diffuse knowledge," to "let all have light," and to assert, bluntly, that habitual self-abuse virtually guarantees the descent of beautiful and accomplished young ladies into idiocy and death.[45]

Like the expert diagnoses Dr. Gregory quoted and endorsed, his prescriptions characteristically stressed a regimen that avoided, or counteracted, excessive stimulation: he counseled work to combat idleness—that fertile soil in which wicked sensual thoughts flourished—a spare diet, habits of early rising and healthful exercise, the cultivation of the intellect, and an avoidance of tight lacing, licentious novels, featherbeds, and similar luxuries. The "valuable testimonials" that Dr. Gregory appended to his little book—from superintendents of lunatic asylums, Baptist conventions, professors of theology, medical journals, and sympathetic reviewers—do more than certify the purity of the author's intentions; they document how deeply his ideas were embedded in his culture. All those who wrote him testimonials agreed with Dr. Gregory: candor was needed, for the facts themselves were frightening enough. Hypocrisy was the worst policy.

French physicians agreed. In 1876, one specialist, Dr. Thésée Pouillet, published a successful "medical-philosophical essay" on female masturbation, in which he presented an exhaustive, neatly classified account of inducements to the habit which listed (among many others) wealth and poverty, misguided confessors and lascivious statues, unhealthy novels and plays, the husband's impotence, dancing, the sewing machine, and other perils spawned by modern civilization. Pouillet's catalogue of consequences included the expected and added some unexpected calamities such as nymphomania and, worst of all, suicide. Individual temperament, the family, social mores, artistic and intellectual influences, technological innovations—late in the nineteenth century the bicycle was added to the list of tempters to orgasm—were all sources of contamination that needed close watching.[46]

Physicians obsessed with the vice of self-abuse and committed to enlightening the public saw themselves surrounded by passions and inundated by practices they sadly lamented and had little hope of controlling. Returning in 1912 to the field of combat he had first entered in 1889 with a manifesto against masturbation, Dr. Rohleder issued an equally

45. Gregory, *Facts and Important Information for Young Women, on the Subject of Masturbation; with Its Causes, Prevention, and Cure* (1847), 5.

46. Thesée Pouillet, *Essai médico-philosophique sur les formes, les causes, les signes, les conséquences et le traitement de l'onanisme chez la femme* (1876; 2nd, considerably enlarged, ed., 1877), Synoptic Table, 136–37.

pessimistic *Outline of Sexual Pedagogy* in which he once more canvassed
the dimensions of the danger. In this study, the sense of alarm joins a
mania for precision. Rohleder cites a medical colleague in Cologne, Dr.
Meirowsky, to the effect that 71 percent of all German secondary-school
students are onanists, while Russian, German, and Hungarian researchers
had discovered even higher, downright appalling percentages of self-
abuse: one Professor Oskar Berger declared the number of adolescent
masturbators in Germany to be 100 percent, while the "famous American
urologist," one Professor "Joung," reached the same total for America's
youth, male and female alike. On his own account, Dr. Rohleder was
slightly less gloomy and somewhat less exact: according to his "fairly
extensive experience," about nine out of every ten German students, boys
and girls, figured among the masturbators. He frankly conceded that perhaps two-thirds of these had "got away without perils for later life."[47]
But even if some crusaders felt compelled to admit that the sin they
combated left most of the sinners unscathed, they persisted in thinking
it a most disagreeable theme. "Solitary indulgence," as an American
physician, Dr. John Ware, put it in 1850, speaking for the fraternity,
was "a subject most painful to dwell upon; one upon which it is hard
to think, to speak, or to write, without seeming to partake in some measure
of its pollution."[48] Still, when duty called, physicians would swallow their
reserve and set aside their disgust, roll up their sleeves and bravely confront the enemy.

The draconian remedies that nineteenth-century medical men thought
suitable as a cure—or, more modestly, a check—for masturbation demonstrate how seriously they took the solitary vice and how depressed they
were by it. The psychoanalyst René Spitz, who made the most comprehensive survey of prescriptions against masturbation, did not hesitate
to call them sadistic. He observes that the classic eighteenth-century
writers from the author of *Onania* to Tissot and beyond restrained their
aggression against their patients, and it is true that they relied principally
on vigorous exercise, soothing baths, hard mattresses, and sensible diet.[49]
The epigones, who drew heavily on the clinical profiles of their admired
forerunners, did not permit the disparity between diagnosis and prescriptions to survive; they matched the terrorism of their remedies to the
terror that the vice inspired in them. After mid-nineteenth century, rela-

47. Rohleder, *Grundzüge der Sexualpädagogik*, 11–12.

48. John Ware, *Hints to Young Men on the True Relation of the Sexes* (1850), in
Dr. Horatio Robinson Storer, *Is It I? A Book for Every Man* (1867), 65.

49. René A. Spitz, "Authority and Masturbation: Some Remarks on a Bibliographical Investigation," *Psychoanalytic Quarterly*, XXI, 4 (October 1952), 490–527.

tively innocuous cures gave way to a war of nerves of priest against penitent, teacher against pupil, doctor against patient. The new remedies included a formidable armamentarium of mechanical restraints resembling nothing so much as medieval torture instruments and surgical procedures like cauterization of the sexual organs, infibulation, castration, and clitoridectomy. Daniel Gottlob Moritz Schreber, father of the famous paranoid lawyer and judge Daniel Paul Schreber, whose case Sigmund Freud was to analyze in 1910, would strap his children into metal contrivances ostensibly designed to teach them good posture but also, though he did not say so, serviceable to keep them from "self-abuse." It was not until after 1900 that gentler methods, notably persuasion, gradually took the ascendancy once more.

Yet in the half-century of terrorism, there was no unanimity, not even a consensus, among physicians on how to combat self-abuse; again and again, texts of the 1860s and later display the more benign temper of earlier years. E. P. Miller, M.D., "Physician to the Hygienic Institutes and Turkish Baths" in New York City, published in 1867 a *Treatise on the Cause of Exhausted Vitality* that could have appeared some decades before. Like all these reformers, Dr. Miller ritually lamented the ignorance from which the world suffered and which his little book was intended to remedy. His own medical experience and that of others proved to him that persons old and young, male and female, abused their "sexual function," by which he meant they engaged in the usual trio: masturbation, promiscuity, and "matrimonial excesses." And ignorance is particularly damaging because children have erotic feelings without the information essential for their deployment and control. "Children inherit strong sexual desires," Dr. Miller wrote three decades before Freud, "of which they do not know the meaning; and, receiving no instructions with regard to these desires, they either fall spontaneously into evil practices, or learn from impure associates habits which eventually prove their ruin." Dr. Miller's list of ailments awaiting the habitual transgressor is wholly derivative; his lyrical expository style rather more his own: the masturbator, "listless, inattentive, indifferent," finds that "his love of books is lost, history become a blank, the glowing pages of romance charm no more, the poet's spell hath lost its power, music's witchery is dead, the beauties of art are passed unheeded by, the loveliest landscape is but an arid desert."[50]

In view of this cheerless, if poetic prognosis, Dr. Miller's recommenda-

50. *A Treatise on the Cause of Exhausted Vitality; or, Abuses of the Sexual Function* (1867), iii, 79–88, 35, 37, 39.

tions are strikingly gentle. He thinks it eminently useful to teach children the truth about sex and about its abuse; to fill their minds with pure ideas to combat the temptations of vicious ones; to have them read good books, keep decent company, eat wholesome food—and bathe frequently: the physician attached to a Turkish bath was not insensible to the purifying properties of water. Above all, he urged, return to religion and come to Christ, who is, it would seem, the most formidable adversary of sexual abuses the world has ever known. And that is all: Dr. Miller emphatically rejects the more drastic methods he must have seen other physicians apply; he had no use for the cauterizing of sexual parts or for such mechanical contrivances as restraining harnesses.[51]

Many other physicians had use for precisely such devices. Some of the most chilling recommendations were actually carried out; Spitz reports the case, far from unique, of a nervous seven-year-old girl who persisted in masturbating after a series of treatments had been tried, and succeeded in tearing the sutures that tied down her clitoris. All else failing, she was subjected to a clitoridectomy. The little girl stopped masturbating; a few weeks after the operation, making one final attempt, she admitted defeat: "You know there is nothing there now," she said with heart-rending reasonableness, "so of course I could do nothing." This happened in 1894, in Cleveland, Ohio. Let the historian record that the presiding surgeon was Dr. Alvin Eyer.[52]

This horror story is true, and I could recite others. But they represent a relatively small number of irreversible interventions. Far more popular than the surgeon's knife were mechanical modes of restraint: modern chastity belts for girls and ingenious penile rings for boys or straitjackets for both, all designed to keep growing or adolescent sinners from getting at themselves. Manufacturers of medical supplies complied with the demand, and their devices, illustrated in their catalogues, survive as vivid symptoms of masturbatory insanity—on the physicians' part. Dr. Deslandes who, as we have seen, believed in the efficacy of frightening his patients, also recommended watchfulness—only the person who is alone for a time can abuse himself—and "coercive" contrivances, such as tying up the hands to "keep them from the sexual organs," and the feet "so as to keep the thighs separated." He also thought highly of special waistcoats "fastened behind," which forced "the arms to rest on the chest," or a "kind of truss," sturdily constructed, to "preserve the sexual parts from external contact."[53] The impulse to vicious habits, which fearful reformers

51. Ibid., 117, 120, 124-26, 121-22.
52. Spitz, "Authority and Masturbation," 125.
53. Deslandes, *Manhood*, 232-34.

personified as a kind of incubus oppressing the young, was vigilant, persistent, and immensely resourceful; the only way to triumph over it was to overmatch it, trait by trait.

The awesome burden of their self-imposed mission induced troubled physicians to enter the arena of public instruction with marriage manuals and religious ruminations; down to the 1870s and 1880s, indeed, the language of medical discourse was so informal that it is often hard to decide whether a physician is speaking to his colleagues or to laymen. Some of these texts, though, left no doubt. Dr. William Alcott, whose widely read manuals on health were a judicious blend of information and uplift, wrote to forestall Satan, whose emissaries spread unsavory doctrine about sexual relations. To outwit him, to guide the innocent and to rescue the fallen, the physician-counselor will inculcate good habits, prescribe proper food, encourage healthful exercise, provide sexual knowledge, and bring the young to the "practical benevolence of the Gospel."[54] Recognizing to a man that mind and matter were inextricably intertwined in the human animal, these pious physicians thought it only right to minister to the souls of their patients and their readers quite as much as to their bodies. They were convinced that to help the one was to help the other.

Alcott's *Physiology of Marriage*, published in 1855, is an attractive specimen in that mixed genre, the medical-religious text, which had so grateful and loyal a following in bourgeois society down to the last decades of the nineteenth century. In it Satan figures as a remote, somewhat shadowy threat, a foil for the exactions of the Christian life, little more than a metaphor for "the licentious doctrines of Byron."[55] In Dr. Cooke's *Satan in Society*, published some fifteen years later, he seems a more palpable presence. The book is a model of unmitigated gloom, a substantial contribution to the pleasures of viewing society with alarm. All of American life, the author tells his readers, is on the road to perdition; its journey to hell began with careless domestic arrangements, went on to secular public schools and seductive boarding schools—"perfect nurseries of vice"—and culminated in the excesses of the woman's movement. *Satan in Society* is not pure lament; it amounts to a substantial treatise embracing most aspects of sexual conduct: abortion, sexual intercourse during pregnancy or menstruation, polygamy, coitus interruptus (it pronounces against them all); and it includes chapters on the condition of women in non-Christian countries and extensive "psychophysiological" comparisons between women and men. But in two of its

54. William A. Alcott, *The Physiology of Marriage* (1855; ed. 1856), 245.
55. Ibid., 45.

eleven chapters, Cooke tackles masturbation in the male and the female, and in three other chapters touches on it—the matter was much on his mind. His verdict is unhesitant: the act is shameful, criminal, frequent, and fatal. But if he found many reasons to despair, he had one ground for hope—religion. Cooke was by no means inhumane; among the "conjugal aphorisms" with which he concludes his book, there is one that sounds like an invitation to an egalitarian view of erotic excitement: "A husband should never indulge in pleasures which he has not the talent to render reciprocal." But worldly pleasure, even if reciprocal, is not enough to guarantee the happy marriage for whose sake he had written his book: "The only recipe for permanent happiness in wedlock," he says in conclusion, is "Christianity."[56]

This conclusion is symptomatic for its time. The churches naturally took an abiding interest in self-pollution. Dr. Carl Capellmann's famous treatise on pastoral medicine, a Latin analysis done into many languages, including German and English, in the 1870s and still available in a new French version in 1926, addressed the question, he hoped, "in complete accord with the doctrines of the Holy Roman Catholic Church." Retaining the Latin whenever the subject seemed excessively indecent, *Pastoral Medicine* bravely surveyed the insalubrious terrain of sexual misconduct and devoted a substantial section to masturbation, which it pronounced "fearfully common." Like secular writers, Capellmann compiled a familiar list of incitements: gymnastics and joint bathing, to say nothing of "evil-minded domestics" and "effeminate education," or "enervating literature" and "immoral art-representations." The world is a dangerous place, since fallen man is naturally sinful: as Dr. Capellmann emphatically notes, in tune with Dr. Samuel Gregory, idleness—the availability of free-floating mental energy—generates wicked thoughts and with them wicked acts. Marriage was "of course" the best remedy, marriage and the recognition that no priest can conscientiously wink at masturbation in any form, at any time.[57]

As physicians did not hesitate to trench on the terrain of divines and educators, these in turn made themselves welcome in the field of medical counseling and joined doctors in issuing the call to arms. There was Sylvanus Stall, D.D., and there was O. S. Fowler, probably America's best-known "Practical Phrenologist," who, not content with writing tracts on self-improvement and on his particular science, published in 1846 a booklet on *Amativeness*, in which he inveighed against the prev-

56. "A Physician," *Satan in Society*, 62, 91, 409, 412.
57. *Pastoral Medicine* (1866; tr. Rev. William Dassel, 1879), v, 70–73.

alence of sensuality and the "filthy practice" of "SELF-ABUSE." Girls "may be less infected" than boys, and yet "woman, young and modest, is dying by thousands of consumption, of female complaints, of nervous or spinal affections, of general debility, and of other ostensible complaints innumerable, and some of insanity, caused solely by this practice." To add gravity to his charge, Fowler leaned on Dr. Alcott's "weighty" authority.[58] The supportive word of a physician was gold coin to the outsider trying to sound like an insider.

O. S. Fowler, Practical Phrenologist, belonged to a veritable tribe that wrote medicine without a license and cited physicians for its own purposes. Much of the authority that Dr. Alcott could claim rested on the widespread custom of lending mutual support. An instructive instance of this logrolling is the Reverend Mr. Smith H. Platt's little book *Queenly Womanhood*, first published in 1877. Adapting his earlier work, *Princely Manhood. For Males Only*, to the use of women, Platt cited his sources more lavishly and covered his pages with quotations more densely than other tractarians, who were rather more fond of their own voices and more secure in their own judgment. And among the experts to whom Platt appeals is "Dr." O. S. Fowler. That "Dr." Fowler appears once again in Platt's slight anthology, as the source of a cautionary tale about a mother who, seeking to warn her three sons against masturbation, found that she was too late with each of them, though the youngest, when she spoke to him about it, was only ten.[59] Mr. Platt, reading what he wanted to read, promoted Fowler on this sensitive issue because Fowler was in tune with respectable physicians. The nineteenth-century crusade against masturbation was not quite so massive as it appears to be; it is easy to overestimate the number, though not the fervor, of its troops. A good portion of the noise it made consisted of echoes.

Educators joined the campaign early. In the 1780s, reform-minded Continental pedagogues, the celebrated "Philanthropists," had already cautioned their charges, and their charges' parents, against touching what the German language so picturesquely called the "parts of shame"— *Schamteile*: "Nothing is more dangerous," Joachim Heinrich Campe wrote in 1783, "than to stimulate or in any way play with those secret parts of our bodies. Do not merely keep them secret from everyone, but also from yourselves; never touch them except when necessary and handle them most circumspectly and most modestly." Campe's catalogue

58. *Amativeness: Or Evils and Remedies of Excessive and Perverted Sexuality: Including Warning and Advice to the Married and Single* (1846), 12, 13, 15, 16.

59. Platt, *Queenly Womanhood, A Private Treatise: For Females Only, on the Sexual Instinct, as Related to Moral and Christian Life* (1877), 21, 25, 119-20.

of the horrendous effects of disobedience—the yielding to momentary pleasure made habitual—is in perfect consonance with the prognoses of Tissot. And a decade before Campe, the great pedagogue Johann Bernhard Basedow had already stigmatized the "unnatural vices," among which he included masturbation, as disgusting and immoral, as well as harmful: they "ruin all hopes of a happy marriage" but also "fill the imagination with revolting and tormenting pictures" which make it hard to "resist this insanity in the future."[60]

More than a century later, writing against a background of unremitting concern among educators, Charles Richmond Henderson, Professor of Sociology at the University of Chicago, could recall these theorists as well as Rousseau, as models whose "line of educational effort" their modern disciples were "simply taking up" once more. Henderson warned against "quack doctors who become rich by advertising their nostrums after exciting the terror of youth," but he remained convinced that "self-abuse is the cause of disorders when it is frequently repeated and long continued." The tone is far less hysterical than it had been for many decades: even educators could be educated. The minority of sensible physicians who had rejected the very notion that masturbation is a vice or a distinct disease had won a hearing; persistent publicists like Havelock Ellis, who denounced the whole campaign as pernicious nonsense, had secured some favorable response. In 1900, Dr. F. R. Sturgis could dedicate his book *Sexual Debility in Man* to "The SEXUAL CRIPPLES OF THE UNITED STATES, whose infirmities have in part contributed to his support," and inveigh, in telling detail and with sharp words, against "the folly" of the "hysterical denunciations" that still pursued the habitual masturbator.[61]

A decade later psychoanalysts added an ironic twist to the great anxiety now winding down: in a systematic canvass of "*Onanie*" conducted in Vienna under Sigmund Freud's informal chairmanship, several of his colleagues, and Freud himself, found the recent exculpation of masturbation rather excessive. Freud could report that the majority of physicians had persuaded themselves that the act is probably harmless. The pendulum of opinion had swung dramatically; too dramatically for Freud and his followers. It seemed plain to them that habitual masturbation actually damaged the masturbator. It generated feelings of guilt and,

60. Campe: *Kleine Kinderbibliothek*, vol. II (1783), in *Kinderschaukel 1: Ein Lesebuch zur Geschichte der Kindheit in Deutschland, 1745–1860*, ed. Marie-Luise Könneker (1976), 85; Basedow: *Elementarwerk* (1774–76), ed. Theodor Fritzsch, 3 vols. (1909), I, 533.

61. *Education with Reference to Sex, Pathological, Economic and Social Aspects: The Eighth Yearbook of the National Society for the Scientific Study of Education* (1909), Part I, 10; Sturgis, *Sexual Debility in Man* (1900), 9.

with that, disagreeable conflicts, particularly in a culture that condemned the act; it served as insulation against desirable love objects in the real world by throwing the masturbator on his fantasy life; and it raised some risks of inflammation or infection of the sexual parts. Masturbation, as Freud put it in his pungent way, "short-circuited" love. This perception had little in common with the nineteenth-century crusade: psychoanalysis removed masturbation from the nebulous realms of morality, religion, and sheer fantasy and placed it where it belonged, among the realities of sociology, psychology, and physiology.[62] Whatever the spectrum of opinions by 1910, the campaign's energy was spent. It had enjoyed a long run.

The persistent panic over masturbation is far easier to document than to explain. Heavily overdetermined, it was a cultural symptom laden with baffling meanings that reached across nineteenth-century society and down into the buried unconscious core of its most troubling preoccupations. Perhaps the most obvious cause of that panic was ignorance: a learned ignorance far more resistant than a sheer lack of knowledge, for that may always be alleviated by pertinent new information. It was an ignorance derived, rather, from the desire not to know, reinforced by a false physiological model constructed on time-honored theories about the human organism going back to Hippocrates—in short, the worst possible kind of ignorance, armored by defensiveness against correctives. A medical model that confined its network of possible causes within the bounds of nature was, to be sure, far from naive; to attribute insanity to autoeroticism was a scientific advance over attributing it to evil spirits.[63] To masturbate—so ran the theory—is to expend energy; while this is obviously true of males, it was thought to hold true for females as well, whether women had a kind of ejaculation, as many physicians believed, or not. Certainly both sexes were seized with fatigue, not to say lassitude, after masturbating, as though they had made an effort, paid out a quantum of energy. It seemed only reasonable to deduce that the young must stay "pure," which is to say celibate, that they must husband their bodily supplies for the single task for which God had implanted the sexual instinct in man: the procreation of children within the sacred precincts of wedlock.

Tissot, that honored prophet, provided suitable guidance to the bourgeois century in this matter as in so much else. "Our bodies are steadily

---

62. *Protokolle der Wiener Psychoanalytischen Vereinigung*, ed. Herman Nunberg and Ernst Federn, vol. II, *1908–1910* (1977), 502–28.

63. See Hare, "Masturbatory Insanity," 11.

losing," he wrote in his book on onanism, "and if we could not repair our losses, we would soon fall into a mortal weakness." The "fabric of our machine" is so constituted that essential body humors like milk or blood need to be continually restored. And among these, the "seminal liquor" is particularly precious: "Physicians of all ages have unanimously believed that the loss of one ounce of that humor is more weakening than that of forty ounces of blood." He was forcing the medical consensus of the past, but there were many who believed him. Amiel for one found Tissot's notion irresistible; he quoted—or rather misquoted—him to the effect that a single seminal emission is the equivalent of four ounces of blood.[64] Without being quite so specific, many nineteenth-century physicians like Dr. William Acton agreed that emissions were the source of serious, sometimes irreparable physical deficits.

No less remarkable than this rescue of an ancient medical superstition into the nineteenth century, and further support for learned ignorance, was the ease with which physicians allowed themselves to make casual imputations on the strength of the most flimsy evidence, or to draw sweeping conclusions from a handful of instances. Benjamin Rush compounded his appalling profile of the masturbator from four cases he had seen in the space of four years. It is true that his catalogue of symptoms antedates by two decades or more the development of social statistics and their epoch-making application to medicine. But good sense alone should have told him that his materials were glaringly inadequate for any clinical picture, no matter how tentative, especially since Rush had no way of showing the pathology he had observed to be the necessary consequence of masturbation. Yet Henry Maudsley, sounding almost exactly like Benjamin Rush, if rather angrier, analyzed "self-abuse" with the same airy confidence half a century later, after the logic of medical inquiry and the uses of statistics for verification had been publicly and intensively studied for twenty-five years or more. If this sort of learned ignorance was wholly, or almost wholly, invincible, that must have been because it was unconsciously cultivated. Henry Maudsley was not an ignorant man.

The application of the economic principle to the expenditures of sexual energy demanded the inference that fornication outside marriage or "excessive" sexual indulgence within it must be as debilitating to the bodily household as masturbation. A number of crusaders were only too eager to draw this conclusion. Some played with numbers: most advised

64. Tissot, *De l'onanisme*, xiv; Amiel, June 13, 1841, *Journal intime*, I, 193.

married couples to show prudent regard for their age, the climate, and the calendar. "In winter time," Dr. Monlau y Roca wrote, paying a physician's tribute to popular wisdom, "and in all months without 'r,' great discretion in sexual relations is proper." Others agreed. "Excessive sexual indulgence," wrote O. S. Fowler, "injures the health" in a variety of ways; it exhausts the body, enfeebles the mind, impairs digestion and circulation, deranges the brain and the nervous system, and engenders depravity in all its forms. But while the perpetrators of "licentiousness" are "eaten up" with "sores and ulcers, nauseating and loathsome beyond description," and while "MATRIMONIAL EXCESS" destroys the health of the wife, to say nothing of the husband's respect for her, none of this can compare with the horrors brought on by self-abuse: the "greatest ruin" was clearly generated by "PRIVATE FORNICATION—TEN TO ONE!"[65] Fowler was something of an intellectual charlatan, but other polemicists, even those far less inclined than he to capitalize on the public's anxieties, insisted that sexual wastefulness was only too real, and very menacing. They carefully established distinctions and hierarchies among its various forms, and agreed among themselves that "self-pollution" was more fateful than fornication which, in turn, had more deleterious effects than marital lust.

Masturbation was not merely the most consequential of sexual vices; it was also the most immoral. And this, in the final analysis, was the heart of the case. With a mere handful of exceptions, physicians and those who followed their lead could not overcome the confusion that the author of *Onania* had introduced: masturbation was more than a medical, it was an ethical and a religious problem. Hence it ranked with syphilis and alcoholism as a malady that nineteenth-century physicians at once treated and called bad names. And while biology and geology, philology and history were fanning strong secular winds, for every striking conversion to materialism caused by a reading of Darwin, there was a quiet return to piety caused by less publicized agents of persuasion. Doubtless, in the nineteenth century pious sufferers called the doctor more quickly and with less conflict than their pious ancestors had done before them, but priesthoods retained ample supplies of professional, and influential, practitioners. The mood pervading the age—uncertainty in the face of change—put morality at a premium and gave the moralist incomparable scope. Whatever its results, there were immense quantities of earnest ethical inquiry, of troubled ethical debate, in the bourgeois century. Physicians

65. Garnier, *Mariage*, 235; Fowler, *Amativeness*, 41, 43, 47.

delivering homilies to their patients and to the world at large were merely joining in the growing chorus of experts who felt called upon, and competent, to improve the public morals.

Still, medical moralizing had its own special quality. The didacticism, the hectoring, the verbal sadism that physicians loosed against their patients on the subject of self-abuse or self-pollution—the very names capsule sermons—were very obtrusive, particularly since these physician-philosophers were, after all, professional men claiming to be scientists and healers, callings to which the role of preacher was, even then, thought to be particularly inappropriate. The notion that scientific truth directly fosters moral goodness—a legacy of gifted but in this respect misguided amateurs of science like Diderot and Goethe—was receding in the nineteenth century before positivistic procedures which sharply differentiated facts from values. Few scientists doubted that knowledge is superior to ignorance and candor to concealment, and to this degree the fearless pursuit of scientific knowledge had moral implications. But the crusaders against masturbation were arguing something very different: here was a sinful affliction that struck simultaneously at the physical and the moral fiber of the sufferer and, in the most unsavory way, demoralized not only him but his spouse as well and, by extension, his society. Hence the masturbator needed, even more than a cure, a lecture. The terroristic prophecies, the ingenious mechanical devices and barbarous operations that doctors inflicted on masturbators, look almost like acts of revenge. In a century in which the sciences were triumphantly emancipating themselves from philosophy and extremely self-conscious about their methods, this was notably bad science.

But the Jeremiahs of masturbation were rarely men of ill-will, almost never salesmen of quack remedies; often they were intelligent and conscientious healers. It follows that the bad science they practiced was fueled, at the deepest level, by anxiety. And it seems that physicians were prey, in the bourgeois century, to two kinds of anxieties: those they experienced as physicians, and those they soaked up from their environment and gave back to society in distilled form.

Nineteenth-century physicians were anxious in part because for decades they often found themselves helpless before diseases and epidemics and, with notable exceptions, were reluctant to resign themselves to their impotence. "More than any other class," O. S. Fowler wrote in the 1840s, physicians "require that liberality of views, that openness of conviction which shall allow them to keep up with the times, and adopt all improvements in the healing art that may be made. No other art is equally imperfect, or more imperiously demands reform and advancement."[66] Dimly, sometimes pointedly, sensing their futility, doctors found themselves obliged to erect an authoritative facade, strikingly at variance with their real sense of themselves. The honest physician knew far better than his middle-class patients that he was only too often merely a privileged and powerless spectator by the bedside.

An age much visited by debilitating, chronic complaints and occasionally devastated by frightful epidemics elevated the prospect of illness and early death into an absorbing preoccupation. In the intimate correspondence and diaries of the nineteenth-century middle-class health is, with the weather, the most expectable of topics; the current condition of the writer and her family, the pathetic duels between faith and doubt in the latest medicine, occupy more space and consume more emotion in these writings than anything else. They are punctuated with declarations of confidence in doctors or, more usually, of abiding distrust. In 1850, as Louisa May Alcott noted in her diary later, her family had been visited by smallpox. "We girls had it lightly, but Father and Mother were very ill, and we had a curious time of exile, danger, and trouble. No doctors, and all got well"—a somewhat cryptic conclusion intimating that perhaps, had the Alcotts had doctors, all might not have recovered.

This skepticism was widespread. Looking back at his long life in 1888, James Hopkinson, that largely self-educated English cabinet-maker, confided in his autobiography that he had high confidence in medical herbalists but very little in physicians: "I have proved beyond a doubt that nature is no respector of persons and that she only requires to be assisted. And that she takes no more notice of a *Latin* Prescription than if it was given in plain English. And as for diplomas I have known the so called Quacks cure cases of disease, where men with diplomas have utterly failed." In his earnest, chapel-going manner, he called upon his readers to "rise above the trammels that surround them" and study "the healing virtues of the Herbs & roots & Bark, which an Allmighty hand has so lavishly spread in every hedge row and in every bank." He was downright cynical about licensed physicians: "During my life many cases of wrong treatment and incapacity on the part of Doctors have come to my knowledge. But however incompetent they may be they are safe under the sanction of their diplomas." What makes these sardonic observations particularly powerful is that while Hopkinson's trust in

66. *Memory and Intellectual Improvement Applied to Self-Education and Juvenile Instruction* (ca. 1845; 25th improved ed., 1846), 219.

herbalists betrays a certain credulity, his hits at physicians were, though at this point out of date, still uncomfortably close to the mark. A little earlier, in May 1885, shortly after suffering a miscarriage, Eleanor Rogers had said much the same thing more laconically. "I have more faith in you than fifty Doctors," she told her sisters, "so tell me what to do and I'll try and do it."[67] It was a familiar cry for help, sounded, regularly and fervently, by educated and open-minded bourgeois.

In an age of professionalization and an increasing unwillingness to practice pious resignation under the blows of fate, middle-class patients seem to have felt entitled to make urgent, often unreasonable demands on their physicians, who could neither realize their fantasies nor dispel them. Among the urban poor and among peasants, resistance to medical interventions was almost second nature, rooted in potent superstitions, the fear of expense, or pious fatalism. But good bourgeois who took pride in their receptivity to science could be almost as primitive as this. The unmeasured hopes and fears of middle-class sufferers were often a none-too-subtle kind of transference. They invested the physician with all the attributes of a caring, all-knowing father, almost a manufactured deity, only to be disappointed over and over again. With them, expectations of the physician's omnipotence alternated with contempt for his impotence, and they irrationally idolized or irrationally execrated him.

This pervasive distrust of the medical profession is not without irony: among the physicians who lowered public confidence were learned and responsible healers who told their patients not to expect miracles. No wonder that many thousands took the casual advice of friends, dosed themselves with patent medicines, or threw themselves at quack healers: the fear of death, especially when it is mixed with hope for survival, wonderfully sharpens man's always keen gift for self-deception. Moreover, the informal technology of complaint—the cheap newspaper, rapid mail service, family visits—vastly improved after the 1830s; it spread criticism of the medical profession, and advertisements of quacks, with sovereign impartiality. There was much to complain about: down to mid-century, and somewhat beyond that, physicians continued to attack their patients' bodies with exhausting bleedings and debilitating purges, infected them on the operating table or in the hospital bed, and could do little as cholera swept through crowded cities and claimed its quota of victims. The vogue of what was called, without irony, "heroic medicine"

67. Alcott: Ednah D. Cheney, *Louisa May Alcott* (1889), 60; James Hopkinson: *Victorian Cabinet Maker: The Memoirs of James Hopkinson, 1819–1894*, ed. Jocelyne Baty Goodman (1968), 70; Rogers: May 28, 1885, box 53, SF. See above, pp. 227–29.

held sway until the 1860s. In this licensed sadism, it was the patient who
was the hero, all too often celebrated posthumously, after the doctor had
done his work. Recalling the years around 1835 in his outspoken autobiography, the distinguished gynecologist J. Marion Sims described the
medicine of his day as "heroic: it was murderous."[68] The most devoted
adherents of homeopathy or other rivals to professional medicine could
not have put it any more forcefully.

All this denigration, some of which was self-denigration, would have
been enough to generate anxiety among the doctors, especially among
the prudent and diligent of the species. But the grounds for uneasiness
were more complicated and more dramatic than this. For all the gratifying
advances that physicians had registered in the age of the Enlightenment,
it is arguable that in the three-quarters of a century between the accession of Queen Victoria and the outbreak of the first World War,
medicine changed more radically than it had in all its previous history.
Some of the doctors' more deplorable failures were necessary prerequi-
sites, stages on the path to progress. This was the century that made
medicine modern; the old sardonic conundrum as to whether it was safer
for the sick to entrust themselves to a physician or to avoid him could
now be resolved, with increasing plausibility, in favor of the physician.

Signs of the new medicine were highly visible everywhere, reassuring
at the least, almost miraculous at best. By the 1870s extended, often
frustrating researches were finally producing the kind of dramatic results
that the public could appreciate, anecdotes could capture, and statistics
could prove. Gradually the doctor, long the butt of hostile jokes, became
a folk-hero of bourgeois culture. True, skepticism survived into the 1880s
and beyond; the human body was too complicated a machine, life still
too precarious, to silence all denigrators of the medical profession. But
the cherished figure of the wise, bearded family physician paternally
feeling a fluttering pulse and making onerous house calls late at night,
or that of the cool, white-coated surgeon saving a life with his expert
interventions were fantasies growing increasingly plausible in the last
decades of the nineteenth century, and based only in part on pious hopes
or magical thinking.

It was precisely this far-reaching and often unpredictable revolution
in the world of medicine, its triumphs even more than its disasters, that
generated disturbing, though often barely visible, psychological conflicts
within its practitioners. As we know from Durkheim and Freud, and as

68. Sims, *The Story of My Life* (1884), 150.

the doctors confirmed in their own lives, good news can be as unsettling as bad. Their besetting anxieties had vast public arenas in which to play themselves out: international medical education, the new teaching hospitals, university clinics, professional meetings, and learned periodicals. The nineteenth-century physician's anxiety, then, was more than the uneasiness of the fool compelled to pose as a sage; it was, rather, the apprehensiveness of the embattled practitioner under immense pressure from his public and his profession at the same time, and trembling on the verge of great conquests. The swings in the moods of physicians express the cost of uncertainty: the touching accesses of great expectations in the midst of bouts with fatalism, of faith in innovation contending against guild conservatism. It is no accident that once the medical profession had safely monopolized the world of healing, settled in with its new associations, schools, and procedures, and regained a solid portion of public confidence at last, it could let up on its campaign against masturbation. Their own potency secure, demonstrated, and gratefully acknowledged, doctors could relax about the potency of others.

But the anxiety which drove physicians into their anti-onanism crusade in the nineteenth century was not simply a response to purely professional pressures. Doctors could not escape their culture. They were husbands and fathers, worried like other bourgeois about the precarious sanctity of their homes and the threatened innocence of their children. They belonged, or, rather more nerve-wracking, aspired, to select social circles and exclusive clubs and hoped to fortify, or to secure, the status of a gentleman. Hence they did not find it prudent to challenge the prevailing, increasingly defensive moral rhetoric of their society. Their susceptibility to fads like the anti-masturbation craze was one of the marks of their insecurity; the faddist is not so much unwilling as unable to defy, let alone correct, current prejudices. In important respects, physicians of the nineteenth century did not rise above common humanity; they felt themselves dependent on the good will of their fellows and their society. As the famous German medical publicist and administrator Christoph Wilhelm Hufeland put it as early as 1836, "For no one is public opinion so important as for the physician. He is, in the essential meaning of the term, *the man of the people*."[69] If a medical writer chose to diverge from the popular and professional consensus on masturbation, he would at most add one wax figure to the well-visited

69. Edith Heischkel-Artelt, "Die Welt des praktischen Arztes," in *Der Arzt und der Kranke in der Gesellschaft des 19. Jahrhunderts*, ed. Walter Artelt and Walter Rüegg (1967), 14.

chamber of horrors. Arrogant and authoritative as they appeared, nineteenth-century physicians were indeed men of the people, unconsciously—and at times consciously—trembling before their verdict.

Some of the anxieties that medical men imposed on their patients were therefore anxieties they had first absorbed from those who consulted them: physicians and patients were nervous together. Professional healers articulated their patients' inchoate fears in language that, as it were, codified them for their time. And yoked to these fears, though not so ostentatiously exhibited, were the hopes of the age. In the nineteenth century, sexuality was on the agenda, particularly for the middle classes; traditions of respectability were on the defensive. People had good reason to expect that physicians would be in the forefront of discovery and reevaluation. With their grasp on professional mysteries, their insights into the secrets of the body, their possession of intimate confidences, doctors were peculiarly called to alleviate sufferings associated with respectable sexual conduct, and to pronounce on the physiological and psychological consequences of irresistible sexual habits. It seemed like a heavy but not unreasonable burden to impose on healers who were, after all, in addition to being ordinary bourgeois, very special individuals.

All this makes doctors exceptionally valuable witnesses to the fantasies of their culture. Derisive twentieth-century commentators have made much of the English colloquialism for having an orgasm—"to spend"—and argued that a high-capitalist culture must naturally regard seminal emissions as a loss and must naturally speak of sexual gratification as though it were a financial transaction. But this rather misses the point. Not only was the idea very old, antedating capitalism by two thousand years and more, but also such language was far from universal across the map of bourgeois culture. What made physicians, in company with their patients, so apprehensive about masturbation in the nineteenth century was that it seemed a pointless and prodigal waste of limited and valuable resources leading, figuratively and often literally, to impotence. It constituted a loss of mastery over the world and oneself. The campaign to eradicate self-abuse was a response to that danger: a way of conserving strength and maintaining control, both highly cherished and maddeningly elusive goals in the nineteenth century. Thus the argument that "self-pollution" was an irresponsible, indeed pernicious, abuse of man's semen and woman's sexual energies was a desperate and in the long run futile attempt to hold on to traditional ways in the face of revolutionary moral possibilities. The demographic evidence is irrefutable: desire won out over duty. But this victory proved Pyrrhic, for it produced a frantic campaign to disseminate sexual information, a symptom far more than a solution.

3. The Flight into Knowledge

The literature on sexual enlightenment flourished in the late nineteenth century as it never had before. It must have eased the trials of thousands of readers, but it is more enlightening about its culture than it is about sexuality, about the vitality of bourgeois repressions now under scattered fire, and about preoccupations that have little to do with sex directly. The genre embraced two seemingly quite disparate types of publication: the philosophical, sociological, and medical treatises addressed to experts, and the exemplary, popular tracts addressed to parents. The first sought to establish the case for enlightenment, the second proposed specific models for procuring it. Both shared a pervasive worry. All insisted, some in so many words, that there was an emergency, and that it was acute. While they conceded that ignorance and misinformation about sex had by no means originated in the bourgeois century, they described their concern about both as virtually unprecedented and insisted on knowledge as the necessary prerequisite to salvation.[70] The speeches of the enlighteners, like their pamphlets, forecast impending disaster; they are shouts of warning and calls to action. "A policy of concealment, silence, ignorance, and quackery," Charles Richmond Henderson wrote in 1909, "has borne its monstrous brood of disease, misery, and moral degradation. A false modesty is guilty of much of this giant wrong."[71] His tone is typical.

Professor Henderson's monition prefaced a substantial and ambitious survey of sex education, of current error and paths to correct pedagogy, enriched with cross-national comparisons. It was designed to serve as the basis for debate at the Chicago meetings of the National Society for the Scientific Study of Education. This, too, was typical: by the first years of the twentieth century, the interest in broadcasting information about sexuality had become intense. It was an international affair, complete with international congresses to exchange information; these gatherings markedly heightened the delegates' sense of mission and provided them with useful feelings of inferiority, or superiority, toward educators

70. William T. Foster, "The Social Emergency," address to the *Sex Education Sessions of the Fourth International Congress on School Hygiene and of the Annual Meeting of the [American] Federation [for Sex Hygiene]* (1913), 45–54 [henceforth, *Proceedings, AFSH*]; Dr. Hugh Cabot, "Education versus Punishment as a Remedy for Social Evils," ibid., 35.

71. *Education with Reference to Sex*, Part I, 7.

in other countries.[72] There was a Society of Sanitary and Moral Prophylaxis in the United States; there was a White Cross Society, founded to advocate the cause of sexual purity, in Great Britain; there was a Society for Fighting Venereal Disease in Germany. In France, Senator René Bérenger, known jocularly as "Père la Pudeur," founded a League against License in the Streets. There were a score of societies with similar names, leading similar crusades, in these and other countries, all earnestly committed to combat ignorance in the name of decency. It was as though concerned and proper professional men and women wanted to make up in a decade what they deplored as the neglect of millennia. The flight from ignorance became a flight into knowledge.

The proceedings of the congresses inevitably bear a strong family resemblance. The speakers are alert to the novelty of their work, proud of the intensity of their worry, and harassed by the need to act with dispatch. The American Federation for Sex Hygiene, to take one of the most active agents of alarm, was founded in 1910. It was an umbrella organization covering twenty-seven constituent societies with over six thousand members, some a little somnolent but most vigorous and excited. It called conferences and distributed literature. In 1913, it held its meetings at Buffalo, as part of the Fourth International Congress of School Hygiene, and its proceedings sum up the underlying impulses, as well as the manifest aims, of the campaign for the dissemination of carnal knowledge. Charles W. Eliot, President of the Federation and President Emeritus of Harvard (these associations were always generously endowed with educators), opened his address by observing that "during my somewhat long, active life I have never seen such a change of public opinion among thoughtful people as has taken place among them within the last ten years on the subject of sex hygiene." For centuries, there had been an almost universal "policy of silence on all the functions and relations of sex, whether normal or morbid." The silence had now been broken. Other speakers agreed with Dr. Eliot and descried a "new interest in sex hygiene." Dr. Thomas M. Balliet, Dean of the School of Pedagogy at New York University, thought that "the necessity of sex education in some form in the case of the young as well as in the case of adults has become, within the last half dozen years, very generally recognized." But recognition had not brought action in its train. Worried enlighteners epitomized prevailing pedagogy in sexual matters with three words:

72. See, for one instance among many, Dr. Laura Satterthwaite, "The Great Need for the Moral Crusade," an address to the National Purity Congress of 1895, in *The National Purity Congress: Its Papers, Addresses, Portraits*, ed. Aaron M. Powell (1896), 58–64.

silence, evasions, lies. Dr. Hugh Cabot, a prominent urinary surgeon, told the meeting that boys got "no systematic training or instruction in the nature of their sexual make-up," and girls got "even less information" than boys, so that most of them had "literally no knowledge of their sexual life, not even of their relation to the function of child bearing." The attitude of parents and teachers to children "has been 'Don't ask.' If they persisted in asking we lied to them, which, of course, constituted a beautiful basis for the teaching of truth."[73] All this, the delegates thought, was old. What struck them as new was that perceptive physicians and pedagogues had finally come to see such failures for what they were, and to understand at the same time that society could no longer afford to make a mystery of the facts of life.

For the disseminators of sex education, the reality, in the United States and in Europe, was manifest: any attempt to keep sexuality a secret from children must fail, and had always failed. Whether they had read Sigmund Freud or not—and most of them had not—sex educators shared Freud's conviction that the sexual curiosity of children is so vigorous and so ubiquitous that it is almost as exigent as an inborn drive. Dr. Cabot spoke for many when he said, bluntly, that it was a mistake to treat children as innocent or ignorant: "There is no such condition as innocence in these children. Let us not start with that assumption. Not one percent of them are ignorant. The question is whether they shall have what they can pick up, or whether they shall have what we can give them."[74]

A decade earlier, the Reverend Edward Lyttelton, headmaster of Eton College, had said the same thing in his polite, troubled *Training of the Young in Laws of Sex*. His previous published work had included studies in the Sermon on the Mount, but, as he observed in the preface, he had felt moved to enter the field of sex education because "the need for some such suggestions as are here ventured is becoming more widely felt each year." It was, he acknowledged, a difficult field, for while the "dangers of speaking are patent to the most superficial reflection, the far greater dangers of reticence are not to be understood without prolonged observation and much thought." Reserve was the real enemy; the most intractable impediment to imparting sound information to growing children was "the shyness of parents, especially of fathers." But ignorance was ruinous in private life: "It is true that good-heartedness, love, and a *felix*

73. Eliot, "Public Opinion and Sex Hygiene," *Proceedings*, AFSH, 13, 16; Balliet, "Points of Attack in Sex Education," ibid., 25; Cabot, "Education versus Punishment," ibid., 36–37.
74. "General Discussion," ibid., 102.

temperamentum will carry many safely through these perils. But still there is a huge amount of woeful and preventable waste of married happiness, due to debased thought and ignorance, which is the direct result of the prevailing reticence on sexual questions." The sexual curiosity of children would break through all barriers; "though to a less extent than formerly," Lyttelton thought, a "vast majority of the young of both sexes are left to gather the knowledge of sexual laws in a haphazard way, either from companions or from books, or from observation of the animal world." Girls, he suggested—a headmaster of Eton could, perhaps, suggest nothing else—needed sexual instruction less than did boys. But they too ought not to be left ignorant. "Should not something be said when the time of possible matrimony is at hand," he asked, "to prevent a young woman from surrendering herself to a husband in ignorance of the full meaning of marriage?"[75]

A year after Lyttelton's book was published, Dr. Friedrich Siebert produced his philosophical guide—*Wegweiser*—to sexual morality and sexual hygiene. Sounding much like Dr. Cabot—sounding, in fact, much like every other authority in this field—Dr. Siebert found "contemporary society" sadly wanting in honesty: "Everything that reminds one of sexual life is kept secret, hushed up, as in a family a memory is buried, the memory of an event of which one would rather not speak, of which one would rather not be reminded. Only in the most extreme emergency do people come to speak of the union of man and wife."[76] Whether German, French, or American, most authors of tracts on sex education were angry at their society and sarcastic at its expense; the earnest expostulations of Edward Lyttelton are exceptional in their gentleness. Yet their arguments are compromised by a pervasive inconsistency: these calls for frankness are reticent; condemning euphemisms, they use little else. Most of this literature evades embarrassing and delicate topics in the most effective way imaginable: by purporting to address them. It is, in the main, a compromise between the concealment it condemns and the candor it professes, with candor more often than not the casualty.

The hesitations of the reformers about their mission often overwhelmed them. The great majority held their meetings and wrote their books to prevent, or contain, social evils rather than chart the way to private pleasures. While a handful of romantic rebels like Paolo Mantegazza or Havelock Ellis proclaimed sensuality to be a divine endowment, bestowed on humanity to be frankly enjoyed, most writers on sex were scarcely

75. Lyttelton, *Training of the Young in Laws of Sex* (1900), vii, 104, 14–15, 3, 65.
76. *Sexuelle Moral und Sexuelle Hygiene*, Preface (n.p.), 35, 62.

praising the erotic life. Few were even cheerful. They extolled purity and excoriated lust. And their anxiety is understandable, for their perception of the desperate necessity for sexual enlightenment generated conflicts between conventional reticence and necessary candor that at times rose to consciousness. They wrote about sex as a duty, with barely masked embarrassment.

Only rarely, then, did sexual enlighteners write to increase the sum of erotic enjoyment. The literature they produced did not work as pornography for those who did not read pornography; it was too anxious for that. Nothing, in fact, made them more nervous than the charge, actual or imagined, that their publications might be a temptation to sensuality; usually they tried to blunt this accusation by confronting it in their prefaces and by acquitting themselves of any intention to abet lust in any way. Lyttelton, who explicitly includes marital happiness among the desirable consequences of acquiring dependable carnal knowledge, spoke for a minority, and in any event his conception of such happiness would have seemed tepid, timid, in short wholly inadequate, to the happiest of Dr. Mosher's respondents. Even he was less concerned with fostering bliss than with preventing misery. Like most of his fellow authors, Lyttelton was a devout Christian, intent on finding an acceptable way of making physical functions consistent with spiritual purity. There were unbelievers among the sexual reformers; Dr. Siebert, for one, was a German chauvinist inclined to the *völkische* ideology of blood and soil, and critical of the Christian dispensation for preaching abstinence and fostering hypocrisy.[77] Even Lyttelton found it tactically useful to separate his pedagogical proposals from the Anglican doctrine he professed, for he wished to appeal, as he ingenuously put it, to "a wider public than could be expected to understand or agree with any one presentment of Christianity."[78]

Among the most indefatigable of the divines laboring in the vineyard of sexual enlightenment was the prolific Sylvanus Stall, whose didactic productions—*What a Young Boy Ought to Know, What a Young Man Ought to Know, What a Young Husband Ought to Know*, and so forth— were vouched for by a roster of "Eminent Men and Women." No whisper of suspicion that he was writing to excite sensual feelings could reach a Doctor of Divinity who had bishops and philanthropists, religious pamphleteers and temperance crusaders, Edward W. Bok (the editor of the *Ladies' Home Journal*) and Anthony Comstock (America's scourge of pornographers and abortionists) testifying to the spotlessness of his inten-

77. Siebert, *Sexuelle Moral*, 36–39, 95.
78. *Training of the Young*, 97n.

tions and the refinement of his execution. Comstock's endorsement, as publisher and author must have been aware, was exceptionally gratifying. Clearly, fundamentalists were no less anxious to repair the ravages of sexual ignorance than were divines with a classical education or pedagogues with scientific training. "I am deeply impressed," Comstock wrote, "with the necessity for instructing the boys of the day," and he was just as impressed with Stall's gift for presenting "delicate subjects" in "such a way as to lift the mind and thoughts upon a high and lofty plane." Like social improvers of other persuasions, Comstock thought that the regulation of sexual life had a direct bearing on the health of the body politic: "There is a great demand for this book, and I hope it may be blessed to the elevation of the thoughts and hearts of the boys of this nation, and to the bringing in of a better and higher social condition."[79] On the high level of public anxiety all parties of sexual enlighteners could meet.

Dr. Stall's books about what young boys and men should know formed part of a series called "Self and Sex." He was in charge of instructing the men. The women were instructed by women, principally by Mary Wood-Allen, M.D., Superintendent of the Purity Department and Lecturer of the National Woman's Christian Temperance Union, wife and mother, quite as pious and as productive as her male counterpart and occasional collaborator. She wrote, among many didactic texts, *What a Young Girl Ought to Know* and *What a Young Woman Ought to Know*. The religious intention of her writings disarmed all skepticism; precisely like Stall's in this and most other ways, they sported highly visible endorsements by faultless celebrities and enthusiastic notices from clerical journals. The purpose of Dr. Wood-Allen's books, like that of Dr. Stall's, was to preserve purity, which is to say, to prevent pollution. The pessimism of this literature about human nature is almost unrelieved. In this critical respect, it mirrors the grave ruminations with which educators entertained and alarmed one another at their conclaves. When vice and virtue clash, virtue unaided will surrender the field to its gloating adversary. A similar gloom shadows the pocket-sized tracts designed for parents. Left on his own, the child all too eagerly listens to evil counsel, imitates wicked actions, believes criminal stories, and falls into deadly sin. To postpone enlightenment is to invite perdition: "I believe it to be a mistake," Dr. Wood-Allen said in *Teaching Truth*, to put off the inquiring child with " 'I will tell you when you are old enough to understand.' This answer but whets his curiosity and induces him to seek fuller infor-

79. Among the "Commendations . . . From . . . Eminent Men and Women," a gathering of one-page tributes to Dr. Stall's book, with a portrait on each page. Sylvanus Stall, *What a Young Boy Ought to Know* (1897), n.p.

mation from any available source, and he often receives it from sources that leave an indelible impress of evil on his innocent soul." She concludes on a note of triumphant alarm, unconsciously enforcing her point with an erotic metaphor: "I would rather tell a child the truth a year before it is really necessary, than to postpone it until five minutes after some one else has sown tares of evil thought in the virgin soil."[80]

Sigmund Freud intensely disliked this kind of equivocation. "J'appelle un chat un chat," he wrote, not without some pride, in the account of the Dora case he published in 1905.[81] But most other writers in those days called a cat by some other name. The pamphlets written directly for parents, pointed little stories or cunning dialogues designed as models for the solemn conversations that fathers and mothers ought to have with their children about the mysteries of human reproduction, carried this inconsistency into the general culture. The humorous characterization of sexual enlightenment as talk about "the birds and the bees" is solidly grounded in the literature of the late nineteenth and early twentieth centuries. Scores of writers, with an evident sense of relief that such comparisons were available, drew heavily on analogies with flowers and birds and domestic animals: "In some quiet hour when the little one, tired of play, comes to the mother's side to enter into confidential intercourse with her, or to beg for a story"—thus Mary Wood-Allen, in her *Teaching Truth*—"let her take advantage of the quiet, receptive state of his mind to talk with him. Let us imagine that she has gathered a few morning-glories, and, showing the child the bright-hued flower-cup, says: 'Would you like to hear the story of Mr. and Mrs. Morning Glory and their children?' "[82] Lyttelton is more sophisticated, less cloying than this, but he too takes refuge in evasion. Here is his suggestion of how to explain sexual intercourse, in its entirety: "On reaching the point where the beginning of conception in the mother is explained, the parent can perfectly well add that the seed of life is entrusted by God to the father in a very wonderful way, and that after marriage he is allowed to give it to his wife, this being on his part an act of the love which first made him marry her." Then comes the expected oblique description of how the sexes differ, and the opportunity for a caution, irresistible and not resisted:

80. Wood-Allen, *Teaching Truth* (1892), 7.

81. "Bruchstück einer Hysterie-Analyse" (1905), *St.A.*, VI, 123; "Fragment of an Analysis of a Case of Hysteria," *S.E.*, VII, 48.

82. *Teaching Truth*, 10–12. Gordon Hart [pseud.], *Woman and the Race* (1907), quotes this "sweet story" in its entirety as a model of how to teach truth to children (pp. 31–32).

"Seldom, I should fancy very seldom, would more than that be required, in the case of girl children. The only difference in the case of boys would be that quite simply and quite delicately use should so far be made of the innate instinct as to indicate with distinctness what portion of his body will have the propagation of life entrusted to it as its natural function; and, based on this instruction, an impressive and much needed warning may be given against misuse."[83] Apparently no one had told Lyttelton that girls masturbate as well as boys; nor had it occurred to him to question the fear of masturbation as the sure road to sickness and early death. Yet he ranks among the sensible, well-informed spirits of his age.

The child, Dr. Wood-Allen once said, is "an animated interrogation point."[84] But the truth that she and other reforming publicists wanted to plant in the virgin soil of his mind was pathetically incomplete. Normally, their brochures begin with a guarded account of gestation: the child is bewildered by the appearance of a little sibling, and the mother takes this opportunity to explain where, and how, the baby grew. This exposition leads into an account of the bodily parts of men and women which omits all of the detail that an observant child could notice for himself. In these favored genteel scenarios, such approved enlightenment moves children to embrace their mothers with fond tears; discovering that they too have lain for nine months in "that wonderful little chamber which is in the mother's body," they love that mother even more.[85] There is no talk or, with rare exceptions, veiled talk about how baby got into that wonderful little chamber. *The Human Flower* by "Ellis Ethelmer," which contains the cozy image of the wonderful chamber, advertises itself in the subtitle as a "Brief and Plain Statement of the Physiology of Birth and the Relations of the Sexes." But Ethelmer's book, like so many others of its kind, does not deliver on its promises: while it is brief, it is not plain. It is evasive, almost wholly silent, on erotic excitement, let alone the mechanics of intercourse. Ellis Ethelmer did not disguise her principal purpose in writing tracts on sexuality: "Yes, indubitably, from fuller knowledge will arise a truer purity." Love, she said in another little book, *Baby Buds*, "is the most precious thing in life," but she was speaking of

83. Lyttelton, *Training of the Young*, 85–86.

84. Wood-Allen, *Child-Confidence Rewarded* (1896), 4.

85. Ellis Ethelmer [pseud.], *The Human Flower: Being a Brief and Plain Statement of the Physiology of Birth and the Relations of the Sexes* (1894), 34. Ellis Ethelmer seems to have been Mrs. Wolstenholme Elmy, and perhaps her husband, Ben Elmy, as well. She was secretary of the Women's Emancipation Union. See J. A. and Olive Banks, *Feminism and Family Planning in Victorian England* (1965), 101n.

pure love: "there are wise thinkers who say that all human love has
sprung in the first place from the love between mother and child."[86] This
was written in 1895. Sigmund Freud would intimate much the same thing
a year or two later. But the import of Ethelmer's definition of love differs
radically from Freud's: it had nothing whatever to do with sexuality.

This is the central fact about the mounting demand for sexual enlightenment which became almost a fad in the days when Freud was making
his first psychoanalytic discoveries: carnal knowledge seemed essential
not for its own sake, but as an instrument for curing social ills by exposing, if not preventing, private vices. The sexual reformers did not create
the malaise that gripped so many writers, artists, philosophers, sociologists,
and pedagogues toward the end of the nineteenth century; they reflected
it. Their calls for urgent reform quite accurately mirrored the general
sense of alarm. The near-panic with which educators preached sex
education and berated parents for their failures as guides to Eros was
their way of responding to fears abroad in their culture, fears with
political, military, biological dimensions. Syphilis, they were sure, was
incapacitating far too many young men, and hence the armies of their
countries stood in danger of being fatally weakened; ignorance about
sexual selection would swamp the "desirable" elements in the population
with inferior stock; uninformed or misinformed young men and women
would infect their loved ones with horrendous diseases and damage, perhaps doom, modern society. What was so offensive about Ibsen's *Ghosts*,
which turns on the ravages of syphilis, was that so many in his audiences
knew precisely what he was talking about. Dr. Hermann Rohleder was
exceptionally strident in his pamphlets, but he only shouted what most
of his colleagues said more quietly. Calling on all the resources of German
typography, spacing his sentences for emphasis and employing boldface
for the essential points, Rohleder pleaded for sexual pedagogy at home
and by teachers, to reduce the incidence of "outbreaks of onanism" in
schools, and to clarify, graphically, the "dangers" of sexual intercourse
for the young. Rohleder described the sexual instinct as one might
describe a ravening savage who must be tamed through fear and diverted
by sports. Private morality, military effectiveness, civilization itself were
endangered by the prevailing sexual ignorance. "Civilization," he wrote,
"is syphilization."[87] Nothing could be plainer than that.

Such manifestos and the debates they generated, curious mixtures of
panic-stricken rhetoric and doctrinaire diagnosis, reverberate with the

86. Ethelmer, *Human Flower*, 35; *Baby Buds* (1892), 42.
87. Rohleder, *Grundzüge der Sexualpädagogik*, 70, 77, 112.

fashionable mythologies of the day; a number of them betray an ominous obsession with racial purity and the threat of race suicide.[88] The alliance for sexual information—Darwinists and bishops, fundamentalists and Anglicans, militarists and utopians—seems ill-assorted, but it was firm. No wonder that Sigmund Freud was inclined to be severe with the literature it produced, with its hesitations, its resounding generalities, its "solemn-bombastic" tone.[89] He was right to suspect that its authors were resisting the very truths they so energetically professed to champion and so half-heartedly tried to disseminate. Some of them, like Dr. Hugh Cabot, glimpsed the inconvenient fact that the young cannot be kept innocent, and know far more than fond and concerned adults like to imagine. Yet ignorance claimed its allies, in the bourgeois century, even among the crusaders for knowledge.

88. "The increase of liberty for all classes of the community seems to promote the rapid breeding of the defective, irresponsible, and vicious." Charles W. Eliot, "Public Opinion and Sex Hygiene," *Proceedings, AFSH*, 16. "Race suicide and divorce are symptoms of a social disorder, doubtless very grave and certainly very evident, whose remedies in my opinion lie in the direction of training both boys and girls for parenthood." Professor Marion Talbot, Dean of Women at the University of Chicago (1908), in Henderson, *Education with Reference to Sex*, Part I, 8.

89. Freud, "Zur sexuellen Aufklärung der Kinder" (1907), *St.A.*, V, 166; "The Sexual Enlightenment of Children," *S.E.*, IX, 137.

⨝ FIVE ⨞

Carnal Knowledge

1. Platonic Libertinism

Sexual intercourse is the most obviously carnal of activities; it presupposes, for its adequate performance, no training and little experience. Yet that performance is also entangled with knowledge acquired in a school to which the flesh is no stranger. "Love," Freud wrote in 1916, "is the great educator."[1] Embedded in biological urges, sexual desire may be relatively autonomous, but it is stimulated, refined, directed, and deflected by education in life, far less by book-learning than by looking around and listening attentively. The sexual fantasies that prompt amorous researches or accompany masturbation elaborate or, far more often, distort provocative scenes one has witnessed, noises one has heard, stories one has read. The young Gustave Flaubert was not the only boy to listen for sounds from his parents' bed. The "Wolf Man," Freud's celebrated patient, was just one among uncounted children to see, or imagine, his parents in the act of intercourse; Havelock Ellis unusual only in recording for posterity how another boy had told him, at eight, about the pleasures of masturbation. Much of the information gleaned in these ways was misinformation, but error is as effective a spur to sexual stimulation as truth, possibly more effective. And by no means all of this erotic education derives from overt sexual activity: children are as aroused by seeing their mother naked as by surprising their parents making love; their sexual history is shaped more by noticing their siblings' genitals

1. "Einige Charaktertypen aus der psychoanalytischen Arbeit" (1916), *St.A.*, X, 232; "Some Character-Types Met With in Psycho-Analytic Work," *S.E.*, XIV, 312.

than by happening upon dogs copulating. Carnal knowledge begins with intimations of the body.

In the nineteenth century, such intimations were everywhere, even for the bourgeoisie, even for virginal girls. There was a good deal of innuendo, often in surprising places, conveying not sexual information so much as an atmosphere of sensuality, of a vague ferment. In 1878, even *Daheim*, that German family periodical of the most unimpeachable respectability, could print an engraving entitled *Wehrlos*; it shows a swarthy and dirt-covered chimney sweep pinching the cheek of a young woman whose arms are full of groceries making her, as the title points out with ponderous jocularity, defenseless against this sexual overture.[2] Actually, bourgeois were not always quite so vulnerable to the assaults of the senses as this. The well-brought up and the comfortable knew rather more than they were willing to reveal to others, or acknowledge to themselves; the most sheltered among them could gather sexual knowledge from a walk in town, an older sister, a school friend, or an opportune story. Somewhat cynically, but not without good grounds, Balzac thought that middle-class girls acquired much tantalizing sexual information, and perhaps some practice, in their boarding schools: "A girl may leave her boarding school a virgin; chaste? No." It is no wonder that in 1895, early in his career as a student of sexuality, Sigmund Freud wondered out loud whether "even adolescents" do not have far more sexual knowledge "than people think or than they trust themselves to have."[3]

Hints of hidden knowledge are everywhere, in the most restrained of decent fictions as in the most worried of pedagogues' treatises. In a much-noted passage in Trollope's *The Eustace Diamonds*, Lizzie Eustace quickly conceals the French novels lying about in her drawing room and replaces them with a Bible as Lady Fawn, the model of propriety, comes to pay a call. One should not read too much into this scene, a happy invention of one among that large school of hypocrite-hunters with which the nineteenth century was provided. But Trollope leaves no doubt that when the Lady Fawns did not intrude upon them, the Lizzie Eustaces of his day took good care to inform themselves about erotic matters. The most prudish allowed that marriage was an admission ticket to the university of life. "Get Dorothea to read you light things," George Eliot has Mr. Brooke, Dorothea's good-tempered and maladroit uncle, say to

---

2. *Daheim*, XIV (1878), 229.

3. Balzac, *Physiologie du mariage* (1829), ed. Maurice Regard (1968), 94; Freud, with Josef Breuer, *Studien über Hysterie* [not in St.A.] (1895), *GW*, I, 195; *Studies on Hysteria, S.E.*, II, 134.

the ailing Casaubon, Dorothea's husband, in *Middlemarch*. "Smollett—
Roderick Random, Humphrey Clinker: they are a little broad, but she
may read anything now she's married, you know."[4]

There was in fact much to read for the respectable, much but not
everything. Toward the end of the century, fairly unbuttoned discussions
of topics as delicate as puberty spread beyond the constricted compass
of medical periodicals to magazines of general circulation. Indeed in
the 1880s, in Paris—it would have to be Paris!—two novelists competed
for the dubious honor of being the first to deal with menstruation in
their fiction. Their battle is not without its involuntary humor. "The
curse" was, in the bourgeois century, a most touchy subject, thought
unfit for polite conversation, let alone for fiction. But then, in 1884,
Edmond de Goncourt published *Chérie*, a carefully researched novel
about the life of a young girl, in which he describes in graphic detail the
"hot awakening of an organism still vegetating," the "terror of the unexpected blood"—her menarche. However, Zola, as careful a researcher
as Goncourt, anticipated his rival by presenting the same decisive awakening in his *La Joie de vivre*, which had begun serial publication in late
1883. Goncourt promptly accused Zola, that "damned assimilator" with
the "cunning of an old peasant," of having stolen that unprecedented
theme from him; Zola, he charged, had asked him if he could read some
of the relevant passages from the manuscript of *Chérie*, an accusation
that Zola hotly denied. The controversy did not make "menarche" into
a household word, nor did it give menstruation license to appear in many
other novels. It remained a subject as unfamiliar to fiction as masturbation.[5] But the quarrel underscored the uncertainties hedging in propriety
during the bourgeois century, and the opportunities open for imparting
carnal knowledge.

The lucky and the alert, in any event, found sufficient sources for that
knowledge. Some newspapers carried lurid accounts of unsavory divorce

4. Trollope, *The Eustace Diamonds* (1873; ed. 1947), 84 [ch. 9]; Eliot, *Middlemarch* (1871–72; ed. 1965), 320–21 [ch. 30].

5. *Chérie* (1884), 137; November 2, 1883, Edmond and Jules de Goncourt, *Journal;
mémoires de la vie littéraire 1851–1896*, ed. Robert Ricatte, 22 vols. (1956–58), XIII,
59. For Zola's denial, see "Etude" by Henri Mitterand, in Zola, *La Joie de vivre, Les
Rougon-Macquart: Histoire naturelle et sociale d'une famille sous le second Empire*,
ed. Armand Lanoux, 5 vols. (1960–67), III, 1767–69. The most explicit representation
of masturbation in nineteenth-century nonpornographic fiction is in Lodewijk van
Deyssel's novel *Een Liefde* of 1887: thinking passionately of her husband, a young
woman, in a near-hallucinatory state, masturbates in her garden in hot summer. The
description, which is graphic and disagreeable, did not find favor and van Deyssel
promptly retreated from his boldness. (I owe this reference to J. W. Smit.)

suits, and court proceedings recording testimony in murder cases with a sexual motive provided alluring details about husbandly impotence, clandestine love affairs, and the most minute circumstances of sexual seductions. More common and doubtless more influential as an educator was the proverbial seductive servant who, if we can trust contemporary accounts, was more than a proverb. The obscene jokes that schoolboys— or, for that matter, the Goncourts and their literary circle—liked to tell performed several functions at once; they served as demonstrations of sexual maturity or sexual prowess, and as emblems of membership in exclusive coteries. But they also carried, almost incidentally, a heavy freight of erotic information. Indeed, in one way or another, many children discovered the distinction between the sexes, and its charged meaning, from other children. In her autobiography, the Norwegian novelist Sigrid Undset describes an encounter that was a particular event —it had, after all, happened to her—but also archetypal in its simplicity, its sensual directness. One day she met a little boy in the neighborhood, "and noticed something sticking out of his breeches in front. All at once the boy shouted: 'Look out! Here comes the water-cart!' and ran out into the road with shuffling steps, stirring up a cloud of white dust all round him. As he ran he sent out a thin jet of water which left a dark zigzag track in the dust." After performing this feat "he came back" and "declared proudly that no girl could do a thing like that, but every boy could." Little Sigrid "realized that he was right" and this, she recalled, made her sad, "but not very much so." She "paid tribute to the superior equipment of boys, meekly and without envy."[6] She must have envied boys more than she later remembered, but she certainly remembered the scene all her life.

For his part, Logan Pearsall Smith, born in 1865 in Philadelphia to a devout Quaker family intent on keeping him from sin, found that by literally keeping his eyes open, he might acquire the very knowledge from which his parents wanted to shield him. When he was a little boy, Barnum's circus came to Philadelphia, and "among the Quakers the question was much debated whether their children should be allowed to witness this entertainment." The sight of exotic animals might "help to enhance their conception of the wonders of creation," but the "scantily clad female acrobats" were quite another matter. The compromise the Smith family reached was to permit the children to look at the animals, but make them keep their eyes closed while the acrobats were on stage. "So there we sat," Logan Pearsall Smith remembered more than six

6. *The Longest Years* (1934; tr. Arthur G. Chater, 1935), 105.

decades later, "a row of Quaker children, staring with all our eyes at the performing elephants, but with our organs of vision closed and our hands before them during the less seemly interludes. But one little Quaker boy permitted himself a guilty peep through his fingers, and gazed on a show of muscular limbs moving, slowly moving, in pink tights." To judge from his later sexual history, the fortuitous junction of muscularity and pink tights helped to engender, or perpetuate, some elementary confusions. In Smith's memory, this glimpse of Sin was so striking that his notion of sin "became coloured in his imagination for a long time with the pinkness of those slowly moving legs." Sometime later, visiting in England for some months, he enjoyed the kind of memorable sight that Sigrid Undset, too, had never forgotten. His companions were for the most part Etonians, hardly models of "unspotted purity." One of them took young Logan "into a walnut tree in his father's park" and treated him "to a display which, though it had no interest for me at the time," was, "as a mark of friendliness from an English to an American boy," nothing less than "a demonstration of international good-will."[7] The charm and light-heartedness of Smith's account should not deceive the reader: the knowledge that Logan Pearsall Smith garnered at that circus performance and in that walnut tree stimulated a fear of powerful females and a taste for virile males that never left him.

Even the mealy-mouthed pseudo-explanations for physical processes that normally served as responses to children's questions were, however distorted, far from uncontaminated by carnal information. What proper nineteenth-century parents thought right for their children to know about the body in general, and sexuality in particular, was more ambiguous in its import than they could have imagined.

Everyone knows the story of the stork and its variants, which made do, in most proper households, as a sufficient explanation for the arrival of a new sibling. But the stork brought its cherished load in an atmosphere of confusion and mystery, among telltale signs of sickness, even violence. When his mother was pregnant, "Little Hans," Freud's famous child patient, was told the usual story by his parents: the stork was about to bring him a little brother or sister. He was then three and a half, beginning to be skeptical of adults' tales. During his mother's labor, as Hans heard her groaning, he asked, "What's mama coughing for?" and answered his own question after a moment: "The stork is coming today for sure." When he saw the physician's bag in the hall, he made the right

7. *Unforgotten Years* (1938), 21–22, 47.

connection: "The stork is coming today." Then, after his little sister Hanna was born, he was invited into the parental bedroom and looked, not at his mother, but at the basins standing on the floor, "filled with bloody water."[8] He sensed, at three and a half, more about the processes of birth than that some antiseptic stork carried babies to expectant households; he had seen the blood and drew his conclusions. Children generally knew more than their parents told them, even if what they knew was confused, fragmentary, and largely wrong. With relatively large families persisting until late in the nineteenth century, and with most babies continuing to be born at home, children had repeated opportunities to discover the body at work, and to discuss it with one another.

The talk of brothers and sisters, though pathetically ill-informed, was often less genteel than the shamefaced lessons that parents reluctantly imparted. The young Gustave Flaubert did not hesitate to use words like "shit" in letters to his sister, or describe wiping himself in letters to his brother, and while Flaubert was exceptionally defiant of polite prescriptions at an early age, exceptionally determined to display his distance from the nauseating bourgeoisie, other boys, less brilliant, less bellicose than he, were quite as foul-mouthed and no less informative.[9] And domestic carnal education at times has aspects far more unsavory than the confidential obscenities uttered by the young. The case books of late-nineteenth-century psychopathologists record harrowing accounts of early seductions, by no means all of them imaginary. Even after Sigmund Freud abandoned his sweeping theory that all neuroses are caused by the seduction of young girls by their fathers, he continued to recognize that reports of such seductions were often enough true. Certainly the incidents that left traces in the medical records represent only a modest fraction of precocious initiations into sexual activity, for most of these never came to the attention of a priest or a psychiatrist. Their victims were inhibited by shame, or had repressed the experience without suffering immediate visible consequences.

Among schools of erotic education, the great cities, and the middling ones, were the most convenient, in fact the most importunate. Prostitutes made themselves into ostentatious ornaments of their notorious quarters,

8. "Analyse der Phobie eines fünfjährigen Knaben" [Der kleine Hans"] (1909), *St.A.*, 16–17; "Analysis of a Phobia in a Five-Year-Old Boy" ["Little Hans"], *S.E.*, X, 10.

9. Gustave Flaubert to his sister Caroline [after December 10, 1842]; to his brother Achille, April 26, 1844, *Correspondance*, ed. Jean Bruneau, 2 vols. so far (1973–   ), I, 135, 206.

and also, in many towns, fanned out to patrol an extensive and thickly populated beat. They sought customers at dances, outside hotels, near the railroad station. At Condet, right outside Limoges, there was a windmill that served as a makeshift brothel "where passers-by and children," the local prefect complained, "behold the most scandalous things." In Berlin, around the turn of the century, the whores inhabiting local bordellos made their morning toilette sitting in the windows "with half-exposed bodies" and "shamelessly gave themselves up to the glances of passers-by. Not a few school boys would skulk past, especially in the morning hours," the better to "satisfy their curiosity." In other cities, whores hounded the theatre or hotel districts accosting pedestrians. Scenes like those in Berlin repeated themselves in varying ways in other metropolitan centers, in the streets, in the newspapers, in the theatres. Amiel, entrusting the impressions of a recent visit to Paris to his journal, confessed that he had been "seduced by the curiosity of the senses and by a kind of Platonic libertinism of the eyes and ears, which swept me away all the while making me blush."[10]

One may leave it to Amiel to find a telling expression for a common experience: Platonic libertinism is precisely what great cities provided for many who lived or visited there—erotic information on which they might act or not as the opportunity presented itself and as their conflicts permitted. With Amiel, as with thousands of other inquirers into sensuality, looking had replaced touching, but that made their investigations, if anything, even more active. And telling spread word of things seen. In early 1865, Joseph B. Lyman described New York to his son Alex, then not yet five: "Some of the people here are very naughty. There is a dancing girl in a cellar who takes off most all her clothes & dances before men. The men eat peanuts and clap their hands." Fortunately, there was a moral the doting father could attach to this sensual vignette: "I am afraid they will all go to that dreadful place where that girl is who had the head of John the Baptist cut off & brought in on the waiter." Of course, New York was not all wicked: "There are a great many good people here too who will go where John went after his head was cut off."[11] Urban life as glimpsed by Joseph Lyman is in itself re-

---

10. John Merriman, *Urbanization, Social Change and Class Politics: Limoges and the French Nineteenth Century* (forthcoming), ch. III; Hans Ostwald, *Das Berliner Dirnentum*, 2 vols. (1907), I, 25; Amiel: October 15, 1851, *Journal intime*, ed. Bernard Gagnebin and Philippe M. Monnier, 4 vols. so far (1976–   ), I, 1071. For prostitution in the bourgeois century, see my next volume, *The Tender Passion*, ch. 5.

11. Joseph B. Lyman to his son Alexander, February 7, 1865, box 3, LF, Y-MA. This passage is a useful reminder that the Bible, which some censors indeed wanted to expurgate, was a handy and explicit guide to carnal knowledge.

markable enough; the erotic excitement provided for one little boy, food for his burgeoning oedipal imagination, is more remarkable still.

In the nineteenth century, the carnal vitality of great cities, for good or ill, was readily enlisted in the popular sport of national self-congratulation or its reverse, self-laceration. Travelers and journalists liked to present little studies of comparative morality, or immorality. Hippolyte Taine, for one, praising the good sense and learning of English girls, found them far superior to the homegrown product, the French girl who was kept in abysmal ignorance about life: "It is too readily believed in France that if a woman ceases to be a doll, she ceases to be a woman."[12] The opposite line, accusing other countries of knowing too much about sensual matters, was more common. In 1872, *Daheim* hit at both French and American sensuality: American children were pushed into society far too early; little boys dressed up in black tie to display their parents' wealth, while little girls, at ten, participated in parties as though they were adults, flirting. And Paris was, of course, wholly immune to the rules of decorum and the promptings of conscience. The press, the stage, and Parisian bourgeois morality in general, *Daheim* was pleased to report, were immodest in the extreme; its correspondent found particular satisfaction in pointing his censorious finger at the "scandalous toilettes" one could see in the streets of the city, and pictures of women, "more impudent, more naked, and more shameless than ever before."[13] In Paris at least, *Daheim* was sure, Platonic libertinism was a broad invitation to a libertinism more consequential, more immoral, than the relatively harmless voyeur's pleasure in watching others.

But the acquisition of erotic information did not depend on seductive or traumatic situations. Obviously, one did not need to be the victim of a rape, the sibling of a Flaubert, the child of a Lyman, to learn much about the body. The innocent discoveries, on public monuments, in the bathtub, at the barnyard, may have been less dramatic than the exciting encounters I have described, but they were also more consequential for the middle-class culture of the nineteenth century. The respectable, young and old, were in conflict. They wanted to know and did not want to know. The Goncourts, cynical as always, were not wholly wrong in 1855: "The world will come to an end the day that young girls stop laughing at scatological jokes."[14]

12. *Notes on England* (1872; tr. Edward Hyams, 1958), 76.

13. "Frühreife Kinder in den Vereinigten Staaten," *Daheim*, VIII (1872), 431; H. K., "Die moderne Pariser Bühne," ibid., 384.

14. September 1855, *Journal*, I, 217.

2. Lessons from the Body

One fine May morning in 1870, the Reverend Francis Kilvert, then a young curate in Radnorshire, walked to a neighboring Welsh hamlet to visit a fellow cleric, only to find two of his daughters "assisting at the castration of the lambs, catching and holding the poor beasts and standing by whilst the operation was performed, seeming to enjoy the spectacle." He, for his part, did not enjoy it. "It was the first time I had seen clergymen's daughters helping to castrate lambs or witnessing that operation and it rather gave me a turn of disgust at first." One of the girls, he added graphically, "was struggling in a pen with a large stout white lamb, and when she had mastered him and got him well between her legs and knees I ventured to ask where her father was. She signified by a nod and a word that he was advancing behind me"—her rural occupation was, then, anything but clandestine, and certainly approved in the household. Kilvert reflected that "the elder members of the family" had probably not "quite expected that the young ladies would be caught by a morning caller castrating lambs, and probably they would have selected some other occupation for them had they foreseen the coming of a guest." This was pure projection. There is, in fact, not a scintilla of evidence that his clerical friend was embarrassed by Kilvert's arrival. Kilvert's response bears the stamp of much genteel moralizing in the bourgeois century: having repressed many of his own childhood experiences, he felt compelled to protect the young from sights from which they thought they needed no protection. He promptly mastered his disgust. "I made allowances for them and considered in how rough a way the poor children have been brought up, so that they thought no harm of it, and I forgave them."[15] There were bourgeois in his age who did not share Kilvert's moral rigorism, and would have found nothing that required forgiveness in this useful domestic occupation.

Not all carnal education involved sexuality quite so directly. But whatever screens anxious pedagogues or doting mothers might place between the child and its world, the world was very much with him. A fainting squeamishness, or the pose of ignorance, far from being universally approved defensive stratagems, were disdainfully treated as affectations; they caught the satirist's eye and prompted the moralist's censure.[16]

15. *Kilvert's Diary*, ed. William Plomer, 3 vols. (reissue 1969), I, 127.
16. Thus Sarah Stickney Ellis wrote in 1839 that among the most distasteful habits of young women in her time were the affectations of refinement and of ignorance. The first made them feign fastidiousness: "They cannot *touch* the coarse material that supplies our bodily wants, or constitutes our personal comfort. They loathe the very

It could not be otherwise. In the world of the nineteenth-century middle classes, as in other times and other classes, babies were born, the sick were nursed, and the aged died at home. This was a world in which Charles Dickens could allow David Copperfield to come upon his still youthful, still lovely mother feeding his half-brother at the breast, and in which Dickens's illustrator, "Phiz," would choose this very moment for an idyllic family portrait.[17]

In general, nursing mothers and wet nurses displayed their breasts with some freedom; if for the most part they were not middle-class women, they often had middle-class witnesses. Writing to his fiancée from Paris in October 1885, Sigmund Freud described wet nurses publicly breast-feeding their charges, and his unembarrassed report to the gently raised Martha Bernays is as instructive as the sight he reported.[18] Charles Dickens, always the supreme test case for what his culture found acceptable, was casual and light-hearted about maternal feedings. When David Copperfield first meets Mrs. Micawber, "a thin and faded lady, not at all young," she has "a baby at her breast." It is, we learn, one of twins, and, the narrator adds in recollection, "I may remark here that I hardly ever, in all my experience of the family, saw both the twins detached from Mrs. Micawber at the same time. One of them was always taking refreshment." Dickens could even use nursing to poke gentle fun at Mrs. Micawber's incurable orotundity. "The twins," Micawber confidentially informs young David Copperfield some time after their first encounter, "no longer derive their sustenance from Nature's founts, in short," he explains himself, "they are weaned."[19] Nursing, then, was a common sight, anything but rare in parks or on railroads; though, as Daumier and other contemporary artists testify, it appeared chiefly in third-class carriages. August Strindberg was being a little provocative perhaps when, in a short story of 1884, he described a husband watching his wife nursing their first baby and allowing sexual thoughts to enter

mention of those culinary compounds, which nevertheless their fair lips condescend to admit; and they shrink with horror from the vulgar notion that the old grandmother-duties of preparing a clean hearth, and a comfortable fireside, for a husband or a brother, could by any possibility devolve upon them." Even more unaccountable, Ellis thought, was the "affectation of ignorance respecting common things," which involved taking pride in "not knowing how any familiar or ordinary thing is made or done." *The Women of England: Their Social Duties, and Domestic Habits,* 2 vols. in 1 (1839), II, 147, 149.

17. *David Copperfield* (1850), ch. 8; the illustration is entitled *Changes at Home.*

18. October 19, 1885, Sigmund Freud, *Briefe 1873–1939,* ed. Ernst L. Freud (1960), 167.

19. *David Copperfield* (ed. 1966), 212, 315 [ch. 9, 18].

his mind: there was "the little red baboon, who smelled of butter, lying at the breast which hitherto had been only his plaything." But in another story published in the same year, depicting a lonely, remote bachelor on a stroll observing a lower-class family picnicking in the park, Strindberg was only noting in print what one could see every day, all across Europe: "a mother with a baby at her breast, a large, rich breast."[20] The scene disgusts the stroller, but that disgust, Strindberg leaves no doubt, is an aberration, a sickly hatred of life.

Modest bourgeois mothers sometimes performed this maternal duty in the presence of friends, providing more carnal knowledge, and far more sexual stimulation, than they consciously intended. One such incident, the twenty-six-year-old Elisa Schlesinger nursing her daughter in front of the fifteen-year-old Gustave Flaubert, was immortalized in literature. The sight haunted the young and infatuated Flaubert, then still a voluptuary only in his imagination, and he inserted it into his early autobiographical story "Mémoires d'un fou" with little or no distortion. "Maria," as he calls Elisa Schlesinger, barely disguised in his tale, "had a child, a little girl; she was loved, she was embraced, she was wearied with caresses and kisses." How he wished he could have "gathered up a single one of these kisses" being lavished on this little girl. His fraternal jealousy was sharpened by an unsuspected and unintended invitation to sexual arousal. "Maria nursed her herself, and one day I saw her uncover her bosom and give her the breast." This, as I have noted, had really happened at the resort of Trouville. "It was a fleshy and round bosom, with brown skin and azure veins one could see under that ardent flesh. I had never seen a naked woman before. Oh! the singular ecstasy into which the sight of that breast plunged me; how I devoured it with my eyes, how I would have liked just to touch that chest!" Flaubert, or his fictional surrogate, had a fantasy of biting it passionately, "and my heart dissolved with delight in thinking of the voluptuous pleasures that this kiss would give me."[21] It was an uncommon response, perhaps, but the sight was common enough.

So were nude bodies, especially at the seaside or the lake. The Lymans took the trouble to find themselves a deserted part of the beach before they shed their clothes to bathe in the sea.[22] But privacy was impossible to guarantee. In 1858, when the Rothschilds were at Scarborough, they

20. "Compensation," in *Getting Married* (1884, 1886; tr. Mary Sandbach, 1972), part I, 129; "Needs Must," ibid., 111.

21. Flaubert, "Mémoires d'un fou," in *Oeuvres de jeunesse inédits*, ed. Conard, 3 vols. (1910), I, 509–10.

22. Joseph Lyman, private memorandum, August 6, 1865, box 4, LF.

discovered nudity "in the full glare of day and sunshine. Here is complete absence of costume," one of the young Rothschild ladies noted in her journal, "as in the garden of Eden before the fall of man, and hundreds of ladies and gentlemen look on, while the bathers plunge in the foaming waters, or emerge from them." It seemed scandalous: "I really think the police should interfere." But the police sagely left the bathers alone. A decade earlier, Amiel had visited the baths on the Rhone and found much to look at: "Water marvelously beautiful; baths miserable; pretty neighbors, glimpsed through a crack in the partition." Gazing at these lovely young women as they "frolicked in the blue waves," he found the sight "poetic," though he saw little enough. "I enjoyed it," he exculpated himself to himself, "as a painter, not as a voluptuary. The bath," he added naively, leaving his historian to draw the inferences, "refreshed me a good deal."[23] There must have been thousands of voyeurs who saw as much as Amiel did, and more. Such displays, far from being difficult to obtain, were, rather, hard to escape, especially among friends. No wonder that Thackeray could have one of his characters, in *Vanity Fair*, describe another, the wily and lovely Becky Sharp, as having "green eyes, fair skin, pretty figure, famous frontal development."[24] Frontal developments, whether famous or not, were far less mysterious in the bourgeois century than critics of that age, including Thackeray himself, supposed.

That century was in fact overrun with evidences of physical realities and reports about facts of life far less pleasing than a young woman's handsome shape: vermin, sickness, destitution, deformity, and death. Warders at Newgate would show visitors plaster casts of the heads of criminals hanged at the prison, and as one contemporary illustration shows, respectable parents brought their young daughters, perhaps no older than eight, to participate in this entertainment. In this atmosphere, lawyers could calmly discuss the merits of whipping and castration as penalties for the crime of rape.[25] Physicians, normally but not always writing for other physicians, described frightful physical malformations or revolting sexual perversions with an eye to detail. Dr. Auguste Ambroise Tardieu, professor of legal medicine at the Faculty of Medicine at the University of Paris, published a popular treatise, *Étude médicale-*

23. Lucy Cohen, *Lady de Rothschild and Her Daughters, 1821–1931* (1935), 93. The author fails to make clear whether the diarist she is quoting is Constance or Annie Rothschild; Amiel: June 8, 1849, *Journal intime*, I, 475 (see also pp. 996 and 1063).

24. *Vanity Fair* (1848; ed. 1950), 190 [ch. 19].

25. Alan Delgado, *Victorian Entertainment* (1971), 69; Simeon E. Baldwin, "Whipping and Castration as Punishment for Crime," *Yale Law Journal*, VIII (June 1899), 371–86.

légale sur les attentats aux moeurs, in which he avoided technical language and cast his exposition in the manner of the catechism. Among the questions he asked himself was whether it is true that one can cure oneself of venereal disease by having sexual intercourse with a little girl. He found it "sad" to have to touch on such a topic, but felt constrained to refute this disgusting superstition explicitly, since he judged it to be widespread and thoroughly engrained in the popular mind.[26] And Charles Dickens could freely speculate whether Sir John Franklin's arctic expedition, which disappeared from view after a well-publicized start in the spring of 1845, had actually resorted to cannibalism—"the dreadful expedient of eating the bodies of their dead companions."[27] Dickens knew his readers could absorb such conjectures.

At times, bourgeois would not merely imagine but witness appalling sights without shrinking. One of the most striking instances I have come across is immortalized in the autobiography that the south-German *Bürger* Ferdinand Weyh set down in 1920, at seventy, to beguile his old age. His exhaustive handwritten account is awash with trivia—his addresses and the rent he paid, the names of servants and their terms of service, and family excursions on foot or on bicycles. It is propelled into feeling only once, as Weyh recalls the death of his only son, Oskar, in World War I: "with his burial all my joy in life, too, was buried." Weyh, officer, bureaucrat, bank clerk, a man of many employments and with many mistresses, had knocked about the world only to settle down in Munich and marry. Late in 1889, while he was still a bachelor, he noticed that his housekeeper, Kathi Lechenbauer, whom he valued as a diligent and competent manager, was beginning to talk strangely of persecutors. As her symptoms of paranoia grew more florid, she would say insistently that she must take her own life to escape her tormentors. Upon her employer's solicitous urging, she agreed to enter a hospital but instead carried out her threat to kill herself. Weyh went to identify the body but was informed that it was already on its way to being dissected in a medical demonstration. Though he had no medical qualifications of any sort, Weyh promptly went to the auditorium, filled with medical students, to see, and instantly recognize, the body of his housekeeper stretched out on the dissecting table, naked. The medical professor who was

---

26. Auguste Ambroise Tardieu, *Etude médicale-légale sur les attentats aux moeurs* (1850s; 6th ed., 1873), 115.

27. "The Lost Arctic Voyagers," *Household Words*, December 2, December 9, 1854, *The Works of Charles Dickens*, National Library Edition, *Miscellaneous Papers, Plays and Poems*, 2 vols. (n.d.), I, 462–92.

lecturing "had just removed the brain from the skull which he had opened with chisel and hammer," and, exploiting the wisdom of hind-sight, was showing his audience a "malformation" which would "surely have led to insanity." Weyh then notes, without further comment, that he had himself introduced to the lecturer, who showed a strong interest in the late Kathi Lechenbauer. That evening, he visited with some companionable friends. The only sign that the day's experience had left any emotional imprint on him is that Weyh did not spend that night at home.[28] There can be no question: one could learn a great deal in the bourgeois century by reading and looking, and many bourgeois were inclined to do both.

The relevance of such horrifying, often unsavory material to the education of the senses is not immediately apparent. But it was one pertinent and in fact indispensable way of clarifying and enriching erotic experience. The child constructs its sexual identity and develops its tentative sexual agenda by observing and touching its body and that of others, noting defects and vulnerabilities quite as keenly as promises of pleasure. And these instructive explorations amount to a continuing training, certainly lasting past puberty. They make for an exposure, however incomplete, to the facts of life. While bourgeois nineteenth-century culture found it far easier to discuss or depict disease and death than details of sexual congress, the candid realism with which the young learned to confront harsh bodily realities made them, at least, into some-thing less helpless than the blushing, fainting ignoramuses of the anti-bourgeois legend, and prepared them for erotic realities. The prudish headmistress of that ladies' seminary in Massachusetts who, according to Captain Marryat, concealed the "*limbs*" of a pianoforte in frilled "modest little trousers"[29] has enjoyed an unwarranted posthumous fame; she has become the favorite witness in the great campaign to expose the bour-geoisie for its prudery and its hypocrisy. But that headmistress, if she ever existed at all, stands not as a representative figure at the center of middle-class culture, but at the most squeamish extreme in the range of permissible behavior, a target of some amused disdain in her own time.

That range was actually very wide. Those who wished to keep the young, especially young women, from the facts of life had to contend with those who insisted on them. Two weeks after Georg Büchner's untimely death at twenty-three, his fiancée, Minna Jaegle, reported on

28. "Erinnerungen," 53, 360–62, Ana 364, Weyh Nachlass, Stabi, Munich.

29. Frederick Marryat, *A Diary in America, with Remarks on Its Institutions*, 2 vols. (1839), II, 45.

her last visit to that brilliant and precocious playwright. Notified that he
had been struck down with a dangerous gastric fever, she wanted to rush
to his bedside, only to be kept from traveling by the absence of a suitable
chaperone. "O paltry discretion!" Finally, she simply insisted on going,
but Büchner's physician did not want her to see the dying man's
distorted face, and warned her: "Be prepared, he will not recognize you."
Nothing could stop her: she bent over him, he knew her, and died.
"I brought him peace. He went to sleep gently, I kissed his eyes closed,
Sunday February 19, at three thirty."[30] And Minna Jaegle, no tremulous,
self-protective maiden, did not think of herself as a heroine.

I have drawn these instances from the literature of fact, and the age,
of course, liked to think of itself as addicted to facts. And there were
unpleasant facts all about. Bodies ill-clothed and misshapen, covered with
vermin and the stigmata of wasting disease, became familiar figures in
government reports on the living conditions of the poor, on the medical
ravages of destitution, and on the scandals endemic in orphanages. These
reports presented their findings with a classical simplicity of diction,
with pungent language to drive home their point and support their call
for remedies. And they were freely available to anyone willing to overcome his defensive repugnance at these candid exposures of the victims
that modern industrial capitalism made.

The literature of the imagination, too, though blinkered and confined,
was far from reticent about the facts of life—or at least some facts of
life. M. E. Braddon, the prolific English sensation novelist, told her editor,
realistically adapting to the facts of the marketplace, that she knew
just what he wanted: "floppings at the end of chapters, and bits of paper
hidden in secret drawers, bank-notes, and title-deeds under the carpet,
and a part of the body putrefying in the coal scuttle."[31] Without literally
following this recipe, Gustave Flaubert dwelt, with sensuous and sensual
delight, on savage orgies and sanguinary battles in *Salammbô*, arousing
no objections; Rider Haggard, a far more conventional writer than
Flaubert, could, in his popular romance *She*, depict in memorable detail
a festive dance of an exotic tribe which employed antique embalmed
mummies as torches: "So soon as a mummy was consumed to the ankles,
which happened in about twenty minutes, the feet were kicked away,
and another put in its place." Walt Whitman's stories of the 1840s are

30. Minna Jaegle to Eugen Boeckel (ca. March 5, 1837), Ernst Johann, *Büchner*
(1958), 160.
31. Winifred Hughes, *The Maniac in the Cellar: Sensation Novels of the 1860s*
(1980), 121.

1

2

(1) Hablot K. Browne ("Phiz"), *Changes at Home*, 1850. For Charles Dickens, *David Copperfield*, ch. 8. The pneumatic portrait on the wall only underscores the mammalian candor of this most Victorian of novels. (2) Carl Jutz, *Memento Mori, Daheim*, 1884. Real cruelty disguised in mock-classical learning.

I

(1) James Ward, *The Day's Sport*, 1826. Unwitting testimony to the kind of scene that nineteenth-century children might witness. (2) V. Morland, *Au Salon de Peinture, Petit Journal pour Rire*, 1882. There were lots of ladies without shirts on view in the Salons. (3) Antonin-Jean-Paul Carlès, *Death of Abel*, 1887.

2

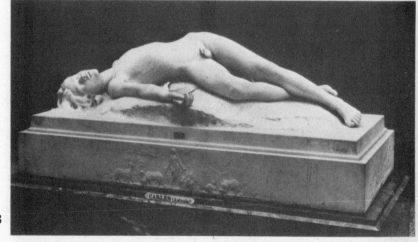

3

1

2

3

4

(1) Ernest Barrias, *Electricity*, 1889. One good example of the modern symbolic nude. (2) Félix Charpentier, *The Bicycle*, ca. 1895–1900. (3) Per Hasselberg, *Magnetism*, ca. 1884. One of a series of life-size high reliefs adorning the Fürstenberg Gallery in Göteborg. Note its placement in the Larsson painting opposite. (4) Carl Larsson, *The Interior of the Fürstenberg Gallery*, 1885. A forest of nudes. The Hasselberg statue (*The Snowdrop*) dominates the center; Raphaël Collin's *Summer* (1884) fills the background. In amusing contrast, Ernst Josephson is shown portraying Göthilda Fürstenberg, stiffly posed and conservatively dressed. Her husband, Pontus Fürstenberg, the donor, appears in front, reading a newspaper.

1

2

3

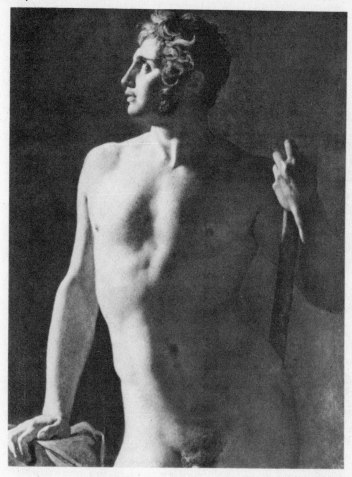

(1) Antonio Teixeira Lopes, *Eça de Queiros*, 1903, Lisbon. Completed three years after the eminent Portuguese novelist's death, the statue depicts the dandified author with a highly symbolic and most pneumatic nude offering herself to him. The inscription on the base is suitably innocuous: "Over the strong nakedness of Truth, the diaphanous veil of Fantasy," the epigraph of Queiros's novel *A Relíquia*. (2) Alexandre Chaponnier, after Pierre-Paul Prud'hon, *Study Guiding the Ascent of Genius*, 1806 or before. From a ceiling painted for the Louvre in 1801. Prepubescent eroticism. (3) August Kiss, *Amazon*. This represents the life-size zinc copy of the 1841 bronze original in Berlin. (4) Jean Auguste Dominique Ingres, *Torso of a Man*, ca. 1800. An instance of male nudity, candid but teasingly incomplete.

(1) Jean Auguste Dominique Ingres, *The Ambassadors of Agamemnon in the Tent of Achilles*, 1801. Frontal male nudity, one nineteenth-century exemplar among many. (2) William Etty, *Venus Now Wakes and Wakens Love*, 1828. Typical of Etty's single-minded concentration on the busty female figure. (3) William Etty, *Andromeda*, ca. 1840. (4) William Etty, *Pandora*, 1824.

2

3

4

Edward Burne-Jones, *Pygmalion and the Image*, 1868–79. Languid and boneless, these modern figures reenact the timeless ritual of man worshiping woman—his own creation (*Above and opposite*).

(1) Jean Léon Gérôme, *Pygmalion and Galatea*, ca. 1881. A characteristically evasive painting, concealing a fascination with the erotic body behind mythological anecdote. (2) Honoré Daumier, *Pygmalion*, 1842. *This* Galatea asks her creator for a pinch of snuff. (3) Jean-Baptiste (called Auguste) Clésinger, *Woman Bitten by a Snake*, after 1847. The bronze reduction of the scandalous marble that aroused considerable emotion when it was first exhibited at the Salon in 1847 (the snake does not appear on this reduction). (4) Alexandre Cabanel, *Nymph Abducted by a Satyr*, 1860. Exhibited at the Salon of 1861, it was promptly bought by Emperor Napoleon III, who loved such art.

3

4

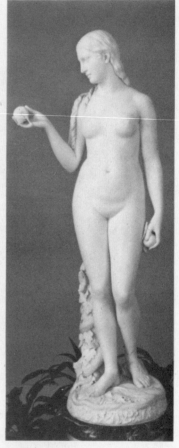

(1) Hiram Powers, *The Greek Slave*, 1843. Probably the most famous nude in nineteenth-century America. Some viewers reported a practically religious experience at her sight. (2) Hiram Powers, *Eve Tempted*, modeled 1842. Less celebrated than Powers's *Greek Slave*, this *Eve* is no less sensual. (3) George Cruikshank, *Making Decent!*, 1822. A moralist lampooning excessive moralizing. (4) A modern Gothic mansion as caricatured in A. Welby Pugin, *The True Principles of Pointed or Christian Architecture, Set Forth in Two Lectures* (1841). Pugin wanted his modern Gothic "truthful," not a pastiche. (5) Sofa with Movable Cushions, from Clarence Cook, *The House Beautiful: Essays on Beds and Tables, Stools and Candlesticks* (1878). Erotic comfort.

3

4

5

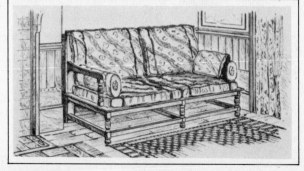

(1) Antonio Canova, *Venus Italica*, 1812. (2) Antonio Canova, *Cupid and Psyche*, 1793. Canova's marbles, which most twentieth-century viewers deride as frigid and frozen, found many admirers in the nineteenth century, including Heinrich Heine and Gustave Flaubert, who thought them exceedingly erotic.

bathed in lurid physicality, with bodies reduced to "a mangled, hideous mass—and rough semblance of a human form—all batter'd and cut, and bloody" and "dabbled over with gore."[32] There were taboos that the age felt compelled to observe; its Podsnaps were, as I have noted, very busy. But there was heavy demand for the body putrefying in the coal scuttle.

In such a culture, the theme of death provided material for heartless humor. In 1885 *Daheim* felt no compunction in printing a picture entitled, with deliberate, whimsical pomposity, *Memento Mori*. In this rustic vignette, a few chickens and a duck stare at the severed black head of another duck. An eloquent stage property, an axe, is visible right behind that head. And the comment on this illustration begins, in mock earnestness, "*Remember that you must die!*"[33] Decapitation, it seems, was a fit subject for families to enjoy together and for the kind of light-hearted solemnity that was the staple of philosophizing in the nineteenth century. Again, when Harriet Beecher asked her sister Catharine to write an epitaph for the parsonage cat, Catharine Beecher suavely complied:

> Here died our kit
> Who had a fit,
>   And acted queer.
> Shot with a gun,
> Her race is run,
>   And she lies here.

No one thought in those years of concealing the hunter's bag or the butcher's meat. In 1826, James Ward documented this candor in painting *The Day's Sport*, which shows children staring at dead game. And in 1859 a popular French periodical, *Le Journal pour Tous*, printed a savage illustration depicting hunters killing a wolf by shoving a knife down his throat. More usually, of course, death was taken to be more somber, and more solemn. At times, it became a pedagogic device. When she was not yet five, the American temperance reformer Frances Willard recalled many decades later, her father had lifted her up to look at "a man who died next door to us," and was laid out, "repellent in death." It was, she remembered, the "first fright my spirit got," as her father held her "quite close down to see what was inside that coffin." The sight traumatized her. "I never had a blow that struck so deep as did that sight;

---

32. Haggard: *She: A History of Adventure* (1887; ed. 1925), 212; Whitman: "Wild Frank's Return," in *Whitman: Poetry and Prose*, ed. Justin Kaplan (1982), 1105.

33. *Daheim*, XXI (1885), 57.

I never had a burn that seared so, nor a pain that tingled like it."[34] This was not, or was not considered to be, sadism; it was education.

In general, dead bodies were a familiar sight, and it was not evaded. In 1829, the Episcopalian minister Harry Croswell, rector of Trinity Church, New Haven, recorded in his journal that he was "informed of the shocking death of one of the workmen at the Church, by the falling of a scaffold." As a matter of course, he "went to see the body," and recorded that "the head was literally crushed by the falling of a mass of stone, which followed him from the scaffold. He was a man of nearly 50, with a family in the country." That duty done, Croswell turned, without transition, to his real business, preparing for his Bible classes: "Spent the remainder of the day, mostly in my study." Five years later, he visited a dying parishioner, as he often did: "Staid till the scene was over." When he was over seventy, and his son died before him at forty-seven, he noted in his bereavement that "the house was opened for the admission of William's friends to see his remains, and there was a continual throng from morning till evening—and never did I behold such tokens of grief."[35] It would have been unthinkable for Harry Croswell not to stay with the dying until it was over, or for William Croswell's friends not to view his body.

That is why Wilhelm Busch, the most quoted and most cherished humorous poet and illustrator of the German Empire, felt free to enliven his popular rhymed tales with a veritable little zoo of bugs, beetles, and mice which he placed, to his many readers' unabashed amusement, in his long-suffering characters' beds, or in their beer. Nor did Busch hesitate to punctuate his work with excrement, generating equally extensive amusement. In a private letter of thanks to a gently reared young girl, his great favorite whom he had known all her life and to whom he was "Uncle Wilhelm," he acknowledged a gift of snipe with a scatological poem complete with a graphic drawing of an obese gourmand dreaming, deliciously, that an angel was shitting on his tongue.[36] He had no intention of shocking her, even mildly; he knew what she knew.

There were, to be sure, in the nineteenth century, as there have always been, particular national and sectarian styles in facetious discourse. Germans were far more addicted than their neighbors to scatology, and

34. Beecher: Kathryn Kish Sklar, *Catharine Beecher: A Study in American Domesticity* (1973), 281; *Le Journal pour Tous*, May 21, 1859; Frances E. Willard, *Glimpses of Fifty Years: The Autobiography of an American Woman* (1889), 6–7.

35. June 16, 1829; July 2, 1834, box 2; November 11, 1851, box 5, Harry Croswell Papers, Y-MA.

36. Wilhelm Busch to Nanda Kessler, December 24, [18]96, *Sämtliche Briefe*, ed. Friedrich Bohne, 2 vols. (1969), II, 84. The drawing is reproduced opposite p. 84.

injected doses of anal humor into their publications that would have offended the Nonconformist conscience in England. Kilvert's young friends would have understood, possibly appreciated, Busch's jokes about bird-droppings, but the English were more given to dwelling on horror than on excrement. Mrs. Montefiore, daughter of a rich land-surveyor and estate-agent, never forgot one picture that her adored father, whom she described as a discriminating patron of painting, included in his collection. It was the scene of "Mlle. de Sombreuil drinking a glass of blood handed her by one of the revolutionaries on the understanding that if she swallowed it her father's life would be spared. The face of the old father aristocrat, the faces of the crowd, and the agony of the girl torn between her love for her father and her shrinking from the revolting ordeal, used to haunt my imagination for nights and days." She reflected that if she "had owned it I would have had it destroyed, but," she added, quickly exculpating her father, "perhaps that thought is the remains of childish impressionability."[37] Francis Fuller, the adored father, did not suffer in her estimation for exposing her to this scene, and it seems never to have occurred to him that the painting might trouble his daughter's fantasy life.

The jocular or the portentous treatment of bodily parts and bodily functions, and of animals, could serve as a genteel defense by preserving distance from the shocking and arousing facts of human physiology. But at the same time it brought them near, into the living room and, through uncounted books and articles, into the kitchen and the nursery. The popular literature of advice to housewives, in fact, demonstrates that the body, with its vicissitudes, was open to the unblinking scrutiny of nineteenth-century bourgeois, probably more to women even than to men. In her best-seller of the mid-Victorian period, *The Book of Household Management*, Isabella Beeton confronts the housewife of her day, on page after page, with blood and bones. The ideal reader of her encyclopedic essay in domestic pedagogy is a wife and mother enjoying at least moderate prosperity and thus enabled to leave some of the housework to others, though not rich enough to delegate the task of superintending her staff. Whatever that reader's financial situation, Mrs. Beeton finds it necessary to tell her how to prepare delicious dishes from calves, turtles, and hogs, omitting no detail. To make mock turtle, one must "Scald the [calf's] head with the skin on, remove the brain, tie the head up in a cloth, and let it boil for 1 hour." Her recipe for turtle soup is no less explicit: "To make this soup with less difficulty, cut off the head of the turtle the preceding day. In the morning open the turtle by leaning heavily with a knife on the shell of the animal's back, whilst you cut this off all round. . . ."[38] There is not a whiff of smelling salts over these pages.

Circumlocutions would in any event have been out of place with most well-brought-up women in the nineteenth century. They were not afraid of dissections. Early in the century, Catharine Beecher, then a young girl, came upon the carcass of a beached whale being cut up for commercial purposes. "It looked like an acre of red meat sunk deep in the sand," she recalled in her autobiography, "and men and boys were cutting it in huge hunks and dragging it off for manure." About eighty years later, young Emily Lytton caught a fish with its own eye. Having landed a "small roach," she had, "in removing the hook brought out the eye with it. The fish, being small, I threw back, and then for fun baited the hook with the eye. A few moments later I had a bite and landed the same small fish with a gaping socket to show where the eye had been."[39] Both of these fairly unpleasant reminiscences were revived, from the distance of maturity, to decorate autobiographical writings, so they must have left a deep mark on these girls' minds. But they were not manifestly horrifying memories, whatever mixed feelings of fascination they deposited. I need not decide whether it was sensual needs that these experi-

---

38. Mrs. Isabella Beeton, *The Book of Household Management; Comprising Information for the Mistress, Housekeeper, Cook, Kitchen-Maid, Butler, Footman, Coachman, Valet, Upper and Under House-Maids, Lady's Maid, Maid-of-all-Work, Laundry-Maid, Nurse and Nurse-Maid, Monthly, Wet, and Sick Nurses, etc. etc. Also, Sanitary, Medical & Legal Memoranda; With a History of the Origin, Properties, and Uses of All Things Connected with Home Life and Comfort* (1861; first serialized in monthly supplements to *Englishwoman's Domestic Magazine* from 1859), 89, 98.

39. Beecher: Sklar, *Catharine Beecher*, 9; Lytton: Lady Emily Lutyens, *A Blessed Girl: Memoirs of a Victorian Girlhood Chronicled in an Exchange of Letters, 1887–1896* (1954), 7.—Late in 1870, when she was not yet fourteen, M. Carey Thomas killed a mouse to get at its skeleton. Bravely she dissected it in the presence of a good friend. The two girls took the dead mouse into the backyard "and commenced operations." Unfortunately, "the horrid mouse's fur was so soft that we couldn't make a hole and besides it made us sick and our hands trembled so we couldn't do a thing. But concluding it was *feminine* nonsense we made a hole and squeezed his insides out. It was the most disgusting thing I ever did. We then took off his skin. It came off elegantly just like a glove." Then the girls boiled the carcass, "picked all the meat off it and saved the tongue and eyes to look through the microscope and then the mouse looked like a real skeleton." For all her evident disgust and counterphobic behavior—being manly lest she be thought feminine—Carey Thomas claimed to enjoy the experiment: "I greatly prefer cutting up mice," she concluded, "to sewing worsted." November 26, 1870, *The Making of a Feminist: Early Journals and Letters of M. Carey Thomas,* ed. Marjorie Housepian Dobkin (1979), 44–45.

ences gratified or aggressive ones; doubtless a mixture of both. What matters is that decorous blushing was the last thing these gentle girls were inclined to resort to, and that they always stood ready to enlarge their store of physical information. For reasons that are easy to surmise, men made it a point of honor to lament women's lack of candor and to praise their own; Amiel spoke for the masculine tribe when he noted in his journal, not without self-satisfaction, that "women, through a complicated modesty of dissimulation, rarely put their words into accord with their thoughts." They were, he thought, duplicitous by nature. And while he was here speaking of sexual flirtatiousness, Amiel generalized his observation to embrace the whole domain of frankness, a domain that was evidently not woman's natural home.[40] Actually, there is good evidence that nineteenth-century women were often less squeamish than men, and that when men were squeamish in their behalf, they were protecting an ideal in their minds, suiting their own needs. While male reviewers exclaimed over the shocking passages in Walt Whitman's poems, women readers found these very passages grounds for wanting to meet him. Indeed, in 1856, when Sara Parton reviewed *Leaves of Grass*, she made her boldness quite explicit: "My moral constitution," she wrote, "may be hopelessly tainted or—too sound to be tainted, as the critic wills, but I confess that I extract no poison from these 'Leaves'—to me they have brought only healing." And she concluded with a weighty metaphor, coupling the freedom to look upon the body with the freedom to read about it: "Let him who can do so shroud the eyes of the nursing babe lest it see its mother's breast."[41] Parton usefully reminded her readers, as she can remind the historian, that the gathering of carnal knowledge begins very early.

Isabella Beeton could thus count on a sympathetic public as she moved, in her businesslike way, from the physiology of animals to that of humans. "All women," she told her readers, who knew from experience that Mrs. Beeton was right, "are likely, at some period of their lives, to be called on to perform the duties of a sick-nurse," and it is best if they prepare themselves, "by observation and reading," for whatever emergency they are called upon to handle. She regarded the "main requirements" for such a nurse to be "good temper, compassion for suffering, sympathy with sufferers," as well as "neat-handedness, quiet manners, love of order, and cleanliness." Once a woman has these qualities, and most do, her wish to "relieve suffering" will help her to "surmount the disgusts which some of

40. November 13, 1851, *Journal intime*, I, 1096; see also 1101.
41. Justin Kaplan, *Walt Whitman: A Life* (1980), 217.

the offices attending the sick-room are apt to create." This is a comment worth noting: Mrs. Beeton does not conceal from her readers that handling bleeding, vomiting, and diarrhea is bound to be unpleasant; she does not advocate a blinkered stoicism that would prepare the sick-nurse for her heroic measures by denying the smells and sights she will encounter. To be sure, like all books of advice, Mrs. Beeton's book, too, is at least in part a hope—a prescription for rather than a description of attitudes. But her perception of her public cannot have differed markedly from that public's perception of itself, and she saw the average literate English housewife as quite knowledgeable about the human animal, as a sturdy rather than a tender plant: "In a civilized state of society," Mrs. Beeton writes, "few young wives reach the epoch that makes them mothers without some insight, traditional or practical, into the management of infants." They will not treat the body, that "beautiful piece of mechanism," as a threatening stranger. But if they need further instruction, Mrs. Beeton is there to impart it, freely. She advises the nursing mother that she should have "a breast pump, or glass tube, to draw off the superabundance that has been accumulating in her absence from the child, or the first gush excited by undue exertion"; she advises her also that if she wants to keep her nipples "sound and unchapped" while she is nursing, and to "avoid what is called a 'broken breast,'" there are several things she can do, and Mrs. Beeton tells her, with calm and competent precision, what they are.[42]

Nursing in general inspired Mrs. Beeton to heights of open-eyed realism, and here once more she was only following, rather than setting, the tone of the times. It is hardly noteworthy that one mother should advise another on this delicate matter: late in 1841, Elizabeth Gaskell urged her sister-in-law Elizabeth Holland to "have a wet nurse if your own milk fails." But that just the year before, William Ewart Gladstone

---

42. Beeton, *Book of Household Management*, 1017, 1060, 1025, 1026, 1036, 1039. There is abundant evidence, from many countries, that Mrs. Beeton appraised her middle-class audience correctly. Not long after she had reported a miscarriage to her sister Sue, Eleanor Rogers told her that her husband Will also needed care. "Will's other lung began to trouble him Sunday and though he has been at the office all day he went to bed as soon as he got home. I still have to paint him with iodine, and mustard pastes followed by chloroform liniment & hot flannels are necessary every day to keep his neck limbered up so he can turn his head." May 28, 1885, SF, Y-MA. And the wife of the German Egyptologist and successful novelist Georg Ebers, who suffered from ill health for the last two decades of his life, kept a meticulous account of her ministrations, filled with his attacks of screaming, vomiting, melodramatic farewells to the family, morphine injections, and so forth. "Georg Ebers' Krankheit. Aufzeichnungen von Antonie Ebers, 1887–1898," box 25, Georg Ebers Nachlass, Stabi, Berlin.

should find room in his austere diary to report *his* sister-in-law in this very predicament, discloses unsuspected candor in Victorian domesticity: "Mary has been obliged to give up nursing." Like Mrs. Gaskell and Mr. Gladstone, Mrs. Beeton thought the matter worthy of the closest attention, and like them, emphatically, she wanted mothers to nurse their own children. Wet nurses, in her day, did not have a good reputation. But when, "from illness, suppression of milk, accident, or some natural process, the mother is deprived of the pleasure of rearing her infant," a wet nurse must be promptly engaged. She must be chosen and inspected with care. "The age, if possible, should not be less than twenty nor exceed thirty years, with the health sound in every respect, and the body free from all eruptive disease or local blemish. The best evidence of a sound state of health will be found in the woman's clear open countenance, the ruddy tone of the skin, the full, round, and elastic state of the breasts, and especially in the erectile, firm condition of the nipple, which, in all unhealthy states of the body, is pendulous, flabby, and relaxed; in which case, the milk is sure to be imperfect in its organization, and, consequently, deficient in its nutrient qualities."[43]

Mrs. Beeton provides these directions with the unselfconscious casualness of someone discussing familiar matters. Implicit in her counsel are, of course, the harsh facts of nineteenth-century class society; few women of means would have discussed, none would have inspected, the nipples of another woman of means. But the point is that Mrs. Beeton expected the commonplace housewife to look at the body of her servant without the slightest twinge of embarrassment. From what I have discovered about her age and class, Mrs. Beeton was quite realistic in her expectations.

The capacity to be comfortable with the body in health and sickness was not the privileged preserve of women writing in their diaries, and to, or for, their intimates. Parents and good friends, to say nothing of husbands, were cheerfully admitted to the inner circle in which carnal knowledge was shared, and thus further developed. Not long after she was married, Sophia Hawthorne reported to her mother that the famous Margaret Fuller had come to visit: "I sprang from my husband's embrace, and found Queen Margaret." And in the 1860s, Lady Duff Gordon, gently born and gently married, went to Egypt for her health—she was, it turned out, suffering from tuberculosis—and shared her adventures

43. Gaskell: [Late 1841], *The Letters of Mrs. Gaskell*, ed. J. A. V. Chapple and Arthur Pollard (1966), 40–41; Gladstone: July 19, 1840, *The Gladstone Diaries*, ed. M. R. D. Foot and H. C. G. Matthew, 8 vols. so far (1968–   ), III, 47; Beeton: *Book of Household Management*, 1022–23.

with her family back in England, in long and intelligent letters. Among other intimate events she witnessed a love affair between her English maid and her Egyptian servant which resulted in an illegitimate pregnancy. Her report on the affair is as circumstantial as it is judicious; she blames her maid for seducing the servant and then putting her mistress to the trouble of delivering the baby. "I must say," she wrote, "she might have spared me the task of being midwife and monthly nurse in a boat and frightened sick by it all. Of course it happened at midnight in a desolate place. However, she was delivered without a twinge and did admirably."[44] If she was indeed frightened, she sturdily overcame it to do a midwife's work—well enough, it would seem—and to write about it without simpering and without moralistic condescension.

The tone of Lady Duff Gordon's letter, quite as much as its content, strongly suggests that at least some among the respectable could confront the consequences of sexuality, the work of the body in its most palpable and scandalous form, with a measure of inner freedom. In a culture in which many women, and some men, spent a good deal of time canvassing the social status and conduct of others, in which some houses would not receive divorcees or unmarried couples living together, there were those who made room for the transgressor. There is no evidence that Lady Duff Gordon lectured her maid for compromising her virtue so ostentatiously. Other women were as uncensorious as she. In early 1877, Mary Foote wrote from California to her cherished friend Helena Gilder about her pregnancy. Her husband Arthur, she reported, was designing a cradle to hang from the ceiling of the piazza, and this meant displacing her maid Lizzie's little boy. "Lizzie's baby sleeps in the hammock on the piazza and I hate to turn him out, poor little fatherless one! There is something very tragic about Lizzie. She has never spoken of her trouble but once as an apology for being short with Georgie." Once Mary Foote had "asked her if it would be any relief to speak," but Lizzie had said that it would not. "Better not begin. I might tell enough if I was to let myself, but it would do no good." When Lizzie sings to her Georgie, Mary Foote goes on, she "never sings songs with any allusion to the *Papa.*"[45] It all sounds very sad, and the dominant note in Mary Foote's confidential report is one of compassion.

This sort of delicacy, all kindness and no shame, was available to men. "May I tell you a queer thing that happened in S.F.," Mary Foote had

44. August 22, 1842, James R. Mellow, *Nathaniel Hawthorne in His Time* (1980), 211; *Letters from Egypt 1862–1869*, ed. Gordon Waterfield (1969), 189.

45. January 28 [1877], Mary Hallock Foote Papers, Special Collections, C. H. Green Library, Stanford University.

written, also to Helena Gilder, just a month before. "It was the beginning of life in my little unknown." She had attended church with two good friends, Mr. Hague and Mr. Ashburner, and during the first part of the service, the "organ made me feel so strangely—Its throbbing seemed to stifle me and for the first time that pulse within me woke and throbbed so strong and it took away my breath." Seated between her two men friends, she felt faint. "Everything grew dark and I did not know anything for a minute—I don't know how long—but came to myself with great drops of perspiration on my lips and forehead—Mr. Ashburner was looking at me very closely—Both Mr. Hague & Ashburner were delicate enough not to allude to it." On the walk home, the three were joined by an acquaintance, who "cheerfully" asked her if she had been ill, for she had looked as though she were going to faint. " 'Ashburner thought so too!'—'Didn't you notice it—Hague'—?" But Mary Foote's friends were not to be ruffled. "Mr. H. said—'I thought she looked a little pale, but the church was very close', and then changed the subject—." Then, preoccupied with the rhythm of life in her body, Mary Foote dismissed the men from her tale. But the historian keeps them in view. She went on to describe that universal, yet *strangest* feeling," that "double pulse—that life within a life—I cannot get used to it!"[46] But evidently Mr. Hague and Mr. Ashburton were used to it; they read her face, understood her feelings, and calmly did the natural thing to protect her privacy without neglecting the warning signals of possible trouble. Learned ignorance could not have acted with so sure a touch, with that felicitous mixture of distance and intimacy.

If friends could unostentatiously mobilize their carnal knowledge, husbands could be expected to be more knowledgeable still, and feel no embarrassment as they cared for their wives' physical needs or spoke of their wives' private parts. Aboard ship to England, Taine had been touched to see "A young woman very seasick: her husband, who appears to be a commercial traveller, held her in his arms, supported her, tried to read to her, in short nursed her with complete freedom and infinite tenderness." That commercial traveler, whose name is lost to history, was not eccentric in his day. In late 1864, while his wife was pregnant with their third child, Joseph Lyman carefully measured her dimensions and meticulously recorded them on a little slip of paper, entitled "Laura at 280 days." And in July 1885, while Mabel Todd was traveling in Europe, her husband sent her a long monitory letter begging her to take care of her health and to drink only boiled water for fear of cholera. "I have

46. 21 [December 1876], ibid.

trusted you alone, darling," he wrote, "but you know you are not so cautious about these things as I am." Then he got to the business that really worried him, "the other physical matter I wrote you—relating to both of us, I mean." He was being oblique not because he was being prissy, but because the two had discussed this troublesome spot before. "I have been studying the matter over a good deal, & it seems likely to have come from some vaginal trouble you had, at or after the time of that severe cold & sore throat. The tendency to repetition of any such thing will be very greatly lessened if you are more frequent in cleansing the vagina."[47] No cant here, no worship of the sacred body, only a blunt reminder from one well-informed marriage partner to another.

David Todd's clinical coolness, which barely masks his anxiety, is less than typical for correspondence between ordinary husbands and wives in his culture. But, to judge from the diary that William Ewart Gladstone kept all his life, carnal candor was certainly not confined to sensualists. Gladstone was an earnest, prayerful, obsessive worker, equipped with a conscience commodious and severe enough to supply a regiment of penitents; he used his daily entries to protocol his erotic temptations, and to measure just how far he had fallen short of the perfection he demanded of himself. He noted his reading, his letter-writing, his political speeches, his acts of charity, his religious observances, and his feelings of unworthiness and guilt. His diaries were also a depository of domesticity, which he experienced as a mixture of sober pleasures and a set of duties that he took as seriously as he took his politics and his Christianity. And the body is not absent from his pages.

Late in October 1842, shortly after her second child was born, Catherine Gladstone developed difficulties with the flow of her milk, an uncomfortable stoppage that threatened swelling and possibly dangerous complications later. We can follow the course of her tribulations in the faithful, if laconic, entries in her husband's diary. The baby was born on October 18, with the mother, we know, brave in her pain and pious in her resolve. For a few days "the dear babe" and her mother were comfortable, but by the twenty-eighth "C." was "very uneasy on one side," and on November 8, after some intermittent improvement, she "suffered most severely from a violent attack of pain in her breast." So, at two in the morning, her husband went for the doctor, and on the next day he could record, "C. better thank God: fights heroically for nature," which is to say that she persisted in her attempts to nurse her daughter herself. By

47. Taine, *Notes on England*, 6; Lyman, box 8, LF; Todd, July 10, 1885, box 36, MLT.

the fourteenth, "Dearest C." still had "her difficulties," baffling her physician, and two days later, two doctors, concurring in the diagnosis, declared "a gathering in the left, & it was bandaged & nursing proscribed." This was painful for the mother in more ways than one: "C. showed me with tears that for the first time she had an abundance—& we got a short reprieve." There was a distinct improvement for a time, but the stoppages returned, and by December 19, after consulting a specialist in Birmingham, the couple resolved, sadly, to wean the baby: "we have now to consider & watch carefully whether hand will do or whether a nurse must be had." Most of the time the hand that expressed the milk lest an abscess ensue was the hand of William Ewart Gladstone.

After the Gladstones' fourth child, Jessy, was born, "C's difficulties with the milk recurred; but relief thank God was obtained at night by the usual means," and then the usual anxieties passed off. With Mary, their fifth, there was some soreness in Catherine's nipples, and when the baby was two days old her husband "rubbed a little for her, almost the first office I have been able to perform about her."[48] After the birth of their sixth child, Helen, he noted with the resignation of an experienced family man that "C. was of course in the meshes of her old difficulties today" and that "aperient medicines tried several times" before had failed. Resignation did not betoken indifference. When manipulations were indicated, Gladstone, a burdened and prominent politician, was there to perform them. "Much rubbing however (by Mrs S[mith] & me) seemed to keep the right organ from getting into an obstinate state." On the following day, he was "much with C. rubbing & otherwise—the medicine has acted, the rubbing too answers & except some soreness everything thank God is well." From then on, improvement was steady: by September 3, he could report, "We have now ceased to rub." With their next child, Henry, Catherine Gladstone's recurrent problem proved somewhat more persistent. "In the aftn. C.s flood of milk troubled her," he wrote in early April 1852, "—& a long rubbing at night in some sort brought it round." Only in some sort: on the next day, he administered "another good rubbing at night—& prayers as usual." Both proved insufficient: "C. kept her ground," he noted three days later, "more rubbing: the difficulty not yet ended." Then, on the next day, "Continued the rubbing with C: who also laboured under some soreness: but better than at any time since 42." Better did not mean quite well; on April 9,

48. October 28, November 8, 9, 14, 16, December 19, 1842; July 28, 1845; November 25, 1847, Gladstone Diaries, III, 234, 237, 238, 239, 247, 472, 671.

there is the final entry before happy normal nursing could resume: "C. improving pretty steadily: rubbing, perhaps the last needed."[49] Confronted with his wife's painful, recurrent problems with nursing, William Ewart Gladstone was not too genteel to offer, and Catherine Gladstone not too genteel to accept, his manual ministrations.

Those homely notations, heartfelt and undramatic, support the conclusion that, if the subtleties of sexual intercourse could pose mysteries for bourgeois husbands in the nineteenth century, its consequences found them involved and well-informed. Many other records, no less homely and no less heartfelt, provide corroborating evidence. The domestic needs and feelings of the nineteenth-century bourgeoisie made, for the married, knowledge of the body a simple necessity, a matter of course. A couple like the Todds were, as we know, unusual in many respects. But in treating one another's bodies as open shrines, they were much like others of their class. Not long after Mabel Loomis Todd was proved to be pregnant, her adoring husband—he was not a scientist for nothing—attempted to establish the sex of the baby she was carrying, by as direct an inspection as was then possible: "Upon Sunday, 28 September," she recalled not long after, "David listened for the tiny heart beats below my own, & heard them distinctly, 146 per minute, which is far above the average for a boy. Subsequently he has heard them several times, once they were oftener than that, twice I think, less frequent, but never below 130," results which they interpreted, correctly enough, to mean that they were going to have a daughter. When Millicent was born, David Todd was naturally present. On February 5, 1880, Mabel Todd, lying beside her husband, awoke at two in the morning, startled by "a singular flow of water coming from me." She put a "large Turkish towel" under herself, but, "the water continuing to flow, I began to think it something serious, & I spoke to David." Looking at the towel under the gaslight, she saw a "small clot of blood," and "upon that, David arose, & said perhaps he had better put the rubber cloth on the bed to prevent the mattress from being wet." So she got up and David Todd "arranged the bed." When, "just before three o'clock David thought probably the little child was coming," he went upstairs to tell his wife's father to stay with her while he went to fetch both nurse and doctor. Her labor pains came periodically, with the pulse of the pain speeding up, but though she cried out repeatedly and "suffered intensely," she found her travail far from unbearable. Still, she did not notice the entrance of Dr. Groot and her

49. August 30, 31, September 3, 1849; April 4, 7, 8, 9, 1852, *Gladstone Diaries*, IV, 151, 152, 418–19.

David, being then intent on the delivery itself and taking little catnaps between contractions—"I was *so* sleepy!" Just before six, her "precious Millicent was born!" and her pain ceased. When the placenta did not come by itself, Dr. Groot, who had been watching his patient intently, "after perhaps five minutes of waiting, gently drew upon the cord, & removed it," then cut the cord. During all of Mabel Todd's labor, her mother had stayed in her own room, since she did not "feel equal to endure the sight of my pain," so that it was the nurse, the physician, her father, and her husband who saw it all.[50]

How intimately David Todd was engaged with the process of childbirth and its attendant carnal realities emerges most plainly in his wife's diary. Mabel Todd's entry for February 4 was completed by her husband; and then for more than three weeks, *he* kept her diary. On February 5, he recorded the birth of his "little Millicent Todd," a "moment or two before six"; two days later, he noted that Dr. Groot was "surprised to find already a very abundant supply of support from the little mother for her little child." He supplemented this agreeable news on the following day, spent at home "with his little wife," by noting that she experienced "almost no pain from giving the young child its food—of which there is an overflowing abundance." It was not until February 27 that Mabel Todd resumed her diary with an exuberant exclamation: "back again!"[51] David Todd's language is labored and circumlocutory; he refrains from using the word "milk," just as William Ewart Gladstone sometimes elided the word "breast" in his diary. But such verbal reserve, though of some diagnostic interest, in no way suggests squeamishness, false gentility. At the vital moments of woman's life, however messy, nineteenth-century husbands were there.

In bourgeois domestic life, the birth of a child was a time less of poetic exaltation than of shared suffering and hard work. When, on June 6, 1869, Siegfried Wagner was born, Richard Wagner witnessed most of Cosima von Bülow's labor. The couple kept separate bedrooms, but on this day, at one in the morning, she awakened him to tell him that her pains were beginning; he walked her back to her bed and watched over her, "in great concern." When the midwife arrived around three, he decided to take a nap to "strengthen himself for the day ahead," but he was too tense to sleep and returned to Cosima, finding her "under the midwife's ministrations, in the most furious pains." Startled by his sudden appearance, Cosima "drove" him out, but he would not stay

---

50. "Millicent's Life," I [pp. 23, 34]; II [pp. 1–3], box 46, MLT.
51. Diary 1880, box 39, MLT.

away; hearing her "moaning," he rushed back and Cosima, in great pain, clutched his arm for a while. Then she asked him to leave her, and he remained in the adjoining room within earshot, hearing "the events of the delivery."[52] The scene is a little hectic, somewhat melodramatic in the action and self-conscious in the telling, but it duplicates in its own heightened way the experience of most nineteenth-century couples.

William Ewart Gladstone's diaries confirm that Richard Wagner's performance was, self-dramatization apart, fairly representative. The birth of the Gladstone children was attended with less theatricality, but with no less emotion. When the first, Willy, was born his father was present at the "slow but favourable labour." It was a new experience for him, as he explicitly noted, but he did not evade it. By the time their second child, Agnes, was born, Gladstone was less of a novice, though no less engaged by the awesome spectacle: "Dearest C.," he writes on October 18, 1842, "had slept well: but had occasional pains thro the early part of the day—we drove at 11 to 12—at 3 she went upstairs & the pains increased very gradually till 6½: then quicker & quicker, 1½ hour very sharp & a girl was born at 8, bigger even than Willy was. Catherine bore the last pains with perfect fortitude & I could not but observe how exceedingly beautiful she looked while this suffering so severe but without bitterness was upon her."[53] It is worth recalling that for Catherine Gladstone there was not, as there would be for many mothers from the 1850s on, chloroform to ease the pain.

What lends such autobiographical jottings their historical credibility is precisely their artlessness, their undisguised roots in the commonplace. Gladstone solemnly and tenderly rubbing his wife's aching breasts and then faithfully noting down his ministrations is being unliterary, repetitive, almost offhand. But he is not recording trivia; he is being a good and loving bourgeois husband taking full responsibility for his, and his wife's, erotic life. And Catherine Gladstone showing her husband "with tears" her abundance of milk makes a dazzling, memorable vignette. So does David Todd putting his ear to his wife's swollen belly to count the heartbeats of his unborn child. Incidents such as these breathe life into the statistics, at best fragmentary and barely legible, that purport to define middle-class sensuality. They elevate anecdotes of domesticity to the stature of a clue to culture, for they lead beyond the particular event to the general climate; they are precious moments of illumination re-

52. Cosima Wagner, *Die Tagebücher*, ed. Martin Gregor-Dellin and Dietrich Mack, vol. I, *1869–1877* (1976), 103–4; Richard Wagner is here writing in her diary (as David Todd had written in Mabel's), but referring to himself in the third person.
53. June 3, 1840, October 18, 1842, *Gladstone Diaries*, III, 33, 231.

sembling nothing so much as a subtle, climactic scene in a novel by Henry James, in which a great deal is clarified by spare gestures and a few words. Vastly though they differ in feeling and form, these humble, oft-repeated incidents open doors to the erotic experience of the nineteenth-century bourgeoisie.

At the same time, they settle very little, certainly nothing conclusively. At times—I suspect very often—the sudden acquisition of carnal knowledge was simply frightening. One evening in 1878, Carey Thomas, then attending graduate school at Johns Hopkins, and two of her close women friends ran through Eliza B. Duffey's *What Women Should Know*, and "about fifteen" of her father's medical books. They thought themselves "old enough to know all about the different forces of life"—Carey Thomas was then twenty-one. And she was determined to enter life without blindfolds; "if passion and sensuality are sure factors I wanted to understand them." After all, "to the pure all things are pure," and surely "natural phenomena" cannot be "degrading." But once these young women had done their clandestine reading, they were horrified and revolted. "I went to bed sick. Absolutely—I had eaten of the fruit of the tree of knowledge of good and evil and it seemed as if there was no such thing as ever believing in purity and holiness again, or ever getting my own mind pure again." What drove her to despair, and, she discovered, her friends as well, was the shock of encountering "this one hateful beastly impulse of men"; she hated to see that "*sense* remains and apparently men are made so."[54] It was not then clear to her, or she quickly repressed the knowledge, that women, too, are made so, and she felt as if she had been violated. Carnal knowledge in itself certainly did not guarantee erotic satisfaction: Carey Thomas's experience documents the rich possibilities for confusion and misery consequent upon the wrong kind of instruction.

Isabella Beeton in the kitchen, then, was a long way from Mabel Todd in the bedroom. Henri Frédéric Amiel picked up a good deal of sexual information by peering through cracks in bath houses and discussing women with intimate friends, but never became comfortable with his sensual needs. Platonic libertinism, in which he and many others indulged, was an uncertain preparation for physical libertinism. The girl who knew how to castrate a lamb or carve a calf's head had not, with this, automatically mastered the varieties of sexual techniques. There are too many variables, notably the psychological history of the sexual partners, to permit easy inferences from knowingness to happiness. If ignorance is not bliss, it does not follow that knowledge *must* be bliss. It is far safer to argue that knowledge is a better guide to sexual gratification than ignorance, and beyond doubt, whatever detractors might say, such knowledge was abundant in the bourgeois century.

3. Readers in Conflict

Short of sexual experimentation itself, the most enticing guide to carnal knowledge in the nineteenth century was, at least on the surface, pornography. It was massively produced and, for the knowing, readily available; booksellers clustering in disreputable neighborhoods stocked obscene prints and books to satisfy the most avid demand. The Paris trade was concentrated around the Palais Royal; London had Holywell Street, a name that by mid-century had become a synonym for obscene publications in general. In 1845, a raid on the premises of one purveyor in Holywell Street yielded 383 books, 351 copperplates, 12,346 prints, 188 lithographic stones, and 3,752 pounds of type font.[55] The sordid shop that Joseph Conrad describes in *The Secret Agent*, with its grimy windows, fly-blown displays, seductive titles, and furtive customers, was a familiar sight in large cities everywhere. While states attempted to check salacious imports at the border—British customs was authorized by an act of 1853 to seize all kinds of "indecent" materials—French and Italian confections crossed frontiers with a certain ease, to supply readers and voyeurs in search of foreign fare. For pornography, as for other merchandise, this was an age of free trade, however imperfect.

Diligent, earnest enforcers of the law interfered with unsavory booksellers; they ruined some and drove others into unrepentant evile or timid conformity. In December 1857, Lord Campbell, Chief Justice of the Queen's Bench and principal architect of England's Obscene Publications Act, passed that year, noted in his diary that the success of his legislation had been "most brilliant. Holywell Street which had long set law and decency at defiance has capitulated after several assaults. Half the shops are shut up and the remainder deal in nothing but moral and religious books." Similar gratifying progress, he added with a glow of satisfaction, had been made in Dublin and "even in Paris."[56] Campbell was being unworldly to the point of naiveté. Pornography continued to be fairly accessible, in new shops at new addresses, or at the same shop, better

---

55. H. Montgomery Hyde, *A History of Pornography* (1964), 167.
56. Diary, December 17, 1857, Hon. Mrs. Hardcastle, ed., *Life of Lord Chancellor Campbell, Lord High Chancellor of Great Britain. Consisting of a Selection from his Autobiography, Diaries, and Letters*, 2 vols. (1881), II, 356.

camouflaged than before. Prosecutions served to advertise spicy titles and efficient publishers of erotica. Theirs was, if one could only survive, a profitable trade. What kept much pornography out of the hands of the impecunious was less the police than the price: the most notorious of these publications, sumptuously bound and lavishly (and graphically) illustrated, were offered in limited editions, too expensive to reach any but rich amateurs. But rich or poor, one could count on the trade. In 1881, summarizing the first eight years of its purifying work, Anthony Comstock's New York Society for the Suppression of Vice reported, with the meticulousness which was his signature, that it had managed to have 27,584 pounds of books destroyed and had confiscated precisely 203,238 obscene pictures, both photographs and etchings, and 1,376,939 catalogues, songs, circulars, and poems.[57] Admittedly, Comstock and his assiduous allies defined pornography very generously, but the numbers suggest that those intent on stimulating their sexual fantasies through reading and looking could satisfy their needs adequately enough.

Defenders of good morals, already in a near-panic about other social evils, grew increasingly nervous about what they perceived to be the rising tide of printed smut. The invention and rapid perfection of the photograph only intensified their alarm. Dismayed moralists found that nineteenth-century technology, the source of so many unquestioned blessings to civilization, also facilitated the dissemination of moral poison. Hence the tempo of prosecutions stepped up markedly in the course of the nineteenth century. The year 1857 is critical; it was in 1857 that Gustave Flaubert, Charles Baudelaire, and Eugène Sue were prosecuted in France for offending public morals and that Britain introduced the Obscene Publications Act.

What came to be called "Victorian" around the same time long ante-dates Victoria, as we know: King George III's much-quoted Royal Proclamation against Vice and Immorality, which bade his subjects to "suppress all loose and licentious prints, books, and publications," dates from 1787; the alert Society for the Suppression of Vice, which instigated a number of successful criminal prosecutions in England, from 1802. A French royal ordinance prohibiting books offending "the purity of morals" goes back to 1751; eighteenth-century officials frequently seized offensive books, and even in the most libertarian phase of the French Revolution, in 1791, municipal police were authorized to bring the sellers of "obscene images" and of books outraging "the modesty of women" before justices of the peace. Decades before the bourgeois

57. James Jackson Kilpatrick, *The Smut Peddlers* (1960), 243.

ascendancy reached its apogee, a succession of regimes acted energetically, if sporadically, to protect morals no less assiduously than church
or state from degradation and subversion. They issued stringent laws,
stern instructions to censors, and administrative directions for local
police officials. But the French Second Empire and early Third Republic,
the German Reich of 1871, late-Victorian England, and the post–Civil
War United States initiated far more house searches, public denunciations, and criminal trials than their predecessors. Pressures in literature
and the arts for liberty—their worried and pious detractors called it
libertinism—coupled with the apprehensiveness attendant upon the breathtaking changes dominating the age generated defensive responses that
went far beyond earlier campaigns to contain obnoxious publications. As
always, there were in these campaigns unmistakable national variations:
Englishmen, appalled at their domestic trade in smut, were even more
appalled at what they denounced, a little complacently, as rampant French
licentiousness. But all, including many Frenchmen, agreed that obscenity
was a modern epidemic which must be eradicated before it fatally infected
all of civilization.

   The anti-smut crusaders energetically turned out literally hundreds of
pamphlets; German readers especially found themselves inundated by
titles proclaiming the nation in danger, calling upon schools to combat
Hintertreppenliteratur, "backstairs literature," in all its malignant forms,
and analyzing pornography as a cause of delinquency and crime. The
general level of irritability was high. Nor was it lowered by the resistance of many German bourgeois to this crusade: in their eyes,
much of the material that the crusaders rather liberally defined as trash
was innocuous, though crude, tales of adventure, and they feared the
philistine venting his nervous rage on experimental literature. But since,
especially after 1900, many little stationery and cigar stores carried
lucrative cheap literature quite openly, the fighters against filth thought
their case well made: "At last people know," Dr. Ernst Schultze wrote
in the preface to his *Die Schundliteratur* of 1909, a typical publication,
"that we have to do with a dangerous enemy—not one that we can
just ridicule." Four years later, Friedrich v. der Leyen, in an essay on
popular literature and popular education, spoke with dismay of the
"uncanny and rapid increase of very wicked literature," an increase that
has "filled the many who care about the spiritual and moral future of
Germany with concern and horror."[58]

   58. Schultze, *Die Schundliteratur. Ihr Wesen, Ihre Folgen, Ihre Bekämpfung* (1909),
7; v. der Leyen, "Volksliteratur und Volksbildung" (1913), special offprint from
Deutsche Rundschau, XIV, 1 (October 1913), 49.

In this atmosphere of pervasive gloom and desperate search for remedies, private associations to combat these seductive evils emerged everywhere. Led by zealots and fluent publicists, often well financed and sponsored by prominent personages, they lobbied for sterner laws, boycotted stores that offended their standards, and brought pressure upon publishers to weed unsuitable materials from their catalogues. Anthony Comstock's widely publicized New York Society for the Suppression of Vice soon had good company in Europe. In 1901, Otto von Leixner, the journalist and editor whose early diaries I have had occasion to quote, founded a Volksbund zur Bekämpfung des Schmutzes in Wort und Bild, while the French had their Ligue française de la moralité publique which, joining its nervous comrades, held its first Congrès des sociétés antipornographiques in 1905. By 1908, these groups had already held their second international congress in Paris. More and more, private citizens denounced sellers of books or photographs they deemed filthy; administrative regulations were brought into play when national legislation seemed unclear or inadequate. The movement to found free public libraries, which left its mark on the urban landscape in England, France, Germany, and the United States late in the nineteenth century, scored impressive successes for as many reasons as there were countries participating in it, but at least one of its incentives, as the polemical literature of the day leaves no reason to doubt, was to provide alternatives to the kind of cheap smut to which the young of all classes were exposed in the world of the rotary press and photogravure. In the campaign against sexually arousing materials, as in others, the last decades of the bourgeois century showed themselves an anxious time.

Many dealers in pornography may have prospered in the nineteenth century, but most of them went underground. The previous century, more intent upon checking sedition and blasphemy, had left obscenity if not free, relatively less obstructed. But in the nineteenth century, pornographers carried on a clandestine business, leaving few traces behind. It is no accident that the most persevering bibliographers have often failed to establish the authorship of best-selling pornographic works, and that a number of eminent nineteenth-century writers including Lord Byron, E. T. A. Hoffmann, Alfred de Musset, Mark Twain, and Guy de Maupassant, to say nothing of such popular, presumably decent publicists as Gustave Droz, had pornographic fictions attributed to them. Attributions of this sort were sometimes accurate enough; more often they were unsubstantiated gossip or brazen, unscrupulous deceptions by dealers in pornography. In this murky, shadowy world it is almost impossible to sort out fact from fancy.

These bibliographical conundrums are only symptomatic of larger and weightier riddles. The definition of pornography was then, as it remains now, almost proverbially elusive. Nor did legislators or judges prove very helpful; rather than settling controversy, they only intensified it. Lord Campbell, soliciting support for his proposed Obscene Publications bill, insisted that it would suppress only those works "written for the single purpose of corrupting the morals of youth" and "calculated to shock the common feelings of decency in a well regulated mind." His announced intentions, reiterated and refined in the face of spirited opposition both in the Lords and in the House of Commons, seemed judicious enough: he was not aiming at sexually explicit classics like Ovid's *Ars Amatoria* or the plays of the English Restoration. Yet J. A. Roebuck, the disputatious radical M.P., unappeased, complained that Campbell's bill "was at attempt to make people virtuous by Act of Parliament," and it was true that his formulations offered generous leeway to subjective and censorious interpretations. It might be easy to identify books written solely to corrupt the young; it was far more difficult to measure the shock administered to, and even to define, well-regulated minds—the two criteria were, in fact, not the same. In 1868, in an authoritative opinion that would set the tone in England and, largely, in the United States for a century, Chief Justice Cockburn gave troubled moralists and ambitious prosecutors still more room for maneuver. "The test of obscenity," he wrote, is "whether the tendency of the matter charged" is "to deprave and corrupt those whose minds are open to such immoral influences, and into whose hands a publication of this sort may fall."[59] Comparable statutes and their interpretation in other countries were no more precise than this. The French law of 1819, codified but neither softened nor further elucidated in 1881 and 1882, tersely condemned "outrages à la morale publique et religieuse et aux bonnes moeurs." Paragraph 184 of the criminal code governing the German Empire was couched in the same vague and resonant language: it prohibited the dissemination of "lewd" publications. Such sententiousness, though apparently adequate to the common understanding, raised interminable questions in the press and the courtroom: the very meaning of "depravation," of "corruption" and "lewdness," even of "distribution," offered rich opportunities to imaginative journalists and astute lawyers.

As Lord Campbell's critics had feared, the well-meaning efforts to contain the outpouring of filth had severe and (at least consciously) unintended consequences everywhere. Neither maker nor distributor of

59. Norman St. John Stevas, *Obscenity and the Law* (1956), 66–70.

erotic literature could expect bureaucrats or judges to have any patience with their pious alibi that the offending work was a covert moral tract excoriating the very vices it was compelled to explore so graphically. When Xavier de Montepin, a mediocre and slippery French sensation novelist, was put on trial for his vast *Les Filles de plâtre* in 1856, he professed, the court derisively noted, "the purity of his intentions, and claimed that his sole design was to blast and expose the mores of a certain social group."[60] He was sentenced to three months in prison. Other judges, and lofty journals like the *Saturday Review* of London, were equally short with such pretensions.

More ominous, the excuse that the questionable work had redeeming literary qualities, that it promised, as it were, to become a Rabelaisian classic of the future, impressed almost no one in authority. Private guardians of public virtue and prosecuting attorneys steadfastly refused to draw fundamental distinctions between works wholly devoted to the mechanical recital of sexual couplings and those containing scattered paragraphs or single verses they judged to be indecent. They came into court armed with lists of offending passages, and many of the verdicts, in fact, called not for the suppression of the whole book but for expurgation: in 1857, Charles Baudelaire and his publisher were ordered to delete six erotic poems from his *Fleurs du mal* while in 1900, after several protracted trials, a German court directed Richard Dehmel, a defiant, often intemperate realist, to strike only one poem from his substantial collection of outspoken and passionate lyrics, *Weib und Welt*. Serious literature calculated, and sometimes intended, to arouse sexual emotions shared the dock with unmistakable pieces of sexual exploitation or, for that matter, with informative, thoroughly aseptic pamphlets. In 1877, during the epoch-making Bradlaugh-Besant trial, the prosecutor denounced Charles Knowlton's *Fruits of Philosophy*, the birth-control tract at issue, as "a dirty, filthy book."[61] Government censors, state attorneys, moral reformers intent on stamping out vice, sustained by their sense of mission and of urgency in the face of danger, used such intemperate epithets quite indiscriminately. To their minds, a sensual lyric poem by Algernon Swinburne, a sober manual on contraception by Robert Dale Owen, and a pornographic story by Anonymous were all the same, all certain to corrupt and deprave the innocent. The most arresting and most controversial obscenity trials of the century were, therefore, not of

60. Alexandre Zévaès, *Les Procès littéraires au XIXe siècle* (1924), 69.
61. S. Chandrasekhar, *"A Dirty, Filthy Book": The Writings of Charles Knowlton and Annie Besant on Reproductive Physiology and Birth Control and an Account of the Bradlaugh-Besant Trial* (1981), 39.

pornographic productions at all, but of candid, realistic erotic poems, plays, and novels.

Certainly not all prosecutions succeeded: Flaubert, after all, was acquitted and saw *Madame Bovary* published integrally. Other poets and novelists in France and in other countries managed to be offensive to the authorities and remain free. Facile though it was, there was something to the observation that a writer's road to fortune lay through notoriety. But the looming threat of fines and prison, the humiliating prospect of having to share the defendants' bench with common criminals, and the financial risks to printers and publishers led to a certain crippling self-censorship, an anxious anticipation of official action that markedly interfered with most writers' intentions to say what they liked about sensuality. Swinburne was induced to withhold his masochistic novel *Lesbia Brandon*; moralistic, influential English lending libraries like Mudie's and railway bookstalls like W. H. Smith exercised a kind of informal censorship against the naturalists of the late nineteenth century; the enterprising publisher Henry Vizetelly was tried for bringing out an expurgated—but not sufficiently expurgated—English translation of Zola's *La Terre* and in 1889, at a second trial, was sentenced to three months in prison. Such instances were by their nature highly public and intimidated more writers than they stung into action. Even the French, who were visibly more tolerant than their neighbors, on occasion demonstrated the dangerous capriciousness of the censor's mind: in 1883, the young Louis Desprez was indicted for a naturalistic, serious novel about rural life, *Autour d'un clocher*. His coauthor, Henry Fevre, was too young to stand trial, but Desprez, despite the outcry among prominent literati like Emile Zola and Alphonse Daudet, and though frail and semi-invalid, was sentenced to a month in jail and a fine of a thousand francs. When Desprez died two years later, his allies in the literary world proclaimed him the victim of official murder. Some of the fury with which the literary and artistic avant-gardes pursued the bourgeoisie of the century stems from this ever-present specter, this intermittent frustration of the artistic will. Acquittals were momentary triumphs, causes for noisy celebration, but never quite enough to reassure the writers of the age. And if writers fared badly in France, they did worse elsewhere.

Some avant-garde experimenters, to be sure, had been exceedingly provocative all along. Insisting on their right to register the varieties of sexual feeling and conduct, they had made easy work for those seeking grounds to suppress them. Swinburne, for one, in *Lesbia Brandon*, dwells with such undisguised relish on the beatings that a virile tutor administers to his young pupil, and repeats these scenes with such frequency and in such detail, that the novel's sadomasochistic appeal is almost as direct as that of a purely pornographic tale of flagellation. And Swinburne's early *Poems and Ballads* of 1866 contains verses that move effortlessly from wounding foreplay to explicit cannibalism.

> I would my love could kill thee; I am satiated
> With seeing thee live, and fain would have thee dead,

as he puts it in *Anactoria.*

> I would find grievous ways to have thee slain.

His masochism is the counterpart to his sadism:

> Ah, wilt thou slay me lest I kiss thee dead?

But, at least in this poem, he prefers killing by making love to being killed:

> Ah that my lips were tuneless lips, but pressed
> To the bruised blossom of thy scourged white breast!
> Ah that my mouth for Muses' milk were fed
> On the sweet blood thy sweet small wounds had bled!
> That with my tongue I felt them and could taste
> The faint flakes from thy bosom to the waist!
> That I could drink thy veins as wine, and eat
> Thy breasts like honey! that from face to feet
> Thy body were abolished and consumed,
> And in my flesh thy very flesh entombed.

Whether the full implications of these rhymed fantasies were appreciated in that pre-psychoanalytic age or not, their outraged reviewers thought to see close and unhealthy affinities to the stuff sold in Holywell Street. It is easy now, from our perspective, to call this righteous reviewing misplaced: no hack writer could have remotely approached the verve, the precision, and the melody of Swinburne's prose and poetry. But his explicit images blurred the distinction between erotic literature and pornographic merchandise, a distinction which, the avant-garde and its spokesmen argued, was perfectly clear. They argued in vain.

The diverse ways in which readers responded to what they read goes far to explain all this confusion. One man's classic was another man's pornography. Amiel who, as we know, could wring sexual pleasure from the Latin definitions in legal dictionaries, enlarged the store of his carnal knowledge with "licentious books," helplessly, compulsively, anguished with shame. "O disgusting human race," he exclaimed in his diary after confessing that he could not stop reading obscene tales which, their mendacious authors to the contrary, would fail to arouse only old men. He berated himself without pity. "How vile we are, how hideous our species must appear to the angels!"[62] Yet the literature that awakened such paroxysms of self-reproach in Amiel included the fables of La Fontaine and the collected works of Montesquieu, both not without their *risqué* moments but scarcely panders to prurient tastes.

William Ewart Gladstone was as contrite about his addiction to "licentious books" as Amiel, and with little more reason. He judged it a sin to read Petronius "for the sake of knowledge." And Gladstone did not trifle with sin; he thought it incumbent upon him to confess that he found such reading, which he had expressly and solemnly undertaken to forswear, "in parts an attractive as well as a repulsive influence." Indeed, his choice of occasion, far more than of titles, bespeaks a kind of obsessive tactlessness. He read some offensive book just after his fifth child had been baptized and his beloved wife Catherine churched: on this day of days, he recorded in his diary, he had in this shameful manner given "proof" of his "ingratitude" for divine blessings received.[63] In Gladstone's unconscious, as in that of others, the sacred and the profane cohabited intimately. But the instruments of temptation, for which he literally flagellated himself, were in general Rabelaisian texts.

It was scarcely surprising that those who frankly enjoyed this sort of sexual stimulation should be no more discriminating. Early in 1887, Thomas Cameron Beer wrote to his brother William, who had evidently asked to have some spicy books forwarded to him. Thomas Beer was then twenty-seven, the son of a circuit judge, responsibly managing his family's property in Ohio. He told William that he would forward a "copy of the 'Devil on two Sticks,'" and, if he liked, "Manon Lescault," published in Berlin. This, he informed William Beer, was "one of the many books not allowed to be pub. in this country"; he had found it at a bookseller in Cincinnati, "& paid all it was worth." Prévost's *Manon Lescaut* put Thomas Beer into a reminiscent mood: "Do you remember," he asked his brother, once borrowing that book from a friend, "& how you got *thunder* from Pap?" Even young men, it would seem, had to be discreet about their choice of reading matter as late as the 1880s. His own library, he added, was "beginning to grow—with such as 'Rabelias' with Ills. by Dore—'Heptameron' by Margaret Queen of Navarre—Boccacio's 'Decameron'—& Aristotle's Famous Masterpiece—Advice to Mid-wives—."

---

62. January 14, 1850, *Journal intime*, I, 627.
63. January 15, December 15, 1847, *Gladstone Diaries*, III, 594–95, 677.

It seems a strikingly conventional, largely predictable list. But Thomas Beer was very proud of his daring. "Did you ever see such a tough collection? I guess I'm no different from other young bachelors."[64]

Precisely because Beer was, in his bold and manly posture, no different from other bourgeois bachelors of his time, his letter is extremely revealing. It is a rare specimen: few among Beer's contemporaries have left evidence of what aroused them. *Gargantua and Pantagruel*, whether illustrated by Doré or not, the *Decameron* and its quieter charming sixteenth-century echo, the *Heptameron*, were suitable fodder for the educated in search of not-too-scandalous sexual suggestion: their coarseness was redeemed by their distance, their sensuality by their wit. While Comstock and his allies counted these very titles among the greatest menaces the young could encounter, they *were* classics. Compared to them, André René LeSage's *Le Diable boiteux*, frequently reprinted and several times translated, is mild indeed, scarcely naughty. A set of picaresque tales loosely based on a Spanish original, this once-famous novel, given its final form in 1725, promises more eroticism than it delivers.[65] It requires an active, suggestive, and probably starved imagination to find LeSage erotically stimulating.

The only entry in Thomas Beer's little catalogue that remotely resembles pornography is *Aristotle's Master-Piece*—but only remotely. It alone among his titles could have supplied the innocent and the curious with abundant carnal knowledge. An informal seventeenth-century compendium often rewritten by a series of anonymous hands and foisted upon Aristotle, it lightened its informative, sometimes even reliable, dissertations on frigidity, impotence, pregnancy, and contraception with jaunty interpolated verses celebrating the joys of sexual congress. First published in the American colonies just before the Revolution, it had run through scores of editions and almost as many versions before Thomas Beer added it to his tough collection.

Beer's library, then, illustrates the susceptibility of nineteenth-century readers to rather tame material, to erotic and scatological scenes em-

64. Thomas Cameron Beer to William Collins Beer, February 8, 1887, box 18, Beer Family Papers, Y-MA. Raiding the stock of a publishing house in New York in 1894, Anthony Comstock found, among other "obscene" books, works by Boccaccio, Rabelais, and Queen Margaret of Navarre. Kilpatrick, *Smut Peddlers*, 46. Beer's list was, by the standards of his time, pretty "tough" after all.

65. The devil Asmodeus, who holds the book together, as George Saintsbury aptly put it in 1917, may be the demon whose particular province is sensuality. But "any fears or hopes which may be aroused by this description, and the circumstances of the action, will be disappointed. Lesage has plenty of risky situations, but his language is strictly 'proper.'" *A History of the French Novel (to the Close of the 19th Century)*, 2 vols. (1917), I, 330n.

bedded in drama, humor, and suspense. It is notorious that those who
need it will convert the most innocuous words and pictures into reasons
for arousal: anything whatever, including technical terms in dictionaries,
may serve as fuel for sexual fantasies. The libido in search of expression
will find, or if necessary construct, what it must have, and weave the
most elaborate masturbatory scenarios around the scantiest and least
probable suggestions. Nineteenth-century bourgeois libidos were no
exception to this human propensity.

The pornography of the age, in short, did not create sexual tastes; it
concentrated, channeled, and liberated inchoate wishes. It doubtless
proved adaptive at certain critical moments on life's way by assisting the
sexual imagination. That explains its appeal to lonely adolescents, frustrated bachelors, and aging roués. The appeal was over-determined:
knowing references to pornographic titles were as much a boost to one's
ego as actual acquaintance with pornographic texts were to one's erotic
fantasies. Many readers were, after all, wholly immune to such texts;
some protected by the reaction formation of disgust which translates
intense desire into intense revulsion, others by their unwillingness to
defy cultural pressures against such salacious reading. Still others did not
need it: they had acquired their sexual education and could obtain their
sexual fodder elsewhere.

The reports of nineteenth-century men seduced by books are therefore
at once infrequent and implausible. Possibly the most circumstantial of
these involves the rich young Englishman Frederick Hankey, who managed to startle the blasé Goncourt brothers when they met him in Paris
in 1862. Hankey was then around thirty, living on a substantial income
and collecting erotica with the discriminating eye of an expert in bindings
and illustrations: it was Hankey who was to supply the English politician
and bibliophile Monckton Milnes with the bulk of his choice library of
erotica. Hankey, talking of special houses in London where customers
could maltreat young prostitutes, or of paying for a good vantage
point to watch an execution while "doing things" to young girls, seemed
to the Goncourts "a madman, a monster" who disclosed, with his incessant
dwelling on abominations "the evil instincts of humanity." This "prodigious and earnest disciple of *Justine*," they noted in their highly colored
and rather unconvincing portrait of him, did not merely preach his
master's doctrines but practiced them. He had, they wrote, read de Sade
at fourteen and remained infatuated with him. But whether Hankey
actually mutilated thirteen-year-olds by sticking pins into them and
collected the skins of young African girls flayed alive, or whether he

merely liked to boast of such pleasures, it is certain that reading de Sade only lowered his inhibitions against thinking thoughts and perhaps performing acts to which he had already been inclined before he had chosen his master.

In nineteenth-century erotic pedagogy, then, pornography played a supporting, modest role. And that is what one might expect. Pornography was written and sold not to impart sexual information but to arouse sexual excitement. Its repetitive and schematic orgies lack all lifelike shadings, all respect for ambiguities. Human sexual experience is a complex and evolving psychological and physiological drama; it mixes failure with success, recaptured memories with fresh attractions, importunate desires with social prescriptions. Dormant unconscious conflicts, revived by aroused appetites, make the course of sexual conquest, like that of true love, anything but smooth. Even the middle-class adolescent's first fumbling experiments—his initiation by a complaisant servant at home or a venal waitress in town—is, in real life, a nest of ambivalences and rationalizations, of confused arousals and bouts of panic. Such debuts became the staple of nineteenth-century pornography, but only in the crudest of caricatures. All pornography could do was demonstrate to its palpitating consumers that any combination of living beings could perform sexual intercourse in a vertiginous diversity of ways. In diminishing its protagonists to sheer engines of fornication, to walking—or, more often, recumbent—genitals, it worked principally as a leering inducement to solitary or shared sexual indulgence, a heavy nudge in the ribs of the timid, the inexperienced, or the perverse. Though programmatically optimistic and cheerful—orgasms in pornography are always moments of supreme, unutterable bliss—there is something desolate about these panders to erotic fantasy, a deadly absence of all human context, and feeling, and differentiation. That is why celebrants of sensuality like D. H. Lawrence were more enraged against the merchants of smut than against the paragons of decency. While the actors in pornographic fictions are presumably engaged in the most liberated play, in the most natural of human pursuits, they appear to be prisoners of some unappeasable appetite, less than natural and less than human at the same time. In the frozen, featureless universe of pornography, one bed, one prick, one cunt, is much like all the others. In its pages the separation of lust from love, which Sigmund Freud was not the first to stigmatize as pathological, is complete. The Goncourts, though a little credulous about their "monster" Hankey, were perceptive enough to sense something of this: Hankey, exquisitely polite, with impeccable aristocratic manners, struck them as afflicted by some "internal lesion" which lent him an air of "impersonality" and the animation of an automaton.[66]

It is easy, therefore, to draw up a set of instructions for the nineteenth-century hack grinding out texts to the specifications of some Holywell Street bookseller. (1) A woman, though she may need to be awakened by her first and decisive sexual encounter, is as passionate as any man, perhaps more passionate. It may be advisable to tell the tale from the woman's point of view, preferably in the first person, since then her assertive and insatiable sexual conduct, especially in fellatio, will prove all the more stirring to the reader. (2) A penis is always gigantic, appearing at once threatening and arousing to the woman who sees and handles it; it is so thick that she can barely get her little hand around it, and— throbbing—a portent of raptures to come. For novices just launched on careers devoted to the uninterrupted pursuit of sexual occasions, the penis may be too ferocious to give immediate enjoyment. But the pain it causes, in itself exciting, will soon turn into pure pleasure as the man drives his formidable instrument, right to the end of its enormous shaft, into her receptive body. (3) The actors are all indefatigable sexual athletes; men are ready to resume intercourse a few minutes after ejaculating and women only too eager to repeat their ecstatic grapplings— not necessarily with the same partner. (4) The customer of pornography is a watcher, stealthily witnessing, as it were, the delicious sexual delirium of others, either passively taking in the scene or actively participating in it through masturbation. One can dramatize his search for knowledge and excitement by introducing a voyeur into as many situations as possible. This reader's surrogate and model, concealed in the shrubbery or peeking through keyholes, will learn the glorious facts of life and promptly incorporate them into his own behavior. (5) The discharge of man's semen, whether into his partner's anus, mouth, or vagina, is a copious stream, a convulsive flood, which is an indispensable culminating element in his partner's satisfaction. Woman, too, has a discharge with orgasm, so that the couple, after ejaculating, is bathed in the sticky, dripping proof of their shared delirium. (6) A woman often has sexual dreams in which she reenacts previous sexual encounters and works herself up to a sweet, trancelike orgasm; the man of whom she is dreaming usually watches her only to awaken her to show her that the reality is even sweeter. (7) While not every story need contain instances of incest, the violation of man's sacred taboo, especially on the part of virile father and pubescent daughter, offers dependable pairings sure to

66. April 7, 1862, *Journal*, V, 89–91.

keep the reader's interest at a high pitch. (8) While it is advisable to stress in each text one line of sexual taste, versatility is always stimulating; foreplay, especially oral, should often emancipate itself to serve as the true climax; couples should extend their activities to others and to groups. Orgies are never boring. (9) Customers with sadistic or masochistic tastes need stories featuring flogging, mutilation, a sense of degradation, and enslavement of one partner by the other. But even conventional tales confined to sexual intercourse between one man and one woman profit from a touch of cruelty: the ruthlessness of the first seduction, the sting of defloration, are good moments to mingle terror with delight. (10) While it may be desirable to sketch in the social and economic background of the leading lovers, such matters have their uses only in so far as they advance arousal: sexual orgies across class lines, much like those violating the incest taboo, add just one more morsel of titillation to the tale. But neither the development of character, nor the complexities of affection, nor the niceties of probability should be permitted to invade the space requisite for the only thing that matters: the sexual encounter.

Nineteenth-century pornographers did not have the time or, for that matter, the talent to bring individuality to bear on their merchandise; their occasional play with tone and style was both timid and mechanical. Numerous texts used scattered sexual and scatological exclamations to whip up the reader with their provocative mimicry of passionate expletives common during actual intercourse. Others introduced playful variations: as the lecherous and sadistic Madame de Chaudelüze is being masturbated by a young man in woman's clothing (I am quoting from *Schwester Monika*, a little sadomasochistic item of 1815, falsely attributed to E. T. A. Hoffmann), she shouts: "VITE! MON ENFANT! HA! PETIT HEROS! VI-TE-AH! JE ME-CON-FONDS!" Still others demurely printed "p——k" or "c——t," this decorum in calculated tension with the uninhibited orgies in which these genitalia performed so brilliantly. Still others, imitating the self-imposed restraint first practiced by John Cleland in *Fanny Hill*, avoided gross or explicit language altogether to evoke sexual parts and sexual congress by means of metaphors, euphemisms, literary circumlocutions. Yet these linguistic games, too, were bound to grow tedious to all but devotees; the names that the most imaginative of pornographers could invent for man's and woman's sexual parts and their employment were not unlimited in number, and all bore a distinct family resemblance. They were predictable variations on a predictable theme. The male part was an instrument, the female a receptacle, both steadily atremble for immediate action. Other stylistic devices held no more surprises: a few nineteenth-century specimens professed kinship to more elevated literature by resorting to "elegant" phrases and pretentiously borrowing epigraphs from the French and English classics. *Suburban Souls*, a voluminous production first published in London in 1901, which dwells in excruciating and explicit detail on fellatio, decorates its chapters with verses from Shakespeare, Musset, Rossetti, and others, and concludes with a blatant reminiscence of Thackeray's *Vanity Fair* by asking "Mr. Prompter" to "ring down the curtain" as the drama concludes, invoking human mortality and the "Great Scene-Shifter." Most, though, disdained such transparent frills, cut all connections with polite culture, and proceeded without delay to the business at hand.

That business was at once flexible and concentrated. Nineteenth-century pornographers catered to all conceivable appetites: pedophilia, fetishism, incest, bestiality, homosexuality, even murder as the climax of intercourse—that is how Musset's *Gamiani* ends. Much like obliging restaurateurs with no culinary style of their own, the purveyors of pornography diversified their menu to capture the largest possible clientele. They knew that their most faithful consumers were specialists who never tired of rehearsing the same scene, and that different specialists had different specialties. Gustave Droz's epistolary tale *Un Eté à la campagne*, published in Brussels in 1868, makes much of the "uncle," an artificial penis with which a married woman consoles herself nightly for the absence of her husband, and with which a young lesbian services a girl she fancies but who prefers men. Such virtuosity was prized but hardly necessary. The orgasm, however reached, was all that mattered.

It is not possible to reconstruct a dependable map across space and time of nineteenth-century pornography: too much has been lost, especially of the cheaper titles, and the expensive collections of rich amateurs which are now behind locked doors in great libraries of the world are not necessarily representative. There are hints of national styles and changing fashions. England, for example, produced and imported vast quantities of the literature of flagellation, mainly addressed to ex–public school boys recalling their floggings with shamefaced delight. But then it was an Austrian, Leopold von Sacher-Masoch, rather than an Englishman, after whom this perversion would be named. And while students of the genre have discerned a certain evolution from dependence on polite literature to total self-referential autonomy, surviving texts published around 1900 and even later mimic literary styles as slyly as books appearing two or three generations earlier had done—I recall *Suburban Souls* of 1901. There seems to be an increasing resort to violence, especially brutality against women; but then the eponymous hero of sadism had died as far back as 1814. Pornography, while it boasts an impressive repertory of acrobatic feats, is the most monotonous kind of literature extant.

It must be so because it serves uniformly and deeply regressive needs. It is written by, and for, those in whom primitive unconscious wishes have erupted into awareness, intermittently or permanently. The pornographic regression dramatically revives archaic desires still surviving, though normally well concealed and well controlled, in the adult's mind. Pornography, in short, bypasses patiently constructed psychological defenses; it undoes the work of sublimation. Such regression can never be an innocent return to earlier modes of mental functioning; the adult always bears the burdens of his years. It is, rather, a furtive reenactment of unfinished business, a recapitulation of unintegrated bits of arousing thoughts and feelings. Freud laid it down in 1905 that the sexual drive is a bundle of component drives which, as the child grows up, come to cluster, as foreplay and supportive excitement, around the principal aim of the adult who has been fortunate enough to navigate the shoals of his development: affectionate genital intercourse with a partner of the opposite sex. In pornography, such mature integration collapses, and infantile sexuality perversely reasserts its rights.

This backward pressure toward the reader's earliest experience makes it seem deceptively easy to move behind the manifest tale to its latent messages. In many respects, these messages are in fact quite open; most obscene texts are quite artless, almost undistorted. Much pornography, in fact, reads like a plagiarism of infantile fantasies. The prevalence of fathers coupling with daughters, unaccompanied by guilt feelings, is one instance; the omnipresence of the voyeur who, in story after story, reenacts his search for the primal scene by watching couples in sexual embraces is another; the delight in soiling, only slightly displaced in substituting discharge from the genitals for discharge from the anus, is yet a third. In *Eveline*, a Victorian instance apparently revised more than once and very popular for decades, a lovely young woman whose specialty is fellatio and who enjoys intercourse with her servants, her brother, and her father at one tense moment masturbates her beloved papa, keeping her new kid gloves on for the purpose: "I knew by all the usual symptoms he was on the verge of climax. It arrived. He straightened himself out. I grasped my victim firmly. He discharged. The hot thick semen came slopping over into my hand. My glove slipped about in the steaming overflow. He pushed upwards to meet my rapid movements until he had emitted the last drops." Here speaks a small child in an adult's body, and with an adult's opportunities.

Nothing offers more persuasive evidence of this infantilism than the stereotypical dreams that nineteenth-century pornographers liked to impose on their female characters. As she lies naked in her bed in *The Three Chums: A Tale of London Everyday Life*, a nymphomaniac recites:

> One night, extended on my downy bed,
> Melting in am'rous dreams, although a maid,
> My active thoughts presented to my view,
> A youth, undrest, whose charming face I knew,
> Stript to his shirt, he sprang to me in white,
> Like a kind bridegroom on the nuptial night,

and so forth, to orgasm. As undisguised wish-fulfillments, like children's dreams, such female sleeping—though scarcely dormant—sexual fulfillments are an epitome of the pornographic enterprise as a whole. Small children wish to possess, dominate, monopolize, incorporate, destroy. Every part of their little bodies may serve as a playground for erotic gratification, and their capacity to differentiate libido from aggression is rudimentary at best. Touching and kissing, stroking, biting and swallowing are, in the constricted universe of the nursery, all acts of love. Freud captured this quality when he said that children are polymorphously perverse. Pornography elaborates this childish capacity for adult consumers.

This polymorphous perverseness—and this is one more demonstration of the regressive fantasies that pornographic writings stimulate—and the conspicuous, total absence of love in pornography testifies to the coexistence of rage with sexual hunger. The violence that "lovers" commit in these tales—mostly men against women—testifies to the infantile sadism that pornography seeks to gratify in its most lurid sexual scenes. The reader's aggressions find outlets in these scenes almost as much as, sometimes more than, his erotic needs. They are still indistinguishable in the rapes, the whippings, the elaborate tortures in which numerous pornographic works specialized.

Still more important, perhaps, the child cannot wait, and once again pornography enacts an infantile mode, which psychoanalysts call primary-process thinking, on the grownup's stage. Pornographic climaxes are moments of uncontrollable impulsiveness. Protagonists often will not even take the time to undress to slake their sexual thirst; and they will brave the risk of discovery, not just to enhance the erotic thrill of their coupling, but simply because they cannot brook delay. Perpetually

brimming with sexual excitement, they exploit the most fleeting interludes alone for yet another round. "But me no buts!" exclaims one impatient, inflamed narrator to her resourceful, indefatigable lover, "I
command you to make haste and do it to the very end, or I will no longer
love you." And a moment later, "Do what I want at once!" Some days
later, as they are out for a stroll with her husband and are left alone for
a few minutes, " 'Angel,' said he, 'let us profit by this moment!' 'You are
mad.' 'No, I love you, let me do as I will.' 'My God, we shall be discovered! I am lost.' 'Not if you hurry. Stoop!' " I am quoting from
Voluptuous Confessions of a French Lady of Fashion, serialized in *The
Boudoir*, an English mid-Victorian pornographic periodical that lasted
for six issues; I could have quoted from countless others. Lovers in such
stories experience the briefest interval between desire and gratification as
a time of torment, of unconscionable deprivation. Postponement of
action, which is the heart of rationality and consideration for others, the
test of love, has no place in their mental universe.

But there must be more to pornography than this—its meanings do not
all lie on the surface. The inescapable fact that the making and consuming of pornography is, after all, an adult activity ensures that its manifest
and latent dimensions do not wholly coincide. Occasional and astonishing bits of gentility—a disinclination of some heroines to perform intercourse during their menstrual period, or some pious endings in which
their sexual prowess gives way to good works—only underscore the
need for deeper analysis. And so does the relative immunity of one
crucial taboo, son-mother incest, to the feverish imagination of the pornographer.

The boy's wish to possess his mother, though complicated by his rage
against her and by his love for his father, is, though in a rudimentary
form, the most thoroughly repressed of his youthful desires. The repression is so effective that it rarely rises to the surface undisguised, even in
pornography, that most—literally—shameless of all writings. When
the nineteenth-century pornographer orchestrates his couplings with
mother-son combinations, it is almost invariably the mother who seduces
her son—another naked wish which, for male readers, assuages their
guilt feelings for having wished it. More often, though, he disguises this
oedipal demand; in all the obscene poems, jokes, anecdotes, and short
novels of *The Boudoir*, for one, such incest is draped in evasions: one
young lover "does it" with his lecherous, experienced, middle-aged land-
lady; another finds an excitable housekeeper of forty who, however, from
vanity and to ward off insinuations, admits to only thirty-three; still

another is inaugurated into the agreeable mysteries of love by a willing French widow of thirty. Elsewhere, it is father-daughter incest that serves as a convenient reversal of that other, that almost unspeakable desire.

The exceptional reticence about son-mother incest lends support to the commonplace, true with some notable exceptions, that pornography was written by men, for men. Certainly the male, in pornography, is in command: the hero dramatizes boyish wishes monstrously enlarged and repetitively granted. His fear of failure is smothered in ceaseless enactments of superhuman successes. His gigantic penis, incomparable in length, thickness, and hardness, displaying its powers in legendary performances, is the emblem of male mastery, as much proof as weapon. While woman's sensuality is greedy, insatiable, women far more than men are made into objects of degradation. They are cruelly deflowered, viciously raped, and, even when they swoon with pleasure, more victim than victimizer. Their aching lubricity is a symptom of their dependence on the superb studs who can best give them what they must have. Women in pornography thus represent, in the most extreme form, the despised half of man's split image of the first, and in some way always most important, woman in his life—his mother. The small boy has not yet integrated his pictures of the cherished being who nourishes and frustrates him: the mother he wants to kill in the afternoon, he wants to marry in the evening. And his wrath at first discovering that his mother, that paragon, does *that* thing with a man, though rapidly repressed, always remains as a ground tone for disillusionment: being no angel, she must be a whore. There are adults fortunate enough to blend their images of mother into a realistic whole—neither angel nor whore, a complex, imperfect, yet lovable being. But the habitual reader of pornography, whether he consciously worships his mother or detests her, is among those who have never healed the harsh infantile division of mother into the purest and the most defiled of women. He is haunted, not merely by unresolved oedipal conflicts, but also by earlier, archaic, pre-oedipal ones. And he must conjure up the grossest, most degraded of females to experience sexual pleasure and enjoy sexual consummation. "The principal protective measure" against impotence that such cripples employ, Sigmund Freud noted in 1912, "consists in the psychological *debasement* of the sexual object." Once they have accomplished this, "their sensuality can freely express itself, and can record considerable sexual performance as well as intense pleasure." And, as Freud adds, significantly, such men "generally have a rather coarse love life; they have retained their perverse sexual aims."[67] This description, though not explicitly intended as a portrait of the reader of smut, fits the addict of pornography to perfection, whether he seeks his outlets in masturbation or with prostitutes. Where he loves, to return to Freud's famous formulation, he cannot desire, and where he desires he cannot love.

None of this makes him less than human. On the contrary. Pornography is, in its perverse way, a tribute to the timelessness and the ultimate simplicity of human nature. All humans harbor the fantasies that pornography spells out in its relentless elaborations. *The Lascivious Hypocrite*, or *Venus im Pelz*, and thousands of productions like them are so many probes into the human unconscious. And to judge from their pronouncements, the fantasies of those most obsessed with the evil of pornography were distorted, slightly sublimated mirror images of the very fictions they were dedicating their lives to extirpating. Their need to scan literature for obscene passages and photographs for obscene postures suggests a wish unconsciously translated into a fear. The crusaders, rarely cursed with introspection, indignantly and sincerely denied such imputations when these hidden affinities were called to their attention.

For they were called to their attention. The underlying pornographic obsessions of the anti-pornographers were not a discovery of the psychoanalysts. That Boston moralist Godfrey Lowell Cabot, assiduous member of the Watch and Ward Society and writer of heated salacious letters to his wife, aroused some derisive comment in his lifetime for his preoccupation with sex. Purity societies, whether religious or secular, found themselves the frequent object of irreverent cartoons. The most grateful target for such malicious ripostes was surely Anthony Comstock; both humor magazines and the most articulate victims of his raids derided him from the onset of his activities as a sick man with a dirty mind, who loved to wallow in the muck. And his language practically invites such vengeful psychologizing: Comstock saw himself "removing swills and slops" from society; he needed to protect the innocent from "impure thoughts" and believed himself an expert on "garbage" which "smells" just as "rank" even if decked out in fine bindings. In 1915, the last year of his life, he returned once again to his favorite image, offal bursting to inundate the world: "If you open the door to anything, the filth will all pour in and the degradation of youth will follow."[68] It was with such

---

67. "Über die allgemeinste Erniedrigung des Liebeslebens" (1912), *St.A.*, V, 202–3; "On the Universal Tendency to Debasement in the Sphere of Love," *S.E.*, XI, 183.

68. See Kilpatrick, *Smut Peddlers*, 36; Robert Bremner, "Editor's Introduction," Anthony Comstock, *Traps for the Young* (1883; ed. 1967), xxviii, xxiv.

smelly, repellent stuff that Comstock had lived for more than four decades to serve the higher good, demonstrating to almost everyone's satisfaction except his own that the pornographer and his nemesis occupied the same mental universe and wrestled with the same primitive sexual problems.

By the turn of the century, when Sigmund Freud provided such invidious analyses with their scientific grounding and their neutral vocabulary, they had become common property among bourgeois put off by the censor's mentality. In the early nineteenth century, Sydney Smith, cleric, magistrate, and incomparable wit, had already noted that "Men whose trade is rat-catching, love to catch rats; the bug-destroyer seizes on his bug with delight; and the suppressor is gratified by finding his vice." The *Saturday Review* made the same point sturdily from its first numbers on. In 1858, severely rebuking the English press for its circumstantial reports of revolting murder trials, it said: "It is an opinion which we have often expressed, and which the publications of which we complain strongly confirm, that there is a very strong current of (probably unconscious) indecency, running through much that piques itself on a certain superfine morality." In 1864 the prolific English novelist Charles Reade, abrasive and litigious, an inveterate writer of letters to newspapers, gave the "pure" partner in this unexpected alliance between moralists and pornographers a name: "the prurient prude." Self-appointed moralists, he argued, read only to find objectionable passages, take them out of context, put obscene constructions on them, exaggerate their importance, and then charge the author with indecency. The prurient prude, as Reade characterizes him—or her—is a "lewd hypocrite, who passes over all that is sweet, and pure and innocent in a book, with genuine disrelish, and fixes greedily on whatever a foul mind can misinterpret or exaggerate into indecency." Then he "makes arbitrary additions to the author's meaning, and so ekes out the indelicacy to suit his own true taste, which is for the indelicate." All this to turn on the author, "whom he has defiled," and call him unclean. "And so," Reade concludes, using the almost inescapable excretory image for polemical purposes of his own, "and so the poor author is. But why? A lump of human dirt has been sitting on him, and discolouring him."[69] His fantasy of Comstocks and Campbells sitting on writers' heads to discharge their

69. Smith: D. R. M. Bennett, *Antony Comstock. His Career of Cruelty and Crime* [a chapter drawn from his *The Champions of the Church* (1878), 1013]; "The Purity of the Press," *Saturday Review*, V (June 26, 1858), 657; Reade: "'A Terrible Temptation,' To the Editor of the 'Daily Globe,' Toronto," October 1871, in *Readiana. Comments on Current Events* (1883; ed. 1896), 261.

excrement on them is striking, original, and more appropriate even than Reade could have known.

In the unconscious, extremes met. Nineteenth-century purists and expurgators—telling names both!—were not, whatever they might claim, authorized spokesmen for the middle-class opinion of their time. Rather, precisely like pornographers, though of course offering very different distortions, they drew a caricature of the prevalent bourgeois concerns with the mastery of passion and the segregation of clean from dirty thoughts; the boundary that the censors and their instigators drew around permissible expression was far too narrow, their threshold of disgust for the public airing of natural processes far too low, to be truly representative of their middle-class culture. They acted like an exigent, punitive cultural superego.

To be sure, the eloquent libertarian manifestos against police repression composed by Algernon Swinburne and George Moore in England, Edmond de Goncourt and Emile Zola in France, and a small army of incensed publicists in Germany were not wholly disinterested. Many of these writers had fallen afoul of the authorities or the lending libraries. But their confident if largely implicit posture of speaking for substantial segments of the educated bourgeoisie was not simply self-serving. They had numerous and influential supporters, readers who were not afraid, for themselves or for their culture, of a good measure of carnal knowledge.

The bourgeois century, in short, presents a jumble of attitudes on the vexed matter of sexual education through fiction, whether decent or indecent. Many among the thoughtful sought in vain to bring their liberal convictions and their moral indignation into harmony, forever redrawing the frontiers between literature they found offensive and literature they wanted the law to suppress. Theirs, I think, was the most characteristic bourgeois perspective, an uncertain, far from consistent liberalism, more likely to respond to events—a scandalous novel or a stupid prosecution—than to shape them. They vacillated, hesitated, and contradicted themselves. But there were, especially from the 1850s on, too many heavy-handed efforts to infantilize fiction—George Moore's splendid philippic of 1885 was entitled *Literature at Nurse*—not to keep the liberal animus alive, and angry. Yet whatever side they took, censors and liberals alike were readers in conflict.

4. The Doctrine of Distance

While reading about sex produced more conflict than information for nineteenth-century bourgeois, looking at nudes in paintings and sculp-

tures, sometimes male though far more often female, proved an almost
wholly agreeable way of improving acquaintance with the human body.
Countless feeble jokes played on this particular pedagogic role of art for
the young. The little boy in Morland's caricature for the *Petit Journal
pour Rire* had many brothers and not a few sisters: staring at a lifesize
standing nude in the Salon of 1882 which he is visiting with his parents,
he ingenuously asks his father: "Who did that lovely lady who's got no
shirt on?"[70] Nudes were in fact on display everywhere throughout the
nineteenth century. They decorated parks and fountains; they were a
commanding presence in public exhibitions and on public buildings.
They stood in niches, covered walls, spread across ceilings. They could
represent, allegorize, celebrate, or symbolize almost anyone or anything·
lying supine, limp genitals prominently proffered to view—the dead
Abel; playful and pneumatic—electricity; exuberant, youthful, dressed
only in seductive long stockings—the bicycle.

In the 1880s, Per Hasselberg, then Sweden's leading sculptor and
known for his sensual nudes, did a group of emblematic sculptures in each
of which a pair of expressive crouching nudes caught in vigorous, even
melodramatic action celebrates an achievement of modern technology:
dynamite, photography, the railway engine, the telephone. And in 1903,
three years after the death of Eça de Queiros, the Portuguese sculptor
Teixeira Lopes commemorated his famous compatriot, an imaginative
realist, with a lifesize group as sensual as anything de Queiros ever wrote:
the novelist, handsome, mature, somewhat dandified, looks down attentively
upon a seductive nude young woman who gazes at him adoringly and
spreads out her arms in a gesture half trusting, half sexual surrender. It
is not surprising that some susceptible viewers should find such sculpted
nudes more exciting than the real thing. "You tell me you don't have a
woman," the young Gustave Flaubert wrote to his intimate Ernest
Chevalier in 1841. "That, by God, is very sensible, considering that I
look upon that species as pretty stupid. Woman is a vulgar animal whom
man has idealized too much. A taste for statuary turns us into masturbators; reality seems to us base."[71] Tastes changed, even in nudes, but the
taste *for* nudes remained untouched by time.

Pierre-Paul Prud'hon's ceiling *Study Guiding the Ascent of Genius* is
a splendid and representative exemplar of the genre. He painted it in
1801, when Napoleon Bonaparte was First Consul, for the room at the
Louvre that then held the *Laocoön*; its popularity outlived Napoleon

70. V. Morland, "Au Salon de Peinture," *Petit Journal pour Rire*, XXVI, 3rd ser.,
No. 347 (1882), 6. I owe this illustration to Dan Sherman.

71. March 28, 1841, *Correspondance*, I, 78.

and, for that matter, Prud'hon, by decades. Napoleon found Prud'hon's delicately sensual allegories precisely to his liking: he showered him with commissions and honors. We may read this somewhat equivocal pairing of a late-latency boy and girl companionably ascending to heaven, the girl holding a suggestive portcrayon, as a revealing specimen of imperial taste. But the middle-class public liked the pair quite as much, right into the days of the Third Republic. The Goncourt brothers, scarcely typical bourgeois, fastidious and discriminating, found Prud'hon puzzling: "Sometimes a great poet, the only poet of the Empire—and sometimes we ask ourselves if he is not deceiving us and is nothing more than a painter of smiling signboards to attract customers to perfumers." The observation neatly captures the ambiguities of Prud'hon's adroit eroticism, but the general run of average art consumers had no such hesitations: Prud'hon's ceiling was copied, and much praised, throughout the century. It was etched, engraved, lithographed. Many decades later, Pierre Gauthiez, one of Prud'hon's biographers, thought it a work "so often, but never enough reproduced, never enough admired," while Charles Clément, another biographer, called it "that admirable work, one of Prud'hon's best known," a "capital and exquisite piece. Here is Prud'hon with all his energy and all his grace, his original and poetic imagination, his highly personal feeling for form, his mellow touch, his charming color. These two children are perfect."[72] They are also unmistakably, frontally, naked.

Nineteenth-century nudes have often jarred twentieth-century taste as grandiloquent or prissy, and for the most part faintly ludicrous. Only a few of them show the genitals complete with pubic hair; one seems to be looking at children too tall, too massive, for their age. Some of these nudes, in fact, appear without genitals altogether. But it is not farfetched to suppose that such genteel distortions awakened heated fantasies in those who saw them when they were first exhibited. The physical information that nudes convey is patent and, in a sense, timeless; while each gives a particular shape to the breasts, the genitals, or the posture of the body, each conveys a piece of carnal knowledge. Yet the feelings they generate vary with the vicissitudes of personal and cultural histories: what one spectator might experience as an inducement to aesthetic contemplation, or, for that matter, to derisive laughter, another might take as an invitation to erotic excitement. We can neither legislate arousal nor predict indifference. Among respectable people in the nineteenth

72. Goncourts: May 28, 1858, *Journal*, II, 239; Prud'hon: Gauthiez, *Prud'hon* (1886), 34; Clément, *Prud'hon. Sa vie, ses oeuvres et sa correspondance* (1872; 3rd ed., 1880), 282–83.

century, many appear to have been inflamed by the glimpse of a trim
ankle, or found food for fantasies in such extravaganzas as the famous
Amazon by Professor Kiss of Berlin, a zinc copy of which graced the
Great Exhibition of 1851. These are scarcely the visual images to rouse
the twentieth-century erotic sensibility, and it takes an act of the
historical imagination to recover how people responded only a hundred
years ago.

The reception of Antonio Canova's cool, once admired marbles documents the varieties of possible aesthetic and sensual responses. Most modern
viewers have dismissed or ridiculed Canova as an expert in depriving his
nudes of any erotic sting; Kenneth Clark summed up this consensus when
he called Canova "a brilliant portraitist and master of contemporary chic"
and accused him of being the fountainhead of mendacious nineteenth-
century nude sculpture with his "mannered classicism" from which "a
mechanical execution had removed the last tremors of excitement. Easier
to get with child a mandrake root than consider the marble Venuses of
the Victorians as objects of desire." It is true that Canova himself is on
record that "the nude, when it is pure and instinct with exquisite beauty,
takes us away from mortal passions" and "lifts our soul to the contemplation of divine things." And Charles Dickens, no doubt unwittingly,
echoed that approving adjective "exquisite," purse-lipped and delicately
asexual, in his appraisal of Canova's statues; Dickens found them exceptional for their "exquisite grace and beauty." But then, at the other
extreme, Heinrich Heine and Gustave Flaubert both testified that they
thought Canova's statues eroticism incarnate. Heine lyrically rediscovered
a living love in Canova's *Venus*: "I often think of this statue now; at
times I dream that she lies in my arms and gradually takes on life and at
last whispers to me with Franscheska's voice." Flaubert's adoration was
even more impulsive: at the Villa Carlotta, he went to study Canova's
Cupid and Psyche often, blind to the rest of the gallery; on his last visit,
he reports, "I kissed under the armpit that swooning woman who
stretches out to Love her two long arms of marble."[73] Heine and Flaubert
were experts in sensuality—or at least wrote as if they were; perhaps
they detected beneath Canova's frozen surfaces the heat that others
were too obtuse to register, perhaps they were projecting their own
sensual needs on Canova's smooth and controlled performances. What-

73. Kenneth Clark, *The Nude: A Study in Ideal Form* (1956), 162; Mario Praz,
"Canova: Ice and Fire," in Thomas B. Hess and John Ashbery, eds., *Academic Art*
(1971), 165–66; Angus Wilson, *The World of Charles Dickens* (1970), 194; Robert M.
Adams, *The Roman Stamp: Frame and Facade in Some Forms of Neo-Classicism*
(1974), 169–70 (translations mine).

ever their true feelings, it is unhistorical to impose our own schedules of arousal on the art of the past. This much is certain: whatever its varied, often baffling effects, the human form was readily accessible to view throughout the age of respectability.

Some nineteenth-century artists are beyond controversy in this matter; they invested their nudes with the carnal vitality of Rubens's fleshy models. Delacroix and Courbet, Manet and Renoir celebrated the female body with such zest that no one could misread their canvases as dutiful academic exercises or as flights into evasion. They are technically accomplished documents of desire. And Degas, intent not on celebrating but on recording life as he saw it, did scores of monotypes depicting middle-aged, obese prostitutes, generally naked except for a velvet band around their throat, slouching on greasy fauteuils waiting for customers, open-legged, unattractive, displaying their bush of pubic hair with a weary indifference. But these artists were, of course, anything but representative bourgeois; they were rebels, or treated as rebels. Whether they intended to offend polite taste or not, polite taste insisted on being offended by their tactless portrayals of carnal contemporaries. The nudes of Courbet or Manet fix moments of sheer sensual pleasure, but we may also read them as messages of protest in their implicit criticism of academic conventionality and primness. Hence they do nothing to disprove the prevalent twentieth-century view that the respectable nineteenth-century bourgeois was prudish and hypocritical.

The nudes that Ingres drew and painted are, however, far more problematic. They raise questions about the bourgeoisie's reputation for denial. The most faultless of academics, laden with all the honors that a succession of French governments could bestow, Ingres was preoccupied with the body from the beginning of his career—that long, uninterrupted march of triumph—to the end. The Paris Baedeker of 1891, which says that he was "unreservedly admitted to be the greatest French painter of his time," notes, without disapproval, that he was "a venerator of antiquity and an enthusiastic admirer of the nude female form." Ingres was not a photographic realist; a pedantic anatomist might find fault with his way of lengthening a model's spine to capture the sinuous curve of her back, or his way of presenting nudes, anticipating Picasso by a century, from more than one perspective at once: he subtly displaces backs, breasts, and bellies as if he were walking around his model to capture her enticing hilly topography. Ingres was a well-instructed classicist thoroughly grounded in the literature and traditions of painting; while Nature was, as he often insisted, the source of his inspiration, he subjected reality to the demands of his art. Unlike his admiring disciples,

Ingres preached the artist's privilege of choice and the primacy of architectural considerations over mere imitation. *La Source*, which the Baedeker for Paris singled out as "perhaps the most perfect specimen of the treatment of the nude among modern paintings,"[74] was a much-revised, long-neglected full-length nude that Ingres began about 1820 and did not complete until thirty-five years later, with the assistance of students, and with some deliberate disregard of realistic proportions. One of his earliest canvases, painted around 1800 while he was still a student of David, is a male torso that offers the body, slightly twisted for animation, to unobstructed inspection; the three-quarter-length format gives Ingres space for a carefully painted triangle of pubic hair—something of a rarity, as I have already noted, in nineteenth-century art. It would be naive to see Ingres's choice of a torso as a conscious evasion of portraying potency; it seems far more appropriate to the atmosphere of this picture to see that choice as a tantalizing incitement to the imagination.

Certainly Ingres's later depictions of the nude are explicit beyond doubt. In the neoclassical canvas with which he won the Prix de Rome, *The Ambassadors of Agamemnon in the Tent of Achilles*, he displays, in the frontal nudity of Patroclus, what he had denied earlier viewers in the studio torso. Just as frankly, and far more frequently, Ingres caressed the outlines and suggested the soft bulk of the female figure, inviting his viewers to travel his model's body and to feel, through their eyes, her lavish delights. *The Turkish Bath*, done, as he himself notes with pride, when he was eighty-two, is less a record of desire than of memory, but it constitutes a convincing anthology of eroticism, complete with the gratifications of the five senses that water, tea, music, perfume, luxuriant stretching and the pressing of female flesh by female hands can provide. His very choice of format, the tondo, exhibits and concentrates the sensual message. This canvas, his most famous painting, was Ingres's testament to beauty as he understood it, a summing up of his art, a characteristic blending of the sensual and the ideal. "Perhaps only M. Ingres, the *petit éléphant bourgeois*," Kenneth Clark had suggested, "with his seat in the Academy, his frock coat, and his absurdly orthodox opinions, could have persuaded public opinion to accept so open an evocation of eroticism," even at "the high-water mark of nineteenth-century prudery."[75] It is an interesting point, but its reverse is more interesting still: it says something about the bourgeois frame of mind

74. Professor Anton Springer, "Remarks on French Art," in K. Baedeker, *Paris and Environs with Routes from London to Paris* (1891), xxxvi; Baedeker, ibid., 120.

75. Clark, *The Nude*, 161.

that so respectable a citizen as Ingres could pursue so sensual an art. In the event, it shocked a few of its viewers and pleased the rest.

There were many in the nineteenth century, by no means all tight-lipped Evangelicals or insular philistines, who denigrated this unapologetic presentation of carnal beauty as typically French, which is to say, predictably immoral. But highly moral artists—Belgian, American, German, even Swiss—far from hoarding their knowledge, imparted carnal information to anyone who had eyes to see. Turner, who sequestered the erotic scenes he sketched in his private notebooks, was an exception, not so much in refusing the general public access to his depiction of sexual intercourse—other artists, like William Mulready, did the same—but in refraining from doing nudes for a wider audience altogether. Most other artists had no such scruples, notably William Etty, the most prolific painter of the nude in nineteenth-century England. To say that the nude was sacred to Etty would be to exaggerate, but only slightly. Born at York in 1787, Etty was a pious Methodist who turned in his later years toward Roman Catholicism, largely on aesthetic grounds. Piety and morality were constantly on his mind. "I have two ambitions," he told his brother Walter, who generously supported him in his younger years, "the first is to become a good man—the next a great painter." The search for goodness and greatness conveniently coincided, for Etty, in the female nude. "Finding God's most glorious work to be WOMAN," he noted in the brief autobiography he published in 1849, the year of his death, "that all human beauty had been concentrated in her, I resolved to dedicate myself to painting—not the Draper's or Milliner's work—but God's most glorious work, more finely than ever had been done." To understand that most glorious of divine works, Etty, contravening both custom and taste, faithfully attended life classes in London and his native York, long after he had become an accomplished and prosperous painter. Not all his aesthetic voyeurism was quite so pure as he liked to protest: "People may think me lascivious," he asserted, a little apologetically, in his autobiography, "but I have never painted with a lascivious motive."[76]

Etty doubtless reported his conscious feelings honestly enough. But art could give him what life was inclined to withhold. An inhibited lifelong bachelor, much attached to his mother, he was both timid and unprepossessing. If he was unhappy in love, one of his nineteenth-century biographers commented, that was not surprising. Socially, he was "a

76. Dennis Farr, *William Etty* (1958), 56, 62–63, 106–7; W. Gaunt and F. Gordon Roe, *Etty and the Nude: The Art and Life of William Etty, R.A., 1787–1849* (1943), 22.

cypher," and his "personal appearance said as little in his behalf as his tongue. Slovenly in attire, short and awkward in body; large head, large hands, large feet, a face marked with the smallpox, a quantity of sandy hair, long and wild," he was a most odd-looking creature to young ladies. No one could have suspected him of being "the creator of works of refined and imaginative beauty." But that refinement was largely in the eye of the biographer. Etty's nudes resembled blowzy dairymaids—nothing classical, let alone divine, in any of them. Certainly he appreciated the female anatomy beyond the call of painterly duty. Once, much to John Constable's amusement, he recommended a "young figure" who was "very desirous of becoming a model," for her contours: "*all in front*," he wrote Constable, "*remarkably fine*."[77] The "famous frontal development" that Thackeray gave to Becky Sharp was William Etty's favorite study. For this amateur of the beautiful, pleasure and duty were one; his superego was not overly exigent.

To do justice to God's work might seem sufficient justification for painting naked women over and over again. But Etty gave another, professional reason: it was his ambition to become a history painter, and history painters, for their renderings of dramatic moments in the past or in mythology, needed intimacy with the human body in all its contortions. It was an ambition that Etty realized; in addition to his canvases of solitary nude women contemplating bowls of fruit, deciding whether to risk a dip in the pond, or just lying there, he produced well-received neoclassical machines with their budgets of nude bodies engaged in animated action or frozen in contemplative postures, and pious—but naked—Magdalens. Etty professed to study nudes the better to do his classical compositions, but I am persuaded that he did classical compositions that he might study his nudes.

This is not simply historical conjecture. In 1875, a quarter-century after Etty's death, the prominent English art critic and editor Philip Gilbert Hamerton published a thoughtful and extensive appreciation of Etty in his periodical, the *Portfolio*, and noted almost in passing that Etty, especially in his mature years, had worked on subjects that "afforded a good pretext" for the nude. "The longer he lived," Hamerton wrote, "the less he felt inclined to abandon his especial superiority of flesh-painting, and so he chose such subjects as old mythology or history, which gave the opportunity for the kind of painting he delighted in." Etty's delight offered Hamerton material for some general reflections.

77. T. F. Thiselton-Dyer, *The Loves and Marriages of Some Eminent Persons*, 2 vols. (1890), I, 279; Farr, *Etty*, 77.

"It has been said that the taste for the nude implies some intellectual inferiority, since it is not the arms and legs, but the face and its expression, which visibly convey to others the intellect of a man. To this it may be frankly answered that Etty was decidedly *not* intellectual, and yet was at the same time quite decidedly artistic; the two orders of mind being separable, as we often see. He therefore sought the subjects which best expressed his simply artistic nature. He was not a painter of thought, but of physical beauty, which to his feeling was most visible in the nude, and a sufficing motive for his art."[78] Hamerton was ready to praise Etty for following his bent in choosing his genre.

Hamerton's innocence is worth pondering for a moment. One might patronize his inability to detect, or his need to deny, the all-too-blatant erotic wishes that informed Etty's passion for the nude. It was not arms and legs, after all, that Etty was principally interested in. But it would be more profitable to recognize Hamerton's generosity toward Etty's "simply artistic nature" as one typical, if little noted, mid-Victorian attitude toward sensuality, an attitude neither prudish nor prurient. Some nineteenth-century critics of Etty, to be sure, while they valued his gifts, at times questioned his taste and doubted his motives. Thackeray, emphatically intent on decency though open to seductive forms, displays the mixed feelings that Etty aroused. He called Etty a "great and original colourist," quite "as luscious as Rubens, as rich almost as Titian." Every year, he noted in 1844, "the exhibition sparkles with magnificent little canvases, the works of this indefatigable strenuous admirer of rude Beauty." This apt and pointed characterization hints at both Etty's admirable and his problematic qualities. Indeed, Thackeray objected that in the "voluptuously beautiful" canvases Etty exhibited in 1844, including his "noblest composition, a classical and pictorial *orgy*," the "female figure is often rather too expansively treated."[79] This was characteristic

78. Hamerton, "Etty," *Portfolio Papers* (1889), 83–84.

79. "May Gambols; or, Titmarsh in the Picture Galleries," *Fraser's Magazine* (1844), in *The Works of William Makepeace Thackeray*, Centenary Biographical Edition, 26 vols. (1910–11), XXV, 298. "Quite unabashed by the squeamishness exhibited in the highest quarter (as the newspapers call it)," Thackeray wrote the following year, "Mr. Etty goes on rejoicing in his old fashion." He found Etty's color superb, though his "Venuses" were expanding "more than ever in the line of Hottentot beauty; his drawing and coloring are still more audacious than they were." But Thackeray greatly admired him—found Etty, in short, a "GREAT painter." "Picture Gossip," *Fraser's Magazine* (1845), in *Works*, XXV, 331. It is easy to quote Thackeray on several sides of the controversies swirling around Etty; nothing illustrates the difficulty of mapping the contours of nineteenth-century middle-class sensuality better than to cull Thackeray for quotations that will substantiate one's case. Thus Eric Trudgill quotes a far more censorious sentence about a *Sleeping Nymph* of Etty's: "so naked, as to be

of the reviews Etty received: enthusiastic praise laced with frowning disapproval.

The painter C. R. Leslie, who was Etty's friend, thought his "treatment and choice of subject" rather "peculiar," and was convinced that "the voluptuous treatment of his subjects . . . recommended them more powerfully than their admirable Art." The painter Thomas Uwins, who was not his friend, caustically explained Etty's substantial income during his last years as profits from pandering to a vulgar crowd of parvenu collectors: "The old nobility and landed proprietors are gone out. Their place is supplied by railroad speculators, iron mine men, and grinders from Sheffield, etc., Liverpool and Manchester merchants and traders." Such consumers do not love the true classics of art. "The voluptuous character of Etty's work suits the degree of moral and mental intelligence of these people, and therefore his success." Art critics, too, though admiring Etty's skill as colorist and draftsman, sometimes censured the nakedness of his nudes. In 1822, reviewing Etty's paintings in an exhibition at the British Gallery, the critic for the *Times* took it upon himself to advise Etty "not to be seduced into a style which can gratify only the most vicious taste." If "naked figures" are painted "with the purity of Rafael," they can be "endured." But "nakedness without purity is offensive and indecent," and Etty's nudes are "mere dirty flesh." These strictures were unabashed moralizing art criticism; Etty should know, the reviewer concluded, "that just delicate taste and pure moral sense are synonymous terms." Six years later, when Etty, to his joy, secured full membership in the Royal Academy, the *Times* rebuked him again: though his *Venus Now Wakes, and Wakens Love* is admirably drawn, and the coloring natural, Etty has handled the subject "in a way entirely too luscious (we might, with great propriety, use a harsher term) for the public eye."[80] Nudity was controversial, even if presented by a skilled and reputable artist, even if his intentions were unmistakably classical. But while Etty's nudes were criticized for being entirely too luscious for the public eye, in the public eye they remained, even in England, even during the years in which the earnest and righteous Nonconformist conscience was at the height of its influence. Etty was a professional artist working in a respectable genre who bent the rules

---

unfit for appearance among respectable people at an exhibition." *Madonnas and Magdalens: The Origins and Development of Victorian Sexual Attitudes* (1976), 4. The conflicts among historians of the nineteenth century only mirror the conflicts within the century they are studying.

80. Gaunt and Roe, *Etty and the Nude*, 22; Farr, *Etty*, 95, 31, 52.

and stepped across the boundaries of artistic liberty. And so his critics, buffeted by conflicting feelings, dealt with them by doing nothing.

The reception of Ingres and Etty only proves that nineteenth-century attitudes toward the nude in art ranged from relaxed acceptance to tense embarrassment. While most of the respectable did little more than supervise their daughters' reading and, perhaps, their museum-going, zealots moved to reshape art in the image of pure morality. After all, as we know, the crusaders against masturbation liked to include lascivious paintings, photographs, and sculptures among the sure incitements to solitary vice. Anthony Comstock was only the most energetic among these uncompromising pessimists about human nature, convinced that "from infancy to maturity the pathway of the child is beset with peculiar temptations to do evil." Perpetual vigilance, therefore, was needed to rescue the young from "artistic and classical traps," which prominently and seductively included painted, sculpted, and—worse—photographed nudes. Of itself, Comstock conceded, "the nude in art is not necessarily obscene, lewd or indecent." Yet it was all too likely to be all three, especially if it was of French provenance. That is why Comstock fulminated against liberals who held that "exposing to public view" the "nude figures of women is an 'educator of the public mind.'" Such exposure, he argued, "may educate the public mind as to the forms of beautiful women, but it creates an appetite for the immoral; its tendency is downward; and it is in many cases a blight to the morals of the young and inexperienced." And that is why Comstock had Herman Knoedler arrested for displaying, in his Fifth Avenue gallery, photographs of "lewd French art—a foreign foe." Yet even Comstock, the humorless fanatic, felt compelled to grant that the nude in art had its place—in a museum.[81]

If even Comstock, who inhabited the extreme frontiers of censoriousness, could make modest room for the nude in his scheme of decent things, one may safely conclude that average bourgeois, less inclined than he to see vice everywhere, less haunted by voyeuristic impulses, made themselves fairly comfortable with the offerings of art, including attractive undraped bodies. The idea that art was a vehicle for carnal knowledge was, after all, an old one; in the 1770s, Basedow had already listed "Statues of Hercules and paintings" among the erotic teachers of the

81. *Traps for the Young* (1883), ed. Robert Bremner (1967), 168–72; *Morals versus Art* (1887), 8–9.

young.[82] Art thus plainly aroused conflicting emotions in middle-class minds, partly because artists, the makers of nudes, seemed so adventurous, so mysterious—so unbourgeois—a breed. It is true that distinguished academic artists traveled in faultlessly reputable circles, often frequented aristocratic houses. They were, for the most part, eligible dinner partners and club members. The most prosperous among them built themselves grandiose villas and kept select company. Even German society, as keen as its neighbors on fine social discriminations, found many painters and sculptors perfectly *salonfähig*, and rewarded the most prominent and inoffensive among them with lucrative commissions, royal command performances, and titles of nobility. Franz Lenbach, who poured out fashionable portraits and was Bismarck's close friend, became Franz von Lenbach; Franz Stuck, painter of violent sensual allegories and Munich's "painter prince" around the turn of the century, Franz von Stuck.

At the same time, bourgeois also allowed themselves to be scandalized —which is to say, tantalized—by musing upon the irregular bohemian lives that many artists must lead, with their late hours, their wild parties, their naked models. The vexed question of the nude model aroused even wilder fantasies and, correspondingly, greater anxiety, than that of the artist's rumored unbuttoned sociability. One friend told Ruskin that "the woman who was made an Academy Model could not be a virtuous woman," a straitlaced opinion that Ruskin duly passed on to his wife Effie, who had sat, as it happened decently garbed, to John Millais more than once. Animated by the same spirit, the Royal Academy in London kept unmarried artists under twenty out of its life classes. Certainly the low reputation of models, by no means wholly undeserved, could be enlisted in the great campaign against sensuality. Conservative painters, or those anxious to please, professed little quarrel with such attitudes: William Mulready, who drew and painted some seductive nudes of his own, thought modeling a "dangerous profession" for which "poor innocent creatures" must be thoughtfully prepared. Yet one man's responsible restraint was another man's incurable viciousness: it was precisely Mulready whom Ruskin singled out for his "degraded and bestial" naked figures. In the United States, too, controversy raged over exposing female flesh to lustful young eyes, all in the name of classical, or classicizing, art: in Philadelphia, all through the nineteenth century, those shocked at nudes done from living models confronted those

82. Johann Bernhard Basedow, *Elementarwerk*, ed. Theodor Fritzsch, 3 vols. (1909), I, 128.

insisting that to go to Nature was the only proper way to paint and sculpt; as early as 1812, *Aurora*, a local periodical, complained of "a species of modesty as it is called, or of prudery or mock modesty as we certainly shall call it," a "pharisaical spirit" that objected to "the exhibition of models of the human figure in chalk or gypsum!" And the reputed earthiness of painters and sculptors made the Pharisees very uneasy indeed. Amiel confided to his journal after a supper with artists that men of sensibility seemed to live uncomfortably close to sensuality —uncomfortably close for him. "It was gay," he wrote, "but alas! without being a puritan, I found this gaiety singularly coarse and broad and even, at moments, ribald." He was "humiliated" to discover "where the representatives of beauty and of art went to find their gratifications," notably to jokes and songs of dubious taste. Perhaps, he speculated, as if to soothe himself, the artist is "generally the natural man, wild stock with its vigor, but with its tartness as well."[83] He was more felicitous in his judgment than he knew: it was precisely because artists, and what they made, were so close to nature that they were so attractive, and so dangerous.

Still, it is noteworthy that for all its sincerity, noisiness, and undoubted influence, the success of the campaign against sensuality was strictly limited. Most respectable citizens, however uneasy, did not adopt Comstock's blunt methods. Nor did they share Amiel's finely tuned sensibilities. They were satisfied with a kind of tacit treaty between artist and audience, setting out what I want to call the doctrine of distance. This doctrine, an impressive exemplar of a cultural defense mechanism at work, holds that the more generalized and idealized the presentation of the human body in art, the more draped in elevated associations, the less likely it is to shock its viewers. In practice this meant abstracting the nude from contemporary and intimate experience by lending it the alien glamor that titles or poses drawn from history, mythology, religion, or the exotic could provide. For some among the pious, even mythology or antiquity were not enough to protect the public from evil thoughts: "Our ladies and gentlemen," William Dunlap wrote in 1834, "only flock *together* to see pictures of naked figures when the subject is scriptural and called moral."[84] Yet many amateurs were

83. John to Effie Ruskin, December 15, 1854, Lutyens, *Millais and the Ruskins*, 54n; Lutyens reports (54) that Effie Ruskin was actually subjected to criticism for allowing herself to pose; Kathryn Moore Heleniak, *William Mulready* (1980), 158; *Aurora*, June 23, 1812, in David Sellin, *The First Pose, 1876: Turning Point in American Art* (1976), 22; Amiel: December 15, 1851, *Journal intime*, I, 1136.

84. *History of the Rise and Progress of the Arts of Design in the United States*, 2 vols. (1834), I, 417–18, in Sellin, *First Pose*, 25.

quite prepared to acquit a nude of low sensuality if the artist could persuade his public that it was "clothed" in a purity of its own.

There is something paradoxical about this ideology, and this is instructive, for where there is a paradox, a conflict often lies concealed. Distance, however generated, made a work of art less erotic and more erotic at the same time. Less erotic, for the viewer was supposed to be responding not to some sexual invitation but, rather, to a historical or literary message; more erotic, for when he saw her draped in its suitable guise he could leer at the nude in ways that more familiar naked bodies could never permit. The nineteenth-century bourgeoisie, in a word, found reassurance in displacing its erotic needs as far from home— literally—as possible. "A picture," as the *Saturday Review* put the case in 1858, "is always to some extent idealized. A Grace, a Nymph, or a Venus, is an unreal, conventional being, whom we associate only with picture galleries."[85] The middle classes found their conflicts over the limits of permissible sensuality hard to resolve. But in unimpeachable guise, with all its concealments and distortions, the nude proved a useful, generally welcome educator for the bourgeois century.

Whatever its limitations and nuances, then, the doctrine of distance was a mechanism for licensing what was impermissible under ordinary circumstances. The bourgeois century, like other centuries, abounded in assertions that "Jewesses" or gypsies or other "exotics" were "hot-blooded" or that redheads were passionate—principally because they were rare creatures. Figures remote in space or time or appearance could release sexual desires and overcome, or at least reduce, inhibitions against erotic fantasies. This self-protective ideology was an institution of civilization, and civilization, as I have said before, is among other things a moat against incest. Remoteness kept the threat of incestuous wishes at bay. A provocative, barely clothed girl lounging in an Algerian doorway was exotic; the same girl in the same attitude in a Parisian doorway would have been obscene. A suggestive nude displaying her flawless body and called "Venus" was a work of art; the same nude in the same posture but obviously of domestic provenance would have outraged many museum-goers. William Mulready, whether with cynicism or in resignation, noted the principle in his sketchbook: "Female beauty and innocence will be much talked about, and sell well. Let it be *covertly* exciting." If it approaches "a more sensual existence," the picture "will be talked more about and sell much better." But it is important to remember that should "excitement appear to be the object," then the "hypocrites will shout and scream and scare away the sensualists."[86] The fashionable Jean-Léon Gérôme could offer, in *Pygmalion and Galatea*, a lithe naked model because she was illustrating a classical tale; Daumier could deflate this stratagem, but its effectiveness remained. The eminent Belgian painter Antoine Wiertz, who specialized in grandiose historical and murky philosophical subjects, could, in *La Belle Rosina*, pose a strapping model bereft of clothing, because he was using her to evoke the somber message of *memento mori*. And Arnold Böcklin, once a favorite among bourgeois art-lovers of German culture, including Sigmund Freud, could, in canvases animated by cavorting, bucolic mermaids, leave few mysteries of the female anatomy unexplored because he elevated his sportive creatures into principal actors in a mythological drama of his own devising.

Persistent and unrepentant offenders against this doctrine could expect to be lectured and denounced. As everyone knows, this was the fate of Manet. The reception of his epoch-making canvases in the early 1860s serves as a reminder that the notion of a France wholly frothy, erotic, corrupt, was an invention of shocked, probably envious, foreigners. Influential segments of the French public were exceedingly straitlaced, and insisted that female flesh could be displayed only in obedience to traditional rules of decorum. Manet offended these circles because the figures in his *Déjeuner sur l'herbe* and *Olympia* were obviously alive and, what was worse, French: the principal objection to his masterly *Déjeuner* was precisely that the nude in the foreground and her two luncheon companions were recognizable portraits of Manet's contemporaries. "A commonplace woman of the demimonde, as naked as can be, shamelessly lolls between two dandies dressed to the teeth" was characteristic of the intemperate reviews that Manet had to read: "This is a young man's practical joke, a shameful open sore not worth exhibiting this way." His *Olympia* fared no better. Despite its manifest debt to Titian's *Venus*, and partly because of it, the canvas was called spicy, indecent, ludicrous, a mockery. And the critics, dwelling with distaste on Olympia's hideousness, her thin body and the serene indifference of her dark eyes, grounded their verdict in the reality of the model. Art criticism here, as so often in this age, faded into moral judgment: the critics who accused Manet of refusing to idealize, or to distance, his naked young woman understood his purposes better than they knew. He was a modern painter offering the public a modern girl, precisely as he saw her. And that was, both aesthetically and ethically, extremely anxiety-provoking for those who, at least in public, liked to have their sexual information diluted or embellished. When in 1867 Emile Zola defended Manet's "new style of paint-ing," he dismissed the charge of immorality as simply irrelevant, by subjecting the *Déjeuner* and the *Olympia* to purely formal analyses. What interested Manet, Zola argued, was the relationship of colors and the intricacy of composition. This was an ingenious defense of Manet, and a refreshing departure from other critics' obsession with the ethical stature of a work of art. But Zola was doing Manet more—or rather less —than justice. Manet was no pure formalist; he was making a point of parading the contemporaneity of his models, and thus, being a great painter, he made history.[87] The doctrine of distance was never quite the same after *Olympia*.

At its simplest, this ideology was a complicated compromise. Etty, after all, was taken to task quite as earnestly for his neoclassical compositions as for his canvases of frankly naked models: there was a measure of sensual exhibitionism that the doctrine of distance was not capacious enough to cover. Try as he might, Etty could never quiet the suspicion that he was playing on his public's erotic susceptibilities, even if he titled his nudes *At the Doubtful Breeze Alarmed*. The breasts of Etty's nudes were too pointed and too prominent for comfort. But most lovers of art, impatient with subtleties, found this permission to view nudes highly satisfactory.

I have called this doctrine a tacit treaty, for the negotiations by and large did not reach the awareness of ordinary viewers. But alert art critics, directors of art institutes which employed models, and anxious moralists were aware of the compromise that this doctrine embodied, and at times uneasy about its boundaries. When Jean-Baptiste Clésinger exhibited his luscious, overpoweringly sensual lifesize nude sculpture *Woman Bitten by a Snake* at the Salon of 1847, Théophile Gautier explicitly commented, though by no means with disapproval, on this violation of an understood and accepted rule: Clésinger, he wrote in his review, "had the daring, unheard of in our time, to exhibit without a mythological title a masterpiece which is neither a goddess, nor a nymph . . . but simply a woman." The snake, Gautier informed his readers, had been an afterthought, designed to supply the kind of cover that the doctrine of distance demanded. Obviously, it was very scanty cover. Frédéric Chopin, by no means the only viewer outraged by Clésinger's erotic realism, wrote that his entry at the Salon "represents a nude woman in an attitude which is more than indecent—so much so that to justify

87. George Heard Hamilton, *Manet and His Critics* (1954; ed. 1969), 45; Peter Gay, *Art and Act: On Causes in History—Manet, Gropius, Mondrian* (1976), ch. 2.

the pose, he had to wrap a serpent around one of the legs of the statue."[88] To an age conversant with Freudian symbolism, Clésinger's narrative subterfuge is not without its irony: a sculpture of a buxom female writhing in sexual surrender was made not less but more erotic by the addition of a phallic serpent. But for his own time that serpent constituted the excuse necessary to make his nude acceptable to the Salon.

Thirty-five years later, the critic Henry Houssaye articulated the doctrine once again. Reviewing the Salon of 1882, he particularly regretted "the absence of scenes from mythology and ancient history because they are the only subjects suitable for the nude."[89] Some cynics among nineteenth-century artists, eagerly pandering to prurient tastes, certainly exploited this doctrine by fabricating esoteric titles or claiming mythological status for scenes nakedly depicting Eros at play. But even artists of relatively pure intentions found the doctrine of distance exceptionally malleable. It was, after all, far less a matter of calculation than of an impulsive response to the general conflict about sensuality, a conflict which painters and sculptors sensed and partly shared, and which guided their brush or their chisel as they made yet another Venus and Cupid, yet another harem scene.

The malleability of this defense proved its worth; some nineteenth-century viewers were scandalized by almost everything, others by very little. Most found themselves somewhere between these polar extremes and were receptive to the lure of the aesthetic, ready to suspend moralizing if they could be persuaded, or persuade themselves, that what they were seeing was elevated art rather than accomplished obscenity. There were layers upon layers of perception and feeling at work in this doctrine—conscious reserve undercut by unconscious needs, acquired prudery clashing with instinctual desire. Contradictions were therefore the order of the day. The most respectable families could introduce large-breasted and highly explicit busts into their parlors. And academic juries could applaud scenes that good sense and unservile judgment would have recognized and condemned as frankly corrupt art. Alexandre Cabanel's *Nymph Abducted by a Faun* of 1860 depicts, to put it plainly, the prelude to a rape. Exhibited in the Salon of that year and promptly purchased by Napoleon III, the painting leaves no doubt of its meaning. The leering faun, dark-skinned and avid, and the reluctant nymph, with her creamy body and flowing hair, are so direct an invitation to sexual

88. Peter Fusco and H. W. Janson, eds., *The Romantics to Rodin: French Nineteenth-Century Sculpture from North American Collections* (1980), 175–76.

89. Hamilton, *Manet*, 253.

arousal as to constitute a piece of polished and astute pornography. What lent this voluptuous canvas the prestige of Art was, of course, its theme. Yet at least one reviewer, Charles Blanc, editor of the *Gazette des Beaux-Arts*, praised the painting precisely because he found the figures charmingly familiar: "These mythological beings," he wrote, "whose forms . . . are choice and whose colors are delicate, have not been brought up in the woods of fable; they come from the city, they are Parisians."[90] The verdict of "pure" or "debased" depended on many things: the way an artist managed his explosive erotic materials, the pressures brought to bear by lobbyists for purity, the dominant mood of a decade, or such accidents as the political ambitions of some government prosecutor. The distances that the doctrine described varied enormously.

Its workings, as well as its flexibility, are beautifully exhibited by one of America's most famous nineteenth-century sculptures, Hiram Powers's lifesize nude *The Greek Slave*. Powers, born at Woodstock, Vermont, in 1805, moved to Florence in 1837, and it was there, six years later, surrounded by classical and neoclassical sculpture, that he had the happy inspiration of doing a nude that would be wholly unobjectionable to the most fastidious moralist. He chose a theme from recent history calculated to arouse the indignation of the sculpture-buying public: during the Greek War for Independence, Powers noted, the Turks had seized Christian prisoners, often "beautiful girls," to sell them "to the highest bidders." Such an inspiring scene, Powers knew, made "entire nudity" imperative: "The Slave," he said, "is compelled to stand naked to be judged of in the slave market;—and this is a historical fact." He made it his study, he added, "to avoid anything that could either by form or import offend the purest mind"; and this required a situation in which the naked girl was wholly unaware of her nudity. He found what he needed in the Greek girl's affliction: her family probably destroyed by the Turks, her feelings for her barbarian captors pure abhorrence, her anxiety over her future acute, but her "reliance upon the goodness of God" a comfort. "Gather all these afflictions together," Powers concluded, "and add to them the fortitude and resignation of a Christian, and no room will be left for shame," and, he implied, no room for wanton ideas in the viewer.[91]

Powers's calculation, less manipulative than it sounds, succeeded brilliantly. The public for his *Greek Slave* grew vast and was, almost

90. *The Second Empire: Art in France under Napoleon III* (1978), 263.
91. C. Edwards Lester, *The Artist, the Merchant, and the Statesmen of the Age of the Medici, and of Our Own Time*, 2 vols. (1845), I, 86–88.

without exception, lyrical and mixed; six full-size versions, three half-size versions, nearly seventy busts, innumerable reproductions in marble, ceramic, Parian ware, engravings and photographs, to say nothing of parodies, gave the piece circulation unprecedented for such a work. Its greatest triumph came at the Great Exhibition in 1851, where it was hailed as "one of the 'lions,'" as "one of the most exquisite objects," as "one of the happiest efforts in modern sculpture." But even before 1851, admirers in England and Italy exclaimed over the purity and sheer beauty of the piece. As one London periodical reported in 1845, "Men gazed on the 'Greek Slave' when they saw it the first time as those men gazed on the Venus de Medici, who dug it up from the earth." In the same year, a visitor to Powers's studio in Florence, C. Edwards Lester, praised the statue, along with Powers's other large unembarrassed nude, *Eve*, for arousing "that beautiful emotion which long lingers around one, like some ideal form that sometimes, in the calm sleep of an early spring morning, flits over the fancy, but cannot be forgotten." The American diarist Philip Hone thought the piece superior to Praxiteles: "I certainly never saw anything more lovely."[92] Such hyperbolic appraisals were accompanied, in many who saw Powers's *Greek Slave*, by a sense of reverence; the distance produced by the chains, or in other versions, manacles, stifled any possible lewd thoughts the girl's nakedness might arouse to generate a delicate aura of sanctity instead. At the same time, the representation of a beautiful girl in shackles, helpless before her sensual onlookers, must have given rise to intimations of sadistic pleasures —at least in some of the *Greek Slave*'s many admirers. But if it did, such speculative satisfactions, remote and considered revolting by the proper, left no traces on public appreciations and remained hidden in the viewer's unconscious.

There were some dissenting, disapproving voices, and they belong on the record. In 1854, one William Peters addressed an indignant pamphlet, *The Statue Question*, to the chairman of the Crystal Palace Company, complaining about the "indecent, intentionally indecent, statues" that had been on show since the Great Exhibition opened in 1851. The most "unquestionably indecorous" of these statues was, to Peters, the *Greek Slave*. Peters had discovered to his horror that "the process for obtaining such fine statues is by copying from the naked figure and moulding from the native form," and he thought it right "to inform the matrons, and through them the daughters of England, that women are habitually hired

92. C. H. Gibbs-Smith, *The Great Exhibition of 1851, Commemorative Album*, (1950; rev. ed. 1964), 129; Lester, *Artist, Merchant, Statesmen*, 12–13; September 13, 1847, *The Diary of Philip Hone, 1828–1857*, ed. Allan Nevins, 2 vols. in 1 (1927), 818.

to expose themselves to the gaze of the penciller." This was something of a shrewd hit; fantasies of naked models seducing, or being seduced by, the artists who depicted them were, as I have noted, part of the imaginative baggage of worried bourgeois. But Peters was a crank, author of a pamphlet against Newtonianism and of another definitively squaring the circle.[93]

Rather more responsible was the reviewer in the *Cosmopolitan Art Journal* who, in 1860, denounced the *Greek Slave* as "more lascivious than anything Greek art has left us." Yet even he was drowned in the avalanche of breathless admiration. Thus Caroline Kirkland, a once well-known writer on Western themes, described the atmosphere at a public showing of the piece—of which there were many: "Men take off their hats, ladies seat themselves silently, and almost unconsciously; and usually it is minutes before a word is uttered. All conversation is carried on in a hushed tone, and everybody looks serious on departing." More than most nudes of the century, Powers's *Greek Slave* invited the saving comment that she was really fully dressed: "The Greek Slave," the Reverend Orville Dewey wrote reverently, "is clothed all over with sentiment, sheltered, protected by it from every profane eye." And, writing in the *Knickerbocker Magazine*, one H. S. C. began a poem with the same thought:

> Naked yet clothed with chastity,
> She stands.

The converse was thought to hold true as well. In 1893, Mary Mac-Monnies showed her sketches for a large mural, intended for the Columbian Exposition in Chicago, to Bertha Palmer, president of the Lady Managers for the Women's Building. When Mrs. Palmer objected to the nudity, MacMonnies defended her design for "Primitive Woman" on the grounds that "timidity and feebleness" were out of place, especially in an exposition for which male sculptors were preparing enormous allegorical nudes. Moreover, she insisted, "A figure draped from head to foot may easily be made more immodest than one entirely nude."[94] The

---

93. *The Statue Question. A Letter to the Chairman of the Crystal Palace Company, Dated 8th July, 1854* (1854), 8–10; see Peters, *Newton Rescued from the Precipitacy of His Followers* (1846), and *The Quadrature and Exact Area of the Circle Demonstrated* (1851).

94. Margaretta Lovell, "Hiram Powers' *The Greek Slave*: Virtue in Chains," in Yale Art Gallery, *American Arts and the American Experience* (n.d.), 27–29; Jeanne Weimann, *Fair Women: The Woman's Building, Chicago, 1893* (1981), 211. I owe this reference to Nancy Cott.—On May 3, 1843, the American sculptor Henry K. Brown, best known for his George Washington in Union Square, New York, wrote to a potential client, E. A. Prentice, that he would soon send him a drawing of a

innocent, engaging sophistry that marks the doctrine of distance could hardly go further than such observations. And, of course, they contain some psychological truth; drapery could be more enticing than nakedness. One could look, then; one was not untroubled, but one could look.

The nineteenth-century middle classes thus found themselves prepared to enjoy the body in art within limits, if ill-defined and porous limits. Flaubert attacked the matter with his characteristic pungency in a letter to his mistress, Louise Colet: "People go about accusing of sensuality sculptors who make real women with breasts that can hold milk and haunches that can conceive. But if, on the contrary, they made draperies stuffed with cotton and figures flat as sign-boards, people would call them idealistic, spiritual. 'Ah yes! true,' they'll say, 'he neglects the form, but he's a thinker!' Whereupon the bourgeois exclaims and forces himself to admire what bores him." Flaubert's judgment is enmeshed in his virulent anti-bourgeois predilections, but, for all its derisiveness, it implicitly, almost involuntarily, allows the bourgeois some dash of sensuality beneath his prudish exterior: those flat chests, those draped signboards that his morality calls for really do bore him. And some good bourgeois admired the undraped form quite openly. Writing to his fiancée from Paris in early 1886, Sigmund Freud described his fellow guests at a reception that Charcot had given; among them had been "Charcot's chief assistant with his wife, who was in a certain state of exposure, for which, however, one cannot blame a beauty. She was, by the way," he added, significantly associating her lovely and highly visible form to the art of sculpture, "as mute as a statue."[95] Yet others among the respectable found that even fig leaves were not enough: the great English caricaturist George Cruikshank, himself no mean moralist, satirized these extremists in 1822 by showing the great Evangelical William Wilberforce covering, with his hat, the genitals of Achilles on that enormous statue erected in Hyde Park in honor of the Duke of Wellington. The joke was that the sculptor had already concealed those genitals behind a fig leaf.[96] Still

---

sculpture he hoped Prentice would buy: "I think you would have but one objection to it, and that is its nudity; it is not draped at all, and I think, should you see it, you would desire it to remain so. It seems to me that no one can look upon it and feel the want of drapery. I think I understand your feelings upon this subject, what you might admire in some situation, you might not wish to place in your parlor." Mss 669, vol. 2, p. 368, Henry Kirke Brown Papers, Art and Architecture Library, Yale University.

95. Flaubert: [September 18, 1846], *Correspondance*, I, 350–51; Freud: February 10, 1886, *Briefe*, 201.

96. "Making Decent—!!" (1822), in Ian Bradley, *The Call to Seriousness: The Evangelical Impact on the Victorians* (1976), after p. 160.

others took far from innocent, though somewhat veiled, pleasure in the unclad bodies of prepubescent girls. Lewis Carroll was only the best known among nineteenth-century photographers to choose eight-year-old girls for his favorite models. The uncomplicated candor of Thomas Love Peacock's Mr. Crotchet was relatively rare; obviously standing in for his author, Mr. Crotchet collected Venuses, admired nude ancient sculpture as "the true school of modesty," and declared himself perfectly willing to let his pretty daughter "sit for a model to Canova." He was, as I have said, rare: in August 1871, when the young Mabel Loomis, not quite fifteen, visited the Boston Atheneum, she "looked into the 'Reading room,' (which is filled with naked figures, . . . Venuses, & the like) and saw Mr. Lovejoy down in one part of the room, reading a newspaper. We were ashamed to be seen in there, so we went out, and sat down."[97] She was ready, even eager, to gather carnal knowledge, but found it improper to have others, especially men, notice her interest. She would not have sat for a model to Canova, not if her parents had known about it.

The very compromise that allowed nudes into decent company had its provocative side. Acceptable undraped females were, by and large, pagan. But while this provenance gave license, it, too, could give offense. I recall the strong-minded unbeliever, Sue Bridehead, in Thomas Hardy's *Jude the Obscure*: walking out of the "ecclesiastical establishment" where she lived in Christminster, she encountered an itinerant peddler and bought from him a Venus and an Apollo, "the largest figures on the tray." It was an act of defiance. "Being of a nervous temperament, she trembled at her enterprise," for they "seemed so very large now that they were in her possession, and so very naked." She carefully wrapped them up and carried her "heathen load into the most Christian city in the country," passing them off as statuettes of St. Peter and St. Mary Magdalen, only to unwrap them at night, shyly glancing at them as she read Gibbon on Julian the Apostate.[98] It is almost—though Hardy neither says so, nor hints at it—as though *The Decline and Fall of the Roman Empire* were pornography, and the very naked little statues incitements to unclean thoughts, and perhaps unclean acts. Those, like Comstock, who thought the nude in art seductive were not wholly wrong.

We have some poignant evidence in some of Edith Wharton's auto-biographical jottings, though, that when the climate was unfavorable, a very forest of nudes provided little, if any, usable information. Wharton's rich and elegant mother was practically phobic on the subject of sexuality

97. Peacock: *Crochet Castle* (1831), ch. 7; Todd: August 25, 1871, Journal I, box 45, MLT.

98. Hardy, *Jude the Obscure* (1896), part 2, section 2.

and refused to acknowledge her daughter's budding senses: "And all the while Life, real Life," Wharton later recalled, "was ringing in my ears, humming in my blood, flushing my cheeks & waving in my hair—sending me messages & signals from every beautiful face & musical voice, & running over me in vague tremors when I rode my pony, or swam through the short bright ripples of the bay, or raced & danced & tumbled with 'the boys.' And I didn't know—& if, by any chance, I came across the shadow of a reality, & asked my mother 'What does it mean?' I was always told 'You're too little to understand,' or else, 'It's not nice to ask about such things.'" Quite early, she remembered, "when I was seven or eight, an older cousin had told me that babies were not found in flowers but in people. This information had been given unsought, but as I had been told by Mamma that it was 'not nice' to enquire into such matters, I had a vague sense of contamination, & went immediately to confess my involuntary offense." For her unquestioning compliance to her mother's rules she got "a severe scolding, & was left with a penetrating sense of 'not-niceness' which effectually kept me from pursuing my investigations farther, & this was literally all I knew of the processes of generation till I had been married for several weeks." She meant precisely what she said. "A few days before my marriage," Wharton recalled, "I was seized with such a dread of a whole dark mystery, that I summoned up courage to appeal to my mother, & begged her, with a heart beating to suffocation, to tell me 'what being married was like.' Her handsome face at once took on the look of icy disapproval which I most dreaded. 'I never heard such a ridiculous question!' she said impatiently; & I felt at once how vulgar she thought me.

"But in the extremity of my need I persisted, 'I'm afraid, Mamma—I want to know what will happen to me!'

"The coldness of her expression deepened to disgust. She was silent for a dreadful moment; then with an effort, & the expression of a person whose nostrils are assailed by a disagreeable smell, she said, 'You've seen enough pictures & statues in your life. Haven't you noticed that men are—made differently from women?'

"'Yes,' I faltered blankly.

"'Well, then—?'

"I was silent, from sheer inability to follow, & she brought out sharply: 'Then for heaven's sake don't ask me any more silly questions. You can't be as stupid as you pretend!'"[99]

99. "Life and I," 33–35, Wharton Archives, Beinecke Library, Yale University. Passages from this long confession appear in R. W. B. Lewis, *Edith Wharton: A Biography* (1975), 53.

The nude pictures and statues she had seen told this troubled girl of
New York high society nothing because she had never known—or,
rather, had felt compelled to repress—what to ask them. There were all
too many Edith Whartons, and their male counterparts, in the nineteenth
century, some of whom ended up in Sigmund Freud's consulting room.
And yet, it is worth recalling that throughout that age, though they
were normally idealized, private parts were public property.

❧ SIX ❧

Fortifications for the Self

Undeniably, the public domain exercised a momentous influence on the shaping of nineteenth-century middle-class sensuality. The wider world teemed with warnings and invitations, with fiascos that strengthened inhibitions and incitements that defeated them. Experience would revive sensual childhood memories to define adult erotic needs, opportunities, and frustrations. In his chronicle of a young man's formation, *L'Education sentimentale*—a title I have borrowed—Flaubert exposes his passive, rather unprincipled protagonist to a parade of instructors in life who are nearly all remote from his parental home: a disillusioning, if not uncharacteristic education of the senses. Society, then, provides extensive, incessantly renewed, often contradictory lessons for maturing egos and superegos; it feeds and thwarts, in a word it educates, the senses.

But since erotic passions and anxieties ripen within the sheltered, partly repressed sphere of personal life, I will now return to the individual after traversing those larger circuits. I will narrow my focus once again to explore the bourgeois' presumed addiction to hypocrisy—mendacious craven compliance with the dictates of despotic public opinion; his never-forgotten teacher, the family; and that silent and discreet solace of his inviolable inner life, the diary. This circular course—from Mabel Todd, as it were, to Mabel Todd—has particular pertinence for the historian of the nineteenth-century bourgeoisie. No other class at any other time was more strenuously, more anxiously devoted to the appearances, to the family and to privacy, no other class has ever built fortifications for the self quite so high.

1. A Search for Safety

Their defensive maneuvers rapidly earned the nineteenth-century middle classes an unenviable reputation for hypocrisy, a reputation which they have never lost. Doubtless, the bourgeois century was amply supplied with teachers of denial instructing their fellows in reticence, evasion, or silence before the facts of life. These strategies left their traces on the accepted taste for art, the instruction of children, sermons of moralists, and, above all, the chary handling of sexuality. Hypocrisy, in its oblique way, also seemed an educator of the senses, issuing instructions on how to disguise feelings and convictions for the sake of social acceptance. In 1911, George Santayana gave that unfortunate Victorian age just past a name which derisively encapsulated this peculiarly middle-class addiction to duplicity. In his much-quoted address "The Genteel Tradition in American Philosophy," whose grasp is far wider than its title, he described polite culture as having suffered for a century from conventionality, the studied escape from life. Once nurtured on the bracing pessimism of Calvinist teachings, Americans had set aside the substance of Calvin's ideas and retained only his rhetoric; more recently swayed by the ambitious formulations of transcendentalism, they had trivialized them into a handy device for overlooking the uncomfortable truths all around them. The consequences lay conspicuously across the American cultural landscape: superficiality, insincerity, disingenuousness, a lack of true seriousness. And Santayana left little doubt that European genteel culture had traversed a very similar course. But he was not pessimistic: his lecture was not a diagnosis but an autopsy. For, he concluded, three remarkable Americans had effectively subverted the dominant self-deceptions of the nineteenth century: Walt Whitman, the bohemian rebel; Henry James, the subtle analyst; and William James, the fearless investigator. "The illegitimate monopoly which the genteel tradition had established over what ought to be assumed and what ought to be hoped for has been broken down."[1]

Santayana's bright hopes for the immediate future stood out against the drab background of nineteenth-century hypocrisy. But in fact circumlocutions and euphemisms were the special preserve neither of the nineteenth century nor of the bourgeoisie. As early as 1634, the English oriental traveler Sir Thomas Herbert had noted that in East India "the women goe most part naked," except for a "loin cloth" to "couer those

---

1. "The Genteel Tradition in American Philosophy," in *Winds of Doctrine* (1913; ed. 1957), 211.

parts, made to be private." And only a few years later, an American woman charged with witchcraft was held to have "an apparent teat in her secret parts."[2] Milton, around the same time, derided "hypocrites" about sexual matters who

> austerely talk
> Of purity and place and innocence,

while La Rochefoucauld immortally defined hypocrisy, which he evidently thought rife in his age, as the "homage that vice pays to virtue." Molière invented Tartuffe, that archetypal hypocrite, during the reign of Louis XIV. The very age of the Enlightenment had its unexamined dusty corners, its accesses of shyness, its coy indirections. We have come to see the canvases of Greuze, which an uninhibited viewer like Denis Diderot valued for their elevated morality, as an art of cunning innocence, of suggestive eroticism in the dress of virginal purity. And blushing reticence, heartfelt or assumed, was highly prized in that candid time. In 1700 a physician named John Jones, describing the sensual pleasures of opium, compared them, "not without good cause, to a permanent gentle *Degree* of that Pleasure, which Modesty forbids the naming of." In *Tristram Shandy* Laurence Sterne, a mocker of hypocrites, thought that in his "canting world," the "cant of hypocrisy may be the worst." It was to stigmatize this cant that in 1798 the playwright Thomas Morton first introduced Mrs. Grundy, that intrusive prude, on the English stage. "Whoever has a wife and children," wrote John Stuart Mill in 1869, "has given hostages to Mrs. Grundy."[3] But that figure of fun and power had been on center stage, lecturing, for more than half a century.

In the bourgeois century itself, aristocrats, so often the targets of middle-class indignation for their presumed indifference to shame and to shrinking sensibilities, found themselves in the camp of the deniers. In April 1839, the young Queen Victoria noted in her diary that Lord Melbourne objected to Dickens's *Oliver Twist*, though she "defended" the book "very much, but in vain." Melbourne would have none of it. "I

---

2. T. H. Esquier [Sir Thomas Herbert], *A Relation of Some Yeares Travaile, Begunne Anno 1626. Into Afrique and the Greater Asia, especially the Territories of the Persian Monarchie: and some parts of the Orientall Indies, and Iles adjacent* (1634), 41; John Putnam Demos, *Entertaining Satan: Witchcraft and the Culture of Early New England* (1982), 82.

3. Milton: *Paradise Lost*, IV, 744–45; La Rochefoucauld: *Réflexions, sentences et maximes morales*, ed. G. Duplessis, after the 5th ed. of 1678 (1853), 60; Jones: *The Mystery of Opium Reveal'd*, in Alethea Hayter, *Opium and the Romantic Imagination* (1968), 24; Sterne: *Tristram Shandy*, book III, ch. 12; Mill: *The Subjection of Women* (1869), 167.

don't *like* those things," he said. "I wish to avoid them; I don't like them in *reality*, and therefore I don't wish them represented."[4] But if nineteenth-century bourgeois were not the first or the only Tartuffes, they combined to make the most concentrated culture of Tartuffes the world had ever known. Or so their disparagers said.

Naturally, the age found eloquent defenders, even among its critics. The *Saturday Review*, that vigorously written and ferociously contentious London weekly, argued from its founding in 1855 that while social mendacity deserved the moralist's whip, the evidence for decency, piety, and truthfulness among the middling orders was creditable, even impressive. "The comparative atrocity of the various cants which are canted in this canting world," one anonymous contributor wrote in 1856, audibly echoing *Tristram Shandy*, "has been a favourable subject of speculation"; undeniably, "external decorum frequently covers the most awful abysses of wickedness." And surely this is a truth of which the canting world "peculiarly needs to be occasionally reminded." But while the *Saturday Review* took credit for urging these realities upon its readers, it had no patience with Jeremiahs who summarily dismissed the civilization of their day "as mere hypocrisy." In fact "the co-existence in any community of much villany with much decorum is anything but surprising." Hence "to publish long accounts of crime and of criminals, professedly with the object of denouncing the hypocrisy of society, and exposing the weak points of 'Our Civilization,' but really for the sake of pandering to that prurient curiosity about wickedness which is one of the lowest appetites of human nature," is in itself "a very unpleasant compound of immorality and hypocrisy."[5] The worst hypocrites, in a word, were those who obsessively hunted out hypocrisy to gratify their own shady needs.

Counterattack may be the best defense, but the calculated equivocations of the *Saturday Review*, though welcome to the educated and affluent who were its faithful readers, did not silence cultural critics. While bourgeois put much stock in denial during the age of Victoria and beyond, hypocrisy also generated a potent reaction in her time, and in their class. Satirical novelists, subversive poets, aristocratic philosophers and tendentious psychologists, all of them derisive, most of them angry, denounced their age as an age of almost intolerable insincerity. The English historian J. A. Froude, writing in 1849, detected an "utter divorce between practice and profession which has made the

4. April 7, 1839, *The Girlhood of Queen Victoria: A Selection from Her Diaries, 1832–40*, ed. Viscount Esher, 2 vols. (1912), II, 144.

5. "Our Civilization," *Saturday Review*, II (June 28, 1856), 195.

entire life of modern England a frightful lie."[6] The letters of Flaubert,
the reportage of Heine, and, a little later, the plays of Ibsen, leave
no doubt that the entire life of France, of Germany, of the Scandinavian
states, especially among the middle classes, seemed no less mendacious
to its unappeasable diagnosticians than that of England. The nineteenth-
century industry of self-criticism, waxing in prosperity with the passing
decades, devoted its finest intelligence and applied its choicest epithets to
the repellent bourgeois practice of doing one thing and saying another.
Through the ages, prophets and philosophers since Isaiah and Socrates
have found their vocation precisely in exposing the pious pretensions of
brazen profiteers and devious sensualists; there is nothing modern in the
disenchanted discovery that men conceal their basest actions behind their
noblest professions and use fine words to shield gross desires. But the
list of nineteenth-century moralists—novelists, poets, and philosophers—
who devoted themselves to the detection and denunciation of hypocrisy
is unusually distinguished and dense with talent: it included that implacable trio Gustave Flaubert, Heinrich Heine, and Henrik Ibsen, as well as
Charles Baudelaire, William Morris and Walt Whitman, John Ruskin,
Georg Brandes and Søren Kierkegaard, Jacob Burckhardt, Thomas
Carlyle and Matthew Arnold, to say nothing of Friedrich Nietzsche
and Karl Marx, Thorstein Veblen and August Strindberg, George Bernard Shaw and Sigmund Freud. Their targets were many and ready to
hand, but their favorite hypocrites were the officious scourges of immorality: Anthony Comstock, the gentlemen of the Society for the
Suppression of Vice, and the rest of their troubled and troublesome race.
The bourgeois century seemed a breeding ground for this disagreeable
type.

Certainly the bourgeois century was an age of unrelenting hypocrite-
hunting. The romantics began early, decades before Queen Victoria
came to the throne. Byron's life and poetry, Stendhal's sardonic social
explorations, E. T. A. Hoffmann's derisive portraits of the safe bourgeois,
were implicit, often explicit, hits at the middle-class hypocrisy that these
enemies of the philistine found at once grating and stifling. "All our
words, manners, religion, morals, and our whole mind and existence in
modern Europe," Byron wrote, "turn upon one single hinge, which the
English in one expressive word call cant." Stendhal was enough taken
with this passage to quote and slyly endorse it in an article for an English audience in the *London Magazine*. Later hypocrite-hunters followed

6. "The Nemesis of Faith," in Walter E. Houghton, *The Victorian Frame of Mind,
1830–1870* (1957), 405.

this line of attack. Humor magazines—*Kladderadatsch* in Germany, *Punch* in England, *Judge* in the United States—drew unflattering caricatures of the utterly respectable plying their canting trade. Douglas Jerrold, for some years the most productive and most popular gadfly for *Punch*, more prolific and more stinging than Thackeray, aimed poisoned darts at worldly bishops, mercenary traders, sanctimonious virgins, at devout churchgoers who ground down their tenants while they prated of charity. In his *Condition of the Working Class in England in 1844*, Friedrich Engels struck at bourgeois hypocrisy with the gusto of the radical who has explored the weak spots of his adversary and delights in what he has found: the rich and the genteel want to know nothing of the social misery for which they are so largely responsible, and take precautions that they may never see it. The very physical arrangement of the great English industrial towns, Engels notes, permits them lives of comfortable denial: the "money aristocracy" of Manchester can walk from its sumptuous houses to its offices without traversing any of the slums that pockmark the city. Engels thought this "hypocritical plan" only too characteristic of his chosen enemy. And he quotes a classic instance, a letter to the *Manchester Guardian*, signed "A LADY." It complained about "swarms of beggars" laying "our main streets" under siege, "human wrecks" who "try to awaken the pity of the passers-by in a most shameless and annoying manner, by exposing their tattered clothing, sickly aspect, and disgusting wounds and deformities." The writer asks plaintively if those who, like herself, pay the poor rates and contribute generously to charitable institutions have not earned the right "to be spared such disagreeable and impertinent molestations." Why can the municipal police not protect her from such sights?[7] Gleefully, Engels swooped down on this letter as a splendid manifestation of the self-protective insincerity common among the bourgeoisie.

Similar charges invaded the arts. Augustus Welby Pugin, the most imaginative and most gifted among the architects sponsoring the Gothic revival in the early years of Victoria's reign, pulled out all the stops of moral outrage to denounce the facility and shallowness of contemporary architecture: "Private judgment runs riot; every architect has a theory of his own, a beau ideal he has himself created; a disguise with which to invest the building he erects." Such departures from the truth of design violate the organic function of shelter. "Styles are now *adopted* instead of generated," Pugin noted with dismay, "and ornament and

---

7. Geoffrey Strickland, *Stendhal: The Education of a Novelist* (1974), 8; Engels, *Condition of the Working Class in England in 1844* (1845; ed. 1892), 46–47, 278–79.

design *adapted to*, instead of *originated by*, the edifices themselves."
Pugin had too much invested in what he cherished as truth in architecture
to be content with the ambiguous triumph of his own favorite style in
his time. Most nineteenth-century Gothic, as it was spread across the
pages of such popular handbooks as Loudon's *Encyclopedia*, seemed to
Pugin inaccurate, inappropriate, and worst of all, corrupt. In his best-
known polemical response, *The True Principles of Pointed or Christian
Architecture*, he lampooned Loudon's fanciful elevations by drawing
an impossible Gothic building of his own, complete with ridiculous
greenhouse, and commented that here "all is mere mask, and the whole
building an ill-conceived lie."[8] In the same way, in Pugin's and Engels's
time, ingenious carvers of bourgeois types—Thackeray, Daumier, Heine,
Dickens—found a large and often appreciative audience which readily
recognized the object of their scorn. I say "often" for Dickens at least
encountered strong and well-informed skepticism among his readers
when he turned from the pleasant humor of *Pickwick Papers* to the
social satire of *Little Dorrit* and the late novels; his imaginative caricatures seemed so remote from reality that they often missed their target
in their time. Yet much anti-bourgeois satire, even Dickens's, hit home.

Surely there was good hypocrite-hunting in the bourgeois century.
Some of it was on a high level of abstraction, and required considerable
philosophical acumen: such hunters could read the cosmic optimism
of Hegel or Ranke, like the contrasting social pessimism of the classical
economists, as sophisticated apologies for inaction. If the world is as it
must be, either as hopeful or as gloomy as philosophers and political
economists choose to paint it, then social action is either unnecessary or
futile, and the powers that be can calmly continue to remain so. Doctrines
borrowed from Malthus and economic liberalism became, for many practical men, sets of convenient rationalizations; no theories surely could be
more comforting, and more bracing, to a captain of industry or lord of
finance than those extolling universal combat or denigrating generosity
as counterproductive and decent wages as contrary to the laws of nature.
For the victims, exploitation lost none of its sting by being called economic liberalism.

But the most vulnerable target was bourgeois attitudes toward sexuality. As Effie Ruskin was about to separate from her husband, John Millais
lamented her patient, silent suffering in an eloquent letter to her mother
in which he blamed the cruel hypocrisy of his day about erotic matters

8. Pugin, *An Apology for the Revival of Christian Architecture* (1843), 1–2; John
Gloag, *Victorian Taste* (1942), 53.

for her travail: "It is only the wretchedness of Society that makes us attach so much importance to disclosures of the kind, making thousands endure a slow inward martyrdom for years rather than suffer a temporary exposure of facts." And Thackeray, taking a nostalgic glance at the robust age of Henry Fielding, told his readers, in the Preface to *Pendennis*, with a movement of envy: "Since the author of *Tom Jones* was buried, no writer of fiction among us has been permitted to depict to his utmost power a MAN. We must drape him, and give him a certain conventional simper. Society will not tolerate the Natural in our Art. Many ladies have remonstrated and subscribers left me, because in the course of the story [of Pendennis], I described a young man resisting and affected by temptation."[9]

Thackeray himself, as his more discriminating readers did not fail to observe, was more comfortable with conventional simpering than he need have been and, for all the apparent vehemence of his satire, might have found a little more freedom, especially about sexuality, perfectly safe. He was "thankful," he wrote with his usual inconsistency, turning for a moment into a very Podsnap, "to live in times when men no longer have the temptation to write so as to call blushes on women's cheeks." As Charlotte Brontë, who much admired Thackeray, complained, employing a subtle sexual metaphor, he was inclined to keep "the mermaid's tail below water."[10] A good deal of nineteenth-century moral censorship was self-censorship.

The boundaries between the permissible and the impermissible, in fact, were uncertain and remained little explored. Others besides Thackeray, both in England and elsewhere, were no less discreet. In 1886, translating *Anna Karenina* into English, Nathan Haskell Dole decorously retained a crucial sentence in the original; facing her lover Vronsky with her shameful and vital secret, Anna Karenina finally yields to his urging and tells him what is troubling her: "Ya béremenna!" As the reader can easily gather from the context, she is imparting the news that she is in what Victorians called an "interesting condition." It was only later translators who thought that the English-speaking reader could be trusted with this information directly. Constance Garnett, in 1901, still chose to be delicate: "I'm with child"; and the full force of the Russian emerged only

9. Millais: April 18, 1854, Mary Lutyens, *Millais and the Ruskins* (1967), 178; Thackeray: *The History of Pendennis. His Fortunes and Misfortunes, His Friends, and His Greatest Enemy* (1850), *The Works of William Makepeace Thackeray*, Centenary Biographical Edition, 26 vols. (1910–11), III, liv–lv.

10. Mario Praz, *The Hero in Eclipse in Victorian Fiction* (1952; tr. Angus Davidson, 1956), 260.

with Louise and Aylmer Maude's version of 1918: "I am pregnant." The German version by Hans Moser, dating from the 1890s, also reached, somewhat like Constance Garnett, for a genteel compromise: "Ich bin gesegnet."[11] German readers would gather without difficulty that being "blessed" meant having been impregnated, but the blunt directness of Anna Karenina's declaration was lost. Such modes of denial swamped candor early in the century and later. In 1824, when De Quincey reviewed Goethe's *Wilhelm Meister*, he priggishly took Goethe to task for his evident pleasure in "personal uncleanliness," and for the descriptive detail he supplied about Mariana's bedroom, which "passes all belief"; De Quincey found Goethe's references to the paraphernalia of woman's dress and cosmetics so disgusting that he judged the whole passage "too bad for quotation."[12]

English critics were not the only readers to accuse Goethe of coarseness. Even Jules Michelet, though not averse to dwelling with a certain lip-smacking enjoyment on the lasciviousness of witches, thought him, though "noble in form, not so in spirit."[13] And Goethe himself, the vigorous, colloquial playwright and poet who called an arse an arse, could flee to euphemisms of his own: translating *Le Neveu de Rameau*, he softened Diderot's famous formulation of the Oedipus complex by rendering "et coucherait avec sa mère" as the less threatening "would dishonor his mother."[14] One did not need to be a bourgeois philistine to discover limits to permissible speech.

In such a climate, not fundamentally different in the 1890s from what it had been in the 1820s, deliberate offenses against accepted conventions of reticence had to expect systematic and furious denunciations. When Ibsen's *Ghosts* was first performed in London in 1891, it was pelted with epithets among which anal images and their derivatives predominated. Obviously this drama, unmasking the sins of the respectable, complete with illicit love affairs and syphilitic insanity, touched a raw nerve. The playwright and producer William Archer, who had been instrumental in bringing Ibsen's plays to England, gathered up a rank bouquet of prudish pronouncements for the *Pall Mall Gazette*, which George Bernard Shaw wickedly reproduced in his *Quintessence of Ibsenism*: a "disgusting representation," one reviewer called the play; "an open drain, a loathsome sore

11. *Anna Karenina* (1875–77), part II, ch. 22. In Dole's translation the passage is on p. 199; in Garnett's translation (1901; 2d ed., 1916), 212; in the Maudes' version (1918; rev. 1939; ed. 1958), 212; in Moser's German version, 2 vols. (ca. 1890), I, 259.

12. Praz, *Hero in Eclipse*, 77.

13. See Michelet, *La Sorcière* (1862), ed. Jules Refort, 2 vols. (1952), I, 25.

14. Goethe's word, not exactly prissy but imprecise, is "*entehrte*."

unbandaged; a dirty act done publicly" were contributions by others. *Ghosts* was "candid foulness" and "gross, almost putrid indecorum," "naked loathsomeness" and "as foul and filthy a concoction as has ever been allowed to disgrace the boards of an English theatre." Ibsen himself was described as "a crazy, cranky being" who was "not only consistently dirty, but deplorably dull." And some reviewers were sure that the unsavory, one hoped vanishingly small, segment of London's theatregoing public who actually liked such filth must be "nasty-minded people who find the discussion of nasty subjects to their taste in exact proportion to their nastiness." Getting to the heart of the matter, they intimated that these lovers of Ibsen's work must be sexual perverts; they must be "the sexless," the "unwomanly woman, the unsexed females, the whole army of unprepossessing cranks in petticoats," to say nothing of "effeminate men and male women."[15] Even technical works were not safe. In 1904, Henry Holt, publishers of Dr. H. Newell Martin's faultlessly professional, widely used textbook *The Human Body*, offered to fill special orders without its concluding chapter, which dealt with human reproduction.

In general, nineteenth-century editors developed sensitive nostrils for what their public would accept. The career of Thomas Hardy's publications was one long tale of compromises exacted by nervous publishers. They would apologetically tell Hardy that *they*, of course, were not prudes, but that their readers, on whose good will their business depended, could not tolerate his explicitness. Even his suggestions were too suggestive. In 1874, Leslie Stephen, then editor of the prestigious *Cornhill Magazine*, admitted to Hardy that he had "deleted a line or two in the last batch of proofs" of *Far from the Madding Crowd*, "from an excessive prudery of wh. I am ashamed; but one is forced to be absurdly particular." Later, in 1886, Mowbray Morris, editor of *Macmillan's*, alerted Hardy to the risks of barely hinting at sexual irregularities: his subscribers, he wrote, are "pious Scottish souls who take offence wondrous easily." Morris also objected to the installments of *Tess of the d'Urbervilles* he had read for exuding entirely too much "succulence."

Hardy, to these cautious souls, was modern, and modern was a synonym for "filthy," for literature apt to corrupt the reader's imagination. Hence, editors would warn Hardy that his novels and stories dealt entirely too much with "those relations between the sexes over which conventionality is accustomed (wisely or unwisely) to draw a veil." Hardy grumbled against "the tyranny of Mrs. Grundy," but obediently

15. Archer, "Ghosts and Gibberings," *Pall Mall Gazette*, April 8, 1891, quoted in Shaw, *The Quintessence of Ibsenism* (1891; ed. 1912), 93–96.

made the changes he was asked to make in his serial publications, reserving most (though not all) of his original formulations for final publication. And while *Tess* offended sensibilities, *Jude the Obscure* enraged them. In August 1894, H. M. Alden, editor of *Harper's New Monthly Magazine*, though protesting to Hardy that he "felt properly ashamed" for his interventions, still found it necessary to remind him that he was "pledged" to publish "nothing which could not be read aloud in any family circle."[16]

While such aggressive timidity about sex marked the overworked Nonconformist conscience in England and fundamentalist prudery in the United States, the French could be as eager for concealment and factitious purity as anyone. Not long after Zola's death, his widow gathered up as much of his correspondence as she could find and bowdlerized it before publishing it; she was particularly ruthless with all the passages revealing that she had lived with Zola for some years before she married him.[17] And Zola's earthiness disgusted some of his fellow-writers. When, around 1890, Zola made the customary visit to the distinguished *littérateur* Xavier Marmier, member of the Académie française, to solicit his vote for a vacant seat in the Academy, Marmier tartly refused. He professed to admire Zola's gifts, his power, his labors to breathe new life into the French novel. "You have made superb books," he told Zola, "but I will not forgive you for having scattered coarseness and horrors among your works. In *La Terre*, in *L'Assommoir*, in *Germinal*, you have soiled admirable scenes with stains which morality and taste condemn."[18] Zola was never elected to the Académie française.

A consistently, rather self-consciously unconventional poet like Walt Whitman, who poured his homosexual pursuits and rather gluey love-making into his work, still chose to reveal his secrets, as he himself put it, by "faint indirections," if at all. His indirections were still too direct for some of his most cultivated and discriminating readers, like Ralph Waldo Emerson. When Emerson suggested that he prune *Leaves of Grass*, Whitman refused: "If I had cut sex out," he said years after,

16. Michael Millgate, *Thomas Hardy: A Biography* (1982), 160, 274, 300–301, 304–306, 349.

17. For details, Zola, *Correspondance*, ed. B. H. Bakker et al., 3 vols. so far (1978–   ), I, 43, 451, and F. W. J. Hemmings, "The Making of a Naturalist," *T.L.S.* (October 3, 1980), 1107.

18. Reported by the journalist Charles Formentin in *Echo de Paris*, September 21, 1890, after an interview with Marmier. See Xavier Marmier, *Journal (1848–1890)*, ed. Eldon Kaye, 2 vols. (1948), II, 49. From the beginning of his career as a novelist, Zola was denounced as obscene, and did not like it. See Zola to Louis Ulbach, September 9, 1872, *Correspondance*, II, 318–19.

sensibly, "I might just as well have cut everything out." And he expressed the animus of all hypocrite-hunters when he deplored the general *"respectability"* of his time and pronounced: "The dirtiest book in all the world is the expurgated book. Expurgation is apology—yes, surrender—yes, an admission that something or other was wrong."[19]

Expurgation might be dirty or apologetic, but it was the custom of the time. Some, like Hippolyte Taine, anticipated their biographers and the prying eyes of posterity by burning their papers and leaving instructions that their "private affairs" be left strictly alone. Most others could count on their authorized biographers to excise embarrassing events, even—or especially—those already in the uncertain public domain of rumor and gossip; editors of collected letters weeded out those they considered to be no one's business. Writers castrated their own work, and their biographers did not complain. In 1889, when Ednah Dow Cheney wrote the biography of Louisa May Alcott, she explicitly noted in her preface that it is "impossible to understand Miss Alcott's works fully without a knowledge of her own life and experience"; fortunately, "herself of the most true and frank nature, she has given us the opportunity of knowing her without disguise." She added, apparently unable to muster the slightest sense of incongruity, that "Miss Alcott revised her journals at different times during her later life, striking out what was too personal for other eyes than her own, and destroying a great deal which would doubtless have proved very interesting."[20] Cheney's sense of regret is very muted indeed: she plainly did not think the public had any right to material that Louisa May Alcott wanted to keep from it.

Charles Dickens was only the most famous victim of such thoughtful protectiveness. He died in 1870; eight years later his sister-in-law, Georgina Hogarth, and his eldest daughter, Mamie Dickens, solicited his letters for an edition to flesh out John Forster's famous, and, to their minds, practically definitive *Life of Charles Dickens*. Working rapidly and efficiently, the editors presented a two-volume selection of Dickens's letters in 1880, followed two years later by a supplement and, in the same year, by a revised and somewhat shortened version. "We have cut and condensed *remorselessly*," Georgina Hogarth wrote in late 1881, "but I hope and think, *wisely* and *well*." Her evocation of *Othello* invites the obvious rejoinder that she and her fellow-editor had, in fact, cut and condensed not wisely but too well. The editors' omissions are an an-

19. Justin Kaplan, *Walt Whitman: A Life* (1980), 235, 249, 252.
20. Taine: Susanna Barrows, *Distorting Mirrors: Visions of the Crowd in Late Nineteenth-Century France* (1981), 82; Alcott: Cheney, *Louisa May Alcott* (1889; reprint of 1890 ed., intro. Ann Douglas, 1980), xxxii.

thology of what they thought too frivolous, or too scandalous, for the late-Victorian public to absorb safely: some fairly elaborate jokes, revealing Carlyle's anti-Semitic bigotry and Dickens's relatively moderate malice directed against a good friend, Dickens's absorbed interest in mesmerism, and his separation from his wife. Letters the editors found "too *entirely* personal" also fell victim to their implacable discretion.[21] Sophia Hawthorne mutilated her husband's journals in the same spirit; Fanny Kingsley amputated her husband's correspondence for the same reason: to protect privacy. These pious editors were shaping materials for a public shrine, not displaying, let alone dissecting, illustrious cadavers.

At times the lust to conceal or correct surviving records reached for a highly idiosyncratic, almost unimaginably stringent reading of Victorian propriety. Alexander Carlyle's edition of his uncle Thomas Carlyle's *Journey to Germany, Autumn 1858* is a caricature of such moralistic editing. When Carlyle notes that on a visit he goes to bed sick, filled with calomel, is waited on by a butler who speaks incomprehensibly, and is treated to castor oil in the morning, his editor suppresses both the butler and the castor oil. When Carlyle, in his own private notes, refuses to spell out the word "whore" and calls Ninon de l'Enclos, the celebrated French courtesan, "that old wh-re," Alexander Carlyle improves on his uncle's discretion by changing "wh-re" to "female." Again, when Carlyle describes the citizens of Liegnitz turning out en masse at the railway station "intent to smell the Prince of Prussia," his nephew decides that it would be more proper for the populace to have gathered to "see" the prince. And when Carlyle dilates in picturesque detail on the statue of St. John of Nepomuk in Prague—"particularly odious to me"; the "whole story is a *premeditated lie*"; the "sprawling *Christkin* in its arms, and the twisted head and thrice-gracious simper looking down on that little gilt phenomenon, has always the physiognomy of an improper-female in breeches"; a "Detestable Humbug; child of the Devil, that, surely"—his bewildered editor, intent on offending no one, chooses to drop the passage in its entirety.[22] Appropriately enough, it was Charles Dickens who exemplified these cultural defense mechanisms, and shrewdly intimated their reason for being, in his brilliantly conceived character of Mrs. General. This is the formidable paragon whom the Dorrits, once they have come into money, hire to teach them gentility:

21. I am indebted in this passage to Madeline House and Graham Storey, eds., *The Letters of Charles Dickens*, Pilgrim Edition, vol. I, *1820–1839* (1965), ix–x.

22. See Thomas Carlyle, *Journey to Germany, Autumn 1858*, ed. Richard Albert Edward Brooks (1940), xvi–xix, 90–93.

"the truly refined mind," she tells her employers and charges, is "one that will seem to be ignorant of the existence of anything that is not perfectly proper, placid, and pleasant." Her doctrine of denial is in sharp, irreconcilable contrast with the stubborn desire of *Little Dorrit*'s protagonist, Arthur Clennam, to discover the truth, however murky, about his past: "I want to know." Dickens intuitively understood, even if he could not clearly articulate, the conflicting needs and ideals that made the bourgeoisie of his day anything but a solid phalanx of hypocrites. Still, in the bourgeois century there were many who did not want to know. Tartuffe, it seemed to exasperated social observers, would have been right at home in Dickens's time.

Molière's Tartuffe was memorable largely because he was a priest, his sensuality and opportunism active beneath his cloak of exemplary piety. Such types were far from unknown to the bourgeois century. In 1870, while he was still an obscure employee in the Bureau of Statistics in the Treasury and happily settled with his Lizzie, Lester Ward drafted a furious letter to a hypocrite who had grievously violated the sanctity of his household—one W. G. Marts, a young man on his way to the Congregationalist ministry. "Sir," Ward curtly began, and plunged into his indictment without polite preliminaries: "Your rascality committed in my house, has long been known to me," but Ward had waited for some time before taking action. "Now however at the especial request of the mother of your mulatto bastard child, who is suffering from want in consequence of your *pious* acts, I write to demand on penalty of exposure and eternal disgrace, that you begin immediately to do what the law requires of such villains and what any but a pious villain like you would do from a sense of honor viz:—namely to send the mother of your child money enough to support it and her comfortably." Ward, an articulate, occasionally eloquent, but scarcely histrionic writer, here employs, overpowered by indignation, the locutions of melodrama; he threatens "exposure and eternal disgrace," and calls Marts a "pious villain." This rhetoric throws some light on the tone of contemporary theatre and fiction: the language of melodrama was not so very remote from the stark realities of Ward's world. Ward offered Marts "a reasonable time" to send the first installment. "If it is not forthcoming I will publish your foul debauchery to the whole world." He threatened to inform Marts's faculty, and to pursue him "till you will pray your God to swallow you up in the earth." For the sake of "the poor ignorant black woman whom you seduced, and of the innocent child of your Christian lust," Ward agreed to keep the whole matter a secret as long as Marts paid "liberally" and continued to pay. "For a while," Ward thought,

Marts must "make up for your neglect thus far. You ought to buy her a house and lot. Think not because she is a black woman you can be allowed to go scot free. In this country," he added, his optimistic egalitarianism running away with him—it was, after all the age of Reconstruction— "there is no distinction on account of color."

Then Ward warmed to his real theme, Marts's "Christian lust." It is evident that he was rather enjoying himself and his outrage. "I shall do all and much more than I have said. I will pursue and ostracize you out of the country. You're a fine specimen of a Christian! member of the Y.M.C.A.! always lecturing everybody to get religion! You hypocrite! Religion! Is that religion, to seduce your landlord's colored servant & then abscond? Christian! Does Christianity teach you to do such dastardly deeds. Member of the Church! Is this the civilizing influence you were always prating about the church's wielding over its members? It speaks bad for that Church even after every possible allowance has been made." And he concluded by reiterating his threat: "I promise you that every person in Washington and out of it too as far as I can proclaim it, who ever heard of you shall know all about your villainy in six months if you dont comply instantly with my demand."[23] Marts survived this episode to marry and to be ordained a Congregationalist minister, but the best jokes of Douglas Jerrold and the most telling caricatures of Charles Dickens pale before Lester Ward's heartfelt indignation.

Among the sardonic witnesses to middle-class hypocrisy was Sigmund Freud. I have already quoted him as saying, in 1898, that "in matters of sexuality we are, all of us, the healthy as much as the sick, hypocrites nowadays." In 1915, thinking about the war then raging, he said it again: as civilized society imposes high moral standards and thus forces people to suppress their instinctual drives, it produces neuroses, character mal-formations, and an almost irresistible pressure for gratification from drives craving discharge. "Whoever is thus compelled to react con-stantly in accord with precepts that do not express the inclinations of his instinctual drives, lives, speaking psychologically, beyond his means and may objectively be called a hypocrite, whether he is clearly con-scious of this incongruity or not." Freud went on to suggest that "it is undeniable that our present culture favors the formation of this sort of

23. May 23, 1870. This is doubtless a draft: I found it in the Lester Frank Ward papers, BU-JHL, and the sum that Ward thought Marts should reasonably pay is left blank, as though Ward were still pondering it. William Gosser Marts was born in 1841, attended Knox College in Galesburg, Illinois, and Yale Divinity School, graduating from the Union Theological Seminary. He died in 1914. (Information from Lynn Metz, curator of the College Archives, Knox College, April 15, 1981.)

hypocrisy to an extraordinary degree." And he conjectured whether "a certain measure of cultural hypocrisy is not indispensable for the maintenance of civilization."[24]

These are promising speculations. And in fact the fundamental idea that all civilization, even the least repressive, exacts sacrifices from the instinctual drives, enforcing the scaling down, postponement, or surrender of certain gratifications, constitutes, we know, the core of Freud's theory of society. Since all cultures whatever, not just nineteenth-century middle-class culture, must impose painful compromises on the individual, all must be felt as a burden since all do some violence to basic human desires. A certain measure of "cultural hypocrisy" is thus, as Freud said, indispensable for the maintenance of civilization. Yet Freud's spacious vistas raise some difficult questions. If "hypocrisy" is a trait essential to all civilization, and if it can be, as Freud suggested, unconscious, the term loses its specificity and all its moral charge. The true hypocrite knows what he is doing, and does it to his own advantage. The unconscious hypocrite is simply man in civilization. And if "cultural hypocrisy" has a historical fate of its own, what the historian wants to understand is not its very existence but its degree, its precise forms, its conscious and unconscious components, and its defensive functions.

While Sigmund Freud supplied the theoretical groundwork for this imaginative perspective on cultural mendacity, he was too busy gathering persuasive instances of it to invent a new, more neutral term. Only two years after he had tersely stigmatized bourgeois sexual hypocrisy, he analyzed, for some months, that late-adolescent hysteric known to psychoanalytic literature as "Dora"; her story provided a most discreditable glimpse into sanctimonious middle-class morality. Herr K., an intimate friend of Dora and her family, had made two blatant sexual advances, the first when she was only fourteen, which she had reported at home only to be told by her father that she had imagined them. Her interpretation, cynical but accurate, was that her father had professed to disbelieve her story because he was at the time carrying on a passionate affair with Frau K.—in short, Dora's father was willing to sell her to Herr K. so that he might keep up his clandestine romance with K.'s wife.

All this, and much else like it, was true for the bourgeois century. When Freud decided to publish his case history of Dora in 1905, he prefaced it with some harsh words for a society that compelled him to make a special point, an unapologetic apology, about speaking freely

---

24. "Zeitgemässes über Krieg und Tod" (1915), *St.A.*, IX, 44; "Thoughts on War and Death," *S.E.*, XIV, 284. And see above, p. 109.

about bodily parts and sexual relations.[25] And a spirit as free as Mabel Loomis Todd confined her erotic delights with her husband, and her rapturous involvement with her lover, to her diary and her journal; though often a little perfunctory about it, she continued to observe the reigning proprieties. Such self-protectiveness was typical, but it did not stop Mabel Todd's age from being one in which it became fashionable, almost obligatory, to call others hypocrites, and to take pride, notably in prefaces, in one's own freedom from hypocrisy. "True modesty," Smith H. Platt, author of improving tracts, wrote in 1877, "springing from pure thoughts, asks for plain words, with definite, undisguised meanings." He warned his readers, whom he suspected of having been made overly sensitive by "the silence of the past," that if they wished to follow him through his frank exploration of human sexuality, they must "lay aside such false delicacy."[26] Such cautionary boasts became commonplace.

Sigmund Freud himself left some fascinating evidence that moments of reticence and evasiveness might illustrate not a policy but a conflict. In *The Interpretation of Dreams* he observes, quite in passing, "We extol childhood as happy, because it does not yet know sexual appetite"—this in the very book that sketches out the Oedipus complex, and from the very scientist who was elevating infantile sexuality into a central proposition in his psychological theory. The statement is a relic of his older, more conventional views, an echo of tenacious self-deceptions sabotaging unpalatable new insights, in the very scientist who was doing more than anyone else to subvert the proverbial Age of Victoria.[27] There is no conceivable duplicity in Freud's disclaimer, no playing up to delicate readers, no hypocrisy, only unconscious resistance.

Some of Freud's most alert contemporaries were by no means insensitive to the psychological ambiguities informing verbal contradictions and apparent insincerity. True hypocrisy, as the English economist and publicist J. A. Hobson put it, as though to elaborate a distinction that Freud was adumbrating in the same years, "implies judgment and calculation," and he was convinced that most manifestly hypocritical conduct springs from deeper sources. "Dishonesty, in the sense of professing to believe what one does not really believe, is very rare at all times."[28] And

25. "Bruchstück einer Hysterie-Analyse" (1905), *St.A.*, VI, 87–89; "Fragment of an Analysis of a Case of Hysteria," *S.E.*, VII, 7–9.

26. *Queenly Womanhood: A Private Treatise: for Females only, on the Sexual Instinct, as Related to Moral and Christian Life* (1877), 7–8.

27. *Die Traumdeutung* (1900), *St.A.*, II, 148; *The Interpretation of Dreams*, *S.E.*, IV, 130.

28. Hobson, *The Psychology of Jingoism* (1901), 70, 99.

it is the second, the unconscious dishonesty that is both far more common and far more interesting than the conscious version.

There is much in Hobson's disclaimer. Many in the bourgeois century doubtless engaged in clandestine sexual activity; many concealed their sexual malaise. Physicians, as Freud charged, would dole out mealy-mouthed pieties about sex and, as we know, frighten their patients with absurdities about the fatal consequences of masturbation or over-indulgence—pieties and absurdities they must have found, in their less anxious moments, scarcely credible. And parents, as we also know, often left their children in the dark about the physiology and psychology of sex. Henry James, himself a master of subtle indirection, charged novel-ists of his day with leaving "love-making" out of their fictions and giving "the constant world-renewal" only "the most guarded treatment" —itself a most guarded way of speaking about intercourse. There were, in these novelists' work, James thought, "many sources of interest neglected—whole categories of manners, whole corpuscular classes and provinces, museums of character and condition, unvisited." But James did not rest content with this complaint, and his diagnosis is more than merely clever. These reticent makers of fiction, he charged, "mistakenly" take it "for granted that safety lies in all the loose and thin material that keeps reappearing in forms at once ready-made and sadly the worse for wear."[29] That is precisely the point. Evasiveness, cant, prudishness, hypocrisy, were cultural defense mechanisms in a time of upheaval, a search for safety.

And that is why the historian, most of all the historian schooled in the ideas of Freud, must wonder how useful "hypocrisy" can be as a diag-nostic instrument for understanding any culture, including that of the nineteenth-century middle classes. Speaking of the secret passions that in his judgment disfigured the lives of most Christians in his age, Dr. Paul Paquin, physician and publicist, asked in 1891: "Can the majority of ap-parent pretenders be justly called hypocrites? Should man struggling in secrecy with the passions ignorantly created within himself, by himself, assisted by exterior environments, be classed among wicked pretenders to virtue?—By no means."[30] This was a little unctuous but by no means imperceptive. It enables the historian to take middle-class denials and contradictions out of the realm of indignant moralizing into that of

29. "The Future of the Novel" (1899), in Henry James, *The Future of the Novel, Essays on the Art of Fiction*, ed. Leon Edel (1956), 40.
30. *The Supreme Passion of Man; or the Origin, Causes, and Tendencies of the Passions of the Flesh* (1891), 53. Director of an insane asylum in North Carolina, Paquin wrote books on personality disorders.

detached observation. Certainly many educated and influential nineteenth-century bourgeois sincerely believed, on what seemed to them sound theological grounds, that sensuality was wicked, and, on the best psychological evidence available to them, that erotic stories or paintings served to seduce the innocent. Freudian ideas of sublimation, reaction formation, and other defenses were still in the future. Nor did every prudish and interfering bourgeois harbor pressing lascivious needs—at least not beyond the budget normal for all human adults.

I am not disposed to deny that moral imposture offered both material and psychological rewards. The ability of the imposter to evade responsibility for his actions, relieved him, at the same time, of the burden that confronting himself would have imposed. It was less punishing than a neurotic symptom, which emerges when an impermissible wish is driven underground and persists in pushing for gratification. But he could not enjoy these rewards in peace. It is characteristic of nineteenth-century middle-class culture that boarding schools, obsessed with the catalogue of sins to which adolescent boys seemed susceptible, stigmatized mendacity as the most abhorrent offense of them all. Charles Kingsley filled out a questionnaire without a doubt on this issue: "The Virtue you most admire? TRUTH. The Vice to which you are most lenient? ALL EXCEPT LYING."[31] Hypocrisy was, often enough, not merely the consequence but also the cause of discomfiting conflicts.

Not even those bourgeois who indulged self-serving cant and ostentatious charity, not even those who espoused doctrinaire purist views on sexuality while keeping a mistress or resorting to prostitutes, were necessarily untroubled frauds. They were, more often than not, at war with themselves. Hobson was right: an authentic hypocrite is a rare animal, more common perhaps in the bourgeois century than at other times, but rare enough even then.

That "divorce between practice and profession" which J. A. Froude so vigorously lamented was, to paraphrase La Rochefoucauld's definition of hypocrisy, the tribute that in the nineteenth century the ego paid to the superego. The bourgeois conscience had never been more exacting, more persecuting, than it was in the Victorian years. That notorious trembling before the specter of public opinion is among its most oppressive symptoms. The pressures of the Other were not purely imaginary; they were embodied in angry nuns punishing their charges for giggling about a mildly lewd joke, indignant readers canceling their subscriptions to

31. David Newsome, *Godliness and Good Learning: Four Studies on a Victorian Ideal* (1961), 47n.

protest too earthy a serialized novel, ambitious prosecutors dragging an
avant-garde poet into the courts. Yet the fear of public opinion was,
much like the feelings of the analysand toward his psychoanalyst, a
manifestation of transference; it ascribed to that abstraction powers it
did not have and invested it with emotions it did not deserve. "You may
talk of the tyranny of Nero and Tiberius," Walter Bagehot, witty and
relevant as usual, wrote shortly after mid-century, "but the real tyranny
is the tyranny of your next-door neighbor." Public opinion, he thought,
"exacts obedience," forcing grown men and women to "think other men's
thoughts, to speak other men's words, to follow other men's habits."
One may, of course, defy such pressures, and no formal banishment, no
cruel penalties will follow, but the offender will be called " 'eccentric' ";
and there will be "a gentle murmur of 'most unfortunate ideas,' 'singular
young man,' 'well-intentioned, I dare say; but unsafe, sir, quite unsafe.' "[32]
Such soft impeachments would not have deterred anyone from holding,
and expressing, any eccentric or unsafe idea had they not hit home somehow, alerting and confirming that ever-present bourgeois sense of guilt.
The nineteenth century, as I have insisted, was an age in which great
promises turned into great threats; in which changes, even changes for
the better, aroused anxiety as they implied that concealed and dangerous
desires might become reality. The dreaded voice of the Other, to be
appeased by outward conformity, was an inner voice projected outward.
But that voice seemed so real, and so threatening, because it had not
always been an internal one; it had first sounded in the child's ears in the
injunctions and scoldings of his omnipotent parents, older siblings,
nurses. It was the hectoring voice of the family, effectively internalized
and then given back to the world magnified and distorted, a voice brimming with irrational and unbounded menace. Against such noisy power,
a search for safety seemed perfectly rational and the place to find it,
precisely where insecurity had begun: at home.

2. Social Science as Cultural Symptom

The family had long presented itself as an institution so ancient, so
ubiquitous, so necessary, that those who thought about it at all thought
it virtually eternal, an unfading fabric without a history. That was to
change in Queen Victoria's day, with its speculations on evolution, its
fascination with cultural comparisons, and its nervous, or delighted,
exploration of the drastic social upheavals that seemed to make everything

32. "The Character of Sir Robert Peel," in Houghton, *Victorian Frame of Mind*,
397.

new, or at least insecure. Since time out of mind, the family had been the organizer of unruly passions, the preserver of cherished beliefs, the chosen instrument of socialization. It had enunciated rules and enforced taboos and directed erotic energies. The middle-class family in the nineteenth century did all these things. Yet in the course of that century, it became controversial. And with good reason: the Victorian bourgeois family presented some subtly distinctive features, setting it off from its ancestors.

The history of the family brings out all the historian's preoccupation with the banal though all-important dialectic of continuity and change. In catering and giving shape to basic human needs, the family is impressively persistent; moving with the deepest currents of human experience, it adapts slowly and reluctantly. Yet in the magnificently diversified palette of its expressive possibilities, in its shifting ways of handling intimacy and distance, discipline and affection, the family bobs on the agitated tides of fashion. It proves, once again, that the essential ingredients of human nature are both fairly simple and very tenacious, but also that there are many ways of doing one thing.

Nineteenth-century poets and painters idealized these ways, social scientists anatomized them, and ideologues put them on trial. A handful of emancipated, radical feminists preferred to do without the family; utopian socialists offered blueprints for its replacement; the Marxists diagnosed it as transient and, by their time, exploitative, hypocritical, and doomed. The most relentless critique of the modern family, however, came not from the left but from the right, from conservatives who discerned little but threats to its integrity and decline from its historic eminence. They chose to see it as both sanctuary and source of infection —as a hiding place from ugliness, materialism, and immorality, progressively contaminated by the decadence it was designed to hold at bay. It is far from accidental that the two founders of family sociology (or, more precisely, its best-known forerunners), Frédéric Le Play and Wilhelm Heinrich Riehl, were merchants of nostalgia and prophets of disaster.

Since Le Play and Riehl were rather different men, their agreement that the family was in dire danger was all the more portentous. Le Play was an engineer turned entrepreneur in sociological research and reform; Riehl a journalist turned academic cultural historian and propagandist. Le Play, an imaginative and consistent methodologist, organized congresses and founded schools and journals to disseminate his views; Riehl, an intuitive impressionist, spun out his social convictions and prejudices in sketches, novellas and in some fluent essays. Le Play did intensive field work, traveling across Europe and Asia, studied budgets, encouraged statistical sampling, and wrote monographs; Riehl occasionally wandered across Germany with his notebook, called for empirical investigations, and wrote treatises.

Yet these self-proclaimed physicians to society also had much in common. They were near contemporaries: Le Play was born in 1806, Riehl in 1823; the first died in 1882, the second in 1897. And the two, experiencing very similar upheavals, became principled and eloquent mourners for the past. In their sentimental rage they were intent on wiping out the French Revolution and a century of social change in separate ways but to the same purpose. The books that made their reputations, the first volume of Le Play's *Les Ouvriers européens* and Riehl's *Die Familie*, both came out in 1855. And neither really got over his picturesque origins: there is as much of the small Norman town of La Rivière-Saint-Sauveur in Le Play's monographs as there is of the small Rhenish town of Biebrich in Riehl's treatises. While their ambitions and their careers propelled them to live in great capitals—Paris and Munich—they somewhat ungraciously exploited them as inexhaustible documents for the social decay of which, they were convinced, the modern middle-class family was a spectacular victim and, sad to say, a conniving agent. Le Play, had he read it, would have heartily endorsed Riehl's terse and unpleasant dictum, "Paris is the continuously festering abscess of France."[33]

While their partisanship explains much of their popularity, both men secured their reputations by embedding their political views in the trappings, and sometimes (especially Le Play) in the actuality of social science. Drawing on conscientiously compiled case histories, Le Play discovered three types of family throughout history and across societies, coexisting and overlapping, but displaying a distinct evolution: the patriarchal family, the stem family, and the unstable family. The first, still common in eastern countries, was authoritarian, traditional, and extended. The second, the *famille souche*, both less ramified and less dictatorial than its patriarchal relative, was the appealing incarnation of responsible care in which three generations lived and two worked together. The third, the nuclear family, stripped down to the bare minimum of parents and children, had—much to its damage—escaped from time-tested extended networks. Isolated, willful, self-centered, it shattered as soon as the children grew up to found new spare unions of their own, indifferent to their siblings and their aged parents alike. And Le Play feared that this modern family, which he had so pointedly named

33. *Land und Leute* (1854), 75.

"unstable," had become paramount in Western civilization, especially among the bourgeoisie. Worse, it was not an anomaly or an accident; the form it had assumed and the values it was transmitting only too faithfully mirrored the social realities of its time: the ravages of large-scale industrialization and the disastrous fashion for individualistic doctrines.

Riehl was only marginally less gloomy. He drew some comfort from reassuring glimpses of tradition-minded German families in the northern regions. *Die Familie* is poised between fitful hope and pervasive discouragement. In 1881, revising the book for its ninth edition, he was pleased to note that the German family had admirably resisted changing along with its state and society; some of the "wishes" he had expressed in 1855 had become, a quarter of a century later, "a prophecy fulfilled." Yet he did not markedly adjust the balance of *Die Familie*: somber analysis continued to serve hectoring exhortation. Riehl wrote far less to communicate scientific findings than to inculcate social ideals and to influence public action: the general title of his work was, instructively, *A Natural History of the People as a Foundation for a German Social Policy.* It is at once an idyll and a lament, idealizing surviving traces of that most precious of jewels, "the German household," and regretting the distant days when families were still true organisms blessed by *Gemütlichkeit* and orderliness, solid morals and sincere piety.[34]

Like Le Play, Riehl recognized three types of families and found the middling size—the stem family, in Le Play's language—the source of social perfections. "In purely patriarchal conditions," Riehl writes, "the individual is virtually destroyed," but in modern times, "with us," the family "is practically dissolved by the unfettered individual." Riehl thought it ominous that modern families lived in impersonal dwellings: *"the organic household has a name; the symmetric one has a number."*[35] As so often in the revolutionary world in which Riehl was compelled to live, quantity had expelled quality, calculation had superseded feeling.

It did not surprise Riehl that the authority of the father, necessary for healthy family life, had been steadily eroding. In the old days the wife had freely accepted her husband's supremacy, symbolizing her surrender to him by giving up her name. And children had acknowledged the father's absolute right to total obedience. The religion that the head of the house professed had been the religion of all. And this had linked the

---

34. *Die Familie* (1855), xiii, 208, viii. This is volume three of his tetralogy, *Die Naturgeschichte des Volkes als Grundlage einer deutschen Sozial-Politik*, of which *Die Familie* is the keystone.

35. Ibid., 140, 194. It is worth noting that Riehl's *Haus* is an ambiguous term, referring both to a house and a household.

first essential of family life, authority, to the second, piety, which Riehl defines as "loving and reverential devotion."[36] In better days, children had been reared at home, by their parents. This domestic pedagogy had inculcated respect, fostered attachments, and guaranteed continuity. But modern middle-class families, seduced by invitations to irresistible self-indulgence, had nearly all yielded to the state this vital element of the household spirit.[37] And this struck Riehl as just another symptom of the perils to which the modern middle-class family had exposed itself.

Much of this analysis is fiction; all of it is tendentious. To give them credit, Le Play and Riehl captured a badly neglected past reality: defying all appearances, family life in early modern Europe had not necessarily been distant, cruel, or calculating. The formal manners prevailing among the educated and the highly placed, the appalling wastage of life among mothers and children, and the almost unlimited legal rights of husbands and fathers had not inhibited affection or prescribed impersonality. Like their nineteenth-century descendants, early modern families often found a place for fondness. Even the Puritans, jibes to the contrary, had been able to love one another, passionately and affectionately. "My sweet spouse," John Winthrop, the distinguished governor of Massachusetts Bay Colony, wrote to his new bride, "let us delight in the love of eache other as the chiefe of all earthly comforts."[38] And Winthrop was not eccentric in his enthusiastic, if piously qualified, commitment to his sweet spouse.

At the same time, preindustrial families had been neither so large, nor so idyllic, as conservative myth-makers portrayed them: the nuclear family, that supposedly modern invention, had been a prominent reality, though scarcely an ideal, among seventeenth- and eighteenth-century households. Moreover, nineteenth-century middle-class families lived at an

36. Ibid., 124–25. Riehl's term for "devotion" is *Hingebung*, which has a slight sensual flavor of "surrender" to it.

37. For Riehl, as for others, the United States was the land of the future, once again showing the way to perdition. "In North America, where family life has almost perished in the race and hunt for monetary gain, domestic education is almost unknown." American women, "generally too grand to conduct their own household," are all the more reluctant to educate, let alone discipline, their "unruly offspring." Riehl, who had been outside Germany just once, on a short holiday to Italy, unhesitatingly joined the ranks of nineteenth-century experts on the United States; American contempt for "the strict exercise of domestic authority as a 'feudal' survival," he thought, had produced the "street youth" of large American cities, "the rudest and most vicious in existence." Ibid., 137.

38. Edmund S. Morgan, *The Puritan Family: Religion and Domestic Relations in Seventeenth-Century New England* (1944; 2nd ed., 1966), 50.

emotional pitch and commanded an emotional range that their denigrators were only too quick to deny them. They cast their net of love and rivalry beyond the immediate household to capture flocks of cousins, aunts, and uncles.

There were gratified contemporaries who sensed all this: the pessimists did not engross informed public opinion on the family. Significantly, nineteenth-century bourgeois could never reach a consensus about the condition and the future of the family; that impressive spectrum of convictions and prejudices which makes nineteenth-century culture so rich and so hard to read prevailed at this point, too. What Le Play and Riehl deplored as decline and isolation, others greeted as improvement and concentrated strength. In the 1820s, Christophe de Villeneuve, a prefect in southern France, noted that prosperous families in Marseilles were thoroughly domesticated. "In former times," he thought, "there was a great distance between husband and wife, between father and children." In those days, "talk came less easily, human ties were less intimate, relationships more distant." But now, the father was glad to come home from business to relax among his loved ones. "Everyone crowds around him. He beams at the children's games; he prides himself on knowing them well and their accomplishments delight him." Villeneuve grew lyrical about this new dispensation: "Family evenings together are," for the father, "a time of the purest and most complete happiness." Four decades later, John Stuart Mill echoed this pleasing diagnosis in a famous passage. "The association of men and women in daily life," he wrote, "is much closer and more complete than it ever was before. Men's life is more domestic. Formerly, their pleasures and chosen occupations were among men, and in men's company," but now, "the progress of civilization, and the turn of opinion against the rough amusements and convivial excesses which formerly occupied most men in their hours of relaxation," combined with "(it must be said) the improved tone of modern feeling as to the reciprocity of duty which binds the husband towards the wife —have thrown the man very much more upon home and its inmates, for his personal and social pleasures." Arguing though he was against the subjection of women and therefore under pressure to exaggerate their plight, Mill, an honest debater, conceded that family life had grown less coarse and more intimate. Sometime earlier Macaulay had canonized this optimistic view in the famous third chapter of his history of England. In 1685, masters had beaten their servants, teachers their pupils, husbands their wives. Now, in the 1850s, all that had changed: "It is pleasing to reflect that the public mind in England has softened while it has ripened, and that we have, in the course of ages, become, not only a wiser, but also a kinder people."[39] Those stereotyped, glowing group portraits that painters, poets, and journalists ground out for the bourgeois trade and published in professionally cheerful periodicals were not pure invention. There really were such Biedermeier scenes, rather touching in their somewhat insecure mood of self-congratulation: well-fed, smiling parents and children, harmoniously gathered around the cozy hearth or in the embracing garden bower, an occasional grandparent benignly looking on, all fixed in companionable attitudes, cordially glancing at one another, busy with common occupations, not a trace of conflict or neurosis anywhere in sight.

These set pieces show just how far the campaign to civilize the family had come across the centuries. It was a campaign that had originated in the books on manners current throughout the Renaissance and culminating early in the eighteenth century in the secular homilies that Addison and Steele scattered through their influential periodicals, the *Spectator* and the *Tatler*. They and their Continental imitators, notably Prévost and Marivaux in France, testify to an unappeased appetite for this sort of moralizing instruction. The Germans explicitly called their versions of the *Spectator* "moral weeklies"—*moralische Wochenschriften*. And all these smoothly written and resolutely complacent periodicals extolled the domestic virtues: sweet reasonableness, decent language, gentlemanly conduct, cordiality to wives, and patience with children. The tone these moralists affected toward women was, and long remained, condescending; it would be among the tasks of nineteenth-century feminists to criticize and, if possible, to modify it. But whatever their hesitations and timidities, the *Spectator* and its progeny contributed to the civilizing work of repression. There had been kind and affectionate families before; now their domestic style was put on the cultural agenda to serve as a model for the rest.

The pedagogues joined in; Locke, Rousseau, and later Basedow and Pestalozzi labored to persuade their bourgeois readers that children are neither little grownups nor little savages, that reason is the last of human capacities to develop, that rote learning or harsh treatment will only produce pliant puppets rather than self-reliant adults. By the nineteenth century, though parents and educators could still speak calmly of breaking the will of children, though corporal punishment continued to be generally practiced and passionately defended, middle-class families

<hr/>

39. Villeneuve: Edward Shorter, *The Making of the Modern Family* (1975), 229–30; Mill: *Subjection of Women*, 175–76; Thomas Babington Macaulay: *The History of England from the Accession of James II* (1848), ch. 3.

increasingly resorted to verbal admonitions and relied on love rather than respect—which had normally meant fear—as the principal agent for securing domestic order. It was enough to drive a believer in stern paternal authority to despair.

The ominous predictions of Le Play and Riehl, then, belong not merely to the history of the family, but also to that massive literature, the legal, theological, medical, and moral advice to men and women about to establish, or hoping to preserve, a household, that flooded the bourgeois century. The conclusions, the argumentation, the very rhetoric of these published and unpublished counsels are notable for their simplicity, their exaltation, and their monotony. The case they made became standard fare for improving and entertaining fiction, for poetry and drama. It supplied texts for thoughtful sermons, many of which found their way into print. It provided inexhaustible materials for lawyers, physicians, and pedagogues with a yearning for authorship. It was taken for granted in uncounted conversations. And it varied little across Western civilization or across the decades, as though its advocates desperately hoped that the sheer weight of their incantations would hold back the tide of destructive modern notions of emancipation and equality. Family ideologues were not original, but they were not intending to be. They repeated themselves, and one another, because they had no fresh ideas of their own and because they counted on the obviousness of their message to ease their work of persuasion. They were internal missionaries taking their texts from a common catechism.

The French, who had gained universal notoriety for their immoral fiction, were also among the most indefatigable propagandists for the domestic pieties. In his set of lectures *La Famille*, published in 1856, the philosopher Paul Janet caught the tone impeccably, and the *Saturday Review* promptly and enthusiastically summarized Janet's message and adapted it to English purposes: "Mistrust the man who speaks jestingly of hearth and home. Not from a corrupt spring can pure waters flow." The lessons that Janet proffered could not be safely ignored. "If we would make fast the foundations of England, and further the reign of peace and happiness, truth and justice, religion and piety, we must do all that in us lies to cultivate a reverence for the household gods. Family, country, humanity, these three—but the greatest of these is Family. Such is the moral we would draw from the work before us."[40]

Janet, emphatically seconded by his uncritical English reviewer, left no doubt that the family he was defending was the patriarchal family.

40. "The Family," *Saturday Review*, I (April 19, 1856), 503.

In a follow-up notice intended to underscore the significance of Janet's book, the *Saturday Review* stressed the "power and authority" which "the head of the family," the father, must wield in obedience to its paramount hierarchical principle. Women have their rights; they are not merely undeveloped men. But the sexes represent "the active and the passive principle respectively." While the man's sphere is "out-of-doors," that of the woman is "at home, by the fireside."[41]

There were literally thousands of such pronouncements, in several languages, scattered across publications in every civilized country. The *Revue des Deux Mondes* said it in the early 1840s, the *Magasine Pittoresque* reiterated it half a century later; so did that eminently respectable English periodical, *The Girl's Own Paper*, launched in 1880 under the solemn auspices of the Religious Tract Society in London. German divines writing tracts of advice for married couples said it in their way, American ministers writing personal letters to their parishioners said it in theirs. Women novelists copied their male counterparts in restating this family ideology. John Ruskin said it and so did W. S. Gilbert: woman's true vocation is the home; she is the guardian angel who turns her little domestic kingdom into the kingdom of God on earth. The hearth is woman's country; the outside world is alien and dangerous terrain for her. To agitate for the emancipation of women from these sacred tasks was to offend against the laws of God and man.[42]

The cement that held all versions of this ideology together was what M. Carey Thomas so angrily called the "stuff and nonsenses" about the nature of the male and female, the self-serving masculine myth of specialization: the two sexes are very different from one another in physical stamina, intellectual equipment, emotional coloring, and moral sensibilities.[43] When each occupies its proper sphere, they work best; for one to invade the other is bound to bring disaster to both. Woman's assignment— managing the household, allocating domestic resources, superintending servants, and raising children—is difficult and dignified; and man has his own drudgery awaiting him in the grinding outside world of the

41. "The Family. Second Notice," ibid., II (May 10, 1856), 43.

42. For a few instances, see Anon., "Les Femmes moralistes," *Revue des Deux Mondes* (1843), IV, 52; Pierre Goy, "La Vocation des femmes," ibid., 355; Rev. C. I. H. Fletcher, *Woman's Equality with Man in Christ*, a sermon preached at St. Mary Magdalene's at Oxford, March 19, 1871 (1871), 1. And see the long monitory letter that the Reverend Anthony Schuyler in upstate New York sent on February 4, 1864, to Alice Loney, a young parishioner whom he had known all her life and who had just got married—a splendid document in male uneasiness. No. 386, Miscellaneous manuscripts, Y-MA.

43. See above, p. 210.

professions, of politics, industry, and trade. In any event, to speak of woman's slavery is to misunderstand the hidden dynamics governing the relations between the male and the female of the human species. Woman at home is free, for there she is fulfilling her destiny; woman in public is the unwitting servant of fashionable philosophy. Besides, woman is as powerful as man, probably more powerful: her influence, quietly exercised behind the scenes, was a trite theme in sly or earnest essays and the subject for innumerable uneasy jokes.

Nineteenth-century men asserted over and over that woman has been endowed by nature with hidden gifts that define her very femininity. Woman vibrates more sensitively than does man to the beautiful and the true; she is, the French woman writer Daniel Stern said, closer to nature than the male can ever be. Feminine intuition, Dr. Otto Funcke, pastor and author, was sure, is nothing less than uncanny; the "feminine instinct" is nearly always right. And when it is wrong, as it occasionally is, woman manages to persuade her husband of the opposite, with guile, favors, and tears. "Women," the Spanish physician Monlau y Roca said at mid-century, speaking for almost everyone, "women are never stronger than when they arm themselves with their weakness."[44]

These spokesmen for the notion of woman's secret power seem to have displaced their awe at the mystery of her sexuality, so neatly concealed in the inward parts of her body and so ominously disclosed during menstruation, onto her impact on the world. The fear of woman on top was, as I have already noted, a popular, platitudinous, yet often hidden theme in the age. "It is easy to tell me," John Ruskin's father wrote to Effie Ruskin's father, that "a man should control and dictate to his wife." He refused to believe "that either you or John could ever" make Effie Ruskin "lead any life but what she was herself disposed to lead." John Ruskin himself would in some famous passages justify his idyll of the obedient domesticated woman precisely on the ground that she already enjoyed as much power as she could safely use. That certainly is what some of Ruskin's faithful readers, like the American theology student Lester Bradner, took away from their master's work. "There is hardly a stronger influence between two persons," he wrote to Edith Murray, with whom he shared his reading and his thoughts, and who was to become his wife, "than that which a woman exercises over any man who

44. Stern: "De la femme," *Revue du Nouveau Monde*, I (1850), 321; Dr. Otto Funcke, *Vademecum für junge und alte Eheleute* (1908); Pedro Felipe Monlau y Roca: *Hygiène de la génération. Le Mariage dans ses devoirs, ses rapports et ses effets conjugaux, au point de vue légal, hygiénique, physiologique et moral*, freely rendered into French, revised and augmented by Dr. P. Garnier (1853; fourth ed., 1885), 140.

cares for her. What he thinks pleases her he will use every effort to do, and so is largely led by her will. If girls would only realize their responsibility in this way, and exercise their true nobility, we should have a different state of things."[45] This was the voice of the average bourgeois speaking.

Many men were ready to be more severe than Ruskin and to assert that woman had not enough but too much power. Was it not true that, as the Duke in Verdi's *Rigoletto* put it, "la donna e' mobile"? And William Ewart Gladstone, though more capable of talking sense to women than most, spoke for the kind of man eager to keep them in their place when he commented in his diary, early in 1840, on a discussion about Ireland and the Irish Church with Lady Braybrooke: "This is the prettiest sight possible: she is so ingenuous, sincere, earnest, acute, playful and incon-sistent: her propositions being founded upon single & reciprocally con-tradictory instincts, never compared & reviewed by the understanding. In short, most characteristically feminine."[46] He was a man who could learn from experience, and later softened his tune. But others, more tenacious and more anxious than Gladstone, stuck to their convictions.

The stifling aura emanating from this trite chorus of defensive mascu-linity was only occasionally relieved by intimations that the respective natures and roles of the two sexes might not be irrevocably fixed and that changing times might serve to change them, too. Some exceptional English clergyman might acknowledge that the woman's movement was a wholly understandable response on the part of middle-class women impatient to widen the circle of their activity; some exceptional well-bred girl might agonize over the question of how career and marriage could be combined. In 1878, the year before she married David Todd, Mabel Loomis fought the issue out in her journal. "I should like to know for what reason God gives women talent? It seems absurd for them to have it, because, in order to make anything of it, to amount to any definite total, they must remain unmarried, and that certainly is not right for all." If talented women remained single, studied, went to Europe, pursued careers in the arts, then only "commonplace women" would become mothers and that would mean the end of "smart, brilliant sons, for the mother makes the child." But if talented women married, they would be compelled to give up "any great work in any way, art, music or what not." She confessed that the question agitated her constantly. "Why, oh

45. Ruskin: April 21, 1852, Lutyens, *Millais and the Ruskins*, 6; Bradner: January 25, 1890, box 1, Lester Bradner Papers, Y-MA.
46. January 3, 1840, *The Gladstone Diaries*, ed. M. R. F. Foot and H. C. G. Matthew, 8 vols. so far (1968–   ), III, 1.

why," she asked, "is one woman given two opposing elements which pull her east & west at the same time? Why do they have talent & affectionate notions too!"[47] It was hard for Mabel Loomis, self-proclaimed radical that she was, even to conceive of a woman's life that would harmonize the full exercise of her talents with wholehearted service to her love.

The issue became ever more troublesome as the years went by, for the possibility of a woman's life outside the domestic sphere became ever more realistic. Even *The Girl's Own Paper* began to run articles on the working woman, praised the active female, refused to look with nostalgia upon bygone days when young ladies did nothing, and looked ahead to the time when the cause of higher education for women had triumphed. In ringing tones, the paper demanded equal pay for equal work and criticized the pervasive male fantasy of wives who were at once hardworking housekeepers and frivolous, pretty playmates.

Yet even such energetic claimants for a new order, though fairly audible by the 1890s, rarely repudiated the reigning family ideology. It took a consistent and courageous feminist to question its tenets. When in 1879, Ibsen's Nora Helmer had walked out of the doll's house that was her marriage, she had stunned not merely her incredulous husband, but a generation of playgoers. The so-called happy ending which kept Nora at home with husband and children, a peculiar compromise forced on *The Doll's House* in many productions, testifies to the tenacity of the ideology and, at the same time, to its fragility. Mabel Loomis, more enterprising than most, only wanted to test her talents, not to assert them at the expense of love. And *The Girl's Own Paper*, with all its youthful drive to open windows onto the world for its female readers, was still inclined to define woman's rights as woman's duty to purify her little domain, to be an angel of mercy in a harsh society. The periodical was even willing to give space to writers wondering out loud whether higher education for women was really so desirable. It was a new age, and these equivocal rebellions helped to dramatize and to advance it.[48] But the family ideology, badly battered and much revised, clung to its place.

Its defenders, though, were in some disarray. In one of his earliest efforts, *Pygmalion and Galatea* of 1871, W. S. Gilbert illustrates how tattered remnants of medieval chivalry could be brought forward to

47. January 6, 1879, Journal II, box 46, MLT, Y-MA.
48. For some representative articles and poems in *The Girl's Own Paper* illustrating these conflicts fought out in print, see M.P.S., "The Disadvantages of Higher Education," III, 112 (February 18, 1882); "Education for Women at Oxford," V, 240 (August 4, 1884); Nora C. Usher, "How to Secure a Situation," XIII, 657 (July 30, 1892); Helen Marion Burnside, "Women's Rights," XIV, 680 (January 7, 1893); "One of Them," "The Girls of Today," XXI, 1040 (December 2, 1899).

support a cause in trouble. "What *is* a man?" Galatea naively asks her maker, and Pygmalion readily responds.[49] A man, he says, is

> A being strongly framed,
> To wait on woman, and protect her from
> All ills that strength and courage can avert;
> To work and toil for her, that she may rest;
> To weep and mourn for her, that she may laugh;
> To fight and die for her, that she may live!

This is light-hearted and almost intentionally ludicrous. When, however, the Goncourt brothers praise as a "fine observation" by a woman of their acquaintance, "Woman must exude a slight perfume of slavery,"[50] man's anxious need to abase her lest she overwhelm him becomes a little more palpable.

Beyond doubt, what Riehl called "family conservatism" was under severe pressure. In a curious coda to *Die Familie*, he sought to deaden his pain at seeing his ideal fade by elaborating a wishful fantasy about a better twentieth century in which the bourgeois family would have regained its old splendid qualities. In this imagined scenario, the middle-class family occupies a whole house, giving room to grandparents, welcoming relatives for extended visits, celebrating reunions, systematically researching its past, embracing servants and apprentices within its compass, making music (Bach and Haydn, not Wagner) together, praying in unison, and marching to church on Sunday mornings, an affectionate troop.[51] He failed to notice that thousands of middle-class families, in Germany and elsewhere, realized his poignant daydream in nearly every respect.

He failed to notice because he was too anxious, busy with other gallant rescue workers stuffing the genie of feminism back into the bottle. Riehl was perfectly explicit about his worries and his remedies. Le Play was more nuanced than Riehl, but in the end he, too, was unequivocal. He sounded not wholly insensitive to the need of nineteenth-century woman to work, but thought it obvious that she worked best at home, for her destiny was that of wife and mother. While he acknowledged that it was impossible to restore the past unchanged, his longing for that past continued to control his program for social improvement. Individual liberty might be desirable, but only if yoked to "the greatest possible

49. *Pygmalion and Galatea, An Entirely Original Mythological Comedy*, in 3 Acts (1871), [Act I], 11–12.

50. February 20, 1858, Edmond and Jules de Goncourt, *Journal; mémoires de la vie littéraire 1851–1896*, ed. Robert Ricatte, 22 vols. (1956–58), II, 200.

51. *Die Familie*, 297–303.

amount of paternal authority." Once "all the feelings that keep the family going" have been forgotten, men will sink to a condition "lower than the brute beasts." This was precisely what was happening in France, where men were abandoning all sense of respect and obedience to "social superiors," a pernicious leveling that had its origins in the steady attenuation of paternal authority.[52]

Le Play did not hesitate to call for the exercise of this male authority over the wife as much as over the children. Feminists are utopians. "The domestic hearth is in several respects a complete world whose governance claims all the care of the mother of the family." Those women who have "deviated from the straight path, are not backward in outdoing the men in perversity, and in becoming the most active auxiliaries to the spirit of evil." It was saddening, Le Play found, to witness modern women attempting to "wipe out the demarcations hitherto maintained between vice and virtue."[53] Shrewdly enough, he attributed the rise of this new woman to the rapidity of changes in society and technology, but his insight only made his regret for the past more pronounced, his anxiety over the modern female harder to assuage.

Riehl voiced the same regrets, only more pointedly, more vulgarly than Le Play. I have quoted his call for an "emancipation from women," from modern masculine ladies, their little flighty heads stuffed with notions of literary fame and political influence and other devouring fancies. "The history of our political misery," he wrote, "runs parallel with our history of the bluestocking." And he expressed his contempt for women "with German names and French habits" who publicly exhibited the ways that "an emancipated woman eats, drinks, smokes, and gets into trouble with the police." It was "high time," he thought, "to clear the air."[54]

Thus the family policies that Riehl, Le Play, and their followers so earnestly urged were fueled by a fear they articulated mainly by means of savage or nervous jokes: that of the new woman. With her lust for publicity, her utter lack of shame, she paraded what in more decent times and within the patriarchal family had remained hidden, under tight control—woman's eternal power over man. This, as I have argued in some detail before, is a very old male obsession but one that the nineteenth century, fostering subjectivity and self-expression, liberally permitted to

52. M. F. Le Play, *Les Ouvriers européens. Etudes sur les travaux, la vie domestique et la condition morale des populations ouvrières de l'Europe* (1855), 286, 18, 287.

53. *La Réforme sociale en France, déduite de l'observation comparée des peuples européens*, 2 vols. (1864), I, 186–90.

54. *Die Familie*, 56–57.

rise to the surface. Women were afraid of men, and had every reason to be. The history of laws and customs is, after all, a history of male dominance, long absolute and often thoughtlessly, even savagely exercised. But within the intimate enclosure of the family, man's legal and traditional authority was vulnerable to psychological warfare, candid or concealed; it could be subverted by man's fond affection or by woman's awesome motherly qualities. On this view, the family was at once cause and cure of male sexual anxieties. What Riehl and his allies wanted, therefore, was one side of family life without the other: the cause turned into a cure. And in this desire they surely spoke for others: they were simply more articulate about their deep-seated fears than their readers. And this makes their social science into an informative cultural symptom.

The oedipal constellation these family sociologists thought desirable—though, of course, they would not have used such terminology—made the mother into the incarnation of purity and the father into the incarnation of power, the one forever out of the son's amorous reach and the other forever safe from that son's aggressive challenge. Their highly elaborated defenses were self-serving but authentic; their regressive longings for the stem family of their nostalgic imagination an effort to ward off emasculation in a perilous world. The loss of male privileges and male dominance loomed as a loss of male power. These nervous scientists of society and givers of advice were no more hypocritical than other mortals; that the threat they faced was essentially imaginary did not make it any less anxiety-provoking.

Much of the indictment against the modern family, particularly the sexual innuendo, was calculated slander. Marx and Engels, we know, could charge that "our bourgeois, not content with having the wives and daughters of their proletarians at their disposal, not to speak of common prostitutes, take the greatest pleasure in seducing each other's wives." Indeed, "bourgeois marriage is in reality a system of wives in common," a vast commerce of mutual seduction "hypocritically" concealing the community of women that had always existed and that the communists were proposing to establish by law.[55] And that indictment was gross, extravagant, not a little absurd. Yet the share of the family in the making of bourgeois sensuality was admittedly as equivocal as it was decisive.

The ambitious pedagogic work of the middle-class family has been a persistent theme in these pages. The Wards, the Gladstones, and their Continental counterparts on whose life histories I have touched were

55. Karl Marx and Friedrich Engels, *The Communist Manifesto* (1848; tr. Samuel Moore, 1888; intr. A. J. P. Taylor, 1967), 101. See above, p. 37.

teachers and students of sexuality in their domestic lives, through the unconscious as much as the conscious messages they sent and received. The Lymans transmitted the amorous atmosphere that was their signature to their little boys. The Todds educated their daughter to the conflicts that the spectacle of philandering and adultery must awaken in a growing, helpless onlooker. There is Joseph Lyman vividly picturing strip-tease dancers in New York for his five-year-old son, encouraging erotic fantasies made no less exciting by the heavy-handed moral lessons that accompanied the report. And Millicent Todd wedged between her buoyant young mother and her mother's elderly lover on their buggy rides into the countryside is a memorable vignette; Millicent was learning all the time, in pain and confusion. Some, like Annie Besant or George Sand, convinced themselves that they had acquired the facts of sexual life in adulthood, though they had certainly picked up the essentials much earlier, only to repress them. In just that way, Carey Thomas first formally studied the terrors of sexual passion when she was more than twenty, with a clandestine reading of the medical texts in her father's library, and those of unwanted pregnancy at about the same time, perusing her aunt's diary. But she had made far-reaching discoveries about sexuality and love as a little girl, as she jealously and impotently watched her mother provide her with siblings, adorable rivals for her parents' attention, year after year.

Domestic lessons for the senses were rarely outspoken instructions in how to pursue moving sexual targets or lie about sexual experiences. They were somewhat more informative, though by and large hopelessly unscientific, about how to avoid perilous sexual temptations. In general, parents bred their children to subtler attitudes, fostering ambition or dependence; they inculcated sensitivity to fine social gradations that would later narrow acceptable choices for love or turn such choices into occasions for internal and familial conflict. Studied paternal or maternal indifference or excessive solicitude often produced incurable erotic cripples; by no means all parental tuition, even that imposed with the best of intentions, smoothed the way to amorous happiness later.

While the adult would continue to feed on the erotic experiences of his childhood, he would find the family he established himself an instructor he could not ignore. Bachelors, whether inhibited like Amiel or worldly like the Goncourts, could obviously not call on it to round out their studies in sensuality. But those who married could apply in their conjugal life the erotic lessons they had learned in their youngest years. David and Mabel Todd taught one another the sensual possibilities inherent in food and warmth, absences and reunions. The Lymans devoted precious hours to pushing back the frontiers of their sexual appetites in teasing letters and stimulating nude baths in the sea. Catherine Gladstone, smiling and stoical amidst the pains of childbirth, gave her watching husband ample food for reflections on the mixed consequences of pleasurable sexual intercourse. George Sand perfected her celebrated erotic style in experiments with a succession of lovers.

Such experiences were variations on common cultural themes. Tolstoy's famous dictum needs amendment: happy families educate themselves in their own way, precisely like unhappy ones. For the family is something of an obstacle course for the emotions, modifying, impeding, distorting the transmission of social values through the special, often neurotic, temperaments of the parents. The war of nerves that physicians, divines, educators—and parents—conducted against habitual "self-abuse" is a telling instance of such diversity. Middle-class fathers and mothers, infected by the tremulous sense of alarm they had helped to generate, would attempt to save their children from the horrendous doom awaiting the "self-polluter" by staging earnest little talks, inflicting corporal punishment for repeated offenses, or strapping their youngsters into devices designed to keep them from getting at their genitals at night. But the precise degree of anxiety, choice of deterrent, and severity of chastisement were particular in each family. If the nineteenth-century family was a private school for love, it had, unlike more professional schools, no coherent program. Nor did it leave a wholly predictable legacy.

3. The Democratization of Comfort

The erotic impact of the family, then, varied with region, status, and religious affiliation, varied even from family to family. Parvenus might pay more minute attention to the eligibility of potential marriage partners than some patricians with long pedigrees. Commercial and industrial entrepreneurs continued to cement the foundations of their prosperity with rational marital alliances at a time when marrying for love was becoming fashionable among bourgeois everywhere. But in general, domestic sensual education took place in an atmosphere of uneasiness, of mingled apprehensiveness and exhilaration at the spectacle of novelty unfolding.

Possibly the most conspicuous new reality that middle-class families had to master was what I want to call the democratization of comfort. Consumer goods and conveniences, inventions enriching and complicating conduct at table, evening entertainments, or moments of intimacy, had been entering Western culture at an impressive pace since the Renaissance—napkins and stoves, cotton stuffs and parquet floors, warm clothing and separate bathrooms. Privacy, that remarkable discovery, became a realistic possibility in the eighteenth century only to sweep all before it, rapidly establishing itself as a necessity for the affluent and an aspiration for the poor.[56] Now, in the nineteenth century, these and other aids to comfort made their way into the hands of prosperous families far beyond the privileged enclaves of the rich; professional men and merchants and civil servants became habituated to commodious houses, wholesome foods, and a generous selection among pieces of furniture, clothing, and decorations. Many of them could afford to work fewer and less utterly wearying hours than before. Those bourgeois, sturdy exemplars of the strenuous Protestant ethic, who kept on driving themselves day and night, generated this compulsion largely from within. But others not so victimized could now claim old luxuries as necessities to which their place in society entitled them: some hours of leisure and relaxation, occasional travel, and above all the blessings of domestic comfort.

Most beneficiaries of comfort would have indignantly, and sincerely, denied that it offered subtle erotic inducements. Yet the sensuality of material artifacts and conditions asserted itself, often in unexpected places. Laura Lyman could tease her absent husband with inviting descriptions of how deliciously clean she was, and how desirable she smelled, after her weekly bath; Mabel Todd could recall the seductions of her cabin on an excursion steamer. Pictures, statuettes, souvenirs, were occasions for titillating or sentimental reminiscences about past amorous moments. Furniture and furnishings provided sensual cues and combined to cater for all the senses at once. They caressed the eye with polished wood and the intricate traceries of Turkish rugs; the ear with yearning melodies sounded on the piano or by companionable voices; the palate with melting candy and succulent grapes; the sense of smell with flowers and sachets and the aroma of food; the touch—always touch—with the surfaces of objects skillfully carved, woven, knitted. To sink into the embrace of a well-upholstered chair was to pamper one's musculature, to regress in the service of the body.

Writers on house and home were sometimes quite frank about the erotic implications of things: in a series of articles for *Scribner's Monthly* gathered into a book in 1878, the popular journalist Clarence Cook

56. Fernand Braudel, *Les Structures du quotidien: le possible et l'impossible* (1979), 269.

surveyed pieces of furniture for every room in the house and bestowed
particular praise on a sofa complete with movable cushions which had
a wooden seat "hollowed, and curved as skillfully as if it had once been
of soft material, and had been molded to its perfection by an owner of
persistently sedentary habits." Cook's description of this gently welcoming receptacle for the body is sensual in the extreme: "the flat arms were
a little broadened and rounded off at the ends, offering a pleasant and
soothing object for the hands to play with."[57] Comfortable surroundings
could become insinuating aphrodisiacs for the most respectable.

In tune with such mild seductions, the fiction of the day brims with a
kind of innocent suggestiveness. Elizabeth Gaskell, a novelist more outspoken than most but scarcely a pander to lust, endowed the heroine of
her novel *North and South* with a discriminating taste for reveling in
creature comforts: Margaret Hale had, Gaskell told her readers, a "keen
enjoyment of every sensuous pleasure," of objects she was too poor to
afford but sensitive enough to covet. And the step from sensuous to
sensual was, even in Victorian times, not very large. The very air that
Margaret Hale breathed aroused her: on a walk, significantly with her
beloved father, she was "ready to dance along with the excitement of the
cool, fresh night air." Modeling clothes for her rich cousin Edith, she
"caught a glimpse of herself in the mirror over the chimney-piece, and
smiled at her own appearance there—the familiar features in the unusual
garb of a princess. She touched the shawls gently as they hung around
her, and took a pleasure in their soft feel and their brilliant colours."
The very act of dawdling over taking off her clothes provided her with
sensual stimulation. "So Margaret rose up and began slowly to undress
herself, feeling the full luxury of acting leisurely." Gaskell does not
reserve this unconscious voluptuousness for Margaret Hale. Mr. Lennox,
one of her suitors, rises to an orgasmic climax in praising the act of
eating pears out of doors: "Nothing is so delicious as to set one's teeth
into the crisp, juicy fruit, warm and scented by the sun. The worst is,
the wasps are impudent enough to dispute it with one, even at the very
crisis and summit of enjoyment."[58] Such language, more appropriate to
the bedroom than the garden, was far from rare and anything but
scandalous in its time. Taken with countless other approving references
to sensual delight in daily objects, it refutes the popular perception of
comfortable bourgeois as anesthetic, as cold machines for profit-making.

57. Cook, *The House Beautiful: Essays on Beds and Tables, Stools and Candlesticks*
(1878), 59–60.
58. Gaskell, *North and South* (1855; ed. 1970), 49, 220, 39, 106–7, 59 [ch. 2, 21,
1, 8, 3].

The Horatian injunction to mingle the agreeable with the useful was in fact an undisputed article of nineteenth-century bourgeois faith. Objects should be pretty as well as utilitarian; an indispensable part of their function was to give pleasure. "A head-dress," the English authority on woman's clothing Eliza Haweis wrote in 1878, "must be—first, becoming —second, beautiful—and third, useful."[59] Decades before her, in his early critique of industrial culture, Thomas Carlyle had already noted that the sensual passion for show immediately followed and often rivaled the very securing of survival: "The first purpose of Clothes," he wrote in *Sartor Resartus*, "was not warmth or decency, but ornament." Once "the pains of Hunger and Revenge" were satisfied, man's "next care was not Comfort but Decoration."[60] Many of Carlyle's affluent contemporaries came to expect comfort and decoration to be not stark alternatives but inseparable companions.

In a word, material comforts bestowed more than material benefits; bourgeois things were vehicles for bourgeois feelings. Writing to Martha Bernays on August 18, 1882, Sigmund Freud demonstrated these intangible dividends in a charming fantasy he wove around prospective domesticity. The couple had been engaged for two months and knew that they had long to wait before their expectations could become realities. Meanwhile, Freud drew up a list of the things he thought would be essential to their "little world of happiness." Once they were married, they would need "two or three little rooms" for themselves and their guests, with a hearth always prepared to make meals, rooms holding "tables and chairs, beds, mirrors, and a clock" and rugs, to say nothing of "an easy chair for an hour of cozy reverie." There would be "linens with dainty ribbons in a chest and little dresses of the latest cut and hats with artificial flowers, pictures on the wall, glasses for daily water and festive wine, plates and bowls," and, usefully, "a little storage room, should sudden hunger or a guest surprise us, a big bunch of keys which must clank audibly." He found much else to look forward to: "the library and the little sewing table and the familiar lamp." While one domestic object would "bear witness to the serious work that keeps the household together," others, less solemn, would testify to "the love of art, to dear friends whom one likes to remember, to cities one has seen, to hours one likes to bring back to mind." Home would be a haven, a repository of memories, a source of pleasure. And all would be pervaded by affection. "Shall we hang our hearts on such small things?" Freud asked, and

59. Haweis, *The Art of Beauty* (1878), 128. I owe this passage to Valerie Steele.
60. *Sartor Resartus: The Opinions of Herr Teufelsdröckh* (1833; ed. 1908), 37. Book 1, ch. 5.

answered that one should, "and without misgivings."[61] No one would accuse Sigmund Freud of being an average or representative bourgeois. But his fond catalogue—the flowered hats, the ready meals, the cherished memories—was pure bourgeois conventionality. Comfort, in his mind and that of thousands of others, would be a setting for love.

Those erotic stimulants of the rich—choice perfumes, seductive music, exotic foods, enticing dress—remained the preserve of the few. But good bourgeois could count on more modest editions of the same agents of arousal and, above all, on that bracing compound of agreeable cleanliness, fair health, and free time so hospitable to erotic contemplation and activity. While illness and invalidism continued to haunt the middle classes in the nineteenth century and worked against sensual ease, bourgeois were in this respect better off than they had been in the past and than their poorer fellow humans.[62]

And the new affluence produced marked and sensually significant shifts in family occupations. Prosperous bourgeois families could afford to exempt the wife from outside occupations altogether. This shrinking in the productive and economic functions of the household was not altogether welcome. Although they had servants to superintend, many wives found housekeeping no less tiring and rather less interesting than sharing responsibilities in a store or small workshop. But as her public presence waned, the wife and mother saw her domestic authority increasing and her decorative charms for her husband subtly enhanced. To be sure, while affluence often invited companionship between husband and wife or parents and children, instruments of segregation like the boarding school or the men's club, the tutor or the governess, show that there were bourgeois who chose not to grasp these unprecedented opportunities for closeness. But many middle-class families established privileged moments for time together, and the erotic consequences of this new intimacy were rich in their implications. William Ewart and Catherine Gladstone, that ideal bourgeois couple, sang of an evening, took long walks, played chess, talked over everything including politics, catechized their children in religion and Latin, and loved one another.

The bourgeois redefinition of permissible aggression and legitimate authority within the family was assisted by the domestication of modern romantic love. This fascinating process aptly illustrates the uses to which

61. August 18, 1882, *Briefe, 1873–1939*, ed. Ernst L. Freud (1960), 29.

62. I shall devote a chapter—the last—of the second volume to this important theme of invidious comparisons; the nineteenth-century bourgeoisie defined itself erotically at least in part by observing the aristocracy, the working class, and the peasants of its time.

ideas can be put in direct contravention of their original purposes. The poems, novels, and philosophical manifestos of European romantics—English, French, German, Scandinavian—around the turn of the nineteenth century and after had been launched as assaults on bourgeois conduct rather than as material for its foundations. The middle classes, the romantics argued, were incapable of love; they were too mean-spirited and too conventional to lift their erotic desires and their marital choices to high levels of the tender passion. And the most subversive among the romantics—Friedrich Schlegel, Percy Bysshe Shelley, to say nothing of Lord Byron—wittily or furiously inveighed against that most sacrosanct of all bourgeois institutions, marriage, and acted out their propaganda in their scandalous, well-publicized private lives. The romantic doctrine of love was a doctrine for the young, a celebration of passionate spontaneity. And the bourgeois, the romantics snidely insinuated, was never young. But the bored and discontented youth who took up the romantic writers, learning their works by heart and at times feebly imitating their imaginative conduct, prominently included bourgeois. Romantic love did not spring out of nothing, from nowhere; it required the health, the leisure, the prized objects of which I have spoken. But this only meant that, as affluence reached wider and wider middle-class circles, passionate love, though often more timid in reality than in rhetoric, was no longer the privilege of a few choice spirits.[63]

Many bourgeois, to be sure, continued to discountenance infatuation as a distraction from the serious business of finding suitable marriage partners. And many wives used their professed inability to experience erotic passions as a form of birth control. But for more and more nineteenth-century bourgeois, inclination became indispensable for marital choices, and parents, though continuing to inject themselves into courtship, learned to practice resignation before the partners their children wanted. Love and profit went hand in hand, as ever: Alfred Tennyson, George Meredith, and others quoted that familiar bit of sage advice to a young man in search of a bride, not to marry for money but to go where the money is. But the majority of middle-class readers eagerly consuming the romantic literature of their day would have disclaimed, and perhaps even refused to practice, such cynical tactics. Nineteenth-century bourgeois invented love as little as they invented sex; the long, immensely rich history of love stories and love poetry attests to that.[64] But they gave affectionate love a consistent and persuasive ideology and

63. I shall explore romantic views of love in the opening chapter of the next volume.
64. See Alan Macfarlane, review of Lawrence Stone, *The Family, Sex and Marriage in England 1500–1800, History and Theory*, XVIII, 1 (1979), 113.

an expressive vocabulary that would have struck their great-grandparents, and even their grandparents, as rather daring and very worldly.

These romantic commitments made for a host of problems, all earnestly discussed. The debate was fought out over nothing less than the nature of human nature. There was no perfect match between secularism and the advocacy of companionship on the one hand, between piety and the defense of patriarchalism on the other. It is true that those who still took the doctrine of human depravity seriously and who read the Fall of Adam and Eve as the decisive event in human history felt obliged to call for order and discipline in the home, and to quote the Scriptures on woman's unchanging domestic, preferably silent, role. "The denial of original sin," Frédéric Le Play wrote in 1881, "is the error that most threatens the future of Europe."[65] But increasingly the religious could draw on liberal theological interpretations of Christian domestic duties and thus grope their way toward the idea of marital partnership—but not without more than a twinge of guilty uneasiness.

For the new comfort and the new intimacy were not safe from the demanding bourgeois conscience. Indulgence in the things of this world, whether perceived as erotic or not, smacked of immoral, downright impious neglect of Christ and of one's charitable obligations; concentration on domesticity, of an irresponsible evasion of what one owed to the public. Social critics like Disraeli sternly warned that the cult of Home was the enemy of community. "Home," he wrote in *Sybil*, "is a barbarous idea; the method of a rude age; home is isolation; therefore anti-social."[66] More alarming still, though less well understood and little remarked, the modern middle-class family was a fertile breeding ground for sexual rivalries. Intimate love, intimate hatred, are timeless; Freud did not name the Oedipus complex after an ancient mythical hero for nothing. But the nineteenth-century middle-class family, more intimate, more informal, more *concentrated* than ever, gave these universal human entanglements exceptional scope and complex configurations. Potent ambivalent feelings between married couples, and between parents and children, the tug between love and hate deeply felt but rarely acknowledged, became subject to more severe censorship than before, to the kind of repression that makes for neurosis. The ideology of unreserved love within the family was attractive but exhausting. Fathers' claims on daughters and mothers' claims on sons, assertions of authority or demands for devotion often masquerading as excessive affection, acquired new potency pre-

65. Le Play, *La Constitution essentielle de l'humanité* (1881), 172.
66. Disraeli, *Sybil, or the Two Nations* (1845; ed. 1926), 197. Book III, ch. 9.

cisely as the legal foundations of authority began to crumble. Increasingly, family battles took place, as it were, not in the courtroom, but in individual minds. The emotional victims whose stories populate physicians' records, court proceedings, and biographers' notebooks were all made within the family. I am not speaking of incest, this most extreme violation of intimacy; that remained the supreme taboo among the middle classes, and a severely pathological exception. I am speaking of subtler wounds.

But, while the closely monitored, highly charged interaction characteristic for most nuclear bourgeois families had its risks and brought its penalties, the nineteenth-century middle-class family was something better than a staging area for emotional conflicts and sexual catastrophes. The husband and father as tyrant, the wife and mother as vampire, were far rarer than dramatic fictions would suggest. The family formed little sensual worlds, laying the foundations for attachments on which later attachments could build, at best amassing resources for autonomous adult ventures in love.

4. The Private Experience

Whether they reveled in it or feared it, contemporary observers could agree that the nineteenth-century middle-class family was the supreme haven of privacy. Behind its sheltered walls one might retreat to shut out meddling magistrates, inquisitive neighbors, even intrusive men of the cloth. Especially in view of the unabashed scrutiny to which sexual conduct had been exposed just two centuries earlier, and was still exposed in frontier settlements here and there, the modern domestic setting offered unsurpassed protection from unwanted witnesses. Some, contemplating this great invention, grew thoughtful, even philosophical. "Behind every man's external life, which he leads in company," wrote Walter Bagehot in 1853, "there is another which he leads alone, and which he carries with him apart. We see but one aspect of our neighbour, as we see but one side of the moon." After all, "we all come down to dinner, but each has a room to himself."[67] Bagehot was musing about the capacity of the "great painters of men"—he was talking about Shakespeare—for solitude. But his homely metaphor was singularly apt. The nineteenth century was an age in which members of the middle classes aspired to rooms of their own.

67. Bagehot, "Shakespeare—The Man," in *Literary Studies*, 2 vols. (ed. 1911), I, 134.

Yet within the fortified precincts of family life, privacy was far from complete, as parents did some prying of their own. They would open their children's letters, oversee their reading, chaperon their visitors, inspect their underwear. If parents exacted truthfulness from their children, this all too often served as a screen for the rude assertion of adult power, as an arrogant, and at times prurient, invasion of young lives. Moreover, like comfort, privacy depended on physical settings and objects, and material conditions were often far from adequate for its realization. Privacy required a door one could close, an hour one could call one's own, a desk one could lock, and many bourgeois, young or old, did not have all, or any, of these advantages. And many who did were not allowed to enjoy them.

Not even diaries, those proverbial incarnations of privacy, were wholly safe from intrusions, whether welcomed or unauthorized. It was not in novels alone that parents or husbands took advantage of the diarist's absence to uncover secrets not meant for their eyes. And the sharing of diaries could be one-sided. In the spring of 1886, Mary I. Barrows, then in boarding school in Connecticut, recorded in her journal: "I was sometime in Etta's room this morning reading her diary & mine." But when Etta asked "to read mine," Barrows would not let her.[68] There were not a few diarists, of course, who wrote with an audience in mind—a husband, a grandchild, posterity. Cosima Wagner kept her copious diary entries as much for Richard Wagner as for herself. The Alcott girls wrote their journals for their family: "In looking over our journals," Louisa May Alcott noted, "Father says, 'Anna's is about other people, Louisa's about herself.'"[69] Mabel Todd had David Todd as her privileged audience—and Austin Dickinson. Yet, however imperfect as protective confessor, the nineteenth-century diary remains a historical artifact; it provides access to one of the defining characteristics of the modern bourgeois experience. Nearly all cultures, we know, draw some line, more or less distinct, between the personal and public spheres. But nineteenth-century middle-class culture was particularly emphatic about this, making the gulf between private and public as wide as it could manage. In such a culture the diary, or its expansive cousin, the journal, were bound to flourish, and it is only just that the nineteenth century should be the golden age for both.

The keeping of diaries and the writing of journals is, to be sure, an occupation with a long and distinguished history. Leonardo da Vinci

---

68. May 8, 1886, Private Record, 1885–1886. (Courtesy of Susanna Barrows.)
69. May 1850, Cheney, *Louisa May Alcott*, 60.

filled his celebrated diary with scientific speculations, architectural designs, financial records, sketches of human bodies, and a single illuminating memory of his childhood; the diaries of John Evelyn and Samuel
Pepys are prized treasures in the English literature of fact; unknown
scores of seventeenth- and eighteenth-century Puritans and Pietists noted
their daily doings or, more anxiously, their progress in piety. James
Boswell recorded his memorable conversations and his sexual exploits
with the evenhanded indiscriminateness of the born collector, preserving
both in meticulous detail and with enviable precision. But in an individualistic, introspective, and reticent century like the nineteenth, the
diary and the journal proved particularly congenial and became almost
obligatory companions to a class endowed with a modicum of leisure.
Teachers would assign diaries as a praiseworthy and healthy activity;
adolescents spread among their friends the taste for this written restricted
form of exhibitionism. And parents presented their children with blank
books, often handsomely bound and decorated, to encourage youngsters
in the habit of chronicling their days and their little adventures.

On March 19, 1874, Edward Tallmadge Root received just such a book
which, as the title page in his mother's hand discloses, was "a birthday
gift from Mama." The diarist's first entry sets the tone, not without
humor. "Today is my 9th birthday, I got this book to write in and a
candy bird A hoop to roll, a box of colored pencils, and some little books,
and a bad cold." On April 8, Mrs. Root gave the same present to Edward's
younger brother Willie, evidently a precocious little boy: "Today is my
birth day," he wrote, letter perfect and remiss only in his punctuation.
"I got this book and a new pair of shoes harmonica and a comb I am seven
year's old." Both brothers wrote mainly about kittens, but did not forget
trips, the weather, visits, and a few exceptional events: "Mr. Golden the
saloon keeper has surrenddered to the Ladies of the Temperance League,"
Edward Root, every inch the preacher's son, recorded on April 12, 1874,
and, on the following day: "The Ladies went down today and got Mr
Golden's pledge to neither sell or drink." He gave space to religion
once again three years later: "This is my Resolve," he wrote solemnly
in April 1877, when he was twelve. "I love Jesus and I mean to serve him
all my life. Edward T. Root." There were thousands of Willie and
Edward Roots across the Western world, scribbling in their books, mainly
in smudgy pencil, berating themselves for not keeping up their entries
more conscientiously, and vowing to do better. "Poor journal." Thus
Edward Root in January 1879. "It is a long time since I last wrote." It
was true enough: he had made the previous entry seven months before.
But he did not reform: in May of that year he ruefully noted, "Poor

journal it is long since I last wrote in you."[70] It was as though he were apologizing to a valued friend he had neglected.

Adults often criticized their own indolence in words much like these. But many diarists were assiduous, faithful to their silent friend. Generally speaking, women were more likely to keep up the habit. Though busy to exhaustion as wives and mothers, they would use their quiet moments to reflect in writing on the day just past. But men, too, kept journals and, more frequently, laconic diaries to fix their experiences, even their inner experiences, for their later perusal.

These personal records performed many services for many people. Some used them as medicine: Harriot K. Hunt, America's first woman physician and the most religious of autobiographers, recalled at least one patient to whom she prescribed a written exercise in inwardness. Cold, isolated, self-centered, depressed, this young patient had turned her back on her mother's moral preachments to lead a fashionable life. "Abandon all medicine," Harriot Hunt told her; "commence a diary; go back into the chambers of the past, catch up your mother's lessons." And the results were nothing short of miraculous. Self-revelations of this sort were much else besides: a benign superego, a preserver of memories, raw material for formal autobiography, an intimate arena for settling troublesome religious, ethical, and sexual conundrums, an aid in rehearsing identifications with idealized figures. Best of all, though sometimes written in obedience to formula or with a self-awareness victimized by self-consciousness, they were someone to talk to: Leonardo addressed himself in his diary in the second person, behaving, as Sigmund Freud put it, like someone accustomed to confessing daily to someone else. So did Henry James, urging himself on to hold converse with his alter ego: "causons, causons, mon bon." It was an exacting genre, to be pursued responsibly, sincerely. A diary, Frieda von Kronoff warned her youthful women readers in the *Töchteralbum* of 1902, should not be a gathering of trivia, a list of beaux and presents, or a storehouse of egotistical and dreamy adolescent fantasies, but rather "a friend who offers truth, who demands truth."[71] There were, in the nineteenth century as at other times,

70. March 19, 1874, Edward Tallmadge Root diary, Root Family Papers, Y-MA; April 8, 1874, Willie Scott Root diary, Root Family Papers; [April] 12, 13 [1877], January 2, May 10, 1879, Edward Root diary.

71. Hunt: *Glances and Glimpses; or Fifty Years Social, Including Twenty Years Professional Life* (1856), 401; Leonardo: Sigmund Freud, "Eine Kindheitserinnerung des Leonardo da Vinci" (1910), *St.A.*, X, 128n; "Leonardo da Vinci and a Memory of His Childhood," *S.E.*, XI, 102n; James: Edmund Wilson, "The Ambiguity of Henry James," *The Triple Thinkers* (1938; ed. 1952), 123; Kronoff: Siegfried Bernfeld, *Trieb und Tradition im Jugendalter* (1931), 129.

wishes and fears so stirring or so frightening that one could not acknowledge them even to oneself, and they reached consciousness only by the detour of dreams or slips of the tongue. There were other confidential matters that could be breathed to a single intimate alone—a favorite sister, a dependable school friend, and, later, a loving spouse. The diary and the journal could stand in for several of these confidants at once. They were discreet, patient, always receptive, and never carping.

There were moments when secret autobiographers did not quite trust their silent friend—or themselves—enough to admit their sexual misdeeds in their own language; diarists from Pepys to Gladstone would employ foreign phrases to record peccadillos they could scarcely bring themselves to utter, or think about. But, whatever residual reserve such recourse to another language might disclose, the diarist normally preferred his diary to the closest of his friends. Henri-Frédéric Amiel, whose enormous, subtle, self-explanatory, and self-tormenting *Journal intime* I have frequently pillaged in these pages, in 1864 called his diary "my conversation, my society, my companion, my confidant." It was "my consolation, my memory, the bearer of my burdens, my echo, the reservoir of my inner experiences, my psychological itinerary, my protection against the mildew of the mind, my excuse for living, almost the only useful thing I can leave behind." Two years after his death in 1881, a stringently abbreviated and thoughtfully expurgated edition of his consolation, echo, and itinerary was published, first in French and then in an English translation by the novelist Mrs. Humphry Ward; a popular success that would have astonished Amiel, who had written for himself, to create a listener to whom he could confess everything. In 1876, a few years before his death put an end to his luxuriating and informal autobiography, he clarified the place of his diary in his life once again: "My journal takes the place of the confidant, that is to say of friend and wife."[72] For Amiel at least, as we know, it did.

In the manner of diary-writers, Amiel often addressed his journal as though it were a partner in conversation. "I have deserted you for a long time, my poor journal," he noted in 1839. And again, in the following year, using almost exactly the same formulation as little Edward Root: "Poor journal! It has been a long time since I have kept you." And he was prompt to blame himself: "I am always the same, forgetful and thoughtless." Apologies of this sort were exceedingly common. "I

---

72. September 20, 1864, *The Private Journal of Henri Frédéric Amiel*, tr. Van Wyck Brooks and Charles Van Wyck Brooks, introd. Bernard Bouvier (1935), xlv; July 26, 1876, *Amiel's Journal: The Journal Intime of Henri Frédéric Amiel*, tr. Mrs. Humphry Ward (1887), 213.

have neglected my friend, the diary, for more than two months," Otto von Leixner, still a student, noted in June 1867. Yet he observed that in confessing to his friend how miserable he had been at a dance, he found extraordinary relief: "It is wonderful—now I feel at least a little easier after I have shared my feelings with my diary."[73] He could have shared them, it would seem, with no one else.

In this atmosphere of shared solitude, diaries became the targets of affection, sometimes of downright sensual infatuation. The famous Russian diarist Marie Bashkirtseff, talented, ambitious, willful, doomed by consumption to die young, lived in, and for, her journal. "My diary!" she exclaimed. "It is half of myself." As she noted a little self-consciously, aware that she would not live long, it was also her legacy to posterity: "The idea that my diary will not be interesting . . . torments me." No less anguished, the Swedish novelist Victoria Benedictsson would open her cherished "Big Book" to pour out her longings for freedom and love: "Dear old book," she called it. Spirits less tempestuous than these could still treat their diaries with real emotion, load them with the kind of affect one usually reserves for real persons: "So little book, goodbye," Mabel Todd concluded her European journal of 1885. "You have been a help & pleasure to me, & a sympathetic though silent friend." In much the same terms, Lady Knightley recalled in a late autobiographical sketch that on her fourteenth birthday, April 25, 1856, "I began to write the Journal which has been my faithful companion ever since."[74] This was more than conventional rhetoric; it discloses an active emotional investment in these sympathetic and silent friends to whom one could entrust pent-up feelings and unrealized wishes.

This innocent but meaningful anthropomorphism finds charming expression in the journals that the precocious Karen Horney started in 1899. "How I come to be writing a diary," she began, "is easy to explain." She was then thirteen. "It's because I am enthusiastic about everything new and now also have the will to carry this through so that in later years I can remember better the days of my youth." They were, as one might expect, days of rash puppy love and quick disappointments, both reported with a sense of trusting intimacy. "To you, my diary,"

73. Amiel: October 14, 1839, October 8, 1840, Henri Frédéric Amiel, *Journal intime*, ed. Bernard Gagnebin and Philippe M. Monnier, 4 vols. so far (1976–   ), I, 137, 154; Leixner: June 10, 1867, January 3, 1868, box 2, Leixner Nachlass, Stabi, Berlin.

74. Bashkirtseff: Dormer Creston [pseud.], *Fountains of Youth: The Life of Marie Bashkirtseff* (1937), 90, 168; Benedictsson: Lucien Maury, *L'Amour et la mort d'Ernst Ahlgren* (1945), 72 (above, pp. 112–17); Mabel Todd: September 27, 1885, Journal IV, box 46, MLT; Knightley: *The Journals of Lady Knightley of Fawsley, 1856–1884*, ed. Julia Cartwright (Mrs. Ady) (1915), 3.

she wrote, "I will confide that I have sent Herr Schulze," an adored teacher, then sick in bed, "6 bottles of wine." Yet only a month later she dismissed her companion with little sentimentality: "Farewell, my diary, there is no room left for you in my trunk." But her infidelity was, as Horney's later diaries show, strictly temporary. In 1901, when she was fifteen, she called the diary she was then keeping "pussy" or "kitten," as she might a school friend on whom she had a crush. And she was, like so many others, contrite when she neglected her kitten: "I had often taken pen in hand to pour out my heart to you, my dear diary, but I never found quiet and time enough."[75] Activity and diary-writing were normally adversaries.

Fortunately for the historian, activity was, in the nineteenth century, rarely engrossing enough to break the habit of diary-keeping entirely. That habit was, after all, symptomatic for bourgeois styles of thinking: it was orderly, though providing space for freedom and individuality, and self-critical, yet open to effusions of hope and self-esteem. Thus it exemplifies the great bourgeois compromise, sometimes pathetic yet often creditable, between the need for reserve and the capacity for emotion. And it exhibits the bourgeoisie's little-regarded gift not merely for experiencing but also for recording erotic excitement. The diary was the resource of the lonely; it was often abandoned upon marriage. It could take the place, as Amiel had said, of friend and wife. Yet great diarists treated their diaries and journals not as substitutes for sexual activity or as rivals to their lovers but as their loyal companions. William Ewart Gladstone kept his diary all through his life, making daily entries in the midst of busy domestic occupations and the most active career any English politician has known. Lester Ward's French journal, to which he confided his most intimate sexual activities, survived into marriage. Mabel Loomis Todd returned to her lyrical and informative journal often and made faithful entries in her diary, both before and during her marriage. Many journal-writers, indeed, found marriage an incentive to more eloquent self-revelations rather than an inducement to stop: the precise place of the diary in the middle-class experience of privacy naturally varied from individual to individual. But together, these records serve to define the boundaries, flexible as they were, between disclosure and reticence in the bourgeois century. Middle-class reserve has lent some support to the suspicion that the nineteenth-century bourgeoisie mounted a conspiracy of silence. But there was no conspiracy and, as

75. June 7, 16, July 7, 1899; April 3, 1901, *The Adolescent Diaries of Karen Horney* (1980), 3, 6, 8, 36.

the diaries prove, no silence. There *was* circumspection, especially about the things that mattered.

What mattered most were issues circling around Eros—sexuality, love, the body, health—and these were off-limits to all unauthorized persons. And good bourgeois, princes of prudence, were inclined to define unauthorized persons as almost everyone other than the loving couple or practically merged siblings. Letters in many languages, mercifully preserved, bear the earnest request that they be kept "Private & Confidential," or, sometimes, destroyed: "Don't read this aloud & burn it up."[76] Perceptions of true propriety lay along a wide spectrum, but the rule that some topics were too delicate, some feelings too sacrosanct for discussion, perhaps even within the family, was fairly strictly observed among the proper. "Dear Sophie," Mrs. Peabody wrote to her daughter, whom she missed greatly, shortly after Sophia Peabody had become Mrs. Nathaniel Hawthorne, "I could fill sheets with what my heart is full of, on several subjects; but I am more and more convinced that this world is not the place to pour out the soul without reserve." Certain personal matters were, almost literally, holy, endowed with all the ambiguous and shadowy power of the taboo. Responding to a love letter from his fiancée, Nathaniel Hawthorne told her that, upon receiving it, he had put it into his pocket, "for I always feel as if your letters were too sacred to be read in the midst of people—and (you will smile) I never read them without first washing my hands!" His acknowledgment that she might smile at his cleansing ritual unintentionally suggests how problematic sexuality had become in Hawthorne's time. It was problematic, and it was private: "How strange, that such a flower as our affection should have blossomed amid snow and wintry winds—accompaniments which no poet or novelist, that I know of, has ever introduced into a love-tale. Nothing like our story was ever written—or ever will be," Hawthorne told Sophia Peabody a little later, "for we shall not feel inclined to make the public our confidant; but if it could be told, methinks it would be such as the angels would take delight to hear."[77]

This was a characteristic stance for lovers to adopt in the nineteenth-century middle classes: they did not deny—on the contrary they cherished—potent emotions, but these were no outsider's affair. Emily Dickin-

76. See John James Ruskin to George Gray, February 16, 1854, Lutyens, *Millais and the Ruskins*, 134; and above, pp. 227–28.

77. [Ca. July 15, 1842], James R. Mellow, *Nathaniel Hawthorne in His Time* (1980), 203; July 15, 1839, January 3, 1840, Hawthorne Papers, Henry E. Huntington Library and Art Gallery, San Marino, Calif.

son, recluse and seer, condensed this social—perhaps, better: anti-social
—style with unmatched economy:

> Tell all the Truth but tell it slant,
> Success in Circuit lies.

The conflicts generated by middle-class definitions of propriety were
exacerbated by banal but often ferocious boundary disputes about the
standards appropriate to men and women. There was little question that
the female, the gentle sex, must carry reserve further than the male, but
how much further was not always clear. In the spring of 1870, the young
social scientist William Graham Sumner, then a promising clergyman,
began to woo Jeannie Elliott and promptly confessed his appetite for
her presence. "Give me at least a crumb of a letter before long," he
wrote her on May 5. "I am modest in my demands but I am very
hungry." Modest as he was, he insisted on his right to correspond, and be
in touch, with her. But it was at this point that frontier skirmishes became almost inevitable. "Your mother, at Guilford," Sumner wrote
Jeannie on May 12, "was quite conservative. She said you might receive
my attentions 'up to a certain point.' What point? I did not ask her to
define."[78] Yet he told his Jeannie that he would have protested against
any restrictions on seeing her.

    This hurdle taken, a far more formidable one, her propriety, barred
his way to consummation. Something of an amateur psychologist, Sumner
wanted Jeannie Elliott to develop into an independent personage in her
own right and open herself to passionate love at her own pace. For more
than a year, practically to the day of their wedding, he pressed her,
firmly, to dismantle the walls of her reserve. She told him in all candor
that it would not be easy. "I am not demonstrative, I never have been."
Yet she hoped to be "a sensible and true woman, even old fashioned
to some extent." He professed to understand. "I know all this new feeling
must disturb you very much," he wrote her in mid-May 1870. "You are
undemonstrative as we have agreed. I saw by your letter yesterday that
you had got so far as to feel that you ought to be and wanted to be
demonstrative." Then he sought to allay her anxieties about her anxiety.
"No woman ever loved a man without having to go through that fear"
—the fear of not loving passionately enough. Yet Sumner was torn,
urgent behind his veneer of self-control. Jeannie had told him that she

78. Box 36, William Graham Sumner Papers, Y-MA.

was dissatisfied with being unable to "give" him more than she did. "Is your heart waking up, Jeannie," he asked her, "and fighting agst. your reserved disposition, and those life-long habits of 'propriety' wh. I talked to you about?" In placing "propriety" between quotation marks he put her defensive habits into question, and he implored her to see that "the time has come for your reserve to break down at least with one"—with him. He attempted to coax her into erotic freedom by resorting to socially acceptable religious language as a cloak for his amorous desires. He could have been "exacting" with her, he told her a little ominously, but had chosen instead to be content with the relatively meager proofs of love she had so far given him. They were enough for him: "I treasure them all the world besides. Some of them are so holy that I can scarcely mention them even to you." Meanwhile she pleaded with him: "be patient with me." And he was, after his fashion. He had observed, and after a time professed to have deciphered, a certain puzzling gesture of hers: it "seemed to me to express just this very perplexity. You used it just after I had said something very tender and affectionate and I guessed that it meant just this doubt or fear."[79]

Sumner's hunger only persisted and grew. "I am afraid that I am insatiable," he wrote on May 23; while, once again, he reassured her that men are ahead of women in erotic impetuosity, he predicted—it was a wish translated into a hypnotic forecast—"you will be swept away at last. . . . You will abandon all your proud reserve." By May 26, obsessively returning to his theme, he was ready to denigrate the respectable defenses taught to gently raised nineteenth-century young women: "When the time comes when your heart prompts you, you will not hold back from any false pride, or false reserve, or false propriety." Much as he protested that he understood and sympathized—he had even, he told her, "pumped" his friends, who all agreed that "during their engagements they found the ladies troubled in just this way"—her coldness was obviously becoming a trial to him. "I want you so much all the time," he told Jeannie Elliott, and while he meant only to say that he missed seeing her, bolder, more pointed longings reverberate in his pathetic declaration. In his frustration, he resorted to the old stereotype about the mysterious female sex. "Woman's heart," he wrote, is an "enigma." And he asked helplessly, "Does it always thus vibrate between hope and fear—peace and anxiety?"[80] He had held her in his arms, but largely, it seems, to reassure and comfort her. The rest had to wait.

79. Jeannie Elliott to William Graham Sumner, May 5, 21, 1870, box 25, Sumner Papers; Sumner to Elliott, [May 15?], May 16, 17, 1870, box 36, Sumner Papers.
80. Sumner to Elliott, May 23, 26, June 10, 8, 1870, box 36, Sumner Papers.

And the rest came, though very imperfect in its enactments. Once married, Jeannie Sumner, perpetuating and intensifying her virginal unresponsiveness, developed debilitating nervous ailments, resorted to drugs, fled to health spas. Her husband remained as fond, as sensually aggressive, as she would let him be, but she deftly defended herself with her illnesses and her bouts of nervous exhaustion. Yet, for all such troubled unions, for all the conspicuous, at times tragic victims of erotic mismatching, the middle classes cultivated their passions.

They often did so maladroitly. Sentimentality disfigured a good deal of published poetry, moralizing tracts, and affectionate correspondence. So did the common defense against it, a kind of embarrassed reticence. Such extremes, though frequent and habitual, did not go unremarked or uncriticized. Not long before their marriage, Nathaniel Hawthorne described to Sophia Peabody what he called, significantly, the "strange reserve, in regard to matters of feelings," that prevailed in his family; his characterization leaves no doubt that he could imagine a reserve less strange, which is to say, less severe: "We are conscious of one another's feelings, always; but there seems to be a tacit law, that our deepest heart-concernments are not to be spoken of. I cannot gush out in their presence—I cannot take my heart in my hand, and show it to them. There is a feeling within me (though I know it is a foolish one) as if it would be as indecorous to do so, as to display to them the naked breast." This sort of reserve dominated many persons, in many conditions: "My father," Alexander Herzen recalled, "disliked every sort of *abandon*, every sort of frankness; all this he called familiarity, just he as called every feeling sentimentality."[81] Hawthorne and Herzen testify to the vitality of feelings in the bourgeois century, even if some could not help repressing them.

It was precisely in defense of these feelings that social commentators ridiculed the purists and the pedants who would put carnal knowledge, like carnal excitement, on short rations. In 1891 *Punch*, scarcely hospitable to advanced moral postures, showed a "Young Bride of Three Hours' Standing (just starting on her wedding Trip)," at a station book stall, pointing with her gloved hand to a book, and exclaiming to her husband: "Oh, Edwin Dear! Here's *Tom Jones*. Papa told me I wasn't to read it till I was married! The day has come . . . at last! Buy it for me, Edwin dear." There is a certain poignancy in a married woman asking her husband to buy her a book instead of buying it herself, but the critical

81. Hawthorne: February 27, 1842, Hawthorne Papers, Huntington Library; Herzen: *My Past and Thoughts: The Memoirs of Alexander Herzen* (tr. Constance Garnett, rev. Humphrey Higgens, abridged and ed. Dwight MacDonald, 1973), 68.

point of the cartoon is, of course, the absurdity of withholding a classic from a respectable young woman. Even William Ewart Gladstone, for decades a pillar of the English religious and political establishment, decided that the passion for privacy had gone too far. Reading the long biography of George Eliot that her husband J. W. Cross had just published, Gladstone complained that "it is not a Life at all. It is a Reticence, in three volumes."[82] When a Gladstone could lament the excesses of reticence, we may be sure that it had exceeded the bounds of rational self-defense.

While lapses into excessive delicacy were common and sometimes ludicrous, their meaning remains hard to read. Once again I turn to the Hawthornes for light. Nathaniel and Sophia Hawthorne's marriage was an ecstatic union of two kindred spirits, as gratifying physically as it was mentally. Sophia Peabody, a highly educated, painfully sensitive young woman, suffering grievously from an assortment of psychosomatic symptoms, found her condition improving upon her engagement; after the wedding some of these symptoms faded away. Once engaged to be married, she could evidently permit herself and her fiancé erotic liberties, apparently short only of intercourse itself. He could write her ardent letters and she could respond almost, if not quite, in kind. "Oh, my dearest," he wrote to her, decently draping his sexual arousal in a few adroit displacements, "I yearn for you, and my heart heaves when I think of you . . . heaves and swells (my heart does) as sometimes you have felt it beneath you, when your head, or your bosom, was resting on it. At such moments it is stirred up from its depths. Then our two ocean-hearts mingle their floods." Sophia Peabody did not object to such prose and replied in tones no calmer than his. She wrote him that she had had a nightmarish dream, in which he had addressed her, in a letter, as "My dear sister," a dream that made him anxious, but no more so than it made her. His erotic imagination was kindled by the frustrations that the bourgeois rules of the courting game inflicted on him, but he did not hesitate to tell her so: "Dove, come to my bosom—it yearns for you as it never did before. I shall fold my arms together, after I am in bed, and try to imagine that you are close to my heart. Naughty wife, what right have you to be anywhere else? How many sweet words I should breathe into your ear in the quiet night—how many holy kisses would I press upon your lips." They were holy, of course, but they were kisses; and Hawthorne translated his wishes into fancied reality by calling his fiancée his wife: "Sophia Hawthorne;" elsewhere, during their engagement, he

82. E. F. Benson, *As We Were* (1930), 111.

referred to one of their embraces as "conjugal." And he told her: "I have a most human and earthly appetite." He was speaking of supper, but he had more rousing food than this on his mind. After a while, he no longer took the trouble to disguise his impatience for consummation. "We have left expression—at least such expression as can be achieved with pen and ink—far behind us." For that matter, "even the spoken word has long been inadequate. Looks—pressures of the lips and hands—the touch of bosom to bosom—these are a better language; but bye-and-bye, our spirits will demand some more adequate expression even than these."[83] There could be no obscurity in his mind just what he meant, or in hers, for that matter.

Marriage, in fact, provided the more adequate expression of love that both had so long desired. They slept wrapped in one another—"I left my Sophie's arms at five o'clock this morning," he noted in his diary, in an entry that his vigilant widow allowed to stand, and Sophia Hawthorne did not lag behind her husband in erotic satisfaction.[84] She noted in her husband's diary, to which she often contributed in the early years, that it is the "inward thought alone" which makes the body "either material or angelical." And, quoting the sacred text, she elaborated: " 'Are ye not the temple of the living GOD?' says the apostle. Ah, yes—also I suppose some persons are the den of the archfiend, through such has this miraculous form come into disrepute. Before our marriage I knew nothing of its capacities, & the truly married alone can know what a wondrous instrument it is for the purposes of the heart." She was severe with those who had married for "convenience or whim"; certainly, "the profane never can taste the joys of Elysium—because it is a spiritual joy, so they cannot percieve it."[85] The miraculous form, the wondrous instrument for the purposes of the heart, the joys of Elysium, whose true possibilities marriage alone can reveal, was lawful and affectionate sexual intercourse.

And yet, when, shortly after Hawthorne's death in 1864, his publisher asked his widow to prepare his diaries for publication, she censored her husband's and her own prose with a ready pen blotting out words, and an equally ready pair of scissors cutting out whole passages. Nudity, even that of their children, was too vulgar to survive her alert eye; some of

---

83. May 26, April 30, September 23, October 3, 1839; January 20, 1842, Hawthorne Papers, Huntington Library.

84. August 24 [1842], *The American Notebooks, Centenary Edition of the Works of Nathaniel Hawthorne*, 16 vols. so far (1962–   ), VIII, 344.

85. Ca. April 11, 1843, M.A. 580, Hawthorne Papers, Pierpont Morgan Library, New York.

her late husband's more pungent expressions, like "whore" or "pimp," or his occasional indulgence in tobacco and liquor, did not pass her rigorous scrutiny. She was, of course, quite as severe, perhaps even more severe, with her own prose: she mutilated her little paean to sexual congress as though it had been a shameful aberration.[86] But her erotic enjoyment appears to have been persistent and relatively unalloyed; if her health remained uncertain, her headaches at least disappeared. And something, perhaps the memory of past felicities, stayed her scissors and allowed at least hints of her gratifications to survive.

And that, of course, is the point—the point of this vignette, of this volume, indeed of the pair of volumes I am devoting to nineteenth-century bourgeois sensuality and love. That treasured, almost miraculous encounter, happy marital sexual intercourse suffused with tenderness, was the business of the lovers alone. Its very mystery, often taken as a symptom of the shame with which prudish bourgeois approached the marriage bed, was something of a tribute to their high regard for loving, erotic pleasures. This much should now be plain: the bourgeois experience was far richer than its expression, rich as that was; and it included a substantial measure of sensuality for both sexes, and of candor—in sheltered surroundings. It would be a gross misreading of this experience to think that nineteenth-century bourgeois did not know, or did not practice, or did not enjoy, what they did not discuss.

The share of enduring affection in erotic enjoyment was obvious but repays emphasis. Good, sober nineteenth-century bourgeois did not treat the conjunction between what Freud called the two currents of love as an empty protestation or a remote ideal. "O sweet love for a worthy object," the German historian of Judaism, Heinrich Graetz, exclaimed in his revealing youthful journal, "how heavenly are your joys, which raise us above low passions."[87] The formulation is a little bombastic, but it was sincerely felt and far from untypical for his class and his time.

Bourgeois reserve, then, modesty, reticence, propriety, to say nothing of prudishness and hypocrisy, gave the middle classes time and space for organizing and reorganizing their responses to a world in flux. Together, these devices amounted to a panoply of defensive tactics that enclosed a privileged space for stirring if unsettling experiences. These devices, at once personal and cultural, kept sensuality alive but out of sight, the mermaid's tail (as Charlotte Brontë had said about Thackeray's writings) below water. And, as I have said, out of sight did not mean out of mind.

86. See Claude M. Simpson, "Historical Commentary," *American Notebooks*, 682–90; Mellow, *Hawthorne*, 584.

87. [1834–35], Graetz, *Tagebuch und Briefe*, ed. Reuven Michael (1977), 8.

Private life became the hidden lair in which men and women bound up their wounds, recouped their forces, and acted out their passions with manageable risks.

These reflections fit the bourgeois education of the senses into a larger framework, that of the individual's place in nineteenth-century middle-class culture. In 1893, quoting an unnamed English writer, Sigmund Freud proposed that the man who first threw an epithet at his enemy instead of a spear was the founder of civilization. By the age of Victoria, especially among the middling orders, the capacity for self-control and sublimation had been very highly developed. The principal themes of this book—the pangs of sex, the pressures of technology, the anxieties of physicians, the risks of pregnancy, the passion for privacy, not to forget man's fear of woman—have all touched on the ways in which nineteenth-century bourgeois organized their lives in a tumultuous time. The specter of the lower orders in revolt embodied in the French Revolution of 1789 and periodically revived in later upheavals across Europe was only the most spectacular, most widely discussed ground for middle-class anxiety. Bourgeois fears of discontented peasants and workers were wholly conscious, out in the open. Other anxieties were less visible, at least partly unconscious. But they were no less potent for that; in the midst of material progress and political successes, the middle classes were apprehensive over social status, moral imperatives, religious traditions, familial conflicts, and, summing them all up, cultural change. They induced the bourgeoisie to deploy some new defenses, or elaborate old ones, defenses that I will explore in the next volume. Bourgeois gave new urgency to the study of love and rehearsed in their fiction the dimensions of love both permissible and forbidden; they devised stratagems giving sensuality respectable credentials and discovered the threat of unorthodox sexual tastes. And they worried over nervousness, which they took to be the archetypal modern ailment, the malaise they deserved.

We may use the bourgeois century, then, as a most severe test of Freud's theories of culture. He argued, as we know, that institutions, whether of society or of the mind, at once control human passions and satisfy human needs. Man cannot live without these institutions, but he cannot live with them in complete, childlike serenity. That is why the constraints they impose are at once indispensable and unpopular. At their best, such constraints will act not to frustrate but to foster personal gratifications. But the best is, of course, very rare, even among well-placed bourgeois.

Precisely because its opportunities were without precedent, the flaws of bourgeois culture were most sensitively probed and most noisily resented. And not all its experiments fencing in sensuality were successful; Freud spoke for others in reading his culture as one in which inhibitions on sexual conduct had gone far beyond the rational. But such maladjustments should have surprised no one. The age, after all, called for largely untried responses to establish, or readjust, the relative shares of freedom and obligation and to regulate anew the relations between man's fundamental, often clashing drives. But there was good cause for optimism, often poignantly disappointed but often cheerfully realized, reason to hope that savagery might be tamed by civilizing Eros, "sensuous force," as George Eliot put it, "controlled by spiritual passion," lust mastered by love.

Appendix

A Note on the Sexual Symbols
in Mabel Loomis Todd's Diaries

Mabel Todd left some highly informative though by no means easily legible signs of her sexual activity. In her diary she recorded her menstrual periods (at first only their onset) with an "x"; later, more precisely, she used a dot enclosed in a circle (her "period") and followed by "st." for "stop." She marked instances of sexual intercourse—worth remembering for prudential as much as for passionate reasons, what with the couple's reliance on a combination of the rhythm method and coitus interruptus—with the symbol for number (#) followed by a numeral progressing through the year. At times, she would add to this numeral abbreviations either explained or self-explanatory ("f.m.," for example, signified "for me"), or rather harder to solve. I believe that "f.m." stood for an orgasm for her, as, most probably, did the letter "o." Thus, on April 28, 1881, she noted: "Happiest of nights with David—my own. #15 (o)," and on May 1: "8:30 A.M. What a life time of happiness I have had since about 5 A.M.," followed at the end of this day by "#16 (o)." (Diary 1881, box 39, MLT.) I take the rhythmic rise and fall of her successive entries as well as some individual ones as confirmation. I have already noted one night marked by two successive symbols (see above, p. 83); here is another, from September 22, 1882, just after David had joined his wife in Washington, D.C.: "I am so glad. . . . #40 f.m., 41 f.m." (Diary 1882, box 39, MLT.)

And yet, her symbolism is not without its conundrums. Thus, on June 30, 1882, David Todd wrote to his wife, asking her to "mark for me

461

against yesterday something of which you know in your little book";
and in her diary we accordingly find on June 29, obviously written in
later: "#25/a." (Diary 1882.) In addition—and this is why I interpreted
David Todd's anticipation of their "first night of love" with some caution,
and suggested that Mabel Loomis went into marriage "technically" a
virgin—there are some symbols (##) followed by numbers that she
entered during her husband's absence and another symbol, "Sem."
followed by a numeral, that appears several times, the first being before
their marriage on March 5, 1879. "Sem. 1" enters her diary on January
14, 1879, and is in her fiancé's hand. On March 7, two days after their
wedding, the entire entry in her diary, written in by him, reads, "A
lovely, quiet marriage afternoon. Sem. 8." May 15 of the same year, the
day on which their daughter was conceived, has "Sem. 28." Then, during
August 1879, while David Todd was on an expedition, Mabel Loomis
Todd used this symbol repeatedly, as, for instance, on August 4, a day
on which she wrote a letter to her husband: "Sem. 45 (A)," and again,
a week later, on August 11, "Sem. 46 (a)." (Diary 1879, box 39, MLT.)

My reading of this latter symbol is that the couple used "Sem." somewhat inconsistently. Before the wedding, I would suggest, it meant heavy
petting leading to orgasm; in March and after, it came to stand for
sexual intercourse; and still later, during their separations, it must have
recorded instances of masturbation, so that "a" or "A" meant something
like "alone." If this is correct, David Todd's letter of June 30, 1882,
would be a request to put down *his* masturbation. That request, as he
knew, and wrote, upset her, and his insisting on it implies an obsession
with his sexual performance that is doubtless deeply personal. But it is,
at the same time, an expression of a view held generally (if not universally) among medical men and "informed" laymen to the effect that male
orgasm, however reached, was an "expenditure" of valuable semen,
which if "excessive," would have serious physical and psychological
consequences.

Bibliographical Essay

This essay is partial in both senses of the term: it is fragmentary—I have consulted far more titles than appear in these pages—and it is polemical; it records my most enduring debts and my most decided dissents. I have written brief polemics, and, in addition, gathered some materials supporting my argument, materials that might have encumbered the footnotes.

General Introduction

Orientations

My principal intellectual obligation is obviously to Sigmund Freud. James Strachey and his fellow translators of Freud's writings did heroic but not flawless work; they are stiffer than that splendid stylist, Sigmund Freud, ever was, and they coined awkward, artificial, rebarbative terms like "cathexis" and "anaclitic." Hence I have made my own translations, but, since the English *Standard Edition* has become just that, I have cited it as well. The German *Studienausgabe*, ed. Alexander Mitscherlich, Angela Richards, and James Strachey, 11 vols. (1969–75), is incomplete and unfortunately arranged topically, but based on *The Standard Edition of the Complete Psychological Writings of Sigmund Freud*, ed. James Strachey et al., 24 vols. (1953–75). The individual writings of Freud and the instructive collections of his letters on which I have drawn will appear in their place. So will other psychoanalytic papers.

Freud's epoch-making letters to Fliess are collected in *Aus den Anfängen der Psychoanalyse: Briefe an Wilhelm Fliess, Abhandlungen und Notizen aus den Jahren 1887–1902*, ed. Ernst Kris et al. (1950); tr. Eric Mosbacher and James Strachey, *The Origins of Psycho-Analysis: Letters to Wilhelm Fliess, Drafts and Notes: 1887–1902* (1954). Both versions omit passages and whole letters; a faithful critical edition is in preparation. For accounts of these early days of psychoanalysis, see Peter Gay, "Sigmund Freud: A German and His Discontents," in *Freud, Jews and Other Germans: Masters and Victims in Modernist Culture* (1978), esp. 36–37, 72–75; Max Schur, *Freud: Living and Dying* (1972), chs. 3 and 4; Ernest Jones, *The Life and Work of Sigmund Freud*, vol. I, *The Formative Years and the Great Discoveries* (1953), chs. 13 and 14—partisan, unstylish, but beautifully informed and still the standard biography. Frank J. Sulloway, *Freud: Biologist of the Mind. Beyond the Psychoanalytic Legend* (1979), overargued, irritatingly self-indulgent, does suggest some revisions of the accepted view of the Freud-Fliess relationship, chs. 5 and 6. The psycho-analyst Bertram Lewin has suggested that Freud's use of Latin, in the letter in which he told Fliess that he recalled seeing his *matrem nudam*, "because it is Latin, testifies to Freud's forthrightness," since it is "doctors' and medical students' argot" suggesting "confidentiality and confraternity." This is in-genious but not convincing; the Latin may have raised a knowing smile in both the writer of this letter and its recipient, but the distancing function of this foreign tongue is, in my judgment, unmistakable and primary. Lewin, "The Train Ride: A Study of One of Freud's Figures of Speech" (1970), in *Selected Writings of Bertram D. Lewin*, ed. Jacob A. Arlow (1973), 377, 371–72.

Freud's most pertinent venture into sociology is the little-known paper "Das Interesse an der Psychoanalyse" (1913) [not in *St.A.*], *G.W.*, ed. Anna Freud et al., 18 vols. (1940–68), VIII, 389–420; "The Claims of Psycho-Analysis to Scientific Interest," *S.E.*, XIII, 165–90. His denial of any real difference be-tween individual and social psychology is in *Massenpsychologie und Ich-Analyse* (1921), *St.A.*, IX, 61–134, esp. 65; *Group Psychology and the Analysis of the Ego, S.E.*, XVIII, 67–143, esp. 69. See Heinz Hartmann, "Psychoanalysis and Sociology" (1944) and "The Application of Psychoanalytic Concepts to Social Science" (1950), both in *Essays on Ego Psychology: Selected Problems in Psychoanalytic Theory* (1964), 19–34, 90–98. W. G. Runciman, "Sociology in Its Place," in *Sociology in Its Place and Other Essays* (1970), 1–44, is a persuasive essay arguing that sociology is essentially parasitic on psychology.

This is not the place for a detailed exploration of psychohistory. I have defended the historian's employment of psychoanalysis rather dogmatically, even aggressively, in a pamphlet, *The Historian as Psychologist* (1983), and expect to elaborate my argument in a forthcoming book, tentatively entitled "Freud for Historians." Some pungent and irritated responses to psychohistory have been only too deserved. The syllabus of errors rehearsing its offenses— including the familiar charges of reductionism and crimes against good sense, scientific procedure, the rules of evidence, and the English language—is not wholly unfounded. Heady speculations on the basis of tenuous evidence or strained interpretations have not improved the psychohistorians' performance, or their reputation. At the same time, the sheer defensiveness that angry historians have displayed in attempting to stifle psychohistory is a tribute less to their acuity than to the dents that psychoanalytically oriented historians have made in their armor. The literature of responsible psychoanalytic history may be small, but it is growing.[1]

1. While it may seem invidious to single out a few titles, I want to list some of those that have, in my judgment, successfully integrated psychoanalytic with historical methods: E. R. Dodds, *The Greeks and the Irrational* (1951), a classic work by a classical scholar, significantly very well received by his colleagues upon its first

In his pioneering though severely flawed *Young Man Luther: A Study in Psychoanalysis and History* (1958), Erik H. Erikson laid down a generous and comprehensive program for reaching beyond the psychoanalytic case to the historical event, to see the great man as an encounter between mind and its time. But neither Erikson nor his followers have fully realized this promise. See Roger A. Johnson, ed., *Psychohistory and Religion: The Case of "Young Man Luther"* (1977), which includes Roland H. Bainton's devastating review. A rejection of reductionism has become an article of faith in psychohistorical ventures: "It is the relationship between Burke's life, personality, and social thought that will be studied here," writes Isaac Kramnick, in the preface to *The Rage of Edmund Burke: Portrait of an Ambivalent Conservative* (1977). And here is Bruce Mazlish introducing his book on the Mills: "John Stuart Mill is not a patient, and psychohistory, as we seek to practice it, does not wish to treat him as one." *James and John Stuart Mill: Father and Son in the Nineteenth Century* (1975), 8. Praiseworthy intentions, somewhat neglected in the execution. William L. Langer's remarkable paper commending psychoanalysis to the attention of historians was delivered as a presidential address to the American Historical Association on December 29, 1957, first published in the *American Historical Review*, LXIII (January 1958), 283–304, and conveniently reprinted in a collection of Langer's papers, *Explorations in Crisis: Papers on International History*, ed. Carl E. and Elizabeth Schorske (1969), 408–32.

Among the many attacks on psychohistory, Jacques Barzun, *Clio and the Doctors: Psycho-History, Quanto-History & History* (1974), and David E. Stannard, *Shrinking History: On Freud & the Failure of Psychohistory* (1980), are particularly unsparing. The latter is a remarkably clever bit of work, but vitiated by its prosecuting fury and its selective way with evidence and documentation. A symposium in *The Psychohistory Review*, IX, 2 (Winter 1980), 136–61, complete with a lengthy reply by Stannard, captures his rage but seems to me inconclusive. Psychohistory has its problems—so does psychoanalysis—but Stannard's is not the way to address, let alone resolve them. In defense, the best texts are Peter Loewenberg's economical survey "Psychohistory," in Michael Kammen, ed., *The Past Before Us: Contemporary Historical Writing in the United States* (1980), 408–32, and Saul Friedländer's modest, persuasive *History and Psychoanalysis* (1975; tr. Susan Suleiman, 1978). H. Stuart Hughes's engaging "History and Psychoanalysis: The Explanation of Motives," in *History as Art and as Science* (1964), 42–67, is eminently worth reading; Hughes suggests that some younger historians be psychoanalyzed or work in a psychoanalytic institute—a suggestion that has found practically no resonance in the historical profession. Intellectually, it is

appearance; Alexander L. George and Juliette L. George, *Woodrow Wilson and Colonel House: A Personality Study* (1956), a modest and convincing psychological interpretation that has survived all challenges from the Woodrow Wilson industry; John Demos, *A Little Commonwealth: Family Life in Plymouth Colony* (1970), brief, unpretentious, responsible, and Demos, *Entertaining Satan: Witchcraft and the Culture of Early New England* (1982), a fine synthetic as well as analytical enterprise; Maynard Solomon, *Beethoven* (1977), a splendid bit of psychoanalytic detective work that does not do violence to Beethoven's genius. There are, of course, others.

on a par with the reasonable demand that the historian inform himself of his terrain, as Samuel Eliot Morison, the great student of Columbus's voyages, reenacted Columbus's bold ventures. The principal objection to Hughes's idea is financial.

The historical study of nineteenth-century middle-class sexuality finds itself today in a curiously paradoxical situation. Our new freedom of speech, which licenses the liberal employment of four-letter words and candid descriptions of sexual activities, including the most picturesque perversions, in serious historical writings, has only served to perpetuate the clichés that rebellious Edwardians and their successors fastened on their "Victorian" parents. What most books now represent as the nineteenth-century reality is a prudish and hypocritical surface and the illicit, often perverse underground, the two forever split apart. Respectable women remain, in these candid exposés, sexually anesthetic; their husbands, bored and frustrated, must seek outlets outside the home. The very titles of some of these books are revealing: Ronald G. Walters, though his introduction (1–18) has some sensible comments, has edited a fairly conventional anthology entitled *Primers for Prudery: Sexual Advice to Victorian America* (1974); Ronald Pearsall, after publishing his bulky panorama *The Worm in the Bud: The World of Victorian Sexuality* (1969), brought out *Public Purity, Private Shame: Victorian Sexual Hypocrisy Exposed* (1976), which (justly) finds it "ill-advised for us to throw too many stones at the Victorians on account of their hypocrisy over sex, impertinent for us to look back in hindsight . . ." (7). But then it goes on, unperturbed, to analyze Victorian "hypocrisy" and the general "conspiracy of silence" (8–9), and to include chapters on "The Cult of Abstinence" and "A Grounding in Hypocrisy." Stephen Kern, *Anatomy and Destiny: A Cultural History of the Human Body* (1975), though filled with interesting detail, falls into the traditional posture when it argues that "those Victorians who dominated public morality came to regard their bodies as a threat to respectability, and their attitude toward them was a combination of denial, distortion, and fear" (1). True for some, not for others. Milton Rugoff, *Prudery and Passion* (1971), presents itself as a pioneering attempt to break through historians' timid silence about "Victorian sexuality," devoting its opening long section to "Prudery: The Denial of Eros," and the last, the third, to "Hidden Fires," designed to reveal "the evasions and more or less furtive escapes from prohibitions and taboos" (7–8). Duncan Crow, in *The Victorian Woman* (1972), stresses "civilizing by ignoring" (22–26) in an extensive "Anatomy of Prudery"; Crow finds it necessary to retell the old, tasteless joke: "Ideally women would produce children by parthenogenesis; failing that, male impregnation should take place in a dark bedroom into which the husband would creep to create his offspring in silence while the wife endured the connection in a coma" (25). In one of the few recent texts to break away from such stuff, *Silent Sisterhood: Middle Class Women in the Victorian Home* (1975), Patricia Branca rightly makes fun of this myth (7). Fraser Harrison, *The Dark Angel: Aspects of Victorian Sexuality* (1977), is, despite its portentous title, somewhat more balanced. See also Eric Trudgill, *Madonnas and Magdalens: The Origins and Development of Victorian Sexual Attitudes* (1976)—modern writers on nineteenth-century sexuality seem to go in for alliterative titles. Intelligent and filled with useful materials, it yet cannot resist sly chapters like "The British Goddess: Sleek Respectability." The information that these monographs convey is often dependable enough, but their emphases and that subtle thing, their tone, are usually grossly misleading: they invite pity for the nineteenth-century bourgeoisie, and not a little contempt. There are some fine independent judgments on female sexuality in Mary S. Hartman's delightful and informative *Victorian Murderesses* (1977). And, for all his hostility to and disdain for the bourgeoisie, E. J. Hobsbawm, *The Age of Capital* (1975), has some understanding pages on bourgeois love (232–37). The reputation of Peter T. Cominos, "Late-Victorian Sexual Respectability and the Social System," *International Review of Social History*, VIII, 1, 2 (1963), 18–48, 216–50, is, for all its merits as an early exploration, not deserved. It overstresses sexual gentility, and draws excessively sociological judgments, a bias scarcely corrected by Cominos's reliance on Erich Fromm. Walter E. Houghton, *The Victorian Frame of Mind, 1830–1870* (1957), is a minor classic; however his chapter on love (and on sex, 341–93), while it amply and informatively documents the darker side of Victorian prudery and reticence, fails to illuminate the (equally important) cheerful aspects of middle-class sensuality. He draws too much on Dr. William Acton (365–68)—see below, p. 468. The contrast between conventional and psychoanalytic scholarship is instructively illustrated in the two contrasting short papers by the historian H. L. Beales and the psychoanalyst Edward Glover, both entitled "Victorian Ideas of Sex," in *Ideas and Beliefs of the Victorians: An Historic Revaluation of the Victorian Age* (1966), 351–58, 358–64. Jeffrey Weeks, *Sex, Politics and Society: The Regulation of Sexuality since 1800* (1981), is only about Britain; a useful overview of the recent literature, it is richly annotated.

There are numerous general histories of sexuality which naturally include sizable chapters on the nineteenth century. These are of varying value, more impressive for their reach than for their grasp. Vern L. Bullough, *Sexual Variance in Society and History* (1976), notably chs. 18 to 20, is useful; Wayland Young, *Eros Denied: Sex in Western Society* (1964), is a vehement but rather informative diatribe against repression; Alex Comfort, *Sex in Society* (1963), is, as one might expect, a briskly written defense of sexuality, with some helpful historical asides. Jean H. Hagstrum's scholarly and enjoyable *Sex and Sensibility: Ideal and Erotic Love from Milton to Mozart* (1980) ranges beyond its announced subject; so does Edward LeComte, *Milton and Sex* (1978). I have also profited from the writings of Jean-Louis Flandrin, notably *Le Sexe et l'occident: évolution des attitudes et des comportements* (1981). As an exemplar of the naive use of historical scholarship in literary history, Russell M. Goldfarb, *Sexual Repression and Victorian Literature* (1970), full of Dr. Acton and Steven Marcus (see below, p. 468), is perhaps unsurpassed. Responsible professional historians have not proved immune to the hardy commonplaces that have so long obstructed our view: speculating on Queen Victoria's intimate life, Pauline Maier has suggested that she must have been troubled by "the prospect of sexual contact, a distasteful obligation for generations of women taught that only abnormal women experienced desire." *New York Times Book Review*, May 16, 1982, 10. This sort of thing dies hard.

The most influential offender in these respects is Steven Marcus, whose widely quoted *The Other Victorians: A Study of Sexuality and Pornography in Mid-Nineteenth Century England* (1966) has immortalized smug twentieth-century condescension about respectable nineteenth-century women's sexual anesthesia. Marcus depends heavily on two sources: the anonymous *My Secret Life*, a vast, obsessively repetitive, in its way gripping account of one man's sexual exploits, and Dr. William Acton's *Functions and Disorders of the Reproductive Organs* (1857, and several times revised). If *My Secret Life* is accurate autobiography, as Marcus seems to assume, it is wholly unrepresentative: the man then would have been a deeply neurotic and incredibly potent sexual athlete. And if it is, as I tend to think, largely a collection of sexual fantasies constructed on a modicum of erotic experiences, *My Secret Life* is a clue less to the sexual life of Victorian England than to the sexual imagination of one Victorian Englishman. As for Acton's view that woman's sexual appetites are normally very limited if active at all, stated both in *Functions and Disorders* and in *Prostitution . . .* (1857), Marcus thinks that this "may be said to represent the official view of sexuality held by Victorian society" (xiii). But this is precisely what it is not. While Acton, a pleasing writer, enjoyed widespread popularity, responsible physicians in his day expressed grave reservations about his opinions, and indeed his competence. Yet the views that Acton championed retain their sway: "In those days," writes Mary Lutyens, normally well informed, referring to the 1850s, "sexually satisfied wives must surely have been very much in the minority however lusty their husbands; it was believed that the bearing of children satisfied all a woman's physical and emotional needs. A woman feels what she is expected to feel by the society in which she lives." *The Ruskins and the Grays* (1972), 216–17. And some historians *still* treat Acton as an authority: "William Acton, the physician," writes Bruce Mazlish, "expressed the typical Victorian conviction [about female sexual anesthesia] in his book, *The Functions and Disorders of the Reproductive Organs*." And Mazlish cites Marcus. *James and John Stuart Mill*, 454. This position has not gone wholly unchallenged. See F. Barry Smith's splendid, economical revisionist essay "Sexuality in Britain, 1800–1900. Some Suggested Revisions," in Martha Vicinus, ed., *The Widening Sphere: Changing Roles of Victorian Women* (1977), 182–98; on Marcus, 184–87. See also the important article by Carl N. Degler, "What Ought to Be and What Was: Women's Sexuality in the Nineteenth Century," *American Historical Review*, LXXIX, 5 (December 1974), 1467–90, to which I am much indebted, and Patricia Branca, *Silent Sisterhood*. I have criticized Marcus in "Victorian Sexuality: Old Texts and New Insights," *American Scholar*, XLIX, 3 (Summer 1980), 372–78. With the work of scholars like Smith, Branca, Degler, and Hartman, I can hardly claim to be wholly alone. I need to note one other, rather odd, "ally": Michel Foucault. In *The History of Sexuality*, vol. I, *An Introduction* (1976; tr. Robert Hurley, 1978), pursuing his usual themes of "discourse" and the "technology of power," Foucault raises questions about what he calls "the repressive hypothesis." He has, of course, a point: my present volume, and its successor, are one long argument against that hypothesis. But his procedure is anecdotal and almost wholly unencumbered by facts; using his accustomed technique (reminiscent of the principle underlying Oscar Wilde's humor) of turning accepted ideas upside down, he turns out to be right in part for his private reasons. (For a far more appreciative view, see Hayden White, "The Archaeology of Sex," *Times Literary Supplement*, May 6, 1977, 565.)

For the "construction of experience," see Clifford Geertz, "The Impact of the Concept of Culture on the Concept of Man" (1966) and "Ideology as a Cultural System" (1964), both in *The Interpretation of Cultures: Selected Essays* (1973), 33–54, 193–233. The psychologist James J. Gibson has beautifully demonstrated the efficiency of sensual perception in *The Senses Considered as Perceptual Systems* (1966). Among psychoanalysts the ego psychologists (who, their somewhat misleading name to the contrary, remained wholly "orthodox" Freudians) have been most valuable to me. I note in particular Heinz Hartmann, *Ego Psychology and the Problem of Adaptation* (1937; tr. David Rapaport, 1958) and "On Rational and Irrational Action" (1947), "Comments on the Psychoanalytic Theory of Instinctual Drives" (1948), "Comments on the Psychoanalytic Theory of the Ego" (1950), and "Notes on the Reality Principle" (1956), all in *Essays on Ego Psychology*, 37–68, 69–89, 113–41, 241–67. Equally important (though more diffuse) are the *Selected Papers of Ernst Kris* (1975), particularly "The Recovery of Childhood Memories in Psychoanalysis" (1956), 301–40. I am deeply indebted to some seminal papers by Hans W. Loewald, which have sharpened (and revised) some of Hartmann's propositions with their analysis of the drives, still fairly undifferentiated at birth and requiring experience to form and develop them. Human maturation, as Loewald shows, is at once a taking in and a spitting out: the infant gradually separates himself from the world, moves from enjoying delusive infantile omnipotence to drawing boundaries between himself and others— thus, in a sense, growing "smaller" as he grows larger. At the same time, the child incorporates the lessons that important figures in his life wittingly and unwittingly convey. See "Ego and Reality" (1951), "On Motivation and Instinct Theory" (1971), and "Instinct Theory, Object Relations, and Psychic Structure Formation" (1978), all in *Papers on Psychoanalysis* (1980), 3–20, 102–37, 207–18. These formulations have their roots (as their authors cheerfully acknowledge) in Freud's late writings, notably *The Ego and the Id* (1923) and *Civilization and Its Discontents* (1930). (See Hartmann, "The Development of the Ego Concept in Freud's Work" [1956], in *Essays on Ego Psychology*, 268–96.) Roy Schafer's lucid and meaty *Aspects of Internalization* (1968) has been important to me. So have two technical studies by Edith Jacobson, *The Self and the Object World* (1964) and *Psychotic Conflict and Reality* (1967).

ONE: The Strain of Definition

Since I am exploring the various incarnations of the bourgeoisie and its reputation in the course of this volume and succeeding ones, I list here only titles that can serve as an introduction to the literature. For all its vast abundance (monographs, biographies, essays) there is as yet no satisfactory general treatment of the nineteenth-century bourgeoisie. "Nothing is more difficult to define than bourgeois, and it must be accepted at the outset that the notion is necessarily a vague one." Theodore Zeldin, *France 1848–1945*, vol. I, *Ambition, Love and Politics* (1973), 12. I agree. "The French bourgeoisie," Richard Cobb has written, thinking of the days of Daumier, "was indeed quite exceptionally selfish, hypocritical, self-satisfied, and, when frightened, unbelievably cruel." "Flaying the Fat," *Times Literary Supplement*, August 14, 1981, 932. This is a representative perception, not confined to the French bourgeoisie, often reiterated and rarely challenged. Yet Cobb's own way with "the bourgeoisie" is an instructive instance of just how hard it is, even for historians program-matically uneasy with generalizations, to do without them. Reviewing Michael B. Miller's *The Bon Marché: Bourgeois Culture and the Department Store, 1869–1920* (1981), Cobb complains that "throughout the book, the author refers to the 'bourgeoisie' as if it were a physical being, endowed with an overriding sense of purpose and a great deal of guile. Professor Miller's 'bourgeoisie' is a busy sort of bee, always up to something or other." *New York Review of Books*, July 16, 1981, 35. I am tempted to mutter something about the mote and the beam.

Among general treatments, Werner Sombart's old *Der Bourgeois: Zur Geistesgeschichte des modernen Wirtschaftsmenschen* (1913; tr. M. Epstein as *The Quintessence of Capitalism*, 1915), with his typical slapdash *obiter dicta*, is interesting only as a curiosity. Charles Morazé's popular *The Triumph of the Middle Classes* (1957; tr. 1966) is a brave but hardly profound survey. J.-F. Bergier, "The Industrial Bourgeoisie and the Rise of the Working Class, 1700–1914" (tr. Roger Greaves), in Carlo M. Cipolla, ed., *The Fontana Economic History of Europe*, vol. III, *The Industrial Revolution* (1973), 397–451, is by necessity summary and devotes only twenty-two pages to the bourgeoisie; Bergier's citing of Sombart's *Der Bourgeois* as a "classic study" (449) only further lowers one's confidence in his argument.

For the name "bourgeois century," see Hansjoachim Henning, cited below, p. 473. While John Seed, "Unitarianism, Political Economy and Antinomies of Liberal Culture in Manchester, 1830–1850," *Social History*, VII, 1 (January 1982), 1–25, concentrates on a particular town and time, his comments on the bourgeoisie in general are stimulating. Paul E. Corcoran, "The Bourgeois and Other Villains," *Journal of the History of Ideas*, XXXVIII, 3 (July–September 1977), 477–85, deals very economically but effectively with some of the terminological problems and the negative appraisals of the middle classes. See also G.D.H. Cole, "The Conception of the Middle Classes," *British Journal of Sociology*, I (1950), 275–90, an attempt to discriminate between middle classes and bourgeoisie, just as Needham does in my text (above, p. 18). There is a balanced comment on the general confusion in William Weber, "The Muddle of the Middle Classes," *Nineteenth-Century Music*, III (1979), 175–85. The kind of vagueness infecting these terms can be documented over and over. Here is one instance: a Danish art historian, J. B. Hartmann, in a book on Copenhagen describes the king of Denmark, Frederick VI (1808–39), as "an absolute though bourgeois ruler who loved his subjects and brilliant uniforms and was a fop, though low in stature and unprepossessing." Quoted in Mario Praz, *Conversation Pieces: A Survey of the Informal Group Portrait in Europe and America* (1971), 121n.

As for theoretical discussions of class, the most accessible compendium of Max Weber's views is in *From Max Weber: Essays in Sociology*, tr. and ed. H. H. Gerth and C. Wright Mills (1948). Marx's mature views are in vol. I of

Capital (1867). Two recent books by Anthony Giddens are most helpful: *Capitalism and Modern Social Theory: An Analysis of the Writings of Marx, Durkheim and Weber* (1971) and *The Class Structure of Advanced Societies* (1973). See also the brief study by R. J. Morris, *Class and Class Consciousness in the Industrial Revolution, 1780–1850* (1979).

Studies of middle classes in individual countries are much better than the overviews. For France there is Adeline Daumard's exemplary thesis on Paris, *La Bourgeoisie parisienne de 1815 à 1848* (1963), also available in an abridgment, *Les Bourgeois de Paris au XIXᵉ siècle* (1970). Zeldin's history *France, 1848–1945*, 2 vols. (1973, 1977), esp. vol. I, chs. 1–8, 11–13, is freighted down with information. Pierre Sorlin, *La Société française*, vol. I, *1840–1914* (1969), is an informal survey that does not neglect the middling orders. Among more specialized studies, Odette Voillard, *Nancy au XIXᵉ siècle, 1815–1871: une bourgeoisie urbaine* (1978), is largely a political and economic survey. See also Charles Morazé's essay *La France bourgeoise, XVIIIᵉ–XXᵉ siècles* (1946), and Régine Pernoud's lengthy historical survey *Histoire de la bourgeoisie en France*, 2 vols. (1960–62), which takes until the second half of her bulky second volume to get to the nineteenth-century French bourgeoisie, which she flatly, and facilely, describes as being "in power" (ch. 10). Looking back from a more recent vantage point, Jesse R. Pitts, "Continuity and Change in Bourgeois France," in Stanley Hoffmann et al., *In Search of France: The Economy, Society, and the Political System in the Twentieth Century* (1963), 235–304, has suggestive comments. Some choice pages in Gordon Wright's textbook, *France in Modern Times, 1760 to the Present* (3rd ed. 1981), are invaluable. While Emmanuel Beau de Loménie, *Les Responsabilités des dynasties bourgeoises*, 3 vols. (1943–54), is speculative, tendentious, and hostile, it is informative on the great banking houses and commercial families of nineteenth-century France. André-Jean Tudesq, *Les Grands Notables en France. Etude historique d'une psychologie sociale* (1964), is a magisterial and monumental study. F. W. J. Hemmings, in *Culture and Society in France, 1848–1898: Dissidents and Philistines* (1971), offers an intelligent survey of the clash between avant-garde culture and—in part—bourgeois society. An interesting essay on the use of "bourgeoisie" as a politically charged vocable is Mechtild Fischer, *Mittelklasse als politischer Begriff in Frankreich seit der Revolution* (1974). Though strenuously popular, Pierre Guiral, *La Vie quotidienne en France à l'age d'or du capitalisme, 1852–1879* (1976), has useful material. So does Marguerite Perrot, *La Mode de vie des familles bourgeoises* (1961). Jean Lhomme, *La Grand Bourgeoisie au pouvoir (1830–1880)* (1960), belongs to the controversy over the "bourgeois century," but is, independently of that, very meaty. For an informative family history, see Pierre Barral, *Les Perier de l'Isère au XIXᵉ siècle d'après leur correspondance familiale* (1964), and, equally informative about an influential individual, Jean Maurain, *Un bourgeois français au XIXᵉ siècle: Baroche, ministre de Napoleon III* (1936). There are good general histories of nineteenth-century France; all inevitably touch on the French bourgeoisie. Best among them all is the collective *Nouvelle Histoire de la France contemporaine*, notably vols. 6 and 7, André Jardin and André-Jean Tudesq, *La France des notables, 1815–1848* (1973); vol. 8, Maurice Agulhon, *1848 ou l'apprentissage de la république 1848–1852* (1973); vol. 9,

Alain Plessis, *De la fête impériale au mur des fédérés, 1852–1871* (2nd ed., 1976); and vol. 10, Jean-Marie Mayeur, *Les Débuts de la IIIᵉ République, 1871–1898* (1973).

For England, the somewhat controversial social history by Harold Perkin, *The Origins of Modern English Society, 1780–1880* (1969), is both informative and suggestive. Asa Briggs's contributions are particularly distinguished by immense learning, good humor, and precise judgments. I single out *The Age of Improvement, 1783–1867* (1959), esp. chs. 4–6, 8, 9. Briggs's article "The Language of 'Class' in Early Nineteenth-Century England," in Briggs and John Saville, eds., *Essays in Labour History* (1967), 43–73, is seminal. Among his other books, *The History of Birmingham*, vol. II, *Borough and City, 1865–1938* (1952), and *Victorian Cities* (1968) are particularly relevant here. I have drawn on other discriminating passages in Geoffrey Best, *Mid-Victorian Britain 1851–75* (1971), and G. Kitson Clark, *An Expanding Society: 1830–1900* (1967). S. G. Checkland, *The Rise of Industrial Society in England, 1815–1885* (1964), is a fresh, beautifully informed synthesis; all parts of the book are helpful, particularly chs. 4 and 8. I have learned much from W. L. Burn, *The Age of Equipoise: A Study of the Mid-Victorian Generation* (1964). Donald J. Olsen, *The Growth of Victorian London* (1976), is elegant, if a little condescending, on the lower middle classes. I also note L. D. Schwarz, "Social Class and Social Geography: the Middle Classes in London at the End of the Eighteenth Century," *Social History*, VII, 2 (May 1982), 167–85, very precise and rich in statistics.

Among general modern histories of England, which do not neglect the middling orders, the best text is R. K. Webb, *Modern England from 1760 to the Present* (2nd ed., 1980); the volumes Elie Halévy completed of his masterly *History of the English People in the Nineteenth Century*, notably his splendid *England in 1815* (1913; tr. E. I. Watkin and D. A. Barker, 1924), remain eminently worth consulting. One minor modern classic is still indispensable: G. M. Young, *Victorian England: Portrait of an Age* (2nd ed., 1953).

On the reluctance of the English to naturalize words like "bourgeoisie," see George Watson, *The English Ideology: Studies in the Language of Victorian Politics* (1973), esp. ch. 10. And on the anti-industrial style of nineteenth-century Englishmen, very relevant to the "bourgeois character," see Martin J. Wiener, *English Culture and the Decline of the Industrial Spirit, 1850–1980* (1981), interesting if perhaps not completely convincing.

German middle-class society and culture await their historian. Meanwhile, we have specialized studies. James J. Sheehan, *German Liberalism in the Nineteenth Century* (1978), has much of importance on the politics and self-perceptions of the German *Bürgertum*. So, though concentrating on the literary precipitate, does Ernest K. Bramsted, *Aristocracy and the Middle Classes in Germany: Social Types in German Literature, 1830–1900* (rev. ed., 1964). It may now be supplemented with Ilsedore Rarisch, *Das Unternehmerbild in der deutschen Erzählliteratur der ersten Hälfte des 19. Jahrhunderts* (1977). The collected essays by Wolfram Fischer, *Wirtschaft und Gesellschaft im Zeitalter der Industrialisierung* (1972), though principally on economic development, are rich in important hints. On that elusive phenomenon, the German public servant, John R. Gillis, *The Prussian Bureaucracy in Crisis,*

1840–1860 (1971), goes beyond its title; Otto Hintze's brilliant essay "Der Beamtenstand" (1911), in *Gesammelte Abhandlungen*, vol. II, *Soziologie und Geschichte* (2nd enlarged ed., 1964), 66–125, remains irreplaceable. On entrepreneurs, see the thorough (though not wholly free of Sombart's facile anti-semitic clichés) Friedrich Zunkel, *Der Rheinisch-Westfälische Unternehmer, 1834–1879* (1962). For a particularly instructive treatment of the educated German bourgeoisie which well complements Zunkel, there is Hansjoachim Henning, *Das Westdeutsche Bürgertum in der Epoche der Hochindustrialisierung 1860–1914. Soziales Verhalten und Soziale Strukturen*, vol. I, *Das Bildungsbürgertum in den Preussischen Westprovinzen* (1972). Henning has also written a brief *Sozialgeschichtliche Entwicklungen in Deutschland, 1815–60* (1977), particularly useful when read in conjunction with his compact anthology, *Quellen zur sozialgeschichtlichen Entwicklung in Deutschland von 1815 bis 1860* (1977). There is much of use in Heinrich Heffter, *Die deutsche Selbstverwaltung im 19. Jahrhundert. Geschichte der Ideen und Institutionen* (1950). So is there in Hartmut Kaelble, *Berliner Unternehmer während der frühen Industrialisierung. Herkunft, sozialer Status und politischer Einfluss* (1972). Ludwig Schrott, *Biedermeier in München: Dokumente einer schöpferischen Zeit* (1963), is an ample collection of testimony about bourgeois life in a royal capital. There are good surveys of the German bourgeoisie in Eda Sagarra, *A Social History of Germany, 1648–1914* (1977); see chs. 13–15, including a discussion on terminology. Ludwig Beutin, "Das Bürgertum als Gesellschaftsstand im 19. Jahrhundert," in *Gesammelte Schriften*, ed. Hermann Kellenbenz (1963), is a justly famous essay.

German urban history needs far more attention than it has so far received. Among the best and, for this chapter, most relevant studies are David F. Crew, *Town in the Ruhr: A Social History of Bochum, 1860–1914* (1979), and Wolfgang Köllmann, *Sozialgeschichte der Stadt Barmen im 19. Jahrhundert* (1960). One revealing local study about patricians is Gerhard Hirschmann, *Das Nürnberger Patriziat im Königreich Bayern, 1806–1918. Eine sozialgeschichtliche Untersuchung* (1971); and see Jürgen Bolland, *Die hamburgische Bürgerschaft in alter und neuer Zeit* (1959); and Helmut Böhme, *Frankfurt und Hamburg. Des deutschen Reiches Silber- und Goldloch und die allerenglischste Stadt des Kontinents* (1968). See also the fine study by Mack Walker, *German Home Towns: Community, State, General Estate, 1648–1871* (1971).

There are few general studies of bourgeoisies in other countries. I have profited, among other titles, from: Joel Mokyr, *Industrialization in the Low Countries, 1795–1850* (1976), a responsible study; E. H. Kossmann, *The Low Countries, 1780–1940* (1978), though it is sadly disappointing for a modern "general" history; Georges-H. Dumont, *La Vie quotidienne en Belgique sous le règne de Léopold II (1865–1909)* (1974), chatty but helpful. The interesting older book by Henri Charriaut, *La Belgique moderne. Terre d'expériences* (1910), has a remarkable section on the middle classes. For Italy, there remains the opinionated Benedetto Croce, *A History of Italy, 1871–1915* (tr. C. M. Ady, 1929); see also Denis Mack Smith, *Italy: A Modern History* (rev. ed., 1969), and J. A. Thayer, *Italy and the Great War: Politics and Culture, 1870–1915* (1964). Alexander Gerschenkron, "Notes on the Rate of Industrial Growth in Italy, 1881–1913," *Journal of Economic History*, XV (1955), 360–75, is, as one may expect, enlightening. Thomas C. Owen, *Capitalism and Politics in Russia: A Social History of the Moscow Merchants, 1855–1905* (1981), is an informative monograph. See also A. A. MacLaren, *Social Class in Scotland, Past and Present* (1976).

On the rich, see the fine, rather terse study by W. D. Rubinstein, *Men of Property: The Very Wealthy in Britain Since the Industrial Revolution* (1981). Bonnie G. Smith, *Ladies of the Leisure Class: The Bourgeoises of Northern France in the Nineteenth Century* (1981), though crippled by such fashionable sociological categories as the "rhetoric of reproduction," has some helpful material on the educational and marital ways of rich young women in the Nord. Tudesq (see above, p. 471) is exceptionally valuable here. Leonore Davidoff, *The Best Circles: Society, Etiquette and the Season* (1973), is brilliant both in substance and in method.

My skepticism about the idea of the ever-rising bourgeoisie is by no means original. See David Thomson, *Democracy in France since 1870* (5th ed., 1969). And, for contrast, Lenore O'Boyle, "The Middle Class in Western Europe, 1815–1848," *American Historical Review*, LXXI, 3 (April 1966), 826–45, responding in part to the ingenious revisionist arguments of Alfred Cobban, *The Social Interpretation of the French Revolution* (1964), and calling forth in turn a brilliant, if not wholly persuasive, response by Cobban, "The 'Middle Class' in France, 1815–48," *French Historical Studies*, V, 1 (Spring 1967), 41–52. For a wry exposure of the legend at work in an earlier century and a single country, see J. H. Hexter, "The Myth of the Middle Class in Tudor England," in *Reappraisals in History* (1961), 71–116. The prehistory of the "risen" nineteenth-century bourgeoisie is, of course, vast. A varied sampling: Isaac Kramnick, "Children's Literature and Bourgeois Ideology: Observations on Culture and Industrial Capitalism in the Later Eighteenth Century," in Perez Zagorin, ed., *Culture and Politics from Puritanism to the Enlightenment* (1980), 203–40, an effort to deal with socialization to bourgeois values. Pierre Goubert, *The Ancient Regime: French Society, 1600–1750* (1969; tr. Steve Cox, 1973), is an excellent, wholly dependable summary (esp. 323–60). Colin Lucas, "Nobles, Bourgeois and the Origins of the French Revolution," *Past and Present*, 60 (August 1973), 84–126, reaches the striking conclusion that "the Revolution made the bourgeoisie even if it was not made by the bourgeoisie" (126). An interesting nineteenth-century appraisal is by Agénor Bardoux, "La Bourgeoisie française sous le Directoire et le Consulat," *Revue des Deux Mondes*, LXXIV (1886), 307–36. Michel and Mireille Lacave, *Bourgeois et marchands en Provence et en Languedoc* (1977), surveys the centuries interestingly, down to the eighteenth. Louis Henry, *Les Familles genevoises* (1956), is a pioneering monograph on a bourgeois city-state by a great demographer.

The seventeenth-century Dutch, that great bourgeois culture, are, of course, fascinating, and no authoritative treatment exists. But the following titles proved most informative: G. J. Renier, *The Dutch Nation: An Historical Study* (1944); Charles R. Boxer, *The Dutch Seaborne Empire, 1600–1800* (1965), a distinguished study; J. H. Huizinga, *Dutch Civilisation in the Seventeenth Century and Other Essays* (tr. Arnold J. Pomerans, 1968), a classic, especially the title essay (1941). See also Violet Barbour, *Capitalism in Amsterdam in the Seventeenth Century* (1950).

On the vexed and related question whether "the bourgeoisie" took political power in the nineteenth century or whether traditional centers of authority, like the aristocracy, remained at least partially in control, the debate remains heated. Some judicious contributions are Michael Brock's authoritative study of 1832 in England, *The Great Reform Act* (1973), and David H. Pinkney's well-reasoned but not wholly convincing argument that the "bourgeois" monarchy of Louis Philippe was really Bonapartist, *The French Revolution of 1830* (1972). The issue is addressed by most articles in the informative anthology *1830 in France* (1975), compiled by John M. Merriman. On the fantasy of integrating the bourgeoisie into the monarchy, see Michel Denis, "Le Monarchisme libéral," *Annales de Bretagne*, LXXVII (1970), 391–415. As I noted in the text, the view remains overwhelmingly (especially for France) that the bourgeoisie was indeed in power after 1830. See, for one additional instance, Jean Bouret, *The Barbizon School and 19th-Century French Landscape Painting* (tr. 1973): "Between 1830 and 1870, the period of the Barbizon school's activity, the bourgeoisie was all-powerful" (10). But (in contrast) see the illuminating article by Patrice C.-R. Higonnet and Trevor B. Higonnet, "Class, Corruption, and Politics in the French Chamber of Deputies, 1846–8," *French Historical Studies*, V, 2 (1967), 204–24, rich in statistics, for continuing aristocratic influence. David Cannadine, *Lords and Landlords: The Aristocracy and the Towns, 1774–1967* (1980), ably documents the involvement of peers and their families in urban politics and culture in England right down to our day. Burn, *Age of Equipoise* (see p. 472), esp. 21, 22, 226, 253, 265–66, 304–12, demonstrates the persistence of aristocratic power in mid-nineteenth-century England. Indeed, Arthur Marwick, *The Deluge: British Society and the First World War* (1965), argues that the English middle classes did not accede to power until after the World War.

The anti-bourgeois campaign is very old: see Jean V. Alter, *Les Origines de la satire anti-bourgeoise en France, moyen âge—XVI siècle* (1966), and the various histories of the bourgeoisie mentioned before (pp. 470–71). For Flaubert, about whom there is a vast literature, suffice it to cite for now the telling excerpts gathered by Victor Brombert in *Flaubert par lui-même* (1971) and his thoughtful *The Novels of Flaubert: A Study of Themes and Techniques* (1966). (I shall be dealing with Flaubert in detail in a later volume.) The best treatments of Heine are Jeffrey L. Sammons, *Heinrich Heine: The Elusive Poet* (1969), and his fine life, *Heinrich Heine: A Modern Biography* (1979), to which I am much indebted. See also the thoughtful book by William Rose, *Heinrich Heine: Two Studies of His Thought and Feeling* (1956). For the general avant-garde attack, see the sociologist Cesar Graña's *Bohemian vs. Bourgeois* (1964) and his collection *Fact and Symbol: Essays in the Sociology of Art and Literature* (1971). Geraldine Pelles's intelligent *Art, Artists and Society: Origins of a Modern Dilemma* (1963) deals with English and French painters between 1750 and 1850. The most interesting general treatment is by Renato Poggioli, *The Theory of the Avant Garde* (tr. Gerald Fitzgerald, 1968), a significant study. For the "opposition," there is the magisterial survey by Helmut Kreuzer, *Die Boheme: Beiträge zu ihrer Beschreibung* (1968). For the special case of Russia, see esp. Nicholas V. Riasanovsky, *A Parting of Ways: Government and the Educated Public in*

Russia, 1801–1855 (1976). It should be read in conjunction with Marc Raeff's fascinating *Origins of the Russian Intelligentsia: The Eighteenth-Century Nobility* (1966), which uses psychological concepts with delicacy.

The charge that the bourgeoisie cannot love is implicit in most of this literature, and explicit in much of it. For a comprehensive array of utopians who (also implicitly and explicitly) criticized the bourgeois way with Eros, see in general Frank E. Manuel and Fritzie P. Manuel, *Utopian Thought in the Western World* (1979). For the Saint-Simonians, there is Frank Manuel, *The New World of Saint-Simon* (1956), while Carel Lodewijik de Liefde, *Le Saint-Simonisme dans la poésie française entre 1825 et 1865* (1927), goes beyond its narrow title. On the French utopian socialist Etienne Cabet and his followers, we now have the impressive monograph by Christopher H. Johnson, *Utopian Communism in France: Cabet and the Icarians, 1839–1851* (1974). As for sexual visionaries, Louis J. Kern, *An Ordered Love: Sex Roles and Sexuality in Victorian Utopias: The Shakers, the Mormons and the Oneida Community* (1981), and, on precisely the same three groups, though somewhat different in treatment, Lawrence Foster, *Religion and Sexuality: Three American Communal Experiments of the Nineteenth Century* (1981). These dreams of organized sexual communities call out for psychoanalytic treatment, but there is at present only one good monograph on Freudian lines: Robert David Thomas, *The Man Who Would Be Perfect: John Humphrey Noyes and the Utopian Impulse* (1977).

I postpone the detailed documentation of bourgeois styles—Manchester vs. Munich—to a later volume.

TWO: Architects and Martyrs of Change

On the psychological question of turning passivity into activity, see the acute papers by David Rapaport, "Some Metapsychological Considerations Concerning Activity and Passivity" (1953) and "The Theory of Ego Autonomy: A Generalization" (1958), in *The Collected Papers of David Rapaport*, ed. Merton M. Gill (1967), 530–68, 722–44. I have dealt with the cultural expression of this turn in the opening chapter of my *The Enlightenment: An Interpretation*, vol. II, *The Science of Freedom* (1969).

In the rich literature on theories of progress, the old study by J. B. Bury, *The Idea of Progress* (1920), retains much validity; it has been only partly supplemented by Robert A. Nisbet, *History of the Idea of Progress* (1980). Morris Ginsberg's article "Progress in the Modern Era," *Dictionary of the History of Ideas: Studies in Selected Pivotal Ideas*, ed. Philip W. Wiener, vol. III (1973), 633–50, is succinct and objective. A special aspect of "progressive thinking" is brilliantly treated in J. W. Burrow, *Evolution and Society: A Study in Victorian Social Theory* (1966; paperback ed. with new introduction, 1970). For Saint-Simon I refer back to Frank Manuel's *New World of Saint-Simon*, to be read in conjunction with his *The Prophets of Paris* (1962).

For anomie as the price of change, see Steven Lukes, *Emile Durkheim, His Life and Work: A Historical and Critical Study* (1972), very full; Robert A. Nisbet, *Emile Durkheim, with Selected Essays* (1965), a diversified anthology;

Raymond Aron's long chapter on Durkheim in *Main Currents in Sociological Thought*, vol. II (1967; tr. Richard Howard and Helen Weaver, 1967), an important critical appraisal. While Sigmund Freud stressed continuity, he had a keen sense of the changes that history imposes. I have noted, in the text, the dramatic instance of his comparison of the Oedipus complex in *Oedipus Rex* and in *Hamlet* in *Traumdeutung*, *St.A.*, II, 265–70; *Interpretation of Dreams*, *S.E.*, IV, 261–66. Richard P. Appelbaum, *Theories of Social Change* (1970), tersely sums up a variety of views; Thomas C. Cochran, the dean of American economic historians, instructively moves beyond economic history in *Social Change in America: The Twentieth Century* (1972). Bruno Bettelheim and Morris Janowitz, in their fascinating *Social Change and Prejudice* (incorporating the older *Dynamics of Prejudice*) (1964) apply psychoanalytic insights to social conflicts. Their stress on reality is congruent with the position I am developing in these volumes.

For a brief analysis of the older anxious view that innovation brings disaster, see Peter Gay, *A Loss of Mastery: Puritan Historians in Colonial America* (1966), 130–31. And see H. G. Barnett, *Innovation: The Basis of Cultural Change* (1953), esp. part IV. There is an illuminating psychoanalytic paper by Harold Searles, moving far beyond its announced subject, "Anxiety Concerning Change, as Seen in the Psychotherapy of Schizophrenic Patients—With Particular Reference to the Sense of Personal Identity" (1961), in *Collected Papers on Schizophrenia and Related Subjects* (1965), 443–64. Sigmund Freud's last view of anxiety is laid down in *Hemmung, Symptom und Angst* (1926), *St.A.*, VI, 227–308; *Inhibitions, Symptoms and Anxiety*, *S.E.*, XX, 77–174. The classic summary of psychological defenses is Anna Freud, *The Ego and The Mechanisms of Defence* (1936; tr. Cecil Baines, 1937).

While I did not want to load down the text with proofs that change was dominant in the nineteenth-century mind, I can adduce two more at this point. In her emotional and banal celebration of modern English poets, Vida D. Scudder noted near the end of the century that "a great poetry has accompanied our century of swift development in thought and deed." *The Life of the Spirit in the Modern English Poets* (1895), 1. In 1873 Auberon Herbert, editor, politician, and philosopher, told the *Times* of London that scientists, the principal engineers of the new, had produced a "moral chaos" and callously destroyed "old landmarks and rules of life." Everywhere, they were hearing "the cry of bewilderment from men and women" but were showing themselves indifferent to "the question how men should face the old fact called life in the new world which has sprung into existence." January 17, 1876, in Richard D. French, *Antivivisection and Medical Science in Victorian England* (1975), 8.

Of the forces making for change—industrialization, urbanization, and others—I want to give a brief sampling on the city. The old quantitative survey by Adna Ferrin Weber, *The Growth of Cities in the Nineteenth Century* (1899), retains its value. H. J. Dyos, ed., *The Study of Urban History* (1968), was a pioneering and is still a profitable collection. So is Stephan Thernstrom and Richard Sennett, eds., *Nineteenth-Century Cities: Essays in the New Urban History* (1969). I also used Charles Tilly, ed., *An Urban World* (1974). John M. Merriman, ed., *French Cities in the Nineteenth Century* (1982), has some fine contributions—the editor's introductory essay places the new and newer urban history into context—and good bibliographies. Some specialized studies are, notably, Lewis Greenberg, *Sisters of Liberty: Lyon, Paris and the Reaction to a Centralized State, 1868–1871* (1971); David H. Pinkney, *Napoleon III and the Rebuilding of Paris* (1958); H. J. Dyos and Michael Wolff, eds., *The Victorian City: Images and Realities*, 2 vols. (1973), which has some splendid articles; and H. J. Dyos, *Victorian Suburb: A Study of the Growth of Camberwell* (1961). And see earlier titles, like Crew (p. 473), Köllmann (p. 473), Olsen (p. 472), and Briggs (p. 472), to say nothing of Daumard (p. 471).

For obvious historical reasons, the "new" middle class has received the most concentrated attention from historians, and not only from Marxists. We know that Marx and Engels had predicted that the *Mittelstand* would sink into the proletariat, simplifying the middle class; the failure of this to happen was one crucial reason why some Marxists became revisionists. See Peter Gay, *The Dilemma of Democratic Socialism: Eduard Bernstein's Challenge to Marx* (1952). For England, see Gregory Anderson, *Victorian Clerks* (1976), and David Lockwood, *The Black-Coated Worker: A Study in Class Consciousness* (1958). From a different perspective, Robert Q. Gray, "The Labour Aristocracy in the Victorian Class Structure," in Frank Parkin, ed., *The Social Analysis of Class Structure* (1974), 19–38, and Geoffrey Crossick, *An Artisan Elite in Victorian Society: Kentish London 1840–1880* (1978).

The early parts of Heinrich August Winkler's judicious and exhaustive monograph *Mittelstand, Demokratie und Nationalsozialismus: Die politische Entwicklung von Handwerk und Kleinhandel in der Weimarer Republik* (1972) deal authoritatively with the evolution of the term *Mittelstand*. Emil Lederer and Jakob Marschak, "Der neue Mittelstand," is older but still useful, as is L. D. Pesl, "Mittelstandsfragen," both in G. Albrecht et al., *Grundriss der Sozialökonomik*, vol. IX, part I, *Die gesellschaftliche Schichtung im Kapitalismus* (1926), 120–41, 40–119.

In view of the unfortunate reputation that the umbrella has acquired as a dismal bourgeois instrument (what with King Louis Philippe carrying one and Daumier showing bourgeois armed with it), a serious study of that implement would be interesting; T. S. Crawford, *A History of the Umbrella* (1970), is only a sketch.

Education of the Senses

BOURGEOIS EXPERIENCES, I:
An Erotic Record

I have drawn the bulk of my materials for this chapter from the splendid, extensive papers of Mabel Loomis Todd and her daughter, Millicent Todd Bingham, and the only less extensive papers of David Peck Todd, Austin Dickinson (intermingled with Mabel Todd's papers), and the Loomis family, all in the Yale Archives and Manuscripts.

On Mabel Todd, see the lucid but uncritical and very brief summary by Millicent Todd Bingham, *Mabel Loomis Todd: Her Contributions to the Town of Amherst* (1935), and also her *Ancestors' Brocades: The Literary*

Debut of Emily Dickinson (1945), which has good material. So does R. W. Franklin, *The Editing of Emily Dickinson: A Reconsideration* (1967).

There are substantial chapters on Mabel Todd in Richard B. Sewall, *The Life of Emily Dickinson*, 2 vols. (1974): I, chs. 6, 9, 10, 12, and Appendix II. A few of the passages I have used in my text are to be found in Sewall's scholarly and exhaustive but genteel study of Emily Dickinson's life, work, and world; he has omitted practically all the erotic material. Even when he prints an amorous passage (see I, 181), he quotes the sentences on love and leaves out the decisive sentences on sexuality. In any event, the interpretation of Mabel Todd in this chapter is my own.

Other somewhat helpful texts include MacGregor Jenkins, *Emily Dickinson, Friend and Neighbor* (1930), especially on Austin Dickinson; Martha Dickinson Bianchi, *Emily Dickinson Face to Face* (1932), which reprints in appendices obituary tributes to Austin Dickinson, most of them going beyond the obligatory pieties. Millicent Todd has a partisan, effusive, but not wholly uninformative account of Mabel Todd's father, *Eben Jenks Loomis, 11 November 1828– 2 December 1912* (privately printed, 1913). And see her *Emily Dickinson's Home. The Early Years, As Revealed in Family Correspondence and Reminiscences, with Documentation and Comment* (1955; corr. ed. 1967).

The nineteenth-century advice literature on fathers and daughters and November-May marriages is fairly bulky. Dr. Gardner's *Conjugal Sins*, which I quote in the text (above, p. 103), depends heavily on the very popular work of Dr. Alexandre Mayer, especially *Des rapports conjugaux, considérés sous le triple point de vue de la population, de la santé et de la morale publique* (1848; 4th corrected and enlarged ed., 1860). For one "victim," see *Margaret Sanger: An Autobiography* (1938), and David M. Kennedy, *Birth Control in America: The Career of Margaret Sanger* (1970). Close father-daughter ties are a staple of nineteenth-century fiction; I cite only Elizabeth Gaskell, *North and South* (1855), whose delicate delineation of an almost fatal attachment of father to daughter has been largely overlooked under the pressure of more obtrusive themes. In the psychoanalytic literature, perhaps the most interesting are Phyllis Greenacre, "Child Wife as Ideal: Sociological Considerations" (1947), in *Emotional Growth*, 2 vols. (1971), I, 3–8, and René Spitz, "Ein Beitrag zum Problem der Wandlung der Neurosenform: Die Infantile Frau und ihre Gegenspieler," *Imago*, XIX (1933), 454–67.

The issue of nineteenth-century engagements needs much further, preferably comparative work. Meanwhile, Ellen K. Rothman, "Sex and Self-Control: Middle-Class Courtship in America, 1770–1870," *Journal of Social History*, XV, 3 (Spring 1982), 409–25, is excellently argued and exhaustively documented for the United States; so is her thesis, " 'Intimate Acquaintance': Courtship and the Transition to Marriage in America, 1770–1900" (Brandeis, 1980).

The general nineteenth-century confusion about the "safe" period for intercourse is lucidly laid out in Carl N. Degler, *At Odds: Women and the Family in America from the Revolution to the Present* (1980), 212–15. See also James Reed, *From Private Vice to Public Virtue: The Birth Control Movement in American Society Since 1830* (1978), detailed and judicious.

My diagnosis of Mabel Todd as a hysteric is tentative. The literature on that protean disorder is vast and uneven. The classic case histories by Freud and

Breuer, *Studies on Hysteria*, S.E., II (1895), now need to be complicated and supplemented. Ilza Veith, *Hysteria: The History of a Disease* (1965), is a sensible and summary overview concentrating on the centuries before Freud; Alan Krohn, *Hysteria: The Elusive Neurosis* (1978), is pedestrian, brief, but dependable, with a selective bibliography; it underscores the variety of ailments that have been called by a single name. I have learned from David Shapiro, *Neurotic Styles* (1965), ch. 4. Otto Fenichel's 1945 text *The Psychoanalytic Theory of Neurosis* is no longer quite up to date, but the relevant chapters on hysteria and conversion (11 and 12) remain eminently worth reading. Of the recent technical literature stressing the complexity of hysteria, I have found most important: Judd Marmor, "Orality in the Hysterical Personality," *Journal of the American Psychoanalytic Association*, I (1953), 656–71; Leo Rangell, "The Nature of Conversion," ibid., VII (1959), 632–62; and in particular, Elizabeth Zetzel, "The So-Called Good Hysteric," *International Journal of Psycho-Analysis*, XLIX (1968), 256–60.

On "delicious" used other than as an adjective describing food, see Charles Dickens, *Our Mutual Friend* (1864; ed. 1953), Book IV, ch. 5, p. 659, for a girl crying for joy. Whitman used "delicious" to characterize American slang phrases. Justin Kaplan, *Walt Whitman: A Life* (1980), 229. Amiel could qualify an episode in a novel as "*délicieux*." And see the diary of Mary I. Barrows, kept while she was a schoolgirl at St. Margaret's in Connecticut: "Geometry is *delicious*." [October] 7 [1885], Private Record, 1885–1886, courtesy of Susanna Barrows.

ONE: Sweet Bourgeois Communions

I have recorded the sources of my conviction that Mabel Todd was not alone, citing the Wards and others in the footnotes. F. Barry Smith, "Sexuality in Britain" (above, p. 468), is again invaluable. There is additional information on Stanton in Lois W. Banner, *Elizabeth Cady Stanton: A Radical for Woman's Rights* (1980); short but dependable. Theodore Stanton and Harriot Stanton Blanch, eds., *Elizabeth Cady Stanton, As Revealed in Her Letters, Diary and Reminiscences*, 2 vols. (1922), is rich, informative, but incomplete. Jocelyne Baty Goodman's edition of Hopkinson's recollections, *Victorian Cabinet Maker: The Memoirs of James Hopkinson, 1819–1894* (1968), is a model. While Leon Harris, *Only to God: The Extraordinary Life of Godfrey Lowell Cabot* (1967), is most informative, the psychoanalytic speculations are my own.

I should note that in interpreting Hopkinson's (or, for that matter, Cabot's or anyone else's) dreams, I am being tentative. I am not trying to evade my responsibilities as an interpreter of the evidence, but I am also alert to the near-impossibility of offering an authoritative interpretation of a dream in the absence of the dreamer adding associations, further details, and memories. High probability and persuasiveness is the best one can hope for.

For Joseph Lyman, see Richard B. Sewall, *The Lyman Letters: New Light on Emily Dickinson and Her Family* (1965), and his *Emily Dickinson*, I, 134–40; II, 422–27 (above, p. 479). Both are scholarly but omit all the sexual material that I found so valuable in the Lyman family papers. The status of phrenology in the Lymans' day is well canvassed in John D. Davies, *Phrenology, Fad and Science: A 19th-Century American Crusade* (1955), and Madeleine B. Stern, *Heads & Headlines: The Phrenological Fowlers* (1971). There are lengthy excerpts from Victoria Benedictsson's diaries and Journals in Frederick Böök, *Victoria Benedictsson och Georg Brandes* (1949), and far shorter ones in Lucien Maury, *L'Amour et la mort d'Ernst Ahlgren* (1945); both offer interesting interpretative details. I have not seen the promisingly titled study of Benedictsson by Tora Sandström, *En psykoanalytisk Kvinnostudie* (1935). For Lester Ward, see Emily P. Cape, *Lester F. Ward: A Personal Sketch* (1922), and Samuel Chugerman, *Lester F. Ward, The American Aristotle: A Summary and Interpretation of His Sociology* (1939). Ch. 4, "Lester Ward: Critic," in Richard Hofstadter, *Social Darwinism in American Thought* (2nd ed., 1955), is terse but brilliant.

On sex researchers in the nineteenth century, a subject that invites more research, see the chapter on Havelock Ellis in Paul A. Robinson, *The Modernization of Sex* (1976). The early biography by Arthur Calder-Marshall, *Havelock Ellis* (1959), now has been superseded by Phyllis Grosskurth, *Havelock Ellis: A Biography* (1980), balanced and impressively informed. For the author of the Mosher Survey, I express once again my indebtedness to Carl Degler's article "What Ought to Be and What Was" (above, p. 468). See also Degler, "Introduction" to *The Mosher Survey: Sexual Attitudes of 45 American Women*, ed. James MaHood and Kristine Wenburg (1980), and Kathryn Allamong Jacob's biographical essay "Clelia Duel Mosher," *Johns Hopkins Magazine*, XXX, 3 (June 1979), 8–16. At least one student of sexuality, Lillian Faderman, has remained unpersuaded by Degler's interpretation of this material and would be by mine; see her *Surpassing the Love of Men: Romantic Friendship and Love Between Women from the Renaissance to the Present* (1981), 440.

The nineteenth-century physician writing on female sexuality who has made the most mischief among historians is Dr. William Acton. Researchers into sexuality working in countries other than England (where his repute was uncertain) obviously enjoyed his message and quoted or paraphrased it at length. Dr. Otto Adler (above, pp. 160–63) uses Acton freely, often without quotation marks; other grateful consumers include Dr. Seved Ribbing, *Sexuelle Hygiene und ihre ethischen Konsequenzen* (1892), 54–55; Dr. Elizabeth Blackwell, *Counsel to Parents on the Moral Education of Their Children* (1878; 4th ed., 1881), 69–71; Dr. Mary Wood-Allen, *Ideal Married Life: A Book for All Husbands and Wives*, ch. xxiv; Dr. Horatio Robinson Storer, *Is It I? A Book for Every Man* (1868), 30–32, 141–43. While Acton's book enjoyed a wide circulation in its day, its recent reputation rests upon the prominent place it occupies in Steven Marcus, *The Other Victorians* (above, pp. 467–68).

The most controversial modern views on female sexuality are certainly those of Freud. The controversy is being conducted within the psychoanalytic community itself. It is significant that Mary Jane Sherfey's important revision of Freud's ideas on female orgasm, *The Nature and Evolution of Female Sexuality* (1972), should first have appeared in the *Journal of the American Psychoanalytic Association*. Harold P. Blum has edited *Female Sexuality: Contemporary Psychoanalytic Views* (1977), which brings the discussion within the fold up to date. The full history of Freud's ideas on women remains to be written. Zenie Odes Fliegel, "Feminine Psychosexual Development in Freudian Theory: A Historical Reconstruction," *Psychoanalytic Quarterly*, XLII, 3 (July 1973), 385–408, gives a dependable account of the spirited debate among analysts on this vexed question in the 1920s, with the young Karen Horney and Ernest Jones championing woman as not a failed man but as developing her own autonomous sexuality. See, above all, Horney, "On the Genesis of the Castration Complex in Women," *International Journal of Psychoanalysis*, V (1924), 50–65, and "The Flight from Womanhood," ibid., VII (1926), 324–39; and Jones, "The Early Development of Female Sexuality" (1927) and "The Phallic Phase" (1933), both in *Papers on Psychoanalysis* (1961), 438–51, 452–84. But Freud's mature position, offered in two short (and somewhat tentative) papers, prevailed: "Einige psychische Folgen des anatomischen Geschlechts-unterschieds" (1925), *St.A.*, V, 253–66; "Some Psychical Consequences of the Anatomical Distinction Between the Sexes," *S.E.*, XIX, 243–58; and "Über die weibliche Sexualität (1931), *St.A.*, V, 273–92; "Female Sexuality," *S.E.*, XXI, 223–43. Psychoanalysts taking his line were, above all, Helene Deutsch, *The Psychology of Women*, 2 vols. (1944–45), and Marie Bonaparte, *Female Sexuality* (tr. John Rodker, 1953). Feminists have been freely and extensively criticizing this position on female sexuality; a representative recent title is Joanna Bunker Rohrbaugh, *Women: Psychology's Puzzle* (1979). In the light of this onslaught, the feminist Juliet Mitchell's *Psychoanalysis and Feminism: Freud, Reich, Laing and Women* (1974), a well-informed polemical defense of Freud, is all the more remarkable.

I must not overlook a fine essay by Nancy F. Cott, "Passionlessness: An Interpretation of Victorian Sexual Ideology, 1790–1850," in Cott and Elizabeth H. Pleck, eds., *A Heritage of Her Own: Toward a New Social History of American Women* (1979), 162–81. I should also note that on the question of whether the moralists took over the debate on female sexuality late in the nineteenth century, I find myself in disagreement with John S. and Robin Haller, *The Physician and Sexuality in Victorian America* (1974), an important monograph from which I have learned (they think the moralists won, I do not).

For Dr. Napheys, see the Biographical Sketch serving as a preface to his *The Physical Life of Woman: Advice to the Maiden, Wife and Mother* (1869; 3rd ed., 1888).

Rosalind Rosenberg's interesting monograph, *Beyond Separate Spheres: Intellectual Roots of Modern Feminism* (1982), came to my attention as I was correcting galley proofs. Her pages on the Mosher Survey (98–99, 180–87) are fascinating; her reading of it is slightly gloomier than mine.

TWO: Offensive Women and Defensive Men

On man's fear of woman, two titles are informative and interesting: H. R. Hays, *The Dangerous Sex: The Myth of Feminine Evil* (1964), and, even more, Wolfgang Lederer, *The Fear of Women* (1968), both moving across ages and cultures. Sigmund Freud's short paper on the terror of the female genitals is important here: "Das Medusenhaupt" (1922) [not in *St.A.*], *G.W.*, XVII, 47;

"Medusa's Head," *S.E.*, XVIII, 273–74. In the other psychoanalytic literature, I found most helpful Edith Jacobson, "The Development of the Wish for a Child in Boys," *Psychoanalytic Study of the Child*, V (1950), 139–52; Géza Róheim, "Aphrodite or the Woman with a Penis," *Psychoanalytic Quarterly*, XIV (1945), 350–90; Karen Horney, "The Dread of Women. Observation on a Specific Difference in the Dread felt by Men and by Women Respectively for the Opposite Sex," *International Journal of Psychoanalysis*, XIII (1932), 348–60; Robert Gessain, "Vagina dentata," *Psychanalyse* [Paris], III (1957), 247–95, and *Le Motif vagina dentata* (1958); and Verrier Elwin, "The Vagina Dentata Legend," *British Journal of Medical Psychology*, XIX (1941), 439–53, this last an impressive anthropological survey. There is also useful material in Daniel S. Jaffe, "The Masculine Envy of Woman's Procreative Function," *Journal of the American Psychoanalytic Association*, XVI (1968), 121–48. Dorothy Dinnerstein's manifesto *The Mermaid and the Minotaur: Sexual Arrangements and Human Malaise* (1976) is suggestive. Joseph C. Rheingold, *The Fear of Being a Woman: A Theory of Maternal Destructiveness* (1964), is a very large and eclectic treatise with much interesting information. The fate of one symbolic woman, Marianne, is traced most intriguingly by Maurice Agulhon, *Marianne into Battle: Republican Imagery and Symbolism in France, 1789–1880* (1979; tr. Janet Lloyd, 1981); a second volume is promised. Natalie Zemon Davis, "Women on Top," in *Society and Culture in Early Modern France* (1975), 124–51, eminently repays reading for the comparative dimension it introduces.

The literature on women's situation, resentments, and aspirations in the nineteenth century is by now very bulky. An enormously comprehensive general survey, taking all the recent scholarship into account, is Priscilla Robertson, *An Experience of Women: Pattern and Change in Nineteenth Century Europe* (1982), with an exhaustive bibliography. Useful also are Louise Tilly and Joan W. Scott, *Women, Work, and Family* (1978), and Lee Holcombe, *Victorian Ladies at Work: Middle-Class Working Women in England and Wales, 1850–1914* (1973). I add the old but still informative Theodore Stanton, ed., *The Woman Question in Europe. A Series of Original Essays* (1884); Marianne Weber's no less instructive survey of women's legal situation, *Ehefrau und Mutter in der Rechtsentwicklung* (1907); and Edith Abbott, *Women in Industry* (1909). For the retreat of women in the early nineteenth century, Ivy Pinchbeck, *Women Workers and the Industrial Revolution, 1750–1850* (1930; new preface, 1969) remains of importance. Doris May Stenton, *The English Woman in History* (1957), is a rapid survey down to the nineteenth century. Mary Roth Walsh, *"Doctors Wanted: No Women Need Apply": Sexual Barriers in the Medical Profession, 1835–1975* (1977), is angry, fair, and rich; I have learned much from it. There are significant and fascinating sidelights in Jean Donnison, *Midwives and Medical Men: A History of Inter-Professional Rivalries and Women's Rights* (1977). Marjorie Housepian Dobkin's edition of Carey Thomas's journals, though quite fragmentary, is electrifying: *The Making of a Feminist: Early Journals and Letters of M. Carey Thomas* (1979). I also recall the remarkable book by Charlotte Perkins Gilman, *Women and Economics: A Study of The Economic Relation Between Men and Women as a Factor in Social Evolution* (1899), ed. Carl Degler (1966).

For governesses, see M. Jeanne Peterson, "The Victorian Governess: Status Incongruence in Family and Society," in Martha Vicinus, ed., *Suffer and Be Still: Women in the Victorian Age* (1973), 3–19, a very meaty essay. And see Katharine West, *Chapter of Governesses: A Study of the Governess in English Fiction, 1800–1949* (1949), and Rosalie G. Grylls, *Queens College, 1848–1948* (1949).

There are several good general accounts of women moving into politics and the professions. I have profited from Richard J. Evans, *The Feminists: Women's Emancipation Movements in Europe, America and Australasia 1840–1920* (1977), terse and dependable. Degler, *At Odds* (above, p. 479), has some good chapters. See also Eleanor Flexner, *Century of Struggle: The Woman's Rights Movement in the United States* (1959); Aileen S. Kraditor, *The Ideas of the Woman Suffrage Movement 1890–1929* (1965); Léon Abensour, *Histoire générale du féminisme des origines à nos jours* (1921); Richard J. Evans, *The Feminist Movement in Germany 1894–1933* (1976), and a fine dissertation by Amy Hackett, "The Politics of Feminism in Wilhelmine Germany 1890–1918" (Columbia, 1976). Hackett has published some of her results: "The German Women's Movement and Suffrage, 1890–1914: A Study of National Feminism," in Robert J. Bezucha, ed., *Modern European Social History* (1972), 354–86. Margrit Twellmann, *Die deutsche Frauenbewegung im Spiegel repräsentativer Frauenzeitschriften. Ihre Anfänge und erste Entwicklung (1843–1888)* (1972), interestingly traces the German feminist movement through its periodicals.

Since women's history is a relatively new field, the anthology both of sources and of articles occupies a central place. Much of the recent scholarship, however combative, has been of high caliber. Good and ample collections of sources include Erna Olafson Hellerstein, Leslie Parker Hume, and Karen M. Offen, eds., *Victorian Women: A Documentary Account of Women's Lives in Nineteenth-Century England, France, and the United States* (1981); Patricia Hollis, ed., *Women in Public, 1850–1900: Documents of the Victorian Woman's Movement* (1979); Janet Murray, ed., *Strong-Minded Women & Other Lost Voices from 19th Century England* (1982), excellent like the others but, as the title shows, a little self-pitying, since the "lost voices" include Queen Victoria and Florence Nightingale; the far briefer William L. O'Neill, ed., *The Woman Movement: Feminism in the United States* (1969); and Julia O'Faolain and Lauro Martines, eds., *Not in God's Image* (1973), a romp through history.

The best collections of modern essays include Martha Vicinus, *Suffer and Be Still*, and her more recent *A Widening Sphere: Changing Roles of Victorian Women* (1977); Nancy F. Cott, *Root of Bitterness: Documents of the Social History of American Women* (1972), and *A Heritage of Her Own* (above, p. 482).

For the "antis," see the economical and wholly persuasive book by Brian Harrison, *Separate Spheres: The Opposition to Women's Suffrage in Britain* (1978). See also Harrison's impressive "Women's Health and the Women's Movement in Britain: 1840–1940," in Charles Webster, ed., *Biology, Medicine and Society 1840–1940* (1981), 15–71. Harrison's collection of essays, *Peaceable Kingdom: Stability and Change in Modern Britain* (1982), has admirable pages on the English women's movement.

Struwwelpeter, that German children's classic, filled with sadism and castration, awaits its psychoanalytic historian. Meanwhile, there is the interesting but tendentious book by Marie-Luise Könneker, *Dr. Heinrich Hoffmann's "Struwwelpeter," Untersuchungen zur Entstehungs- und Funktionsgeschichte eines bürgerlichen Bilderbuchs* (1977). On castrating females in the bourgeois literature of the nineteenth century, see Mario Praz's magisterial *The Romantic Agony* (1930; 2nd ed., tr. Angus Davidson, 1951), on which I have relied. For Pater, see esp. Michael Levey, *The Case of Walter Pater* (1978). The complex female anti-feminist Mrs. Linton is examined in Herbert Van Thal, *Eliza Lynn Linton: The Girl of the Period* (1979), and in the older G. S. Layard, *Mrs. Lynn Linton: Her Life, Letters and Opinions* (1901). Linton's strange autobiographical "novel" in which she adopts a male persona, *The Autobiography of Christopher Kirkland* (1853), repays study.

For some of the artists I consider in the text, I single out from a far larger literature: Robert Rosenblum, *Ingres* (1967), a seminal text; Jean Paladilhe and José Pierre, *Gustave Moreau* (1972); David Sonstroem, *Rossetti and the Fair Lady* (1970); Virginia Surtees, *The Paintings and Drawings of Dante Gabriel Rossetti (1828-1882)*, 2 vols. (1971), a most revealing catalogue raisonné; Henrich Voss, *Franz von Stuck, 1863-1928. Werkkatalog der Gemälde mit einer Einführung in seinen Symbolismus* (1973); *Edvard Munch: Symbols and Images* (1978), informative with some brilliant essays by various hands and Introduction by Robert Rosenblum; Ulrich Weisner, ed., *Munch: Liebe, Angst, Tod: Themen und Variationen* (1980), a splendid catalogue; Max Schmid, *Klinger* (1901), badly dated but not useless; *Max Liebermann in seiner Zeit* (1979), with essays by Matthias Eberle and others, a truly exhaustive catalogue of that once very famous German-Jewish painter.

THREE: Pressures of Reality

On chloroform and its pioneers, see Myrtle Simpson, *Simpson the Obstetrician* (1972), and J. A. Shepherd, *Simpson and Syme of Edinburgh* (1969). For Dr. Ignaz Semmelweis's dramatic struggle to make childbirth in hospitals safer, there is the substantial biography by Sir William J. Sinclair, *Semmelweis: His Life and His Doctrine: A Chapter in the History of Medicine* (1909), to be supplemented by Sherwin B. Nuland's interesting study of medical politics, "The Enigma of Semmelweis—An Interpretation," *Journal of the History of Medicine and Allied Sciences*, XXXIV, 3 (July 1979), 255-72, and by Erna Lesky, *Ignaz Philipp Semmelweis und die Wiener Medizinische Schule* (1964). Reliable details on individual life-and-death stories explored in my text can be found in Sarah Freeman, *Isabella and Sam: The Story of Mrs. Beeton* (1978); Mary Lutyens, *The Ruskins and the Grays* (1972), esp. appendix III for the fate of the Gray children. For the English royal family, among a rich harvest, Cecil Woodham-Smith, *Queen Victoria: From her Birth to the Death of the Prince Consort* (1972). William Gladstone's eloquent diary (*The Gladstone Diaries*, impeccably edited by M. R. D. Foot and H. C. G. Matthew, 8 vols. so far [1968-   ]) can be read in conjunction with S. G. Checkland, *The Gladstones: A Family Biography, 1764-1851* (1971), and Deryck Schreuder, "Gladstone and the Conscience of the State," in Peter Marsh, ed., *The Con-*

science of the Victorian State (1979), 73-134. The family history of the
Lenbachs is briefly canvassed in Siegfried Wichmann, *Franz von Lenbach und
seine Zeit* (1973).

For the great statisticians of the nineteenth century, there is Maurice Halb-
wachs, *La Théorie de l'homme moyen: essai sur Quetelet et la statistique
morale* (1912), to be supplemented by Paul F. Lazarsfeld, "Notes on the
History of Quantification in Sociology: Trends, Sources and Problems," *Isis*,
LII (1961), 277-333, and Lazarsfeld and David Landau, "Quetelet, Adolphe," in
International Encyclopedia of the Social Sciences (1968), XIII, 247-55. Farr is
adequately treated in John M. Eyler, *Victorian Social Medicine: The Ideas and
Methods of William Farr* (1979); the old anthology, *Vital Statistics: A
Memorial Volume of Selections from the Reports and Writings of William
Farr*, ed. Noel A. Humphreys (1885), is full and judicious.

Freud touched on the relationship of sexual precautions to mental well-being
all along the way; see his early paper "Über die Berechtigung, von der
Neurasthenie einen bestimmten Symptomenkomplex als 'Angstneurose' abzutrennen" (1895), *St.A.*, VI, 25-49; "On the Grounds for Detaching a Particular Syndrome from Neurasthenia under the Description 'Anxiety Neurosis,'"
S.E., III, 87-117, for anxiety in men practicing abstention or coitus interruptus
and suffering from unconsummated excitement. See also Freud, "Die Sexualität
in der Ätiologie der Neurosen" (1898), *St.A.*, V, 11-35; "Sexuality in the
Aetiology of the Neuroses," *S.E.*, III, 261-85. His important short later paper
"Die 'kulturelle' Sexualmoral und die moderne Nervosität" (1908), *St.A.*, IX,
9-32; "'Civilized' Sexual Morality and Modern Nervous Illness," *S.E.*, IX,
181-204, anticipates many of his central arguments on civilization as sacrifice in
Civilization and Its Discontents (1930).

Among psychoanalytic studies of pregnancy I have learned most from
Therese Benedek, "On the Organization of the Reproductive Drive," in
Psychoanalytic Investigations: Selected Papers (1973), 408-45; Grete L.
Bibring, "Some Considerations of the Psychological Processes in Pregnancy,"
Psychoanalytic Study of the Child, XIV (1959), 113-21, and Bibring, Thomas
F. Dwyer, Dorothy S. Huntington, and Arthur F. Valenstein, "A Study of the
Psychological Processes in Pregnancy and the Earliest Mother-Child Relation-
ship," ibid., XVI (1961), 9-72. For "Anna O.," really Bertha Pappenheim, see
Breuer's own circumstantial case history (with Sigmund Freud) in *Studien
über Hysterie* (1895), *G.W.*, I, 77-312; *Studies on Hysteria*, *S.E.*, II, 21-47;
Freud's comments are in "Zur Geschichte der Psychoanalytischen Bewegung"
(1914), *G.W.*, X, 44-45; "On the History of the Psychoanalytic Movement",
S.E., XIV, 11-12. Lucy Freeman, *The Story of Anna O.* (1972), is a popular
account of this famous patient; Marion A. Kaplan, *The Jewish Feminist Movement in Germany: The Campaigns of the Jüdischer Frauenbund 1904-1938*
(1979), deals with Bertha Pappenheim's fascinating later career. A different,
anthropological perspective is to be found in Sheila Kitzinger, *Women as
Mothers* (1978).

Historians and demographers have in the last four decades or so paid close
attention to the elusive question of birth control. Among the pioneers, those
most influential for historians have been Louis Henry, esp. his *Anciennes
familles genevoises. Etude démographique, XVIᵉ-XXᵉ siècles* (1956), *Manuel*

de démographie historique (1967), and, with M. Fleury, *Des régistres paroissiaux à l'histoire de la population. Manuel de dépouillement et d'exploitation de l'état civil ancien* (1965); David V. Glass, *Population Policies and Movements in Europe* (1940), and Glass, ed. with D. E. C. Eversley, *Population in History: Essays in Historical Demography* (1965), which contains important methodological as well as detailed historical papers. E. A. Wrigley's little gem "Family Limitation in Pre-Industrial England," first published in the *Economic History Review* [Utrecht], 1966, has often been anthologized, best in Michael Drake, ed., *Population in Industrialization* (1969), a fine collection paying special attention to recent controversies. See also Wrigley, *Population and History* (1969), and T. H. Hollingsworth, *Historical Demography* (1969). Perhaps the earliest modern demographic study, usable both as a document for, as well as an exploration of, the early nineteenth century, is Christoph Bernoulli, *Handbuch der Populationistik oder der Völker- und Menschenkunde nach statistischen Erhebnissen* (1841). Derek Llewellyn-Jones, *Human Reproduction and Society* (1974), ably and thoroughly canvasses our current knowledge of reproductive forces.

For general summaries of recent work and its results see André Armengaud, "Population in Europe, 1700–1914," tr. A. J. Pomerans, in Carlo M. Cipolla, ed., *The Fontana Economic History of Europe*, vol. III, *The Industrial Revolution* (1973), 22–76; Jacques Dupaquier, "Population," in *The New Cambridge Modern History*, vol. XIII, *Companion Volume*, ed. Peter Burke (1979), 80–114. Herbert Moller, ed., *Population Movements in Modern European History* (1964), contains fine short essays on Sweden, France, urbanization, industrialization, nineteenth-century Germany, and others. Edward Shorter's controversial and, to me, unpersuasive and somewhat coarse *The Making of the Modern Family* (1975) has material on historical demographic findings. How controversial the application of such findings to history can be emerges from Robert I. Rotberg and Theodore K. Rabb, eds., *Marriage and Fertility: Studies in Interdisciplinary History* (1980), which pits a number of historians like Shorter and Flandrin against their critics. George D. Sussman's interesting "Parisian Infants and Norman Wet Nurses in the Early Nineteenth Century: A Statistical Study" is part of that collection (249–65).

The point that the desire for contraception is ancient, and that the nineteenth-century "revolution" was but its more or less incomplete satisfaction, is forcibly made in that ungainly but indispensable, richly annotated classic, Norman E. Himes's *Medical History of Contraception* (1936; ed. 1970). Another classic, more graceful, is John T. Noonan, Jr., *Contraception: A History of Its Treatment by the Catholic Theologians and Canonists* (1965), which is wider than its title. See also Frédéric Sipperstein, *La Grève des naissances en Europe et ses problèmes* (1939).

Among studies of individual nations I have found useful, for France: the old, polemical Emile Levasseur, *La Population française*, 2 vols. (1888–92); K. A. Wieth-Knudsen, *Natalité et Progrès: Synthèse économique, démographique et biologique* (1908; French. tr. 1938), particularly useful in debunking earlier imprecise, often slipshod French estimates. The classic controversial studies done within the time-span of this book are mainly by Arsène Dumont, *Dépopulation et civilisation: étude démographique* (1890) and *Natalité et démocratie* (1898), Jacques Bertillon, *La Dépopulation de la France* (1911), and Paul Leroy-Beaulieu, *La Question de la population* (1913). Worried Frenchmen had denounced the two-child family even earlier; note Henri Medile Gourrier, *L'Avenir du mariage ou l'usage et l'abus dans l'union des sexes. Propositions et développements rédigés aux points de vue médical, philosophique, et théologique* (1871). The debate is well summarized in Theodore Zeldin, *France* (see above, p. 471), vol. II, *Intellect, Taste and Anxiety*, ch. 19.

French Malthusianism and its enemies have been rewardingly studied: see Hélène Bergues et al., *La Prévention des naissances dans la famille, ses origines dans les temps modernes* (1960). The "strike of the bellies" is well analyzed in Francis Ronsin, "Liberté—Natalité; Réaction et répression anti-malthusiennes avant 1920," *Recherches*, 29 (December 1977). Modern demographic studies (which of course deal with contraception) include Philippe Ariès, *Histoire des populations françaises et de leurs attitudes devant la vie depuis le XVIIIe siècle* (1948; abridged but also slightly augmented ed., 1979), and the authoritative works by André Armengaud, *Les Français et Malthus* (1975), and *La Population française au XIXe siècle* (1971). The pre-nineteenth-century history of French birth control is discussed in some remarkable essays by Jean-Louis Flandrin, *L'Eglise et le contrôle des naissances* (1970), and, in conjunction with more general themes, in his *Families in Former Times: Kinship, Household and Sexuality* (1976; tr. Richard Southern, 1979). And see Orest and Patricia Ranum, eds., *Popular Attitudes Toward Birth Control in Pre-Industrial France and England* (1972).

For Zola and *Fécondité*, F. W. J. Hemmings, *Emile Zola* (1953, 2nd ed., 1966), 290–96; and the psychological study by John C. Lapp, "The Watcher Betrayed and the Fatal Woman: Some Recurring Patterns in Zola," *P.M.L.A.*, LXXIV (1959), 276–84, as well as the intriguing essay by Chantal Bertrand-Jennings, *L'Eros et la femme chez Zola. De la chute au paradis retrouvé* (1977).

Himes has, of course, much material on England, which has been abundantly studied, though here too the controversies have not died down. J. A. Banks, *Prosperity and Parenthood: A Study of Family Planning Among the Victorian Middle Classes* (1955), and J. A. and Olive Banks, *Feminism and Family Planning* (1964), suggestively attempt to tie birth control to social structures and ideas. Himes's article "Bentham and the Genesis of Neo-Malthusianism," *Economic History*, III (1937), 267–76, somewhat overstates Bentham's clarity and commitment; for a corrective, see William L. Langer, "Origins of the Birth Control Movement in England in the Early Nineteenth Century," *Journal of Interdisciplinary History*, V, 4 (Spring 1975), a masterly summing up. Two informative recent studies deal with infant and maternal mortality in conjunction with social attitudes: A. J. Youngson, *The Scientific Revolution in Victorian Medicine* (1979), and F. B. Smith's (to me important) *The People's Health, 1830–1914* (1979). D. E. C. Eversley, *Social Theories of Fertility and the Malthusian Debate* (1959), is excellent. The evolution of the organized English Malthusians has been well presented by Rosanna Ledbetter, *A History of the Malthusian League 1877–1927* (1976); it can be supplemented with F. D'Arcy, "The Malthusian League and the Resistance to Birth Control Propaganda in Late Victorian Britain," *Population Studies*, XXXI (1977), 429–48. The great Bradlaugh-Besant trial, covered in the Bankses' volumes and elsewhere, now has its own documentation, S. Chandrasekhar, *"A Dirty, Filthy Book": The Writings of Charles Knowlton and Annie Besant on Reproductive Physiology and Birth Control and an Account of the Bradlaugh-Besant Trial* (1981). Angus McLaren, *Birth Control in Nineteenth-Century England* (1978), is stronger on ideas than figures. John W. Innes's older study, *Class Fertility Trends in England and Wales, 1876–1934* (1938), makes important social discriminations and remains worth reading. R. Sauer, "Infanticide and Abortion in 19th-Century Britain," *Population Studies*, XXXII (1978), 81–94, argues that abortions increased as they got safer.

For the pre-nineteenth-century history of contraception, see the work of Peter Laslett and his colleagues at Cambridge, notably his path-breaking *The World We Have Lost* (1965) and *Family Life and Illicit Love in Earlier Generations: Essays in Historical Sociology* (1977). There is much that is informative in the book edited by Laslett, Karla Oosterveen, and Richard M. Smith, *Bastardy and Its Comparative History: Studies in the History of Illegitimacy and Marital Nonconformism in Britain, France, Germany, Sweden, North America, Jamaica and Japan* (1980).

There are some authoritative studies for the United States: James C. Mohr, *Abortion in America: The Origins and Evolution of National Policy* (1978), is a legal history from which I have borrowed; one good supplement is R. Sauer, "Attitudes to Abortion in America, 1800–1973," *Population Studies*, XXVII (1974), 53–68. And see James Reed's informative *From Private Vice to Public Virtue: The Birth Control Movement and American Society Since 1830* (1978). Linda Gordon, "Voluntary Motherhood; The Beginnings of Feminist Birth Control Ideas in the United States," in Mary Hartman and Louise W. Banner, eds., *Clio's Consciousness Raised: New Perspectives on the History of Women* (1974), 54–71, is excellent. So is her book, *Woman's Body, Woman's Right: A Social History of Birth Control in America* (1976). Again Degler, *At Odds* (above, p. 479), esp. chs. IX and X, is informative. Daniel Scott Smith, "Family Limitation, Sexual Control, and Domestic Feminism in Victorian America," *Feminist Studies*, I (1972–73), 40–57, suggests what he calls an emerging "domestic feminism" around the issue of contraception. While David Kennedy, *Birth Control in America: The Career of Margaret Sanger* (above, p. 479), is a little prone to credit "anti-Victorian" clichés about nineteenth-century sexuality, it says what needs saying on the American birth-control pioneer.

Germany was rich in alarmist (often statistically exhaustive) literature on contraception before World War I. There were among others Reinhold Seeberg, *Der Geburtenrückgang in Deutschland. Eine sozialethische Studie* (1913); Elias Schrenk, *Notsignal für das deutsche Volk* (1913); Felix A. Theilhaber, *Das Sterile Berlin. Eine volkswirtschaftliche Studie* (1913); Julius Wolf, *Der Geburtenrückgang* (1913); Jean Bernhard Bornträger, *Der Geburtenrückgang in Deutschland. Seine Bewertung und Bekämpfung* (1913); Max von Gruber, *Ursachen und Bekämpfung des Geburtenrückgangs in Deutschland* (1914). Fritz Winters, *Die deutsche Beamtenfrage* (1918), carefully marshals evidence on just what each child cost a German government employee, complete with inferences to show that these bureaucrats and their wives got the point and acted accordingly.

Recent studies on Germany include John E. Knodel, "Natural Fertility in Pre-Industrial Germany," *Population Studies*, XXXII (1978), 481–510, which persuasively argues that villagers did not on the whole practice birth control; his important book *The Decline of Fertility in Germany, 1871–1939* (1974), and Toni Richards, "Fertility Decline in Germany: An Econometric Appraisal," *Population Studies*, XXXI (1977), 537–54, which suggests industrialization as the principal cause for that decline. Studies of other regions or themes that have proved illuminating to me include J. Sanders, *The Declining Birth Rate in Rotterdam* (1931), which takes the figures back to the 1880s; Ph. Van Praag, "The Development of Neo-Malthusianism in Flanders," *Population Studies*, XXXII (1978), 467–80, which has much on the Roman Catholic counterattack; and Michael Drake's informative *Population and Society in Norway 1735–1865* (1969). Theodore Cianfrani, *A Short History of Obstetrics and Gynecology* (1960), has much of interest. William Petersen, *The Politics of Population* (1964), collects a number of stimulating essays, notably "Notes on the Socialist Position on Birth Control," 90–102. On this issue, see also R. P. Neuman, "Working Class Birth Control in Wilhelmine Germany," *Comparative Studies in Society and History*, XX, 3 (July 1978), 408–28.

The literature on Malthus is large; I have profited from the useful review of the arguments in Kenneth Smith, *The Malthusian Controversy* (1951); see also the somewhat surprising defense by George F. McCleary, *The Malthusian Population Theory* (1953); and, above all, D. V. Glass, ed., *Introduction to Malthus* (1953). Some of Petersen's essays in *Politics of Population*, esp. "Malthusian Theory: A Commentary and Critique" (26–45) and "Marx versus Malthus: The Symbols and the Men" (72–89), are particularly pertinent, as is his book *Malthus* (1979).

For the reformer Henry Wright, see Lewis Perry, *Childhood, Marriage, and Reform: Henry C. Wright, 1797–1870* (1980).

FOUR: Learned Ignorance

One leading psychoanalyst specializing in adolescents has written: "The consolidation at the close of adolescence is accompanied by repressions, producing a state of amnesia reminiscent of the beginnings of the latency period. However, there is an essential difference between the two: at the end of early childhood, memories are closer to the emotions experienced, and the facts are deeply repressed. In contrast, at the end of adolescence, memories contain precise factual details, but the emotions experienced are repressed." Peter Blos, *On Adolescence: A Psychoanalytic Interpretation* (1962), 189. See also his *The Young Adolescent: Clinical Studies* (1970) and Samuel Ritvo, "Adolescent to Woman," *Journal of the American Psychoanalytic Association*, XXIV, 5 (1976), 127–37.

The literature on repression is vast; the concept is, of course, central to all psychoanalytic thinking. The classic is Sigmund Freud's celebrated metapsychological paper, "Die Verdrängung" (1915), *St.A.*, III, 103–18; "Repression," *S.E.*, XIV, 141–58. And see again Ernst Kris, "The Recovery of Childhood Memories" (1956) in *Selected Papers of Ernst Kris* (1975), 301–40; Hans Loewald, "On Internalization" (1973), in *Papers on Psychoanalysis* (1980), 69–86. For the difficult notion of primary repression, see Alvin Frank and Hyman Muslin, "The Development of Freud's Concept of Primal Repression," *Psychoanalytic Study of the Child*, XXII (1967), 55–76; Edward Glover, *The Technique of Psychoanalysis* (1955), ch. 4, and once again Anna Freud's orderly *The Ego and the Mechanisms of Defence* (above, p. 477).

Nineteenth-century innocence about lesbian arrangements (which was just as marked as that about male homosexual ones) is canvassed in the intelligent if strident book by Lillian Faderman, *Surpassing the Love of Men* (above, p. 481). I shall deal with this issue in detail in my next volume, *The Tender Passion*, ch. 3.

For the story of Emily Lytton, later Lutyens, see her moving correspondence with an elderly confidant, *A Blessed Girl: Memories of a Victorian Girlhood, 1887–1896* (1953), Mary Lutyens, *Edwin Lutyens* (1980), and Elizabeth Longford, *A Pilgrimage of Passion: The Life of Wilfrid Scawen Blunt* (1980), esp. 303–21. Annie Besant's early and vigorous *Autobiography* (1893) should be supplemented with Arthur H. Nethercot, *The First Five Lives of Annie Besant* (1960) and *The Last Four Lives of Annie Besant* (1963). The history of Effie Gray Ruskin is well reported in the trilogy by Mary Lutyens, really a copious selection of letters with abundant commentary: *The Ruskins and the Grays* (1972), *Young Mrs. Ruskin in Venice* (1966), and *Millais and the Ruskins* (1967). John Ruskin has proved irresistible to anthologists and biographers. Of the latter, I have found most useful John D. Rosenberg, *The Darkening Glass: A Portrait of Ruskin's Genius* (1961), and Joan Abse, *John Ruskin: The Passionate Moralist* (1981).

What George Sand "knew" has been much debated. Joseph Berry, *Infamous Woman: The Life of George Sand* (1977), 76–81, 392, argues that her early erotic life with her husband was perfectly satisfactory; he quotes from some of her letters to suggest that it was very passionate. André Maurois, *Lélia, ou la vie de George Sand* (1952), 79, calling upon the letter to her half-brother that I have quoted in the text, takes the opposite point of view. Berry has the better of the argument and yet—. For the ambivalence of the Victorians about this most controversial figure, see Paul G. Blount, *George Sand and the Victorian World* (1979).

For the vexed question of male fiasco, see William A. Hammond, *Sexual Impotence in the Male* (1883). Four years later he brought out a second edition expanded to take in women as well: *Sexual Impotence in the Male and Female* (1887). See also Freud's Preface to Maxim Steiner, *Die psychischen Störungen der männlichen Potenz* (1913) [not in *St.A.*], *G.W.*, X, 451; "Preface to Maxim Steiner's *The Psychical Disorders of Male Potency*," *S.E.*, XII, 345–46. Wilhelm Stekel, *Die Impotenz des Mannes* (2nd enlarged ed., 1923), is wild but not useless. I owe much on this point to Dr. Richard Newman.

Modern social historians have in recent years paid much profitable attention to nineteenth-century medicine; the scholarly literature is sizable and excellent. My chief debt is to Richard Harrison Shryock, *The Development of Modern Medicine: An Interpretation of the Social and Scientific Factors Involved*

(1936; ed. 1948), an illuminating extended essay, and Shryock, *Medicine and Society in America, 1660-1860* (1960). Among other highly instructive monographs I single out: M. Jeanne Peterson, *The Medical Profession in Mid-Victorian London* (1978), William G. Rothstein, *American Physicians in the Nineteenth Century: From Sects to Science* (1972), and Jacques Léonard, *Les Médecins de l'ouest au XIXᵉᵐᵉ siècle*, 3 vols. (1978). Léonard's little anthology, *La France médicale au XIXᵉ siècle* (1978), is most satisfactory. For some special issues, see James V. Ricci, *One Hundred Years of Gynecology, 1800-1900* (1945), Jean Donnison, *Midwives and Medical Men* (above, p. 483), and, once again, Haller and Haller, *The Physician and Sexuality in Victorian America* (above, p. 482). Among numerous physicians' autobiographies, I found J. Marion Sims, *The Story of My Life* (1884), most startling. And see Edith Heischkel-Artelt, "Die Welt des praktischen Arztes," in Walter Artelt and Walter Rüegg, eds., *Der Arzt und der Kranke in der Gesellschaft des 19. Jahrhunderts* (1967), 1-16. Most of the other contributions to this interesting symposium deal with the physician in literature. Erna Lesky's bulky *The Vienna Medical School of the 19th Century* (1964; tr. L. Williams and I. S. Levij, 1976), is stodgy but authoritative. Charles E. Rosenberg's collection of thoughtful essays, *No Other Gods: On Science and American Social Thought* (1976), ranges more widely than medicine, but illuminates that, too. I postulated what I call the "Recovery of Nerve" in the eighteenth-century Enlightenment, visualized as a kind of medical enterprise and prelude to the nineteenth-century medical revolution, in *The Enlightenment: An Interpretation*, vol. II, *The Science of Freedom* (1969), ch. 1.

For Tissot, there are Ch. Eynard, *Essai sur la vie de Tissot* (1839), and E. Cochet, *Etude sur S.-A. Tissot. 1728-1797* (1902), a doctoral thesis in the Faculty of Medicine at Paris. It is sobering to note that Cochet, specifically referring to Tissot's anti-masturbation views, can still call him (16) a "profound moralist and well-informed philosopher." A modern study would be welcome. Meanwhile, there is a revealing collection of letters, *Albrecht von Hallers Briefe an Auguste Tissot, 1754-1777*, ed. Erich Hintzsche (1977). On masturbation in general, especially its nineteenth-century "fame," see the wicked and telling third chapter in Alex Comfort, *The Anxiety Makers: Some Curious Preoccupations of the Medical Profession* (1967), "The Rise and Fall of Self-Abuse." Havelock Ellis, *Studies in the Psychology of Sex*, vol. II, *The Evolution of Modesty, the Phenomena of Sexual Periodicity, Auto-Eroticism* (1900), esp. 199-231, is a storehouse of information on which all later literature (including this book) has heavily drawn. René A. Spitz, "Authority and Masturbation: Some Remarks on a Bibliographical Investigation," *Psychoanalytic Quarterly*, XXI, 4 (October 1952), 490-527, is an important article reprinted in *Yearbook of Psychoanalysis*, IX (1953), 113-145. Despite its brave bibliography of 314 items, this essay is, though rich, not exhaustive. And see E. H. Hare, "Masturbatory Insanity: The History of an Idea," *Journal of Mental Science*, CVIII (January 1962), 1-25, as well as the brief, informative article by John Duffy, "Masturbation and Clitoridectomy: A Nineteenth-Century View," *Journal of the American Medical Association*, CLXXXVI (1963), 246-48. There are some instances of surgical interventions in G. J. Barker-Banfield, *The Horrors of the Half-Known Life: Male Attitudes Toward Women and Sexuality in Nineteenth-Century America* (1976), 124–31.

For psychoanalytic views of masturbation, see "Die Onanie, Diskussionen der Wiener Psychoanalytischen Vereinigung" (1912), with Freud's comments, [not in *St.A.*], *G.W.*, XIII, 332–45; "Concluding Remarks" to a *Discussion on Masturbation* (1912), *S.E.*, XII, 241–54. This can be read in conjunction with the evening discussions of the Vienna Psychoanalytic Society of May 25, June 1, and June 8, 1910, with contributions by Freud; summarized in *Protokolle der Wiener Psychoanalytischen Vereinigung*, ed. Herman Nunberg and Ernst Federn, vol. II, *1908–1910* (1977), 502–28. Among other psychoanalytic literature, I cite only Annie Reich, "The Discussion of 1912 on Masturbation and Our Present-Day Views," *Psychoanalytic Study of the Child*, VI (1951), 80–94; Ernst Kris, "Some Comments and Observations on Early Autoerotic Activities," ibid., 95–116; and Jeanne Lampl-DeGroot, "On Masturbation and Its Influence on General Development," ibid., 153–74.

For Freud's famous Schreber case, see his analysis, "Psychoanalytische Bemerkungen über einen autobiographisch beschriebenen Fall von Paranoia (Dementia Paranoides)" (1911), *St.A.*, VII, 133–203; "Psycho-Analytic Notes on an Autobiographical Account of a Case of Paranoia (Dementia Paranoides)" *S.E.*, XII, 3–82. William G. Niederland has written a fascinating commentary, *The Schreber Case: Psychoanalytic Profile of a Paranoid Personality* (1974).

The "flight into knowledge" requires far more historical study. Meanwhile, there is David J. Pivar's scholarly *Purity Crusade: Sexual Morality and Social Control, 1868–1900* (1973), reliable but to my judgment excessively committed to the notion of social control. Joseph R. Gusfield, *Symbolic Crusade: Status Politics and the American Temperance Movement* (1963), follows Richard Hofstadter's socio-psychological thesis of status anxiety. And chs. 1 and 2 of Paul S. Boyer, *Purity in Print: The Vice-Society Movement and Book Censorship in America* (1968), are relevant here. Aaron M. Powell, ed., *The National Purity Congress: Its Papers, Addresses, Portraits* (1896) is revealing mainly as a symptom. Franz Xaver Thalhofer, *Die sexuelle Pädagogik bei den Philanthropen* (1907), is a brief but useful study of the late-eighteenth-century educational reformers. See also in this connection Charles Richmond Henderson, *Education with Reference to Sex, Pathological, Economic and Social Aspects: The Eighth Yearbook of the National Society for the Scientific Study of Education* (1909).

FIVE: Carnal Knowledge

Sigmund Freud wrote some influential papers on children's search for sexual knowledge; see esp. "Zur sexuellen Aufklärung der Kinder (Offener Brief an Dr. M. Fürst)" (1907), *St.A.*, V, 159–68; "The Sexual Enlightenment of Children (An Open Letter to Dr. M. Fürst)," *S.E.*, IX, 129–39; "Über infantile Sexualtheorien" (1908), *St.A.*, V, 169–84; "On the Sexual Theories of Children," *S.E.*, IX, 205–26; and "Der Familienroman der Neurotiker" (1909), *St.A.*, IV, 221–26; "Family Romances," *S.E.*, IX, 235–41. And see Selma Fraiberg, "Enlightenment and Confusion," *Psychoanalytic Study of the Child*, VI (1951), 325–35; as well as Eleanor Galenson and Herman Roiphe, "The Impact of Early Sexual Discovery on Mood, Defensive Organization, and Symbolization," ibid., XXVI (1971), 195–216. Phyllis Greenacre has made the family romance (especially of writers) her own, esp. in her papers "The Childhood of the Artist: Libidinal Phase Development and Giftedness" (1957) and "The Family Romance of the Artist" (1958), both in *Emotional Growth*, II, 479–504, 505–32 (above, p. 479). Linda Joan Kaplan's survey of the literature, "The Concept of the Family Romance," *Psychoanalytic Review*, LXI, 2 (1974), 169–202, with an exhaustive bibliography, is most informative. Maynard Solomon's fine biography, *Beethoven* (1977), works out the family romance of one famous exemplar.

As is only too well known, Sigmund Freud developed his theory about the centrality of fantasies in mental life by learning to discount the reports of his female hysterical patients that they had been seduced by their fathers. Nothing, though, that Freud wrote in 1897, when he made the discovery that these confessions were indeed fantasies, or anything he said later, led him to complete skepticism about such reports. Freud to Wilhelm Fliess, *Aus den Anfängen der Psychoanalyse*, 229; and Peter Gay, "Sigmund Freud: A German and His Discontents," in *Freud, Jews and Other Germans*, 86–87; above, pp. 463, 464. Freud's record on the issue is complicated by his denying twice—in two early case histories of hysteria—that it had been the patient's father who had assaulted or mistreated her. He made amends, with some severe self-criticisms, in the second edition in 1924; see *G.W.*, I, 195n, 238n; *S.E.*, II, 134n, 170n.

In addition to the titles in the footnotes on the individuals I instance, there is, for Logan Pearsall Smith, the fascinating family study by Barbara Strachey, *Remarkable Relations: The Story of the Pearsall Smith Family* (1981).

The delicate subject of menstruation in literature and public discussion requires more work. Janice Delaney, Mary Jane Lupton, and Emily Toth, *The Curse: A Cultural History of Menstruation* (1976) is a first step; it ranges widely among anthropological studies. Patricia Crawford, "Attitudes to Menstruation in Seventeenth-Century England," *Past and Present*, No. 91 (1981), 47–73, offers some interesting comparisons with earlier days. Some brief comments on the taboo (with scathing references to Drs. Clarke and Maudsley) are in Elaine and English Showalter, "Victorian Women and Menstruation," in Vicinus, *Suffer and Be Still* (above, p. 484), 38–44. Hays, *Dangerous Sex*, and Lederer, *Fear of Women* (above, p. 482), are pertinent here. Amid the psychoanalytic literature (not very rich on this subject) perhaps the most interesting is Judith S. Kestenberg, "Menarche," in Sandor Lorand and Henry Schneer, eds., *Adolescents: Psychoanalytic Approach to Problems and Therapy* (1965), 19–50.

Public nursing on the railroad is immortalized in several portrayals by Daumier; and see the picture in Paul Hastings, *Railroads: An International History* (1972), 99. Eric Trudgill has further evidence on unashamed nude bathing in Victorian England in *Madonnas and Magdalens* (above, p. 466), 5–7. On the decline of public hanging, complete with a depiction of the last one in 1868, see David D. Cooper, *The Lesson of the Scaffold: The Public Execution Controversy in Victorian England* (1974); the illustration precedes p. 165.

Death was something of a staple in children's stories, of which the notorious gruesome scene in Mrs. Sherwood's *The Fairchild Children* is only the most egregious: the father takes his children to see the rotting corpse of a hanged thief to enforce some moral lesson. See David Gryllis, *Guardians and Angels: Parents and Children in Nineteenth-Century Literature* (1978).

On how to read advice-literature, in addition to Freeman's biography of Mrs. Beeton listed above (p. 485), once again note the judicious comments by Patricia Branca, *Silent Sisterhood* (above, p. 466).

Marryat's "report" on those prudish American ladies draping the "limbs" of their pianos in frilly trousers made history. Carl N. Degler was among the first to establish Marryat's responsibility for this myth, and lists a number of recent historians who have actually taken this story seriously. This peculiar bit of prudishness is either wholly fictitious, unique, or very rare. Degler, "What Ought to Be," above, p. 468. He could have added G. Rattray Taylor, who writes that to call a chicken leg a "leg" was offensive to the Victorians; to call a chicken breast a "bosom" was "at least as applied to chickens" an "American refinement, as was the fitting of piano legs with crinolines—though not, it seems, chair-legs, which presumably were too thin to inspire lascivious thoughts." *Sex in History* (1954), 215. There is also Duncan Crow, *The Victorian Woman* (1971), 29. The myth is also treated as true by Bonnie G. Smith: "The sexual symbolism of the home is perhaps most famously illustrated by the Victorian ladies who recognized the sexual potency of table legs and covered them from sight." *Ladies of the Leisure Class* (above, p. 474), 83. It was widely credited by the middle of the nineteenth century. In 1860, in a scathing notice of Walt Whitman's *Leaves of Grass*, the London *Saturday Review* scornfully referred to the United States as "the country where piano-legs wear frilled trousers." X (July 7, 1860), 19.

The historian of pornography runs the risk of taking it not seriously enough or too seriously. Extremists of either camp claim sophistication: the first insisting that it is philistine to despise "dirty" books when they simply celebrate sensuality; the second, that it is vulgar, indeed pretentious, to elevate such boring, monotonous stuff to the level of art. That the erotic may legitimately call itself art is certainly amply demonstrated in the nineteenth century—I think of Flaubert, of Browning, among many others. At the same time, some fiction, normally of scant (or no) literary merit, was produced in that century with the sole mercenary purpose of stirring up sexual excitement, and in the most mechanical way. It is this sub-literature I have called "pornography" in the text.

The scholarship on the subject, though growing, remains limited and its results, so far, frustrating. Most work remains to be done on the publishers of smut (or "erotica"), whether cheap or fanciful and expensive. And references to the consumption of pornography and its psychological impact are hard to come by. Even the Institute for Sex Research (Kinsey Institute) at Bloomington, Indiana, though immensely rich in primary material, has very little scholarship on such questions in its holdings. An instructive instance of just how hard it can be to establish authorship of pornographic works is *Schwester Monika erzählt und erfährt* . . . (1815), often attributed to E. T. A. Hoff-

mann, but wrongly. See, for a cautious verdict, Claudio Magris, "Das andere
Elixir des Teufels: E. T. A. Hoffmann und die Schwester Monika," in *Die
andere Vernunft. E. T. A. Hoffmann* (1980), 109–18.

The most important source of information for nineteenth-century (and
earlier) pornography remains Pisanus Fraxi [Henry Spencer Ashbee], *Index
Librorum Prohibitorum: Being Notes Bio-Biblio-Icono-graphical and Critical,
on Curious and Uncommon Books* (1877), followed by *Centuria Librorum
Absconditorum* (1879) and *Catena Librorum Tacendorum* (1885), a trio of
gold mines. See Steven Marcus, *The Other Victorians*, which I have criticized
for its ventures into cultural history (above, pp. 467–68), ch. 2. Marcus is also rewarding in his analyses of individual pornographic works (esp. chs. 5 and 7),
though I do not agree with his account of a historical development from dependence on polite literature to self-enclosed autonomy. David Foxon's well-
known articles on early erotica, "Libertine Literature in England, 1660–1745,"
Book Collector, XII, 1, 2, 3 (Spring, Summer, Winter, 1963), 21–36, 159–77,
294–307, are impressively informative. General histories are necessarily anecdotal
and slight, and prone to copy from one another. H. Montgomery Hyde, *A
History of Pornography* (1964), is the best that I have read. Vern Bullough's
Sexual Variance (above, p. 467) has some useful scattered comments, as does
Wayland Young, *Eros Denied* (above, p. 467), esp. 54–58, 87–92, 361–67.

Compendia of value (in addition to those of "Pisanus Fraxi" just listed) include Eduard Fuchs, *Geschichte der erotischen Kunst*, 3 vols. (1912–26), richly
illustrated, and Jules Gay, *Bibliographie des ouvrages relatifs à l'amour, aux
femmes et au mariage*, 6 vols. (1871–73).

For incest, the older and bulky psychoanalytically oriented study of literature
by Otto Rank, *Das Inzest-Motiv in Dichtung und Sage* (1912; 2nd ed., 1926),
retains its interest. Henry Miles, *Forbidden Fruit: A Study of the Incest Theme
in Erotic Literature* (1973), does not live up to its promising title; it veers between angry denunciations and extensive quotations from pornographic books.
Eberhard and Phyllis Kronhausen, *Pornography and the Law* (1959; rev. ed.,
1964) seeks to discriminate between the psychology of "erotic realism" and that
of hard-core pornography. The distinction works fairly well, and the book
attempts, in addition to dealing with legal issues, to offer a psychological
profile of pornography. Gardner Lindzey's informative paper "Some Remarks
Concerning Incest, the Incest Taboo, and Psychoanalytic Theory," *American
Psychologist*, XXII (1967), 1051–59, has important comments on the rarity of
mother-son incest.

The Kronhausen book shows the interest in the legal history of forbidden
books. For Germany there is the encyclopedic work by H. H. Houben,
Verbotene Literatur von der klassischen Zeit bis zur Gegenwart, 2 vols.
(1924, 1928). For France, see Paul Lapeire, *Essai juridique et historique sur
l'outrage aux bonnes moeurs par le livre, l'écrit et l'imprimé* (1931), a dry and
specialized thesis. The lively, judicious pages in F. W. J. Hemmings, *Culture
and Society in France* (see above, p. 471), esp. ch. II, "The Blue-Pencil Regime,"
are most helpful, as is Alexandre Zévaès, *Les Procès littéraires au XIXe siècle*
(1924), which narrates and documents such famous trials as those of Flaubert
and Baudelaire and some more obscure ones. The best treatment of the English
law (and cultural temper), from which I have learned much, is Norman St.

John-Stevas, *Obscenity and the Law* (1956), with a most helpful bibliography. It may be usefully supplemented with Alec Craig, *The Banned Books of England and Other Countries: A Study of the Conception of Literary Obscenity* (1962), which brings in the comparative dimension. A report by the Working Party set up by a conference convened by the Chairman of the Arts Council of Great Britain, with a foreword by John Montgomerie, *The Obscenity Laws* (1969) is most interesting, containing testimony from clergymen, psychologists, and other experts. For the United States, see James Jackson Kilpatrick, *The Smut Peddlers* (1960); Rugoff, *Prudery and Passion* (above, p. 466), 124–25, 316–19, is not very revealing. Ludwig Marcuse, *Obszön: Geschichte einer Entrüstung* (1962), is a German publicist's exercise in indignation against the censors; it contains lively retellings of familiar cases, like the attacks on Friedrich Schlegel's *Lucinde*, the trials of *Emma Bovary* and *Les Fleurs du mal*, and others—useful mainly for those new to the subject.

The vexed moral issues raised by this kind of literature are canvassed in many of the titles just cited. Additional comment may be found in Harry M. Clor, *Obscenity and Public Morality: Censorship in a Liberal Society* (1969), which seeks a middle way between censoriousness and utter permissiveness. Michael J. Goldstein and Harold S. Kant, with John J. Hartman, have explored the difficult issue of the psychological effects of obscene literature in *Pornography and Sexual Deviance* (1973). It lists many recent studies. A study of the collectors of erotica would repay the labor; there are only a few (useful if slightly apologetic) pages on that side of the subject in James Pope-Hennessy, *Monckton Milnes: The Years of Promise, 1809–1851* (1949), and *Monckton Milnes: The Flight of Youth, 1851–1885* (1951).

The fury of feminists at pornography is easy to understand; in recent years, the number and imaginative fervor of cruel acts against women in these publications seem to have greatly increased. See Don Smith, "Sexual Aggression in American Pornography: The Stereotype of Race" (1976), as cited in Laura Lederer, ed., *Take Back the Night: Women on Pornography* (1980, ed. 1982), 210–11; the whole anthology, though repetitive and polemical, is valuable. It raises, once again, the vexed question of whether reading is a stimulus inviting imitation or a catharsis making imitation unnecessary. While a good psychoanalytic study of the moral fanatic remains a desideratum, there is the amusing but scholarly and responsible biography by Heywood Broun and Margaret Leach, *Anthony Comstock: Roundsman of the Lord* (1927); while Robert Bremner's edition of Comstock's *Traps for the Young* (1883; ed. 1967) has a good if rather short introduction.

Two of Swinburne's erotic tales, of which the masochistic *Lesbia Brandon* is of special interest, were issued in 1963, with an introduction by Edmund Wilson: *The Novels of A. C. Swinburne*. Cecil Y. Lang's splendid edition of *The Swinburne Letters*, 6 vols. (1958–62), has fascinating material. Among particular studies I note Clyde Kenneth Hyder, *Swinburne's Literary Career and Fame* (1933), and Hyder's compilation *Swinburne: The Critical Heritage* (1970). The best biographies are Georges Lafourcade, *Swinburne: A Literary Biography* (1932), and Jean Overton Fuller, *Swinburne: A Critical Biography* (1968). George Moore's angry *Literature at Nurse: or Circulating Morals* (1885) is worth reading. On the censorship role of the English lending libraries, there is Guinevere L. Griest, *Mudie's Circulating Library and the Victorian Novel* (1970). See also Amy Cruse, *The Victorians and Their Books* (1935), and G. R. Pocklington, *The Story of W. H. Smith & Son* (privately printed, 1921).

Finally, but not least, there is Weston LaBarre's judicious statement on the relativity of the obscene in "Obscenity: An Anthropological Appraisal," in "Obscenity and the Arts," a symposium published in *Law and Contemporary Problems* (Autumn 1955), 533–43.

The naked body in art has garnered a certain amount of scholarly attention. The (justly) most-cited modern title is Kenneth Clark, *The Nude: A Study in Ideal Form* (1956), learned, valuable, opinionated. See also Jean Cassou and Geoffrey Grigson, *The Female Form in Painting* (1953), a useful historical sweep; and the older book by Julius Lange, *Die menschliche Gestalt in der Geschichte der Kunst* (1903). Edward Lucie-Smith, *Eroticism in Western Art* (1972), races through the centuries; not without its uses, it overstates the general conscious cynicism: he observes "how instinctively" successful nineteenth-century academic artists "responded to the needs of the contemporary public that supported them, and how ingenious were some of the formulae which they discovered for combining titillation with respectability" (121). I grant the instinct at work; I find the ingenuity arguable. Fuchs, *Geschichte der erotischen Kunst* (above, p. 496), is relevant here. For the painter of the most controversial nudes of the nineteenth century, Edouard Manet, see my *Art and Act: On Causes in History—Manet, Gropius, Mondrian* (1976), ch. 2, with an annotated bibliography. See also Beatrice Farwell, *Manet and the Nude: A Study in Iconography in the Second Empire* (1973), and George Heard Hamilton's informative *Manet and His Critics* (1954; ed. 1969), which has taught me much. Stephen Kern has some comments on nineteenth-century aesthetic conventions, including that of omitting pubic hair, in his *Anatomy and Destiny* (above, p. 466). A number of artists, including Johann Heinrich Fuseli, who did not, after all, scruple to imagine (or remember) some very erotic postures, would on occasion draw naked males without genitals at all. See Fuseli's pencil drawing *A Naked Warrior Attacking with a raised Sword* (between 1805 and 1810), reproduced in the *Times Literary Supplement*, March 13, 1981, 281.

For Prud'hon, see Jean Guiffrey, *L'Oeuvre de P.-P. Prud'hon* (1924), which supplements such revealing earlier appraisals as Pierre Gauthiez, *Prud'hon* (1886), and Charles Clément, *Prud'hon. Sa vie, ses oeuvres et sa correspondance* (3rd ed., 1880). For frontal nudity resembling the Prud'hon I reproduce, see M. Mercie's *Le Génie des arts guidé par la France*, obviously borrowed from Prud'hon's invention. Henri Havard, *L'Art à travers les moeurs* (1882), 399.

For Canova, in addition to a few comments in Clark's *Nude*, there is Mario Praz, "Canova: Ice and Eros," in Thomas B. Hess and John Ashbery, ed., *Academic Art* (1971), 165–66, and Robert M. Adams, *The Roman Stamp: Frame and Facade in Some Forms of Neo-Classicism* (1974), esp. 162–83. Among earlier informative appraisals of Canova, the best are J. S. Memes, *Memoirs of Antonio Canova with a Critical Analysis of His Works, and an Historical View of Modern Sculpture* (1825); and Quatremère de Quince, *Canova et ses ouvrages, ou Mémoires historiques sur la vie et les travaux de ce célèbre artiste* (1834).

There is useful material in Ennio Francia, ed., *Delfina de Custine, Luisa Stolberg, Giuletta Racamier a Canova. Lettere inedite* (1972).

Of the ample literature on other nineteenth-century nudes, I single out Eugenia P. Janis, *Degas Monotypes* (1968). Courbet's explicit nudes are so familiar as to require no discussion. Jean-François Millet, too, drew some candid nudes, including a pair of lovers. See Robert L. Herbert's catalogue *Barbizon Revisited* (1962), nos. 60, 62. For that celebrated painter of smooth, hairless, but seductive nudes, Ingres, I recall Rosenblum's study, above, p. 485.

That once-celebrated but now little-regarded English painter of nudes, William Etty, has been well served by Dennis Farr, *William Etty* (1958), and by W. Gaunt and F. Gordon Roe, *Etty and the Nude: The Art and Life of William Etty, R. A., 1787-1849* (1943). See also Philip Gilbert Hamerton, "Etty" (1875) in *Portfolio Papers* (1889), 39-101. In his biographical sections, Hamerton leans heavily on Alexander Gilchrist, *Life of William Etty, R.A.*, 2 vols. (1855). For Mulready, see Kathryn Moore Heleniak, *William Mulready* (1980).

Hiram Powers is quoted at length in C. Edwards Lester, *The Artist, the Merchant, and the Statesmen of the Age of the Medici, and of Our Own Times*, 2 vols. (1845), I, 86-88. Amid a sizable body of work on Powers, the most important are William H. Gerdts, "Marble and Nudity," *Art in America*, LIX, part I, January-June 1971 (May-June), 60-67; Linda Hyman, "*The Greek Slave* by Hiram Powers," *Art Journal*, XXXV, 3 (Spring 1976), 216-23; Neil Harris, *The Artist in American Society: The Formative Years, 1790-1860* (1966), 100, 132-39. There are also important comments and illustrations in Gerdts, *American Neo-Classic Sculpture: The Marble Resurrection* (1973), 30-34, 52-55, and Margaretta Lovell, "Hiram Powers' *The Greek Slave*: Virtue in Chains," in Yale Art Gallery, *American Arts and the American Experience* (n.d.), 27. For Powers in London, see C. H. Gibbs-Smith, *The Great Exhibition of 1851*, Commemorative Album, Victoria and Albert Museum (1950; ed. 1964), 129. American nudes are interestingly explored by David Sellin, *The First Pose. 1876: Turning Point in American Art* (1976).

Amid a growing literature on naked children, see esp. Morton N. Cohen, *Lewis Carroll, Photographer of Children: Four Nude Studies* (1978). The illustrated booklet on rather erotic pre-pubertal girls by Graham Ovenden, *Nymphets & Fairies: Three Victorian Children's Illustrators* (1976), is suggestive (in more ways than one). There is another interesting example by Thomas Couture, *A Young Bather* (1849), in Albert Boime, *Thomas Couture and the Eclectic Vision* (1980), 336.

Peter Fusco and H. W. Janson, eds., *The Romantics to Rodin: French Nineteenth-Century Sculpture from North American Collections* (1980), is an informative catalogue. For Clésinger's model, and a good instance of a naivete that treats the snake as harmless, see (for the first) Edmond and Jules de Goncourt, *Journal; mémoires de la vie littéraire 1851-1896*, ed. Robert Ricatte, 22 vols. (1956-58), I, 117, and (for the second) the editor's note (117n). See also the important sculpture section in the exhibition catalogue *The Second Empire, 1852-1870: Art in France under Napoleon III* (1978). Benedict Read's excellent, exhaustively documented *Victorian Sculpture* (1982) has nudes scattered throughout, esp. in ch. 2; John Gibson's *The Tinted Venus* (illus-

trated on 42) is a remarkable instance of an attempt at reproducing classical
Greek painted sculpture and (as one contemporary critic put it) of a "naked,
impudent English woman" (25).

For Hasselberg, the Swedish sculptor, there is the copiously illustrated but
rather skimpy memorial volume, *Per Hasselberg, 1850–1894* (1898).

SIX: Fortifications for the Self

By far the most useful treatment of nineteenth-century "hypocrisy" I have
read—though my conclusions, grounded in psychoanalytic thinking, are rather
different—is ch. XIV of Walter Houghton's *Victorian Frame of Mind* (above,
p. 467). I have drawn on its rich materials. Houghton divides Victorian hypocrisy
into conformity, moral pretension, and evasion and gives space to "anti-
hypocrisy." Like Houghton, I have derived much from George Eliot's spirited
attack on the Evangelicals in "Evangelical Teaching: Dr. Cumming," *Westminster Review*, LXIV (1855), 436–62. Lionel Trilling's suavely combative
Sincerity and Authenticity (1972) is marginal to my argument but repays
study. The titles I have discussed under attitudes toward sexuality (those by
Walters, Pearsall, Rugoff, Crow, Fraser Harrison, Trudgill, Hobsbawm,
Cominos, Beales, and Glover—above, pp. 466–67) are informative but (except
for the last-named) too censorious to capture the unconscious conflicts beneath
the self-satisfied surface. In contrast, Mario Praz's imaginative and compendious
Romantic Agony (above, p. 485) contains some splendid analytical pages,
especially on Thackeray. The best general biography of this key figure is
Gordon N. Ray, *Thackeray: The Uses of Adversity, 1811–1846* (1955), and
Thackeray: The Age of Wisdom, 1847–1863 (1958). Ray's earlier, compact
*The Buried Life: A Study of the Relation Between Thackeray's Fiction and His
Personal Life* (1952) is illuminating. Theodore Zeldin has some comments on
hypocrisy in France in *France 1848–1945*, vol. II (above, p. 488). A recent
analysis of the Evangelical mind is Ian C. Bradley, *The Call to Seriousness: The
Evangelical Impact on the Victorians* (1976). Among biographies and studies of
the hypocrite-hunters, I only list a few I have found most helpful: Alan Bell,
Sydney Smith: A Biography (1980), authoritative but, in view of the subject's
wit, not long enough; Richard M. Kelly, ed., *The Best of Mr. Punch: The
Humorous Writings of Douglas Jerrold* (1970), an ample anthology; again
Kaplan, *Whitman* (above, p. 480); Alastair Buchan, *The Spare Chancellor: The
Life of Walter Bagehot* (1959), the best biography of the brilliant editor,
publicist, and economist whom G. M. Young thought the archetypal Victorian.
For Lester Ward see the entries above, p. 481. There is good literature on Pugin,
notably Phoebe Stanton, *Pugin* (1971), Michael Trappes-Lomax, *Pugin: A
Medieval Victorian* (1932), an outstanding study; and Henry-Russell Hitch-
cock, *Early Victorian Architecture in Britain*, 2 vols. (1954). Christopher
Ricks's clever and amusing *Keats and Embarrassment* (1974) deals with the
things that made nineteenth-century people blush—or not. August Strindberg's
concerted assault on "hypocrisy" (and not just in Sweden) still aches for a
monograph; meanwhile, there is a brief anthology, *Ein Lesebuch für die
niederen Stände*, ed. Jan Myrdal (1977).

In his informative study of German small and middle-sized towns, principally in the eighteenth century, Mack Walker paints a convincing portrait of strict morality, much of it "hypocritical," which is to say, dictated less by internalized feelings of guilt than by fear of social disapproval: "Hometownsmen would not buy their sausages from an adulterer, a liar, a blasphemer, a cheat, if only for fear of what their neighbors would say if they did; and if a neighborhood butcher was one of those things they would know it and his business would fail." *German Home Towns* (above, p. 473), 101.

The controversies surrounding Dickens's ventures into social criticism are lucidly laid out in George H. Ford, *Dickens and His Readers: Aspects of Novel-Criticism Since 1836* (1955), and anthologized in Philip Collins, ed., *Dickens: The Critical Heritage* (1971). The best-known and most extensive biography, Edgar Johnson, *Charles Dickens: His Tragedy and Triumph*, 2 vols. (1952), is reliable on facts but naive on Dicken's critique of society. Humphry House, *The Dickens World* (1941; 2nd ed., 1942), is a brilliant corrective for such earnest superficiality.

Hardy's travail with editors, publishers, and the public is best summarized in Michael Millgate, *Thomas Hardy: A Biography* (1982), which I have quoted. Robert Gittings's slightly earlier biographies, *Young Thomas Hardy* (1975) and *The Older Hardy* (1978), are also excellent. Merle Mowbray Bevington, *The Saturday Review 1855-1868: Representative Educated Opinion in Victorian England* (1941), is a dependable treatment of a conservative, vehement, influential Victorian periodical, equally relevant to social critics and the Victorian family ideology. All of David Newsome's delightful *Godliness and Good Learning: Four Studies on a Victorian Ideal* (1961), but particularly 46–48, reveals the nineteenth-century passion for truthfulness.

The family has in recent years enjoyed considerable vogue among historians. I shall concentrate, of course, on titles dealing with, or at least including, the bourgeois family. For the "prehistorians" on whom I concentrate in the text, see Michael Z. Brooke, *Le Play: Engineer and Social Scientist* (1970), terse but informative; Andrée Michel, "Les Cadres sociaux de la doctrine morale de Frédéric Le Play," *Cahiers Internationaux de Sociologie*, XXXIV (1963), 47–68; the collection *Recueil d'études sociales publié à la mémoire de Frédéric Le Play* (1956); and the anthology *Frédéric Le Play (1806–1882). Textes Choisis* (1947), ed. Louis Baudin, with a substantial introduction (3–61). Riehl haunts books on the origins of Nazism, but the full treatment remains to be done. On those origins and Riehl, see George L. Mosse, *The Crisis of German Ideology: Intellectual Origins of the Third Reich* (1966), esp. 19–24. Victor v. Geramb, *Wilhelm Heinrich Riehl. Leben und Wirken (1823–1897)* (1954), is a vast labor of love—or, better, of adoration. All the facts are there, but drowned out by embarrassing rhapsodies. There are some fleeting comments in Ernest K. Bramsted, *Aristocracy and the Middle-Classes in Germany: Social Types in German Literature 1830-1900* (1937; 2nd ed., 1964), and a refreshingly scathing section in Klaus Bergmann, *Agrarromantik und Grosstadtfeindlichkeit* (1970), 38–49, which treats Riehl as the father of a pernicious agrarian romanticism. But see also Georg Schwägler, *Soziologie der Familie. Ursprung und Entwicklung* (1970), which intelligently compares Le Play and Riehl in the early chapters. In fairness I add George Eliot's long appreciation of Riehl's *Land und*

Leute and *Die bürgerliche Gesellschaft* in "The Natural History of German Life: Riehl," *Westminster Review*, LXVI (July 1856), 51–79 (an article I owe to Peter Demetz); it recognizes Riehl's conservatism but lauds his sense of the concrete. For another tradition in German sociology, see A. Oberschall, *Empirical Social Research in Germany, 1848–1914* (1965).

Essential to finding one's way among the thickets of recent debates is Michael Mitterauer and Reinhard Sieder, *The European Family: Patriarchy to Partnership from the Middle Ages to the Present* (1977; tr. Karl Oosterveen and Manfred Hörzinger, 1982), rational, persuasive and, in the English version, equipped with comprehensive, valuable bibliographies. "The transition from the large to the small family in the course of industrialization that is presumed by family sociologists," Mitterauer notes tersely, "is a phenomenon that can be disproved statistically" (27). (In the Preface, Peter Laslett cannot deny himself the sneer, "it is a delicious irony that . . . Viennese historians should have demonstrated that the Oedipus phenomenon cannot be called a human universal, but belongs historically to the imperial Vienna where Sigmund Freud himself resided" [viii]. The book, in my judgment, demonstrates no such thing, but Laslett's comment underscores once again the uneasiness of most historians with psychoanalytic propositions.) Laslett's own work has been invaluable, beginning with *The World We Have Lost* (above, p. 489). All, or practically all, of the titles I listed in the pages dealing with population and birth control (above, pp. 486–90) are pertinent here. So is John R. Gillis, *Youth and History: Tradition and Change in European Age Relations 1770–Present* (1974; expanded ed., 1981), especially the first half of the book; an important monograph.

Among sociological studies of the family, I single out Talcott Parsons and Robert F. Bales, *Family, Socialization and Interaction Processes* (1955). And Carl Degler's *At Odds* (above, p. 479) also belongs in this section.

English nineteenth-century historians deal with the family as a matter of course. A number of titles cited before, notably Perkin, Briggs, Best, Kitson Clark, Checkland and Burn (above, p. 472) are valuable here. I add J. F. C. Harrison, *The Early Victorians: 1832–51* (1971). Zeldin, *France, 1848–1945*, esp. I, chs. 11–13 (above, p. 471) is informative on the French family; the footnotes are exceptionally helpful in locating other sources or monographs. Earlier works, no less interesting as symptoms than as informants, include Miss Betham-Edwards, *Home Life in France* (1905), and Barrett Wendell, *The France of Today* (1907; 2nd ed., 1909). For the family life of the rich in the Nord, see Bonnie Smith, *Ladies of the Leisure Class* (above, p. 474). Mary P. Ryan's stimulating *Cradle of the Middle Classes: The Family in Oneida County, New York, 1790–1865* (1981) documents the survival of the stem family and communal intrusiveness right into the nineteenth century.

Most of these titles, and those I am about to list, have informed my estimate of the pre-nineteenth-century middle-class family, which recent historical writing has at once clarified and thrown into confusion. I owe much to Norbert Elias's long-neglected and now-celebrated *The History of Manners: The Civilizing Process* and *The Civilizing Process: Power and Civility* (both orig. 2nd ed., 1969; tr. Edmund Jephcott, 1982). Still the best psychoanalytic treatment, though somewhat dated, is J. C. Flügel, *The Psycho-Analytic Study of the Family* (1921). My own judgment, based on wide if somewhat impressionistic reading, must be tentative. Lawrence Stone's bulky and ambitious *The Family, Sex and Marriage in England 1500–1800* (1977) teems with interesting details, but its general scheme—from the open lineage family to the restricted patriarchal family to the closed domesticated family—though hedged with qualifications, is not convincing; nor is its bleak assessment of early modern coarseness and intrafamilial cruelty. Stone's *The Historical Origins of the Modern Family* (1982), a lecture printed as a pamphlet, offers further cautious disclaimers but leaves the structure of his argument intact. Edward Shorter's slangy *Making of the Modern Family* (above, p. 487) takes the same view. I must plead guilty to having propagated the idea of the callous early modern family until the evidence persuaded me otherwise. In my edition of *John Locke on Education* (1964), I quoted Montaigne's notorious remark, "I have lost two or three children in their infancy, not without regret, but without great grief" (in "Of the Affection of Fathers for Their Children") and commented on his inability to recall the very number: "Even in Locke's time," I wrote, "and after, a child's survival was so problematical that parents usually covered their losses in advance, by refusing to invest too much emotion in their offspring" (2). But, first, Montaigne was probably not typical and, second, his remark may really be a successful defense against a deep sense of loss.

Stone has been taken to task, briskly by Charles and Louise A. Tilly, "The Rise and Fall of the Bourgeois Family, as Told by Lawrence Stone and Christopher Lasch," Center for Research in Social Organization Working Paper No. 191 (January 1979), politely by Keith Thomas, "The Changing Family," *Times Literary Supplement* (October 21, 1977), 1226–27, and very sternly by Alan Macfarlane, reviewing Stone's book in *History and Theory*, XVIII, 1 (1979), 103–26. Both Thomas and Macfarlane (who calls Stone's big book a "disaster," 124) offer ample evidence to force serious amendments to Stone's thesis, if not its total abandonment. Macfarlane has buttressed his case in *The Family Life of Ralph Josselin: A Seventeenth-Century Clergyman* (1970) and in his speculative and aggressive revision of English social history, *The Origins of English Individualism: The Family, Property and Social Transition* (1978)—note esp. 59–60. Several essays in R. B. Outhwaite, ed., *Marriage and Society: Studies in the Social History of Marriage* (1981), challenge Stone's (and Shorter's) conclusions. Edmund Morgan's brilliant, pioneering *The Puritan Family: Religion and Domestic Relations in Seventeenth-Century New England* (1944; new ed. 1966) should have effectively demolished the old cliché of cold, prudish premoderns head-on—but evidently has not. See also, on the American theme, Bernard Bailyn's masterly essay *Education in the Forming of American Society* (1960) and John Demos's fine Eriksonian monograph *A Little Commonwealth* (above, p. 465n). G. R. Quaife, *Wanton Wenches and Wayward Wives: Peasants and Illicit Sex in Early Seventeenth Century England* (1979), is unfortunately titled, for it is a sober, highly instructive study of the sexual lives of the rural populations of Somerset between 1601 and 1660; it firmly asserts that "there was no privacy" (16) but insists that even the poor knew about love—an explicit refutation of Shorter's and Stone's views (see "Conclusion," 243–49, and the ample documentation throughout). While Quaife concentrates on "peasants," his conclusions on affection must hold *a fortiori* for the middling orders. In this connection, too, Jean-Louis

Flandrin's writings, most notably his essays in *Le Sexe et l'occident* and *Families in Former Times* (above, pp. 467, 488), are subtle and largely persuasive. On the other side, see Miriam Slater, "The Weightiest Business: Marriage in an Upper-Gentry Family in Seventeenth-Century England," *Past and Present*, No. 72 (August 1976), 25–42, which supports Stone on the central role that interest played in early-modern English marriage alliances. The books are not yet closed.

One interesting clue to the history of the family is obviously the treatment of children. It naturally appears in practically all the titles I have listed. Philippe Ariès's seductive *Centuries of Childhood: A Social History of Family Life* (1960; tr. Robert Baldick, 1962) long held the field; its account of the "discovery of childhood" as a fairly recent phenomenon seemed overwhelmingly convincing. One significant result was David Hunt, *Parents and Children in History: The Psychology of Family Life in Early Modern France* (1971), which added Erik Erikson to Philippe Ariès. The heavy reliance of both on the journal of Dr. Jean Héroard, physician to the young Louis XIII, the journal that contains some fairly fantastic assertions about the little prince's sexual play, has raised some questions, and the "discovery of childhood" remains controversial. As for Erikson, his early, "tough" work, of which *Childhood and Society* (1950; 2nd ed., 1963) is a good instance, is superior to his later work in which childhood sexuality takes a more marginal place. Among recent work on childhood, J. H. Plumb's beautifully informed "The New World of Children in Eighteenth-Century England," *Past and Present*, No. 67 (May 1975), 64–95, is outstanding. Peter Coveney, *The Image of Childhood: The Individual and Society. A Study of the Theme in English Literature* (1967), confronts the literary evidence. Ivy Pinckbeck and Mary Hewitt, *Children in English Society*, 2 vols. (1969, 1973), particularly the second, *From the Eighteenth Century to the Children Act, 1948*, are strong on class, economic, and legal aspects. For France, there is still the old Charles de Ribbe, *Les Familles et la société en France avant la révolution*, 2 vols. (1879), as much document as source, and Edmond Pilon, *La Vie de famille au dix-huitième siècle* (1923). And see George Boas, *The Cult of Childhood* (1966), an elegant intellectual historian's view. Lloyd de Mause, ed., *The History of Childhood* (1974), is something of a mixed bag; the editor's bulky introduction proposes a kind of psychoanalytic Whig history, with things getting better and better. Individual contributors take children through the ages; Priscilla Robertson, "Home as a Nest: Middle Class Childhood in Nineteenth-Century Europe" (407–31), is most relevant to this volume.

Dieter Claessens, *Familie und Wertsystem. Eine Studie zur "zweiten, soziokulturellen Geburt" des Menschen und der Belastbarkeit der "Kernfamilie"* (1962; 3rd ed., 1972), canvasses the fate of the nuclear family. Among German sociologists working on the family none has been more effective than René König; see esp. *Materialien zur Soziologie der Familie* (2nd ed., 1974), "Soziologie der Familie," in René König, ed., *Handbuch der empirischen Sozialforschung*, vol. II (1969), 172–305, and *Die Familie der Gegenwart. Ein interkultureller Vergleich* (1977). There is no sound or substantial history of the German family; Ingeborg Weber-Kellermann, *Die deutsche Familie. Versuch einer Sozialgeschichte* (1974), is well meaning but shallow. For the "prehistory" of the nineteenth-century German family, see Helmut Möller, *Die kleinbürgerliche Familie im 18. Jahrhundert. Verhalten und Gruppenkultur* (1969), the model of a monograph and revealing on sexual ideals and conduct. G. A. Ritter and Jürgen Kocka, eds., *Deutsche Sozialgeschichte. Dokumente und Skizzen*, vol. II, *1870–1914* (1974), is a helpful anthology. Richard J. Evans and W. R. Lee, eds., *The German Family: Essays on the Social History of the Family in Nineteenth- and Twentieth-Century Germany* (1981), is characteristic of recent social history in that only one of its nine papers (Karin Hausen, "Family and Role Division," 51–83) deals with the middle classes. For France, see again Flandrin, *Families in Former Times* (above, p. 488). Prerevolutionary times are briefly but well treated by James Traer, *Marriage and Family in Eighteenth-Century France* (1980); Roderick Phillips, *Family Breakdown in Late Eighteenth-Century France: Divorces in Rouen, 1792–1803* (1980), an excellent monograph; and two fine French demographic and legal studies well worth reading: Maurice Garden, *Lyon et les Lyonnais au XVIIIᵉ siècle* (1970), and Yves Castan, *Honnêteté et relations sociales en Languedoc au XVIIᵉ et XVIIIᵉ siècles* (1976). Richard Sennett's interesting study *Families Against the City: Middle Class Homes of Industrial Chicago 1872–1890* (1970) has much on "the intensity of family life" in the second half of the nineteenth century. There are some good essays in Virginia Tufte and Barbara Myerhoff, eds., *Changing Images of the Family* (1979), dealing with the family in Europe and in the United States, with facts and fictions. Another informative anthology is Anthony S. Wohl, ed., *The Victorian Family: Structure and Stresses* (1978). See also the collection *The Family*, *Daedalus*, CVI (Spring 1977), as well as John Demos and Sarane Spence Boocock, eds., *Turning Points: Historical and Sociological Essays on the Family* (1978), varied and often interesting; see especially the paper by Carroll Smith-Rosenberg, "Sex as Symbol in Victorian Purity: An Ethnohistorical Analysis of Jacksonian America" (212–47), and the introductory essay by Glen H. Elder, Jr., "Approaches to Social Change and the Family" (1–38), which ably surveys recent work (and controversy) in family history. Theodore K. Rabb and Robert I. Rotberg, eds., *The Family in History: Interdisciplinary Essays* (1971), is also useful; Tamara K. Hareven discusses "The History of the Family as an Interdisciplinary Field" (211–26). The "Bibliographical Note" by C. John Summerville (227–35) is invaluable. See also *Geschichte und Gesellschaft. Zeitschrift für Historische Sozialwissenschaften*, I, 2–3 (1975), a special number devoted to historical family research and demography. There is a fascinating brief study of a nineteenth-century Danish family by Ellen Damgaard and Poul H. Moustgaard, *Et Hjem—en familie* (1970), with an English summary. Incidentally, Michael Anderson, *Approaches to the History of the Western Family* (1980), very critical of Shorter and others, repays study.

For *The Girl's Own Paper*, see Wendy Forrester, *Great-Grandmamma's Weekly: A Celebration of "The Girl's Own Paper" 1880–1901* (1980), a light-hearted compilation that first called my attention to this material. Another characteristic product of the time, mirroring the changes that had taken place and the reluctance to take pride in them, is a volume edited by Annie Nathan Meyer, the moving force in the founding of Barnard College, *Woman's Work in America* (1891), patterned after Theodore Stanton's *The Woman Question*

in Europe (above, p. 483). The guidelines that the editor set down for her contributors suggest the maturity the woman's cause had achieved in half a
century: "Facts and History rather than eloquence; Truth before picturesque-
ness; A total absence of railing against the opposite sex" (v–vi). At the same
time, the book is not free of pathetic catalogues of distinguished women in
this field or that.

The great nineteenth-century combat between fathers and sons deserves
more study than it has had. Howard R. Wolf, "British Fathers and Sons, 1773–
1913: From Filial Submissiveness to Creativity," *Psychoanalytic Review*, LII, 2
(Summer 1968), 197–214, which deals with the Mills, Gosse, D. H. Lawrence, is
very thin; Kurt K. T. Wais, *Das Vater-Sohn Motiv in der Dichtung bis 1880*
(1931) and *Das Vater-Sohn Motiv in der Dichtung 1880–1930* (1931), are far
richer; full of suggestions, these compact volumes are somewhat compromised
by a polemical, rather angry anti-Freudian animus. Bruce Mazlish's study of
the Mills, father and son (above, p. 465), takes on a promising theme but is disappointing. Stephen Kern's psychoanalytically informed essay, "Explosive
Intimacy: Psychodynamics of the Victorian Family," *History of Childhood
Quarterly*, I, 3 (Summer 1974), 437–61, touches all the right bases but is, in
my judgment, too relentlessly critical; it notes the strains but overlooks the
felicity in middle-class nineteenth-century families. Otto Rank, *Inzest-Motiv*,
already mentioned (p. 496), is an exhaustive compendium by a maverick
psychoanalyst which goes beyond literature. I conclude with several
informative articles in the *Psychohistory Review*, not all of them pure
psychohistory by any means but valuable in their own right: Renée Neu
Watkins, "The Renaissance Pater Familias—'Be Ye Perfect,'" IX, 2 (Winter
1980), 91–110, analyzes two "father-figures," Gianozzo in Alberti's *Della
Famiglia* and Polonius in Shakespeare's *Hamlet*; Nancy F. Cott, "Notes Toward
an Interpretation of Antebellum Childbearing," VI, 4 (Spring 1978), 4–20,
makes large and beautifully documented claims for the centrality of an understanding of child-rearing for the historian; a special issue on "psychohistorical
Study of the American Family," VI, 2–3 (Fall–Winter 1977–78), has a number
of rewarding essays, esp. Cushing Strout, "Fathers and Sons," 25–31.

The history of comfort needs to be written; it is, of course, implicit in all
histories of furniture and furnishings. But there is good material in John Corn-
forth, *English Interiors 1790–1848: The Quest for Comfort* (1978), and John
Gloag's earlier, not yet superseded *Victorian Comfort* (1942). Jean and
Françoise Fourastié, *Histoire du confort* (n.d.), is brief but helpful; the two
also collaborated in an important chapter in Jean Fourastié's *Machinisme et
bien-être. Niveau de vie et genre de vie en France de 1700 à nos jours* (ed.
1969). See also Jennie Calder, *The Victorian Home* (1977), alert to the strains
within the comfortable family, but harsher than I have been. Siegfried Giedion's
classic *Mechanization Takes Command: A Contribution to Anonymous History*
(1948) remains immensely informative. The best survey of Biedermeier, that
style both maligned and sentimentalized out of all recognition, is Georg
Himmelheber, *Biedermeier Furniture* (1973; tr. Simon Jervis, 1974), which
successfully avoids both extremes.

Fernand Braudel has made the comfort—or discomfort—of the centuries
preceding the nineteenth his own. His bulky and eccentric three-volume work

Civilisation matérielle, économie et capitalisme, XVe–XVIIIe siècle, 3 vols. (1979), esp. vol. I, *Les Structures du quotidien: le possible et l'impossible* (tr. Sian Reynolds, *Civilization and Capitalism, 15th–18th Century* [1981]), provides much detail. The English translation of an earlier version of that work, *Capitalism and Material Life, 1400–1800* (tr. Miriam Kochan, 1973), has made its way among social historians. "Privacy," Braudel there says flatly (224) "was an eighteenth-century innovation." Robert Mandrou, *Introduction à la France moderne. Essai de psychologie historique, 1500–1640* (1961), offers much fascinating material, especially on the history of the senses in early modern Europe, in Part One. See also Michel and Mireille Lacave, *Bourgeois et marchands en Provence et en Languedoc* (1977), which has interesting details on the uncomfortable bourgeois domestic styles of life down to the eighteenth century (chs. VIII–X).

The Germans seem to have been particularly voluble on the need to rethink, and perhaps reform, the institution of marriage. Especially in the 1890s, stimulated by the reality of the "new" woman and by such controversial philosophers as Nietzsche, they poured out tract after tract. I list a small bouquet. Maximilian Schacht, *Sociologische Studien*, vol. II, *Versittlichung der Ehe* (1895), argues that love, not rigid legal prescriptions, should govern; the rest will follow. Dr. Phil. Reinhold Günther, a Swiss philosopher, in *Weib und Sittlichkeit. Studien und Darlegungen* (1898), defends "moral sensuality" and praises woman as naturally chaste and naturally a lover of children. Otto Caspari, a professor of philosophy, in *Das Problem über die Ehe! vom philosophischen, geschichtlichen und socialen Gesichtspunkte* (1899), worries about the increasing sexual immorality of the unmarried. But the Germans, of course, had no monopoly on such troubled surveys. See, for one French instance, Count A. de Gasparin, *L'Ennemi de la famille* (1874).

For one of the few psychologically sophisticated treatments of diary-keeping, see Siegfried Bernfeld, *Trieb und Tradition im Jugendalter. Kulturpsychologische Studien aus Tagebüchern*, Beiheft 54 for the *Zeitschrift für angewandte Psychologie* (1931). There is also Peter Blos, *On Adolescence* (above, p. 490). Macfarlane's *Family Life of Ralph Josselin* (above, p. 503) has some good pages on diary-keeping (esp. 4–8). A highly specialized but fascinating paper by Willie Hoffer psychoanalyzes "Diaries of adolescent schizophrenics (hebephrenics)," *Psychoanalytic Study of the Child*, II (1946), 293–321. See also M. Leleu's "characterological" study, *Les Journaux intimes* (1952), Robert A. Fothergill, *Private Chronicles: A Study of English Diaries* (1974), P. A. Spalding, *Self Harvest: A Study of Diaries and the Diarist* (1949), and Gustav René Hocke, *Das Europäische Tagebuch. Beiträge zur vergleichenden Literaturgeschichte* (1963), a large (over 450 pp.) anthology of snippets from diaries and journals introduced by a long (over 500 pp.) and rather pretentious though by no means uninformative introduction.

John Mack Faragher has suggested that men kept terse, businesslike records while women ran to the emotional, domestic, and expansive. This doubtless holds for his sample—mid-nineteenth-century Americans trekking westward—but less strictly for cultivated bourgeois on the American East Coast or in Europe. *Women and Men on the Overland Trail* (1979), esp. 14, 128–33. Dr. William Alcott in 1839, in *The Young Husband*, urged husbands and wives to keep a journal to express their private feelings—see Haller and Haller, *Physician and Sexuality* (above, p. 482), 227. For Mrs. Humphry Ward's translation of Amiel's diary and the English reception, see William S. Peterson, *Victorian Heretic: Mrs. Humphry Ward's "Robert Elsmere"* (1976), 90–101. Bashkirtseff's famous diary is generously excerpted in Dormer Creston [pseud.], *Fountains of Youth: The Life of Marie Bashkirtseff* (1937). Gladstone's contemporary appreciation is of great interest: "Journal de Marie Bashkirtseff," *Nineteenth Century*, XXVI (October 1889), 602–7. For Victoria Benedictsson, see above, p. 481. James R. Mellow's fluent and intelligent *Nathaniel Hawthorne in His Time* (1980) makes good use of the Hawthornes' intimate writings and I have found it helpful.

For the Sumners' marriage, and especially Jeannie Sumner's health problems and sexual malaise, see Bruce Curtis, "Victorians Abed: William Graham Sumner on the Family, Women and Sex," *American Studies*, XVIII (1977), 101–22; Joy and Bruce Curtis, "Illness and the Victorian Lady: The Case of Jeannie Sumner," *International Journal of Women's Studies*, IV, 5 (1981), 527–43. The subject of women's use of the sickbed as a form of securing contraception remains a matter of controversy. It is affirmed in Barbara Ehrenreich and Deirdre English, *For Her Own Good: 150 Years of the Experts' Advice to Women* (1978), but can have been only one strategy among many.

Illustrations and Sources

Measurements in inches, width preceding height

Antoine Wiertz, *La Belle Rosina*, also called *Two Young Girls*, 1847, Oil on canvas, 39 x 54.6. Antoine Wiertz Museum (dept. of the Royal Museums of Fine Arts of Belgium), Brussels. Inv. No. 1935. Photo copyright A. C. L., Brussels.

Mabel Loomis Todd, February 1882, photograph. Todd-Bingham Picture Collection, Yale University Library.

Eben J. Loomis, 1895, photograph. Todd-Bingham Picture Collection, Yale University Library.

David Peck Todd, ca. 1890, photograph. Todd-Bingham Picture Collection, Yale University Library.

William Austin Dickinson, ca. 1890, photograph. Todd-Bingham Picture Collection, Yale University Library.

Sir John Tenniel, *Woman's Emancipation*, *Punch*, XXI (1851), 3.

Edward L. Sambourne, *The Angel in "The House"; Or, The Result of Female Suffrage*, *Punch*, LXXXVI (1884), 279.

Modern Hothouse Plants, *Fliegende Blätter*, I, 6 (1845), 46.

Mrs. Professor, *Fliegende Blätter*, IV, 85 (1846), 102.

The Poetess, *Fliegende Blätter*, IV, 89 (1846), 135.

Honoré Daumier, "*Pardon me, Sir, if I disturb you a little,*" lithograph from *Les Bas bleus*, *Le Charivari*, March 8, 1844. Yale Sterling Library.

Heinrich Hoffmann, *History of a Thumb-Sucker*, *Struwwelpeter* (1844–45, ed. ca. 1900).

Phyllis Riding Aristotle, before 1300. Bronze Mosan aquamanile, 13 3/16. The Metropolitan Museum of Art, New York, Robert Lehman Collection, 1975.

Dante Gabriel Rossetti, *Venus Verticordia*, 1864. Oil on canvas. Russell-Cotes Art Gallery and Museum, Bournemouth.

Dante Gabriel Rossetti, *Pandora*, 1879. Colored crayon on paper, 24½ x 38. Fogg Art Museum, Harvard University, Gift—Grenville L. Winthrop.

Max Liebermann, *Samson and Delilah*, 1902. Oil on canvas, 83.5 x 59.5. Städelsches Kunstinstitut, Frankfurt a. M. Photograph Ursula Edelmann.

Franz von Stuck, *Sin*, 1893. Oil on canvas, 37.6 x 49. Bayerische Gemäldesammlung, Munich.

Edvard Munch, *Harpy*, 1894. Drypoint, 8⅝ x 11⅙. Munch-Museet, Oslo.

Edvard Munch, *Vampire*, 1895. Hand-colored lithograph, 21⅝ x 15 1/16. Munch-Museet, Oslo.

Edvard Munch, *The Death of Marat*, ca. 1905–7, later reworked. Oil on canvas, 78⅝ x 59 1/16. Munch-Museet, Oslo.

Edvard Munch, *Salome II*, 1905. Etching. Munch-Museet, Oslo.

Aubrey Beardsley, *The Climax*, 1894, Line block, 8¼ x 6. Illustration for Oscar Wilde, *Salome*. Beinecke Rare Book and Manuscript Library, Yale University.

Aubrey Beardsley, *The Battle of the Beaux and Belles*, 1895–96. Ink drawing, 6.8 x 9.9. Illustration for Alexander Pope, *The Rape of the Lock*. Barber Institute of Fine Arts, The University, Birmingham.

Gustave Moreau, *Oedipus and the Sphinx*, 1864. Oil on canvas, 41¼ x 81¼. The Metropolitan Museum of Art, New York, Bequest of William H. Herriman, 1921.

Franz von Stuck, *The Kiss of the Sphinx*, 1895. Oil on canvas, 57 x 63. Szépművészeti Museum, Budapest.

Edvard Munch, *Sphinx*, ca. 1927. Drawing. Munch-Museet, Oslo.

Four-Pointed Urethral Ring, from J. L. Milton, *Pathology and Treatment of Spermatorrhoea* (London, 1887), 127. Courtesy of the Wellcome Trustees, Wellcome Institute for the History of Medicine, London.

Apparatuses against onanism, from Maison Mathieu catalogue, 1904. Courtesy of the Wellcome Trustees, Wellcome Institute for the History of Medicine, London.

Hablot K. Browne ("Phiz"), *Changes at Home*, 1850, for Charles Dickens, *David Copperfield*.

Carl Iutz, *Memento Mori*, *Daheim*, XX (1884), 57.

James Ward, *The Day's Sport*, 1826. Oil on canvas, 51¼ x 39½. Yale Center for British Art, Paul Mellon Collection.

V. Morland, *Au Salon de Peinture*, *Petit Journal pour Rire*, XXVI, 3rd series (1882), 6.

Antonin-Jean-Paul Carlès, *Death of Abel*, 1887. Musée du Luxembourg, Paris.

Ernest Barrias, *Electricity*, 1889. Plaster, destroyed. Photo Giraudon.

Felix Charpentier, *The Bicycle*, ca. 1895–1900. Terracotta, whereabouts unknown. Photo from Peter Fusco and H. W. Janson, eds., *The Romantics to Rodin* (1980), 69.

Per Hasselberg, *Magnetism*, ca. 1884. Plaster. Fürstenberg Gallery, Göteborgs Konstmuseum, Göteborg.

Carl Larsson, *The Interior of the Fürstenberg Gallery*, 1885. Oil on canvas, 22¼ x 30⅝. Göteborgs Konstmuseum, Göteborg.

Antonio Teixeira Lopes, *Eça de Queiros*, 1903. Marble. Lisbon. Courtesy of Portuguese Consul General, New York.

Alexandre Chaponnier, after Pierre-Paul Prud'hon, *Study Guiding the Ascent of Genius*, 1806 or before. Stipple engraving in color, 8½ x 10⅞. In the possession of the author.

August Kiss, *Amazon*, 1841. Engraving representing the life-size zinc copy exhibited in the Great Exhibition in London. From *The Art-Journal, Illustrated Catalogue, The Industry of All Nations, 1851* (1851), 37.

Jean Auguste Dominique Ingres, *Torso of a Man*, ca. 1800. Oil on canvas, 31½ x 39⅜. Ecole des Beaux-Arts, Paris.

Jean Auguste Dominique Ingres, *The Ambassadors of Agamemnon in the Tent of Achilles*, 1801. Oil on canvas, 61 x 43¼. Ecole des Beaux-Arts, Paris.

William Etty, *Venus Now Wakes and Wakens Love*, 1828. Oil, 24 x 20. Russell-Cotes Art Gallery and Museum, Bournemouth.

William Etty, *Andromeda*, ca. 1840. Oil, 20 x 26⅜. Lady Lever Art Gallery, Port Sunlight, Merseyside.

William Etty, *Pandora*, 1824. Oil on canvas, 44⅛ x 34¾. City Art Gallery, Leeds.

Edward Burne-Jones, *Pygmalion and the Image*, 1868–79. Oil on canvas. Courtesy of Birmingham Museum and Art Gallery.

Jean Léon Gérôme, *Pymalion and Galatea*, ca. 1881. Oil on canvas, 29¼ x 37¼. The Metropolitan Museum of Art, New York, Gift of Louis C. Raegner, 1927.

Honoré Daumier, *Pygmalion*, lithograph, *Le Charivari*, December 28, 1842. Yale Sterling Library.

Jean-Baptiste (called Auguste) Clésinger, *Woman Bitten by a Snake*, after 1847. Bronze reduction of marble original. Los Angeles County Museum of Art, Private Collection.

Alexandre Cabanel, *Nymph Abducted by a Satyr*, 1860. Oil on canvas, Musée des Beaux-Arts, Lille.

Hiram Powers, *The Greek Slave*, 1843. Marble, Yale University Art Gallery, Olive Louise Dann Fund.

Hiram Powers, *Eve Tempted*, modeled 1842. Marble, National Museum of American Art, Smithsonian Institution, Washington, D.C.

George Cruikshank, *Making Decent!*, 1822. Etching. British Museum.

A modern Gothic mansion, from A. Welby Pugin, *The True Principles of Pointed or Christian Architecture, Set Forth in Two Lectures* (1841), 58.

Sofa with Movable Cushions, from Clarence Cook, *The House Beautiful: Essays on Beds and Tables, Stools and Candlesticks* (1878), 59.

Antonio Canova, *Venus Italica*, 1812. Marble, Pitti Palace, Florence. Photo Alinari.

Antonio Canova, *Cupid and Psyche*, 1793. Marble. Louvre, Paris. Photo Alinari.

Acknowledgments

In writing this book, which has been in the making for a decade, I have accumulated obligations which it is a pleasant duty to discharge. I can only hope that, with the innumerable encounters I have enjoyed at lectures and at conferences, I have forgotten no one. That anonymous graduate student at Berkeley who steered me to the diary of Heinrich Graetz, and the friend (but which of them I can no longer remember) who informally gave me a title, "Glandular Christianity," which I will be using in the second volume, remind me just how far-flung and manyfold my debts are.

I have been immensely fortunate in invitations to test out my ideas in the making. I was privileged to be the first Ena H. Thompson Lecturer at Pomona College in 1980, and attempted, in these genial surroundings, to spell out the direction this study would take. Three years earlier, in 1977, I had the honor of delivering the Martin Rist Lectures at the Iliff School of Theology in Denver, renewing valued acquaintance with old friends and familiar places and rehearsing my thoughts on bourgeois culture in the nineteenth century. Harvey H. Potthoff put me in his debt, as always. The Whitten Lectures I gave at McMaster University in Hamilton, Ontario in the same year on the "Bourgeois Century" considerably assisted me also. A very different formulation of my ideas served me for the Christian Gauss Lectures in Criticism at Princeton in 1979, where I underwent the kind of friendly, constructive grilling for which this lectureship is justly famous. The four Freud Lectures that I delivered at Yale in 1980 under the sponsorship of the Western New England Institute of Psychoanalysis and the Humanities Center at Yale University touched on some themes that I have canvassed in this volume. I also enjoyed the hospitality of the Concilium on International and Area Studies and of the Program on Modern Studies at my university. Lectures elsewhere, dating all the way back to the Spring of 1971, when I organized the first version of my thoughts about the bourgeois century under the auspices of the Institute of Historical Research in London, have proved exceedingly helpful in formulating and reformulating my ideas and in giving me the benefit of discussion, suggestions, and dissent, from the floor. In 1972, I spoke at the University of Indiana at Bloomington, at Western Michigan University at Kalamazoo, and at Goucher College, in Towson, Maryland, on such topics as gentility and repression in the nineteenth century. In 1974, I returned to my alma mater, the University of Denver, to speak on "Modernism." Among later talks particularly relevant to the present volume, I single out the University of Connecticut at Storrs in 1980; the same year I had a stimulating day at Harvard Center for European Studies debating my views. More recently, in 1982, I spoke at Concordia College in Montreal and at Arizona State University in Tempe. I also recall with pleasure repeated visits to the University of California at Berkeley and at Los Angeles and, in the mid-1970s, to the Johns Hopkins University. Equally pleasant and productive were my lecture-visits at the University of Wisconsin in Madison, at Kenyon College at Gambier, Ohio, at Tufts University, Medford, Massachusetts, and at the Institute for Advanced Study in the Humanities, University of Massachusetts at Amherst. In October, 1982, I gave the introductory lecture at a Conference on sexuality at Cornell University. All these intellectual exercises combined, in true Horatian fashion, the useful with the agreeable.

Money is time. This book—and its successors, of which one, the second volume, is already very far along—required long stretches of "leisure" for visiting archives, reading at home, discussing a variety of issues with patient and forthcoming colleagues everywhere, for writing—and rewriting. I feel exceptionally fortunate in having received two substantial grants from the Research Division of the National Endowment for the Humanities, the first stretching from 1973 to 1975, the second from 1981 to 1984, which allowed me some invaluable intervals to myself, and financed trips to archives in several countries. Generous fellowships from the Humanities Division of the Rockefeller Foundation and the John Simon Guggenheim Memorial Foundation bought further indispensable time, and I am grateful to both. I must particularly thank the Rockefeller Foundation yet a second time for its swift and most unbureaucratic understanding of the needs of a scholar in search of matching funds. I am also happy to acknowledge the aid of the Fund for Research of the American Psychoanalytic Association, the more so since this endowment normally concentrates on far more technical work than mine has proved to be. The Deutsch-Amerikanische Austauschdienst (known to all as DAAD) and the Fritz Thyssen Stiftung supplied funds aiding me in visits to German archives and in xeroxing rare materials. At Yale, I have had the benefit of repeated benefactions from the Council on West European Studies of the Concilium on International and Area Studies, as well as from the A. Whitney Griswold Fund, both of which supported travel and costs of typing and xeroxing.

I am in general beholden to my university, and to my department, for its supportive attitude toward my work. My colleague Howard Lamar, Dean of Yale College, worked out the unorthodox schedule permitting me at once to do valued teaching and to take some equally valued time for these books. Joseph Warner and Linda Downey at the Grants and Contracts Administration guided my way through complex applications and regulations, far beyond the call of duty; Richard S. Field and Debra N. Mancoff at the Yale Art Gallery were forthcoming in finding and providing illustrations. Loueva Pflueger smoothed the ways of the scholar in her inimitable manner. Gay Walker resolved some technical conundrums. Marjorie Wynne of the Beinecke Library clarified a picture puzzle. Robert Balay and his rightly famous crew of reference librarians solved some intractable riddles for me. Betty Paine did better than type my often hardly legible pages, more than once; she also supplied me with interesting pictures and pertinent anecdotes, and made this manuscript very much her own. I want also to thank the helpful professionals at the Yale Manuscripts and Archives, notably Judith Schiff. In addition, my thanks go to Ferenc Gyorgyey, Historical Librarian at the Historical Library, Yale Medical School.

I owe much to archivists elsewhere, for answering my letters and directing me to the right sources, thus saving me much time. This was true in Cologne, Hamburg, Munich (both in the Staatsbibliothek and the Monacensia), the Schiller Institute at Marbach, Karlsruhe, Berlin (West-Berlin, of course), as it was in Cambridge, Oxford, Oslo, Lille, Paris, and Göteborg. I am especially grateful to the information gladly supplied by Mrs. Ingvari Desaix of the Göteborgs Konstmuseum. In this country, I want to thank Herbert Cahoon at the Pierpont Morgan Library, New York; Rita H. Warnock at the John Hay Library, Brown University; Richard J. Wolfe at the Francis A. Conway Library of Medicine in Boston; Lynn Metz, Curator of the College Archives, Knox College, at Galesburg, Illinois; Dorothy Green and Susan L. Boone, Sophia Smith Collection, Smith College, Northampton, Massachusetts; Ruth James, Amherst Historical Society, Amherst, Massachusetts; Eva Moseley, Schlesinger Library, Radcliffe College, Harvard University, Cambridge, Massachusetts; Sara Timby, Manuscripts Division at Stanford University, Stanford, California; Susan Matusek at the Institute for Sex Research, Indiana University, Bloomington, Indiana; Peter Fusco at the Los Angeles County Museum of Art; Sara S. Hodson, Huntington Library, San Marino, California.

My debt to the Western New England Institute for Psychoanalysis, where I have completed my seven-year stint as a Research Candidate, is very great and very obvious. While it would be invidious to single out one or another among my teachers, I want to record a special, unforgettable obligation to Dr. Richard Newman, for reasons he knows as well as I, and to Ernst Prelinger, whose immense and imaginative learning in the psychoanalytic corpus first enabled me to see the critical role of reality in the making of minds. And my classmates, I am glad to say, were individually and collectively patient with my sometimes rather oblique interests.

I have thanks to render to a number of students, colleagues at Yale and elsewhere, acquaintances, strangers coming up to me after a lecture, who have all assisted me in more ways than I can record or even recall. I trust they will not mind my expressing my gratitude in a simple alphabetical listing for the way they informed me of some elusive personage, supplied a telling story, translated a Russian word, offered a title I did not know, or just listened to me: James Albisetti, Madelon Bedell, John Blum, John Brewer, Michael Burns, Paul Bushkovitch, Ruth Butler, Susan Chitty, Judy Coffin, Stefan Collini, Marian F. Conway, Nancy Cott, Angela Covey-Crump, Carl Degler, Peter Demetz, Betty Anne Doebler, Teri Edelstein, Richard Ellmann, Jane Fulcher, John Garraty, Sophie Glazer, Raymond Grew, Sir Ernst Gombrich, Fred Grubel, Robert Harding, Brian Harrison, Judith Hughes, Isabel Hull, Julie Iovine, Jane Isay, Steven Kablick, Herbert Kaplan, Jay Katz, Carl Landauer, Tim Lang,

Tom Laqueur, Lisa Lieberman, Peter Loewenberg, Gene McAfee, Jeffrey
Merrick, Ellen Messer, Marc Micale, Sir Ralph Millais, James Mohr, David
Musto, Thomas Nipperdey, Harry Payne, Janet Polasky, Barbara Corrado
Pope, Jules Prown, Howard A. Reed, Monika Richarz, Samuel Ritvo, David
Roberts, Jeffrey Sammons, C.J. Scheiner, Steven Scher, Alexander Shenker,
Daniel Sherman, Quentin Skinner, Pamela and Wim Smit, Albert Solnit,
Valerie Steele, Mary Lee Townsend, Frank Turner, Heinrich Voss, Malcolm
Warner, Sharon White.

Since 1972, several students have done research for me, especially among
foreign periodicals. I am grateful to them all: Karen Bradley, Joseph Koerner,
Jay Lutz (who translated from the Swedish for me), Georges Magaud, Harry
Payne, Debra Perry, Becky Saletan, Sally Tittman.

I am also happy to acknowledge the help of my friends and editors at Oxford
University Press: Sheldon Meyer, whose faith in this enterprise has sustained
my own; Nancy Lane, who has helped me in more ways than she might know;
Stephanie Golden, a patient and penetrating editor, at once respectful and
critical when it counts.

And then my readers! Vann Woodward, to whom I have dedicated this book,
gave my long introduction a critical and constructive reading at a time when I
needed his assistance most; Jerome Meyer, my classmate at the Psychoanalytic
Institute, cast an informed eye on the whole manuscript and at once encouraged
and corrected me in the finer points of the Freudian dispensation; Carol Payne
offered some skeptical queries especially in the third chapter; my old friends
Dick and Peggy Kuhns gave the manuscript a sensitive, sympathetic, and
psychologically informed reading from which it greatly benefited; my two
former students and research assistants, now close friends, Susanna Barrows
and Henry Gibbons, went over every word of this manuscript most thoughtfully, and supplied invaluable information, support, and criticism in happy
proportions. My colleague and friend John Merriman engaged me in a series
of spirited and highly productive disagreements and was particularly helpful in
spelling out the claims of reality. And Bob Webb, as always, studied my manuscript with a historian's fund of information and an editor's fine eye, much
improving what he read. Given the learning and the care of such readers, I am
tempted to blame on them any errors that remain.

Ruth Gay deserves a paragraph of her own. She did not only read these pages
more than once, often more than twice, with impressive patience and exceptional sense; in a very real way she made the book possible by bringing home
trophies from the archives which her infallible eye had discovered, and which
allowed me to think of this enterprise in psychological detection at all. In the
midst of important and exhausting work of her own, she has been critic, editor,
researcher and enthusiast all in one. She has made this book in a very real sense
a collaboration.

                                                                        PETER GAY

Index